THE
AMERICAN REPUBLIC

for Christian Schools®

the AMERICAN

Rachel C. Larson, M.A.
Pamela B. Creason, M. Ed.
Michael D. Matthews, M. Ed.

REPUBLIC

for Christian Schools®

Second Edition

Bob Jones University Press
Greenville, SC 29614

This textbook was written by members of the faculty and staff of Bob Jones University. Standing for the "old-time religion" and the absolute authority of the Bible since 1927, Bob Jones University is the world's leading Fundamentalist Christian university. The staff of the University is devoted to educating Christian men and women to be servants of Jesus Christ in all walks of life.

Providing unparalleled academic excellence, Bob Jones University prepares its students through its offering of over one hundred majors, while its fervent spiritual emphasis prepares their minds and hearts for service and devotion to the Lord Jesus Christ.

If you would like more information about the spiritual and academic opportunities available at Bob Jones University, please call
1-800-BJ-AND-ME (1-800-252-6363).
www.bju.edu

NOTE:
The fact that materials produced by other publishers are referred to in this volume does not constitute an endorsement by Bob Jones University Press of the content or theological position of materials produced by such publishers. The position of Bob Jones University Press, and the University itself, is well known. Any references and ancillary materials are listed as an aid to the student or the teacher and in an attempt to maintain the accepted academic standards of the publishing industry.

THE AMERICAN REPUBLIC for Christian Schools©
Second Edition

Authors
Rachel C. Larson, M.A.
Pamela B. Creason, M.Ed.
Michael D. Matthews, M.Ed.

Contributing Authors
Terri L. Koontz
Thomas G. Luttmann
Jill M. Blackstock, M.Ed.

Consultants
John A. Matzko, Ph.D.
 Professor, Department of History,
 Bob Jones University
Steven N. Skaggs
 Supervisor, Secondary Authors
Daniel P. Olinger, Ph.D.
 Strategic Planning Coordinator,
 Bob Jones University Press
Mark Sidwell, Ph.D.
 Director, Fundamentalism File
David Fisher, M.A.
 Instructor, Bob Jones Academy
Elizabeth Olsen, M.Ed.
 Instructor, Bob Jones Junior High School

Compositor
Nancy C. Lohr
Designers
Ellyson Kalagayan
John W. Bjerk
Editor
Manda Kalagayan
Photo Acquisition
Terry R. Latini

"I Have a Dream" speech reprinted by arrangement with The Heirs to the Estate of Martin Luther King, Jr., c/o Writers House, Inc. as agent for the proprietor. Copyright 1963 by Martin Luther King, Jr., copyright renewed 1991 by Coretta Scott King

Produced in cooperation with the Bob Jones University Departments of History and Social Studies of the College of Arts and Science, the School of Education, and Bob Jones Academy and Junior High School.

for Christian Schools is a registered trademark of Bob Jones University Press.

ISBN 1-57924-312-6

©2000 Bob Jones University Press
Greenville, South Carolina 29614
First Edition ©1988, 1993

Printed in the United States of America

CONTENTS

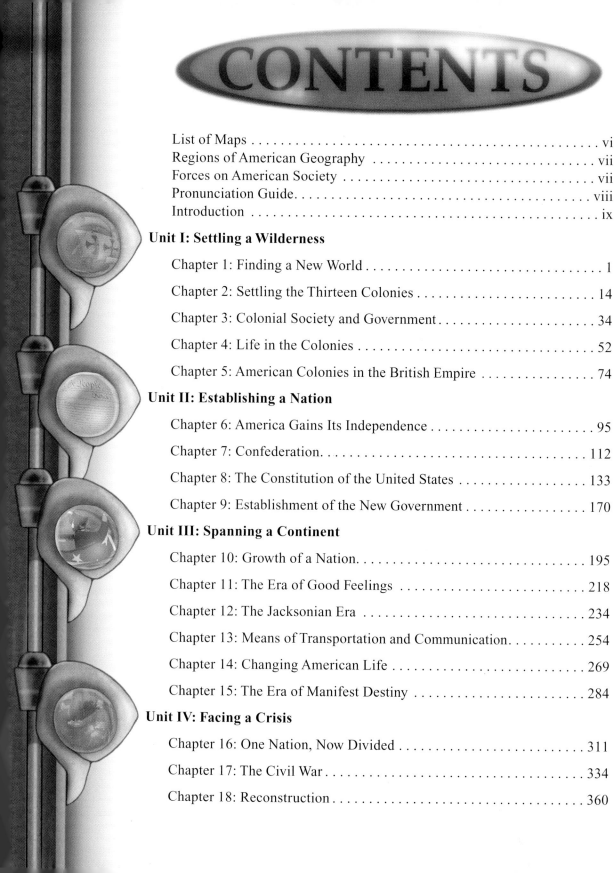

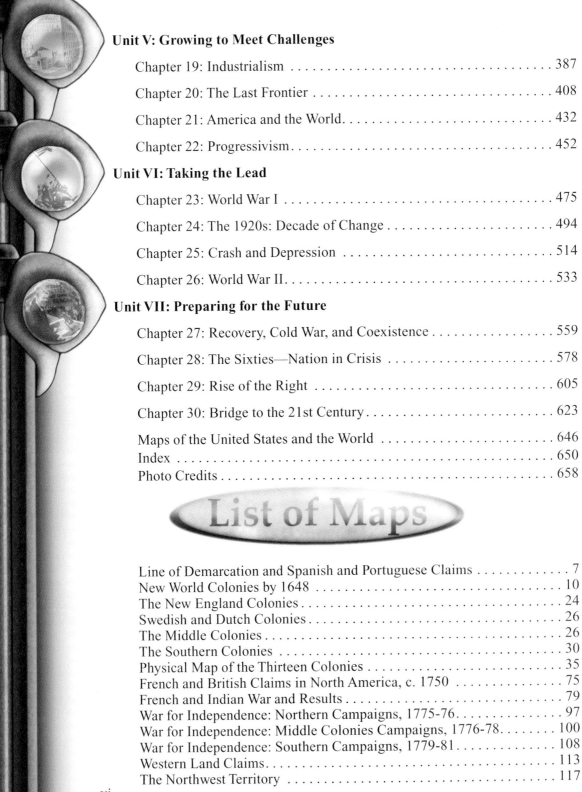

List of Maps

Regions of American Geography

Forces on American Society

Pronunciation Guide

The pronunciation key used in this text is designed to give readers a self-evident, acceptable pronunciation for a word as they read it from the page. For more nearly accurate pronunciations, consult a dictionary.

Syllables with primary stress appear in LARGE CAPITAL letters. Syllables with secondary stress and one-syllable words appear in SMALL CAPITAL letters; for example, Afghanistan appears as (af GAN uh STAN). Where two or more words appear together, hyphens separate the syllables within each word; for example, the Rub al Khali appears as (ROOB ahl KHAH-lee).

Most sounds are readily apparent. Here are the possible exceptions:

SYMBOL	EXAMPLE	SYMBOL	EXAMPLE
g	get = GET	th	thin = THIN
j	gentle = JEN tul	th	then = THEN
s	cent = SENT	zh	lesion = LEE zhun
a	cat = KAT	i-e	might = MITE
ah	cot = KAHT	eye	icy = EYE see
ar	car = KAR	oh	slow = SLOH
aw	all = AWL	ou	loud = LOUD
a-e	cape = KAPE	oy	toil = TOYL
ay	paint = PAYNT	u	some = SUM
e	jet = JET	uh	abet = uh BET
		oo	crew = CROO
		oo	push = POOSH

Introduction

A Baptist minister asked a Midwestern audience in the 1930s, "Who, knowing the facts of our history, can doubt that the United States of America has been a thought in the mind of God from all eternity?" Indeed, Christians must realize that nothing in history is accidental; our sovereign God directs the affairs of men and nations to accomplish His will. As you begin your study of the history of the United States, keep in mind that God has likewise directed—and is still directing—America's history. The story of the United States is but one part of God's overall design for the ages. You will read about human failure and weakness, but remember that God superintends all things for His glory and purpose. "For of him, and through him, and to him, are all things: to whom be glory for ever. Amen." (Romans 11:36)

UNIT 1

Settling a Wilderness

1770: Tensions began to rise between the colonies and their mother country. Provoked by a colonial mob, British soldiers in Boston opened fire, killing five and wounding six others.

x

1741: The preaching of Jonathan Edwards helped restore colonial America to its spiritual foundations during the Great Awakening.

1492: Though he believed the island he named San Salvador was part of the Orient, Columbus had actually paved the way for the exploration and development of a New World.

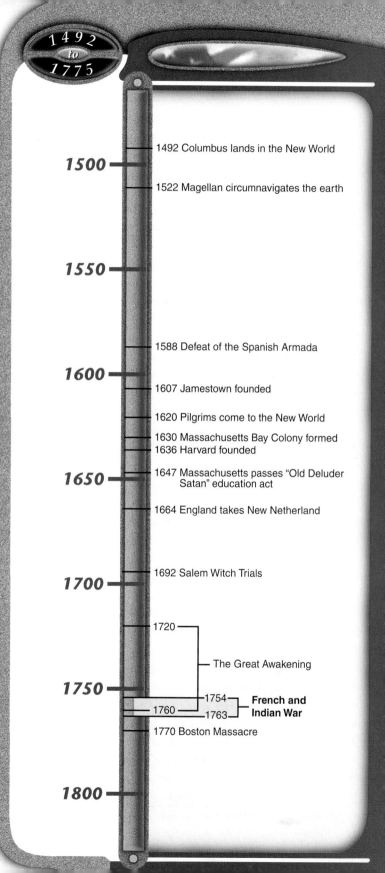

1492 to 1775

1500
1492 Columbus lands in the New World

1522 Magellan circumnavigates the earth

1550

1588 Defeat of the Spanish Armada

1600
1607 Jamestown founded

1620 Pilgrims come to the New World

1630 Massachusetts Bay Colony formed
1636 Harvard founded

1650
1647 Massachusetts passes "Old Deluder Satan" education act

1664 England takes New Netherland

1692 Salem Witch Trials

1700

1720

The Great Awakening

1750
1754
1760
1763
French and Indian War

1770 Boston Massacre

1800

Unit I: Settling a Wilderness

William Bradford's Account of the Founding of Plymouth

Governor Bradford wrote *Of Plymouth Plantation,* the most famous account of the early years of Plymouth Colony. After you read about the Pilgrims' arrival in December, answer the questions that follow.

Being thus passed the vast ocean, and a sea of troubles before in their preparation, they had now no friends to welcome them nor inns to entertain or refresh their weatherbeaten bodies; no houses or much less towns to repair to. . . . Savage barbarians, when they met with them (as after will appear) were readier to fill their sides full of arrows than otherwise. And for the season it was winter, and they that know the winters in that country know them to be sharp and violent, and subject to cruel and fierce storms, dangerous to travel to known places, much more to search an unknown coast. . . .

What could now sustain them but the Spirit of God and His grace? May not and ought not the children of these fathers rightly say: "Our fathers were Englishmen which came over this great ocean, and were ready to perish in this wilderness; but they cried unto the Lord, and He heard their voice. . . ."

They chose, or rather confirmed, Mr. John Carver (a man godly and well approved amongst them) their Governor for that year. And after they had provided a place for their goods . . . and begun some small cottages for their habitation; as time would admit, they met and consulted of laws and order, both for their civil and military government. . . .

In these hard and difficult beginnings they found some discontents and murmurings arise amongst some, and mutinous speeches and carriages [conduct] in other; but they were soon quelled [quieted] and overcome by the wisdom, patience, and just and equal carriage of things, by the Governor and better part, which clave faithfully together in the main.

But that which was most sad and lamentable was, that in two or three months' time half of their company died, especially in January and February, being the depth of winter, and wanting houses and other comforts; being infected with scurvy and other diseases which this long voyage and their inaccommodate condition had brought upon them. So as there died some times two or three of a day in the foresaid time, that of 100 and odd persons, scarce fifty remained. And of these, in the time of most distress, there was but six or seven sound persons who to their great commendations, be it spoken, spared no pains night nor day, but with abundance of toil and hazard of their own health, fetched them wood, made them fires, dressed them meat, made their beds, washed their loathsome clothes, clothed and unclothed them. In a word, did all the homely and necessary offices for them which dainty and queasy stomachs cannot endure to hear named; and all this willingly and cheerfully.

1. How many people died during the first few months?
2. According to Bradford, what saved the colonists?
3. What was Bradford's opinion of the first governor?
4. List four hardships that the colonists faced.

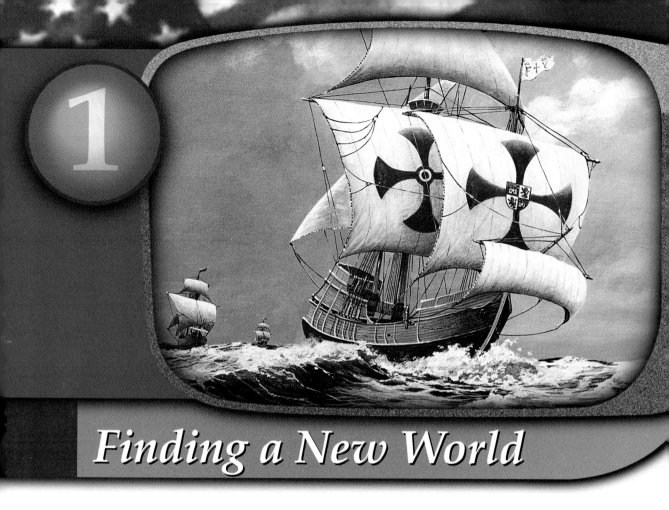

Finding a New World

After sailing nearly three thousand miles, ninety men and boys in three small ships searched the horizon for land. The sailors were reluctant to sail on into the unknown waters far to the west of Europe, but their leader, Christopher Columbus, was determined to find the riches of the Orient. He was sure that he could reach the lands of spices and gold in the East by sailing west.

At ten o'clock that night, Columbus saw a dim light on the horizon. It may have been the moonlight reflecting on an island beach or cliff, or it may have been a fire used by natives on an island. Columbus pressed toward the light, and four hours later, in the early morning of October 12, 1492, Columbus, his men, and his three ships, the *Niña,* the *Pinta,* and the *Santa Maria,* reached sight of land. Later that day Columbus went ashore on the island he named San Salvador (Holy Savior).

Debate still continues over which of several small islands in the Bahamas Columbus saw first, but Columbus believed it was an island in the Orient, perhaps in the East Indies. Therefore, he called the natives "Indians." Even after four voyages to the "New World" he had found, Columbus continued to believe he had reached the Far East. He failed, however, to find the spices and riches he sought, and he died in 1506, poor and powerless. Nevertheless, Columbus's discovery of America opened the door to the exploration and development of two continents and gave the United States of America an important piece of its early heritage.

The New World Before Columbus

Columbus introduced Europe to the Americas, but those lands were not empty and unknown before his discovery.

The First Americans

Almost everywhere Europeans explored in the New World, they came into contact with the people whom Columbus mistakenly called "Indians." It is still uncertain how and when these first Americans came to North and South America. They probably came to the land shortly after the scattering of the nations at the Tower of Babel in Genesis 11. Perhaps they crossed a land bridge that may have linked Asia to Alaska. However they came to America, it is clear they lived in the New World centuries before the Europeans came.

Spread out across North and South America, the Indians were not a unified people. They were divided into hundreds of clans or tribes, each with its own language, lifestyle, and leader, or chief. Some Indians were **nomadic,** constantly on the move in search of game, fish, and wild plants. Other groups settled in one area and farmed the land, raising crops such as maize (corn), potatoes, squash, and beans. The various groups lived in different kinds of shelters. The nomadic Indians often lived in portable shelters such as the cone-shaped tepees covered with animal hides. But more often Indians lived in more permanent housing such as dome-shaped wigwams covered with leaves and bark, or adobe houses built of sun-dried bricks.

Although most Indians throughout the Americas lived in small villages, there were three groups that built large civilizations before the white man came. In Central and South America, the **Mayas,** the **Aztecs,** and the **Incas** lived in large cities and developed many skills. The Mayan (MAH yuhn) civilization, located on the Yucatan (YOO kuh TAN) Peninsula of Mexico and in Guatemala, flourished from A.D. 300 to 900. The Mayas were amazing builders; they built their temples, for example, on top of large stone pyramids. Unlike most Indian groups, they developed a system of writing and of mathematics. They also studied

Although intellectually developed, the Mayas worshiped pagan gods with human sacrifices in temples like this one.

the stars and the planets. Their calendar was more accurate than the one used in Europe at the time of Columbus.

Although the Mayan civilization had fallen five hundred years prior to Columbus's arrival, the Aztecs and the Incas were strong when he came. The Aztecs (AZ TEKS) were fierce warriors who conquered other Indian tribes in what is now Mexico. They built their capital city, Tenochtitlán (teh NOCH tee TLAN), on an island in the middle of Lake Texcoco (tay SKOH KOH) in central Mexico. It was a beauti-

An artist's idea of how Tenochtitlán may have looked

ful city with large plazas, pyramid temples, and adobe houses. A network of canals flowed through the city. Connecting the capital to the mainland were massive earthen bridges. An estimated one hundred thousand people lived in the city at the time of the arrival of the first Europeans. Today, Mexico City, the present-day capital of Mexico, is located in the same area.

The Incas built an empire in the mountainous region of present-day Peru. They looked on their ruler, "the Inca," as a god. Like the Mayas and Aztecs, the Incas were excel-

lent builders. Ruins of their well-planned cities and roads still exist. Inca craftsmen produced fine metalwork, textiles, and pottery.

White Men Before Columbus

Although the Indians lived in America long before the arrival of the first Europeans, it is not known when the Indians first saw a white man. Columbus is generally regarded as the "discoverer" of America, but almost certainly he was not the first European to see the Americas.

Many theories exist about who arrived first. Stories are told of Phoenician (fih NISH un) sailors who came to the New World centuries before the birth of Christ. There is a legend of Madoc, a Welshman who founded a settlement among the Indians during the Middle Ages. Legends of Welsh-speaking, blue-eyed Indians persisted from the 1600s to the 1800s. Many explorers, such as Lewis and Clark, looked for these Welsh-speaking Indians. Other tales tell of Irish monks who visited America over a thousand years ago.

Evidence indicates that the **Vikings** visited America around A.D. 1000. The Vikings, or Norsemen, were courageous seamen from northern Europe. They planted colonies in Iceland and Greenland. From Greenland, the Vikings sailed their brightly painted ships westward to America. The best known of the Viking adventurers is **Leif Ericson,** the son of Eric the Red, who colonized Greenland. Ericson found "the strange land to the west" and called it "Vinland." Archaeologists have uncovered some evidence of the Vikings visiting eastern Canada.

Other Vikings journeyed to America after Ericson. But the rest of Europe was unaware

Columbus proposes his voyage to Cathay (China) to King Ferdinand and Queen Isabella.

of their voyages. Their discoveries went unnoticed and had no lasting effect on Europe or the New World. It was not until Columbus's "discovery" that a new era dawned for both Europe and the Americas. This was the age of exploration and discovery.

Columbus's Contribution

Europe had entered a new era of exploration in the late 1400s. The Europeans had new ship designs and new instruments to help them sail the seas. Much of the early exploration centered on finding new routes to the Orient (the Far East), where spices and wealth were readily available. Europeans greatly desired the spices of the East, which would help them improve the taste of their food. They also wanted the fine products of the East—silk, porcelain, gems, and precious metals. Because great profits could be made by obtaining these goods for Europe, merchants and rulers were willing to search for new trade routes. While some, like the

Portuguese, tried to find a way eastward around Africa, others wondered whether the Orient could be reached by sailing west. It was this belief that led to the discovery of the New World.

The Italian sailor **Christopher Columbus** was convinced that by sailing west he could reach the rich lands of the Indies. For many years he tried to persuade the Portuguese king to finance his voyage. Having no success, he turned to Portugal's rival, Spain, for help. There he secured the support of **King Ferdinand** and **Queen Isabella.**

In August of 1492, Columbus set sail on his historic voyage with his three ships. Each day his men grew more anxious and impatient. Some of the sailors, who believed the earth was flat, feared that they would sail off the edge. Others, who believed the earth was round, feared that the ships would sail "downhill" so far that they would not be able to sail back "uphill" to Spain. There was also the fear of "sea monsters." Who could know what great beasts lived in unexplored seas? Despite their fears, Columbus was able to keep his concerned crew on course until land was in sight.

Columbus made his discovery that October and then returned to Spain with news of what he thought was the Far East. Soon swarms of other explorers came to investigate the lands across the Atlantic. Before long they realized that what Columbus had found was really a roadblock in their path to the Orient. One of the first to suggest that these lands were not the East was an Italian merchant and explorer named **Amerigo Vespucci.** Having made several voyages westward, Vespucci offered proof that the lands were not the Orient but instead a "new world." A German mapmaker included the new land on his map and named it after Amerigo. The map became popular and with it the name "America." Thus Columbus was denied the honor of having the two continents of the Western Hemisphere named after him.

Nonetheless, Columbus had pointed the way for European countries to explore the lands to the west. His voyages encouraged Spain and other countries to seek out the extent and the riches of these lands. Without a courageous adventurer like Columbus to lead the way, discovery, further exploration, and settlement of the Americas would have been postponed.

SECTION REVIEW

1. What were the two general types of Indian lifestyles?

2. What three groups of American Indians had built impressive civilizations before the Europeans arrived?

3. What Viking adventurer set out to find the strange land west of Greenland? What did he call this area?

4. What prompted early explorers to risk their lives exploring uncharted seas?

5. What nation financed Columbus's voyage to prove his theory that by sailing west he could reach the Orient in the east?

6. Name the Italian explorer who offered proof that Columbus had in fact discovered a new world and not a new route to the Orient. How was he honored?

 Why were the early Americans called "Indians"?

Claiming a New World

With Columbus's discovery, Spain got off to a fast start in the exploration of the Americas. Other countries, however, soon saw that there was much to be gained by making claims in the New World. The resulting struggle for the lands of the New World helped shape the heritage of the United States.

Spanish Conquests

Spain's original goal had been to find the wealth of the Orient. Because Columbus had not found great treasures in the New World, a desire for Oriental trade remained; so Spain continued to search for a route around the Americas to the Far East. Such desire led to further exploration such as **Vasco de Balboa**'s crossing of the Isthmus of Panama (1513) and **Ferdinand Magellan**'s circumnavigation of the earth (1519-22). (*Circumnavigation* means "sailing around.") Even so, Spain continued to explore the Americas in hopes of finding treasure there.

Conquistadors—Spain's early expeditions to the New World remained primarily along the coastal region of Central and South America. However, they eventually pushed inland. The inland explorations were led by **conquistadors** (conquerors). The colonies established by these conquerors became the backbone of the Spanish empire in the New

World. The land they claimed extended over most of South and Central America and into what is today Florida, Texas, and the Southwestern United States. The two most famous conquistadors were **Hernando Cortés** and **Francisco Pizarro.**

Cortés landed in Mexico the same year that Magellan began his famous voyage. With a small army he marched to Tenochtitlán, the capital of the mighty Aztec empire. Montezuma, the Aztec king, welcomed Cortés, thinking that he was a god. Cortés, however, took Montezuma captive. He then defeated the Aztec warriors, destroyed their capital, and built on its site Mexico City.

Pizarro had accompanied Balboa on his journey across Panama and had later settled there. But on hearing of the wealth of the Incas in the Andes Mountains of South America, he organized an expedition and traveled south. With only 180 men he conquered the entire Inca empire.

Both the Aztecs and the Incas were brave and intelligent, but they could not stand against the Spanish guns, armor, and horses. By defeating these two great civilizations, the Spanish finally found what they wanted from the New World—treasures. The Spanish confiscated gold, silver, and gems from the Indians and then forced the Indians to mine more of the precious metals and stones. This wealth kept the Spanish interest primarily in Central and South America instead of North America, which lacked large deposits of these treasures.

Before the Aztecs, the Olmec, Toltec, and Mayan civilizations dominated Central America.

As we look at Latin America today, we can still see the strong influence of the Spanish culture there. The Spaniards implanted their language, customs, and the Roman Catholic religion in the New World. But to gain such a stronghold on those New World lands, the conquistadors were often cruel and ruthless. They killed or mistreated the Indians and plundered their wealth, often under the guise of converting them to Roman Catholicism. The Spanish also set up governments in the Americas controlled by officials called viceroys, and these men were often corrupt and self-seeking. The Spanish came to take as much as they could from the New World; they rarely sought to improve it and make it their home.

A Portuguese Agreement—Portugal began its voyages in search of the Orient before Spain did. With Vasco da Gama's trip around Africa to India in 1497-99, the Portuguese were actually successful first. But Spain's discovery and exploration of the New World made the two countries realize that if they both continued their exploration, they would have territorial conflicts. Since these two nations were Roman Catholic, they called in the pope to "settle" their growing disputes. In 1493 the pope drew an imaginary line, called the **Line of Demarcation** (DEE mahr KAY shun), dividing the world in half.

According to the pope's decree, Portugal was free to claim all the lands east of the line, and Spain was free to claim those to the west. The following year, the line was slightly altered when the two countries signed a treaty moving the line farther west. This alteration eventually allowed Portugal to claim the South American land of Brazil.

The pope's Line of Demarcation offered only a temporary solution, however. In his decree he had recognized only Spain and Portugal. It was only a matter of time before other European countries would rise up to challenge this Portuguese and Spanish supremacy in the New World.

English Rivalry

Throughout the 1500s, tension between Spain and England mounted. The Spanish objected to English intrusion into the New World, which they had claimed as their own. They were especially angered by the plundering activities of the English **"Sea Dogs."**

The Sea Dogs were a group of bold and daring English sea captains who struck at the heart of Spanish power. Acting as pirates, they disrupted the flow of gold and silver from the New World to Spain. They raided coastal towns, destroying Spanish harbors and ships. They also seized Spanish ships full of treasure and took their booty back to England.

The most courageous of the Sea Dogs was **Sir Francis Drake,** a favorite of **Queen Elizabeth I.** In 1577 he sailed down the coast of South America, plundering Spanish ports and capturing treasure ships. His ship was soon weighted with gold and silver. To escape the Spanish patrols, Drake sailed around South America, across the Pacific, and returned to England by sailing around the Cape of Good Hope. He duplicated the feat of Magellan, becoming the first Englishman to circumnavigate the earth.

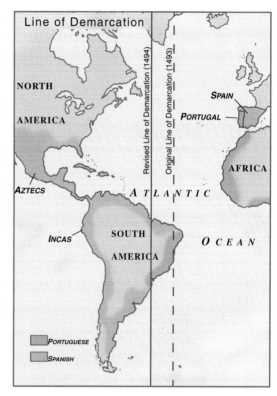

Drake became the hated enemy of the Spanish. They called him "the master thief" and "the dragon." But in England he became a popular hero. Queen Elizabeth I, who had secretly encouraged his pirating raids, now openly knighted him on board his ship, the *Golden Hind.*

Perhaps the most significant difference between Spain and England was their difference in religion. The Reformation, started by Martin Luther, had spread to England, and the nation had shifted toward Protestantism and had renounced the authority of the pope. Spain, on the other hand, was the bitter enemy of the Protestant Reformation. The king of Spain, Philip II, was the strongest champion of Roman Catholicism in Europe. He wished to restore England to the Catholic fold.

The "Rediscovery" of God's Word

At the same time that the explorers were discovering the New World, Europeans were also "rediscovering" God's Word. The invention of movable-type printing made copies of the Scripture readily available, and the revival of learning spawned by the Renaissance helped more people learn to read and write. As a result, people began to explore God's Word for themselves. This "exploration" revealed the errors taught by the Roman Catholic Church and encouraged a spiritual revival.

Almost twenty-five years after Columbus stood before Ferdinand and Isabella to proclaim that the earth was round, Martin Luther stood before their grandson Charles V to proclaim his faith in God's Word. Luther's actions turned men's attention back to the Bible as the source of authority and exposed the accepted, but false, teachings of Rome. Other preachers also began to proclaim the truth of God's Word. As is often the case, however, revival was followed by persecution for many European Christians. But God had provided the New World as a "way of escape." It seemed as though He had prepared America through the centuries for the time when His people would need to flee the religious persecution in Europe.

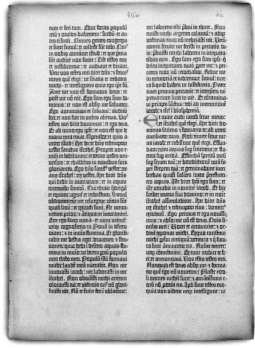

Movable-type printing made the Scripture available for all men to read.

To conquer his political and religious rival, Philip II organized a large invasion force known as the "Invincible Armada." In 1588 his proud fleet of 130 ships sailed toward England. The English navy, ably commanded by Sea Dogs such as Francis Drake, met the Spanish Armada in the English Channel. The lighter and faster English ships inflicted heavy damages on the Spanish galleons. The battered armada fled back to Spain, but fierce storms wrecked even more ships along the way. Only about half of the Spanish ships returned to Spain.

The English leaders praised God for destroying the powerful Spanish navy. Spain never recovered, and England eventually took her place as "the Mistress of the Seas." The weakening of Spanish sea power opened the door for English colonization in the New World. Spain could no longer threaten English activity in most of North America. Thus a Protestant land gained the opportunity to settle what would become the United States. Had it not been for the defeat of the Spanish Armada, Spain might have kept control of the New World, and North America might have become Spanish-speaking and Roman Catholic just as Central and South America are today.

French Activity

The French were also interested in the Americas. Because the Spanish had a strong hold on the Caribbean area, however, France concentrated on exploring parts of North America. Like Spain and other countries, France hoped to find a water passageway through America to the Far East. **Jacques Cartier** (KAHR tee AY), France's representative, sailed in search of such a waterway and, in the process, found the St. Lawrence River. His exploration of this important river of eastern Canada helped to give France a claim to a large section of North America. Other French explorers added to that claim. Most significant was **Robert de La Salle**'s claim to the Mississippi River and the land that it drained.

France was slow to develop its claims in the New World. The French were preoccupied by European affairs and did not find gold and silver as did their Spanish counterparts to the south. It was almost a century after the first French explorers laid claim to North America that the French began to explore the land in earnest.

Throughout the seventeenth century the French settled up and down the major rivers, especially the St. Lawrence and the Mississippi, and around the Great Lakes. The lakes and rivers served as "roads," opening up the interior to French traders. Trading tools, trinkets, clothing, axes, and pots for the skins of fox, moose, otter, wolverine, and beaver became a lucrative business for the French in the land that they called "New France."

The French did not establish well-organized towns as the English did. The most permanent signs of French civilization were the military forts, missions, and trading posts built at key places to protect the traders and trappers. These outposts—such as Quebec, Montreal, Detroit, and New Orleans—became centers of French culture and religion in the New World.

Because of the lack of opportunity for quick riches or prosperous farms, French colonies did not attract as many settlers as did the English. The French colonies were under the strict control of the French king. There was no local government or self-rule. In addition, the early traders monopolized the fur market, discouraging others who might have come to seek their fortune. Furthermore, beginning in the mid 1600s, only French Roman Catholics were allowed to settle in the French colonies. They excluded their own highly skilled, industrious group of Protestants, called **Huguenots** (HYOO guh NOTS). These French Protestants were eventually forced to flee France because of religious persecution. When they fled, many of them settled in English territory.

A few other countries, most notably the Netherlands, sent explorers to the New World in hopes of gaining land and treasures. Yet the Spanish, French, and English ended up with most of the claims. While the Spanish concentrated on mining the New World's riches and the French cornered the fur trade market, the British would take another approach to developing their land in the Americas.

SECTION REVIEW

1. Name two men who conquered outstanding Indian civilizations.

2. How did Spain and Portugal settle their disputes about territories in the New World?

3. What famous English sailor circumnavigated the globe?

4. What effect did the defeat of the Spanish Armada have on England and the future United States?

5. How did France profit from its New World claims?

 Why did French colonies not grow significantly in population?

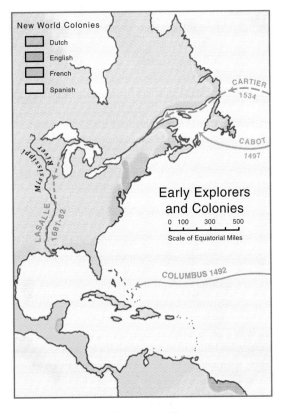

New World Colonies

- Dutch
- English
- French
- Spanish

CARTIER
1534

CABOT
1497

Mississippi River

LASALLE
1681–82

Early Explorers and Colonies

0   100   300   500

Scale of Equatorial Miles

COLUMBUS 1492

The English Come to Stay

The English had begun to explore the eastern coast of what is now the United States long before they defeated the Spanish Armada. In fact, the explorer **John Cabot** had laid claim to the Atlantic coast of North America for England in 1497 and 1498. In less than a century, some Englishmen were very interested in founding an English colony in this new land.

The Lost Colony

Although he did not go to the New World himself, **Sir Walter Raleigh,** an English nobleman, organized several colonizing expeditions to Roanoke Island off the coast of North Carolina. The first attempt, in 1585, failed because of poor leadership, Indian attacks, and famine. After one year the settlers returned home.

In 1587 Raleigh tried again. John White was placed in charge of the new group sent to found a colony. Shortly after they landed, White returned to England for supplies, but his return to America was delayed for three years by war with Spain. When he finally returned, the colony had disappeared. Along with the other colonists, White's daughter and baby granddaughter were missing. The baby, Virginia Dare, had been the first English baby born in the New World. The only clue to the disappearance of the colonists was the word *Croatoan* carved in a tree. It was thought that the nearby Croatan Indians had taken the people captive, but to this day no one knows what happened to the "Lost Colony" of Roanoke Island.

Jamestown

Nearly twenty years later the English established their first permanent colony. In May 1607 three small ships containing just over one hundred men and boys sailed into Chesapeake Bay. These colonists had been sent by a group of London merchants to establish a money-making colony. Full of hope, they sailed up the James River and selected a site near the Virginia coast to build a settlement. They named it **Jamestown** in honor of their king, James I.

Reconstructed Jamestown gives visitors an idea of how early settlers lived.

The settlers had trouble right from the start. Many were noblemen who considered themselves too good to work; they preferred to spend their time searching for gold. Those who labored to plant crops were discouraged when all their harvest was placed into a common storehouse. As a result, these men stopped working, and soon there was a shortage of food. Disease also took its toll among the settlers. Their drinking water was impure, and malaria-carrying mosquitoes bred in the swampy areas that surrounded Jamestown.

One man who helped Jamestown survive was **John Smith,** a rough, hard-talking soldier who demanded obedience. In keeping with the teaching of II Thessalonians 3:10, he declared that any man who did not work could not eat. Soon everyone was busy planting, hunting, or building.

When Smith was injured in a gunpowder explosion and had to return to England, problems mounted once again. There were Indian attacks, fires, and disease. But most devastating was a terrible famine that plagued the settlement during the winter of 1609-10. It was called the "starving time" because so many men died. The colonists ate anything they could find—horses, dogs, snakes, and even mice. In the first year and a half, six hundred men had settled in Jamestown; by the end of the "starving-time," only sixty were left.

In the spring of 1610, the few remaining settlers decided to abandon the settlement and return to England. Just after they had made this decision, however, ships arrived from England with more men and supplies. Encouraged, they decided to stay. Soon they

learned to plow and plant crops that could support the colony. Although it proved to be an unhealthful product, the tobacco plant, introduced by colonist John Rolfe, became a profitable money crop for the early colonists.

Their troubles were not over; there were more Indian attacks, more sickness, and more hunger. But the colony continued to grow. In 1608 Mistress Forrest and her maid Ann Burras became the first women in the colony. However, eleven years later several more women arrived from England. Many of these women married settlers and began to raise families. They were an important influence on the colony, for with the families came stability and morality that the colony had lacked before. Few women had come to the New World colonies of Spain and France, but the English quickly settled in to make this new land their home. Jamestown was the first success, but the English soon planted many successful colonies.

The Virginia **House of Burgesses,** the first representative government in America, began meeting in Jamestown in 1619. The burgesses, representatives of the people, gathered to pass laws for the good of the colony. In this way Jamestown provided the beginning of the American republic.

SECTION REVIEW

1. What Englishman sponsored two colonizing attempts on Roanoke Island? What happened to those colonies?

2. Why did the earliest Jamestown settlers not have enough food? What man helped the colony survive?

3. What event of 1609-10 almost ended the Jamestown colony?

4. What was the first body of representative government in America?

 How did the arrival of women change the colony of Jamestown?

SUMMARY

Columbus's discovery of America in 1492 was not the beginning of American history. Indians had lived in the Americas for centuries; the Mayas, Aztecs, and Incas had built great civilizations. Vikings had come to North America about five hundred years earlier, but Columbus opened the way for European exploration and colonization of the New World.

The Spanish took great interest in the gold, silver, and gems that they found in Central and South America. They concentrated their colonizing efforts in those regions, spreading their culture and Roman Catholicism. The French, also Roman Catholics, made their claims in North America, where their chief activity became the fur trade. The English grew as a sea power in the late 1500s and were free to explore and settle along the east coast of North America. In contrast to the Spanish and the French, the English were mostly Protestant. Thus, while Roman Catholicism claimed much of the New World, the English preserved a part of North America for more religious freedom and the influence of the Bible. Jamestown, Virginia, founded in 1607, was the first successful English settlement.

Chapter Review

People, Places, and Things to Remember

nomadic
Mayas
Aztecs
Incas
Vikings
Leif Ericson
Christopher Columbus
King Ferdinand
Queen Isabella

Amerigo Vespucci
Vasco de Balboa
Ferdinand Magellan
conquistadors
Hernando Cortés
Francisco Pizarro
Line of Demarcation
"Sea Dogs"
Sir Francis Drake

Queen Elizabeth I
Jacques Cartier
Robert de La Salle
Huguenots
John Cabot
Sir Walter Raleigh
Jamestown
John Smith
House of Burgesses

Review Questions

Answer the following questions.

1. On what date did Columbus discover America?
2. What were the names of Columbus's three ships?
3. What did Columbus name the island on which he first landed?
4. Which Indian group built a large capital in central Mexico?
5. Which Indian civilization grew in the Andes Mountains of South America?

Name the persons described below.

6. He came to America five hundred years before Columbus.
7. They helped Columbus finance his voyage.
8. The new lands were named after him instead of Columbus.
9. He crossed the Isthmus of Panama.
10. He captained the first ship that circumnavigated the earth.

Fill in the blank.

11. _____ was a conquistador who conquered the Aztecs.
12. The Line of Demarcation temporarily settled claim disputes between Spain and _____.
13. _____ explored the St. Lawrence River for France.
14. _____ gave the English claim to the Atlantic coast of North America.
15. In 1607 the first permanent English settlement, _____, was founded.

Questions for Discussion

16. What do you think might have happened to Columbus if he had failed to find land?
17. How might the colonization of the Americas have been different if the Spanish Armada had defeated England?

Settling the Thirteen Colonies

In the early 1600s Spain and France held or claimed most of North America. With the defeat of the Spanish Armada, however, England gained new boldness to challenge their claims. Although plagued by hardships, early attempts at settlement inspired other Englishmen to cross the Atlantic. England brought to the New World her customs, laws, and language; and she established thirteen colonies that would later separate from England to become the United States of America.

To Build a Colony

The Spanish and French had restricted those who could go to their New World colonies. The Spanish sent mainly noblemen, soldiers, slaves, and priests to their colonies, while the French permitted only approved citizens to go to New France. (Non-Catholics, such as the Huguenots, were among those who could not go.) In contrast, England allowed almost anyone who wanted to leave to go to its North American colonies. This opened up the New World to Englishmen who had many reasons for starting a life in that new land.

Reasons the English Came

There were many motives for the founding of the English colonies. In Jamestown and other settlements, the desire for profit was a major concern. Like the Spanish and French, many Englishmen came to the New World hoping to find gold and silver. Investors, with the same desire for personal gain, paid the expenses of new colonies settled by their countrymen. These Englishmen hoped that raw materials from the colonies would repay their investment and return to them a healthy profit.

Another reason for settlement was the chance to own land. In England, wealthy families held most of the land, and tradition kept a family from selling it to anyone else. Thus, unless Englishmen inherited land from relatives, they had little hope of owning any. Many were forced to rent farmland or work for a large landholder. In America, however, there was plenty of land. The opportunity to own land of their own drew many farmers to the New World.

Still another motive was the desire for employment. About the time the colonies were fully established, many English landowners started turning their farmland into pastures for sheep. The farmers who had rented these lands were evicted, and they found themselves with neither homes nor jobs. Many of these men found a new life in America, where they could farm or practice a trade without worrying about landlords.

The desire for political freedom was another important reason for English colonization. The English had gained some voice in their government. The *Magna Carta,* a document signed by King John in 1215, had limited the power of the English monarch and had guaranteed certain basic rights to the English people. In later years the English had gained more freedoms from their kings, and they had elected representatives to serve in the English Parliament, or legislature. However, in the early 1600s two kings, James I and Charles I, tried to strengthen royal power and restrict some of the people's freedoms. As a result, many Englishmen went to America, where they could be far away from the strict rule of these kings.

Although many of the earliest settlers desired political freedom, even more came to America in search of religious freedom. It was this reason for settlement that helped to give the colonial heritage of the United States a great distinction. English monarchs had established the Church of England, or Anglican

Original pages from the Fundamental Orders of Connecticut. This early document helped establish a pattern of freedom in America.

Church, as the official church of the land. Everyone in England supported that church with taxes, and everyone was supposed to belong to it. The Church of England had embraced the Protestant Reformation and had renounced the authority of the pope, but it kept some of the Roman Catholic practices. A number of Englishmen were dissatisfied with the church because they believed it did not fully follow biblical practice. Those who refused to support or belong to the church lost many privileges, and some were severely persecuted for their beliefs. Consequently, these Englishmen looked on the New World as a haven where they could freely worship God according to their beliefs.

One more reason that some of the English settlers came to America was a desire for adventure. The fact that the New World was unknown and there was much to explore made it attractive to some. However, the hardships usually overshadowed the excitement. As it turned out, many of America's early settlers who came to begin a new life found plenty of adventure, whether they wanted it or not.

Difficulties of Colonization

Moving to a new American colony in the 1600s and early 1700s was not easy. The men and women who decided to go had to face many challenges. Not only did they have to find a way to finance their voyage, but also they had to survive the long and uncomfortable trip across the Atlantic. Many had to endure hardships such as hunger and sickness while they were finding a way to make a living in a land that was still a wilderness. The early settlers also had to establish law and order among themselves and their colonial neighbors. Although promoters sometimes billed America as a paradise on earth, those who were led to the colonies by such promises soon found that the new land held many difficulties.

Financial Support and Colony Organization—Founding a new colony was not a cheap activity. It was not easy to raise the money needed for ships and supplies. For example, Sir Walter Raleigh risked his personal fortune to found a colony at Roanoke. In the end he had nothing to show for his efforts. Such prospects made the wealthy reluctant to sponsor colonization.

To provide a solution for the financial needs involved in settling a colony, English investors began to form **joint-stock companies.** These businesses, the forerunners of our modern corporations, were specifically developed for the purpose of helping colonies get started. Groups of Englishmen pooled their money to form a company. To get even more money, they allowed others to invest in the company by buying "shares of stock" at a certain price. Then they invested the money from the sale of stock in a colonization attempt in hopes that the colony would prosper and make money for the investors. This idea not only helped provide the initial cost of setting up the colony, but it also provided money to maintain the settlement awhile. If the venture failed, each investor lost only the amount he had put in. If it became profitable, the profits were split among the investors according to the number of shares each held.

One joint-stock company was the Virginia Company, formed by a group of Englishmen who wanted to get raw materials from the New World. The company was divided into two parts: the London group and the Plymouth group. It was the London group that financed Jamestown, the first permanent English settlement in North America. The Plymouth group never established a colony.

The king gave joint-stock companies a charter for establishing their colonies. The charter, which contained the regulations gov-

THE AMERICAN COLONIES

COLONY	SETTLED	TYPE
Virginia	Jamestown, 1607	Charter; became royal colony, 1624
Plymouth	Plymouth, 1620	Charter; absorbed by Massachusetts, 1691
Massachusetts	Salem, 1628 Boston, 1630	Charter; became royal colony, 1686
Rhode Island	Providence, 1636	Charter
Connecticut	Hartford, Wethersfield, & Windsor, 1633-36	Charter
New Hampshire	Odiorne's Point, 1623	Proprietary (John Mason); absorbed by Massachusetts, 1641; made separate royal colony, 1679
New York	Settled as New Netherland by Dutch; Fort Orange (Albany), 1624; conquered by English, 1664	Proprietary (Duke of York); became royal colony
New Jersey	A part of New Netherland; early settlement by Swedes	Proprietary (John, Lord Berkeley and Sir George Catteret); became royal colony, 1702
Maryland	St. Marys, 1633	Proprietary (George Calvert, Lord Baltimore; transferred to his son, Cecilius Calvert)
Pennsylvania	Philadelphia, 1682	Proprietary (William Penn)
Delaware	Settled as New Sweden by Swedes; Fort Christina (Wilmington), 1638; annexed by New Netherland, 1655; conquered by English, 1664	Proprietary (the duke of York transferred it to William Penn, 1682); separated from Pennsylvania, 1704
North Carolina South Carolina	Settlers from Virginia moved near Albemarle Sound, 1654; Charles Town (Charleston), 1670	Proprietary (eight English nobles received grant, 1663); separated to form two colonies, 1712; both became royal colonies, 1729
Georgia	Savannah, 1733	Proprietary (James Oglethorpe); became royal colony, 1751

erning where the colony would be located and how it would be administered, was the official permission for founding the colony. Thus, colonies founded under these conditions were called **charter colonies.** There were also two other kinds of colonies. **Proprietary colonies** were those which had been given to individuals or groups by the king. The men who received these colonies from the king were called proprietors, and they could govern their colonies as they pleased. The king took control of some of the colonies. These **royal colonies** fell under the direct supervision of the king.

Hardships of the Early Settlers—If the colonist survived the hazardous voyage to

America, he probably faced many dangers in the new land. Food and shelter were his immediate needs. Those who lacked adequate nourishment and protection often did not survive the long and cold months of winter. Over half of the original Jamestown colonists in 1607 died of scurvy, fever, or exposure before they had spent three months in the New World. Casualties such as these were common in the early years of settlement.

Indians were another problem. Although some were friendly, many began to turn against the white man when they saw he was taking their land. In 1622 an Indian attack wiped out over three hundred settlers around Jamestown, and in 1675-76 Indians raided and burned many settlements in Massachusetts and surrounding colonies. The Indian threat had lessened in the more populous colonies by 1700, but regions in the southern colonies and along the western frontier remained in danger.

With these dangers came many other difficulties as the colonists learned to support themselves in a new land. But as these people learned to deal with the challenges of life in the colonies, they developed their own culture and abilities. Separated from life in England, these Americans would one day found their own new nation.

SECTION REVIEW

1. How did English colonists differ from Spanish or French colonists?

2. List six reasons that English colonists went to America.

3. Name the three types of colonies.

4. List at least three hazards faced by the early colonists.

 What benefits did a joint-stock company offer to potential investors in a colony?

The New England Colonies

Religious freedom was the dominant factor in the founding of the New England colonies. Many English Christians were unhappy with the Church of England. They believed that it was still too much like the Roman Catholic Church, whose practices they thought were unscriptural.

Among those who disagreed with some of the practices of the Anglican Church were the **Puritans.** They called themselves *Puritans* because they hoped to purify the church from various Roman Catholic practices and ceremonies. They believed that laymen should be able to participate in the governing of the church, and they stressed the authority of Christ over that of the church. A second group, called **Separatists,** did not believe that the Anglican Church could be "purified." As a result, they chose to separate themselves from the church and to hold their own worship services.

Plymouth Colony

Because of persecution, a group of Separatists left their village in Scrooby, England, and went to the Netherlands, where their religious beliefs would be tolerated. Led by their pastor, John Robinson, they settled in Leyden, Holland, in 1609. After a few years the parents in this group became concerned that their children were learning the worldly ways of the Dutch children and were losing sight of their English heritage.

These Separatists, who are known in history as the Pilgrims, decided to go to the New World, where they could live as Englishmen but still have religious freedom. Too poor to finance such a venture themselves, they arranged for financial support from a group of English businessmen. These businessmen were to receive any profits the colony made in its first seven years. The Pilgrims were also to receive permission from the London group of the Virginia Company to settle in Virginia, just north of Jamestown.

In September, 1620, the Pilgrims set sail from Plymouth, England, in a ship named the *Mayflower*. With them went other Englishmen who wanted to share in founding the new colony. Since these people were not Separatists, the Pilgrims called them "Strangers." The two groups got along fairly well because both the Pilgrims and the Strangers believed in religious freedom and because both groups had skills that the colony needed in order to survive.

After more than two stormy months at sea, the *Mayflower* arrived in America. Because of the storms, however, it had landed far north of its destination. Instead of being just north of Jamestown, it was off Cape Cod in what is today Massachusetts. The Pilgrim leaders were troubled; they had no authority to settle that far north. With winter coming on, there was no time to sail south to where they had originally intended to settle. So before leaving the ship to begin their new colony, the men gathered to write and sign an agreement calling for a government to be formed in Massachusetts. Called the **Mayflower Compact,** this agreement became the first document providing for self-government in the New World. Thus it was an important contribution to the heritage of the American republic that would later arise.

After electing one of their leaders, **John Carver,** to be governor, the Pilgrims began to build their colony. They named it **Plymouth,** after the port in England from which they had sailed. Like those at James-

This statue of a Pilgrim stands in Plymouth as a reminder of the colonists' faith and determination.

town, the Plymouth settlers had a difficult first winter. Since they had landed at Plymouth in December, there had been no time to plant crops. Weak, sick, and hungry, nearly half the colonists, including Governor Carver, died the first winter.

When spring came, however, things began to improve. An Indian named Squanto (SKWAHN toh), who had learned English from coastal fishermen, showed the Pilgrims how to plant corn and squash. He helped them start a trading industry with the other Indians, who were of the Wampanoag (WAM puh NOH ahg) tribe. For times when the Indians were not so friendly, Miles Standish, one of the Strangers, trained the men to defend their colony.

Despite hardships, the Pilgrims had much to be thankful for at the end of the first year in Plymouth. They had survived and prospered. Their new governor, **William Bradford,** called for a celebration of thanksgiving to God, following the biblical example set forth in Deuteronomy 26:10—"I have brought the firstfruits of the land, which thou, O Lord, hast given me." They invited the Indians to this feast, and for three days the settlers and their Indian friends rejoiced together.

Why did Plymouth do so much better than Jamestown in its first year, despite the greater harshness of the winter? One reason was that entire families came to Plymouth, whereas Jamestown had only men for its first twelve years. The presence of families forced the colonists to make the area livable for women and children, thus civilizing the colony more quickly; also, the men had to work to provide not only for themselves but also for their wives and children.

through difficult times. For these reasons, Americans should be grateful for these forefathers.

Massachusetts Bay

Puritan attempts to reform the Church of England met with little success. Weary of the rising tide of persecution and increased taxation, twenty-six Puritan businessmen decided to follow the example of the Pilgrims. They formed a company, the **Massachusetts Bay Company,** to establish a colony in America. After receiving a charter from the king, the

Another reason was that the Pilgrims were all used to hard work; none of them refused to work, as some of the "noblemen" at Jamestown had. But the most important reason was the motives of the colonists. Those at Plymouth had come for religious freedom; they had devoted their lives to God, and they lived to be His servants. They wanted this new land to be their home where they could serve and worship God. Those at Jamestown were not so dedicated, and they let their selfish desires hinder the colony's welfare.

By 1627 the Plymouth Colony was doing well. The settlers had repaid their debt to the English businessmen who had sponsored them. They were finally on their own, and their labor in agriculture and business was supplying their needs.

Plymouth was never a large or rich colony. In fact, after seventy years it became part of its larger neighbor, the Massachusetts Bay Colony. As a result, Plymouth did not become one of the colonies that formed the United States. However, the Pilgrims became a major part of America's heritage because of the example they set. They practiced religious toleration; they set up a responsible self-government; and they worked hard, persevering

To stay true to the original colonial construction, this thatcher works to restore a roof on a building at Plymouth Plantation.

leaders of the Massachusetts Bay Company began recruiting settlers.

In 1630 a fleet of seventeen ships carrying nearly one thousand settlers arrived in Massachusetts Bay. These settlers joined other Puritans who had previously founded the town of Salem. Soon new towns and villages such as Boston, New Towne (later called Cambridge), Watertown, and Dorchester began to thrive. The colony grew rapidly during the 1630s as over fifteen thousand new colonists arrived, giving this period in the colony's history the title "the Great Migration."

Like the Pilgrims, the Puritans came to the New World seeking religious freedom, and they wanted to make a good home for themselves and for their children. For the most part, the Puritans who came were wealthier and better educated than the Pilgrims. Learning from the mistakes of others, they were able to bring many supplies with them from England. Among those who came were merchants and craftsmen, doctors and preachers. Because the Puritans believed the Bible to be the Word of God and stressed that God spoke to men through it, they valued education as a means of learning to read and obey Scripture. They had more college-educated settlers than did any other colony. Most of the colonists, however, were farmers.

The charter gave to the stockholders, or "freemen," full powers to govern the colony. Of the original twenty-six stockholders, only twelve were actually interested in going to America. Those twelve bought the shares of the other fourteen and took the charter and control of the colony with them to America. Thus all those in charge of the company governed the colony from America, and England did not interfere during the early years of the colony.

Not everyone who eventually settled in the Massachusetts Bay Colony was a Puritan. Puritans were not even in the majority. Yet it was the Puritans who established the government, built the churches, and set up the schools. The Puritan leaders had a high goal for their settlement. They wanted to establish an ideal state based on biblical principles, one that would be a model for other governments. Their leader, Governor **John Winthrop,**

This model of an Indian dwelling reminds visitors to Plymouth that other people inhabited the land prior to the Pilgrims' arrival.

hoped that Massachusetts would be "a city set upon a hill" to bear witness to all the world of the wisdom of biblical government as they interpreted it.

Because of this aim, church and state leaders worked closely together. The state, in an attempt to assist the church in promoting godliness in society, required everyone to attend church—even non-Puritans. Likewise, the state enforced a strict standard of moral conduct on everyone in the community, on the unsaved as well as the saved.

The leaders of the colony did not want to let control of the colony fall into the hands of the ungodly. Thus only church members were given the right to vote. Others were free to live in the community as long as they did not disrupt Puritan teaching or authority. In 1634 the colony became too big for all the voters to participate effectively in every decision. It was decided that each town would elect two delegates to attend the General Court, which governed the colony. This representative body functioned much like the House of Burgesses in Virginia.

Puritanism, firmly planted in Massachusetts Bay, soon spread to other areas of New England. As the population increased, many settlers went out from this colony to establish new ones. Some left to seek better farmland, where they could enjoy greater prosperity; others left to find more religious liberty. They did not wish to, or were not allowed to, remain in the Massachusetts colony because they disagreed with the way the colony was run. As new colonies were established, however, they could not help resembling in some way the "mother" colony of Massachusetts Bay.

Rhode Island

One of the first to disagree openly with the Puritan leaders was **Roger Williams,** a pastor in Salem, Massachusetts. Although he was generally a Puritan in belief, Williams disagreed with them on three points. First, he believed that the church and state should be separate, that is, that the government should not try to force a particular religion on society. This idea ran directly against the whole purpose of the Massachusetts Bay Colony. The Puritan leaders wanted their colony to be governed by the Bible as they interpreted it. Second, Williams believed that the Indians owned all the land in the colonies. Thus the colonists had no right to stay unless they paid the Indians for the land. This, too, most Puritan leaders denied. Finally, he believed that the Puritans should not try to "purify" the

The Governor's Wife

She described herself in a letter as "a fierce spirit, unwilling to submit to the will of God." Yet two sentences later she honestly asserted her fervent desire that the will of God be done. Such was Margaret Winthrop, the wife of John Winthrop, the first governor of Massachusetts.

Margaret was born in England in 1591. When she was twenty-six, her father was murdered. The next year—on the heels of that tragedy—Margaret married John Winthrop, a

Church of England from within, but, like the Pilgrims, should leave the church.

In 1635 Williams was brought to trial for "newe and dangerous opinions." To preserve the peace, the Puritans exiled him from Massachusetts. Puritan leaders offered to let him stay through the winter. But fearing that he would be kidnapped and sent back to England, he left.

He spent the bitterly cold winter with the Narragansett Indians, who considered him a friend. In the spring he traveled south to Narragansett Bay, where he bought a tract of land from the Indians and founded a village. He named it Providence as a testimony of God's protection, guidance, and comfort in his lawyer who was no stranger to sorrow himself. At the age of thirty-one, he was already twice a widower. His second wife had died after less than a year of marriage. Along with her husband, Margaret gained a country estate in England called Groton Manor. She also gained four children from John's first marriage, children she would love as her own. She and John also had eight more children, but only four lived to adulthood.

Life at Groton Manor was prosperous but lonely. John's law practice kept him in London most of the time. The love letters the two exchanged give us great insight into the times in which they lived. In fact, Margaret's letters have made her famous. In them she beautifully expresses the proper foundation for love: "I have many reasons to make me love thee, whereof I will name two, because thou lovest God, and secondly because that thou lovest me. If these two are wanting all the rest would be eclipsed."

As John contemplated moving to the New World, Margaret constantly assured him of her support and of her willingness to give up all the wealth, security, and familiarity of home. When he did finally decide to go to Massachusetts, Winthrop left his wife behind for a year until he could get settled.

On November 4, 1631, Margaret arrived in Boston. She was greeted with a six-cannon salute and a day of feasting and thanksgiving. Margaret Winthrop would spend the last sixteen years of her life in Massachusetts. During most of that time her husband was governor of the colony. There were, no doubt, many difficult and exciting times. Her duties as the governor's wife were numerous, not to mention her duties as a mother. Yet she seems to have handled it all exceedingly well. Those who knew her best—her husband and children—never recorded a word of complaint. Often they wrote to her seeking advice and aid. Always, it seems, she was ready to help.

In 1647, after one day of illness, Margaret Winthrop died. In less than a year, John Winthrop passed away too. God had obviously provided John Winthrop with the right wife for the challenge of establishing a Puritan colony in the New World. In her life Margaret had learned to submit her will and could say with confidence, "As for God, his way is perfect" (Ps. 18:30).

---

time of trouble. Williams was determined that his settlement would have religious freedom, including separation of church and state. He welcomed all, regardless of their religion, to settle nearby. Several of the people from his old church in Salem joined him.

By 1644 the English Parliament recognized four settlements, including Providence, as the colony of Rhode Island. Soon the colony drew up a constitution guaranteeing that the government would have authority "only in civil [nonreligious] things."

Connecticut

Unlike that of Rhode Island, the settling of Connecticut did not arise from controversy.

Despite the strict rule in Massachusetts Bay, settlers kept arriving, and that colony was soon crowded. As a result, several settlers decided to move west to the fertile Connecticut River Valley. There they settled Windsor (1633) and Wethersfield (1635). In 1636 **Thomas Hooker,** a pastor in New Towne, Massachusetts, received permission to move. He journeyed with his congregation to Connecticut and founded the town of Hartford. In 1639 these three newly settled villages merged to form the colony of Connecticut, naming Hartford as its capital. Connecticut, like Massachusetts and Rhode Island, would survive as a colony and later help form the United States.

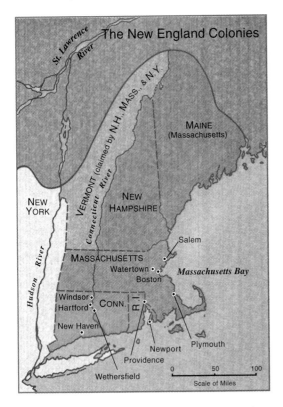

The New England Colonies

Scale of Miles 0 50 100

In 1639 the settlements in Connecticut adopted a plan of union called the **Fundamental Orders of Connecticut.** This document is usually regarded as the first written constitution, or plan of government, drawn up in America. According to the orders, the authority behind government lay in the "free consent of the people." For the most part, Connecticut's government copied that of Massachusetts. One main difference was that the orders did not make church membership a requirement for voting. The orders became a model for future state constitutions and the United States Constitution of 1787.

New Hampshire

Besides moving south and west into Rhode Island and Connecticut, Massachusetts colonists also moved north into New Hampshire and Maine. These areas were proprietary colonies for a while, but they experi-

enced little success. As the number of Puritans increased in this region, Massachusetts extended its control over the settlements established there. In 1679 several towns received a royal charter for New Hampshire, making it a separate colony from Massachusetts. Thus New Hampshire was one of the four New England colonies that would later become one of the thirteen original states of the new nation. Maine did not become a separate colony but remained a part of the Massachusetts colony until 1820, when it became a state. Vermont, also in this New England area, was largely under French influence until New York and New Hampshire were able to gain some control. Like Maine, Vermont never became one of the thirteen English colonies, but in 1791 it became the first new state added to the union.

SECTION REVIEW

1. What was the main reason for the founding of the New England colonies?

2. How did the Puritans and the Separatists differ?

3. Why did the Pilgrims believe it necessary to write the Mayflower Compact? What is the significance of the document?

4. Who had the right to vote in the Massachusetts Bay Colony?

5. List Roger Williams's three criticisms of the Massachusetts Bay Colony. What colony was formed as a result of his belief, and what was its first settlement?

6. What plan of government is considered the first written constitution drawn up in America?

7. List the four New England colonies that eventually became states.

 How were the governments of Massachusetts Bay and Connecticut different? Which was more like the present American government?

The Middle Colonies

New England was settled primarily by the English, who shared a common heritage. Unlike New England, several of the middle colonies were influenced first by other nations. The Dutch and the Swedes had claimed and settled part of this region decades before the arrival of the first Englishmen. By the time England gained control, there was a diversity of language, ideas, religion, and culture in these colonies. However, they did share the common goal of carving out a civilization from the wilderness. Gradually their differing cultures blended into a common American culture.

New York and New Jersey

An Englishman named Henry Hudson explored for both the Netherlands and England. While sailing for the Netherlands in 1609, Hudson discovered the river that now bears his name, and he sailed up it to the present site of Albany, New York. His exploration gave the Dutch claim to the region that became the colony of New York, although then they called it **New Netherland.**

Dutch efforts to settle in the New World were primarily directed by government-approved companies. Merchants organized these companies to establish settlements from which they hoped to profit.

In 1624 a Dutch ship brought thirty families from the Netherlands to America. They landed on Manhattan Island (now part of New York City), but most settled up the Hudson River near the present site of Albany. Two years later a settlement was begun on Manhattan Island. The governor of the colony, **Peter Minuit** (MIN yoo wit), purchased Manhattan from the Indians. The town that grew there, later called New Amsterdam, became the capital of New Netherland.

The Dutch promised large grants of land to anyone who could bring fifty settlers to the New World. Those who received these large grants were called **patroons.** People who could not bring fifty settlers received as much land as they could farm themselves. Although many of the farmers were successful, the development of the new land did not bring as much profit as the Dutch investors had hoped. Soon the Netherlands began to neglect its colony, sending few new colonists and offering little aid.

The English Take Control—The Dutch settlements along the Hudson River, however, made the English envious. At New Amsterdam, the Dutch had one of the finest harbors on the Atlantic coast. Moreover, New Netherland stood between New England and the southern colonies, thereby preventing England from controlling the entire Atlantic coastal region.

John Cabot had claimed the Atlantic coast of North America for England in 1497. Before long, England pressed her claim that New Netherland was her rightful territory. In 1664 the king of England gave the land that was the Dutch colony to his brother, the **duke of York,** as a proprietary colony. The duke sent warships to capture the colony. The settlers in New Amsterdam, who were already dissatisfied with the Dutch administration, saw the fleet and decided to surrender. Thus this Dutch colony passed peacefully into the hands of the English, who renamed it New York.

The Founding of New Jersey—The duke of York gave the southern portion of his new territory to two of his friends: **Sir George Carteret** and **Lord John Berkeley.** In order to attract settlers to their new colony of New Jersey, they offered cheap land, full religious liberty, and a measure of self-government. Trouble plagued the colony for a time, and it was divided into East and West Jersey. It was later reunited as a royal province under the direct rule of the English king. The name New Jersey comes from the island of Jersey in the

English Channel, of which Sir George Carteret was governor.

Pennsylvania

Pennsylvania, like Plymouth, was established because of religious persecution in England. The Society of Friends, commonly known as the **Quakers,** separated from the Church of England. They believed in and practiced few of the accepted religious ceremonies of the Church of England, but they did practice many "good works." They viewed all men as equal regardless of race, color, or social status. They opposed war and refused to take oaths. Unfortunately many trusted in these works for their salvation, and they believed that they had an "inner light" that told them God's will apart from the Bible. These beliefs made them unpopular both in England and in the American colonies.

One Quaker, **William Penn,** came from a wealthy English family. King Charles II owed

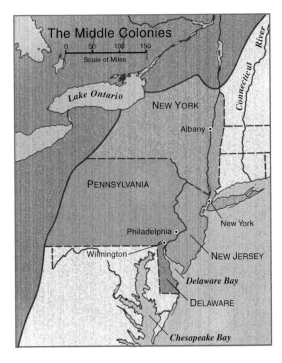

Penn's father a large sum of money. When Penn's father died, the debt was to be paid to William. In 1681 the king agreed to pay Penn by giving him a large piece of land in America. Penn called it "Sylvania," Latin for "woodland"; the king called it "Penn's Sylvania." Although the land was Penn's by royal grant, Penn wisely bought the land from the Indians. In doing so he made friends with them and avoided the attacks that plagued other colonies.

Penn hoped to use the proprietary colony to provide a haven for himself and his persecuted Quaker friends. He referred to his colony as a "Holy Experiment." His goal was to establish a colony ruled by "brotherly love," the fruit of which would bring peace and prosperity. He began by setting up laws granting religious freedom to all who believed in one God. There was no established church to obstruct people from worshiping God in

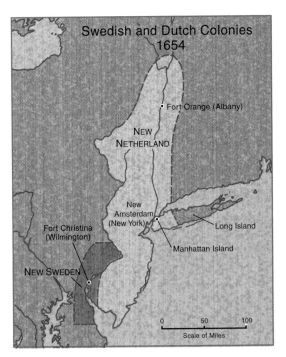

their own way. This freedom attracted other persecuted religious groups from Europe. Many of the people who came to Pennsylvania were from Germany. They called themselves *Deutsche* ("Germans"). Others, however, called them the "Pennsylvania Dutch."

With many industrious people and more fertile land than that of New England, Pennsylvania became the most prosperous colony in North America. By 1776 its capital, Philadelphia ("city of brotherly love"), was a bustling city. Only one city in the entire British empire, London, was larger.

William Penn practiced the good works he preached by establishing good relations with the Indians of Pennsylvania.

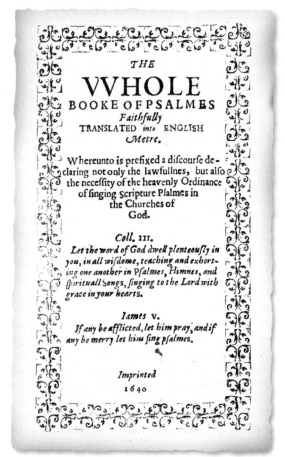

The Bay Psalm Book *became an important tool for colonial worship.*

Delaware

Penn's land also included what is now Delaware. This region had originally been settled by the Swedes. In 1638 they founded Fort Christina (now Wilmington, Delaware) and named it after the Swedish queen. Their colony, known as **New Sweden,** later passed into the hands of the Dutch and then to the English. The duke of York granted this territory to Penn in 1682. Although the settlements of Delaware were later allowed a separate assembly, they remained under the governor of Pennsylvania until 1776.

1. How were the people that settled the middle colonies different from those in New England?

2. Why did England want New Netherland? What nobleman was responsible for taking it?

3. Name the two men to whom New Jersey was given.

4. Why did King Charles II give the territory of Pennsylvania to William Penn? What religious group did Penn hope to protect?

5. What colony's control passed from the Swedish to the Dutch to the English?

 Why was "Philadelphia" a good name for the capital of Penn's new colony?

The Southern Colonies

The five southern colonies—Virginia, Maryland, North Carolina, South Carolina, and Georgia—were, like New England, settled mainly by the English. While they shared some concerns and characteristics with the middle colonies and New England, the southern colonies developed differently.

Virginia

In the last chapter we looked at the early English attempts to settle Virginia. The first permanent settlement was Jamestown, but this settlement did not live up to the high expectations of its financial backers. Instead of providing quick profits, the colony became a financial burden for the profit-minded company. Hunger, disease, dissension, and Indian attacks drained the life from the colony.

From the Indians the Virginia colonists learned how to grow tobacco. John Rolfe, the husband of an Indian woman named Pocahontas, cultivated tobacco and sold it in England, where tobacco products were popular. (People in that day were less concerned with the health dangers of tobacco, although it had already been called "a noxious weed.") As the demand for tobacco products increased, the tobacco industry grew. Tobacco became

This painting records a romantic version of the marriage of Pocahontas and John Rolfe.

Scenes from Williamsburg, Virginia: The Governor's Mansion shows early colonial architecture and graceful living while another location displays the more common task of weaving.

the one major crop of the Virginia colonists and eventually was so valuable that it sometimes served as money for payment of taxes and wages.

By the 1620s Virginia was a prospering colony. However, bickering among the leaders of the London Company made the king of England displeased with the way the colony was being managed. As a result he revoked the company's charter and made Virginia a royal colony. The king then took control and appointed a colonial governor and council. However, he allowed the House of Burgesses (the colonial representative assembly) to continue to meet.

Throughout the seventeenth century, settlers branched out from the original Jamestown settlement. New towns and plantations were established. When fire destroyed much of Jamestown toward the end of the century, the capital of the colony was moved to Williamsburg, just a few miles away. This colonial city became a leading center of government and culture among the thirteen colonies.

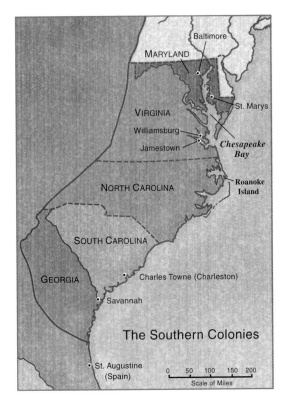

The Southern Colonies

Maryland

Roman Catholics, as well as Separatists, Puritans, and Quakers, suffered persecution in seventeenth-century England. However, Charles I, the English king who ruled from 1625 to 1649, was sympathetic to the Catholics. He gave the land of Maryland as a gift to his friend **George Calvert,** known as Lord Baltimore. Calvert, a Roman Catholic, wanted a place where other Catholics could be free from the persecution they faced in England. He also wanted to make money by investing in a colony in the New World. The king named the territory Maryland in honor of his queen, Henrietta Maria.

George Calvert died before he could begin his settlement, but his son **Cecilius Calvert,** also called Lord Baltimore, led the first settlers across the Atlantic. In 1634 they founded

a town called St. Marys. According to the king's charter, Calvert was to be the proprietor of Maryland, but all the landowners were to have a part in making the laws.

Soon Protestants also began to settle, and eventually they outnumbered the Catholics three to one. The Catholics began to fear that they might face new persecution in their own colony. So in 1649 the lawmakers passed the Act of Toleration, which guaranteed religious freedom to all who believed in the Trinity. This was the first written law of religious freedom in the colonies, although Rhode Island already had unwritten laws of religious freedom.

The Carolinas

After a period of turmoil and civil war in England, Charles II came to the English throne. He wished to reward those who had been loyal to the royal family during the time of trouble. In 1663 he granted to eight English noblemen a tract of land that they named Carolina after the king, whose name in Latin was *Carolus.*

In 1670 a large group of settlers began the settlement of Albemarle Point. Ten years later they moved to a better site nearby, founding the port city of Charles Towne (now Charleston, South Carolina). Because of its fine harbor, the city became an important colonial commercial center. Soon other settlers were attracted to the region. French Huguenots, Scots-Irish, and Englishmen from the islands in the West Indies moved to the new colony.

A much smaller group settled on the Carolina coast far to the north, near Virginia. These distant settlements grew, but they had little in common. In 1712, less than fifty years after receiving its charter, the colony of Carolina was divided: the northern portion became North Carolina; the southern portion, South Carolina.

Both of the Carolinas followed Virginia's example of raising a large cash crop. Tobacco became that crop in North Carolina, but South Carolina found its coastal lands and climate to be suitable for growing rice. **Indigo,** a plant from which a popular blue dye could be made, added a second cash crop for South Carolina.

Georgia

Georgia, the last of the thirteen colonies, had an unusual beginning. Because the English government worried about the Spanish forts in Florida, Parliament wanted to use the land between the Carolinas and Florida as a buffer zone to keep the Spanish at a distance. While Parliament was considering this idea, a wealthy English general named **James Oglethorpe** (OH gul THORP) asked for permission to found a colony. He was unhappy with the way debtors were treated in England. If a man owed a debt, he could be thrown into prison until he paid. But if he were in prison, he could not work to pay off the debt. Oglethorpe thought that such men should be allowed to work and have an opportunity to

Indigo became an important cash crop in South Carolina.

31

repay their debts. King George II finally gave Oglethorpe and some other trustees title to the new colony of Georgia, which could both serve as a new home for debtors and provide protection for the colonies that lay farther north.

Parliament agreed to Oglethorpe's plan, and it even contributed money for the project. The first settlers arrived in 1733 and founded the city of Savannah under Oglethorpe's direction. Oglethorpe worked hard to ensure the colony's success. He built forts along the coastal islands for protection from Spanish attack, and in 1742 a Georgia force defeated a small Spanish force that came against them. Realizing that the Creek Indians, a powerful tribe in West Georgia, might also be a threat, Oglethorpe sought to maintain peace with them.

Only a few debtors ever settled in Georgia, defeating Oglethorpe's original purpose, but other Europeans came to the colony.

After only a few years Georgia became a royal colony and began to resemble the other southern colonies.

SECTION REVIEW

1. What crop became the staple crop of Virginia?

2. What city became the center of government in Virginia after Jamestown?

3. Who was the proprietor of Maryland? What was the first settlement?

4. What was the first written law of religious freedom in the colonies?

5. What colonies had eight English noblemen as proprietors?

6. For what two reasons was Georgia founded? By whom was it founded?

 Why did the people of Maryland believe they needed a written law of religious freedom?

SUMMARY

The English colonists came to America for many reasons—profit, land ownership, employment, political freedoms, religious freedoms, and adventure. They established the original colonies as either charter colonies, proprietary colonies, or royal colonies.

The first colony in New England was Plymouth, established by Separatists in 1620. Plymouth eventually merged with Massachusetts, a strong colony built with Puritan leadership. Colonists from Massachusetts helped to build three other New England colonies: Rhode Island, Connecticut, and New Hampshire.

The Dutch originally settled New York and New Jersey as their own colony of New Netherland, and Swedes settled Delaware as New Sweden. However, the English took control of these colonies in 1664. Those colonies, along with William Penn's Pennsylvania, became the middle colonies.

The southern colonies found much of their prosperity by growing cash crops of tobacco or rice and indigo. Jamestown, Virginia, was the first permanent English settlement in North America, and Lord Baltimore founded Maryland as a colony that would welcome Roman Catholics. North Carolina and South Carolina were one proprietary colony until their division in 1712, and James Oglethorpe tried to make Georgia a refuge for debtors.

Chapter Review

People, Places, and Things to Remember

joint-stock companies
charter colonies
proprietary colonies
royal colonies
Puritans
Separatists
Mayflower Compact
John Carver
Plymouth
William Bradford

Massachusetts Bay
  Company
John Winthrop
Roger Williams
Thomas Hooker
Fundamental Orders of
  Connecticut
New Netherland
Peter Minuit
patroons

duke of York
Sir George Carteret
Lord John Berkeley
Quakers
William Penn
New Sweden
George Calvert
Cecilius Calvert
indigo
James Oglethorpe

Review Questions

Name these twos and threes.

1. Three kinds of colonies
2. Two religious groups that settled in the Massachusetts area
3. Two important documents for colonial government
4. Two countries that colonized the middle colonies before England
5. Three important southern colonial crops

Match each man with the appropriate colony.

6. Cecilius Calvert
7. James Oglethorpe
8. William Bradford
9. Roger Williams
10. John Winthrop
11. Thomas Hooker

  a. Plymouth
  b. Massachusetts
  c. Rhode Island
  d. Connecticut
  e. Maryland
  f. Georgia

Name the colony most closely associated with the following:

12. Quakers
13. Roman Catholics
14. patroons
15. debtors

Questions for Discussion

16. How was the joint-stock company like modern corporations?
17. Why was Plymouth Colony important to America's heritage even though it did not survive as a separate colony?

3

Colonial Society and Government

eople of all kinds left Europe to come to the British colonies. Preachers, paupers, wealthy landowners, merchants, thieves, and plenty of farmers were among the thousands who sailed the ocean to find their new home. The average crossing took over four months, and the passengers usually spent their time in crowded, damp conditions. No doubt many of these new colonists took their minds off their present discomforts by thinking about the new land that awaited them. What would life be like in the colonies?

Occupations: How the Colonists Made Their Living

Some settlers came prepared for what they found in the New World. Those who settled in Plymouth and Massachusetts Bay, for example, generally brought necessary materials, tools, and supplies. They found the land and climate of New England similar to that of their home in England. Most of those enroute to America, however, were unaware of the variety of land and climate that the colonies would hold. Plains and mountains, forests and grasslands, warm and cold climates—all were

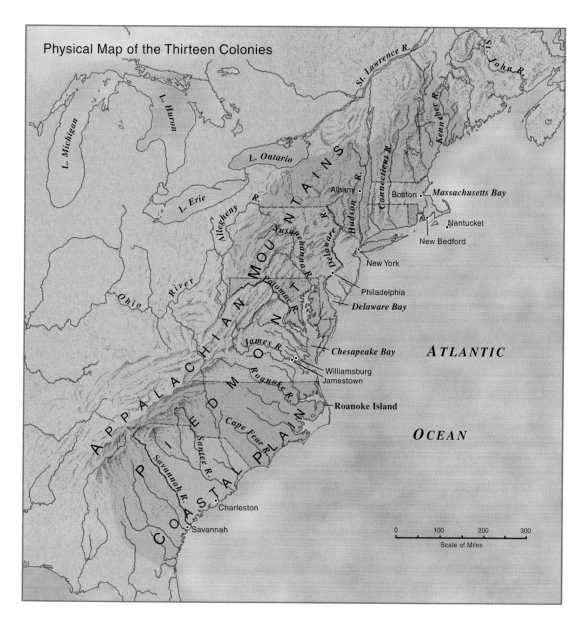

Physical Map of the Thirteen Colonies

available in this land they were to settle. In many areas of the colonies, these people had to learn to adjust to a land that was different from their homelands in Europe.

The climate and resources of the land were very important to the early settlers.

Today at our local grocery store, we may buy foods brought from many parts of the country or even imported from other countries. In our department stores, we may buy merchandise manufactured all over the world. The colonists, however, had to depend mainly on what would grow on their own land or what they could make from other available materials to meet their other needs. This was especially true for the farmers, who made up over ninety percent of the colonists. The vast majority of these were **subsistence farmers,** who were able to raise just enough crops and livestock to provide their families with adequate food and clothing. Even colonists who were not farmers themselves had to depend on locally grown food, and many also used local resources for their work—carpenters and shipbuilders used trees from nearby forests, and smiths often used metals from nearby deposits.

Because geography influenced the lifestyle of the colonists, definite patterns arose in the three colonial regions we have already learned about—New England, the middle colonies, and the southern colonies. As we learned in Chapter 2, colonies within each

Fishing and whaling supported much of the New England economy.

of these regions shared some similar features in their founding and settlement. They also shared some similarities in the climate and resources that influenced the activities of the colonists. Although all three regions would eventually band together as the United States, they developed their own special characteristics.

The New England Colonies

The geography of New England is rough and cold in comparison to the other regions. Although a wide coastal plain extends along most of the Atlantic coast, only a narrow piece extends into New England. As a result, the remaining landscape bulges with hills and low mountains. The region lacks not only flat farmland but also fertile and abundant soil. It has only a thin, rocky cover of soil that makes farming difficult. In addition, New England has only a short growing season and long, cold, snowy winters.

Because New England's geography was not favorable for extensive farming, nearly all the colonists who were farmers were subsistence farmers. With little hope for profit in agriculture, many New Englanders looked to the ocean for other work. Fishing opportunities along the New England coast and codfish off the Grand Banks of Newfoundland soon made fishing an important industry. The fish were caught, salted, and exported to the middle colonies, the West Indies, and Europe. Whaling also became important to New England. Because whales were processed for their oil and bone in New Bedford and Nantucket, Massachusetts, these became busy whaling ports.

At first, fishermen and whalers sailed on British ships, but soon the Americans began building their own and even supplying ships for England. The region had plenty of timber for the shipbuilding industry. By 1776 nearly one-third of the British trading ships were made in the colonies. Most of the products the ships carried were raw materials from America or manufactured articles from England. Although New England settlers manufactured some products at home during the winter, most produced only enough for their own family's use. The colonies did not export many manufactured products until sometime later.

Almost all of the early settlers of New England were British, so it was natural for them to take up many of the industries that were common in the mother country. Britain, as an island country, had built much of its wealth in sea trade and related activities. New Englanders, with their limited land resources, also made sea activity profitable. Because these colonists looked to the sea, harbors became important points of settlement and centers of trade.

Pennsylvania's colonial policy of religious freedom allowed groups such as the Amish to flourish. Here a couple is married in an Amish ceremony.

The Middle Colonies

Life in the middle colonies was influenced by its diverse peoples and its geography. These colonies were "melting pots." Immigrants from many different European countries, not just the British Isles, came to this region, and the colonists blended their various cultures. Pennsylvania, although opened to settlement by English Quakers, also became the home of Scotch-Irish Presbyterians from Northern Ireland. Moravians had come from Czechoslovakia by way of Germany; Mennonites came from Switzerland. The Pennsylvania Dutch settled from Germany. New York had descendants of the Dutch as well as Englishmen within her borders. New Jersey's settlers were mostly Dutch or Swedish. As a result of such diverse cultures, the settlers in the middle colonies were less strictly bound to British traditions.

Geography offered two other strong influences on the middle colonies. One was the abundance of navigable rivers. The Hudson River helped settlers move to inland New York and New Jersey. On the banks of the Delaware River, Philadelphia grew from four thousand people in 1690 to more than forty thousand by 1775. The Susquehanna (sus kwuh HAN uh) and Allegheny (AL ih GAY nee) Rivers also opened paths into Pennsylvania. These and other rivers served as water highways to inland settlements and farms, providing transportation routes for trade.

The second geographic advantage was that the middle colonies had rich, thick soil. Although the region had plenty of hills and mountains, it also had fertile coastal and river plains. Settlers could grow an abundance of cereal grains like corn, oats, barley, and wheat. For this reason the middle colonies were also called the **bread colonies.**

Farming became the major activity in the middle colonies. And, although most farmers raised food primarily for their own needs, some were able to sell extra farm produce for profit. Abundant pasturelands fed cattle and horses, and livestock became an export. Other industries arose to meet the needs of the farmers. Coopers and wainwrights used lumber from the forests to produce barrels and wagons. Merchants in the towns bought the farmers' produce and in return sold them all kinds of needed supplies.

Settlers in the western areas of the colonies, where few whites lived, trapped animals for their fur and traded with the Indians for more furs. Those settlers could then trade in the towns and make large profits. Albany, New York, became an early fur-trade center because of its location on the Hudson and its closeness to the Iroquois Indian tribes.

The Southern Colonies

The rich soil and long growing seasons of the southern colonies prompted agriculture to become the dominant activity. Although some corn, wheat, and other basic food crops were grown, the colonists found other more profitable crops. They could grow and export tobacco, rice, and indigo because those crops were in demand in Europe. Since greater profits could be made if these crops were raised in large fields and tended by unskilled laborers, large farms called **plantations** became a major part of southern culture. A few port cities and river towns grew to meet the transportation and trading needs for the plantations and other farms, but few other industries grew.

The geography of the southern colonies suited plantation agriculture. A wide coastal plain gave these colonies plenty of flat farmland, and the money crops thrived in the warmer climate. Most of the early colonists were English, and the wealthy planters set up their plantations to resemble the large country estates in Britain. Far more of the southern colonists, however, were not so wealthy. Because their small farms could not compete with the plantations, many of them became subsistence farmers in the inland "Piedmont," or foothills of the Appalachian Mountains.

Southern Money Crops—Tobacco became the first important money crop for the southern colonies, despite some drawbacks. From the bitter experience of starvation at Jamestown, the colonists had learned that it was more important to grow food than tobacco. Furthermore, the English recognized that tobacco contained some type of habit-forming substance. Nonetheless, economic gain finally overruled better judgment, and tobacco production increased rapidly. Although tobacco was difficult to grow and depleted the soil, it became the leading cash crop in Maryland, Virginia, and North Carolina.

Rice was raised in the **tidewater** (areas along coastal rivers and inlets), where tides could be used to raise and lower water levels in rice fields. At high tide farmers opened floodgates to cover the fields with water. Later as the tide ebbed, the floodgates were opened again to lower the water level. The fields were flooded twice each season, and the rice was finally dried for harvest in September.

Indigo proved a good second crop because it grew off-season from both rice and tobacco. Thus the workers could stay busy all year. Harvested indigo was laid in vats to ferment. When the leaves had decayed enough, the water was drained out and the plants beaten. Limewater was added to bring out the indigo's rich blue color. One drawback of handling indigo was that the fermenting leaves gave off an unpleasant odor. Indigo and rice were especially important crops in South Carolina.

Corn—The largest and most important food crop in all the colonies was corn, also known as maize. The Indians had taught the colonists to grow this valuable New World plant. Corn could grow almost anywhere, was easy to hoe and weed, and grew quickly. It could be ground into meal for johnnycake or cornpone, cooked with lima beans to make

Not all early colonists lived in mansions, but they did have access to the bounty of the new land.

The Frontier

All the early settlements in the colonies were on or near the Atlantic coast, and settlement moved inland slowly. The Appalachian Mountains, which lie inland from the coast, helped to form a western barrier for the British colonies for over one hundred years. Even so, all three colonial regions constantly had a frontier. The **frontier** was the undeveloped area at the edge of the settled areas. As settlements moved west, the frontier moved west too. Easterners also called the frontier the "back country."

Most frontier people were hard working and God fearing. But they were joined by others, the riffraff of society—people whom Easterners wanted out of the way. Wife-deserters, escaped convicts, and debtors running from bill collectors came to live on the edge of society. Some of the riffraff remade their lives; others failed again. But on the frontier few questions were asked. Men and women worked at backbreaking tasks for hours to keep themselves fed and clothed. Only a few became wealthy.

The frontier settler claimed land almost anywhere he wished. Since the land had to be cleared, few farms exceeded two hundred

succotash, sweetened with sugar to make Indian pudding, or roasted in unshucked cobs. Soaked in lye, it became hominy; dried hominy was ground to make grits, a favorite in the South. Dried corn could be stored until needed; cornstalks could be used to stuff mattresses, to make children's toys, or to feed to livestock. Dried cobs could be used to kindle fires. Virtually every part of the corn plant was put to some practical use.

acres. The farmer grew a patch of corn and perhaps some peas, potatoes, and wheat. He had a cow or two and a hog—animals that lived off the land. The farmer did not have time to clear land to grow food for the animals. Because he was a subsistence farmer, he had little to sell—perhaps a little flax, wheat, tobacco, or indigo. With the little money he earned from selling his surplus he could buy a new sickle, a cooking pot, some salt, or some cloth for his wife to make a dress. He lived on pork and hominy, ate from wooden "trenchers" (platters), and drank from wooden "noggins" (mugs).

Despite the frontier's problems and dangers, its population grew. The Wilderness Road, begun in 1769, enabled people to cross the Appalachians more easily than before. The Great Wagon Road, stretching seven hundred miles from Salisbury, North Carolina, to Lancaster, Pennsylvania, became the main north-south highway. Parliament made it illegal to settle beyond the Appalachians after 1763, but by 1776 more than 250,000 settlers had found their way to the frontier. A few brave souls headed even farther west.

The upper class of society in the colonies enjoyed many of the luxuries of the aristocrats in the Old World.

 Why did plantations develop in the southern colonies?

SECTION REVIEW

1. What was the occupation of most of the colonists?

2. Why was farming not the primary source of profit in the New England colonies?

3. What three occupations provided the main sources of income for the New England colonists?

4. What two geographic characteristics were advantages to the middle colonies?

5. What was the nickname of the middle colonies? How did they get this name?

6. List three major money crops in the southern colonies.

7. What was the frontier?

Social Classes: Who Was Who in the Colonies

The colonists were much more concerned about a person's social class than we are today. John Winthrop, the first governor of Massachusetts Bay, wrote, "God Almighte in his most holy and wise providence hath soe disposed of the Condicion of mankinde, as in all times some must be rich, some poore, some highe, and eminent in power and dignitie; others mean and in subjection." Even the young students were affected by colonial class structure. Students were called on to recite not by academic grade or alphabetical arrangement, but by the father's income and social class. Diplomas were given out in the same manner. Even so, class structure was less permanent in the colonies than in England. If a man started out in a lower class, he could work his way into a higher class if he made the effort.

The Upper Class

All three colonial regions had their upper-class people, who were sometimes called **aristocrats** because of their refined tastes and manners. In New England the upper class generally included merchants, traders, and clergymen. Names such as Mather, Winthrop, Faneuil (FAN yul), and Hancock meant wealth. In the middle and southern colonies the upper classes were those who owned large pieces of land. A few gained their positions by holding high government offices or by marrying someone wealthy. In colonial New York the Roosevelts (ancestors of two presidents) and the Van Rensselaers (VAN REN-suh-LEERZ) were in the upper class. Plantation owners in the South included the Byrds, Lees, and Pinckneys.

In all three regions, the upper-class families enjoyed more comforts and luxuries than the lower classes. Usually the upper class imported much of their clothes, furniture, and other possessions from Europe. Their sons received good educations. Servants helped the family perform the household chores. Most of these wealthy colonists, however, were not at all lazy. They worked hard to earn their money, and they worked hard to keep it.

The Middle Class

The middle classes were those colonists who were neither wealthy nor poor. Many had gradually made their way up the social ladder in the New World. They generally owned some

land and had a reasonably comfortable home. But they lacked the servants and the luxuries that the aristocrats could afford. The middle classes included small independent farmers, clergy, shopkeepers, ship captains, carpenters, and blacksmiths.

The Lower Classes

The colonies had few extremely poor people. Land was available to almost everyone, and a good effort at farming would usually feed and clothe a family. Nonetheless, there were a good number of servants who, while they served, owned no land and had few material possessions. And at the very bottom of the social scale was the growing number of slaves.

Servants—The two bottom rungs on the social ladder in white society were occupied by redemptioners and indentured servants. **Redemptioners** usually came from continental Europe rather than the British Isles. They brought their families and possessions. Because they could not pay for all of their passage, they hoped to find a relative or friend to pay the remaining fees after they arrived. If they did not, the fees were paid by some wealthy colonist who required two to four years of service as repayment.

Indentured servants were usually single men from ages eighteen to thirty. Most agreed to be servants to gain passage to the colonies, but a few became servants to repay debts or to learn a trade. By the year 1636 indentureships were so common that those who applied received a printed form with blanks to be filled in. The master paid the servant's passage to America, and then the indentured servant in return worked for the master for four to seven years. A servant could not marry without his master's consent. Few masters consented, for they would have to pay the cost of rearing children that might result from such a marriage. Indentured servants who ran away from

Blacks were sometimes indentured servants, but even when they were freed from their indenture, they were rarely treated as equal members of colonial society.

their masters usually paid with additional years of service. Sometimes they were whipped as well. Some of the servants lived in relative comfort, but others lived difficult lives.

When his service was completed, the indentured servant received land and his "freedom dues"—a new suit, an ax, a hoe, and even cash. Most of these people moved quickly into the middle classes, and some indentured servants became quite successful. For example, former indentured servants include Charles Thomson of Pennsylvania, who became the secretary of the Continental Congress, and Matthew Thornton, who signed the Declaration of Independence for New Hampshire.

Slaves—The first blacks in the mainland colonies were brought against their will to Jamestown by the Dutch in 1619. Even though they were received as indentured servants, before long the practice of enslaving black servants became common. As the supply of European indentured servants failed to meet the demand for more laborers in America, white colonists began to want more and more of these Africans. The average slave cost about five times as much as an indentured servant, but the slave would work for the master for the rest of his life—and he would have children who would also become the "property" of the master.

Understanding the social structure of Europe at the time helps us understand the behavior of these early colonists without condoning it. Europe's rich and prosperous citizens were used to having others work for them. European lower classes had few rights. The virtual slavery of serfdom was a not-too-distant memory, and later conditions for English workers in the factories owned by the rich were bad even until the 1800s. Greed and selfishness often cause people to justify their wrong behavior in order to gain success. But the Bible says in Proverbs 16:25, "There is a way that seemeth right unto a man, but the end thereof are the ways of death." The trouble that the colonists reaped for themselves, the Africans they enslaved, and the future of America was not worth the profits that seemed important at the time. Even if it had been worth the trouble, it was wrong.

Most estimates say that Europeans transported about nine or ten million slaves from Africa to the New World. Traders sold about half a million African people in what became the United States, but the majority went to the Caribbean and South America. By 1730 thirty percent of the population south of Pennsylvania was black. By 1760, blacks comprised sixty percent of South Carolina's population. The number of slaves grew higher in the South because the South based its economy on agriculture—cash crops. Large numbers of workers increased the amount of land that could be planted and harvested by a single owner. The greater the harvest, the greater the profits. The shorter growing season in New England and the middle colonies allowed farmers to plant and harvest during only a small portion of the year, making large farms less profitable. Northerners used slaves most often as servants in upper-class homes.

Although people in other groups could move up the social ladder and benefit from English policies and a free economic system, slaves could not. Freed black men and women in the South had to carry papers to prove they were free; furthermore, they lacked many privileges assumed by the white colonists. Land ownership, occupational and religious choice, education, voting, and holding office were only a few of the rights denied to black people.

Most slaves worked six days a week, fifteen to sixteen hours a day in the summer and fourteen hours a day the rest of the year. Many free workers in those days kept similar hours—even the masters. However, the free workers and masters were working for pay and were free to spend their time and money as they wished. No one can put a value on those freedoms. Colonial law set the maximum hours slaves could work in most colonies, but it is doubtful that those laws were either monitored or strictly adhered to. It was the common sense and compassion of the masters that determined how well slaves were treated.

Slavery is a dismal chapter in American history. Later chapters of this book will reveal the continuing problems it produced in the United States and for this country's people.

The interior of an armory shows rows of weapons for defending the colony.

Local men trained to serve in their colony's militia, which was similar to the modern-day National Guard.

SECTION REVIEW

1. Name four groups that probably were part of the upper class in the colonies.

2. How was the upper class better off than the middle class?

 How was the position of a redemptioner or indentured servant more hopeful than that of a slave?

Government: Establishing Law and Order

Because of man's natural selfish desires, God ordained that governments should rule over man to keep him from doing evil to his neighbors. The early colonists recognized their need for government, and they set up their own governments when leadership from Europe was not provided. The principles of their colonial and local governments were a pattern for the later establishment of the government of the United States.

Colonial Governments

We have already learned that colonies were established and governed under three different plans of authority. One was the royal colony, where the king kept control; one was the proprietary colony, where the king gave the colony to one or more proprietors; the third was the charter colony, in which the king signed a charter, which gave permission and regulations for a joint-stock company or other group to establish a colony. These different colonies had different types of government.

Governors and Legislatures—Some governments were more powerful than others. The charter colonies (Massachusetts, Connecticut, and Rhode Island) elected their own government and legislature. They had the least interference from Britain. In proprietary colonies such as Pennsylvania and Carolina, the governor was appointed by the proprietor or his heirs, if the king approved. In royal colonies—sometimes called crown colonies—the king chose the governor himself. Often the governor stayed in England and sent a lieutenant governor to rule for him. In most colonies the governor served five years. He was responsible to members of the British government. Sometimes the colonists tried to influence those officials in Britain to give them a new governor or force the old one to be more cooperative. Benjamin Franklin, for example, lived in England for several years while he served as an agent for Massachusetts, Pennsylvania, New Jersey, and Georgia.

In all but the charter colonies, the governor was quite powerful. He could veto laws that the legislature passed, regulate land grants, and command the local army, called the **militia.** But the legislature had **"the power of the purse"**—they paid the governor's salary and financed government activities. If the governor did not do what they wanted him to do, they could refuse to pay for his programs or even refuse to pay his salary. All the colonies developed their own legislatures or assemblies similar to the House of Burgesses in Virginia. All free men in the colonies who owned some property were generally able to vote for representatives to these colonial assemblies. Thus a representative or republican government became an early feature of American life.

The Courts—Most of the ideas for the colonial court systems came from England, but they were changed to meet local needs. Governors appointed **justices of the peace** to try those accused of crimes and to settle disputes between citizens. The justices also collected taxes, granted licenses, recorded deeds to property, and served other public needs.

Sometimes the justices even conducted the elections. This system usually worked well because the justices knew the people in their communities. They rendered justice to each person, guided by the spirit of the law.

Taxes—The colonists paid for their governments by paying taxes. The main tax was a property tax. Anyone who owned land or other

From the House of Burgesses, the governor of Virginia oversaw the political workings of the colony.

valuable property paid a certain amount to the colony, depending on how much he owned. Some colonies had poll taxes that citizens paid before they could vote. A Massachusetts poll tax required every voter to pay except the governor and lieutenant governor; the president, faculty, and students at Harvard; and ministers, schoolteachers, and invalids. A poll tax in New York in 1702 was a graduated tax—that is, wealthier people had to pay more than poorer people. For example, those who wore wigs, a common fashion for the rich in colonial times, paid more. Other forms of taxes were tried, but eventually property taxes became the main source of income for the government in all the colonies.

Local Governments

Most of the colonies were divided into counties. These areas of a colony, along with the communities that developed, needed their own special organizations of government. Although the British government sometimes exerted some control in the colonial governments, the colonists ran their own towns and county governments with little interference from England.

In New England the basic unit of government was the **township.** At announced times all the **freeholders** (property owners) attended town meetings. The town meeting was the purest form of democracy, or direct government, by the people in America. The average citizen had his own say in a town meeting, and he did not have to rely on an elected representative to speak for him. Some towns still use this system today.

At a town meeting local issues were settled by majority vote. Each new settler was given citizenship and allowed to own land in the township by vote of his fellow townsmen.

Election Day in the Colonies

In New England the rights to vote and hold office were usually given only to free adult male church members who owned property (usually fifty acres or fifty British pounds of personal property). If a colonist met qualifications such as these, he could participate in the elections.

Voting in a colonial election was very different from going to the polls today. If the candidate had no opposition, he might be elected "by view" at a meeting. The voters just raised their hands, in the same way that we often vote on simple matters in the classroom.

When there was more than one candidate, the sheriff or justice of the peace opened the polls on election day by standing in front of the door and reading the official notice of election. When each voter came in, his name was called out, and the sheriff cried, "How vote ye?" The voter then answered aloud, and the town clerk recorded the vote. Sometimes each candidate stayed at the polls. When someone voted for him, he stood, bowed, and thanked the voter. When the sheriff thought all the voters had come, he went to the door and called, "Gentlemen, freeholders, come into the court and give your vote, or the poll will be closed."

Election day was often a day of celebration. Those who lived far from the voting place had to travel some distance to vote; so they often took care of other business in town as well. They stayed part of the day, visiting friends, gathering news, and perhaps celebrating the results of the election.

Other issues were settled as well. For example, the citizens appointed night watchmen to protect the town. At first all able-bodied men over sixteen were expected to take turns serving night watch. Wealthy people who did not want to serve paid someone to serve for them. Besides patrolling the streets, the watchman was sometimes expected to call out the time of night and tell the state of the weather.

At a town meeting citizens also considered ways to help the poor. The simplest type of relief was to send a poor person "round the town" to live several weeks with each family. Another was "putting out"—a single family provided food and shelter and received money from the town for giving it. If a poor person could work at all, he was bound out like an indentured servant. He then worked for the person who paid for his care. Larger towns built almshouses, where both the "honest poor" and the criminals lived. Most people considered poverty a shame and had to be totally desperate before asking for help. The town wasted little sympathy on the lazy or beggars. Idlers were indentured, jailed, or even whipped and expelled from the town.

In the southern colonies, where there were fewer towns and the population was mostly rural, local government was organized more by counties. Sometimes, however, counties were divided into smaller areas called parishes. Elections were generally held to elect officials for the counties and parishes, and the prominent plantation owners were usually the winners. Then these officials acted on most of the matters of local government themselves. The middle colonies had local governments similar to both those in New England and those in the southern colonies.

SECTION REVIEW

1. List the three types of colonies and tell who had the authority to establish a government for each type.

2. What official was in charge of holding court in the colonies?

3. What is a poll tax?

4. Why was the town meeting considered the purest form of democracy in America?

5. Who usually had the right to vote and hold office in the colonies?

 What prevented colonial governors from becoming too powerful?

SUMMARY

The English colonies shared many similarities, but they also had geographic and cultural differences that affected their development. The New England colonists, who lacked good farmland and a warm climate, turned to sea industries for most of their livelihood. The middle colonies used their good farmland to grow much grain, and the southern colonies grew large money crops on their plantations.

Although the colonists respected social class, opportunities for people to climb into the middle and upper classes were common. Hard work was respectable and necessary in the colonies. Unfortunately, the practice of black slavery developed because of the need for more workers.

Governors and legislatures provided government for the colonies. Most of the colonies set up legislative assemblies that represented the people and their wishes. However, colonial power was kept in check in the royal and proprietary colonies by appointed governors. Even so, all the colonies were able to establish their own local governments without British interference.

Chapter Review

People, Places, and Things to Remember

subsistence farmers
bread colonies
plantations
tidewater
frontier

aristocrats
redemptioners
indentured servants
militia
"the power of the purse"

justices of the peace
township
freeholders

Review Questions

Tell whether each of the following statements best describes New England, the middle colonies, or the southern colonies.

1. also known as the bread colonies
2. had a variety of cultures
3. had the most slaves
4. developed many sea industries
5. could also be called "plantation colonies"
6. had thin and rocky soil

What do you call the things described below?

7. the basic area ruled by a local government in New England
8. property owners who were allowed to vote in town meetings
9. a colonial army
10. the kind of farmer who raised only enough food for his family
11. the kind of servant who worked for a master for a limited time
12. the power that the colonial legislatures had over the governors
13. upper-class people
14. large southern farms
15. people who worked as servants to pay for their passage to America

Questions for Discussion

16. Why do you think so many people were subsistence farmers in colonial times?
17. How would you explain the fact that the frontier moved west?

History Skills

Time Lines

Time lines are helpful tools for the study of history. A time line shows at a glance the most significant events and people of a period and provides a good memorization tool.

A time line also helps you to discover relationships by showing the sequence of events in a period of time. For example, the German invasion of Poland took place immediately before the start of World War II in Europe. Seeing the two events together on a time line should lead to this question: Did World War II start because Germany invaded Poland? Not all events that occur close together in time are related in some other way, but many are. Looking at a time line, therefore, can often help you understand why things happen.

Using the time line at the beginning of Unit 1, page xi, answer the following questions. Try to think like a historian, looking for possible relationships between events.

1. In what year was the first English settlement founded?

2. The House of Burgesses was established in 1619. Had the Pilgrims arrived in the New World yet?

3. How many years passed between the founding of the first colony (Jamestown) and the charter of Georgia in 1733 (the last of the thirteen colonies)?

4. What war began toward the end of the Great Awakening?

5. How old is Harvard University?

Thought Questions

6. Which colony seemed especially to encourage education?

7. How many years passed between the landing of the Pilgrims and the start of the Great Awakening?

8. What does the answer to #7 show about changes in American colonists?

Regions of American Geography
The Northeast

Location

The Northeast includes Connecticut, Delaware, Maine, Maryland, Massachusetts, New Hampshire, New Jersey, New York, Pennsylvania, Rhode Island, and Vermont. The region extends from the far northeastern corner of the United States south to the Chesapeake Bay and west to Lake Erie. Canada and the Great Lakes border the region on the north. The Atlantic Ocean forms the eastern border.

Climate

Most of the region has a humid continental climate with temperatures varying based on latitude—the farther north, the colder the weather. Residents enjoy four distinct seasons including warm, humid summers and cold, snowy winters. However, the clash between the cold, dry air coming down from Canada and the warm, wet air coming up from the Gulf of Mexico produces unpredictable weather from severe thunderstorms to blizzards.

Topography

The Appalachian Mountains cut through the region, leaving a narrow coastal plain in the northeast that widens as it moves south. In the nation's early days, the fall line lies where the coastal plain meets the rolling hills of the Piedmont. In the nation's early days, the fall line not only was the farthest that boats could travel upriver into the interior of the nation, but also was where fast-moving rivers could turn waterwheels to power machinery. The region also features easily navigable rivers such as the Hudson, the Delaware, the Susquehanna, and the Potomac, as well as a number of large bays such as the Chesapeake, the Delaware, Cape Cod, and Long Island Sound. Along these bays are many excellent harbors.

Natural Resources

Before the colonies were founded, European countries discovered the rich fishing grounds off the coast of New England. These waters continue to provide seafood to the nation. Maine is especially famous for its lobster. In the north, where the region's coastal plain is rugged and infertile, logging, along with granite and marble quarrying, provides industry for the economy. As the coastal plain widens in New Jersey, it provides fertile ground for farming. Western Pennsylvania has the nation's largest anthracite coal deposits. With this fuel source available nearby, Pittsburgh, Pennsylvania, soon became home to the nation's largest steel industry.

Geography and Culture

In the Northeast, industry sprang up along the fall line, creating major cities. This industry, combined with the abundance of good harbors, allowed the region to become a major center for trade. New York City, Philadelphia, Wilmington, and Baltimore continue to transport millions of tons of cargo in and out of their ports. The cities in the Northeast are so close to each other that from Boston to Washington, D.C., they almost run together. Large suburbs on the outskirts of one city blend into the suburbs of the next city, giving the chain of cities the title megalopolis (great city).

Though early settlers in the Northeast were Protestants seeking religious freedom, the Northeast has strayed far from its original religious roots. The great religious schools such as Princeton and Harvard long ago left their original Bible teaching. These Ivy League schools continue to be among the most distinguished in the nation for their high academic standards. However, high academics are not enough to help the region cope with the problems associated with large cities. Much of the political concern of the region deals with social problems such as crime, drugs, and poverty.

With nine of the original thirteen colonies represented in the region, the area is steeped in history. Museums, historic sites, Revolutionary War battlefields, and national treasures remind visitors of the foundations of our nation.

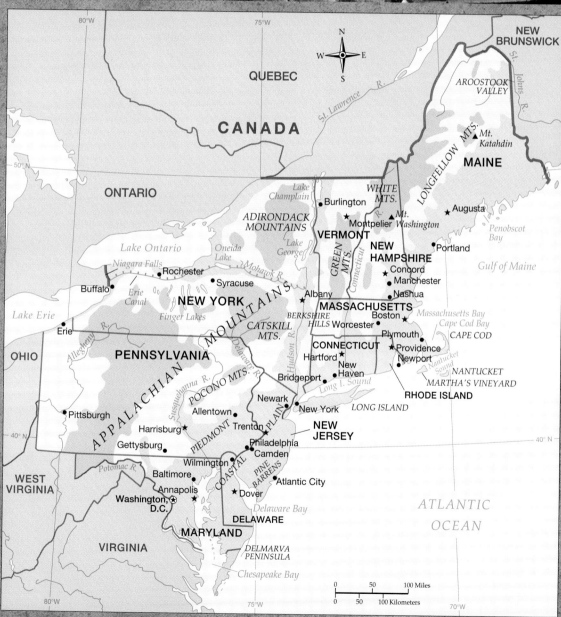

QUEBEC

CANADA

ONTARIO

NEW BRUNSWICK

AROOSTOOK VALLEY

St. Johns R.

St. Lawrence R.

Mt. Katahdin ▲

LONGFELLOW MTS.

MAINE

Lake Champlain

ADIRONDACK MOUNTAINS

WHITE MTS.

● Burlington

Augusta ●

Lake Ontario

Oneida Lake

Lake George

VERMONT

Montpelier ★

Mt. Washington ▲

NEW HAMPSHIRE

Penobscot Bay

Niagara Falls

Rochester ●

Mohawk R.

GREEN MTS.

Connecticut R.

Concord ★
Manchester ●

Portland ●

Gulf of Maine

Buffalo ●

Erie Canal

Syracuse ●

NEW YORK

Albany ●

Nashua ●

Lake Erie

Finger Lakes

Allegheny R.

Erie ●

CATSKILL MTS.

BERKSHIRE HILLS

MASSACHUSETTS

Worcester ●

Boston ★

Massachusetts Bay
Cape Cod Bay

CAPE COD

OHIO

APPALACHIAN MOUNTAINS

PENNSYLVANIA

Delaware R.

Hudson R.

CONNECTICUT

Hartford ★

Plymouth ●

Providence ★
Newport ●

Nantucket Sound

NANTUCKET

Pittsburgh ●

Susquehanna R.

POCONO MTS.

Allentown ●

New Haven ●

Bridgeport ●

Long I. Sound

RHODE ISLAND

MARTHA'S VINEYARD

Harrisburg ★

PIEDMONT

Newark ●

New York ●

LONG ISLAND

Gettysburg ●

Trenton ★

Philadelphia ●

Camden ●

NEW JERSEY

Potomac R.

Wilmington ●

COASTAL PLAIN

PINE BARRENS

Atlantic City ●

WEST VIRGINIA

Baltimore ●

Annapolis ★

Dover ●

Delaware Bay

ATLANTIC OCEAN

Washington, D.C. ✪

DELAWARE

VIRGINIA

MARYLAND

DELMARVA PENINSULA

Chesapeake Bay

N
W E
S

80°W   75°W   70°W

50°N

40°N

0   50   100 Miles
0   50   100 Kilometers

4

Life in the Colonies

ife in colonial days lacked many of the conveniences we take for granted today. There were no electric lights, only the light of a fireplace, candles, or perhaps a whale oil lamp. Of course there were no airports, train stations, or superhighways; there were not many roads either. Those that did exist connected only major towns and were dusty or muddy depending on the weather. The fastest way to travel between two towns like Boston and Philadelphia was by ship along the coast, but that took over a week. Today we can make the three-hundred-mile trip by car in a few hours.

Life has changed greatly from colonial times to today, but the people themselves were just like us today. The colonists had spiritual needs as well as a desire for learning and for expressing themselves through their arts and crafts. As they pursued these interests, they added much to the heritage of America.

Religious Backgrounds of the Colonies

Religion was important in the early colonies. It was, after all, the reason some of the colonies had been founded. But religious beliefs in the colonies varied greatly, mainly because the colonists had different religious backgrounds.

Puritan New England

In New England the Puritan groups were most influential. Most of the Puritans came to be called **Congregationalists** because the members of the congregations had more say in church affairs. (Anglican, Presbyterian, and other churches had bishops, elders, or other leaders who ruled in church affairs.) Religion dominated every aspect of the Puritans' life and society. Their emphasis on diligent work (the work ethic) and the need for godly education set a good example for future Americans. They tried to build their government on biblical principles, but they soon found that they could not force unwilling colonists to abide by godly standards.

The Puritan Congregationalists faced the same problem found in some Christian homes today: not all their children accepted Christ. These unsaved young people grew up, married, and reared their own children. They continued to attend services, but inwardly many were unconcerned about spiritual truths. Church membership was important in most of the New England colonies because only church members could vote in colonial government elections. Each Puritan was accepted for church membership after his conversion when he "proved up" (showed evidence of his conversion before his pastor and congregation). But what about the growing number of unsaved in the church? Should they be allowed to vote even if they did not "prove up?"

The Puritans tried to solve this problem by adopting the **Halfway Covenant** in 1662. They decided to accept the children of church members even if the applicants or their parents were not saved. But only the genuinely converted could take communion. The clergymen hoped that the "halfways" might be saved if the church accepted them. This unfortunate compromise did not succeed. The church reformed few sinners, but the sinners affected

Built in 1682, the First Congregational Church in Lynn, Massachusetts served as a place to worship and to conduct town business.

the churches. Eventually some unsaved men became part of the clergy, and the influence of Puritanism steadily declined. When Massachusetts was rechartered as a royal colony in 1691, Puritan leaders lost control of the colony, and the Anglican Church became the established church. The decline of Puritan influence definitely created a need for revival.

The Southern Colonies

The Church of England, or the Anglican Church, was the official church in every southern colony. The Bishop of London was the Anglican Church leader who was responsible for the churches in America. Although he never came to the colonies himself, he appointed *commissaries,* or official substitutes, to report on the conditions, advise American pastors, and promote education. The two best-known commissaries were

Thomas Bray and James Blair. Bray is noted for his work in establishing good libraries for churches in Maryland, and Blair helped establish William and Mary College in Virginia.

The Anglican Church was strongest in the cities. Each church served a neighborhood or area called a parish, but there were too few ministers to serve in the colonies, especially in all the rural areas. The Anglican rector, or pastor, received the use of a home and sometimes a small farm; he also received a small salary collected from taxes (usually on tobacco), as well as wedding and funeral fees. South Carolina raised money by taxing non-Anglicans. North Carolina collected so little money that it could pay the salaries of only two Anglican clergymen.

The early English settlers were the ones who attended the Anglican churches in the southern colonies. Many of the members were planters, merchants, and other wealthy colonists. As other Europeans moved in— Germans, Scots-Irish, French Huguenots, and others—they increased the numbers of non-Anglican colonists. Although it had few members, the Anglican Church did little recruiting among these other peoples. It remained the church of the "upper class." In 1701 King William III chartered the Society for the Propagation of the Gospel in Foreign Parts to support Anglican missions among Indians, slaves, and non-Anglican whites, but it met little success in the American colonies. Other religious groups were permitted to settle in the South as long as they paid taxes to the state church and followed certain rules. The Scots-Irish on the frontier were strongly Presbyterian. Baptists also settled there. Huguenots were numerous on the Carolina coast. Most Huguenots were skilled artisans, refined and industrious people who contributed greatly to colonial life.

The Supernatural

Colonial Christians were much more conscious of God's working than most Christians today. They looked for direct evidence of God's working, both in nature and in themselves. Thomas Prince, a Puritan preacher in Boston, said,

God does not confine himself to act according to his common Course of Nature, but most wisely and justly reserves the Liberty of acting otherwise on all Occasions when he sees most fitting. . . . In this Manner, he may in the most proper Seasons send both Droughts and Rains, and Sicknesses and Health, to particular Places; he may point his Lightnings to particular Persons; he may raise a storm to disperse a fleet, and give additional Powers to a Gust of Wind to overset a Vessel, or to the waves to break her. . . . And so in Multitudes of other Cases.

Unusual events usually gained considerable attention. In 1646, after a calf was born with three mouths, three noses, and six eyes, John Winthrop confessed, "What these . . . portend [mean] the Lord only knows, which in due time he will manifest." Comets in 1665 and 1666 caused great excitement. Thunderstorms and crop failures were considered warnings of God's displeasure. Earthquakes in 1727 and 1755 caused some to examine their hearts. The events, interpreted as signs of God's judgment, brought changes in some lives, but most of the changes were short-lived.

Another interesting religious group in the colonies was the **Moravians,** followers of the early reformer John Huss. The group was called *Moravians* after Moravia, the place in eastern Europe where Huss's early followers had lived. Searching for refuge from religious persecution, the Moravians had settled in Germany. When they met persecution there, they came to Georgia in 1732. They were not well received in Georgia, however, because they did not believe in fighting wars, even against the Indians. Consequently many of the Moravians moved on to Moravian settlements in North Carolina and Pennsylvania, where the group grew and prospered.

The Moravians wanted to come to America to do missionary work among slaves, Indians, and German settlers. Probably no other Christian group of the colonial era made as great a missionary effort as did the Moravians. The Moravians also influenced American church music. They used string, brass, and woodwind instruments in their services. Benjamin Franklin described a visit to a Moravian church, "I was entertained with good musik, the organ being accompanied with violins, hautboys [oboes], flutes, clarinets, etc." A beautiful Moravian service took place every Easter morning when the

Buildings in the Moravian settlement of Old Salem, North Carolina

Moravians gathered at their cemeteries, "God's acres." There, with appropriate festival music, they were reminded that Christ will resurrect those who have died in Him.

The Middle Colonies

The middle colonies had the greatest religious diversity. Most of the traditional denominations and some sects were found there. Anglicans, Lutherans, Dutch Reformed, Presbyterians, and Quakers all settled in the middle colonies.

Jews also migrated there, but their freedoms were limited. Because the Jews were not "Christians," the Protestants of early America treated them as pagans. Although the Jews could trade and buy land, they could not be shopkeepers or skilled tradesmen. At first they could not meet in their own synagogues. One influential Jewish family was the Levys. Along with nineteen other

Moravian influence went far beyond the buildings of Old Salem, North Carolina.

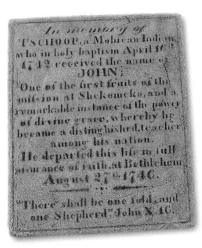

In memory of
TSCHOOP, a Mohican Indian,
who in holy baptism April 16,
1742 received the name of
JOHN;
One of the first fruits of the
mission at Shekomeko, and a
remarkable instance of the power
of divine grace, whereby he
became a distinguished teacher
among his nation.
He departed this life in full
assurance of Faith, at Bethlehem,
August 27th 1746.

"There shall be one fold, and
one Shepherd." John X. 16.

Huts of Peace, Huts of Grace

The story of the Delaware Indians shows the dramatic influence the gospel can have on people. The missionary work of a Moravian named David Zeisberger (ZICE berg ur) persuaded this group of Indians to accept Christ and abandon their pagan customs and even to adopt the unpopular Moravian conviction that a Christian should not bear arms. These Indians refused to go against their beliefs, even after many years of severe persecution from other Indians and white men alike.

In 1743 Zeisberger established a mission in Shamokin, Pennsylvania, where sixty-three Indians were soon converted. However, within months the first of many political difficulties disrupted the Christian community. The British, fearing French influence, closed the work until the end of King George's War in 1748. They then required the Indians to take an oath of allegiance, which the Indians refused on religious grounds. The angered Englishmen promptly moved them. The Indians went west and built two successful villages called Friedenhutten ("huts of peace") and Gnadenhutten ("huts of grace").

However, the outbreak of the French and Indian War brought more threats to the new Moravian villages. In January 1754 the French burned Gnadenhutten. The Indians did not retaliate; instead, they quietly rebuilt their homes. When peace finally came, the illegal westward movement of whites stirred up local Indians led by Chief Pontiac of the Ottawas. The Moravian Indians, caught between, were easy targets for the whites who said, "The only good Indian is a dead Indian." In 1763 soldiers guarding a traveling Indian party got drunk and murdered the Indians they were guarding. Citizens in the area, fearing reprisals, threatened to destroy all the villages. The Christian Indians, influenced by Zeisberger's preaching, did not fight back as expected. Instead they fled to a stockade at the village of Bethlehem. Then they willingly gave up their fields and weapons to travel under guard to Philadelphia. As they passed through cold November rains, angry village mobs hurled insults, stones, and garbage at them. Yet the Moravian Indians sang hymns and prayed for their enemies.

The colonists placed them in filthy, crowded buildings on Providence Island, where, despite everything, the men knelt and gave thanks to God for their safety. By December public pressure forced them to leave on a three-week pilgrimage through New Jersey and New York. But neither state received them. So they returned home in a savage January snowstorm, praising God for their opportunity to spread the gospel. A group of white people proved the tribe's innocence and allowed them to stay in their village. After a long year and a deadly smallpox epidemic, the Indians decided to move west. On the banks of the Ohio River, they built the first Protestant schoolhouse and the first Protestant church west of the river. The "Golden Age of Indian Work" followed. For ten years Indians visited from all over. Many were saved, and everyone marveled at the town's strict discipline.

Hopes of lasting peace ended with the coming of the War for Independence. When the Delaware Indians refused to "take up the hatchet" against the colonists, the British offered rewards for the scalps of their leaders and missionaries. In 1781 the British destroyed their fields and took the people prisoner. Zeisberger went north to Detroit to face trial as a spy. When the troops guarding him were called away, he proceeded faithfully on to the trial on his own. The judge released him when the guarding officer returned and vouched for his innocence.

Nevertheless, a bitterly cold winter brought the Indians to the point of starvation. They had to send a relief party south for supplies. Before returning, the party offered to share their goods with some American militia in the area. Little did they know that the soldiers wanted revenge for the recent murder of a white family by Indians of another tribe. The soldiers took the weapons from the unsuspecting Indians and voted to kill them. After a time of prayer and preparation, the innocent Indians went two by two to their deaths. Ninety-six died in the massacre. The event brought a revival among the remaining Indians because they searched their hearts to see why God had spared them.

After the war a government commission showed that the Moravians had done more with the Indians in a few years than colonial government had been able to do in more than one hundred. The new Confederation Congress offered to pay for the wrongs of the war by granting the Delaware a tract of land. The Indians returned to the Ohio and built the town of Goshen. But the aging Zeisberger could no longer protect them from evil influences. Liquor entered and morality declined. Eventually the Delaware moved, intermarried with the Cherokee, and lost their national identity. But their story remains a living testimony of what the gospel can do. God's power was able once again to transform unregenerate people into Christians with the character and conviction to endure great affliction for their beliefs.

families, Asser Levy helped set up a synagogue in New York and also influenced Jewish settlements in Baltimore and Philadelphia in the mid-1700s. Pennsylvania, a Quaker colony, allowed more religious toleration than any of the other middle colonies. The Schwenkfelders, a mystical group, settled in Philadelphia in 1734. Amish Mennonites settled in large numbers in Lancaster County. The Dunkers (a German group) founded a secluded colony at Ephrata (EF ruh tuh) in 1745. Some of the Dunkers, including those at Ephrata, denounced marriage, kept Saturday as the sabbath, and baptized by triple immersion, face forward. Christopher Sauer, a German printer and Dunker leader, printed America's first Bible in a continental European language in 1743. He also edited and printed the first German newspaper in America.

A group of Moravians from Georgia bought land in Nazareth, Pennsylvania, and began settling in the area. On Christmas Eve, 1741, the Moravians named their most important settlement in the Pennsylvania colony Bethlehem.

SECTION REVIEW

1. What religious group dominated every aspect of life and society in New England? Why was its name changed to Congregationalist?

2. What church was strongest in southern cities? How was it usually supported?

3. Whom did the Anglican Bishop of London appoint as his representatives in America?

4. What group followed the teachings of John Huss? Why did they want to come to America?

5. What colonial region had the greatest religious diversity? Name some groups that settled that region.

 How did the Halfway Covenant affect Puritanism?

The Great Awakening

As the years passed in the colonies, the people suffered more and more spiritual poverty. Puritan churches had lost their spiritual strength, and fewer churches in the southern or middle colonies preached the gospel.

Many ministers were unsaved; colleges lost their spiritual emphasis; the people grew less interested in spiritual things. The nation stood in need of revival. That revival began in the 1720s. It was so powerful that even non-Christian historians call it the **"Great Awakening."**

Leaders of the Great Awakening

The revival first came in New Jersey. There Theodore Frelinghuysen (FREE ling HIGH zen) preached in Dutch Reformed churches, and William Tennent and his son Gilbert preached to Presbyterians. Gilbert and fifteen other young men had been trained by William Tennent in a log cabin later called "the log college." The log college graduates became God's instruments to spread revival

God used Jonathan Edwards's quiet preaching to change hearts in New England.

throughout the middle colonies, especially New Jersey and Pennsylvania. The revival also spread to the South when William Robinson, a log college graduate, preached in western Virginia and North Carolina. Samuel Blair also preached in the South, but the greatest figure in the southern Great Awakening was probably **Samuel Davies** in Virginia.

Jonathan Edwards played a key role in the Great Awakening. Edwards, who was from Massachusetts, entered Yale at the age of thirteen. In 1727 he became associate pastor of his grandfather's Congregational church in Northampton, Massachusetts. Two years later he became the pastor. Edwards described the conditions in the town of Northampton:

> Licentiousness [lie SEN shus ness; lack of moral restraint] for some years greatly prevailed among the youth of the town; there were many of them very much addicted to night walking and frequenting the taverns, and lewd practices wherein some by their example exceedingly corrupted others. It was their manner to get together in assemblies of both sexes, for mirth and jollity, which they called frolics; and they would often spend the greater part of the night in them, without regard to order in the families they belong to; indeed family government did too much fail in the town.

In 1737 Edwards began preaching sermons on justification by faith. Conversions began first among the young and later among the older people as well. Within two years over three hundred were saved. The New England revival reached its peak in 1741. That July, Edwards preached what is probably the best-known revival sermon of all time, "Sinners in the Hands of an Angry God." As he calmly and clearly preached the judgment of God, the listeners' guilt increased. Conviction of sin was so great that Edwards had to stop several times when the cries of the people threatened to drown out the sermon. In all his preaching Edwards stressed not only the love of God to save men but also the wretchedness of sin in the light of God's holiness. A hatred for sin brought genuine repentance and godly living.

Edwards later served as a missionary to the Indians, and then in 1757 he became president of the College of New Jersey (later Princeton University). But after only a few months at the college he died from smallpox. Historians have ranked Edwards with Benjamin Franklin as "one of the two most outstanding minds in America of the early eighteenth century." One author says that as a philosopher and theologian, Edwards "had no peer [equal] in his own time."

One other important preacher of the Great Awakening was not an American but an Englishman. **George Whitefield** (WHIT feeld) had attended Oxford, where he had been a close friend of John and Charles Wesley. Whitefield became an evangelist, and his evangelistic preaching brought him across the Atlantic seven times in his thirty-four-year ministry. It is estimated that he preached at least eighteen thousand times (an average of once every seventeen hours). He was often forced to preach in open fields because established churches refused to let him use their pulpits. But his resonant voice reached greater crowds outdoors than could have gathered in even the largest church buildings. Once he preached to a crowd of twenty thousand without even a megaphone. When Benjamin Franklin heard him preach in Philadelphia, he estimated that thirty thousand people could have heard him at one time.

Whitefield was concerned for all men, but he had a particular burden for children. In 1740 he founded what is today America's oldest orphanage, Bethesda (meaning "house of mercy"), near Savannah, Georgia. He preached to slaves, wrote a gospel tract for American Indians, and had an indirect influence in starting several colleges. Whitefield died during a preaching tour of New England.

Preaching the truth of God's Word, George Whitefield traveled throughout the colonies.

He is buried beneath the pulpit of a church in Newburyport, Massachusetts.

Enemies of the Great Awakening, then and since, have attacked preachers such as Edwards and Whitefield because they preached the Scriptures plainly and emphasized the truths of the gospel. We should not forget that unsaved men who are not spiritually discerning usually fail to grasp spiritual truths. "The natural man receiveth not the things of the Spirit of God: for they are foolishness unto him: neither can he know them, because they are spiritually discerned" (I Cor. 2:14).

Effects of the Great Awakening

The Great Awakening produced far-reaching results. It has been said that the Great Awakening knew no boundaries—political,

Nassau Hall, the first building constructed on the present Princeton University campus, was completed in 1756.

Third, the Great Awakening affected American higher education, for as orthodox Christians parted company with religious unbelievers, they established new schools to train their pastors and missionaries. The College of New Jersey—an outgrowth of Tennent's "log college"—was established by Presbyterians in 1747, Kings' College (Columbia) by Anglicans in 1754, Brown University by the Baptists in 1764, and Queen's College (Rutgers) by the Dutch Reformed in 1766. Dartmouth was founded in 1770 to train young men to reach the Indians.

Fourth, the Great Awakening helped increase the gap between church and state. Roger Williams and others had already helped establish the principle of separation between church and state. Now many people realized that their churches could exist without the support of government. Although a few government-sponsored churches remained in some colonies, the end of established state churches would come after the War for Independence.

Fifth, the revival increased the colonists' desire for political freedom. Pastors and evangelists stressed man's worth and personal responsibility before God. If individuals were so important in God's plan that Christ died for them, then they were important enough to the state to be equal under the law. If an individual man was responsible to accept or reject Christ, then he should also be responsible to guide his own government. It is significant to note that in atheistic, communistic countries, the individual is not important and is subjected to the wishes of the government.

social, or geographic. The most obvious result was the great number of converts. Between 1740 and 1742 more than thirty thousand were added to churches in New England alone—out of a total population of only three hundred thousand.

Second, the Great Awakening increased the number of American missionary works. The best-known missionary to the Indians following the Great Awakening was David Brainerd, who worked in New York, New Jersey, Pennsylvania, and Massachusetts. He died from tuberculosis in 1747 at the age of twenty-nine. Brainerd's diaries have continued to inspire others to devote their lives to missionary service.

Another missionary, Samuel Kirkland, began his work in 1764 with the Iroquois tribes. Simon Horton, a Presbyterian, worked among the Indians on Long Island. The Moravians carried on works among the Indians throughout the colonial era.

Samuel Davies and the Southern Great Awakening

Samuel Davies, a major leader of the Great Awakening in the southern colonies and perhaps the greatest American pulpit orator of his day, was born to Welsh parents on November 3, 1723. His mother gave him the name "Samuel" because, like Samuel of the Bible, he had been "asked for of the Lord." Davies's mother had prayerfully dedicated her son to the Lord to preach. However, Davies related that until the age of fifteen he was "not particularly concerned with things of a religious nature." But while studying at St. George, Delaware, under an itinerant preacher, Davies awoke "to solemn thoughtfulness and anxious concern about [his] eternal state." Saved shortly thereafter, he made a practice of secret prayer and ended his prayers with the plea that he might be "suitably prepared to enter the gospel ministry."

That preparation was aided by a gift of money made to William Robinson, a Presbyterian preacher who was serving in Hanover County on Virginia's frontier. There was no regular minister, and out of grateful hearts for the services Robinson had held, the people gave him a gift of money. Robinson did not feel right about accepting it for himself but told the group,

There is a very promising young man, now studying divinity . . . whose parents . . . find great difficulty in supporting him at his studies. I will take this money and it shall be given him to help him through—and when he is licensed, he shall come and be your preacher.

After finishing his training, Davies was ordained as "an evangelist to all congregations without preachers in Virginia but especially in Hanover County." Except for a fourteen-month interval when Davies went to England to raise money for the College of New Jersey and a two-year period when he served as its president just before his death, he devoted all his preaching years to this needy area.

For almost twelve years Davies held services in seven churches in five different counties and traveled by horseback over the whole state of Virginia organizing revival meetings. He also gave young preachers practical training, traveled from plantation to plantation preaching to slaves, organized his church members to teach slaves to read so that they would be able to study the Scriptures, and served as a distributor of books to frontier homes and slave dwellings. He also influenced the founding of two schools in the Hanover Presbytery: Hampden-Sydney College and Washington (later Washington and Lee) College.

Moreover, because the Anglican Church was still the established church in Virginia, he worked for more freedom of religion in the colony. He told his people that loyal patriotism would encourage government leaders to give them more religious liberty, and the Virginians found his advice to be sound.

In his pastorate Davies was always conscious to challenge his people by example. He sought to have balance in his ministry and in his preaching. He preached to meet men's needs. He said that preaching "had to help the people in the things that most affected them; it had to help them solve the problems of life and ever prepare them to face death."

Finally, the Great Awakening strengthened the moral fiber of the American people. This strength helped them to withstand the perils of two upcoming wars.

Opponents of the Great Awakening

The Great Awakening changed the religious thinking of many Americans, but it was not the only influence on eighteenth-century minds. Many Americans, especially those educated in Europe, were influenced by a movement called the **"Enlightenment."** This movement exalted rational thinking and critical reasoning. Unfortunately, man's ability to think often seemed more important to eighteenth century people than God's truths as revealed in Scripture. If a man disagreed with God's truths, he discarded them. Although such men prided themselves in casting off "old prejudices," they merely showed man's inability to understand the wonders of God. "Hath not God made foolish the wisdom of this world?" (I Cor. 1:20).

Deism—One important philosophy that grew out of Enlightenment thinking was **deism.** Deists taught that God created the universe in a perfect and balanced manner. But then He allowed the world to function under certain laws of nature and never intervened in man's affairs again. Deists pictured God as the great Watchmaker who made the watch (the earth), started it running, but then just let it run without touching it again. Thus there was no way to know God or have fellowship with Him. God was just a distant power without any concern for man's present needs. But according to the Bible, God does intervene in our lives. His Holy Spirit convicts of sin, and He offers salvation through His Son, Jesus Christ. God also guides and protects us day by day.

Deism argued that miracles mentioned in the Bible did not take place because they violated the "unchangeable laws" of God's created universe. For instance, Christ could not have walked on the water as Matthew 14:25 states because a man is heavier than water and will sink. Such a belief, however, fails to recognize that a powerful and wise God who could create the world and the basic laws of nature can also overrule those laws when it suits His divine purpose. Nevertheless, deists denied the inspiration of the Scriptures. They believed that their own reason showed them all they needed to know about God and their own moral duties. By the end of the colonial era, many prominent men—Benjamin Franklin, Thomas Jefferson, Ethan Allen, and others—were deists. Although their view of God was unbiblical, many deists did have high moral principles that aided them as they helped to found a new American nation.

Unitarianism—A second unbiblical philosophy that originated during this time was **Unitarianism.** This religious movement asserted the "unity" of God by denying the doctrine of the Trinity. Unitarians denied the deity of Jesus Christ, insisting that He was only a great man. Although Unitarians claimed to believe the Bible, they denied man's need of salvation through the blood of Christ. According to Unitarianism, people needed only to live a moral life. The influence of Unitarianism continued to grow even after the War for Independence. Unitarianism became especially strong among some American intellectuals, and it influenced American writers for many years.

False teachings have always been part of history. Studying such teachings can remind us of our responsibility to test the new ideas of every age to be certain that they are consistent with the Word of God. Paul cautions us to "beware lest any man spoil you through philosophy and vain deceit, after the tradition of men, after the rudiments of the world, and not after Christ" (Col. 2:8).

SECTION REVIEW

1. In what decade did the Great Awakening begin?
2. What Puritan preacher played a key role in the Great Awakening in New England?
3. What English preacher was also instrumental in the Great Awakening?
4. List the six major results of the Great Awakening.
5. What is deism?
6. What is Unitarianism?

 Why was Enlightenment thinking dangerous?

Colonial Education

In seventeenth- and eighteenth-century Europe, education belonged almost exclusively to the rich. Common people rarely had access to schools or books. They labored at their occupation from the time they were children until they died, without having time or money to learn about the world around them. In the American colonies an education was still a privilege. But Americans, especially those in New England, began to want all children to go to school. They believed children should have the opportunity to learn about God by reading the Bible and to learn about His world by reading other books.

Grammar Schools

Grammar schools were similar to our elementary schools. Children learned to read and write, but they learned far more at a grammar school in the colonial era. Older students learned to read Greek and Latin. These subjects, along with math and natural philosophy, were difficult, but they disciplined the mind. The upper social classes also believed that correct grammar, acceptable accent, fluency in Greek and Latin, and some knowledge of ancient classical literature set them and their

children apart from average people. Grammar school studies took seven grueling years. If a student did well and had the financial support, he might be able to enter college while still in his early teens.

Spelling was not on the list of subjects for grammar school. Since Noah Webster's *Blue-Backed Speller* was not published until 1783, there was no consistent model for spelling words. The way people spelled sometimes depended on how they felt at the time or on how much reading they had done. Some schoolmasters used the King James Version of the Bible as their spelling model.

Most colonial children first learned to read from a hornbook, a printed sheet posted on a board that looked much like a paddle. It was called a "hornbook" because it was covered with a thin transparent sheet of animal horn. Hornbooks always had the alphabet on them; sometimes they also contained a list of

Colonial children started their formal education reading from a hornbook.

vowels, some syllables to sound out, or the Lord's Prayer. Children from the upper class sometimes had fancy hornbooks engraved on brass or pewter plates. As they learned from their hornbooks, a common way for students to practice forming their letters was to trace them with a stick in the hearth sand. (Sand was put in front of the fireplace to catch sparks and prevent fires.)

If you had lived in colonial days, you might already be preparing for your graduation exercises. And graduations *were* exercises! Graduates gave memorized speeches in Latin or Greek and then debated, using all the knowledge they had gained in grammar school.

Schools in New England—In the earliest colonial days parents were responsible to teach their children to read and write at home. In 1642 the Massachusetts General Court passed a law ordering parents to teach their children "to read and understand the principles of religion and the capital laws of the country." If a child did not learn to read, his parents could be fined. Parents sometimes gave the task of education to widows or single ladies, who established simple schools in their homes. These were called **"dame schools."**

By 1647 there were only eleven grammar schools in New England. In that year the General Court of Massachusetts passed an act "to prevent that Old Deluder Satan" from keeping men "from the Knowledge of the Scriptures." The act required all towns of fifty or more families to appoint a schoolmaster to teach the children to read and write. Other New England towns gradually began to follow Massachusetts's example and established town schools.

By 1750 Latin grammar schools were being replaced by academies. In addition to keeping the emphasis on Latin and Greek, these schools also included English composi-tion and literature, math, modern languages, and natural science. Private schools taught much the same subjects but also included skills such as letter writing, civil government, navigation, gunnery, and even fencing and shorthand.

Schools in the Middle and Southern Colonies—Some of the middle colonies established public schools, but most of the schools were organized by church groups. The Dutch Reformed Church established some schools in New Netherland, and the Quakers founded seventy schools in Pennsylvania, admitting students from all social classes.

In the middle and southern colonies, however, there were fewer schools than in New England. Because long growing seasons required children to help on the farms during many months of the year, schooling was difficult. Government officials did not value education either. In 1671 Governor Berkeley of Virginia noted that "there are no free schools nor printing in Virginia . . . for learning has brought disobedience, and heresy, and sects

Single women and widows sometimes opened "dame schools" in their homes.

into the world, and printing has divulged them, and libels against the best government. . . . God keep us from both!" Some planters or wealthy farmers joined to hire a schoolmaster and provide a school for several families. Others could afford private tutors for their children. Either way, usually only the children of the upper classes were able to receive such an education.

Higher Education

The first chartered institution of higher learning in the colonies was **Harvard College** in Cambridge, Massachusetts. Puritans founded it in 1636 "to advance learning and perpetuate it to Posterity." The Puritans did not want "to leave an illiterate Ministry to the Churches when our Present Ministers shall lie in the Dust." Three years later the college got its name when John Harvard, a young minister in nearby Charlestown, died of tuberculosis. He left half of his estate and his handsome library of four hundred books to the young school. Although the sum Harvard left was not large, the high cost of books and the purchasing power of the money made his donation important and led to the college's taking the name of its early benefactor.

College students followed a strict schedule. Their days frequently began at 5:00 A.M. and included study, prayers, lectures, recitations, chapels, and meals along with two short breaks daily. To enter college, students had to be able to write, speak, and translate in Latin since college books were written in Latin and lectures contained much Latin. There was no

A Prospect of the Colledges in Cambridge in New England

Harvard College made it unnecessary for young colonists to travel overseas for an education.

definite end to a class; a course of study ended when the tutor believed that his students had mastered the subject. Students and teachers often lived in the same building, ate their meals together, and studied and worshiped together.

Yale and Dartmouth were started when New England Puritans saw that Harvard had been affected by the liberal ideas of the Enlightenment. Other schools were fostered by the Great Awakening. Although they were begun primarily to teach preachers of the gospel, they did not keep their original, godly goals. Today these schools have a totally secular emphasis.

William and Mary, founded in 1693 in Virginia, was the only college in the southern colonies for many years. Many southern planters and other wealthy people from all of the colonies, however, continued to send their sons across the Atlantic for college education.

This practice helped keep Americans interested in the current discoveries and fashions in science and thought in Europe.

Vocational "Schools"

Formal schooling was not the only way for colonial young people to learn. Farm and shop training were also valued. The **apprenticeship** system was used to teach trades. Apprenticeships usually lasted seven years or until the apprentice turned twenty-one. The apprentice was supposed to be moral and serve his master faithfully.

Benjamin Rush, future doctor and signer of the Declaration of Independence, was apprenticed to a Philadelphia physician, Dr. John Redman. He had little free time. In 1766 Rush wrote that during a five-and-a-half-year apprenticeship, "I was absent from Redman's business but eleven days and never spent more than three evenings out of his house." Apprenticeships were often means to wealth, and men who completed them were able to reach positions of high esteem. In addition to Rush, several other signers of the Declaration of Independence had once been apprentices. Roger Sherman of Connecticut began as a shoemaker's apprentice; George Taylor had served as an iron maker in Chester County, Pennsylvania; and Benjamin Franklin had been a printer.

SECTION REVIEW

1. What were the early elementary schools called?

2. What was a hornbook?

3. Which colonial region most emphasized education?

4. What system was used to teach trades?

 How were schools such as Harvard and Yale different in colonial times from what they are today?

Colonial Arts and Crafts

Although many colonists enjoyed artistic beauty, making a living in a new and rugged land allowed little time for such enjoyment. One New Englander summed it up by saying, "The plowman that raiseth grain is more serviceable to mankind than the painter who draws only to please the eye." Nonetheless, the colonists often expressed artistic ideas in their daily lives—in dishes, furniture, and architecture. If a colonist had to make something, he often made it attractive as well as practical.

Glassware

The first glassworks in America was in Jamestown, Virginia. It was started in 1608, just one year after the colony was founded. By the late 1630s glass factories in Massachusetts and New York made window glass and bottles that compared favorably with European glass. Two German immigrants established glassworks in the colonies. Caspar Wistar (WIS tur), who at first made brass buttons in Philadelphia, later established his first glass factory in Salem County, New Jersey in 1739. Henry Stiegel (STEE gul) started his factory in Lancaster, Pennsylvania, in 1763. Stiegel made a rich, deep blue glass that is still admired. Glassware became the first manufactured product to be exported from America.

Metalworking

Pewter, which the colonists called "poor man's silver," was an alloy of tin, lead, and copper. Pewter was used to make plates, mugs, and porringers (shallow bowls). During the War for Independence, pewter became scarce because lead supplies were needed for bullets.

The first recorded American silversmith was Thomas Howard, who lived in Jamestown in 1620. Although Boston boasted twenty-four silversmiths by 1776, including the famed Paul Revere, much of the silver in America's early years was imported from

England. But over the years Americans began to produce more silver. Silverware soon replaced wooden and pewter tableware because it lasted longer. The first American forks had two tines, but by 1725 four-tine forks were in use. The "teaspoon" dates from the early 1700s, when British traders introduced tea drinking to the colonists.

Local ironworks were usually located near sources of bog iron. They produced pots, kettles, cooking cranes for fireplaces, nails, and hinges. Colonists on the frontier sometimes pounded nail heads into their doors to protect them from Indian tomahawks. They arranged the nail heads in geometric designs to make decorative doors. Hinges could be simple or ornate. Wind vanes also gave the ironmaster or blacksmith a chance to show his artistic talents. Joseph Jenkins, sometimes called the "father of the iron industry," invented the boot scraper, which colonists used to clean the mud from their shoes before entering buildings. Since there were no paved roads or sidewalks, this device was much appreciated. Two famous early ironworks were the Saugus Iron Works in Lynn, Massachusetts, and Hopewell Forge in Pennsylvania. The Saugus (SAW gus) works, begun in 1646, employed 185 men—ironworkers, miners, woodcutters, and boatmen. Two years later Governor John Winthrop noted, "The Furnace runnes 8 tun per weeke, and their barre Iron is as good as Spanish."

Clocks

Colonists made and repaired all kinds of clocks. Since most people did not use bedside tables, alarm clocks were made to be fastened to the high bedposts. Because of the cost of producing metal pieces for clocks, Eli Terry invented a clock with all wooden workings. In 1807 he formed a partnership with Seth Thomas and Silas Hoadley to mass produce clocks. They harnessed nearby waterfalls for power and in three years produced four thousand clocks. Eventually Seth Thomas founded his own company at Thomaston, Connecticut. His thirty-hour clock originally sold for $15.00, but

Colonial weathervanes not only showed wind direction, but also gave decorative flair to rooftops.

Colonists developed American furniture styles.

by efficient production methods and high sales, he brought the price down to $5.00. His company still exists today.

Three brothers, sons of seventeenth-century clock maker Simon Willard, settled in Roxbury, Massachusetts. They specialized in church, hall, and gallery clocks. Willard clocks were so finely made that some are still working today, after two hundred years. The banjo clock, so called because of its shape, was probably the most unusual Willard clock.

Furniture

Most settlers made their own furniture. They usually did so in the winter, when they could not work in the fields. They made cupboards (hutches), chests, tables, chairs, and other needed items. Ever eager to save time, some enterprising settlers fashioned bedsteads with cranks on the footboards. By tying the quilt to the crank and rotating the crank in the morning, one could tidy up the bed quickly.

By the late 1600s furniture craftsmen became established. Although other native

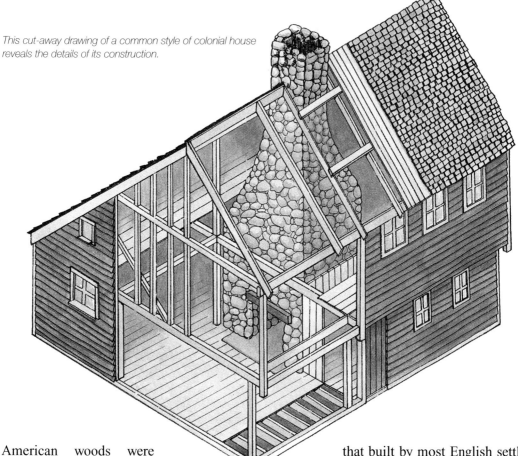

This cut-away drawing of a common style of colonial house reveals the details of its construction.

American woods were often used, mahogany came into use for construction of the best furniture. The strength of mahogany permitted a refinement of style. **Duncan Phyfe** (FIFE) was probably the most famous furniture maker. He made furniture of top-quality mahogany, sometimes paying up to $1,000 for a single log. His furniture commanded high prices, but much of it has lasted for generations.

Architecture

Colonial houses varied in style, depending on the climate, the type of building materials at hand, the builder's training, and the money available. The most common early style was that built by most English settlers. It had a large central chimney with a kitchen on one side and a parlor or living room on the other. An overhead loft, reached by a ladder, held two sleeping rooms. A lean-to might be added in back to store farm implements. Some houses had clapboard siding, made of split logs.

Log cabins, introduced by the Swedish settlers along the Delaware River, proved practical because they did not require any nails, which were always rare. Brick was used where clay was abundant, especially in areas where fire had devastated earlier dwellings. Boston had a disastrous fire in 1679 and was rebuilt mostly of red brick.

Georgian architecture became popular from 1725 to 1750, during the reigns of Kings George I and George II. Georgian houses had a balanced arrangement of windows and doors. Inside there were cornices over the windows, paneling on some of the walls, and fancy mantlepieces. The houses were usually rectangular and were two or three stories tall. Most were plain on the outside and more ornate inside.

Painting

Early painters, called "limners" (from the word *illuminate*), usually painted in a style called American Primitive—a simple style unaffected by European styles of the day. Most pursued art as a sideline while they worked at some other trade for a living.

They produced three main types of works: portraits, landscapes, and historical scenes. Since cameras had not been invented, portraits were especially popular. While religious art was popular in Europe, not much of it was done in America. Puritans believed that divine things were understood by the mind rather than pictured to the eye. In America more people could read the Bible for themselves and did not need pictures. Five of these American painters are especially well known. **John**

Benjamin West's Esau and Jacob Presented to Isaac, *The Bob Jones University Collection*

Singleton Copley has been called "the greatest painter ever to work in colonial America." He created a famous painting of Paul Revere. Charles Willson Peale traveled with the army during the War for Independence and painted many battle scenes, including *Cornwallis's Surrender at Yorktown.* Although blind in one eye, John Trumbull also painted battle scenes, including *The Battle of Bunker Hill.* Four of his paintings hang in the rotunda of the United States Capitol. Benjamin West lived in England during the War for Independence, but he became one of the best-known American painters. Gilbert Stuart is remembered most for his "unfinished portrait" of George Washington—the portrait that appears on the one-dollar bill.

SECTION REVIEW

1. Of what inexpensive metal were many of the colonists' utensils made?

2. Who was one of the best furniture craftsmen in the colonies?

3. Who introduced log cabins? Why were they practical?

4. List the five well-known colonial painters.

 Why was religious art not popular in America?

SUMMARY

Religion was an important part of life in the colonies. In New England the Puritan Congregationalist influence was greatest, while the Anglican Church was established in most of the southern colonies. The middle colonies saw many religious groups settle in the region. Although many of the colonists were very religious, many were far from God in the early 1700s. But the Great Awakening brought a revival to parts of the colonies, and many were saved. Even so, other Americans turned away from God to the ideas of the Enlightenment, embracing deism and Unitarianism.

Educational opportunities grew, especially in New England, where grammar schools and colleges multiplied. Many colonists served as apprentices to learn trades. America soon developed many talented craftsmen and educated leaders.

Chapter Review

People, Places, and Things to Remember

Congregationalists
Halfway Covenant
MoravianGreat
  Awakening
Samuel Davies
Jonathan Edwards

George Whitefield
Enlightenment
deism
Unitarianism
grammar schools
dame schools

Harvard College
apprenticeship
pewter
Duncan Phyfe
John Singleton Copley

Review Questions

Match the group with its description.

1. Anglicans
2. Congregationalists
3. deists
4. Moravians
5. Unitarians

a. believed God had no personal concern for man
b. denied the Trinity
c. Puritans
d. strongest in southern cities
e. supported much missionary activity

Who was he?

6. English preacher of the Great Awakening
7. "the greatest painter ever to work in colonial America"
8. the greatest figure in the southern Great Awakening
9. famous Boston silversmith
10. preached "Sinners in the Hands of an Angry God"
11. famous furniture maker

Fill in the blanks in the following paragraph with the appropriate words.

Not everyone could receive an education in the colonies, but some children were able to go to (12) ,where they learned to read, write, and study literature. Some schools were operated by single ladies or widows and called (13) . As the students learned to read, they used a (14) that contained the alphabet and other simple information. Instead of going to school, some colonial young people became (15) so that they might learn a trade from a master.

Questions for Discussion

16. Would you say that Enlightenment ideas are still common today? Why or why not?
17. What are some of the differences between education in colonial times and education today? Was a good education as important then as now? Why or why not?

History Skills

Reading Tables

No library would be complete without a copy of the *Statistical Abstracts of the United States*. It is the most widely used source of U.S. statistics available. The U.S. government has been keeping detailed information about the states and the nation ever since the first census in 1790. Whenever you have doubts about statistics quoted on television or in the newspaper, you might want to compare them to a table in the *Statistical Abstracts*.

Below is a table taken from the abstracts, or summaries, of U.S. statistics. The information appears in columns (that run down the page from top to bottom) and rows (that run across the page from left to right.) Look at the table carefully and answer the questions that follow.

Colony	1630	1650	1670	1690	1700	1750	1770
New Hampshire	500	1,305	1,805	4,164	4,958	27,505	62,396
Vermont							10,000
Plymouth	390	1,566	5,333	7,424			
Massachusetts	506	14,037	30,000	49,504	55,941	188,000	235,308
Rhode Island		785	2,155	4,224	5,894	33,226	58,196
Connecticut		4,139	12,603	21,645	25,970	111,280	183,881
New York	350	4,116	5,754	13,909	19,107	76,696	162,920
New Jersey			1,000	8,000	14,010	71,393	117,431
Pennsylvania				11,450	17,950	119,666	240,057
Delaware		185	700	1,482	2,470	28,704	35,496
Maryland		4,504	13,226	24,024	29,604	141,073	202,599
Virginia	2,500	18,731	35,309	53,046	58,560	231,033	447,016
North Carolina			3,850	7,600	10,720	72,984	197,200
South Carolina			200	3,900	5,704	64,000	124,244
Georgia						5,200	23,375
Total	4,646	50,368	111,935	210,372	250,888	1,170,760	2,725,369

1. What was Plymouth colony's population in 1630? in 1690?

2. What is the first year for which statistics are available for Pennsylvania?

3. What colony had the largest population in each of these years—1630, 1700, 1770?

4. Which colony had the smallest population listed in 1670? By 1770 how did this colony's population compare to the other colonies'?

5. Which colony was not included on the chart until 1770? Do you know why?

6. Which colony was dropped from the chart in 1700? Do you know why?

7. Give the rank (first, second, and so on) of the five largest states in 1770. Was New York one of them?

5

American Colonies in the British Empire

Britain's power was growing in the 1700s. It was expanding its empire in the Americas and in India. It was also acquiring islands in the Pacific and territory on the continent of Australia, as well as many other lands that would become a part of the British Empire. The thirteen American colonies, as a part of this empire, were allied with Britain in its growth and development. Yet while Britain attended to other needs in its empire, it had given the thirteen colonies much independence in handling their own affairs. Although the colonists were still willing to fight side by side with the British against common enemies, they were not willing to give up the liberty they had enjoyed.

The French and Indian War

At the outset of the eighteenth century, France and Britain were the two leading European powers. Both nations were actively involved in building overseas empires. By establishing new colonies, they hoped to increase their wealth and power. The intense rivalry between the two led to a series of wars.

Background to the Struggle

North America was important to both the French and the British. French colonists had settled along the St. Lawrence River, in the Great Lakes region, and by the Mississippi River, while British colonists had settled along the Atlantic seaboard. Both, however, laid claim to the whole continent. Both wanted control of the fur trade in the vast, unsettled territory west of the Appalachian Mountains. In addition, they both wanted control of the rich fisheries off the coast of Newfoundland. It was not long before their rival interests led to open conflict.

***French Advantages and Disadvantages*—** The French had many advantages in their struggle against the British. Their government exercised strong and unified control over her colonists. Furthermore, the French were actively building forts at strategic spots along America's inland waterways. They also had a well-trained army and the support of many Indian tribes who hated the British. Despite these advantages, however, the French had one major weakness: New France was a vast territory with widely scattered and sparsely populated French settlements. To defend such a large region was difficult.

***British Advantages and Disadvantages*—**The British colonies had a few advantages as well. They had nearly fifteen times the population of New France. In addition, they had the support of the **Iroquois** (IR uh KWOY), the strongest confederation of Indian tribes in America. The English navy was also the strongest in the world.

Perhaps Britain's greatest weakness was a lack of unity among the colonists. There was no central colonial organization, and there was little cooperation among the thirteen colonies or between the colonies and the British government. Each colony preferred to

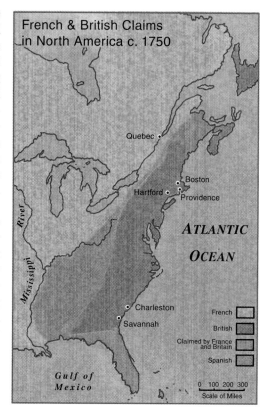

French & British Claims in North America c. 1750

Quebec

Boston
Hartford   Providence

ATLANTIC OCEAN

Charleston
Savannah

French
British
Claimed by France and Britain
Spanish

Gulf of Mexico

0   100 200 300
Scale of Miles

protect its own special interests rather than the interests of the colonies as a whole. When faced with the threat of Indian uprisings and French expansion, many colonists did not want to help unless they themselves were immediately threatened. Only then were they willing to take action to defend their homes, families, and livelihood.

***Earlier Wars*—**Between 1689 and 1763 the rivalry between France and Britain led to four wars. The first three conflicts broke out in Europe and spread to America. (They were "King William's War," 1689-97; "Queen Anne's War," 1702-13; and "King George's War," 1744-48.) The results of these three wars were indecisive; neither side was able to gain an upper hand. The fourth war, however, decided who would control the North American continent. In this last war, fighting broke out in America two years before it began in Europe. Europeans named it the "Seven Years' War." The American colonists called it the **"French and Indian War"** because the French and Indians joined forces against the British.

The Outbreak of War

The immediate cause of the French and Indian War was a struggle for control of the Ohio Valley. The British hoped to open the region to settlement. This alarmed the French, who feared that British settlers would disrupt their fur trade. Furthermore, if the French could gain control, they could stop further British expansion and keep the British colonists hemmed in along the Atlantic coast.

The key to the region was the point where the Allegheny and Monongahela (muh NON guh HE luh) Rivers joined to form the Ohio River (the present site of Pittsburgh, Pennslvania). Here in 1754 some Virginians began building a fort. The governor of Virginia sent a force under the leadership of **George Washington** to protect them. But before they arrived, the French attacked the unfinished fort and drove off the Virginians. The French completed the fort and named it Fort Duquesne (doo KANE) in honor of their new Canadian governor.

As Washington and his troops advanced to the fort, they met and defeated a small French force. Learning of a larger French force nearby, Washington fell back and hastily constructed a stockade called Fort Necessity. A much larger French force was sent out to meet the British colonial troops. After a valiant defense Washington's outnumbered men were forced to surrender. The French allowed them to return to Virginia. This fighting on July 3, 1754, marked the beginning of the French and Indian War.

Early War Activity

During the early years of the war, the French successfully drove the British from the Ohio Valley. Indian tribes in league with the French used a style of fighting that was effective in the wilderness. They hid behind trees and brush, ready to ambush the British. In contrast, the British went to battle European style, dressed in full uniform and marching in rank. These rows of colorfully dressed soldiers made easy targets for Indians hiding in the forests.

The Albany Plan of Union—Both the British and the colonists were concerned about the Indian threat to the colonies. In particular they were afraid that the Iroquois Indians would also join the French in their fight. A meeting was called to deal with this concern, and in June of 1754 delegates from several American colonies met at Albany, New York. At this Albany Congress these leaders met with some of the chiefs and persuaded the Iroquois to support the British.

The congress was more important for another reason, however. During the conference the delegates adopted a plan of union to submit to the colonies. The **Albany Plan of Union,** primarily the work of Benjamin Franklin, called for the creation of a grand council made up of delegates from all the colonies. The assembly would be empowered to raise an army, build forts, and govern Indian affairs. Nevertheless, both Britain and the colonial legislatures rejected the plan. Britain feared that such a union would threaten her control of the colonies. Individual colonies likewise feared that they might lose some of their freedom to such a union. Even so, the plan was significant because it was the first attempt of the American colonies to unite.

With his coonskin hat, Benjamin Franklin charmed the French, who thought all Americans were backwoodsmen.

Braddock's Road—The first major step the British took in the war was an attempt to capture Fort Duquesne. British General **Edward Braddock** took about fifteen hundred British soldiers and about a thousand colonials in his march northward from Virginia. George Washington served as an aide to Braddock on the mission. Braddock moved his men slowly, clearing a roadway and building bridges as they marched. When Braddock's forces finally met the French near Fort Duquesne on July 9, 1755, Braddock suffered not only a defeat but also a fatal wound. The loss discouraged the British and left the colonists uncertain about future British support. However, it did leave the colonists with a new road that would be useful in future settlement of the frontier.

William Pitt's System—In 1756 the war broadened into a worldwide conflict, with

British and French troops battling on three continents: North America, Europe, and Asia. To meet the new challenges, the struggling British placed the war effort in the hands of **William Pitt.** His energetic leadership brought a dramatic change in the war. Pitt turned Britain's halfhearted, defensive tactics in America into aggressive action. He named young, talented generals to replace older, incompetent ones appointed because of their social and political standing. Pitt also agreed to pay for the outfitting of colonial soldiers to aid the British. Now backed with the full support of the British government, British troops, teamed with American colonials, began their assault on French strongholds in America.

One by one French posts began falling to the British. Late in 1758 a British force ousted the French from Fort Duquesne. The British rebuilt the badly damaged fort and renamed it Fort Pitt. The following year the British began preparation to capture Quebec, the crucial blow planned by Pitt to defeat the French.

The Battle of Quebec

Quebec was the strongest city of New France. Perched high above the St. Lawrence

Employing the aid of warring Indians, the English and French fought one another in the bloody battles of the French and Indian War.

Results of the War

Although the British would not capture Montreal until a year later, for all practical purposes the fall of Quebec spelled the defeat of New France. The struggle for North America was over, but the war in Europe continued until 1763. In that year the Peace of Paris was negotiated. France gave up her claim to all territory east of the Mississippi River except New Orleans. Britain retained control of Canada and also received Florida from Spain, a French ally. To compensate Spain for the loss of Florida, France gave her the Louisiana Territory.

A rough drawing shows the French fort at Quebec. Well-placed and well-planned, the fort seemed invincible.

River and protected by steep cliffs, it was a seemingly invincible fortress. The British, under the command of General **James Wolfe,** laid siege to the city. The French, however, were content to stay within the safe confines of their stronghold and wait out the siege.

After several unsuccessful attempts to take the city, General Wolfe decided on a daring plan. Under cover of night, British troops crossed the river downstream from the fort. By morning on September 13, 1759, more than four thousand British troops had silently scaled the cliffs protecting Quebec. They took up battle positions on a plain called the "Plains of Abraham" a short distance from the fortress. When the surprised French commander **Marquis de Montcalm** (mar-KEE deh mont-KAHM) learned what the British had done, he ordered an immediate attack, hoping to defeat the British before they could become entrenched. But the British routed the French and their Indian allies. Both Wolfe and Montcalm were mortally wounded in the battle. With their commander dead and their troops disorganized, the French surrendered Quebec.

SECTION REVIEW

1. Why did France and Britain both want North America?

2. What war settled the question of who would have control? What was this war called in Europe?

3. What advantages did the French have in fighting the war? What advantages did the British have?

4. What river valley did both countries seek to control?

5. Why was the Albany Plan of Union significant?

6. What man's leadership turned the tide, helping the British win?

7. What battle became the turning point of the war, giving the British certain victory?

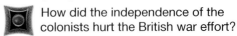 How did the independence of the colonists hurt the British war effort?

New British Policies

Britain emerged from the war as the strongest nation in the world. Her colonial empire reached from India to America. To administer such a large empire, Britain sought to tighten her hold on her colonies, including

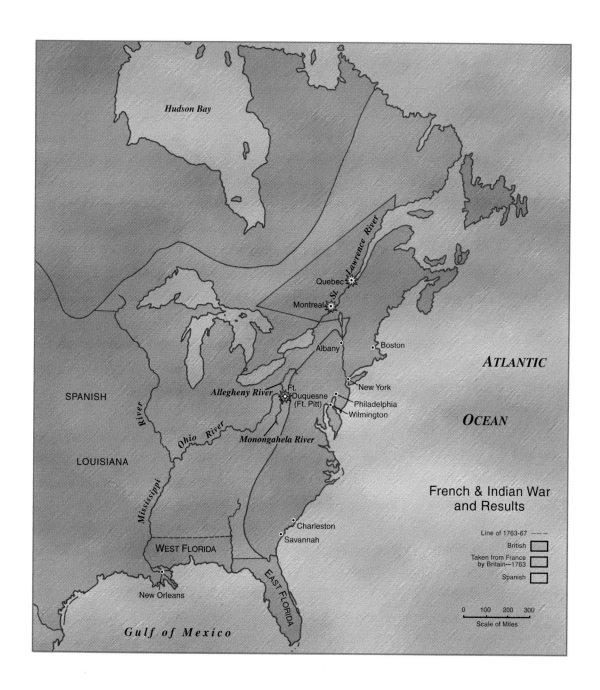

Hudson Bay

St. Lawrence River

Quebec

Montreal

Albany

Boston

ATLANTIC

New York

Allegheny River

Ft.
Duquesne
(Ft. Pitt)

Philadelphia

Wilmington

OCEAN

SPANISH

River

Ohio River

Monongahela River

LOUISIANA

Mississippi

French & Indian War
and Results

Charleston

Savannah

Line of 1763-67 – – –
British
Taken from France
by Britain—1763
Spanish

WEST FLORIDA

EAST FLORIDA

0   100   200   300

Scale of Miles

New Orleans

Gulf of Mexico

those in America. An added reason for tightening control on these colonies was that many leaders in Britain were upset that the colonies had only halfheartedly provided troops and supplies to assist in the war effort. Likewise they were angered that colonial merchants had traded with Britain's enemies during the war. Some members of Parliament decided that the colonies had been allowed too much independence, and they enacted policies aimed at bringing America under closer supervision of the mother country. These policies took many forms, including trade regulations, the closing of western lands, and new taxes. What members of Parliament failed to recognize was that they had previously fostered the colonists' attitude of independence by allowing them to handle their own local affairs. The new imperial policy created growing tension between Britain and its American colonies.

The Closing of Western Lands

After the war the colonists thought the frontier would be safe to settle. Consequently some trappers, settlers, and speculators moved into the region. But **Pontiac,** an Ottawa Indian chief, had organized the tribes from Canada almost to the Gulf of Mexico to stop the entrance of the white man. The Indians captured British forts and terrorized settlers along the frontier. The British, who finally put down Pontiac's revolt, took steps to prevent further problems in the West.

The king issued the **Proclamation of 1763,** forbidding colonial settlement west of the Appalachian Mountains. The British government did not want traders or settlers stirring up unrest among the Indians; therefore, it closed this region to colonial settlement. Settlers already there were asked to leave. Trappers and traders were allowed into the region only with official licenses. Such actions angered the colonists. They had fought to open the frontier to colonial expansion. Besides, Britain had violated colonial charters that promised the colonies the land from the Atlantic to the Pacific.

Quartering British Troops

To defend her holdings, Britain left ten thousand troops in America. This force could put down Indian uprisings and enforce British policies if the colonists refused to obey. The colonists viewed the presence of these troops as a violation of their rights. Many saw the British troops as a greater threat to their liberty than either the French or the Indians. Objections grew when the Quartering Act of 1765 ordered colonists to house the troops and provide them with firewood, salt, and drink. Colonies where large numbers of British

Chief Pontiac of the Ottawa nation made a brave effort to prevent the colonists from spreading further inland.

Mercantilism

Throughout the 1600s and 1700s, most European nations were guided by an economic system known as mercantilism (MUR kun tee LIZ um). According to this system, wealth was measured by the amount of gold and silver a nation possessed. Competing for control of the world's wealth, European nations tried to become self-sufficient. They disliked purchasing goods from rival countries because this drained their own supply of gold while enriching their rivals'. Most European nations sought to remedy this problem by establishing colonies and building empires.

Mercantilistic countries viewed their colonies as a source for raw materials for the industry of the mother country. They also viewed their colonies as markets where goods from the mother country could be sold, increasing the homeland's wealth and power. By regulating the economies of their colonies, the mother countries profited—but often at the expense of the colonies. By strictly controlling the trade of the colonies and by heavily taxing colonial trade and activities, the mercantilistic country could reap large short-term gains from its empire.

troops were kept were especially outraged because of the extra expense they suffered.

Navigation and Trade Acts

The **Navigation and Trade Acts** were one series of Britain's mercantilistic policies. These acts regulated trade between the colonies and Britain's foreign competitors. Such regulations were supposed to help British manufacturers and raise revenue for the British treasury. The acts were not effective, however, and were quickly outdated. Also, the British did not enforce these acts strictly, a fact that encouraged colonial merchants to smuggle in goods from other countries.

Such trade had not only helped Britain's enemies during the French and Indian War but had also deprived Britain of badly needed revenue. Following the war, British officials changed their habits and began enforcing the colonial trade laws strictly. The British sent customs officials with **writs of assistance** (general search warrants) to search for smuggled goods anywhere—even in homes. Several colonial leaders protested these writs that gave British officials unlimited authority to search private property. James Otis, a Boston attorney, held that these searches violated the rights of Englishmen, arguing that a man should be "as secure in his house, as a prince in his castle."

Taxes

The colonists had been paying taxes to support their colonial and local governments, but they had not been required to pay taxes to the British Parliament. This policy also changed as the British began to impose taxes on the colonies.

The Sugar Act—In April 1764 Parliament passed the **Sugar Act.** Through it Britain sought to gain money to help pay for protecting the colonies. The Sugar Act placed duties (taxes on imported goods) on such items as sugar, molasses, coffee, silks, and indigo. The American colonies were importing these items from the West Indies.

The Stamp Act of 1765—To raise additional revenue for the defense of the colonies, Parliament proposed another tax—a stamp tax. It differed from the duties on imported goods because it directly affected colonial businesses and therefore every colonist. The

Stamp Act of 1765 required colonial businessmen and lawyers to purchase special stamps and place them on items that were taxed. This in turn raised the price that the colonists had to pay for these items. Among the items taxed were legal documents, newspapers, calendars, and playing cards. Without a stamp, such items were considered illegal.

Opposition from the Colonists

A storm of controversy erupted in the colonies over the Stamp Act. The protest was not over the amount of the tax, for the new tax amounted to only a few pennies per colonist. Compared to their counterparts in England, who had paid the tax for some time, the colonists were paying little. The issue was whether Parliament had the right to tax the colonies at all. The colonists argued that since they had no representation in Parliament, Parliament could not tax them. "No taxation without representation" became a colonial rallying cry. Taxing lawyers and printers, the most vocal of the colonists, proved to be an unwise policy for Britain, since these colonists spread their views quickly.

Throughout the colonies, groups called Sons of Liberty organized and held rallies to protest the Stamp Act. These groups, however, often resorted to intimidation and violence to obtain their ends. They threatened to tar and feather stamp agents, hoping to force them to resign. Sometimes those agents who refused to resign had their homes destroyed by rioting mobs. Of course, use of violence was not a proper response even to injustice.

A more conservative protest arose from an assembly commonly known as the **Stamp Act Congress.** This general colonial congress met at the urging of Massachusetts's **Samuel Adams.** In 1765 delegates from nine colonies gathered in New York. They sent a petition to **King George III** and affirmed their loyalty to him. However, they insisted on their

Stamps like these raised the prices of goods purchased by the colonists.

rights as English citizens to be taxed by their own representative bodies. When the king did not grant their requests, they responded by advocating a boycott.

Throughout the colonies, people refused to buy English merchandise. Colonial merchants would not unload goods from British ships. This boycott hurt British trade, and as a result, many factories in England closed and workers were laid off. Soon British merchants and workers joined the colonials in calling for the repeal of the Stamp Act. In response to the mounting opposition, Parliament finally did so. The repeal brought rejoicing in both Britain and the colonies, and trade between the colonies and their mother country was quickly restored.

SECTION REVIEW

1. Give three reasons for the tightening of British control over her American colonies.

2. Why did the British issue the Proclamation of 1763?

3. What were writs of assistance?

4. What tax act led to the strongest protest in the colonies?

5. What action did the colonists take against Britain to ruin her trade when the king did not give in to their requests?

 Explain the meaning of the colonial rallying cry "no taxation without representation."

The Breach Widens

The Townshend Acts

The storm of controversy seemed to have ended with the repeal of the Stamp Act. But a change in the leadership of Parliament brought renewed efforts to tax the colonies. Parliament passed the **Townshend Acts** in 1767, placing new duties on such items as glass, paper, lead, and tea. Once again the colonists protested by boycotting British goods.

Again some colonial merchants sought to avoid the new duties by smuggling goods past British customs agents. The British in turn stepped up their efforts to find the smugglers by widening the use of writs of assistance. Resentment between colonial merchants and British agents mounted. Samuel Adams and the Massachusetts legislature denounced the Townshend Acts as a violation of their rights. Adams wrote a letter urging united colonial action, and this letter was sent to all the colonial legislatures. In several port cities British troops were called in to maintain order, but the presence of troops only deepened colonial resentment.

The Boston Massacre

Distrust between the colonists and British soldiers was especially evident in Boston. Here two regiments of British soldiers were called in to try to calm what was already a hotbed of colonial resistance. The citizens resented having British troops stationed in their city. They showed their resentment by booing the troops as they marched down the streets. Some patriots even dared to throw rotten eggs and seashells at the soldiers.

The situation came to a climax on the night of March 5, 1770. A crowd of men and boys began taunting seven soldiers by throwing snowballs and stones at them. The troops fired into the mob, killing five people and

Colonist Samuel Adams loudly protested British injustices.

because of the very high moral standards it had, was known as "the dullest court in Europe"—a fact of which King George was proud.

King George tried to bring the American colonies under tighter rule. His insistence that the British not give in prolonged the War of Independence that was to come. The defeat of his armies and the independence of the colonies was a great embarrassment to him because they thwarted his dreams of restoring the power of the monarchy. When William Pitt the Younger came on the scene, the king withdrew from politics for the most part and left the government in Pitt's hands.

From 1786 on he survived several assassination attempts. His forgiving spirit toward some of the attackers gained him some measure of popularity. But he began having periods of madness around 1788, and by 1810 he was permanently insane. Many believe the insanity was a hereditary condition. His son—whom he despised because of his loose living and poor moral character—took over the throne in 1811.

How do historians sum up the character of America's last king? He was a man of great personal bravery, calm in a crisis, sincere, and highly principled. America's last queen was just as highly principled. Charlotte, North Carolina, and Charlottesville, Virginia, today bear her name.

America's Last King and Queen

America's last king, George III, came to the throne in 1760 at the age of twenty-two. He married Charlotte Sophia, who remained loyal to him throughout his life. Early in their marriage he purchased Buckingham Palace for her, and there they reared their fifteen children.

When George III came to power, he had three goals: to curb the power of the Whigs (one of the major British political parties), to cleanse British politics of corruption, and to restore royal powers that had been lost. As a result of these goals, he upset British politics during his early years as king; and his court,

wounding six others. It is still uncertain who gave the command to fire. Their leader, Captain Preston, defended by lawyer John Adams, was later cleared of all charges. Two soldiers were branded on the hand, and the rest were acquitted.

News of the incident quickly spread throughout the colonies. Most accounts of what happened, however, were exaggerated by radicals who hoped to rouse public sentiment against the British. They labeled the incident the **"Boston Massacre"** and praised those killed as patriot "martyrs."

The Boston Massacre and Boston Tea Party heightened tensions between the British and Americans.

Harboring Resentments

Faced with renewed colonial opposition, Parliament repealed the duties on everything but tea. The British hoped this would restore peace in the colonies. But this action only divided the colonists. Some thought that Britain had conceded enough. Others, however, raised again the cry "no taxation without representation."

The Committees of Correspondence—Samuel Adams, perhaps the most prominent leader of colonial opposition, urged Boston to adopt a **Committee of Correspondence.** Soon eighty Massachusetts towns followed Boston's example. These committees were organized to promote opposition to Britain and became important in alerting the colonists to British threats on liberties throughout the colonies.

The Tea Act of 1773 and a Tea Party—Little happened to stir up the public for about three years. But then Parliament passed the Tea Act of 1773. This act gave the struggling

British East India Company a monopoly on tea trade to America. The monopoly enabled the company to bring cheaper tea to the colonies in spite of the tax on tea. This was a blow to American tea merchants, who could not compete with such a monopoly. The Committees of Correspondence joined the protests of the merchants.

When the first tea ships arrived, the colonists refused to unload them. In Boston a group of fifty or sixty men dressed like Indians boarded the ships and threw the tea overboard. A crowd along the shore watched this **"Boston Tea Party"** in silence.

Passage of the Intolerable Acts

News of the Boston Tea Party angered the British. They viewed the incident as an act of defiance. Many believed the colonists had gone too far and called for swift retaliation. This retaliation came through passage of several parliamentary acts.

The Boston Port Act and the Quartering Act—During 1774 Parliament passed a series of acts, which the colonists called the **Intolerable Acts,** designed to punish unruly Massachusetts. The Boston Port Bill Act closed the port of Boston until the destroyed tea was paid for. Parliament also made changes in the colony's charter, giving British officials more control over the government. Massachusetts colonists lost their right to conduct town meetings, elect representatives, name judges, and select juries. Another act allowed royal officials charged with crimes to be tried in London or in another colony to ensure a fair trial. Parliament also passed a new Quartering Act. This gave colonial governors power to requisition whatever supplies or buildings were needed to house British troops in the colonies.

The Quebec Act—In that same year Parliament passed the **Quebec Act.** This act was not meant to punish the colonists, since it dealt with the newly acquired territory in Canada, not the colonies. Nevertheless, many colonists viewed this act as even more "intolerable" than the others. Not only did it allow French law to be used in civil cases, but it extended the borders of Quebec south to the Ohio River. The colonists feared that this would further shut off westward expansion. Parliament also gave Roman Catholicism, the leading religion in Quebec, a recognized status. The colonists resented Parliament's granting favored status to French law and Roman Catholicism. If Parliament could do that in Quebec, what would stop it from doing the same in the colonies?

SECTION REVIEW

1. What goods were taxed by the Townshend Acts of 1767?

2. How did the merchants avoid the Townshend taxes?

3. Unrest between colonists and British troops led to what deadly incident on March 5, 1770?

4. What organizations were formed to unify colonial opposition to British policies?

5. What three acts did the British pass following the Boston Tea Party? What did each act do?

 Knowing that tea had gone down in price, why did the colonists protest the Tea Act of 1773?

The Colonies Unite for Action

The tide of discontent over the Intolerable Acts spread beyond the port of Boston. Other colonies became concerned that their liberties would be taken away too. The Virginia House of Burgesses declared the day the port of Boston was to be closed a day of fasting and prayer. Angered by this show of sympathy for the "rebels" in Massachusetts, the royal governor of Virginia dissolved the House. Its

Liberty or Death

It was March 23, 1775. One hundred twenty delegates from across Virginia had gathered at St. John's Church in Richmond to discuss what action Virginia should take in pressing the controversy with Britain. Among the delegates was George Washington, who had distinguished himself as a military leader in the recent French and Indian War. Also in attendance was young Thomas Jefferson. But they were not the center of attention on this day.

A tall, stooped gentleman in the third pew rose to his feet. With a commanding voice and bold gestures, he addressed the convention: "They tell us, sir, that we are weak—unable to cope with so formidable an adversary. . . . Three millions of people armed in the holy cause of liberty, and in such a country as that which we possess, are invincible by any force which our enemy can send against us."

He viewed the events of recent months with great alarm and wished to motivate the convention to action.

> There is no retreat, but in submission and slavery! . . . The war is inevitable—and let it come! . . . Gentlemen may cry, peace, peace—but there is no peace. The war is actually begun. The next gale that sweeps from the North will bring to our ears the clash of resounding arms! Our brethren are already in the field! Why stand we here idle? What is it that gentlemen wish? What would they have? Is life so dear, or peace so sweet, as to be purchased at the price of chains and slavery?

> Forbid it, Almighty God! I know not what course others may take; but as for me, give me liberty or give me death!

The speaker took his seat. His words, however, lingered on in the hearts of the delegates. Their complacency now turned to action as they, too, became willing to say with **Patrick Henry,** "Give me liberty or give me death!"

Statues such as this remind Americans of the bravery of early patriots.

members, however, gathered at the nearby Raleigh Tavern in Williamsburg, where they called for a general colonial congress to address the complaints of the colonies.

First Continental Congress

On September 5, 1774, more than fifty delegates, men from every colony except Georgia, gathered at Carpenter's Hall in Philadelphia. The delegates were united in their opposition to the Intolerable Acts but were divided in deciding what action to take against the British. Those who wanted to retain the benefits of British protection and trade urged conciliation. Others, however, believed that to yield would be to lose their right of self-government.

Sessions of this **First Continental Congress** lasted more than a month. The delegates adopted a formal statement of protest, a Declaration of Rights and Grievances. This declaration voiced their objections to the recent acts of Parliament, which they called "unjust, and cruel, as well as unconstitutional, and most dangerous and destructive of American rights."

The congress also organized the Continental Association. Its members pledged not to import any goods from Britain after December 1, 1774, nor to export any goods to Britain after September 10, 1775. They also refused to participate in the English slave trade. The delegates affirmed thus: "We do solemnly bind ourselves . . . to adhere to this association, until such part of the several acts of Parliament passed since the close of the last war . . . are repealed."

Throughout the congress the delegates declared their loyalty to the king. They sent him their petitions, hoping he would correct the injustices of Parliament's actions. The congress, however, called for another meeting for the spring of 1775 if the pleas went unheeded.

The colonists fully expected Britain to repeal the Intolerable Acts. After all, Britain had responded to earlier colonial protests by repealing the Stamp Act and the Townshend Acts. But this time Britain was determined to force the "rebellious" colonists to submit. Additional troops were sent to Boston. Further restraints were placed on colonial trade. King George III wrote to his chief minister, "The die is now cast; the Colonies must either submit or triumph; I do not wish to come to severer measures, but we must not retreat."

"The British Are Coming!"

In rural towns surrounding Boston, the colonists began storing arms and ammunition in case armed resistance against the British became necessary. The British commander, General Thomas Gage, learned of a stockpile in nearby Concord and ordered a detachment of British soldiers to destroy it. He also gave orders to arrest two colonial leaders in nearby Lexington: Samuel Adams and John Hancock.

On the night of April 18, 1775, British troops left Boston and began their march toward Lexington and Concord. They hoped to surprise the colonists, but their departure did not go unnoticed. William Dawes and **Paul Revere** rode through the countryside warning that the British were coming. As the soldiers marched, the alarm was spread—bells rang and guns fired. Early the next morning the soldiers reached **Lexington.** In the middle of the town square, they encountered about seventy colonial militiamen, or minutemen. No one knows who fired first, but shots rang out. Eight colonials lay dead; ten more were wounded. The rest of the militiamen scattered.

The British continued to **Concord,** where they destroyed what military supplies they could find. But more minutemen gathered and another brief skirmish occurred at Concord Bridge. The British advanced no further but began a retreat to Boston. All along the way colonial minutemen from other towns harassed the British. They fired at the British

In this reenactment, "colonists" march to fight "redcoats" once again.

"redcoats" from behind trees, buildings, and fences. The British made it back to Boston but suffered heavy casualties.

The skirmishes at Lexington and Concord mark the beginning of the War for Independence. The British force suffered 273 casualties, nearly three times that of the colonials. Word of the conflict spread quickly throughout the colonies. Colonial militiamen from other colonies rallied to Massachusetts's aid. They set up a siege around Boston. But they could not drive the British out. The first shots had been fired, and a war that neither side wanted nor was prepared to fight had begun.

SECTION REVIEW

1. Why did colonies other than Massachusetts become concerned about the Intolerable Acts?

2. Where did colonial delegates meet to decide what to do about British actions? What was the body of delegates called?

3. For what two reasons did Thomas Gage send British soldiers out toward Lexington and Concord?

4. What two men warned the colonists of the approach of the British?

5. What were the colonial militiamen called who came to stop the British on short notice?

 How was the British reaction to the Declaration of Rights and Grievances different from what the colonists had expected?

Redcoat reenactors prepare for battle.

SUMMARY

During the French and Indian War (1754-63), British and colonial troops fought side by side to defeat their French and Indian enemies. They won control of most of North America for Britain. But shortly after the war, Britain began tightening her control over the colonies. The colonists resented the threat to their liberty, and soon a conflict was in the making between the colonies and the mother country.

Chapter Review

People, Places, and Things to Remember

Iroquois
French and Indian War
George Washington
Albany Plan of Union
Edward Braddock
William Pitt
James Wolfe
Marquis de Montcalm
Pontiac
Proclamation of 1763

mercantilism
Navigation and Trade Acts
writs of assistance
Sugar Act
Stamp Act
Stamp Act Congress
Samuel Adams
King George III
Townshend Acts
Boston Massacre

Committee of
 Correspondence
Boston Tea Party
Intolerable Acts
Quebec Act
Patrick Henry
First Continental Congress
Paul Revere
Lexington
Concord

Review Questions

Choose the word or words that make each of these statements true.

1. The (Iroquois/Pontiacs) were Indian supporters of the British.

2. Another name for the French and Indian War was (Queen Anne's War/
   the Seven Years' War).

3. Both the British and the French wanted to build a fort where the
   (St. Lawrence River/Ohio River) formed.

4. The Albany Plan of Union was (accepted/rejected).

5. The British defeated the city of (Quebec/Toronto).

Match these men with their descriptions.

6. George Washington   a. most prominent leader of colonial opposition

7. Edward Braddock   b. defeated by the French at Fort Necessity

8. Samuel Adams   c. British general who built a road

9. William Pitt   d. warned the colonists of approaching troops

10. Paul Revere   e. British leader who organized the war effort

Give the year that each of these events occurred.

11. The Boston Massacre

12. The Battles of Lexington and Concord

13. Proclamation closed the West to settlement

14. Meeting of the Stamp Act Congress

15. The Boston Tea Party

Questions for Discussion

16. What do you suppose would have happened if the French had won the
    French and Indian War?

17. What do you think the British could have done to keep the colonies a con-
    tented part of their empire?

Establishing a Nation

1787: The Constitutional Convention drew up a new plan for American government that would at once be specific enough to solve the problems of the Articles of Confederation and general enough to adapt to the needs of the future.

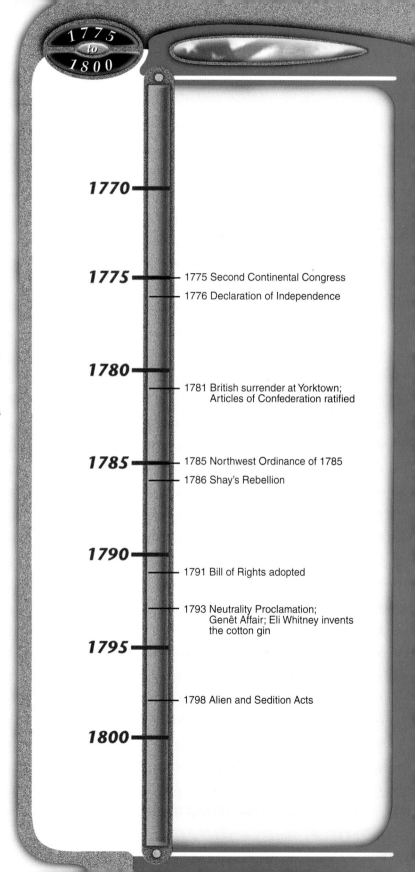

1770

1775 — 1775 Second Continental Congress

1776 Declaration of Independence

1789: Having won America's freedom as commander-in-chief of the Continental Army, George Washington was given the responsibility of setting the nation's direction as its first president.

1780

1781 British surrender at Yorktown; Articles of Confederation ratified

1785 — 1785 Northwest Ordinance of 1785

1786 Shay's Rebellion

1790

1791 Bill of Rights adopted

1781: Cornwallis's surrender at Yorktown helped the American colonies establish the status they had already claimed: free and independent states.

1793 Neutrality Proclamation; Genêt Affair; Eli Whitney invents the cotton gin

1795

1798 Alien and Sedition Acts

1800

Unit II: Establishing a Nation

John Adams's Account of the Drafting of the Declaration of Independence

John Adams, America's second president, was on the committee that drafted the Declaration of Independence (1776). Read his own account of the process, written in 1822. Then answer the questions below.

You inquire why so young a man as Mr. Jefferson was placed at the head of the Committee for preparing a Declaration of Independence? . . . It was the Frankfort advice to place Virginia at the head of everything. . . .

Mr. Jefferson came into Congress in June, 1775, and brought with him a reputation for literature, science, and happy talent of composition. Writings of his were handed about, remarkable for the particular felicity of expression. Tho' a silent member in Congress, he was so prompt, frank, explicit, and decisive upon committees and in conversation, not even Samuel Adams more so, that he soon seized upon my heart; and upon this occasion I gave him my vote, and did all in my power to procure the votes of others. . . .

The subcommittee met. Jefferson proposed to me to make the draft. I said, "I will not." . . . "What can be your reasons?" "Reason first—You are a Virginian, and a Virginian ought to appear at the head of this business. Reason second—I am obnoxious, suspected, and unpopular. You are very much otherwise. Reason third—You can write ten times better than I can." "Well," said Jefferson, "if you are decided, I will do as well as I can." "Very well. When you have it drawn up, we will have a meeting."

A meeting we accordingly had, and conned the paper over. I was delighted with its high tone and the flights of oratory with which it abounded, especially that concerning negro slavery, which, tho' I knew his Southern brethren would never suffer to pass in Congress, I certainly never would oppose. There were other expressions which I would not have inserted, if I had drawn it up, particularly that which called the King tyrant. I thought this too personal; for I never believed George to be a tyrant in disposition and in nature; I always believed him to be deceived by his courtiers. . . . I consented to report it, and do not now remember that I made or suggested a single alteration.

We reported it to the committee of five. It was read, and I do not remember that Franklin or Sherman criticized anything. We were all in haste. Congress was impatient, and the instrument was reported, as I believe, in Jefferson's handwriting, as he first drew it. Congress cut off about a quarter of it, as I expected they would; but they obliterated some of the best of it, and left all that was exceptionable, if anything in it was.

1. List three reasons Jefferson was selected.
2. How many years after the event did Adams write his account?
3. Did Adams record the exact words of his conversation with Jefferson?
4. What difference between Adams and Jefferson appears in paragraph four?

6

America Gains Its Independence

Two days after the incidents at Lexington and Concord, twenty-two thousand angry Americans gathered at Cambridge near Boston. They were ready to put a stop to any British actions. General Gage's force of four thousand English redcoats seemed to be isolated in Boston. A conflict was in the making, and Americans were ready and willing to take action if necessary.

Moving Toward Independence

Although the colonists' determination to stand up and fight against British assaults was growing, there was not yet a confirmed desire for total independence. Most still hoped to convince the king and Parliament that the colonies wished to be a loyal part of the British Empire. The colonists merely wanted their rights as Englishmen to be acknowledged. Events would soon prove, however, that America would separate from Britain.

The Second Continental Congress Meets

On May 10, 1775, the **Second Continental Congress** convened in Philadelphia. The delegates first sent a letter to the king, asking him to preserve their rights as Englishmen. The tone of the petition was so conciliatory that it became known as the Olive Branch Petition. (The olive branch is a symbol of peace.) However, the Second Congress was not optimistic and continued preparing for war.

The Continental Congress put the army at Boston under its command and asked the colonies for war supplies and troops. The Congress decided to call the troops the **Continental army** and made George Washington of Virginia its commander-in-chief.

The king refused to receive the colonial agents bearing the Olive Branch Petition from the Congress. Instead he ordered the army to suppress the rebellious colonists, asserting that peace could be restored only when they were willing to submit. Compromise was impossible.

To make matters even worse, Parliament—at the urging of the king—issued the Prohibitory Act. This act cut off British trade to the colonies and stated that Britain would no longer protect them. Colonial ships were now subject to capture, and their cargo became the "lawful prize" of the captors.

Early Military Action

Even before the Congress had met, the colonists were stirred by the events in Boston and the stubbornness of the king and Parliament. Many were ready to take up arms, and some did.

Forts Ticonderoga and Crown Point—The news of Lexington and Concord had quickly traveled to western New England. There, **Ethan Allen,** the leader of the Green Mountain Boys—a unit raised to defend the New Hampshire land grants—decided to capture the British outposts of Fort Ticonderoga (TY kon duh ROE guh) and Crown Point. Since these forts were on Lake Champlain, getting them into American hands would prevent the British from cutting off New England from New York and the rest of the colonies.

Meanwhile, **Benedict Arnold** had set out from Massachusetts on the same mission. Allen and Arnold met en route and argued about who should lead the expedition. Unable to decide, they both served as commanders. These unwilling partners captured **Fort Ticonderoga** without a shot at dawn on the same day that the Second Continental Congress first met. In addition to gaining a strategic location, they seized the fort's artillery. The following day the same forces captured Fort Crown Point, clearing the way for an invasion of Canada.

The Battle of Bunker Hill—Meanwhile, back in Boston, the conflict continued to grow. While the Second Continental Congress debated proposals vital to the American cause, the Boston patriots took possession of Bunker and Breed's Hills on the Charlestown peninsula, just across the bay from the city. Colonel William Prescott then ordered his men to build trenches in case of attack.

The British general Gage wanted to force the Americans from these hilltop positions. Reinforced by **William Howe** and his three thousand men, Gage ordered Howe to capture the hills. The

Monuments memorialize militia leaders such as Ethan Allen, who were vital to the American war effort.

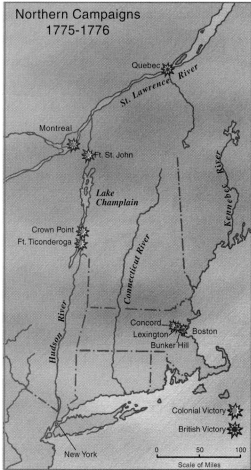

**Northern Campaigns
1775-1776**

Quebec

St. Lawrence River

Montreal

Ft. St. John

Lake Champlain

Kennebec River

Crown Point
Ft. Ticonderoga

Connecticut River

Hudson River

Concord
Lexington
Bunker Hill
Boston

Colonial Victory
British Victory

New York

0   50   100
Scale of Miles

after the German region from which most of them came.

A Canadian Invasion—The colonists hoped that they could rally Canadians to the patriot cause and thus win Canada easily. If the British lost Canada as a base for their operations, it would be harder for them to attack elsewhere. The colonists were optimistic about Canadians coming to their aid for two reasons. Some Canadians were French and had never liked the British. Others had suffered many of the same injustices the colonists had suffered. Congress approved a two-front approach. General Philip Schuyler (SKY lur) was to advance along Lake Champlain northward to take Fort St. John and Montreal. While Schuyler was moving, Benedict Arnold was to trek across Maine and southern Canada to Quebec. Schuyler would then join Arnold at Quebec for an assault on that city.

During November Schuyler became ill, and Richard Montgomery, a former British officer, assumed command and captured Fort St. John and Montreal. Crippled by cold and hindered by the freezing waters of the Kennebec (KEN uh BEK) River, Arnold's

first two assaults were driven back. On the third attempt the colonists ran out of ammunition and were forced to retreat. Howe had won, but his casualties were heavy.

The British were determined to put a stop to colonial resistance, and they quickly stepped up their military action. To prevent any trade of weapons and supplies between colonies, the British ordered a blockade of New England. They also hired several thousand troops to help them. These hired soldiers, or **mercenaries** (MUR suh NAIR eez), were called Hessians

Revolutionary battles copied the European technique of fighting in ordered ranks.

forces did not reach Quebec until late December. Montgomery joined Arnold for an attack on Quebec on New Year's Eve. The Americans waged the attack—a disastrous failure—in a driving snowstorm. Montgomery was killed, Arnold was severely wounded, and one-third of the American force was captured. Smallpox also broke out among the troops, forcing them to pull back to Fort Ticonderoga. The Americans had gained a healthy respect for the British army, and although reinforce-

Thomas Paine helped stir American patriotism.

ments came in the spring, the Continental army never again attacked Canada.

Common Sense

As the months passed, more and more people saw that they would have to choose either to submit to the British or to fight against them. One factor that influenced their thinking was a pamphlet written by **Thomas Paine** called ***Common Sense.*** Although Paine had been in America less than two years, he had quickly embraced the American cause. Here he saw a land of greater opportunity and less poverty than England. He believed that America was a place where the eighteenth-

century ideas of a just society could work.

In one of the most influential political tracts in history, Paine built a case for American separation from Britain. He tried to convince the masses that Britain had become unfit to rule them. He noted tyrannical acts of the king and Parliament and used these facts to show that to separate from Britain was the "common sense" thing to do. Within six months after the publication of *Common Sense,* the Declaration of Independence was signed.

Paine wrote a second pamphlet called *The American Crisis.* This essay was first read to Washington's troops on December 10, 1776. The pamphlet rallied the men amid their hardships to complete or even stay beyond their enlistments. These men then went on to victories in New Jersey, proving that they were not the mere "summer soldiers" or "sunshine patriots" the pamphlet had scorned.

Freeing Boston

During the winter of 1775-76, American efforts centered on getting the British out of Boston. Colonel Henry Knox, a Boston bookseller turned soldier, performed one of the most amazing feats of the war. Using forty-two sledges pulled by eighty teams of oxen, the twenty-five-year-old Knox and his men hauled sixty tons of artillery (cannon and ammunition) from Fort Ticonderoga to Boston. They did it in forty-seven days over mountains, snow, and ice, covering a distance of about three hundred miles. The Americans placed the cannon on Dorchester (DOR chuh stur) Heights overlooking Boston on the night of March 1.

When the British army saw the cannon looming over them, they evacuated the city and sailed south to New York on March 17. About a thousand **Loyalists**—colonists who favored Britain's cause—also left Boston, sailed to Halifax, Nova Scotia, and settled there.

Declaring Independence

During the fall of 1775 and the winter of 1776, the Continental Congress took steps toward declaring independence from Britain by creating an American navy, purchasing more war supplies, and welcoming unofficial French aid. On May 15 Virginia's House of Burgesses endorsed a resolution for independence. The other colonies were also ready to make such a move. Only Pennsylvania and New York were reluctant.

On June 7 Richard Henry Lee of Virginia introduced a resolution to the Continental Congress "that these United Colonies are, and of right ought to be, free and independent states." A committee of five men was appointed to write the declaration. (Other committees were to design a plan of union, or confederation, and to consider making foreign alliances.) On July 2 the resolution came up for a vote. All the delegations except New York's voted for the declaration. The document, written primarily by **Thomas Jefferson,** was polished for two days. On July 4, 1776, the Congress unanimously approved the **Declaration of Independence.**

The Signing of the Declaration of Independence *by John Trumbull records America's official break with England.*

 What was Thomas Paine's role in America's fight for independence?

Battling for Independence

The Declaration of Independence forced Americans not already committed to the cause to declare themselves either patriots or Loyalists. The number of patriots grew toward the end of the war, but throughout most of the struggle, about one-third to one-half of the colonists were in this group.

Another one-fourth to one-third of the population were Loyalists, sometimes called Tories after the British political party that was strongly loyal to the crown. Around a hundred thousand Loyalists were either uncomfortable enough or unsure enough about the future that they fled the colonies and went to England, Canada, or the British West Indies. Most Loyalists stayed behind, probably because they did not want to risk losing valuable properties. To stay out of trouble, they often kept their opinions to themselves. Other Tories, about fifty thousand, fought directly for

---

SECTION REVIEW

1. What name was given to the petition the Second Continental Congress sent to the king? What was the king's response?

2. What two commanders led their men in the strategic capture of the British forts Ticonderoga and Crown Point?

3. What were the colonists who favored the British cause called?

4. When did the Continental Congress finally approve a declaration of America's independence?

Britain, especially during periods when Britain seemed to be winning. These colonists aided the British by selling them food and supplies. Some even led Indian parties raiding the settlements. Others became spies or propagandists.

There were good men on both sides. Many Loyalists, seeing the king as God's authority over them, believed it wrong to rebel against the British Empire. On the other hand, many patriots believed that Britain had relinquished her authority over the colonies and that they should thus "be subject" to the colonial government.

The remaining colonists were indifferent. Some were neutral for business reasons, fearing financial hurt if they chose sides. Others lived in remote areas and were not greatly concerned with the conflict.

Washington's Action

With Boston secure in American hands, Washington moved his army south to New York in April. The Americans assumed that New York would be the British target and committed troops to its defense. Because of its sea access, islands, and rivers, however, New York proved impossible to defend. Throughout July seven hundred British ships brought an army of 34,000 from Nova Scotia to New York under General Howe's command.

Trouble in New York—Outnumbered four to one, Washington could not defeat the British. However, he could outmaneuver them in battle. If he did not, he would lose his army. Howe had broken through the American outer defense on Long Island, forcing the Americans to flee to Brooklyn Heights by the East River. There seemed to be no way of escape for the colonial army. But Alexander McDougall, one of Washington's aides, hurried across the East River to New York City and returned with a motley fleet of fishing boats, rowboats, and sailing ships. A rainy

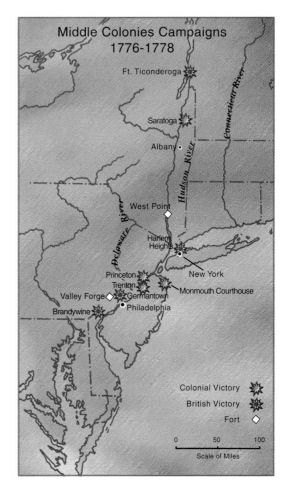

Middle Colonies Campaigns 1776-1778

Ft. Ticonderoga

Saratoga

Albany

West Point

Harlem Heights

Princeton

Trenton

New York

Monmouth Courthouse

Valley Forge

Germantown

Brandywine

Philadelphia

Delaware River

Hudson River

Connecticut River

Colonial Victory
British Victory
Fort

0   50   100
Scale of Miles

night followed by a heavy morning fog permitted the American army to be ferried to temporary safety on Manhattan Island.

After making a stand at the battle of Harlem Heights on Manhattan, Washington managed to get most of his troops across the Hudson River to relative safety in New Jersey and later across the Delaware to Pennsylvania.

Washington Attacks Trenton and Princeton—Howe settled down in New York for the winter but sent Hessian soldiers to Trenton, New Jersey, to keep an eye on Washington. Since the Americans had been forced out of New York and had not won a major battle in seven months, their morale was low. Moreover, the troop enlistments were to expire December 31, 1776. If these men left, Washington would have only fourteen hundred men—unless, of course, he gained some new recruits. He needed a victory to attract more men to the cause.

Responding to the challenge, he and his men crossed the ice-filled Delaware River on Christmas night, surprised the Hessians at **Trenton** the next morning, and captured over nine hundred of them.

The British responded quickly and sent a superior force under **Charles Cornwallis** to confront Washington. Washington left decoy campfires burning, slipped out of camp, went around Cornwallis's camp, and marched north to Princeton. There he overcame a small British force.

He then turned toward Morristown, the location selected for his winter headquarters. His daring, unconventional moves had freed most of New Jersey from British occupation and had given new hope to Americans. A British observer wrote, "A few days ago they had given up the cause for lost; . . . now they are liberty mad again."

Victory at Saratoga

Because the British believed that a mere show of force might end the colonial rebellion, they had not been overly aggressive in 1776. In 1777, however, they developed a plan of attack that they thought would quickly end the war.

According to the British plan, General **John Burgoyne** (bur GOIN) would lead an army south from Montreal into New York while General William Howe went up the Hudson River from New York City. General Barry St. Leger (SAINT LEJ-ur) would go down the St. Lawrence from Montreal to Lake

Ontario and then cut east across the Mohawk River valley. The three generals were to meet at Albany. Their offensive, had it been successful, would have cut off New England and upper New York, centers of colonial resistance, from the rest of the colonies.

In trying to execute their plan, the British made disastrous mistakes. Instead of moving up the Hudson, Howe sought the war minister's permission to pacify Pennsylvania. Washington met him unsuccessfully at Brandywine Creek west of Philadelphia and at

Emanuel Leutze gives a romantic representation of Washington's crossing of the Delaware River.

Germantown. Howe then wintered in the luxury of Philadelphia and missed the fall action at Albany.

St. Leger made some initial progress, but as he worked his way east, he found New York militiamen to be tougher than he expected. St. Leger's force was made up of about two thousand Indians and Tories, and the Indians were difficult to control. When Benedict Arnold's carefully planted rumors about American strength reached their ears, many Indians deserted. Because his force was crippled by the desertions and by an American attack, St. Leger retreated to Lake Ontario.

Nathan Hale: The Schoolmaster Who Gave His Life

One problem Washington faced in New York was that he desperately needed information about the British plans and troops on Long Island. When officers were asked to volunteer for this dangerous task, there was only one volunteer: a schoolteacher from East Haddam, Connecticut, named **Nathan Hale.**

Hale had no special training for such a mission. He did have his Yale diploma, however, which enabled him to travel as a schoolmaster. He was thus able to work his way south from Connecticut to Long Island in a few days.

But Hale had no sooner gotten information on Long Island when Howe forced the Continental Army across to Manhattan. Because his information about Long Island would now be of less value, Hale pursued the British army up Manhattan Island. There, on the night of September 21, he was captured. The information he was carrying implicated him, and Howe ordered him hanged the next morning without even a trial.

On his way to the gallows, Hale supposedly said, "I only regret that I have but one life to lose for my country." It is not certain whether Hale indeed said these words. It is possible, however, for they were a paraphrase from *Cato,* an eighteenth-century play by Joseph Addison. It is reasonable to assume that a schoolmaster of Hale's caliber could readily recall the quotation. In any case, Captain Frederick Mackenzie, a British officer who described Hale's death, wrote, "He behaved with great composure and resolution." He added that Hale's last words were, "It is the duty of every good officer to obey any orders given him by his commander-in-chief."

Marching southward, Burgoyne recaptured Ticonderoga on July 5. From that point on, however, his progress was slowed. First, General Philip Schuyler's men felled trees and dammed streams to block him. Soon Burgoyne ran short of supplies and draft animals.

He sent a foraging party of seven hundred men—mostly Hessians—east to Bennington, Vermont, where he had heard there was a stockpile of American military supplies. But his soldiers were met by a force of more than fifteen hundred New Hampshire militiamen under John Stark. They had been angered by the shooting and scalping of Jane McCrea, a settler's wife, and Burgoyne's pardon of her murderer. The patriots captured all of the foraging party and most of the relief party sent to rescue the British troops.

Burgoyne needed either to crush the Americans speedily or to wait for rescue by Sir Henry Clinton, who was in New York City. On September 19 he attacked the Americans under Horatio Gates at Freeman's Farm near Saratoga (SEHR uh TOE guh). The British suffered heavy casualties. Thinking that Gates would divide his forces to go after Clinton, Burgoyne took the offensive a second time three weeks later at Bemis Heights. Again Burgoyne lost heavily. Low on supplies, he surrendered on October 17, 1777.

This battle of **Saratoga** knocked one British army out of the war and forced Britain to give up any hope of taking the northern colonies. Alarmed, the British changed their strategy. They would now focus on the South, where the population was more scattered and where there were supposedly more Loyalists. Meanwhile, in the North they would only continue the naval blockade and make coastal raids.

Besides giving renewed hope to Americans, the battle at Saratoga officially brought France into the war on the American side. French military and financial aid proved helpful as the war continued.

The Bad Winter of 1777-78

Although the victory at Saratoga offered Americans new hope, it did little to change the physical condition of Washington's men. Acute supply problems had left them hungry, cold, ill-clothed, and sick at **Valley Forge,** Pennsylvania, in late 1777 and early 1778. Baron Von Steuben (STOO bun), a drill master from Prussia, gave military training to those who were well enough. The pride and skill he instilled helped the men to focus less on their hardships and more on the cause. A new army quartermaster, General **Nathanael Greene,** tried to solve the supply problem, but it improved little. Congress had no power to tax and little money for purchasing supplies. Those supplies sent by the states often never reached the men because of poor transportation or theft. Collapse of the paper money system also added to the financial crisis. Eventually some New Jersey troops mutinied, two Connecticut regiments demonstrated, and Pennsylvania troops marched off to the state house to negotiate their pay.

The slim pocketbook of the Continental army was replenished by some donations. Robert Morris, head of the Department of Finance, was able to ask for money and supplies from the states and for a loan of four million dollars from France. Morris also used the banking system to stretch the government's resources.

In June 1778, **Sir Henry Clinton,** who took Howe's place in the North, moved from Philadelphia toward New York, hoping to use its harbor as a base for sea raids. Washington

The Battle of Saratoga is brought to life by reenactment volunteers.

Joseph Brant: Mohawk Loyalist

Joseph Brant, a Mohawk chieftain, first gained recognition during the French and Indian War, when he fought under Sir William Johnson against the French. After the war Johnson sent Brant to Eleazar Wheelock's Indian school in Lebanon, Connecticut, where Brant became a devout Christian. During Pontiac's Rebellion, Brant again fought with the British. In the meantime he had been serving as a missionary to his people.

When the War for Independence began, Brant sided with the Loyalists. In his opinion as a Christian, the colonies were wrong to rebel against the king, whom God had placed in power. His influence brought many other Indians to the Loyalist cause as well. Commissioned a captain, he led several raids on American settlements in the Cherry Valley. The colonists soon feared his men.

After the war Brant encouraged peace. For his help during the war, the British gave his people land and money to settle in Ontario. Brant returned to his missionary work and translated the Gospel of Mark into the Mohawk language. He never took up arms again.

As an Indian statesman he negotiated treaties with other tribes and traveled in the American West in an effort to form an all-Indian confederacy.

Joseph Brant was a man who gave his all to whatever cause he believed to be right. He was an Indian whom even modern historians are forced to recognize as a man of convictions and a devout Christian.

The winter of 1777 tested the determination of the troops at Valley Forge.

The War in the West

The British, Loyalists, and Indians were also active in the West. In 1778 some settlers in the Wyoming Valley of Pennsylvania and Cherry Valley, New York, were massacred. General John Sullivan drove the Tories back to their base at Fort Niagara, but he never gained the fort itself.

Settlements in the Ohio River valley were also raided. British colonel Henry Hamilton, who had been nicknamed "Hair Buyer" because he paid bounties for American scalps, was responsible. **George Rogers Clark** organized a force of 175 men to go into the Ohio Valley to drive Hamilton out. Braving dark forests, swamps, and icy rivers, as well as the threat of Indians and Tories, Clark captured two frontier outposts—Kaskaskia (kus KAS kee uh) in Illinois and Vincennes (vin SENZ) in Indiana. This meant that later the United States could lay claim to lands bordering the Mississippi River.

The War at Sea

Throughout the war America was involved in fighting at sea. America did not have a navy at the beginning of the war. The early navy

followed him and attacked at Monmouth Courthouse, New Jersey. The American effort was unsuccessful, however, and the British army made it to New York. Washington and his men spent the winter of 1778-79 at White Plains, New York, hoping at least to keep Clinton in the area.

consisted mostly of **privateers,** merchant vessels outfitted to fight.

Since Great Britain had a strong navy, Americans faced an almost impossible task on the seas. After France came into the war, the Americans hoped that French sea power would come to their aid. America could, and did, use French ports as bases of operation and even used French ships to attack the British.

The most famous American naval officer was **John Paul Jones.** A Scotsman by birth, Jones gained his greatest fame by defeating the British ship *Serapis* (SEHR up pis) in the North Sea. He used a French ship rechristened the *Bonhomme Richard* (BON-om RICH-urd), after Benjamin Franklin's *Poor Richard's Almanac.*

SECTION REVIEW

1. What was the difference between the patriots and the Loyalists (Tories)?

2. What two victories virtually freed New Jersey from British occupation and gave new hope to Washington's men?

3. What American victory forced the British out of the North?

4. What American leader won important victories in the West?

5. What were the privateers, and what part did they play in the War for Independence?

6. Who was the most famous American naval officer in the War for Independence?

 Why did the Continental army have supply problems?

Women at War for Independence

There were several women who contributed to the patriot cause on the field of battle. Some helped in a moment of crisis; others fought throughout the struggle. From the front lines to the frontier, however, these women of the War for Independence took the call to arms seriously. They were not afraid to fight for the cause their family and friends believed in—no matter what the danger or the cost.

Margaret Corbin: This young lady went to war with her husband. At the British attack on Fort Washington, she began firing a cannon when the man working it was killed. Then her husband, who was firing the cannon next to her, was killed. Margaret took over his position and continued firing until she was shot and wounded. Her wound was so severe that she was an invalid for the rest of her life.

Mary Ludwig Hays McCauley: This woman warrior became known as Molly Pitcher. She served as a water carrier for her husband and the other patriot soldiers during the Battle of Monmouth.

When her husband was wounded, Mary took charge of his cannon and fired it for him.

Betty Zane: In an Indian and Loyalist attack on Fort Henry, the patriot defenders found themselves running low on gunpowder. They knew

Mary Hays, better known as Molly Pitcher

Winning Independence

After the loss at Saratoga, the British turned their interest toward the South. In the fall of 1778, Clinton's force set sail for the major southern port city of Savannah, Georgia. It was captured easily, as was Augusta, Georgia. In 1780 the British besieged Charleston, South Carolina, from March until May, when it also fell. Clinton believed that the British could recover everything back up to the Hudson "unless a superior fleet shows itself."

Southern Successes

The Continental Congress sent Horatio Gates south from Saratoga. He engaged Lord Cornwallis at Camden, South Carolina, and suffered a crushing defeat. Gates then fled to Charlotte, leaving his men behind. He was soon replaced by General Nathanael Greene. British colonel Banastre Tarleton used his forces to harass the southern soldiers as they tried to regroup. Although the situation seemed bleak for the patriots, success would soon come.

---

that some was available in a cabin about one hundred yards away. To go after the powder appeared suicidal, but Betty Zane convinced the men that she could make it. She reasoned that since she was a woman, the Indians might be more interested in capturing her than in shooting her. Leaving the stockade, Betty calmly walked across the line of fire to the cabin. There she put the powder into a tablecloth and headed back. On her return trip the Indians and Loyalists saw what she was doing and began firing at her. Running all the way, she arrived safely at the fort.

"Mad Anne" Bailey: This adventurous woman served as a scout and messenger for the patriots on the frontier. She was given her nickname by the Indians because they thought that either she had special protection from the Great Spirit or she was insane. Her husband had been killed in an Indian attack. Once, when being chased by Indians, she hid in a hollow log. After the Indians left, she trailed them to their camp and that night took back everything they had stolen from her. Several times she traveled alone through areas infested by Indians to get gunpowder for a fort running low on it.

Nancy Hart: The Indians fighting for the British in Georgia called her the "War Woman." Once she helped a patriot escape from several Loyalists by having him gallop right through her house so that he wouldn't leave a trail. When the six Loyalists returned from their futile search, they forced Nancy to prepare a meal for them. While doing so, she sent her daughter for help. Then while they were eating, she took their muskets, killed two of the men, and held the rest at gunpoint until help arrived.

Women did much for the cause of independence.

In September of 1780, British colonel Patrick Ferguson sent a proclamation to the frontiersmen of the Carolina Piedmont region. The proclamation stated that the men should come to Ferguson to lay down their weapons or he would "lay waste the country-side with fire and sword." Those who had been indecisive about freedom were now furious. The men crossed the mountains in search of Ferguson and his Tory forces at **Kings Mountain**. On October 7, 1780, these "over-mountain men," as they are called, met Ferguson's challenge by killing or capturing the entire force of a thousand men. Ferguson himself was killed and buried on the battlefield.

Nathanael Greene then divided the small patriot army in the South and had Daniel Morgan fake a retreat. Tarleton took the bait and came after him. On January 17, 1781, at **Cowpens,** South Carolina, Morgan and his men killed or captured most of Tarleton's force.

Greene lured Cornwallis northward away from Morgan and crossed the Dan River, faking a move into Virginia. Then on March 15, 1781, he dropped back down to challenge Cornwallis at Guilford Courthouse near Greensboro, North Carolina. Although Cornwallis won the battle, his victory proved expensive, and the cost of the win contributed to his ultimate defeat.

British Surrender at Yorktown

As Cornwallis moved across the Carolinas chasing Greene, his supply lines lengthened. Guerilla fighters—such as Francis Marion, Thomas Sumter, and Andrew Pickens—attacked those lines and harassed British troop movements at every turn. A frustrated Cornwallis pulled out of the Carolina midlands and Piedmont and headed for coastal southeastern Virginia. There, he reasoned, the British navy could keep him supplied, and he could devise a new strategy. Cornwallis

When asked to surrender by the captain of the Serapis, *John Paul Jones answered, "I have not yet begun to fight!"*

believed he could subdue Virginia, the source of patriot supplies. Then his troops could menace the South once more. The only threat to Cornwallis seemed to be a twenty-four-year-old French volunteer, **Marquis de Lafayette** (mar-KEE deh lah-fee-ET), whom Washington had sent to the area with troops. Cornwallis met very little resistance from these troops as he headed for Yorktown, where he planned a well-fortified base. British general Clinton, a rival, did little to help him.

Cornwallis was unprepared for what happened next. The patriots had pleaded repeatedly for French naval help. Suddenly Admiral de Grasse (GRAHSS), now in the West Indies, was ready to help with his twenty-eight ships. The British did not expect this show of strength, and they thought that when an attack

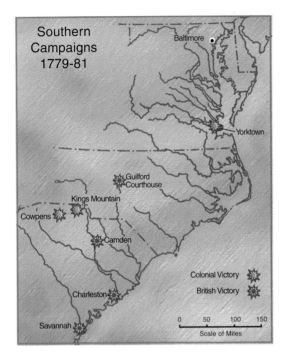

Southern
Campaigns
1779-81

Baltimore

Yorktown

Guilford
Courthouse

Kings Mountain

Cowpens

Camden

Colonial Victory

British Victory

Charleston

Savannah

0   50   100   150
Scale of Miles

did come it would be at New York City rather than at Yorktown.

Washington slipped out of New York with most of his forces to help trap Cornwallis in Virginia. De Grasse's French troops arrived to reinforce Lafayette's and Washington's men and help prevent Cornwallis's escape. Eight additional French warships prevented any of the remaining British ships from leaving for New York. Now Cornwallis was trapped at **Yorktown** without the hope of support from the British navy. Outnumbered more than two to one, Cornwallis offered only brief resistance, and on October 18, 1781, he surrendered. With his surrender came the British recognition that the Americans had won. Although the British had formally surrendered one army, they still occupied some American territories. They were especially active in the Northwest and still controlled some forts there. The conflict between Loyalists and patriots continued for some time.

Treaty Negotiations

Since France had been America's major ally, the peace talks were held in Paris. Benjamin Franklin, John Jay, and Henry Laurens were chosen as the American negotiators. While on his way to Paris, Henry Laurens was captured by the British and imprisoned in the Tower of London. He arrived in time for only the signing. Franklin, meanwhile, suffered a kidney stone attack, leaving John Jay as the chief negotiator.

The **Treaty of Paris,** signed September 3, 1783, ended the eight-year war with Britain. It formally granted the United States of America its independence and gave the new nation all lands that had not already been occupied east of the Mississippi. It also set the northern boundary from the Great Lakes to Lake of the Woods in Minnesota.

The fighting between the United States and Britain had stopped in April 1783. The last British troops left New York City on November 25, 1783. The war was officially over. But now, as an independent nation, the United States faced enormous problems. Independence would bring change—and many new challenges.

SECTION REVIEW

1. What brought the "over-mountain men" out to fight the battle of Kings Mountain?

2. What battle did Cornwallis "win" that was so costly it ultimately contributed to his defeat?

3. Where did Cornwallis surrender?

4. What treaty officially ended the war with Britain?

 How were the colonists able to defeat Cornwallis?

The Surrender of Lord Cornwallis *by John Trumbull*

SUMMARY

Although the War for Independence had begun with the battles of Lexington and Concord in 1775, the colonies did not officially declare their independence until a year later. The early years of the war brought only a few victories to the Continental army, but the British defeat at Saratoga in 1777 began to turn the tide. Victories for the Americans in the South led to the eventual entrapment of Cornwallis's British army at Yorktown in 1781. After that, only scattered resistance remained until the peace treaty was signed two years later. America's independence was won.

Chapter Review

People, Places, and Things to Remember

Second Continental
  Congress
Continental army
Ethan Allen
Benedict Arnold
Fort Ticonderoga
William Howe
mercenaries
Thomas Paine
Common Sense

Loyalists
Thomas Jefferson
Declaration of
  Independence
Trenton
Charles Cornwallis
John Burgoyne
Nathan Hale
Saratoga
Valley Forge

Nathanael Greene
Sir Henry Clinton
George Rogers Clark
privateers
John Paul Jones
Kings Mountain
Cowpens
Marquis de Lafayette
Yorktown
Treaty of Paris

Review Questions

Supply the name of the missing man or location in these statements.

1. Ethan Allen and _?_ captured Fort Ticonderoga from the British.

2. General Gage and _?_ defeated the colonists at Bunker Hill.

3. General Henry Knox brought cannons from _?_ to drive the British from Boston.

4. _?_ crossed the Delaware River to defeat the Hessians at Trenton.

5. The Americans defeated General Burgoyne at _?_.

6. Washington spent a hungry, cold winter with his men at _?_.

7. _?_ defeated "Hair Buyer" Hamilton in the West.

8. America's most famous Continental naval officer was _?_.

9. The Americans trapped the British general _?_ at Yorktown.

Match the following terms to their descriptions.

10. Hessians

11. Loyalists

12. Marquis de Lafayette

13. privateers

14. Thomas Paine

15. Treaty of Paris

a. author of *Common Sense* pamphlet

b. backed the British in the war

c. Frenchman who aided the Americans

d. mercenary troops who fought for the British

e. officially ended the War for Independence

f. trading ships equipped for warfare

Questions for Discussion

16. What do you think would have happened if Canada had sided with the Americans?

17. Why do you suppose the patriots won their victory at Kings Mountain?

History Skills

Reading Maps

If you want to follow events in U.S. history, you need to be able to see in your mind the places where the events occurred. You can't understand history without maps. When "reading" each map, notice the scale. A scale shows the distance between two points on the map. To visualize distances, try to think of places that are similar distances from your home. Another essential element on many maps is the legend. A legend, or key, shows what the map's colors and symbols represent. For example, the legend for "Early Explorers and Colonies" (p. 10) shows the colors that correspond to the colonizers—Dutch, English, French, and Spanish.

Look closely at the maps in Chapters 1-6 to answer the questions below.

1. Look at the map of Early Explorers and Colonies, page 10. What country is green in the legend? How many regions are green on the map?

2. Look at the map of the Middle Colonies on page 26. What is the approximate distance between New York and Philadelphia?

3. Look at the map of Swedish and Dutch colonies on page 26. Why is the name *New York* shown in parentheses?

4. Compare the three maps of the American colonies on pages 26 and 30. Do they all have the same scale?

5. Look at the physical map of the thirteen colonies on page 35.
   a. What are the three main land features labeled on the map?
   b. Does the map give any hints that the western borders of the colonies were unsettled?

6. Compare the maps on pages 75 and 79.
   a. Which country controlled the land west of the Mississippi River in 1750? in 1763?
   b. Which country controlled East Florida in 1750? in 1763?

7. Compare the three campaign maps on pages 97, 100, and 108.
   a. What two symbols appear on every key?
   b. Which map shows four British victories and four colonial victories?
   c. Which map shows the location of the photograph on page 103?
   d. Which battle—Bunker Hill, Yorktown, Vincennes—is not shown on any maps in this chapter? Why is it impossible to show this battle on these maps?

Confederation

Before and during most of the War for Independence, the First and Second Continental Congresses along with state assemblies governed the colonies. Although the people had been reluctant to grant extensive political power to any centralized government, the crisis convinced the patriot leaders that they needed a more permanent form of government. Cooperation among the colonies in financing and fighting the war was essential. Many colonial leaders questioned whether the Continental Congresses even had the authority to wage war. Consequently, a committee was appointed in 1776 to submit a new plan for an improved system of government. The new form suggested was a **confederation,** a loose association, or league, of states.

Organization and Achievements of Confederation

The new plan, drafted in 1777, was called the **Articles of Confederation** and was written largely by Delaware's John Dickinson. Under this plan the government had one governing body, a congress, whose members were to be elected yearly.

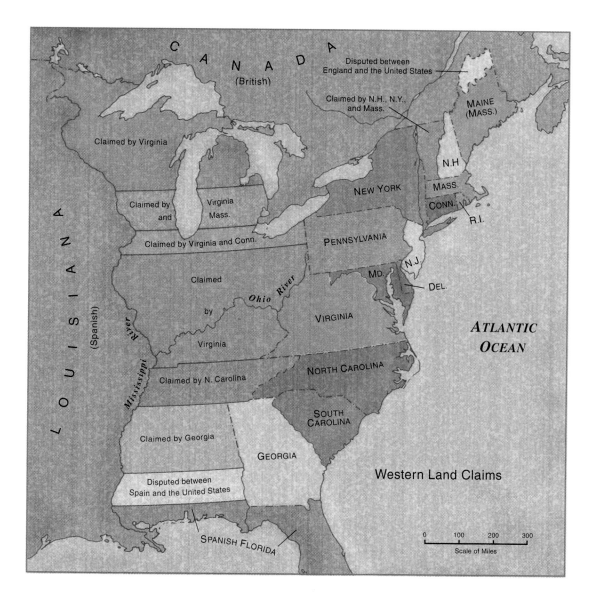

Western Land Claims

Adoption of the Articles of Confederation

Before the articles could become law, however, each state had to **ratify** them (give them formal approval). The articles were presented to the states in November 1777, but it took almost four years to complete the ratification process. Maryland, a smaller state, refused to ratify the plan until power was given to Congress to dispose of western lands. Some states objected to this idea for two main reasons. First, the states with western land claims did not want to give them up. Second, influential land speculators were upset that they would be unable to make huge profits reselling the cheap land they had purchased.

The states compromised. The Confederation Congress gained control of the western lands, but in return each state, no matter how small, was given an equal vote in the Congress. Also, to satisfy the large southern states, tax assessments in the slave states were based on the value of improved lands rather than on the population. Virginia, the state with the largest western land claim, held out on the compromise until January of 1781 when it offered to give up its claims north of the Ohio River. In response, Maryland ratified the Articles the same month. Finally, on March first the plan was adopted by the Confederation Congress.

Under the new plan laws could be passed when nine of the thirteen states approved them. The Articles themselves could be changed only with the unanimous consent of the states.

The Powers of Congress

Although the Confederation Congress lacked some crucial powers, especially the power to tax, it did have more powers than the makeshift Continental Congresses. For example, the Confederation Congress could raise and maintain an army, declare war, make treaties with foreign countries, manage Indian affairs, establish a postal system, and borrow and coin money. These powers, however, were not held exclusively by Congress. The states, without congressional consent, could also coin their own monies, issue bills of credit, deal directly with foreign governments, and even declare war.

In addition, certain powers were held only by the states. The states, for instance, controlled both domestic and foreign trade; had the right to act in economic matters involving debts, contracts, and family affairs; and had the right to tax citizens.

The states also agreed to cooperate in some matters. First, they agreed to give full faith and credit to public civil acts of other states. Thus each state would respect the others' birth, marriage, and death certificates and wills. Second, they agreed to return, at the request of a state's governor, criminals and runaway slaves who crossed state lines. Third, they agreed to settle their differences by arbitration. This meant that two states involved in a dispute would let a mutually acceptable third party help them reach a solution.

Lasting Achievements

Although the Confederation government lasted only eight years, it did take some legislative actions that are noteworthy. Several important ideas of government were established, some of which are still being followed today.

Probably the most important legislation passed by the Confederation Congress dealt with the western lands. Until 1890 the West was a constantly changing land area. In the 1780s the term *West* meant the land west of the thirteen colonies. Thomas Jefferson, who penned most of the Declaration of Independence, also drafted two pieces of legislation dealing with these lands: the Northwest Ordinance of 1785 and the Northwest Ordinance of 1787.

The Northwest Ordinance of 1785—The Confederation Congress had first gained control of the lands that lie north of the Ohio River and between the Mississippi and the Appalachian Mountains. The Congress quickly made provision for the settlement of this land, which was called the **Northwest Territory.** The **Northwest Ordinance of 1785** provided for surveying and selling the western lands that the Articles of Confederation had placed under the Congress's control. This government land totaled almost a quarter billion acres of excellent land and was eventually divided into five states.

The ordinance provided for the land to be divided into areas six-mile square, called

townships. Each township was then divided into thirty-six smaller parcels (each one-mile square) called sections, with each section containing 640 acres. (See the illustration.) Second, the ordinance provided for the sale of the land at auctions. The minimum acceptable price was one dollar an acre, and the buyer had to purchase at least one section, or 640 acres.

Although Congress could have made more money by setting a higher price or by using a different method of sale, it wanted to give people of modest means the opportunity to purchase the land for family farms. Many did, but others either could not raise the necessary $640 or saw no need to purchase parcels so large. Consequently, Congress, ever short of cash, sold the land at wholesale prices to several large land companies, the Ohio Company being probably the best known.

Another condition placed on the sale of the land was that Congress had to have legal title to the land before selling it. That is, Congress had to make treaties with the Indians to buy the lands they claimed before any of that land could be sold. Congress hoped this would prevent Indian uprisings like Pontiac's Rebellion (1763-66).

The orderly, practical system established by the Ordinance of 1785 has had a lasting effect on America. Not only the states of the Northwest Territories but also other new territories and states were surveyed according to

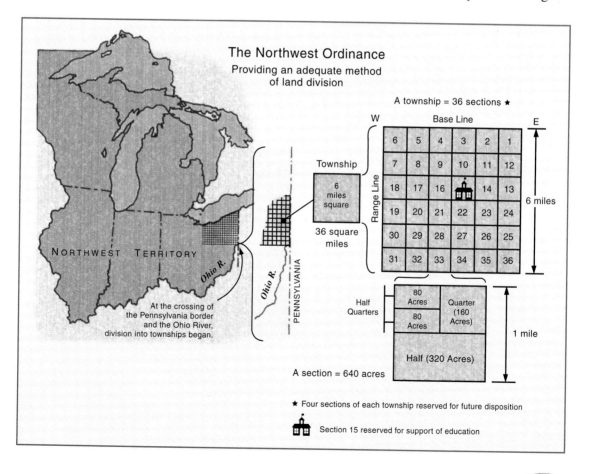

The Northwest Ordinance
Providing an adequate method of land division

A township = 36 sections ★

A section = 640 acres

At the crossing of the Pennsylvania border and the Ohio River, division into townships began.

★ Four sections of each township reserved for future disposition

Section 15 reserved for support of education

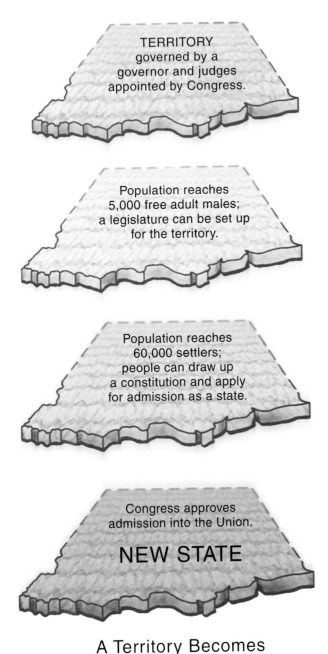

TERRITORY
governed by a
governor and judges
appointed by Congress.

Population reaches
5,000 free adult males;
a legislature can be set up
for the territory.

Population reaches
60,000 settlers;
people can draw up
a constitution and apply
for admission as a state.

Congress approves
admission into the Union.

NEW STATE

A Territory Becomes
a State

its demands. A look at the map of the fifty states (see the map of the United States in the back of the book) shows that unless there was a natural waterway like a river or lake to form a boundary between states, the boundaries were usually drawn as straight lines. In addition, a flight over land west of the thirteen colonies shows an almost checkerboard arrangement of farms, with the roads running as straight lines with right angle turns. The Land Ordinance of 1785, with its system of surveying western lands, is responsible for both of these features.

The Northwest Ordinance of 1787— A second piece of legislation, called the **Northwest Ordinance of 1787,** provided a means for governing these large tracts of western land. Originally, the ordinance applied only to those lands in the Northwest Territory, an area bounded on the east by the original thirteen colonies, on the west by the Mississippi River, on the north by the Great Lakes, and on the south by the Ohio River.

Under this ordinance the land was divided into territories. Each one had a governor to preside over its affairs, three judges to handle the courts and legal matters, and a secretary. All these officers were appointed by Congress, and the people living in the territory had no voice in their government.

When the population of any territory reached 5,000 adult white free males of voting age, however, that region could elect its own territorial legislature, but Congress would still select its governor. This governor, like governors in colonial days, had the power to approve or veto acts of the legislature.

When the population in a territory grew to 60,000, the people could write a constitution and submit it to Congress. If they submitted a constitution that guaranteed a republican form of government, they could be accepted as a state. Each new state would have the same powers and rights as the original states.

The Northwest Ordinance allowed Congress to accept no fewer than three and no more than five states from these western lands. A look at the map shows that five entire states and part of a sixth (Minnesota) came out of the Northwest Territory.

The Northwest Ordinance also included what one historian called "a mini-bill of rights." For example, this legislation guaranteed freedom of religion. Perhaps the most surprising point was that the ordinance forbade slavery in the Northwest Territory, thereby making the Ohio River the dividing line between slave states and free states.

The legislation was wise. It allowed new states to come into the Union on an equal footing with the old. Instead of becoming an empire controlled by the original states, the United States became one growing republic with new states gaining a full representation in the government. As a result the legislation helped unite the nation and did more to further the ideals of the union than any other political document except the Constitution.

Other Helps for the Nation—The Confederation Congress also set other important examples for future government. For example, it published its proceedings, an official record of what was done in the Congress. Started as monthly publications, these journals developed into today's *Congressional Record.* Congress also used the decimal system for the money it coined. This system, based on tens and hundreds, is the basis of the money system Americans use today.

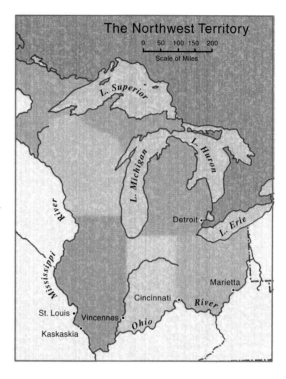

The Northwest Territory

0   50   100 150   200
Scale of Miles

L. Superior
L. Michigan
L. Huron
L. Erie
Detroit
Marietta
River
Cincinnati
Ohio River
St. Louis
Vincennes
Kaskaskia
Mississippi River

SECTION REVIEW

1. What two groups were responsible for governing the colonies before and during the War for Independence?

2. What convinced the leaders of the need for a more permanent form of government?

3. Who wrote much of the Articles of Confederation?

4. What were the two main reasons some states objected to Congress's disposing of western lands?

5. What did the Northwest Ordinance of 1785 provide for western lands?

6. What did the Northwest Ordinance of 1787 provide for western lands?

 What steps did a region take as it moved toward statehood?

Before a national currency was used, each state had its own money.

Organizational Weakness

The primary organizational weakness of the Articles was that the Confederation Congress did not have any power to enforce the laws that it made. There were no executive or judicial branches to enforce or interpret the laws, allowing the national government's decrees to be ignored or disobeyed with little chance of punishment.

Economic Weaknesses

There were serious economic weaknesses as well. For example, Congress could not levy taxes. The Confederation Congress could, and did, ask the states for help. However, the states seldom complied. Because Congress lacked the power to tax, it lacked the necessary funds to run the government and to pay war debts. This meant that debts owed to soldiers, to foreign nations, and to those who had bought war bonds all went unpaid.

Congress also lacked the power to regulate domestic and foreign trade. France eagerly waited to pick up the foreign trade the British had lost, while the states argued over whether they should tax one another's imports.

In addition, Congress did not have the sole authority to coin money or to regulate its value. Gold and silver, needed for coinage or to back the paper money in circulation, were scarce. As a result, states printed paper money with so little backing that it was almost worthless. When this money was not accepted by creditors, people who owed debts couldn't repay them. In some places creditors got control of state legislatures and levied heavy taxes

Weaknesses of Confederation

The Confederation Congress had not only several notable accomplishments but also a few failures. However, most of these failures resulted from the weaknesses in the Articles of Confederation themselves, not from what Congress did or did not do.

to pay off state debts. When the small farmers could not pay the taxes, the courts moved in and took their property.

Poor Foreign Relations

A lack of respect for the political power of the new government produced more problems for the Confederation Congress both at home and overseas.

Problems with Britain—Although the Treaty of Paris, signed in 1783, called for all British troops in the colonies to return to England, the British kept their troops in western forts that they had held before the war. The British reasoned that since Americans could not pay the debts they owed British subjects, Britain would continue her fur trade in America as a way to collect the money owed. Moreover, since no American army was available to dislodge the troops, Britain saw no real need to call them home.

The Treaty of Paris had also required the fair treatment of Loyalists. Many Americans, however, were still bitter toward those who had supported Britain, and they did not treat them well despite the provisions of the treaty. The patriots sometimes kept Loyalist property and even lynched some Loyalists. The British government was justifiably annoyed.

In addition, before the war American shipping enjoyed the protection of a strong British navy because America was a part of the British Empire. Now the British navy was stopping American ships, especially those that still used old British trading routes. Since the American navy was small, it could not rescue these ships. The only option was to find new trade routes where the British did not operate. On their own, however, American ships had little protection from pirates. This was particularly true in the Mediterranean, where the Barbary pirates thrived by preying on unprotected shipping and by forcing the payment of tribute (money paid to protect the ships from

harassment as they passed by). Such treatment was an insult to the United States because it implied that the country was too weak to protect itself.

Problems with France and the Netherlands—Since France had been an ally during the war, the United States continued to court her friendship. But with the states' failure to supply the money requested by Congress, the United States could not pay even the interest owed on its debt to France. When Americans turned to France for more loans, they were refused. As a result, French merchants who thought they would gain from the decline in America's trade with the British were disappointed.

The United States also owed the Netherlands, which had given financial aid to the war effort. Although the Dutch pursued claims with less vigor than others, the debt did not decrease through silence.

Problems with Spain—Relations with Spain had been uneasy for years. Although Spain fought against Britain in the war, she could hardly be labeled a close ally. Spain still held land in North America, and it now eyed the new nation nervously. Because American expansion into the Southeast was a direct threat to Spanish holdings along the Mississippi River and in Florida, Spain retained its forts in the Southeast. Spain easily convinced the local Indians that the Americans would deprive them of their lands and urged them to raid American frontier settlements. Spain hoped these raids would discourage further American settlement so that it could keep the land.

Another dispute with Spain involved American use of ports on the lower Mississippi for exporting. American flatboats floated down the rivers to New Orleans regularly. The Americans expected to have the **right of deposit,** the freedom to stockpile

John Jay attempted to make a treaty with Spain to allow Americans to use ports on the lower Mississippi River.

Lack of Respect

The Confederation Congress had not gained much respect at home either. In the summer of 1786, discontent rose markedly among the farmers of western Massachusetts. The pledge of the Massachusetts Assembly to repay war debts meant levying heavy taxes on the state's citizens to raise the funds. Since crop prices at the time were low, the tax burden was heavier than many farmers could bear. Some fell behind on their taxes; others were forced into bankruptcy. A state law also required that business transactions, even small ones, be recorded by the courts and an appropriate fee paid to the court official for his efforts.

By late summer farmers in four western counties had organized angry mobs that kept the county courts from convening. Despite the state's efforts to lift the tax burden, the mobs continued to show the same spirit they had shown in earlier years against the redcoats. **Daniel Shays,** a veteran officer of the Continental Army, led the mob. As the news of their movement spread eastward, citizens feared that the government would be thrown into turmoil, and many began to panic. The state's governor raised a militia to subdue Shays, who by this time had marched his men toward Springfield, where a federal arsenal (a storage place for weapons) was located. Instead of taxing the people to pay for the militia, rich Bostonians gave to what might be termed a "fright fund." Shays's mob of twelve hundred met the state troops in January, 1787. One volley of shots dispersed the rebels, and there was no property damage or loss of life.

Recognition of Weaknesses

Nevertheless, **Shays's Rebellion** underscored the weakness of the Confederation. When George Washington heard of it, he was "mortified beyond expression," for he believed it made the young nation look "more

goods until ships came to transport them overseas, but Spain wanted to deny them that privilege. Congress gave its experienced treaty maker, **John Jay,** the task of working out the problem. But the Spanish minister had been told not to yield on the right of deposit. The resulting treaty pleased no one, and Congress did not *ratify* (approve) it. Americans retained the right of deposit, but they paid dearly for it with high **tariffs** (charges on imported goods).

Spain also disputed the placement of America's southern boundary. The Americans drew the boundary at the 31st parallel; Spain placed it one hundred miles farther north. Disputes with Spain flared until 1795, when the Pinckney Treaty officially settled them.

Mann's Tavern in Annapolis, Maryland, was the site of the Annapolis Convention.

contemptible" than ever. Congress voted to call a convention to create a government better able to cope with such difficulties. The result was the **Philadelphia Convention**—a meeting that would settle the question of what kind of government America should have.

The government of the United States under the Articles of Confederation was in severe trouble. Something had to be done to strengthen it, and most of America's leaders recognized the need. Their concern would lead to the Philadelphia Convention and a new Constitution. Before this action came, several other meetings laid the groundwork for the Philadelphia Convention.

Preparation for Change—The first important step leading to change came in 1785, when delegates from Maryland and Virginia met at Mount

Independence Hall in Philadelphia

Vernon (George Washington's home). They met regarding the use and navigation of the Potomac River and Chesapeake Bay. Encouraged by their success, they issued an invitation to Pennsylvania and Delaware to join them. They hoped to discuss tariffs on imports, the use of paper money, and other common commercial problems. Some Virginia legislators who were more open to a stronger union seized the opportunity and called for a meeting of all the states to be held at Annapolis in September 1786.

Because only five states showed up, the **Annapolis Convention** did not resolve any commercial disputes as its leaders had hoped. Yet with a vision of a better union that went beyond the moment, three delegates—New York's Alexander Hamilton, Virginia's James Madison, and Delaware's John Dickinson—

persuaded the others to ask the Confederation Congress for a convention of the states to be held on May 14, 1787, in Philadelphia. The purpose of the Philadelphia convention would be to revise the Articles of Confederation so that the national government would be strong enough to govern the country.

When the Philadelphia Convention opened, however, scarcely a dozen men had arrived. Eleven uneasy days went by until finally the delegates from seven states, a bare majority, showed up, and the meeting was convened on May 25.

Eventually fifty-five delegates attended the meeting, coming from twelve states. Only Rhode Island failed to send representatives. The meeting was held in Independence Hall, the same building in which the Declaration of Independence had been signed. George

William Pierce described the authors of the Constitution as "the wisest council in the world."

Washington, already respected because of his leadership during the war, was elected convention chairman. The delegates wisely decided to keep their discussions secret. This gave them the freedom to speak their minds, and also to change them, without fear of public criticism. It also helped avoid the pressures of special-interest groups whose members might have besieged the delegates had they been aware that important matters were being discussed. The secrecy also made it more likely that the states could ratify the document when it was presented to them, for had the people been aware that the delegates had not been in unanimous agreement on the content, their faith in the resulting Constitution might have been shaken.

Men Who Brought Change—God in His wisdom brought the right men to Philadelphia at the right time. Rarely in American history has such a talented, brilliant group of men been assembled in one place. Major William Pierce, a delegate from Georgia, called it "the wisest council in the world" and believed he was greatly privileged to be able to serve with men of such outstanding ability. Proverbs 15:22 reminds us, "Without counsel purposes are disappointed: but in the multitude of counsellors they are established."

George Washington led the Virginia delegation. Some have said that his presence in Philadelphia made the convention a success. As chairman he provided the control and balance necessary. His colleague, **James Madison,** who is called "America's first political scientist," was the single most influential member of the convention, and he has often been called the "Father of the Constitution." Madison, a lawyer by profession but also a keen student of government, kept a diary of the proceedings that is the most accurate source of information about the event. Another Virginia delegate, George Mason, had written the constitution and bill of rights

James Madison has been called the "Father of the Constitution."

for Virginia. The preamble of that bill had served as a model for the preamble of the Declaration of Independence.

The leader of the Pennsylvania delegation was the philosopher-scientist **Benjamin Franklin.** At age eighty-two, he was the oldest delegate, and his sense of humor helped relieve tension. One of Franklin's Pennsylvania colleagues was James Wilson. Major William Pierce wrote of him, "Government seems to have been his peculiar study; all the political institutions of the world he knows in detail, and can trace the causes and effects of every revolution from the earliest stages . . . down to the present time." Wilson's broad knowledge of history and

Alexander Hamilton favored a strong central government.

Companies. Today the city of Dayton, Ohio, bears his name.

Some of the men who were key leaders during the War for Independence were absent from the convention. Thomas Jefferson was serving as minister to France, while John Adams was minister to Great Britain. Thomas Paine was in England seeking to interest the British in his design for iron bridges, and Samuel Adams had not been selected for his state's delegation. Well-known patriot leaders John Hancock and Patrick Henry had not been selected either. Some stayed away because they believed the convention had become an upper-class, conservative effort. The more "radical" elements from the war years were less welcome as ideas had mellowed.

government made him a great asset to the convention. A third noteworthy Pennsylvanian was Gouverneur Morris. He was a captivating speaker and persuasive debater. His gifts as a writer gave the Constitution much of its literary grace.

Alexander Hamilton led New York's delegation. Hamilton favored a strong central government, "one," he said, "that could stand like a Hercules." He believed that the states should have little power and that the national leader should appoint the governor for each state.

The youngest delegate, twenty-six-year-old Jonathan Dayton from New Jersey, later became a proprietor of the Ohio Land

SECTION REVIEW

1. What was the organizational weakness that caused most of the failures of the Confederation Congress?

2. What was to be the source of income to run the government under the Articles of Confederation? What was the result of the Congress's insufficient income?

3. What uprising of 1786-87 protested a heavy tax burden in Massachusetts?

4. What two meetings prepared the way for the Philadelphia Convention?

5. When did the Philadelphia Convention begin? Where was it held? Who was the chairman? What was its original purpose?

6. What were three benefits of keeping convention discussions secret?

7. Name six notable men who were at the convention.

 Why did the United States have problems with nations that had supported the War for Independence?

Stepping Beyond a Confederation

The men who met at Philadelphia soon realized that the Articles of Confederation could not be changed to make an effective government. Edmund Randolph suggested that what was needed was the creation of a completely new plan of government. The others agreed, and they set about to devise a new government for the United States by writing its Constitution.

Why Not a Democracy?

Why did the leaders who wrote the Constitution choose to form a republic rather than a democracy? They had learned from their many experiences in colonial, revolutionary, and confederation days that what the people wanted could change and that their wants could be easily manipulated. The writers did not want the wishes of small groups to be overrun by the changing attitudes of the majority. In other words, they did not want a government based on mob rule. Thus they specified in the Constitution what each branch of the government could and could not do. These men knew that in a true democracy the rules for governing could change whenever the wishes of the majority changed. But in a republic the rules could be changed only by changing the Constitution. Consequently these early leaders concluded that a republican form of government would best insure the freedoms of all the American people. The republican form of government they developed was different from all the forms of government tried before. Their new American republic, however, would become a model for many governments that followed.

Points of Agreement

As the process of writing the Constitution got underway, there were several items on which the delegates agreed. They agreed that a stronger central government was needed. They reasoned that a stronger federal government could be given the power to handle certain matters while allowing state and local governments to solve those problems affecting only their citizens. Thus there would be a division of powers to limit the power of the federal government.

They also agreed that the government established would be a **republic.** In a republic, elected representatives govern the people. The power of these representatives, as well as that of the government as a whole, is limited by the Constitution. (Many people mistakenly refer to the United States government as a democracy, which is rule by the people directly.)

The writers believed in the separation of powers, that no branch or level of government should have all the power. They had learned this principle while suffering under the tyrannical rule of Parliament and the king. Most of the delegates also knew of *Spirit of the Laws,* a work written by the French philosopher Montesquieu (MON tuh SKYOO). In his book Montesquieu outlined three branches of government: executive, legislative, and judicial. Each of these branches had specific functions.

As Montesquieu had also suggested, these men desired a balance of power. They wanted each branch of government to have powers that would balance and control the powers delegated to the other branches. In this way no one branch of government could become more powerful than the others.

As had been evident in the Declaration of Independence, these men wanted to preserve the rights of the individual and his property. And finally, the delegates realized that in order to produce a document acceptable to all the states, compromises would be necessary.

The Virginia
(Large-State) Plan

The New Jersey
(Small-State) Plan

Representation in Congress
based on Population

Same number of Congressmen
from each state

The Great Compromise

CONGRESS

SENATE

Virginia   New Jersey

Same number from each State

HOUSE OF REPRESENTATIVES

Virginia   New Jersey

Based on Population

The convention members adopted so many compromises in writing the Constitution that it has sometimes been called "a bundle of compromises." Yet even with its compromises, William Gladstone, a prime minister of Britain in the nineteenth century, deemed it "the most wonderful work ever struck off at a given time by the brain and purpose of man." Christians realize that the Constitution was no accident.

Convention Compromises

The disputes at Philadelphia involved two groups. First, the large and small states disagreed about the number of votes each state should have in Congress. Second, the northern and southern states argued over slavery and commerce.

The Great Compromise—Two different plans were submitted in an effort to solve the controversy over voting and representation. Edmund Randolph, a delegate from Virginia, submitted Madison's **Virginia Plan** (also called the Large State Plan). According to this plan, the new government would have two legislative houses with membership in both of them based on a state's population.

Meanwhile, the small state of New Jersey proposed a plan written by William Paterson. (It became known as the **New Jersey Plan** or the Small State Plan.) This plan advocated one legislative house with all the states having the same number of representatives. During the debate, Roger Sherman of Connecticut proposed the **Great Compromise** (or Connecticut Compromise). The compromise provided for two legislative assemblies. In the upper house, called the Senate, all states would be equally represented, with two senators per state. In this way the power of the small states would be preserved. In the lower house, called the House of Representatives, representation would be based on population. The larger the population of a state, the larger would be its representation. This part of the compromise favored the large states. Every ten years the federal government would determine the population of the states by taking a **census,** a count of the population. The people would elect the members of the lower house, while the state legislatures would elect the senators.

The Three-Fifths Compromise—The differences over slavery revolved around how the slaves should be counted for taxation and representation. Since a state's taxes were levied according to population, if the census included the slaves, the South's tax burden would be heavy. The North, of course, was not upset by this prospect. On the other hand, when figuring the number of representatives each state would have, the South, by counting the slaves, could have a greater influence than the North in the House of Representatives.

The matter was settled through the **three-fifths compromise.** A slave would be counted as three-fifths of a free person in figuring both taxes due and the number of representatives. Unfortunately, the compromise also included a promise that for twenty years Congress would make no laws interfering with slavery. But many people believed slavery was becoming less profitable, and many hoped that it would die out by itself. Therefore, the delegates agreed to the three-fifths compromise, believing it to be only a temporary measure.

The Commerce Compromise—The commerce disputes centered on whether the nation needed to pass navigation and tariff laws. The northern states wanted Congress to pass such laws to protect their industries from foreign competition. The South, on the other hand, had few factories and produced mostly raw materials. Hence southerners believed that navigation and tariff laws would lead to higher prices on goods the South needed to buy. Southerners reasoned that countries would have less money to buy the South's raw materials if tariffs made it more difficult for those countries to sell their products in the United States. Consequently, the South wanted to require a two-thirds vote to pass navigation laws or tariffs. Since the southern states totaled five of the thirteen, they figured that they would be able to block any laws that would be to their disadvantage.

The Commerce Compromise favored the North by allowing navigation laws to be passed by a simple majority. It favored the South by forever forbidding states to levy taxes on one another's exports. This insured the development of a large home market and made the United States less dependent on foreign trade.

Ratifying the Constitution

Instead of amending the Articles of Confederation, the men at the Philadelphia, or "Constitutional," Convention had drawn up a remarkable new plan for the government of

Roger Sherman:
Big Man from a Small State

It was Roger Sherman of Connecticut who seconded a motion by Franklin for prayer as they began the Philadelphia Convention. The second oldest delegate at the convention, the tall, lean, brown-eyed man had an outstanding reputation. John Adams spoke of him as "that old Puritan, honest as an angel." Jefferson told a visitor to the Congress, "That is Mr. Sherman of Connecticut, who never said a foolish thing in his life." Sherman had learned the lesson of Proverb 29:11—"A fool uttereth all his mind: but a wise man keepeth it in till afterwards."

Born in Massachusetts, Sherman was apprenticed as a youth to his father, a shoe-maker and farmer. Although his formal education was only that given by the grammar schools, Sherman acquired a love of books. Patrons of his shoe shop said there was always a book lying on the cobbler's bench. He showed special interest in mathematics, law, and politics. His most enduring interest, however, was the Bible, and he read it constantly. He had a deep interest in theology and studied the works of Richard Baxter, an important Puritan writer. Cautious in making big decisions, Sherman did not join the Congregational Church until he was twenty-one. From that time on he was active in church work and served many years as a deacon.

After his father's death, Sherman left Stoughton, Massachusetts, and walked about two hundred miles to New Milford, Connecticut, carrying his tools on his back. He had learned surveying and hoped to make that his living, but it took several years before he prospered. He joined his brother in a country store and continued to run it after his brother's death. He gathered information and published a series of almanacs. Sherman pursued his study of law and was admitted to practice in 1754. He was elected to local offices, including town clerk, mayor, and superior court judge. He was also elected to the legislature and later to Connecticut's upper house.

After moving to New Haven, Connecticut, he became actively involved in the affairs of Yale University, including giving and raising money for the Yale University Chapel. The War for Independence next demanded his time. Although he had monetary reasons for supporting the war, his biggest concern was a religious one: he believed that if the British won, his church would have to submit to Anglican bishops.

He represented Connecticut in the Continental Congresses, was on the committee of five who drafted the Declaration of Independence, and was selected for the committee on the Articles of Confederation. Although his ideas for the Articles were commendable, few were accepted. This was probably because he pushed for a strong currency system, for Congress to have the power to tax, and for a supreme court. Although these ideas were unpopular at the time, all were included in the United States Constitution some ten years later.

In 1787 he went to the Philadelphia Convention "disposed to patch up the old scheme of government." But soon he too saw the need for an entirely new system. Although he favored a strong national government, he was the leading member of the compromise group. On June 11 it was he who introduced the famous Connecticut Compromise. Sherman signed the Constitution and the other two great documents of America's early history: the Declaration of Independence (1776) and the Articles of Confederation (1777).

He returned to Connecticut and there led the campaign to have the new Constitution ratified. In the new government he served first in the House and then in the Senate. Sherman died on July 23, 1793. Because of the years of service he had given his state and nation, sometimes with little or no pay, Sherman never gained much worldly wealth. Historian Clinton Rossiter, in judging the wealth of the delegates, listed Sherman as a man "of very modest means" and among the three poorest delegates. But to Sherman, honest devotion to God-given duty was more important than any material gain. His epitaph aptly described him as "a man of approved integrity; a cool, discerning judge; a prudent sagacious [wise] statesman; a true, faithful, and firm patriot."

the United States. On September 17, 1787, the delegates gathered for their last session and signed the Constitution. (Because the Constitution was signed on this day, it has been called Constitution Day.) The delegates then returned to their home states with a big job, promoting the new Constitution so that the states would approve it. Three of the delegates—George Mason, Edmund Randolph, and Elbridge Gerry—refused to sign the Constitution because they wanted a Bill of Rights to be added first.

Those who favored the adoption of the Constitution were called **Federalists.** They persuaded their states to ratify through a series of newspaper essays, *The Federalist Papers.* Written by Alexander Hamilton, John Jay, and James Madison, this collection of essays stated the most common objections to the Constitution and then systematically refuted them. A number of American leaders opposed the Constitution because they believed it would rob the states of their power. These - people worked against ratification and were called **Anti-Federalists.**

Nine states were required to accept the Constitution before it could be approved. New Hampshire became the ninth state to ratify in July 1788. Although the two largest states, New York and Virginia, had not ratified by this time, they did so before the new government met.

Elections for the new republic were held early in 1789. In January the **electoral college,** the system established by the Constitution to elect the president, unanimously named George Washington as president and John Adams as vice president. Not long after, the new Congress passed the **Bill of Rights,** a specific listing of the personal and civil rights and freedoms of every citizen. The Bill of Rights became the first ten amendments to the Constitution, and it went into effect on December 15, 1791.

Among other freedoms, the Bill of Rights has given Americans a freedom to worship God and to preach the gospel. Christians should be very thankful that the writers of the Constitution wisely added these amendments.

Portrait of George Washington

1. What is a republic?

2. What two principles of government were suggested by Montesquieu's writings?

3. What was the difference between the Virginia Plan and the New Jersey Plan?

4. Who proposed the Great Compromise, and what was his proposition?

5. What was the three-fifths compromise?

6. Why did the North and the South have different views on navigation and tariff laws?

7. Who were the Federalists? Who wrote *The Federalist Papers*, and what did the publication contain?

8. Who were the Anti-Federalists, and why did they take their position?

 How is a republic better than a true democracy?

SUMMARY

With independence declared and a war to maintain that independence in progress, the new country needed a plan of government. The Articles of Confederation served to unite the states in a loose confederation. Unfortunately, the national government under this plan was kept weaker than the state governments. With no power to enforce its laws and no taxes to finance the nation's debts and operations, the Confederation government was doomed. Finally, the nation's leading statesmen met at Philadelphia in 1787. They realized the articles could not be revised satisfactorily, and so they drew up a new plan of government for the country. That plan was the United States Constitution.

Chapter Review

People, Places, and Things to Remember

confederation
Articles of Confederation
ratify
Northwest Territory
Northwest Ordinance of
  1785
townships
Northwest Ordinance of
  1787
right of deposit

John Jay
tariffs
Daniel Shays
Shays's Rebellion
Philadelphia Convention
Annapolis Convention
James Madison
Benjamin Franklin
Alexander Hamilton
republic

Virginia Plan
New Jersey Plan
Great Compromise
census
three-fifths compromise
Federalists
The Federalist Papers
Anti-Federalists
electoral college
Bill of Rights

Review Questions

Write the appropriate word or phrase for each blank.

After declaring independence, American leaders drew up a new plan of government called the (1) . The plan kept the national government very weak. To strengthen the government, a convention was organized in the city of (2) . There leaders wrote a new Constitution and presented it to the states for ratification. Supporters were called (3) . Some Americans refused to accept it until certain freedoms were guaranteed by a (4) . The first ten amendments satisfied this need.

Fill in the blank with the appropriate term.

5. The _____ divided western land into townships.

6. The _____ was established to elect the new president.

7. The _____ established the method for territories to become states.

8. The _____ proposed representation based on population in both houses.

9. The _____ proposed equal representation in one house.

10. _____ were written to encourage the adoption of the Constitution.

Short Answer

11. What are charges or taxes paid on imported goods called?

12. A delegate from which state devised the Small State Plan?

13. What is an official count of the population called?

14. What three men composed the *The Federalist Papers*?

15. Who was the oldest delegate at the Constitutional Convention?

Questions for Discussion

16. How would the Confederation government have been different if the Congress had had the power to tax?

17. How did Shays's Rebellion in Massachusetts show the weakness of the Confederation?

History Skills

Comparison and Contrast: The Articles of Confederation to the Constitution

Fearing a strong central government, Americans created a loose confederation of states. However, they discovered that weakness can be just as bad for a nation as strength. The need for change eventually became apparent. Representatives of the states met together to discuss problems with the Articles of Confederation and possible solutions. Summarize their discussions by drawing and completing this chart on your own paper. For each weakness of the Articles given, describe the solution reached under the Constitution. The last one is challenging.

Weakness Under Articles	Solution Under Constitution
One vote for each state in Congress	
No power to enforce laws	
Lack of funds to run the government and pay war debts	
State disputes over the taxing of imports	
Worthless money printed by states	

The Constitution of the United States

The two most important documents in American history are the Declaration of Independence and the Constitution with its Bill of Rights. The Declaration of Independence stated that the United States would no longer be under British rule and affirmed the rights and universal principles of justice on which the new republic would be built. The Constitution put these principles into practice and is the written law by which the United States has been governed ever since.

America's Amazing Document

The United States Constitution is now more than two hundred years old. No other nation's constitution has lasted as long. Nearly two-thirds of the approximately one hundred sixty national constitutions in the world have been adopted or revised since 1970 alone.

Only fourteen were written before World War II. While Norway's 1814 constitution is the second oldest constitution in continual use, it has not had the influence outside its own borders that America's Constitution has had. One law professor said, "The United States Constitution is this nation's most important export." The constitutions of many other nations have been modeled after it. The Constitution is remarkable not only because it has lasted but also because it has worked so well with so few changes. Although others have copied its ideas, few have been able to make the principles work so effectively.

Reasons for Its Success

One reason that the Constitution has been successful is that its writers included some biblical principles and practices. Even though their debt to Scripture may not have been known to them or may not even have been intended in every case, they saw from experience which principles worked. Bible principles work and make life operate more smoothly even for unbelievers.

A second reason for success was that Americans put forth much patient effort to make the Constitution work. They decided to abide by its laws and follow its precepts. When certain parts of the Constitution did not seem to work as planned because they were flawed or circumstances outdated them, Americans did not throw out the document and revolt. They modified the document through a formal amendment process. If America's form of government is to continue, it is essential that the laws be respected and followed. Disrespect for authority and government undermines any form of government.

A third reason for the success of the Constitution is that while it outlines broad principles and some specifics, it has also been flexible enough to deal with changing times. The Constitution is a living, working docu-ment. In the past two hundred years, the Constitution has been amended only twenty-seven times. Ten of the amendments were passed as the Bill of Rights in 1791, so there have been only seventeen changes since that date. Of course, some changes in the interpretation of the Constitution have also been made through court decisions.

Principles in the Constitution

It is important, as our study of this document begins, to recognize some of the principles that the writers used to form it. Because these ideas are important and are seen throughout the document, not just in one specific item, they will be listed and described here. But as you read the Constitution, you will want to note where they appear and how they are applied.

Written Law—Under the Constitution, rule is by written law. The powers of government leaders cannot be changed by their own desires. The Constitution has limited those powers, establishing what government may and may not do. Thus the Constitution gives the United States a limited government that may not step beyond the powers given to it. The only ways the written law of the Constitution can be changed are by amendment or by a change in interpretation by the courts. Because these changes are somewhat difficult to bring about, major changes in constitutional law are rare.

The written law of the Constitution helps to protect Americans from the rise of cruel dictators as well as from unconstitutional governmental action. This protection depends, however, on the constitutional knowledge of American citizens. If Americans are unaware of the limitations of government, they may unknowingly allow the government to overstep them. This thought should motivate us to study the Constitution carefully.

Separation of Powers—As we learned in Chapter 7 (p. 122), the powers that government does have are divided among three branches: executive, legislative, and judicial. With this **separation of powers,** no one branch has too much power. Congress, which is the legislative branch, makes the laws. The executive branch, led by the president, is responsible for enforcing the laws. And the courts of the judicial branch interpret the laws as they apply them to specific cases. These are the major, separate responsibilities of the three branches of government.

Checks and Balances—There is also a system of **checks and balances** that keeps each of the three branches of government from going beyond its powers. Each branch has been given one or more powers that limit or check the powers of the other two branches. Such a safeguard is useful because government leaders may be tempted to take added powers for their own selfish purposes. These checks, however, keep the powers of each of the branches balanced or in proportion to those of the other branches.

A Federal System—Under the Articles of Confederation, the states operated almost as

LEGISLATIVE BRANCH   EXECUTIVE BRANCH   JUDICIAL BRANCH

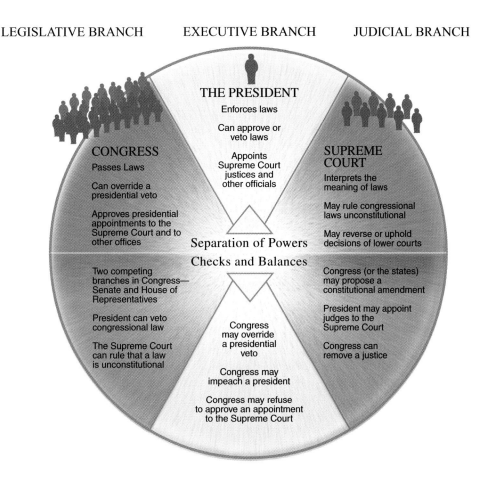

THE PRESIDENT
Enforces laws
Can approve or veto laws
Appoints Supreme Court justices and other officials

CONGRESS
Passes Laws
Can override a presidential veto
Approves presidential appointments to the Supreme Court and to other offices

SUPREME COURT
Interprets the meaning of laws
May rule congressional laws unconstitutional
May reverse or uphold decisions of lower courts

Separation of Powers

Checks and Balances

Two competing branches in Congress—Senate and House of Representatives
President can veto congressional law
The Supreme Court can rule that a law is unconstitutional

Congress may override a presidential veto
Congress may impeach a president
Congress may refuse to approve an appointment to the Supreme Court

Congress (or the states) may propose a constitutional amendment
President may appoint judges to the Supreme Court
Congress can remove a justice

though they were independent nations. The government allowed them to keep most powers for themselves, while the Confederation Congress had only a few powers. The Constitution sought to strengthen the power of the national government, but it did not intend to take away all the powers of the states. To do this, the Constitution established a **federal system** that divided the powers of government between those given to the national government and those reserved for the states.

Under a federal system the duties and powers of government are assigned to the level of government best equipped to handle them. No single level has total power. Under the federal Constitution, the national government is given powers over things of importance to the whole nation. For example, waging war and providing for the common defense involve the whole nation and are powers given to the national government. Other powers, such as many of those relating to health, safety, education, most election regulations, and punishment for most crimes, are left to the state and local governments. You would not call the White House, for example, to report a stolen bicycle.

The system of national, state, and local government, each with its own powers, is called a federal system. However, you should not be confused if you hear the term used in another way. The national government in Washington, D.C., is often called the federal government, and things that are related to the national government are also described as "federal." Federal employees, federal regulations, and federal agencies are some examples.

A Republic

When Benjamin Franklin left the final meeting of the convention, someone asked him, "What have you given us?"

He answered simply, "A republic, if you can keep it."

The old statesman knew that the ideas of the Constitution were good, but it would be up to the American people to make them work. Although the ideas of the Constitution have proved to be sound for over two hundred years, it still remains the responsibility of the American people to continue to make them work.

SECTION REVIEW

1. What two documents are the most important in American history?

2. What are three reasons for the success of the Constitution?

3. What are the two ways of making changes in the Constitution?

4. What keeps one branch of government from getting too much power?

5. What system divides the powers of government between the national government and the state governments?

 What is meant by this statement: "The United States Constitution is the nation's most important export"?

THE CONSTITUTION OF THE UNITED STATES

Preamble

We the people of the United States, in order to form a more perfect union, establish justice, ensure domestic tranquillity, provide for the common defense, promote the general welfare, and secure the blessings of liberty to ourselves and our posterity, do ordain and establish this Constitution for the United States of America.

Article I: The Legislative Branch
Section 1

All legislative powers herein granted shall be vested in a Congress of the United States, which shall consist of a Senate and House of Representatives.

Section 2

1. The House of Representatives shall be composed of members chosen every second year by the people of the several states, and the electors in each state shall have the qualifications requisite for electors of the most numerous branch of the state legislature.

2. No person shall be a representative who shall not have attained to the age of twenty-five years, and been seven years a citizen of the United States, and who shall not, when elected, be an inhabitant of that state in which he shall be chosen.

3. Representatives and direct taxes shall be apportioned among the several states which may be included within this Union, according to their respective numbers, which shall be determined by adding to the whole number of free persons, including those bound to service for a term of years, and excluding Indians not taxed, three-fifths of all other persons. The actual enumeration shall be made within three

The **Preamble** introduces the Constitution. First it states the source of government's power: "We the people." Second, the Preamble lays out six purposes of government: (1) to form a more perfect union (a workable united government), (2) to establish justice (fairness), (3) to insure domestic tranquillity (keep peace within the nation), (4) to provide for the common defense (protect from enemies), (5) to promote the general welfare (benefit the people), and (6) to secure the blessings of liberty to . . . our posterity (the generations that follow us).

Article 1 deals with the legislative branch of government, whose primary function is to make laws. This power belongs to Congress, which has two houses, an upper house called the Senate and a lower house called the House of Representatives. A two-house legislative system is called a **bicameral system.**

Members of the House are elected every two years and serve two-year terms. The House has always been elected directly by the people.

Qualifications: members of the House of Representatives must be (1) at least twenty-five years old, (2) American citizens for at least seven years, (3) residents of the state they represent.

The number of representatives each state receives is determined by its population. Also, any direct federal taxation of the states must be distributed according to population. Amendment 16, however, makes the income tax an exception to this rule. Special arrangements were made for counting slaves, indentured servants, and Indians in the population; but these rules no longer apply since the end of slavery and the beginning of Indian citizenship. Today the House membership has been set at 435. A counting of the population, called a census, is taken every ten years to determine how many of these representatives each state receives.

years after the first meeting of the Congress of the United States, and within every subsequent term of ten years, in such manner as they shall by law direct. The number of representatives shall not exceed one for every thirty thousand, but each state shall have at least one representative; and until such enumeration shall be made, the state of New Hampshire shall be entitled to choose three, Massachusetts eight, Rhode Island and Providence Plantations one, Connecticut five, New York six, New Jersey four, Pennsylvania eight, Delaware one, Maryland six, Virginia ten, North Carolina five, South Carolina five, and Georgia three.

4. When vacancies happen in the representation from any state, the executive authority thereof shall issue writs of election to fill such vacancies.

5. The House of Representatives shall choose their speaker and other officers; and shall have the sole power of impeachment.

Section 3

1. The Senate of the United States shall be composed of two senators from each state, chosen by the legislature thereof, for six years; and each senator shall have one vote.

2. Immediately after they shall be assembled in consequence of the first election, they shall be divided as equally as may be into three classes. The seats of the senators of the first class shall be vacated at the expiration of the second year, of the second class at the expiration of the fourth year, and of the third class at the expiration of the sixth year, so that one-third may be chosen every second year; and if vacancies happen by resignation, or otherwise, during the recess of the legislature of any state, the executive thereof may make temporary appointments until the next meeting of the legislature,which shall then fill such vacancies.

The head of the House is called the Speaker of the House; he is elected by the House members. The House has the sole power of **impeachment**— the filing of charges against a major federal official. Each state has two senators, who serve six-year terms. Originally, state legislatures elected senators. Since the passage of Amendment 17 in 1913, the people have directly elected senators. One-third of the senators are up for election every two years. By this method, there are always experienced people in the Senate.

3. No person shall be a senator who shall not have attained to the age of thirty years, and been nine years a citizen of the United States, and who shall not, when elected, be an inhabitant of that state for which he shall be chosen.

4. The Vice President of the United States shall be President of the Senate, but shall have no vote, unless they be equally divided.

5. The Senate shall choose their other officers, and also a president pro tempore, in the absence of the Vice President, or when he shall exercise the office of President of the United States.

6. The Senate shall have the sole power to try all impeachments. When sitting for that purpose, they shall be on oath or affirmation. When the President of the United States is tried, the chief justice shall preside: and no person shall be convicted without the concurrence of two-thirds of the members present.

7. Judgment in cases of impeachment shall not extend further than to removal from office, and disqualification to hold and enjoy any office of honor, trust or profit under the United States: but the party convicted shall nevertheless be liable and subject to indictment, trial, judgment and punishment, according to law.

Section 4

1. The times, places and manner of holding elections, for senators and representatives, shall be prescribed in each state by the legislature thereof; but the Congress may at any time by law make or alter such regulations, except as to the places of choosing senators.

2. The Congress shall assemble at least once in every year, and such meeting shall be on the first Monday in December, unless they shall by law appoint a different day.

Qualifications: senators must be (1) at least thirty years old, (2) citizens for at least nine years, (3) residents of the state they represent.

The head (president) of the Senate is the vice president of the United States. He votes only in case of a tie.

The Senate also elects its own **president pro tempore** (proh TEM-puh-ree), who serves as leader of the Senate when the vice president is absent.

The Senate acts as a trial court for impeachment cases. Two-thirds of the senators must vote for conviction in order to remove the official from office. If the president is impeached, the chief justice of the Supreme Court presides over the trial rather than the vice president.

When the House impeaches an official and the Senate tries and confirms the charges, Congress may punish him only by removing him from office and barring him from holding any government offices in the future. Even so, the person can be tried in a regular civil or criminal court afterwards and be sentenced to further punishment if found guilty.

State legislatures have the right to administer congressional elections in their states, but they must follow any regulations established by Congress. For instance, national law requires that secret ballots be used in these elections. Congressional elections are held on the Tuesday following the first Monday in November in even-numbered years.

Congress is to meet at least once a year. Originally it began its meeting on the first Monday in December. Now it first meets at noon on January 3, since the date was changed by the Twentieth Amendment.

Section 5

1. Each house shall be the judge of the elections, returns and qualifications of its own members, and a majority of each shall constitute a quorum to do business; but a smaller number may adjourn from day to day, and may be authorized to compel the attendance of absent members, in such manner, and under such penalties as each house may provide.

Each house judges its own elections. A *quorum* (KWAWR um) is the minimum number needed to transact business, and a simple majority (just over one-half the members) is a quorum.

2. Each house may determine the rules of its proceedings, punish its members for disorderly behavior, and, with the concurrence of two-thirds, expel a member.

A disorderly member can be expelled by a two-thirds vote of the body he has served in.

3. Each house shall keep a journal of its proceedings, and from time to time publish the same, excepting such parts as may, in their judgment, require secrecy; and the yeas and nays of the members of either house on any question shall, at the desire of one-fifth of those present, be entered on the journal.

Each house keeps a journal or record of what it does each day. Today this is called *The Congressional Record.* A written record of the vote is kept if one-fifth of those present request it.

4. Neither house, during the session of Congress, shall, without the consent of the other, adjourn for more than three days, nor to any other place than that in which the two houses shall be sitting.

Since the houses work together to pass legislation, one cannot adjourn (go out of official session) for more than three days without the permission of the other.

Section 6

1. The senators and representatives shall receive a compensation for their services, to be ascertained by law, and paid out of the Treasury of the United States. They shall in all cases, except treason, felony and breach of the peace, be privileged from arrest during their attendance at the session of their respective houses, and in going to and returning from the same; and for any speech or debate in either house, they shall not be questioned in any other place.

Senators and representatives are public employees paid salaries by the U.S. Treasury. They cannot be arrested going to or from the House or Senate, nor can they be arrested for what they say on the floor of the House or Senate. This precaution gives congressmen the freedom to voice even unpopular ideas without fear of being arrested to prohibit their participation in Congress.

2. No senator or representative shall, during the time for which he was elected, be appointed to any civil office under the authority of the United States, which shall have been created, or the emoluments where-of shall have been increased during such time; and no person holding any office under the United

A congressman must give up any other federal offices he holds to become a congressman. He cannot take any federal office created by his house of Congress until his term is ended, and until his term is expired, he cannot take an office for which Congress has increased the pay during his term. This precaution prevents Congress from giving themselves offices with increased salaries.

States, shall be a member of either house during his continuance in office.

Section 7

1. All bills for raising revenue shall originate in the House of Representatives; but the Senate may propose or concur with amendments as on other bills.

2. Every bill which shall have passed the House of Representatives and the Senate, shall, before it becomes a law, be presented to the President of the United States; if he approves, he shall sign it, but if not, he shall return it with his objections to that house in which it shall have originated, who shall enter the objections at large on their journal, and proceed to reconsider it. If after such reconsideration, two-thirds of that house shall agree to pass the bill, it shall be sent, together with the objections, to the other house, by which it shall likewise be reconsidered, and if approved by two-thirds of that house, it shall become a law. But in all such cases the votes of both houses shall be determined by yeas and nays, and the names of the persons voting for and against the bill shall be entered on the journal of each house respectively. If any bill shall not be returned by the President within ten days (Sundays excepted) after it shall have been presented to him, the same shall be a law, in like manner as if he had signed it, unless the Congress by their adjournment prevent its return, in which case it shall not be a law.

3. Every order, resolution, or vote to which the concurrence of the Senate and House of Representatives may be necessary (except on a question of adjournment) shall be presented to the President of the United States; and before the same shall take effect, shall be approved by him, or being disapproved by him, shall be passed by two-thirds of the Senate and House of Representatives, according to the rules and limitations prescribed in the case of a bill.

Bills dealing with money must start in the House, but the Senate may make changes if it desires.

In order for a bill to become a law, it must be passed by both houses and signed by the president. This is a part of the system of checks and balances. If the president opposes the bill, he may return it to the body where it started, stating his objections. This is a **veto**. Congress may override the president's veto with a two-thirds vote of both houses, and the bill becomes law. If the president does not sign a bill that comes to him and does not veto it, it becomes law in ten days as long as Congress remains in session. If he does not sign a bill and Congress adjourns within ten days, it is vetoed automatically. This is called a **"pocket veto."**

The ideals that the patriots fought for are contained in the Constitution.

All other acts requiring approval of both houses of Congress (except the decision to adjourn Congress) require the signature of the president or the overriding of his veto by a two-thirds vote of both houses.

Section 8

1. The Congress shall have the power to lay and collect taxes, duties, imposts and excises, to pay the debts and provide for the common defense and general welfare of the United States; but all duties, imposts, and excises shall be uniform throughout the United States;

2. To borrow money on the credit of the United States;

3. To regulate commerce with foreign nations, and among the several states, and with the Indian tribes;

4. To establish a uniform rule of naturalization, and uniform laws on the subject of bankruptcies throughout the United States;

5. To coin money, regulate the value thereof, and of foreign coin, and fix the standard of weights and measures;

6. To provide for the punishment of counterfeiting the securities and current coin of the United States;

7. To establish post offices and post roads;

8. To promote the progress of science and useful arts, by securing for limited times to authors and inventors the exclusive right to their respective writings and discoveries;

9. To constitute tribunals inferior to the Supreme Court;

These are the enumerated (numbered and listed) powers of Congress; they are specifically stated.
(1) *It has the power to tax.* Congress can lay (impose the amounts or system) and collect taxes, duties (taxes on imports), imposts (taxes on duties), and excises (internal taxes on production, sale, or consumption of certain items such as telephones).
(2) *It has the power to borrow money.* The government usually borrows money by selling bonds (certificates that it pledges to repay with interest).

(3) *It has the power to regulate trade with foreign nations, within the country, and with the Indians.* Indians were dealt with as independent nations.
(4) *It has the power to regulate naturalization and bankruptcy laws.* **Naturalization** is the process by which a foreign-born person gains citizenship. **Bankruptcy** is the way a debtor is declared unable to pay his creditors. These laws must be uniform so that it is not easier or harder to gain citizenship or declare bankruptcy in one state than in another.

(5) *It has the power to control the nation's currency and the standard weights and measurements.* These values need to be the same throughout the nation.
(6) *It has the power to punish those who illegally interfere in the currency system.* **Counterfeiting** means making copies of something (often money) and using them illegally.

(7) *It has the power to provide needed offices and roads for the postal service.* Post roads are roads for delivering the mail. They became the basic roads of the U.S. highway system.

(8) *It has the power to issue copyrights and patents.* **Copyrights** protect authors or their heirs from having their works copied by another person. (Today the length of the copyright is the lifetime of the author plus seventy years.) **Patents** protect inventors from having their ideas taken by another person for use or profit.
(9) *It has the power to establish federal courts other than the Supreme Court.*

10. To define and punish piracies and felonies committed on the high seas, and offenses against the law of nations;

(10) *It has the power to determine what acts committed at sea are crimes and to commit offenders to federal courts for trial.* "Offenses against the law of nations" include piracy, terrorism, and hijacking.

11. To declare war, grant letters of marque and reprisal, and make rules concerning captures on land and water;

(11) *Congress alone has the power to declare war.* Letters of marque and reprisal permitted private citizens to outfit vessels to fight in wartime and to capture enemy goods and people. Such permissions are no longer granted.

12. To raise and support armies, but no appropriation of money to that use shall be for a longer term than two years;

(12) *Congress may create an army, but it cannot vote to use money to support the army more than two years ahead of time.* The limit of two years helps prevent a takeover or misuse of power by the military.

13. To provide and maintain a navy;

(13) *It has the power to create a navy and to vote for money to support it.*

14. To make rules for the government and regulation of the land and naval forces;

(14) *It has the power to make the rules for the armed services.*

15. To provide for calling forth the militia to execute the laws of the Union, suppress insurrections and repel invasions;

(15) *It may call the state militias (now the National Guard) into service for the national government under certain conditions.*

16. To provide for organizing, arming and disciplining the militia, and for governing such part of them as may be employed in the service of the United States, reserving to the states respectively, the appointment of the officers, and the authority of training the militia according to the discipline prescribed by Congress:

(16) *It has the power to organize, arm, and discipline the militias, while the states appoint the officers and train these troops.* When called into national service, however, the militia is under federal control as a part of the armed forces.

17. To exercise exclusive legislation in all cases whatsoever, over such district (not exceeding ten miles square) as may, by cession of particular states, and the acceptance of Congress, become the seat of the government of the United States, and to exercise like authority over all places purchased by the consent of the legislature of the state in which the same shall be, for the erection of forts, magazines, arsenals, dock yards, and other needful buildings; and

(17) *It has the power to make laws for the District of Columbia and for all federal properties such as military installations or bases.* This also includes historic sites, national cemeteries, national forests and parks, and fisheries.

18. To make all laws which shall be necessary and proper for carrying into execution the foregoing powers, and all other powers vested by this Constitution in the government of the United States, or in any department or officer thereof.

This "necessary and proper clause" of the Constitution lets Congress do what it believes is necessary and proper to carry out any listed power. This clause is sometimes also called the **elastic clause**. To borrow money, for example, it can sell bonds and even create a bank. The Supreme Court can check this power by deciding whether the laws Congress passes by this authority are really necessary and proper.

Section 9

1. The migration or importation of such persons as any of the states now existing shall think proper to admit, shall not be prohibited by the Congress prior to the year 1808, but a tax or duty may be imposed on such importations, not exceeding ten dollars for each person.

Powers Forbidden to the Federal Government:
(1) *Congress could not interfere with slavery until after 1808.* Nor could it tax slavery out of existence by levying heavy taxes on slaves.

2. The privilege of the writ of habeas corpus shall not be suspended, unless when in cases of rebellion or invasion the public safety may require it.

(2) *Congress may not take away a person's right to the writ of* **habeas corpus** *except in times of extreme danger. Habeas corpus,* Latin for the first words in the writ, forces authorities to charge a person with a crime if he is held in jail. Because of this right, a person cannot be held prisoner unless a charge of a crime is made against him.

3. No bill of attainder or ex post facto law shall be passed.

(3) *Congress cannot pass a* **bill of attainder,** *which permits punishment without a trial, or an* **ex post facto law,** *which makes a law retroactive.* Acts that were legal when they were done cannot be made illegal afterwards.

4. No capitation, or other direct tax shall be laid, unless in proportion to the census or enumeration hereinbefore directed to be taken.

(4) *Congress cannot levy a direct tax that is not equal for all citizens.* For example, it could not make Californians pay a special tax of one hundred dollars when people from Ohio have to pay only fifty dollars. Amendment 16 made the income tax an exception.

5. No tax or duty shall be laid on articles exported from any state.

(5) *Congress cannot tax the exports of the states.* This means that neither goods exported to other nations nor those exported to other states may be taxed.

6. No preference shall be given by any regulation of commerce or revenue to the ports of one state over those of another: nor shall vessels bound to, or from one state, be obliged to enter, clear, or pay duties in another.

(6) *Congress cannot give preference to any port or state through its laws, and it cannot tax trade between the states.*

7. No money shall be drawn from the treasury, but in consequence of appropriations made by law; and a regular statement and account of the receipts and expenditures of all public money shall be published from time to time.

8. No title of nobility shall be granted by the United States: and no person holding any office of profit or trust under them, shall, without the consent of the Congress, accept of any present, emolument, office, or title, of any kind whatever, from any king, prince or foreign state.

Section 10

1. No state shall enter into any treaty, alliance, or confederation; grant letters of marque and reprisal; coin money; emit bills of credit; make anything but gold and silver coin a tender in payment of debts; pass any bill of attainder, ex post facto law, or law impairing the obligation of contracts, or grant any title of nobility.

2. No state shall, without the consent of the Congress, lay any imposts or duties on imports or exports, except what may be absolutely necessary for executing its inspection laws: and the net produce of all duties and imposts laid by any state on imports or exports, shall be for the use of the treasury of the United States; and all such laws shall be subject to the revision and control of the Congress.

3. No state shall, without the consent of Congress, lay any duty of tonnage, keep troops, or ships of war in time of peace, enter into any agreement or compact with another state, or with a foreign power, or engage in war, unless actually invaded, or in such imminent danger as will not admit of delay.

(7) *Money from the treasury can be spent only if Congress approves, and a record of income and expenditures must be published.*

(8) *The United States cannot grant titles of nobility (duke, earl, baron, etc.), nor can our citizens accept titles or honors from foreign countries without the permission of Congress.*

Powers Denied to the States:
States are forbidden from doing many of the things the federal government can do. They are also given some of the same prohibitions that the federal government has. By limiting state powers, the Constitution makes the central government stronger and produces a more united government. In addition to the topics already described in Section 9, states are forbidden to keep troops or ships (except a state militia), make alliances with foreign powers, or declare war. However, states may respond to attacks if invaded.

Questions on Article I

1. What is the primary function of the legislative branch?
2. What are the two houses of Congress called?
3. What is a bicameral system?
4. How much older does a senator have to be than a representative?
5. Who is the head of the House? Who selects him?
6. How many senators does each state have? How long are their terms?
7. Who is the head of the Senate? How often does he vote?
8. What function does the Senate play in impeachment? What is the punishment (judgment) for impeachment?
9. When can a pocket veto be used?
10. What federal areas or properties does Congress control?
11. What is another name for the "necessary and proper clause"?
12. What is a writ of habeas corpus?
13. In addition to the things forbidden Congress, list four things that states are forbidden to do.

Article II: The Executive Branch
Section 1

1. The executive power shall be vested in a President of the United States of America. He shall hold his office during the term of four years, and, together with the Vice President, chosen for the same term, be elected as follows.

2. Each state shall appoint, in such manner as the legislature thereof may direct, a number of electors, equal to the whole number of senators and representatives to which the state may be entitled in the Congress; but no senator or representative, or person holding an office of trust or profit under the United States, shall be appointed an elector.

The electors shall meet in their respective states, and vote by ballot for two persons, of whom one at least shall not be an inhabitant of the same state with themselves. And they shall make a list of all the persons voted for, and of the number of votes for each; which list they shall sign and certify, and transmit sealed to the seat of the government of the United States, directed to the president of the Senate. The president of the Senate shall, in the presence of the Senate and House of Representatives, open all the certificates, and the votes shall then be counted. The person having the greatest number of votes shall be the President, if such number be a majority of the whole number of electors appointed; and if there be more than one who have such majority, and have an equal number of votes, then the House of Representatives shall immediately choose by ballot one of them for President; and if no person have a majority, then from the five highest on the list the said House shall in like manner choose the President. But in choosing the President, the votes shall be taken by states, the representation from each state having one vote; a quorum for this purpose shall consist of a member or members from two-thirds of the states, and

Article II deals with the executive branch of government. Its primary function is to carry out the nation's laws. Both the president and vice president serve four-year terms.

The president is still elected by this electoral college. The original design was modified by the Twelfth Amendment in 1804.

The Senate and House of Representatives oversee the counting of the electors' votes. When no candidate receives a majority of the votes, the House of Representatives votes by state to choose the new president.

George Washington became the first president of the new nation.

a majority of all the states shall be necessary to a choice. In every case, after the choice of the President, the person having the greatest number of votes of the electors shall be the Vice President. But if there should remain two or more who have equal votes, the Senate shall choose from them by ballot the Vice President.

3. The Congress may determine the time of choosing the electors, and the day on which they shall give their votes; which day shall be the same throughout the United States.

4. No person except a natural born citizen, or a citizen of the United States, at the time of the adoption of this Constitution, shall be eligible to the office of President, neither shall any person be eligible to that office who shall not have attained to the age of thirty-five years, and been fourteen years a resident within the United States.

5. In case of the removal of the President from office, or of his death, resignation, or inability to discharge the powers and duties of the said office, the same shall devolve on the Vice President, and the Congress may by law provide for the case of removal, death, resignation, or inability, both of the President and Vice President, declaring what officer shall then act as President, and such officer shall act accordingly, until the disability be removed, or a President shall be elected.

6. The President shall, at stated times, receive for his services, a compensation, which shall neither be increased nor diminished during the period for which he shall have been elected, and he shall not receive within that period any other emolument from the United States, or any of them.

7. Before he enter on the execution of his office, he shall take the following oath or affirmation:—"I do solemnly swear (or affirm) that I will faithfully execute the office of President of the United States, and will to the best of my ability, preserve, protect and defend the Constitution of the United States."

Congress determines the time for the president's election. Election day is the first Tuesday after the first Monday in November.

Qualifications: the president must be (1) a natural-born citizen, (2) at least thirty-five years of age, (3) a resident of the U.S. for at least fourteen years.

Presidential Succession: In 1948 Congress established the present line of succession: (1) the vice president (as stated in the Constitution), (2) the Speaker of the House of Representatives, (3) the president pro tempore of the Senate, and (4) members of the president's cabinet in order of the creation of their departments. The State and Treasury Departments are the two oldest.

The president's salary stays the same throughout his term.

Section 2

1. The President shall be commander in chief of the army and navy of the United States, and of the militia of the several states, when called into the actual service of the United States; he may require the opinion, in writing, of the principal officer in each of the executive departments, upon any subject relating to the duties of their respective offices, and he shall have power to grant reprieves and pardons for offenses against the United States, except in cases of impeachment.

2. He shall have power, by and with the advice and consent of the Senate, to make treaties, provided two-thirds of the senators present concur; and he shall nominate, and by and with the advice and consent of the Senate, shall appoint ambassadors, other public ministers and consuls, judges of the Supreme Court, and all other officers of the United States, whose appointments are not herein otherwise provided for, and which shall be established by law: but the Congress may by law vest the appointment of such inferior officers, as they think proper, in the President alone, in the courts of law, or in the heads of departments.

3. The President shall have power to fill up all vacancies that may happen during the recess of the Senate, by granting commissions which shall expire at the end of their next session.

The president's oath of office is dictated by the Constitution. The word "affirm" is offered because some religious groups object to the use of the word "swear." (See Matt. 5:34.) George Washington added the words "so help me God" to the end of the oath, and that addition has become a tradition.

Powers and Duties of the President:
The phrase "in each of the executive departments" became the basis for the president's cabinet. **Reprieve** means a temporary postponement of punishment; **pardon** means a complete forgiveness of a crime and its consequential punishment.

Treaties must be approved by a two-thirds majority of the Senate. The president appoints ambassadors, ministers (usually to foreign countries), consuls, judges, and other officers as allowed by Congress with approval of the Senate.

The president can fill vacancies in offices without Senate approval if the Senate is out of session.

Section 3

He shall from time to time give to the Congress information of the state of the Union, and recommend to their consideration, such measures as he shall judge necessary and expedient; he may, on extraordinary occasions, convene both houses, or either of them, and in case of disagreement between them, with respect to the time of adjournment, he may adjourn them to such time as he shall think proper; he shall receive ambassadors and other public ministers; he shall take care that the laws be faithfully executed, and shall commission all the officers of the United States.

Section 4

The President, Vice President, and all civil officers of the United States shall be removed from office on impeachment for, and conviction of, treason, bribery, or other high crimes and misdemeanors.

Duties of the President:
(1) The information the president gives Congress is called the State of the Union message. It is usually given near the end of January.
(2) The president can suggest that Congress pass certain legislation. He can influence opinion.
(3) He can convene (call into official session) both houses. This has been done to deal with national emergencies.
(4) If the House and Senate cannot agree on adjournment, the president can intervene.
(5) Receiving ambassadors and public ministers is important to the presidential power in foreign affairs. If the president fails to recognize diplomats of a certain country, it may mean the United States is about to declare war.

The Process of Impeachment:
The president can be impeached—have charges filed against him with the intention of removing him from office—for treason (aiding an enemy), bribery (giving or accepting money, gifts, or favors illegally), high crimes (serious crimes), or misdemeanors (bad behavior).

Questions on Article II

1. What is the primary function of the executive branch?
2. How long does the president serve?
3. What are the qualifications of the president of the United States?
4. Concerning treaties and appointments, what check does the Senate have on the president?

Article III: The Judicial Branch
Section 1

1. The judicial power of the United States shall be vested in one Supreme Court, and in such inferior courts as the Congress may from time to time ordain and establish. The judges, both of the Supreme and inferior courts, shall hold their offices during good behavior, and shall, at stated times, receive for their services, a compensation, which shall not be diminished during their continuance in office.

Section 2

1. The judicial powers shall extend to all cases, in law and equity, arising under this

The function of the judicial branch is usually defined as "to interpret the law." This function is not listed in the Constitution; it was established through the court case *Marbury v. Madison* under Chief Justice John Marshall. The nation's highest court is the Supreme Court. Inferior or lower courts may be and have been created by Congress. They include Circuit Courts of Appeal and Federal District Courts as well as tax, claim, and military courts. Federal judges do not have specific terms of office and may serve as long as they serve responsibly—usually for the rest of their lives unless they resign.

This section lists the cases that the federal courts must decide. No other courts can have jurisdiction in these cases.

Constitution, the laws of the United States, and treaties made, or which shall be made under their authority; to all cases affecting ambassadors, other public ministers and consuls; to all cases of admiralty and maritime jurisdiction; to controversies to which the United States shall be a party; to controversies between two or more states; between a state and citizens of another state, between citizens of different states, between citizens of the same state claiming lands under grants of different states, and between a state, or the citizens thereof, and foreign states, citizens or subjects.

2. In all cases affecting ambassadors, other public ministers and consuls, and those in which a state shall be party, the Supreme Court shall have original jurisdiction. In all the other cases before mentioned, the Supreme Court shall have appellate jurisdiction, both as to law and fact, with such exceptions, and under such regulations as the Congress shall make.

3. The trial of all crimes, except in cases of impeachment, shall be by jury; and such trial shall be held in the state where the said crimes shall have been committed; but when not committed within any state, the trial shall be at such place or places as the Congress may by law have directed.

Section 3

1. Treason against the United States shall consist only in levying war against them, or in adhering to their enemies, giving them aid and comfort. No person shall be convicted of treason unless on the testimony of two witnesses to the same overt act, or on confession in open court.

2. The Congress shall have power to declare the punishment of treason, but no attainder of treason shall work corruption of blood, or forfeiture except during the life of the person attained.

Original jurisdiction (joor is DIK shun) means that this court has first opportunity to hear and decide the case. With **appellate** (uh PEL it) **jurisdiction,** a case, which has already been brought to trial at least once, is sent up from a lower court, and the court hears the case on appeal.

Trials for crimes occur where the crime was committed, unless the person cannot get a fair trial there. (If a fair trial is considered unlikely at the location of the crime, a *change of venue* can be obtained, and the trial will be moved to another location.) The common method for trial is by jury.

Treason is defined specifically so that no one can be accused unjustly. To be convicted of treason, the accused must either confess to it or have two people who saw it testify in an open court.

The punishment for treason extends only to the life of the person himself, not his family.

Article IV: Interstate Relations
Section 1

Full faith and credit shall be given in each state to the public acts, records and judicial proceedings of every other state. And the Congress may by general laws prescribe the manner in which such acts, records and proceedings shall be proved, and the effect thereof.

Section 2

1. The citizens of each state shall be entitled to all privileges and immunities of citizens in the several states.

2. A person charged in any state with treason, felony, or other crime, who shall flee from justice, and be found in another state, shall on demand of the executive authority of the state from which he fled, be delivered up to be removed to the state having jurisdiction of the crime.

3. No person held to service or labor in one state under the laws thereof, escaping into another, shall, in consequence of any law or regulation therein, be discharged from such service or labor, but shall be delivered up on claim of the party to whom such service or labor may be due.

Section 3

1. New states may be admitted by the Congress into this Union; but no new state shall be formed or erected within the jurisdiction of any other state; nor any state be formed by the junction of two or more states, or parts of states, without the consent of the legislatures of the states concerned as well as of the Congress.

Questions on Article III

1. What is the primary function of the judicial branch?
2. What is the nation's highest court and the only one specifically established by the Constitution?
3. What branch of government was given the power to create inferior or lower courts?
4. How long is the term of a federal judge?
5. Where is a case normally tried?
6. Except in impeachment cases, what is the method of trial?
7. To prevent unjust accusations, what is necessary to convict a person of treason?

Full Faith and Credit Among States: Each state is to respect the public civil acts of other states. Thus items like marriage licenses, wills, and contracts are respected among the states. This clause does not apply to police acts; thus each state can control its own long-term licensing for barbers, beauticians, lawyers, teachers, and doctors.

Mutual Duties of States: If a person passes through another state or moves there, he still has all his rights as an American citizen.

A governor can request that a criminal who flees to another state be returned to the state where the crime was committed to stand trial. The process of returning the criminal is called **extradition**.

Runaways—applied to slaves—were to be returned to their owners.

New States
(1) Congress admits new states to the Union.
(2) If a state is formed out of another state or by the combination of two states, the legislatures of the states involved must approve.

2. The Congress shall have power to dispose of and make all needful rules and regulations respecting the territory or other property belonging to the United States; and nothing in this Constitution shall be so construed as to prejudice any claims of the United States, or any particular state.

Congress regulates the territories. (Today this applies to Puerto Rico, Guam, and other American possessions.)

Section 4
The United States shall guarantee to every state in this Union a republican form of government, and shall protect each of them against invasion; and on application of the legislature, or of the executive (when the legislature cannot be convened) against domestic violence.

When it submits its constitution, each state is to have a republican form of government. The federal government will protect the states from invasion or handle riots or domestic violence when a state legislature, a governor, or the president requests it.

Questions on Article IV
1. What does Article IV address?
2. Give some examples of public civil acts that are respected from state to state.
3. What branch of government admits new states to the Union?
4. What kind of government are new states required to have?

Article V: Amending the Constitution
The Congress, whenever two-thirds of both houses shall deem it necessary, shall propose amendments to this Constitution, or, on the application of the legislatures of two-thirds of the several states, shall call a convention for proposing amendments, which in either case, shall be valid to all intents and purposes, as part of this Constitution when ratified by the legislatures of three-fourths of the several states, or by conventions in three-fourths thereof, as the one or the other mode of ratification may be proposed by the Congress; Provided that no amendment which may be made prior to the year 1808 shall in any manner affect the first and fourth clauses in the ninth section of the first article; and that no

Two-thirds of both houses of Congress or two-thirds of the states in convention propose amendments. Ratification—approval to put an amendment into effect—requires a vote of three-fourths of the state legislatures or three-quarters of the states in conventions.

state, without its consent, shall be deprived of its equal suffrage in the Senate.

Questions on Article V

1. What groups have the power to propose amendments?

2. How much support is required to propose an amendment?

3. How much approval is needed to ratify an amendment?

4. What provision can never be changed unless a state would consent to it?

Article VI: Constitutional and National Supremacy

1. All debts contracted and engagements entered into, before the adoption of this Constitution, shall be as valid against the United States under this Constitution, as under the Confederation.

2. This Constitution, and the laws of the United States which shall be made in pursuance thereof; and all treaties made, or which shall be made, under the authority of the United States, shall be the supreme law of the land; and the judges in every state shall be bound thereby, anything in the constitution or laws of any state to the contrary notwithstanding.

3. The senators and representatives before mentioned, and the members of the several state legislatures, and all executive and judicial officers, both of the United States and of the several states, shall be bound by oath or affirmation, to support this Constitution; but no religious test shall ever be required as a qualification to any office or public trust under the United States.

The United States Constitution is the supreme (highest) law of the nation. The order of authority in the United States is (1) the American Constitution (as interpreted by the Supreme Court), (2) the laws of the U.S. Government (Congress), (3) constitutions of the states, (4) state laws, and (5) local laws (city and county).

All national and state officers affirm to support the Constitution. Holding specific religious beliefs is not a requirement for holding public office.

Questions on Article VI

1. What was to happen to debts contracted before the adoption of the Constitution?

2. What is considered the supreme law of the land?

3. How does the adoption of the Constitution ensure that state officers will support it?

Article VII: Ratifying the Constitution

The ratification of the conventions of nine States shall be sufficient for the establishment of this Constitution between the States so ratifying the same.

Done in convention by the unanimous consent of the states present the seventeenth day of September in the year of our Lord 1787, and of the independence of the United States of America the twelfth. In witness whereof we have hereunto subscribed our names.

George Washington, President and Deputy from Virginia

Nine of the thirteen states had to ratify the Constitution to start the new form of government.

New Hampshire
John Langdon
Nicholas Gilman

Massachusetts
Nathaniel Gorham
Rufus King

Connecticut
William Samuel Johnson
Roger Sherman

New York
Alexander Hamilton

New Jersey
William Livingston
David Brearley
William Paterson
Jonathan Dayton

Pennsylvania
Benjamin Franklin
Thomas Mifflin
Robert Morris
George Clymer
Thomas Fitzsimons
Jared Ingersoll
James Wilson
Gouverneur Morris

Delaware
George Read
Gunning Bedford Jr.
John Dickinson
Richard Bassett
Jacob Broom

Maryland
James McHenry
Daniel of St. Thomas Jenifer
Daniel Carroll

Virginia
John Blair
James Madison Jr.

North Carolina
William Blount
Richard Dobbs Spaight
Hugh Williamson

South Carolina
John Rutledge
Charles Cotesworth Pinckney
Charles Pinckney
Pierce Butler

Georgia
William Few
Abraham Baldwin

Questions on Article VII

1. How many states had to ratify the Constitution before it became the law of the land?
2. On what day was the Constitution signed?

Amendments to the Constitution

The first ten amendments, known as the Bill of Rights, went into effect December 15, 1791. House member James Madison introduced these amendments, and they were ratified two years and three months later. The immunities listed in the Bill of Rights were already in existence, but the amendments insured them. The Constitution and Bill of Rights made the people's liberties secure. The amendments illustrate the principle of limited government.

Amendment I: Five Freedoms

The First Amendment insures five freedoms: religion, speech, press, assembly, and petition. At first the limitations in the Bill of Rights applied only to the central government and not to the states. For example, Massachusetts levied state taxes to support a state church until 1833. But the courts have been using the "due process" rule of Amendment XIV to apply the Bill of Rights to states.

Congress shall make no law respecting an establishment of religion, or prohibiting the free exercise thereof;
or abridging the freedom of speech or of the press;

Congress cannot establish any church or denomination as a state-sponsored church. But people are free to worship as they choose.

Freedom of speech is important to our political system because it permits criticism of misdeeds of those in power. Freedom of speech is not, however, unlimited. Slander, defaming a person by word of mouth, and libel, defaming a person in writing, are not protected.

or the right of the people peaceably to assemble, and to petition the government for a redress of grievances.

Without the right of assembly, there could be no clubs, churches, or other private organizations except those approved by the government. People would be unable to unite to change the government by legal means. Lack of the right to assemble often leads to dictatorships.

Amendment II: The Right to Bear Arms

A well regulated militia being necessary to the security of a free state, the right of the people to keep and bear arms shall not be infringed.

The Second Amendment forbids Congress from infringing on the right of citizens to keep weapons.

Amendment III: No Quartering of Troops

No soldier shall, in time of peace, be quartered in any house, without the consent of the owner, nor in time of war but in a manner to be prescribed by law.

The Third Amendment protects the people from military intrusion into their homes. In colonial days, Americans resented being forced by Britain to take soldiers into their homes during times of war.

Amendment IV: No Unreasonable Searches

The right of the people to be secure in their persons, houses, papers, and effects, against unreasonable searches and seizures, shall not be violated, and no warrants shall issue, but upon probable cause, supported by

The Fourth Amendment guarantees the privacy of homes from illegal searches. It does not keep authorities from conducting legal searches or seizures with search warrants.

oath or affirmation, and particularly describing the place to be searched, and the persons or things to be seized.

Amendment V: Rights of the Accused

No person shall be held to answer for a capital, or otherwise infamous crime, unless on a presentment or indictment of a grand jury, except in cases arising in the land or naval forces, or in the militia, when in actual service in time of war or public danger; nor shall any person be subject for the same offense to be twice put in jeopardy of life or limb; nor shall be compelled in any criminal case to be a witness against himself, nor be deprived of life, liberty, or property, without due process of law; nor shall private property be taken for public use without just compensation.

A grand jury determines whether there is enough evidence against a person to warrant a jury trial for guilt or innocence. This amendment ensures that no citizen can be forced to give evidence against himself. It protects citizens from being tortured or brainwashed to force information from them.

Jeopardy means danger or risk. No person can be tried twice for the same crime.

A person cannot be imprisoned, have his property taken away, or be sentenced to death without a fair and proper trial (due process of law).

Private property can be "condemned [taken] for the public good," but it has to be paid for. For instance, government can take land needed for the building of a new highway, but it must pay the owner a fair price for that land.

Amendment VI: Rights of the Accused in Criminal Trials

In all criminal prosecutions, the accused shall enjoy the right to a speedy and public trial, by an impartial jury of the state and district wherein the crime shall have been committed, which district shall have been previously ascertained by law, and to be informed of the nature and cause of the accusation; to be confronted with the witnesses against him; to have compulsory process for obtaining witnesses in his favor, and to have the assistance of counsel for his defense.

Because some political trials in England had been held in secret and lasted for years (and the accused remained in jail for that time), the Bill of Rights guaranteed the right to a speedy public trial. An accused person has the right to see and face his accuser and his witnesses. The court will require witnesses to appear by serving a subpoena (suh PEE nuh), a document requiring a person to appear in court as a witness. A counsel for the defense (lawyer) is provided even at public expense.

Amendment VII: Rights of Citizens in Civil Trials

In suits at common law, where the value in controversy shall exceed twenty dollars, the right of trial by jury shall be preserved, and no fact tried by a jury shall be otherwise reexamined in any court of the United States, than according to the rules of the common law.

A litigant in any court case involving money or property of twenty dollars' value or more can demand a trial by jury.

Amendment VIII: Cruel, Unusual, and Unjust Punishments

Excessive bail shall not be required, nor excessive fines imposed, nor cruel and unusual punishments inflicted.

Amendment IX: Unlisted Rights

The enumeration in the Constitution of certain rights shall not be construed to deny or disparage others retained by the people.

Amendment X: Unlisted Rights Go to States or to the People

The powers not delegated to the United States by the Constitution, nor prohibited by it to the states, are reserved to the states respectively, or to the people.

Amendment XI: Suing States (1798)

The judicial power of the United States shall not be construed to extend to any suit in law or equity, commenced or prosecuted against one of the United States by citizens of another state, or by citizens or subjects of any foreign state.

Amendment XII: Separate Ballots for President and Vice President (1804)

The electors shall meet in their respective states, and vote by ballot for President and Vice President, one of whom, at least, shall not be an inhabitant of the same state with themselves; they shall name in their ballots the

Bail, money held by the court to ensure an accused person's appearance at a court of trial, may be required, but it is not to be excessive. Unusual punishments included whipping, hanging by the heels, branding, and stocks. Such abuses were here outlawed for federal offenses. The courts decide when bail and fine are excessive and punishments cruel or unusual.

The fact that the Constitution does not list a specific right does not mean the right does not exist. For example, the rights to move and settle somewhere and to choose an occupation are unlisted rights, yet we still have them.

The states or people have any rights that the Constitution does not forbid them to have. The federal government cannot take such rights away from them.

Questions on Amendments 1-10

1. What are the first ten amendments usually called?
2. What do these amendments address?
3. What five freedoms are included in the First Amendment?
4. What are three rights you have if accused, according to the Fifth Amendment?
5. Why was a speedy public trial important?
6. What does the Eighth Amendment ensure about any punishments or fines?
7. To whom do rights not listed in the Constitution go?

Seventeen other amendments have been passed since 1791. Some amendments have corrected problems or more fully explained subjects touched upon by the Constitution. Some of the amendments are related to one another, such as those passed during Reconstruction, and they deal with problems or ideas from a given time. Others deal with single issues or ideas. The Eleventh Amendment states that a citizen of another state or a foreign country may not sue a state in a federal court without that state's consent. Suits must be in the state's own courts.

Instead of voting for two persons, electors are to vote separately for the president and vice president. Thus the possibility of a tie between the president and vice president, which had occurred in 1800, was eliminated.

person voted for as President, and in distinct ballots, the person voted for as Vice President, and they shall make distinct lists of all persons voted for as President and of all persons voted for as Vice President, and of the number of votes for each, which lists they shall sign and certify, and transmit sealed to the seat of the government of the United States, directed to the President of the Senate; the President of the Senate shall, in the presence of the Senate and House of Representatives open all the certificates, and the votes shall then be counted; the person having the greatest number of votes for President, shall be the President, if such number be a majority of the whole number of electors appointed; and if no person have such majority, then from the persons having the highest numbers not exceeding three on the list of those voted for as President, the House of Representatives shall choose immediately, by ballot, the President. But in choosing the President, the votes shall be taken by states, the representation from each state having one vote; a quorum for this purpose shall consist of a member or members from two-thirds of the states, and a majority of all the states shall be necessary to a choice. And if the House of Representatives shall not choose a President, whenever the right of choice shall devolve upon them, before the fourth day of March next following, then the Vice President shall act as President, as in the case of the death or other constitutional disability of the President. The person having the greatest number of votes as Vice President shall be the Vice President, if such number be a majority of the whole number of electors appointed, and if no person have a majority, then from the two highest numbers on the list, the Senate shall choose the Vice President; a quorum for the purpose shall consist of two-thirds of the whole number of senators, and a majority of the whole number shall be necessary to a choice. But no person constitutionally ineligi-

ble to the office of President shall be eligible to that of Vice President of the United States.

Amendment XIII: Slavery (1865)

Section 1. Neither slavery nor involuntary servitude, except as punishment for crime whereof the party shall have been duly convicted, shall exist within the United States, or any place subject to their jurisdiction.

Section 2. Congress shall have power to enforce this article by appropriate legislation.

Amendment XIV: Citizenship (1868)

Section 1. All persons born or naturalized in the United States, and subject to the jurisdiction thereof, are citizens of the United States and of the state wherein they reside. No state shall make or enforce any law which shall abridge the privileges or immunities of citizens of the United States; nor shall any state deprive any person of life, liberty, or property, without due process of law; nor deny to any person within its jurisdiction the equal protection of the law.

Section 2. Representatives shall be apportioned among the several states according to their respective numbers, counting the whole number of persons in each state, excluding Indians not taxed. But when the right to vote at any election for the choice of electors for President and Vice President of the United States, representatives in Congress, the executive and judicial officers of a state, or the members of the legislature thereof, is denied to any of the male inhabitants of such state being twenty-one years of age, and citizens of the United States, or in any way abridged, except for participation in rebellion, or other crime, the basis of representation therein shall be reduced in the proportion which the number of such male citizens shall bear to the whole number of male citizens twenty-one years of age in such state.

Section 3. No person shall be a senator or representative in Congress, or elector of President and Vice President, or hold any

Amendments 13-15 were all ratified during or just after the Civil War and deal with problems of that era. Amendment 13 abolished slavery. It restricted the states as well as the national government.

All persons, regardless of race or former status as slave or free, born in the United States or naturalized, are both American citizens and citizens of the state in which they live. A state cannot deprive any person of life, liberty, or property without due process (a fair trial based on just laws). States that deny voting rights could have their representation in Congress denied, but this has never been done.

Sections 2, 3, and 4 deal with restrictions and provisions made for the states that were in the Confederacy during the Civil War as they took back their responsibilities in the national government.

office, civil or military, under the United States, or under any state, who having previously taken an oath, as a member of Congress, or as an officer of the United States, or as a member of any state legislature, or as an executive or judicial officer of any state, to support the Constitution of the United States, shall have engaged in insurrection or rebellion against the same, or given aid or comfort to the enemies thereof. But Congress may by a vote of two-thirds of each House, remove such disability.

Section 4. The validity of the public debt of the United States, authorized by law, including debts incurred for payment of pensions and bounties for services in suppressing insurrection or rebellion, shall not be questioned. But neither the United States nor any state shall assume or pay any debt or obligation incurred in aid of insurrection or rebellion against the United States, or any claim for the loss or emancipation of any slave; but all such debts, obligations, and claims shall be held illegal and void.

Section 5. The Congress shall have power to enforce, by appropriate legislation, the provisions of this article.

Amendment XV: Black Voting Rights (1870)

Section 1. The right of the citizens of the United States to vote shall not be denied or abridged by the United States or by any state on account of race, color, or previous condition of servitude.

Section 2. The Congress shall have power to enforce this article by appropriate legislation.

Amendment XVI: Income Tax (1913)

The Congress shall have power to lay and collect taxes on incomes, from whatever source derived, without apportionment among the several states, and without regard to any census or enumeration.

Race, color, or past service as a slave should not prevent any citizen from voting.

Amendment XVII: Direct Election of Senators (1913)

The Senate of the United States shall be composed of two senators from each state, elected by the people thereof, for six years; and each senator shall have one vote. The electors in each state shall have the qualifications requisite for electors of the most numerous branch of the state legislature.

When vacancies happen in the representation of any state in the Senate, the executive authority of such state shall issue writs of election to fill such vacancies; *provided,* that the legislature of any state may empower the executive thereof to make temporary appointments until the people fill the vacancies by election as the legislature may direct.

This amendment shall not be so construed as to affect the election or term of any senator chosen before it becomes valid as part of the Constitution.

Amendment XVIII: Prohibition (1919)

After one year from the ratification of this article, the manufacture, sale, or transportation of intoxicating liquors within, the importation thereof into, or the exportation thereof from the United States and all territory subject to the jurisdiction thereof, for beverage purposes is hereby prohibited.

Amendments 16-19 are sometimes called the Progressive Amendments because most were passed at the height of the progressive era (1900-1920).

Rather than using state apportionment to set a tax base so that each state paid a tax equal to the percentage of its population, Congress was given the power to tax incomes.

The people rather than the state legislatures gained the right to elect their two senators. Anyone who is qualified to vote in a state house of representatives election is also qualified to vote in a United States Senate election. Senate vacancies may be filled by special election or by a state governor, who can appoint a senator if state law allows it.

Prohibition refers to forbidding the manufacture, sale, or transportation of liquor. Congress passed the Volstead Act to define "intoxicating liquor" and to enforce the amendment. The Twenty-first Amendment repealed the Eighteenth in 1933.

The Congress and the several states shall have concurrent power to enforce this article by appropriate legislation.

This article shall be inoperative unless it shall have been ratified as an amendment to the Constitution by the legislatures of the several states, as provided in the Constitution, within seven years from the date of submission hereof to the states by Congress.

Amendment XIX: Women's Suffrage (1920)

Freedom in the United States allows people, such as these early suffragettes, to demonstrate for causes that they hold dear.

The right of citizens of the United States to vote shall not be denied or abridged by the United States or by any state on account of sex.

The Congress shall have power to enforce this article by appropriate legislation.

Amendment XX: Lame Duck Amendment (1933)

Section 1. The terms of the President and the Vice President shall end at noon on the 20th day of January, and the terms of Senators and Representatives at noon on the 3rd day of January, of the years in which such terms would have ended if this article had not been ratified; and the terms of their successors shall then begin.

Section 2. The Congress shall assemble at least once in every year, and such meeting shall begin at noon on the 3rd day of January,

Questions on Amendments 11-18

1. According to the Fourteenth Amendment, who besides the federal government cannot deprive a person of life, liberty, or property without due process of law?

2. What is meant by "due process of law"?

3. What amendment makes income taxes constitutional?

4. What amendment gives voters rather than state legislators the right to elect senators?

5. What does the Eighteenth Amendment prohibit? When and by what amendment was this repealed?

Women were hereby given the vote. The right to vote is also called **suffrage**.

The dates for starting terms for the president, senators, and representatives to take office were changed. Presidential terms begin on January 20 every fourth year; terms for senators and representatives begin on January 3 and are six and two years respectively. This amendment shortens the length of time between the November elections and the taking of office.

unless they shall by law appoint a different day.

Section 3. If, at the time fixed for the beginning of the term of President, the President-elect shall have died, the Vice President-elect shall become President. If a President shall not have been chosen before the time fixed for the beginning of his term, or if the President-elect shall have failed to qualify, then the Vice President-elect shall act as President until a President shall have qualified; and the Congress may by law provide for the case wherein neither a President-elect nor a Vice President-elect shall have qualified, declaring who shall then act as President, or the manner in which one who is to act shall be selected, and such person shall act accordingly until a President or Vice President shall have qualified.

Section 4. The Congress may by law provide for the case of the death of any of the persons from whom the House of Representatives may choose a President whenever the right of choice shall have devolved upon them, and for the case of the death of any of the persons from whom the Senate may choose a Vice President whenever the right of choice shall have devolved upon them.

Section 5. Sections 1 and 2 shall take effect on the 15th day of October following the ratification of this article.

Section 6. This article shall be inoperative unless it shall have been ratified as an amendment to the Constitution by the legislatures of three-fourths of the several states within seven years from the date of its submission.

If the president-elect dies before taking office, the vice president-elect takes his place until another president qualifies.

Amendment XXI: Repeal of Prohibition (1933)

Section 1. The Eighteenth Article of amendment to the Constitution of the United States is hereby repealed.

Section 2. The transportation or importation into any state, territory, or possession of the United States for delivery or use therein of intoxicating liquors in violation of the laws thereof, is hereby prohibited.

Section 3. This article shall be inoperative unless it shall have been ratified as an amendment to the Constitution by conventions in the several states, as provided in the Constitution, within seven years from the date of the submission thereof to the states by the Congress.

This amendment repealed prohibition, but states and territories could prohibit the sale of alcohol within their borders.

Amendment XXII: Presidential Terms (1951)

No person shall be elected to the office of the President more than twice, and no person who has held the office of President, or acted as President, for more than two years of a term to which some other person was elected President shall be elected to the office of the President more than once.

But this article shall not apply to any person holding the office of President when this article was proposed by the Congress, and shall not prevent any person who may be holding the office of President, or acting as President, during the term within which this article becomes operative from holding the office of President, or acting as President during the remainder of such term.

This article shall be inoperative unless it shall have been ratified as an amendment to the Constitution by the legislatures of three-fourths of the several states within seven years from the date of its submission to the states by the Congress.

Presidents can be elected for only two terms in their own right. If elevated from the vice-presidency during the second half of a previous president's term, a vice president who becomes president could serve a maximum of ten years.

Amendment XXIII: Voting for Washington, D.C. (1961)

Section 1. The District constituting the seat of Government of the United States shall appoint in such manner as Congress may direct:

A number of electors of President and Vice President equal to the whole number of Senators and Representatives in Congress to which the District would be entitled if it were a state, but in no event more than the least populous state; they shall be in addition to those appointed by the states, but they shall be considered, for the purpose of the election of President and Vice President, to be electors appointed by a State; and they shall meet in the District and perform such duties as provided by the twelfth article of amendment.

Section 2. The Congress shall have power to enforce this article by appropriate legislation.

Residents of the District of Columbia can vote in presidential elections, and the district has three electoral votes.

Amendment XXIV: No Poll Tax (1964)

Section 1. The right of citizens of the United States to vote in any primary or other election for President or Vice President, for electors for President or Vice President, or for Senator or Representative in Congress, shall not be denied or abridged by the United States or any State by reasons of failure to pay any poll tax or other tax.

Section 2. The Congress shall have the power to enforce this article by appropriate legislation.

The payment of a poll tax to a state in any federal election was forbidden. A **poll tax** was a tax some states charged people before they let them vote.

Amendment XXV: Presidential Succession (1967)

Section 1. In case of the removal of the President from office or of his death or resignation, the Vice President shall become President.

Section 2. Whenever there is a vacancy in the office of the Vice President, the President shall nominate a Vice President who shall take office upon confirmation by a majority vote of both Houses of Congress.

If the vice-presidency becomes vacant, the president can appoint a new vice president with the approval of both the House and the Senate.

Section 3. Whenever the President transmits to the President Pro Tempore of the Senate and the Speaker of the House of Representatives his written declaration that he is unable to discharge the powers and duties of his office, and until he transmits to them a written declaration to the contrary, such powers and duties shall be discharged by the Vice President as Acting President.

Section 4. Whenever the Vice President and a majority of either the principal officers of the executive departments or of such other body as Congress may by law provide, transmit to the President Pro Tempore of the Senate and the Speaker of the House of Representatives their written declaration that the President is unable to discharge the powers and duties of his office, the Vice President shall immediately assume the powers and duties of the office as Acting President.

Thereafter, when the President transmits to the President Pro Tempore of the Senate and the Speaker of the House of Representatives his written declaration that no inability exists, he shall resume the powers and duties of his office unless the Vice President and a majority of either the principal officers of the executive department or of such other body as Congress may by law provide, transmit within four days to the President Pro Tempore of the Senate and the Speaker of the House of Representatives their written declaration that the President is unable to discharge the powers and duties of his office. Thereupon Congress shall decide the issue, assembling within forty-eight hours for that purpose if not in session. If the Congress, within twenty-one days after receipt of the latter written declaration, or, if Congress is not in session, within twenty-one days after Congress is required to assemble, determines by two-thirds vote of both Houses that the President is unable to discharge the powers and duties of his office, the Vice President shall continue to discharge the same

The president can transfer his duties to the vice president when he is unable to perform them. He may do this, for example, when he is undergoing surgery and therefore under anesthetic and unable to make decisions.

as Acting President; otherwise, the President shall resume the powers and duties of his office.

Amendment XXVI: Eighteen-Year-Old Vote (1971)

Section 1. The right of citizens of the United States, who are eighteen years of age or older, to vote shall not be denied or abridged by the United States or by any state on account of age.

Section 2. The Congress shall have power to enforce this article by appropriate legislation.

Amendment XXVII: Congressional Pay Raises (1992)

No law, varying the compensation for the services of the Senators and Representatives, shall take effect, until an election of Representatives shall have intervened.

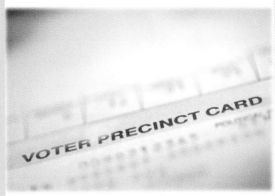

Eighteen-year-olds were given the right to vote. (Previously the voting age was twenty-one.)

Any vote for a raise for senators and representatives cannot take effect until after the next election.

Questions on Amendments 19-27

1. Who was given the right to vote in each of the following?
   a. Amendment 15
   b. Amendment 19
   c. Amendment 26

2. According to the Twentieth Amendment, when is the president to be inaugurated?

3. What section of the country got the right to vote for president in 1961?

4. If the vice president becomes president, who picks a new vice president, and how is he approved?

SUMMARY

The United States Constitution has served as the foundation of American government for over two hundred years. It has provided a written law for the land, and it contains features that have helped it to adjust and endure as the nation and its needs have changed through the years.

Chapter Review

People, Places, and Things to Remember

separation of powers
checks and balances
federal system
Preamble
bicameral system
impeachment
president pro tempore
veto
pocket veto

naturalization
bankruptcy
counterfeiting
copyrights
patents
elastic clause
habeas corpus
bill of attainder
ex post facto law

reprieve
pardon
original jurisdiction
appellate jurisdiction
extradition
suffrage
poll tax

Review Questions

Match the following constitutional terms to their best description.

1. appellate jurisdiction
2. bicameral system
3. bill of attainder
4. counterfeiting
5. elastic clause
6. extradition
7. habeas corpus
8. impeachment
9. naturalization
10. pardon
11. patent
12. reprieve
13. suffrage
14. veto

a. prevents imprisonment without a criminal charge
b. temporary postponement of punishment
c. a foreigner's becoming a citizen
d. presidential rejection of a bill
e. protection for inventors and their inventions
f. Congress can do anything "necessary and proper"
g. a legislature with two houses
h. file charges against a major federal official
i. making phony money
j. document permitting punishment without a trial
k. complete forgiveness of a crime
l. the right to vote
m. send a criminal to another state for trial
n. court's right to hear a case already tried in a lower court

Question for Discussion

15. What do you think will be necessary for the continued success of the Constitution?

History Skills

Analysis: Unconstitutional Laws and Actions

You are a young federal judge. Your job is to uphold the Constitution as the highest law in the land. To do so, you must apply constitutional principles to the actual cases that you encounter.

Practice your decision-making abilities by evaluating each of the following situations. Write a *C* if the hypothetical case is constitutional and a *U* if it is unconstitutional. Give the article and section or the amendment in the U.S. Constitution that supports each of your conclusions.

Example: Maine has elected a man who is only twenty-four years old to the U.S. House of Representatives. *U; Art. I, Sec. 2*

1. The U.S. representatives have voted to extend their terms to four years.
2. The House of Representatives has set its membership at 435.
3. The Senate has proposed a revenue bill to pay for a new highway.
4. Congress overrode the president's last veto by a simple majority in both houses.
5. Congress has banned imports from China.
6. Against the wishes of the governor, congress is using Alabama's militia to enforce a new law in the state.
7. Congress has given Miami the privilege of being a "free port" where no tariffs apply.
8. Alaska has decided to coin its own money to help pay its debts.
9. Texas has declared war on Mexico because of illegal drug traffic.
10. The new U.S. president was born a German citizen, but he has been an American citizen for fourteen years.
11. The president has granted pardons to three federal officials who were convicted of embezzlement against the U.S. Treasury.
12. At the president's request, Congress has voted to remove all Supreme Court justices over the age of seventy-five.
13. Illinois does not give full faith and credit to marriage licenses from New Mexico.
14. Congress has formed a new state within the jurisdiction of California without the consent of California's legislature.
15. Congress has passed a law barring churches from preaching the gospel.

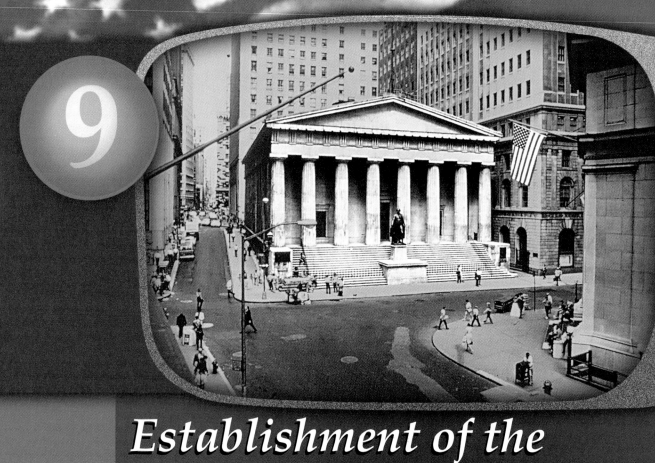

9

Establishment of the New Government

Just before noon on April 30, 1789, a solemn George Washington stepped out on the balcony of Federal Hall on the corner of Wall and Broad Streets in New York City, the capital at that time. Washington's **inauguration,** the formal ceremony that officially begins a president's term, began precisely at noon. He placed his left hand on the Bible and raised his right hand to take the oath of office. He then repeated the thirty-five words required by the Constitution:

I do solemnly swear that I will faithfully execute the office of President of the United States, and will to the best of my ability preserve, protect, and defend the Constitution of the United States.

At the end of the oath, Washington added a phrase of his own: "so help me God." He realized that he could not do his job without God's help. The oath of office taken, he entered the Senate Chamber to give his inaugural address before both houses of Congress.

Washington had good reason to be solemn. At that time the United States had only four million people, seven hundred thousand of whom were slaves. Other world governments were ruled by kings unfriendly to the United States and her new form of government. The nation had no money in its treasury and lacked a strong army and navy. The Constitution had outlined a framework for the new government but lacked many of the exact details.

Challenges of the New Government

The government that Washington was going to supervise was completely new. No country had a working republic to act as an example for Washington and the other leaders. They had to find out how to make this new government work, so Washington began to build an administration that could help him meet the problems that would come. His first challenge was to set up a **cabinet,** a group of advisors, to help him with his responsibilities.

Establishing a Cabinet

Although Article II, Section 2, of the Constitution (see p. 148) provided for executive departments to give advice, nothing was said about how to pick leaders or how to organize the departments. Washington benefited from the counsel of James Madison, his unofficial administrative assistant. Washington established four departments of government and placed men he trusted at their heads. The department of state was headed by Thomas Jefferson, the treasury by Alexander Hamilton, that of defense by Henry Knox, and what has come to be called the Justice Department by Attorney General Edmund Randolph. Washington also appointed Samuel Osgood to head the post office. These department leaders became Washington's cabinet, advising him on policies and problems of the government.

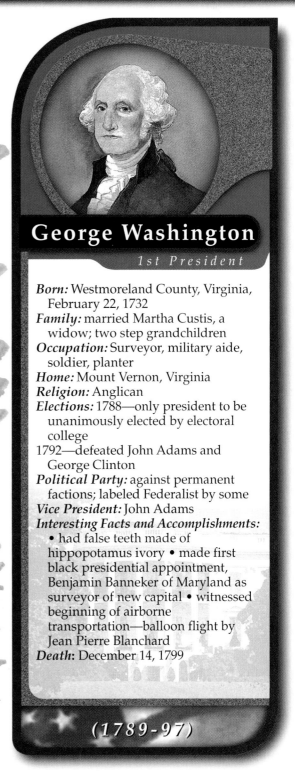

George Washington
1st President

Born: Westmoreland County, Virginia, February 22, 1732
Family: married Martha Custis, a widow; two step grandchildren
Occupation: Surveyor, military aide, soldier, planter
Home: Mount Vernon, Virginia
Religion: Anglican
Elections: 1788—only president to be unanimously elected by electoral college
1792—defeated John Adams and George Clinton
Political Party: against permanent factions; labeled Federalist by some
Vice President: John Adams
Interesting Facts and Accomplishments:
• had false teeth made of hippopotamus ivory • made first black presidential appointment, Benjamin Banneker of Maryland as surveyor of new capital • witnessed beginning of airborne transportation—balloon flight by Jean Pierre Blanchard
Death: December 14, 1799

(1789-97)

Edmund Randolph
Attorney General

Alexander Hamilton
Secretary to the Treasury

George Washington .
President

Thomas Jefferson
Secretary of State

Henry Knox
Secretary of War

National Finances

There was little federal income. This meant that there was almost no money to pay for government. The cost of operating the government in 1789 seems ridiculously low to us today. Washington's annual salary was to be $25,000, but he agreed to serve for his expenses. Members of the House and Senate received $6.00 per day. The Speaker of the House received $12.00 per day. Cabinet members made $3,500 annually. At first the government had much difficulty paying these salaries because the government had not organized its finances. The war debts owed to individuals and states could not be repaid either. Even the interest owed on those debts was not paid. Of course, the government's inability to meet its obligations caused lack of respect for the government, just as a Christian's inability to fulfill obligations leads to a lack of respect for Christianity in the eyes of the world.

Hamilton's Plan—Secretary of the Treasury Alexander Hamilton designed a financial program to make the new nation capable of paying its debts and meeting its obligations. First, the government would have to levy (impose and collect) taxes to obtain the needed revenue. To raise money a tariff of eight percent was levied on foreign imports, and an **excise tax** (a tax paid for the manufacture or sale of certain goods and services within a country) was levied on whiskey. Second, the government would repay the money borrowed during the Revolution. To settle this debt, it had to repay Americans who had purchased bonds to finance the war. The Continental Congress had not been able to pay this debt, and most of the bond owners doubted that they would ever be repaid. However, news of possible repayment by the new government leaked to speculators, who began to purchase many bonds. Because some of the owners thought the bonds to be worthless, they sold them to the speculators for a fraction of their value. When the Funding Bill of 1790 passed, it arranged for repaying the bonds at their printed value plus interest. Some innocent citizens who had sold bonds for small sums were hurt. Nonetheless, the act helped the government stand by its promises. The debt was paid.

Third, Hamilton wanted the federal government to take over responsibility of repaying the debts of the states. By repaying the states as well as the citizens, the federal government hoped for an increase in the states' loyalty to the federal government. This idea resulted in the Assumption Act of 1790. Fourth, the federal government should establish a **national bank**. The bank could hold the tax money the government collected in one place, and the nation's financial transactions could be handled through the bank. The major share of the bank would be owned by private citizens while the federal government would retain only a twenty-percent interest. Thus the bank was largely a private business operation. Accordingly, Congress set up the Bank of the United States in 1791.

Differing Views—Several of Hamilton's ideas brought widespread disagreement, particularly the assumption of state debts and government involvement in banking. A group opposed to both emerged under Thomas Jefferson's leadership. He and many southerners opposed the assumption of state debts because the southern states had already paid most of their debts. They did not wish to help pay those of the northern states. They also opposed the national bank because its business

Precedents

Washington knew that "many things which appear of little importance in themselves and at the beginning, may have great consequences." He wrote James Madison: "At the first everything . . . will serve to establish a precedent. It is devoutly wished on my part, that these precedents may be fixed on true principles."

Even the way in which Washington took office became a precedent for other presidents to follow. Presidents since Washington have continued to put their hand on the Bible and say "so help me God." Washington realized the importance of being a good example even in little things.

That first government faced many problems. His solutions to them set precedents—models for doing things—that were so wise they have been followed ever since.

Congress argued over what to call the new chief executive. Vice President Adams suggested "His electoral Highness." The Senate suggested "His Highness, the President of the United States of America,

and Protector of their Liberties." The House's idea was "President of the United States." Although their idea was adopted, and this is the way the president is introduced, it became the custom to call him simply "Mr. President."

Washington established a cabinet, a group of executive advisors, to help him with his responsibilities. Other presidents have since used and expanded the cabinet and their executive departments. Washington also traveled through the country as president and gave many Americans the opportunity to see him.

Washington served the United States as president for two four-year terms. No president served more than two terms until Franklin Roosevelt broke that tradition almost a hundred and fifty years later. Belatedly, seeing the wisdom of Washington's precedent, Congress passed the Twenty-second Amendment to the Constitution. When it was ratified in 1951, it made the two-term tradition law.

operations would help northern industries but not southern agriculture.

Despite this opposition, Hamilton's plan was implemented. The Assumption Act was passed because of a compromise. In return for Jefferson's and southern support of the debt assumption, the federal capital would be located in the South. Maryland and Virginia gave land along the Potomac River for a federal district to be named after Columbus and George Washington. Today's Washington, D.C., is built on the land given by Maryland. Regardless of the criticisms, Hamilton's plan did work, and the nation's credit and reputation were restored.

Although Washington himself had expressed hope that there be no political parties, the groups that had formed around Hamilton and Jefferson during the debates over Hamilton's plans eventually became the basis of America's two-party political system. Hamilton's party was called the **Federalist Party;** Jefferson's party received the name **Democratic-Republican Party.** (Its members were called "Republicans" for a few years, but later they became known as the "Democrats.")

The Whiskey Rebellion

The excise tax on whiskey led to a controversy that tested Washington and the federal government. On the western frontier, in addition to being used as a foodstuff for man and animals, corn was fermented and then distilled into whiskey. Because there was a shortage of money and a desire for whiskey, some people used whiskey in place of money. Westerners resented the tax that affected many of their purchases. If a man paid for a pig with a gallon of whiskey, he was still charged the tax on the whiskey. If he refused to pay the tax and was arrested, he had to go to a federal court for trial. The federal courts were sometimes miles away in cities close to the coast.

In the summer of 1794 in western Pennsylvania, a federal marshal sought to serve papers on a whiskey distiller who had not paid the tax. Angry farmers attacked the marshal, burned the home of a tax inspector, and tarred and feathered other officials. Soldiers arriving to stop the violent outbursts gave up when they encountered armed resistance. President Washington tried to get the state of Pennsylvania to handle the problem, but the state's governor refused. Washington offered the rebels amnesty, a group pardon, if they would agree to abide by law, but his offer was ignored. The president then called about thirteen thousand militiamen out as a federal force, and he commanded the rebels to disperse by September 1 or the militia would move in.

Washington moved forcefully. A larger group of volunteers than he had ever had at his command during the Revolution rode with the president himself on September 30, 1794. He told the troops to "combat and subdue all who may be found in arms in opposition to the national will and authority." Washington, then sixty-two, soon realized he was too old to sit in a saddle all day, but he went almost halfway before he decided to return to Philadelphia. When the rest of the troops arrived at the scene, some rebels were arrested; two of them were condemned to death, but Washington later pardoned them. In using federal force to put down the **Whiskey Rebellion,** Washington established another precedent and let the public know that he would allow no disobedience of national laws.

Establishing the Federal Court System

Although Article III, Section I (see p. 149) of the Constitution had established by name only one court, the Supreme Court, it did give Congress the power to set up lesser courts. Under the Judiciary Act of 1789, Congress provided the mechanics of a working court system. The Supreme Court would have five associate justices and one chief justice. Washington appointed John Jay as the first chief justice.

There would also be thirteen federal district courts, one per state. Most cases involving violation of federal laws could be tried in these courts. Three circuit courts were set up to hear cases sent up and appealed from the district courts and state supreme courts. Today's federal court system follows a similar pattern.

Congress provided for federal courthouses to be located in each state. This early courthouse was located in Williamsburg, Virginia.

Ratification of the Bill of Rights

The Philadelphia Convention had already discussed a bill of rights. They rejected it because they believed that the rights listed in it already belonged to the people and that the federal government really had no power over such matters. Yet others were uneasy and believed that failure to guarantee rights might lead to the loss of their rights. As a result, in the struggle to ratify the Constitution, the Bill of Rights became an issue. Four states had agreed to ratify it only if the first Congress would give adoption of the Bill of Rights first priority.

When the first Congress convened, a debate erupted over the Bill of Rights. The bill left the House with sixteen amendments. By the time the Senate finished with it, there were fourteen left. A House-Senate Conference Committee agreed on twelve, and on September 25, 1789, they released them to the states. In December of 1791, ten were ratified.

Fighting Indians on the Frontier

Americans desired to move into the lands of the Old Northwest but found such movement blocked by Indians. The British in the Northwest Territory had been urging the Indians to attack Americans. Sometimes the Indians were openly promised British help if they would halt the spread of American settlements.

The government made several unsuccessful attempts to put a stop to the Indian attacks. Finally in 1794, war hero **Anthony Wayne** and a well-trained force moved into what is now northwestern Ohio. They defeated a band of Indians and their allies at **Fallen Timbers,** near modern Toledo. Following the defeat the Indians came to a peace conference at Fort Greenville in 1795. There they gave up their claim to about one-half of the state of Ohio in return for gifts and annual payments.

Despite the fear of hostile Indians and other obstacles, pioneers went west. During the 1790s three new states met congressional standards for admission as outlined by the Northwest Ordinance of 1787: Vermont (1791), Kentucky (1792), and Tennessee (1796). Also, Ohio and the western sections of New York, Pennsylvania, and Georgia made population gains during this decade.

The battle at Fallen Timbers brought the Indians to the peace table.

SECTION REVIEW

1. Give three reasons Washington was solemn on his inauguration day.

2. What were the four departments of government that Washington established, and who was head of each?

3. List the four parts of Hamilton's financial program.

4. What brought about the first political parties in the United States?

5. Where did Anthony Wayne's forces defeat a band of Indians?

 What precedent did Washington set with his handling of the Whiskey Rebellion? Why was the precedent important?

Foreign Threats to the New Government

Although the United States had established its independence with its victory in the Revolution, other world nations were not sure of its strength. European powers doubted that the United States would be able to protect its rights. The young country had yet to prove that it could not be bullied.

America and the French Revolution

By late summer of 1789, word reached American shores that the French had revolted against the government of King Louis XVI. Americans cheered, identifying with the French slogan "Liberty, Equality, and Fraternity." They supported the French because the French had aided America during the War for Independence, and at first they gave approval to the French revolutionaries. Lafayette, who temporarily served as the French leader, even sent George Washington the key to the Bastille, a French prison. The fall of the prison had symbolized the start of the French Revolution. But by 1793 Americans were horrified. Lafayette had been imprisoned, and France was bathed in blood. The French government, although professing to be a republic, was highly unstable, and citizens suffered from a reign of terror. Furthermore, the French campaigned against

Washington used his home, Mt. Vernon, to entertain foreign dignitaries.

religion, and infidel thinkers became popular. During that riotous time, France and Britain became involved in a war.

America's Position of Neutrality—The Americans had joined the French in 1778 in a "perpetual" Treaty of Alliance and a trade pact. The Federalists now urged Washington to denounce both. A Federalist from Massachusetts named Fisher Ames denounced revolutionized France as "an open hell, still ringing with agonies and blasphemies, still smoking with sufferings, and crimes in which we see . . . perhaps our own future state." The Democratic-Republicans, however, agreed with the more liberal Thomas Jefferson, who said that he was willing to see "half of the earth devastated" to insure "the liberty of the whole." But when it appeared the devastated half might include the American portion of the sphere, even the secretary of state gave in to Washington's desire to announce neutrality. On April 22, 1793, Washington issued his **Neutrality Proclamation,** urging Americans to be "impartial" toward all possible foreign foes and to cease actions that would involve the United States in foreign wars.

Citizen Genêt—Meanwhile, a young French diplomat decided to test the proclamation. **Edmond Charles Genêt** came to Charleston, South Carolina, to set up a base for French land and sea operations against Spain and England. Genêt unwisely tried to hire war hero George Rogers Clark and other veterans to fight Spain in Spanish-owned Florida and Louisiana. He also outfitted American private ships to attack Spanish and British shipping. When the president refused Genêt's pleas to call Congress into special session to vote aid for France, he announced that he would go over Washington's head and appeal to the American people. Since the American press did not agree on the matter, he was sure that he would find a sympathetic audience.

Genêt managed to equip twelve privateers, who captured eighty British vessels before Jefferson could see Washington's point that this citizen was dragging the United States into "war abroad and anarchy at home."

Washington asked France to recall Genêt, and Congress passed laws to prevent other foreign agents from causing such trouble. However, just as Genêt was to be deported, the French government changed hands. Since the new faction said that it would behead Genêt, Washington kindly let him stay in America.

But the end of the Genêt affair also meant the end of Jefferson's career as secretary of state. Ever locked in disputes with Hamilton and pressing Washington and the newspapers to take sides, Jefferson finally resigned his position.

Trouble with the British

Although the Neutrality Proclamation and the silencing of Genêt may have helped calm England's fears of America's siding with France, the threat of another United States war with Britain continued. The nations disagreed over what rights neutral countries—namely the United States—might have at sea. The United States, with an ever-growing trade fleet, had opened up trade with the French West Indies and France, Britain's enemies. To retaliate, Britain invoked an old law, the "Rule

French diplomat, Edmond Genêt, caused international problems when he tested the Neutrality Proclamation.

of 1756," which said that trade not open in peace could not be opened in war. Thus she seized two hundred fifty American ships with their cargoes and crews.

Impressment—The British also were offended when their own sailors, who had been subjected to bad food and harsh discipline, jumped ship in ports where American ships were also docked. These sailors deserted to American ships for higher pay and better treatment. To regain their lost sailors, the British retaliated by seizing American sailors and forcing them to serve the British, a practice called **impressment.** Although these disputes led to a session around a peace table in 1795, the issues really were not settled by the treaty signed there. Instead, they were factors that would lead to a war in 1812.

The Jay Treaty—To avoid war, Washington appointed Chief Justice John Jay to head a peace mission to Britain. Since Britain was a strong world power and the United States was a small new republic, Jay was at a disadvantage from the start. The United States agreed to limit trade with France, Britain's enemy, and to pay British citizens what Americans owed them. The British agreed to abandon their forts in the Northwest, pay the United States for ships seized, and open some ports in the British West Indies to American trade.

The **Jay Treaty** did not really settle the issues of neutral rights at sea or of Indian attacks. Congress and the American public were angry with it and with Jay; but since there was no other option except war, the Senate ratified the treaty. The House of Representatives tried to block the treaty by voting down monies needed to carry it out. President Washington stepped in, insisting that a treaty ratified by the Senate was already law and had to be honored. The House was silenced, and ever since, presidential treaties have been free of House influence. But the

John Jay's treaty with England enflamed public opinion against him.

public called Jay "an archtraitor worse than Benedict Arnold." Jay remarked that he could have found his way across America by night using the light from the many burning effigies of himself.

Settling Differences with Spain

Spain still controlled Florida, and it had temporary control of the Louisiana Territory (the land west of the Mississippi River; see map on p. 113). Spain's interference in America's frontier regions remained an unsettled issue. Now westerners clamored for the government to solve their problems. If the government did not help them, the settlers announced, they would take matters into their own hands and make their own treaty with Spain.

Washington responded by sending Thomas Pinckney of South Carolina to Spain to negotiate the dispute. Pinckney successfully made a treaty with Spain in 1795 that gave the United States the right of deposit at New Orleans and made the thirty-first parallel of

latitude the southern boundary of the United States. The treaty, called the **Pinckney Treaty** in America, was also called the Treaty of San Lorenzo. Unlike the Jay Treaty, the Pinckney Treaty was popular, and Pinckney became an instant hero.

SECTION REVIEW

1. Disillusioned with the French Revolution, America in 1793 took what official position toward European conflict?

2. What Frenchman sought to alienate Washington from the American people?

3. For what two reasons did Britain seize American ships and impress American sailors?

4. What two issues were settled by the Pinckney Treaty, and with what country was that treaty made?

 What precedent did Washington set when the House tried to block the carrying out of the Jay Treaty? Why was this precedent important?

Continuation of the Government

Washington's presidency was a time of great trials for the new government, but the young nation survived. Now it was time for a new administration to take over and continue what Washington had begun.

Washington's Farewell

On September 19, 1796, six months before he officially left office, Washington gave what is now called his "Farewell Address" to David Claypoole, a newspaper publisher, to print. Although some people thought that Washington should run again, Washington said that two four-year terms were enough.

In addition to asserting the two-term tradition, the address gave advice for future years. Washington warned against disputes that would divide both politicians and people into factions. He urged caution in making any permanent alliances with foreign countries. This warning helped lead the United States to a century-long policy of isolationism. He encouraged maintaining the nation's credit and implied that America should stay out of debt.

Washington was sixty-six years old when he returned home to his beloved Mount Vernon. After eight years of the pressures of the presidency, the Washingtons enjoyed the change. But they had only a little over two years to enjoy their retirement. Weakend by the common medical practice of bleeding, Washington died December 14, 1799, when his throat swelled shut from infection. The

Martha Washington capably supervised the work at Mount Vernon during her husband's absence, first during the Revolution and later, during his terms as president.

country mourned him. His name and memory were greatly honored. He is the only American for whom a state was named, and seventy other places bear his name—the most places named for any individual. In addition, his image appears on many postage stamps and other national emblems and memorials. George Washington is, in the words of fellow Virginian Henry Lee, still "first in war, first in peace, and first in the hearts of his countrymen."

The Election of 1796

Since Washington had faced no opposition, had not campaigned for office, and had not had to deal with political parties in his elections, there were no real precedents to follow for the election of 1796. There were, however, political parties. The party leaders met and chose their candidates. Everyone expected the Republicans to choose Thomas Jefferson, and they did, with Aaron Burr to run for vice president. The Federalists, however,

disagreed on their choice. The High Federalists, or pro-Hamiltonians, favored Thomas Pinckney, while the moderates of the party selected John Adams.

John Adams won the most votes in the electoral college. But the split in the Federalist votes allowed Jefferson to come in second and to win the vice-presidency. This meant that the president and vice president were from different parties, a situation that hindered the creation of a unified administration.

In Washington's Shadow

Few presidents came to office as well equipped as John Adams. A lawyer and a diplomat, he had never really sought or expected popularity, but his service in both of the Continental Congresses had won him the respect of other legislators. In addition, his twelve years as minister in France and England had won the new nation respect overseas and had equipped Adams to deal with foreign affairs. As the nation's first vice president, John Adams called that office "the most insignificant ever contrived by man." His only constitutionally stated duty was to preside over the Senate, where he cast votes only in case of ties. Yet he did use his office to observe the problems of the new government firsthand. It was natural that, when Washington decided not to run for a third term, Adams was suggested as his successor.

Following Washington as president, however, was no easy matter. On the day Adams took office, the cheering for Washington was louder than that for him. There were tears of sadness in people's eyes for a great man that was leaving and little praise for another that had arrived. On what was probably the biggest day of Adams's life, his inauguration day in Philadelphia, his wife, Abigail, was not there to share it. Fearing public criticism, Abigail had stayed home on their farm in Massachusetts. Thus, his "dearest and best

friend," as Adams called her in his letters, shared the experience only by letter.

Adams did not appoint a new cabinet but left Washington's cabinet in office. Although he did not know it, the cabinet was consulting with Alexander Hamilton, who was no longer in office, before they made decisions that opposed the new president's wishes. This opposition frustrated several of Adams's policies. Criticisms from his political adversaries throughout his term of office caused Adams to lose the admiration of many Americans. Even though John Adams sought the best interest of his country in his actions as president, he could never be as popular as George Washington.

To people outside his own family, Adams often seemed reserved and aloof. Had he perhaps made an effort to be more outgoing with the American people, Adams's presidency

John Adams came to the office of president amid the people's sorrow at Washington's departure.

Abigail Adams

If any president ever found the perfect helpmate, it was John Adams, the second president. His wife, Abigail Smith Adams, loved him unfailingly through fifty-four years of marriage. She would have done anything for him. He was often gloomy and uncompromising, but her charm would cheer him up and soothe his impatience. She sacrificed her personal pleasures for the good of his career and the benefit of their estate. She stood by him when all others were against him. She was a humble, dutiful wife but certainly no mindless slave. Her husband always delighted in her wit and opinions. Her many letters addressed him in all seriousness as "my dearest and best friend."

From their first meeting, he loved her ability to talk on a wide range of issues. Although she never had a formal education, she became one of the nation's best-educated women. She took every opportunity to learn, whether from her father's library or from the rigging on a ship. She would not let any obstacle keep her from marrying John. Her parents disliked him because he was nine years her elder, because he was born into a poor, lowly family, and because he was a lawyer. She, on the other hand, could claim a long line of noble ancestors. Her father was a parson, and he considered law a dishonest and unworthy profession. Nevertheless, he agreed to let them marry after a three-year courtship had proved their love. He chose for his wedding sermon the amusing text: "For John came neither eating bread nor drinking wine, yet ye say 'He hath a devil.'" The nineteen-year-old bride moved to a cottage in Braintree, Massachusetts. For ten years she managed the farm and raised five children while her husband rode his circuit of courts.

She wrote him often during this time. But it was not until John entered the political activities of the War for Independence that her writing was in earnest. It was at this time she proved to be the most outstanding woman correspondent of the period. The first of several separations came in 1774, when John left home to represent his state in the Continental Congress at Philadelphia. Her letters were essential sources of encouragement when he became disheartened by the course of the war and by his loneliness. She discussed politics as well as life on the farm. Her letters, written as often as three times a day, kept him up-to-date on the military and political situations at home. She was a keen observer, who fully realized the historical importance of the times. She kept up his faith in the colonies; she told her husband to declare a complete break from Britain.

She did not let the hardships at home depress her. She sacrificed her energy in running the farm, caring for needy American soldiers, and ordering the household. She never faltered, despite outbreaks of smallpox in the area and her own poor health.

John Adams's house in Braintree (now Quincy), Massachusetts

She took great care in the rearing of her children. She prodded her talented son John Quincy to make the most of himself. In order to teach John Quincy Latin, Abigail learned the language herself. When he became gloomy later in life, she would remind him, "These are times in which a genius would wish to live. It is not in the still calms of life . . . that great characters are formed."

John returned home briefly in 1778, but he was soon sent to France as an ambassador. She did not try to stop him: "I found his honor and reputation dearer to me than my own pleasure and happiness." She let him take the ten-year-old John Quincy, believing the boy would profit from the experience. For six years, except a short leave in 1779, the couple was separated. Her many letters reveal much about her wide scope of interests. She scolded her husband when he failed to write or when his letters were too short. When she joined him in 1784, they had to send their son back home to Harvard. She kept in constant contact with John Quincy, showering him with motherly advice.

The next year, John took his wife with him to London as the first ambassador from the colonies. She rejoiced when he resigned in 1788 and they returned to Braintree: "I have learned to know the world and its value. I have seen high life. I have witnessed the luxury and pomp of state, the power of riches, and the influence of titles. Notwithstanding this, I feel that I can return to my little cottage and be happier . . . and if we have not wealth, we have what is greater—integrity." But in nine short months, national duty again called her husband away to New York to be vice president under Washington. He presided over the Senate and shared everything with her. When he was away, which was often, he said that her letters kept him going:

"There is more good thoughts, fine strokes, and mother wit in them than I hear in the whole week." She and her friend Martha Washington helped their husbands to work well together.

When Abigail became the First Lady following John's election in 1796, she was extremely well suited for her role. She had traveled around the world, had been active in politics from the beginning, and took her duties very seriously. Experienced with running a large estate, she knew how to spend money wisely. Her receptions were smaller than those that the Washingtons had been able to afford, but the atmosphere was more informal and pleasant. She dressed modestly but with the dignity befitting a president's wife. Her day started at 5:00 A.M. She kept the family budget, directed thirty servants, read, wrote, planned entertainments, received visitors, and made public appearances.

Four months before John was to leave office, he decided to move into the unfinished building called the Executive Mansion (later called the White House), even though the stay was temporary and only six rooms were completed. The stairs were unfinished, the plaster was not up, and she had to yell for her servants because the bells had not yet arrived. Every day thirteen fires were kept burning in a vain attempt to dry out the walls. She even had to use the audience chamber to wash and hang the family wash. Yet she was a perfect hostess. She prepared the drawing room for a New Year's reception, the first of its kind given in the White House.

The couple left Washington and politics to spend sixteen years together at their farm. It had become a great success due to Abigail's wise management. The year she died, her son John Quincy had been appointed secretary of state. The future president wrote of his mother, "She had been fifty-five years the delight of my father's heart, the sweetener of all his toils, the comforter of all his sorrows, the sharer and heightener of all his joys."

might have been more effective. However, he did have a strong sense that it was his God-given duty to serve others, regardless of the personal cost. This idea he passed on to his own children. His descendants have continued to serve their nation, state, and city for over two hundred years.

Although Adams's one term as president was not particularly impressive in some matters, it was very important in one respect. The new government, which was passed from the "Father of Our Country," George Washington, to Adams, was safely kept and passed on to be continued to our day.

SECTION REVIEW

1. When he left office, in what three areas did Washington advise that caution should be exercised?

2. Name the Federalist and the Democratic-Republican candidates for president in the election of 1796.

3. What was unusual about the outcome of the election of 1796?

 What things hindered the effectiveness of Adams's presidency?

Difficulties for President Adams

Even though George Washington had set a good example as first president and the country was growing stronger, Adams still had a difficult job ahead of him.

The XYZ Affair

Although the British were still seizing American ships when Adams took office, the greatest problem came from America's recent ally, France. A new French government, angered by the Jay Treaty with Britain, became hostile. The French ordered their navy to raid American shipping. They seized more than three hundred American sailors found on British ships and threatened to hang them. To add to the insult, they refused to receive Charles Cotesworth Pinckney, the American minister to France.

American Envoys Meet French Agents—Although some Federalists believed Adams should break relations with France and perhaps even declare war, he first chose to try negotiating. He sent John Marshall and Elbridge Gerry to assist Pinckney. The trio sought a hearing with Talleyrand, the French minister of foreign affairs, but after nine months they had yet to see the man. However, the Americans did meet his three agents. The agents implied that the Americans could have recognition if they would give a $250,000 bribe and insure a $10 million loan for France.

Adams, still a lawyer at heart, went to Congress to expose this insult to the United States. He laid out every piece of evidence before an open session of Congress. To protect the three American envoys, Adams substituted the letters *X, Y,* and *Z* for the names of the French agents. Soon the whole episode was dubbed **"the XYZ affair."**

A Call to Arms—Congress was angered by the evidence and took measures to arm the country for action against France. They voted, over Republican opposition, to make the navy a separate department and to build forty ships, a far cry from the three-vessel fleet of Washington. The most famous of the new frigates was the U.S.S. *Constitution.* The size of the army was tripled. Washington, still alive at that time but reluctant to lead an army again, was recalled as commander-in-chief. He asked for Alexander Hamilton, Thomas Pinckney, and Henry Knox—to be ranked in that order—as his commanders.

Although open war was never declared, by the fall of 1800, ninety French vessels had been captured while the Americans had lost but one ship. (Because there was some actual

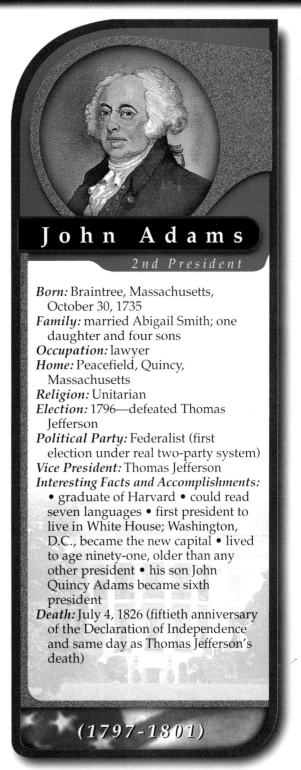

John Adams
2nd President

Born: Braintree, Massachusetts, October 30, 1735
Family: married Abigail Smith; one daughter and four sons
Occupation: lawyer
Home: Peacefield, Quincy, Massachusetts
Religion: Unitarian
Election: 1796—defeated Thomas Jefferson
Political Party: Federalist (first election under real two-party system)
Vice President: Thomas Jefferson
Interesting Facts and Accomplishments:
 • graduate of Harvard • could read seven languages • first president to live in White House; Washington, D.C., became the new capital • lived to age ninety-one, older than any other president • his son John Quincy Adams became sixth president
Death: July 4, 1826 (fiftieth anniversary of the Declaration of Independence and same day as Thomas Jefferson's death)

(1797-1801)

fighting, this conflict is sometimes called a "quasi-war.") The public cheered the victories and pressured for real war. But Adams was hesitant. He believed that a full-scale war was unwise and that the United States was unprepared to fight.

War Avoided—Meanwhile the French formed still another government; Napoleon Bonaparte took over in 1799. Napoleon, who could see that the United States might be a stronger enemy than was commonly thought, grew nervous. With France's defeat by Lord Nelson at the battle of the Nile and the entrapment of the French army in Egypt, Napoleon sent word he would move to a peace table. Although Adams wanted Napoleon to pay the damages, he settled for the signing of a new agreement called the **Convention of 1800.** Adams had avoided war. But few of his countrymen recognized the benefit. Dismayed Federalists now sided with the Republicans and denounced him. But Adams considered this his single most important contribution to America. He requested that his epitaph (the engraving on his tombstone) read: "Here lies John Adams who took upon himself the responsibility of peace with France in the year 1800."

Federalist Opposition to Adams

Adams, who responded to duty and was a statesman rather than a politician, had done little to win the favor of the Federalist Party leaders on domestic matters. Adams began to pay a high price for his restraint even before the conflict with France became an issue. In 1798 Adams angered the majority of his party when he disagreed with them on some of their legislation.

The Alien and Sedition Acts—In 1798, against Adams's wishes, the Federalists passed four laws called the **Alien and Sedition Acts.** Although the Federalists claimed that the laws would help the whole country, the acts were intended to harm the Democratic-Republican Party and to keep it from gaining power.

The first of the laws, the Naturalization Act, extended the time required to gain American citizenship from five to fourteen years. Since most immigrants joined the Democratic-Republican Party, the supposed party of the "common man," this act would keep them from voting. However, because states controlled their own elections, and the Republicans had control in many states, the law had little effect.

The Alien Enemies Act and the Alien Act allowed the president to imprison or expel any foreigners deemed "dangerous to the peace and safety of the United States." The first act gave this power during times of war or invasion, and the second allowed him to deport any aliens thought to be dangerous even if war had not been declared. The laws were purposely though dangerously vague. "Peace and safety" were not defined, nor was

The Capitol Building in 1800 looked quite different from today's version.

Although Napoleon had many military successes in Europe, he decided that the war with the United States would be dangerous.

"war." Adams, aware of the dangers of the acts, never enforced them.

The last act, the Sedition Act, however, was enforced. It said that any person found guilty of saying, writing, or publishing anything false or malicious against the government or its officials could be fined $2,000 and imprisoned for up to two years. The Republicans rightly saw this act as an attempt to stop both their mouths and pens. They protested that the law was a violation of their freedom of the press and speech. Although numbers of people were arrested under this law, only twenty-five were brought to trial, and scarcely a dozen were convicted.

Opposition to the Alien and Sedition Acts—The Republicans worked hard to overrule the Alien and Sedition Acts, and a few Federalists sympathized. Republicans James Madison and Thomas Jefferson wrote **Virginia and Kentucky Resolutions** for those two state legislatures. Each set of resolutions asserted the right of **nullification,** the ability of a state to nullify, or declare void, any federal law within its boundaries. Jefferson and Madison held that the union of states had come from an agreement in which the states freely gave up their independent rights to a central government. But the states were still sovereign, holding powers of their own. This fact should allow states to rule on whether actions of the federal government were constitutional in their opinion. Supporters of nullification based their thinking on Article VI of the Constitution. (See p. 153.) However, those who opposed nullification read the same article to mean supremacy of the national government over the states.

Although the Kentucky and Virginia Resolutions were never put into effect, the idea that they expressed, nullification, resurfaced several times over the next sixty years. Eventually it led to the temporary breakup of the federal union and a civil war. The immediate effect of the Resolutions, when coupled with the Alien and Sedition Acts, was a Republican victory at the polls in 1800.

The Disputed Election of 1800

Despite their dislike of Adams, the Federalists chose him to run for reelection in 1800, and they selected Charles Cotesworth Pinckney of South Carolina as his vice-presidential running mate. The Republicans chose Thomas Jefferson for president and **Aaron Burr** of New York to run with him.

However, the ballots for that election did not state which man was running for which office. This omission had caused a problem in 1796, and it did again in 1800. Each of the electoral college members was allowed to cast two votes. When the 1800 vote came in, Jefferson and Burr both received equal numbers of votes, more than Adams or Pinckney, but there was no designation that Jefferson was the one who was supposed to be president.

The Constitution stated (see p. 144) that in a tie the president would be selected by the House of Representatives. Each state was to have one vote, and the winner was to have a majority of votes cast (nine at that time).

Burr, ever a political opportunist, refused to defer to Jefferson and say he was really running for vice president. Many of the Federalists decided to vote for Burr. They believed that if they helped him win, he would later be more favorable to their party. Some also believed that if there was a deadlock, Adams or Pinckney might win as a compromise candidate.

The states voted: Jefferson took eight states, but he did not get the needed majority.

Monticello, home of Thomas Jefferson

The election dragged on for a week and through thirty-five ballots. Finally on the thirty-sixth ballot, James Baynard of Delaware shifted his vote to Jefferson.

SECTION REVIEW

1. How did the French react to Jay's treaty with England?

2. What incident led America to prepare for war against France? Name three steps Americans took to defend themselves.

3. What agreement averted war between America and France? What French leader sought this peace settlement?

4. What did the Sedition Act say? Why did the Democratic-Republicans feel this law unfair?

5. Under the nullification theory, what power would the states have?

 What weakness of the electoral college system was demonstrated by the election of 1800?

Strengthening the Courts

One of John Adams's accomplishments was the appointment of a new chief justice to the Supreme Court. His appointment had far-reaching effects on the power of the court.

The Appointment of John Marshall

During Adams's term the health of Oliver Ellsworth, chief justice of the Supreme Court, failed. Ellsworth resigned shortly before Adams left office, giving him the rare opportunity of appointing a new chief justice and extending the influence of his administration far beyond his term as president. On January 20, 1801, Adams nominated **John Marshall,** and the Senate confirmed Marshall a short time later.

John Marshall agreed with Alexander Hamilton, who had earlier called the judicial branch "the weakest of the three departments of power." Marshall believed the national gov-

Although political enemies, Thomas Jefferson and John Adams corresponded with each other until their deaths on July 4, 1826.

ernment's power could be made stronger through the courts. He believed the nation's future was closely tied to the Constitution's ability to adapt to changes in American life. The courts could be guardians of the past as well as guides of future change.

Marshall wasted no time in starting to strengthen the court system. First, he believed the Supreme Court looked weak in the eyes of the people. Every justice had been writing his own ideas on each case rather than issuing a group opinion for the majority. Marshall unified the court by having the justices hold private conferences and by having them issue one opinion to support their decision, usually called the majority opinion. If some justices disagreed, they could still write dissenting opinions telling why.

The Judiciary Bill and the Midnight Judges

Just six days before Adams left office, Congress passed the Judiciary Act of 1801. Until this time the Supreme Court justices had been serving as circuit court judges too. This required them to move from place to place, as the cases demanded. The new act created sixteen new circuit judgeships to aid in administration of the law. It also cut the number of court justices from six to five and allowed a number of justices of the peace to be appointed.

Since John Adams signed the commissions that appointed fifty-eight judges to full-time positions late the night before he left office, the judges have often been called **"the midnight judges."** Although the Republicans were highly critical and later repealed the act, Adams was within the law in naming his judges. Moreover, the Senate had to approve his choices, so he would have their backing for these appointments if they were accepted.

Marbury v. Madison

Federalist William Marbury had been appointed as one of Adams's midnight judges. The commission for his job was not delivered before Adams left office, however, and James Madison, the Republican secretary of state, refused to release it. Marbury sued for his job, believing that it was Madison's duty to deliver that commission.

Chief Justice Marshall decided the case of *Marbury v. Madison.* He realized that if he gave Madison the order to deliver the document, he would probably ignore it. This would weaken the image of the Supreme Court. Instead Marshall ruled that Madison did not have to deliver the commission because the section of the federal law that granted such power was unconstitutional. Although the Supreme Court had earlier declared state laws to be unconstitutional, this was the first time the court had declared a federal law unconstitutional. Thus the court took the power of **judicial review,** which the Constitution provided for state laws, and applied it to federal laws as well. This was an extension of the court's power.

Despite the favorable decision in *Marbury v. Madison,* Jefferson probably would have challenged Marshall's use of judicial review in later cases in an attempt to reduce Marshall's power. Marshall, however, outfoxed him. He never again used the power himself, and it would be 1857 before another chief justice would assert judicial review.

SECTION REVIEW

1. Whom did Adams nominate to be the chief justice of the Supreme Court?

2. Who were the "midnight judges"?

 What was the significance of the *Marbury v. Madison* case?

SUMMARY

As first president of the United States under the Constitution, George Washington helped to establish a sound government for the young nation. His administration overcame foreign and domestic threats to the country's stability and passed a functioning government on to the second president, John Adams. Although not a popular figure like Washington, Adams also provided needed leadership to steer the government through the problems of the era.

Chapter Review

People, Places, and Things to Remember

inauguration	Fallen Timbers	Alien and Sedition Acts
cabinet	Neutrality Proclamation	Virginia and Kentucky
excise tax	Edmond Charles Genêt	Resolutions
national bank	impressment	nullification
Federalist Party	Jay Treaty	Aaron Burr
Democratic-Republican	Pinckney Treaty	John Marshall
Party	John Adams	the midnight judges
Whiskey Rebellion	the XYZ affair	*Marbury v. Madison*
Anthony Wayne	Convention of 1800	judicial review

Review Questions

Identify each of the following people or terms.

1. This French citizen hoped to gain American support for France.

2. The president is "advised" by this group of presidential advisors.

3. Marbury tried to get his commission from this secretary of state.

4. This political party reflected Hamilton's views.

5. Adams appointed these judges at "the last minute."

6. The British forced American sailors to serve in their navy by this method.

7. This war hero stopped Indian attacks in the Northwest Territory.

8. Some claimed that states had this right to declare a federal law to be void.

9. Adams appointed this man to be chief justice of the Supreme Court.

10. This secretary of the treasury planned the nation's finances.

11. John Marshall used this type of review to declare a federal law unconstitutional.

12. This diplomat made a popular treaty with Spain.

13. This formal ceremony begins a president's term.

14. Indians of Ohio came to a peace conference following this defeat.

Questions for Discussion

15. Why do you think George Washington became such a distinguished and respected president in America's history?

16. Why was the Sedition Act dangerous?

UNIT

3

Spanning a Continent

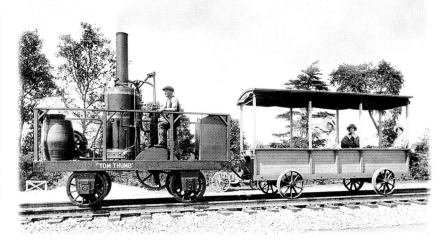

1830: Peter Cooper's steam engine, the Tom Thumb, proved that the train could pull its weight and more. By 1860 there were over 30,000 miles of track in the country.

1836: One hundred eighty-three men were killed as they defended a huge abandoned mission, the Alamo, at San Antonio, Texas. Their deaths rallied the Texans to fight for their independence from Mexico.

1844: On May 24 Samuel F. B. Morse tested his telegraph at the U.S. Capitol. The telegraph allowed immediate communication throughout the country.

1850: Daniel Webster and fellow compromisers Henry Clay and John C. Calhoun worked to preserve the Union. By 1852 all three had died, and the nation moved closer to conflict.

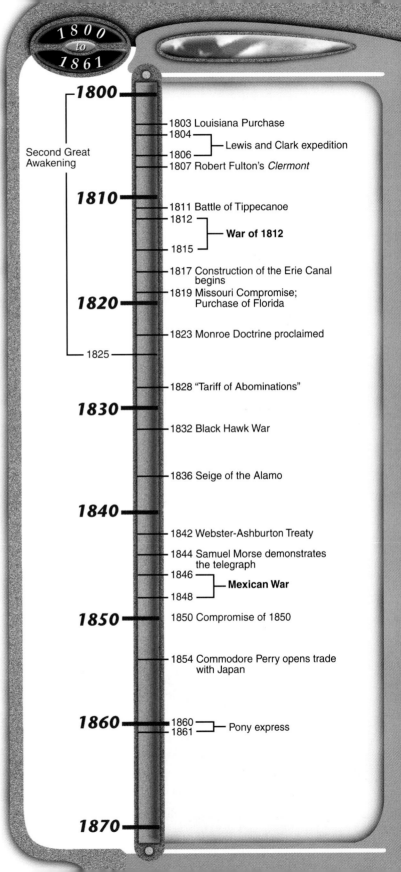

1800
to
1861

1800

1803 Louisiana Purchase
1804 —
— Lewis and Clark expedition
1806 —
1807 Robert Fulton's *Clermont*

1810

1811 Battle of Tippecanoe
1812 —
— **War of 1812**
1815 —

1817 Construction of the Erie Canal begins
1819 Missouri Compromise; Purchase of Florida

1820

1823 Monroe Doctrine proclaimed

1825 —

1828 "Tariff of Abominations"

1830

1832 Black Hawk War

1836 Seige of the Alamo

1840

1842 Webster-Ashburton Treaty

1844 Samuel Morse demonstrates the telegraph
1846 —
— **Mexican War**
1848 —

1850 1850 Compromise of 1850

1854 Commodore Perry opens trade with Japan

1860 1860 —
1861 — — Pony express

1870

Second Great Awakening

Unit III: Spanning a Continent

The Journals of Lewis and Clark

The journals of Lewis and Clark are filled with exciting stories. Along with their adventures and discoveries, we can see their endurance through many hardships. Read these excerpts, and answer the questions at the end.

[May 14, 1804] Rained the fore part of the day. I set out at 4 o'clock, P.M., in the presence of many of the neighboring inhabitants and proceeded under a gentle breeze up the Missouri to the upper point of the first island, 4 miles, and camped on the island.

[November 4] A fine morning. We continued to cut down trees and raise our houses [at Fort Mandan]. A Mr. Charbonneau, interpreter for the Gros Ventre nation, came to see us. This man wished to hire as an interpreter. Great numbers of Indians pass, hunting.

[February 11, 1805] The weather was fair and cold. Wind N.W. About five o'clock this evening, one of the wives of Charbonneau was delivered of a fine boy. It is worthy of remark that this was the first child which this woman had born, and as is common in such cases her labor was tedious and the pain violent.

[April 13] We saw many tracks of the white bear of enormous size, along the river shore. We have not as yet seen one of these animals, though their tracks are so abundant and recent. The men, as well as ourselves, are anxious to meet with some of these bear. The Indians give a very formidable account of the strength and ferocity of this animal, which they never dare to attack but in parties of six, eight, or ten persons; and are even then frequently defeated with the loss of one or more of their party.

[June 28] The white bear have become so troublesome to us that I do not think it prudent to send one man alone on an errand of any kind, particularly where he has to pass through the brush. They come close around our camp every night but have never yet ventured to attack us, and our dog gives us timely notice of their visits. I have made the men sleep with their arms by them as usual, for fear of accidents.

[June 29] A torrent of rain and hail fell, more violent than ever I saw before. The rain fell like one volley of water from the heavens and gave us time only to get out of the way of a torrent of water which was pouring down the hill into the river with immense force, tearing everything before it, taking with it large rocks and mud.

[August 17] Captain Clark arrived [at the camp where Sacajawea said her people stayed in the summers] with the interpreter, Charbonneau, and the Indian woman, who proved to be a sister of the chief Cameâhwait. The meeting of these people was really affecting, particularly between Sacajawea and an Indian woman who had been taken prisoner with her, and who had afterwards escaped and rejoined her nation.

[November 7] Great joy in camp. We are in view of the ocean, this great Pacific Ocean which we have been so long anxious to see, and the roaring or noise made by the waves breaking on the rocky shores (as I suppose) may be heard distinctly.

[March 23, 1806] At 1:00 P.M. left Fort Clatsop on our homeward-bound journey. At this place we had wintered and remained from the 7th of December, 1805, to this day, and have lived as well as we had any right to expect, and we can say that we were never one day without three meals of some kind a day, either poor elk meat or roots, notwithstanding the repeated fall of rain which has fallen almost constantly.

1. When did Sacajawea give birth to her baby?
2. List three hardships that the expedition faced.
3. Lewis and Clark were the first white men to see a grizzly bear. What did they call it?
4. When did the expedition come in view of the Pacific?

10

Growth of a Nation

aptain William Clark wrote in his notes on November 7, 1805, "Ocian in view! O! the joy." After nearly fourteen months of hardship, toil, and peril, William Clark, Meriwether Lewis, and their band of rugged adventurers had crossed through America's western wilderness to the Pacific. The Lewis and Clark expedition was only one of the challenging experiences that the early years of the nineteenth century held in store for the United States.

Triumphs of a Growing Nation

The election of 1800 had brought the Democratic-Republican Party into power. Many Americans believed that the Federalists had used the government for the greater benefit of the Northeast's wealthy merchants and industrialists. Thomas Jefferson's presidency was thought to be a victory for the common people.

Jefferson took his oath of office on March 4, 1801. He was the first president to be inaugurated in Washington, D.C., the nation's new but still unfinished capital. New York and

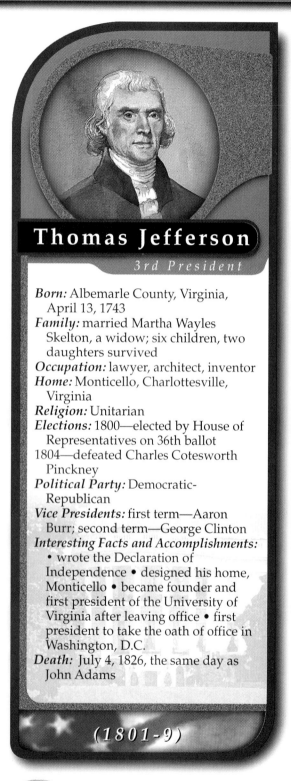

Thomas Jefferson
3rd President

Born: Albemarle County, Virginia, April 13, 1743

Family: married Martha Wayles Skelton, a widow; six children, two daughters survived

Occupation: lawyer, architect, inventor

Home: Monticello, Charlottesville, Virginia

Religion: Unitarian

Elections: 1800—elected by House of Representatives on 36th ballot
1804—defeated Charles Cotesworth Pinckney

Political Party: Democratic-Republican

Vice Presidents: first term—Aaron Burr; second term—George Clinton

Interesting Facts and Accomplishments:
• wrote the Declaration of Independence • designed his home, Monticello • became founder and first president of the University of Virginia after leaving office • first president to take the oath of office in Washington, D.C.

Death: July 4, 1826, the same day as John Adams

(1801-9)

Philadelphia, the two previous capitals, were older, more elegant cities. Washington, D.C., in 1801, however, did not look like the beautiful city we know today. For example, the land around the partly finished Capitol was a forest. Members of Congress reached the White House by using a muddy track though the trees. There were no paved streets labeled with street signs. The new city was almost wilderness.

Although some historians have suggested Jefferson's presidency meant great change—a Jefferson Revolution—for the common man, such suggestions are overblown. The new president stressed simplicity and informality, but this may have resulted from necessity rather than design. In his inaugural address, President Jefferson seemed eager to bind the nation's factions together. "Let us then fellow-citizens unite with one heart and one mind. . . . We have called by different names brethren of the same principle. We are all [Democratic-] Republicans; we are all Federalists."

Reversing Federalist Policies

During his first term Jefferson increased his popularity in a variety of ways. He began by ousting only those Federalists who had abused their powers, especially those who had enforced the Sedition Act.

Rather than having the Alien and Sedition Acts repealed, Jefferson let them expire in 1801. He pardoned those jailed under the Sedition Act and wrote personal letters of apology to the victims. The five-year residence requirement for citizens was restored, thus repealing the Naturalization Act, which had required a residence of fourteen years.

Gallatin, Jefferson's secretary of the treasury, was a frugal financier. He and Jefferson wanted to rid themselves of the debt incurred when the nation's defenses were increased during the XYZ affair. Jefferson opposed a strong standing army and navy, fearing they could be sources of too much federal power. Instead he chose to rely on state militias, which were cheaper to maintain because they were part-time and because they were not federally funded. By doing this, he decreased the national debt by one-half, which in turn allowed him to abolish the whiskey tax.

At Jefferson's request Congress reversed itself and repealed the Judiciary Act of 1801. Consequently, many of the midnight judges never served. Jefferson then attacked the Federalist courts from another angle. According to the Constitution, judges were to be appointed to office for life. But the Constitution also said that judges could be impeached for "treason, bribery, or other high crimes and misdemeanors." Before taking power the Jeffersonians had claimed to take the Constitution literally; now they wished to use the language loosely.

First, the Jeffersonians impeached John Pickering, a district court judge from New Hampshire. Because Pickering was both an alcoholic and insane, they were able to get the House to file the charges and two-thirds of the Senate to vote to remove him.

But the next target, Federalist Supreme Court justice Samuel Chase, was another story. Although Chase was not a great jurist, his attacks on Republicans were hardly a crime. The Senate, sensing that Jefferson was threatening to destroy the Supreme Court's power and independence, refused to remove Chase. Jefferson's attacks on the judiciary probably made some judges more responsive to public opinion, but after this defeat Jefferson never again attacked the courts.

Retaining Federalist Benefits

Jefferson was wise enough to leave some Federalist policies alone. Although he had opposed the founding of a national bank, he now left it intact because it was working well. He also retained the Federalist plan for repaying war debts. Jefferson, who had charged others with hypocrisy in earlier years, now began to see how difficult it was to be a truly consistent politician. Although he had often denounced the growth of the government's power when Washington and Adams were president, he came to realize that power was not necessarily bad, if used for good ends. Since he believed his ends were good, he became skillful in his use of presidential powers. He soon extended presidential powers further than his predecessors had.

The Barbary Pirates and the Tripolitan Wars

A foreign challenge came to America from the small Muslim countries in North Africa, known as the Barbary States. These countries gained money by charging tribute to ships that sailed on the Mediterranean. This piracy hampered trade in the Mediterranean Sea. While he had been secretary of state, Jefferson had suggested that the United States organize an international blockade to shatter the system. But the two-million-dollar annual tribute seemed small compared with the cost of a possible war.

Now, however, the Barbary States increased their tribute fees, and Jefferson refused to pay them. The pasha (ruler) of Tripoli then declared war. Jefferson sent Commodore Richard Dale and later Stephen Decatur to the region to protect American interests and to deal with the terrorists. Dale tried a local blockade. On February 16, 1804, Decatur boldly sailed into Tripoli's harbor and seized the American frigate *Philadelphia,* which had been run aground and captured. Rather than let Tripoli have the ship, he burned it. Over the next decade Decatur led other expeditions in the area. The tribute dispute was settled in 1815 when a combined British-American force moved in on the pirates.

The **Tripolitan War** increased the respect of foreign countries for the United States. It also allowed American naval commanders to stay in practice and to be prepared for the much larger conflict with England that was soon to come.

The Louisiana Purchase

The port of New Orleans was of great importance to American settlements west of the Appalachians. Three-eighths of American trade in 1800 passed through this port in Spanish-owned Louisiana Territory. In 1800 Spain ceded Louisiana back to France, its original owner. France, however, was no longer the ally who had helped win American independence. In the years since the French Revolution, she had given up republican ideals and was under the rule of Napoleon. Jefferson accurately suspected that Napoleon, who had been forced into a temporary truce with Britain, was planning a New World empire. Napoleon's brother-in-law, Charles LeClerc, and large numbers of troops had arrived in Haiti, an easy launching point for an invasion of North America. At the same time another French force moved to a Dutch port to await the signal to embark across the Atlantic.

Jefferson told Robert Livingston, the American ambassador to France, to try to buy New Orleans and East and West Florida. Jefferson then put the nation on war footing. Secretary of War Henry Dearborn set up recruiting centers for soldiers, rushed troops to Fort Adams near Natchez, Mississippi, and sent more guns and ammunition to battle LeClerc's forces.

A series of events forced Napoleon to reconsider. First, a yellow fever epidemic in Haiti doubled his heavy war losses. Second, winter ice stranded his other army in Holland. At the same time he was told that Jefferson did not want the Louisiana Territory because it would divide the American nation into eastern and western factions. (This was an idea that Jefferson had purposely planted.) Napoleon reasoned that he should defeat Britain first. If England were soundly defeated, he could control the seas and then handle a divided America. Besides, the money he needed to fight Britain could come from the sale of Louisiana.

Initially, Napoleon's foreign minister, Talleyrand, had rejected Livingston's offer for New Orleans. Then, nine months later, in May 1803, Talleyrand suddenly asked the American if he wanted to buy the entire Louisiana Territory. After several bargaining sessions, Livingston settled on $15 million for what was later discovered to be 529,911,680 acres—making the cost only 2.8 cents per acre. Livingston and the other envoys working on the negotiations nervously wrote Jefferson to inform him of "a truly noble acquisition." They hoped Jefferson would not be angry because they had exceeded their original instructions.

Jefferson's feelings about the **Louisiana Purchase** were mixed. There were over fifty thousand French and Spanish Creoles in Louisiana. Would his action make them citizens? Did he have the right to make them citizens without their consent? Did he have the right to buy land for the nation when the Constitution did not give him the power?

Jefferson hesitated, but only briefly. His first thought was to ask Congress to pass an amendment making such a land purchase legal. This would insure the bargain and preserve his principles. But he feared that the restless Napoleon might change his mind before three-quarters of the states approved the amendment. Jefferson decided to call Congress into special session, ask for the purchase, and not bring up any of the constitutional questions concerning the bargain. In doing so, Jefferson again extended governmental powers beyond those that the Constitution specifically gave. The Senate approved the purchase and rushed the money to France on the fastest ship available. On December 20, 1803, the Stars and Stripes was raised over Louisiana.

The Western Expeditions

The Lewis and Clark Expedition—Even before the Louisiana Purchase was made, Jefferson was interested in learning more about the West. He recruited his private secretary, **Meriwether Lewis,** to lead the first of two expeditions to explore the West. Lewis chose **William Clark,** under whom he had fought in the Indian wars in the Northwest Territory, to go with him. Although Clark lacked the classical education of Lewis, Clark's wilderness experience and interests made him a good surveyor, mapmaker, and naturalist. Lewis and Clark went west to seek the source of the Missouri River and to explore lands of what became ten western states.

Jefferson sent Lewis a detailed letter of instructions and advice. Lewis and Clark were to make careful studies on the geology, botany, and zoology of the region and to gather detailed information on any natives they met. They were to search for the source of the Missouri River, report on any commercial possibilities, and seek for evidence of British soldiers or forts in the vast area.

Lewis hurried to Philadelphia where he took crash courses under five leading scientists. He learned celestial navigation, geology, and medicine. He even learned to perform emergency surgery.

Congress approved an expense of $2,500 for the expedition to buy the needed supplies and to pay men who were to be out twenty-eight months, covering more than nine thousand miles. The trip actually cost $39,000. For repeatedly risking their lives during more than three years of work, Lewis and Clark each received sixteen hundred acres of public land.

Lewis and Clark led the expedition to seek the source of the Missouri River.

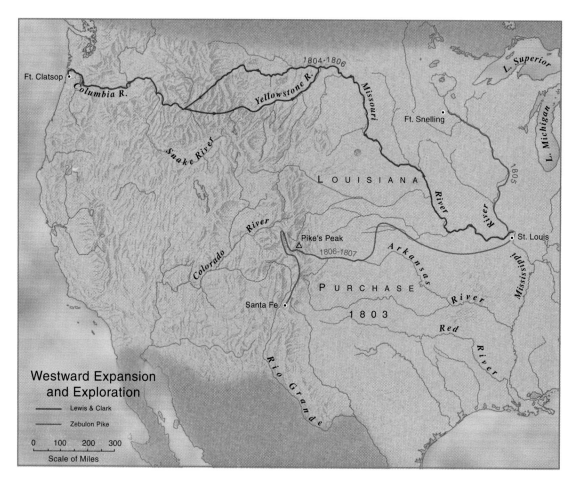

Westward Expansion
and Exploration

——— Lewis & Clark

——— Zebulon Pike

0   100   200   300
Scale of Miles

The party left St. Louis on May 14, 1804 (five months after the Louisiana Purchase had been made), using a fifty-five-foot keelboat and two flat-bottomed dugouts. The keelboat had a cannon mounted at the bow and lockers, whose heavy lids could be raised to protect the men. But when the Missouri River became shallow farther upstream, all the boats were abandoned.

There were twenty-nine men in the official party, along with seven soldiers and nine river men who acted as guards. York, Captain Clark's personal slave, came with his master. Among the Indians he was an object of curiosity. Some of them had seen white trappers and

fur traders before, but none had ever seen a black man. They wanted not only to look at him but also to feel him. The Indians thought York was painted and tried to scrub his skin.

The trip west took the group from St. Louis on the Mississippi River to the site of Astoria, Oregon, on the Pacific coast. The men followed the Missouri, Snake, and Columbia Rivers most of the way. At Fort Mandan, in what is now North Dakota, a French fur trapper named Charbonneau (shahr bohn NOH) joined the expedition. His wife, Sacajawea (sak uh juh WEE uh), also came along. She was a Shoshone Indian who had been stolen from her tribe as a child. When the explorers had no means of transportation and desperately needed horses, they met a group of Shoshones, including Sacajawea's brother, now a chief. They received thirty horses from the Shoshones. Eventually they had to kill some of the horses for food. Sacajawea helped the expedition through the Bitterroot Mountains with her guiding abilities and her skills as an interpreter.

The expedition usually moved ten miles a day, sometimes less. The scenery was breathtaking. The trip to discover the falls of the Missouri River was worth the view, but it meant carrying their boats and everything else for sixteen miles. Clark nearly lost his life when he encountered a bear that was more than seven feet tall. Ten shots were needed to bring it down. He named it the "grizzly" bear. Later Lewis was mistaken for an elk and was shot in the leg. He had difficulty continuing the journey. The party split up to explore the two branches of the Missouri on their return trip. Lewis navigated the upper Missouri while Clark's group followed the Yellowstone. The group met on the Missouri above Fort Mandan, and the trip back to St. Louis was completed uneventfully on September 23, 1806.

Lewis and Clark were celebrities of their day. They were acclaimed just as early aviators and astronauts were in the twentieth century. In their explorations, the team had discovered twenty-five varieties of fish (including the anchovy), six kinds of birds, five reptiles, and four amphibians. Clark used his artistic talent to illustrate the flowers, plants, animals, and Indians he had seen on the trip. Their journals did much to stir interest in western settlement. Lewis and Clark were also among the last white men to contact western Indians who were mostly unaffected by the white man's way of life. They found the Indians to be

This statue honors Sacajawea, the Shoshone woman who accompanied Lewis and Clark on their expedition.

friendly and curious. In a few years the western Indians would have reason to become suspicious of, if not openly hostile to, whites.

The Pike Expedition—The second expedition, under **Zebulon Pike,** was accomplished in two different trips. On the first, in 1805, Pike followed the Mississippi in search of its source. He also let the British know that the American flag would fly over the Louisiana Territory, although he did not have enough military force to oust the British from their forts.

Pike's second trip, in 1806-7, went up the Arkansas River into Spanish-held territories. He explored the Rockies of Colorado and sighted the peak that today bears his name. He used the Rio Grande for his return trip but was captured by the Spanish. They imprisoned him and took his diaries, but he was later released. Other explorers followed him into the region in preparation for the later settlement of these mountainous lands.

SECTION REVIEW

1. What was unique about Jefferson's inauguration? What did he stress in his inauguration speech?

2. Why did the United States pay tribute fees to the Barbary States?

3. Why was the city of New Orleans vital to the settlers west of the Appalachian Mountains? Who regained control of the city in 1800?

4. What territory did Jefferson want Robert Livingston to buy? What did America actually purchase?

5. Who led an expedition to the Pacific coast and back? What mountain range did Zebulon Pike explore?

 What were some of the benefits and dangers of the Louisiana Purchase?

Troubles of the Growing Nation

In his reelection in 1804, Jefferson and his new running mate, New Yorker George Clinton, carried every state but Connecticut and Delaware. Burr, who had alienated Jefferson in the election of 1800, had been ignored most of the first term and was dropped as his running mate.

Neutral Rights at Sea

During Jefferson's second term as president, the defense of neutral rights at sea again troubled America. The years to come held many of the same frustrations faced earlier by Washington and Adams. France and Britain were again at war. Americans, determined to make money from the war, traded with both war powers. Huge stocks of goods from French colonies in the West Indies found their way to American ports. The British also found a ready market in growing America. While the warring countries were busy fighting each other, they did not bother American shipping.

With Lord Nelson's victory over the French fleet at Trafalgar on October 21, 1805, Britain kept her supremacy at sea. Napoleon's armies, however, controlled much of Europe, having defeated Austria, Prussia, and Russia. By 1807 the war was a stalemate. Both countries now planned to win by destroying the economy of the other. The United States was soon caught in the middle of this strategy.

British and French Actions—The British blockaded all French-controlled European ports, and they proclaimed their **Orders in Council** in 1807 to make it illegal for neutral nations to trade in European ports unless they first stopped at a British port for inspection. Britain hoped that limiting European trade with America would cause so much dissatisfaction that the conquered nations would revolt against Napoleon.

Whatever Happened to Aaron Burr?

Aaron Burr, a grandson of Jonathan Edwards, had risen to fame through his heroism and service under Washington during the War for Independence. Some predicted a promising career for the man, and he did achieve the vice-presidency in 1800. It would not have been surprising for him to have become president. But further glory never came for Burr.

Because Burr had tried to usurp the presidency in the election of 1800, Jefferson ignored Burr while he was vice president. Burr resented his exclusion and believed that his talents were not being recognized.

In 1804, while still vice president, Burr decided to run for governor of New York. Alexander Hamilton campaigned for Burr's rival, and the two men became bitter enemies. Biting words from both appeared in the press. Burr demanded Hamilton take back his statements. When Hamilton refused, Burr challenged him to a duel. Burr killed Hamilton in the duel, and many considered it murder because Hamilton had fired into the air.

Scorned in the East, Burr fled west while he was still vice president. He became involved in a scheme to set up an empire in Louisiana. Some think that he planned to conquer Mexico and become its emperor. Jefferson had him charged with treason. Burr was brought east to face trial, but he was acquitted (cleared of charges) because there was only one witness who would attest to his treason in open court.

After the trial Burr became an outcast, suffering personal loss and rejection. Burr could not win respect in America, and he also failed in England. Burr could have served his country with distinction; instead he died disgraced. His life was ruined by his inability to deal with his pride. He was not willing to wait until people recognized his genuine talents but pushed himself into positions and used people. He had not learned the truth of I Peter 5:6-7: "Humble yourselves therefore under the mighty hand of God, that he may exalt you in due time: casting all your care upon him; for he careth for you."

France meanwhile hoped to keep Britain from getting necessary supplies, forcing her to surrender. To stop the flow, the French ordered a blockade of British ports. In 1807 Napoleon issued the **Berlin and Milan Decrees,** which stated that neutral ships trading with Britain or obeying the Orders in Council could be seized. The potential profits were so high, however, that Americans risked defying both powers. If only one of three trade vessels got through, the ship owner still made a profit.

The *Chesapeake* and the *Leopard*—Both Britain and France seized ships and cargoes. The British also seized American sailors, as they had in the 1790s. More than ten thousand Americans were impressed by the British. (See p. 178.) Although forty percent were released once they arrived in England, the practice was greatly resented.

Things worsened because the British believed American officials were encouraging His Majesty's sailors to desert. Many of the desertions took place around Chesapeake Bay,

The Jefferson Bible

He saith unto them, But whom say ye that I am? And Simon Peter answered and said, Thou art the Christ, the Son of the living God. (Matt. 16:15-16)

In 1804 Thomas Jefferson began work on the first of two of his own editions of the Bible. Among many other things, Jefferson had studied religions and religious figures of the past. He wrote, "Of all the systems of morality, ancient or modern, which have come under my observation, none appear to me so pure as that of Jesus." Although he was impressed by the precepts of Jesus, he did not believe Jesus to be the Son of God.

It was this erroneous view of Jesus that led Jefferson to put together his own editions of the Bible. His first work was a forty-six-page extract called *The Philosophy of Jesus of Nazareth*. It contained the moral teachings of Jesus in nugget form, organized by topic. Believing it suffered from being "too hastily done," he then started on a fifteen-year project to distill the gospel of where the many inlets gave the deserters refuge. A few even enlisted in the United States Navy. One deserter, Jenkin Ratford, served on the U.S.S. *Chesapeake,* based at the Norfolk navy yard. The British found out where he was when he insulted his old officers, who were on shore leave in Norfolk.

Jesus—what he thought Jesus actually did and said, rather than what others in Scripture said about Him. He sent to Ireland for two English New Testaments, and he also used Greek, Latin, and French translations. He then assembled them in columns, each language side by side.

Jefferson did not believe the miracle stories, nor could his reason grasp supernatural events. Thus in Jefferson's Bible there are no verses telling of Jesus' walking on the water, healing the sick, or being raised from the dead. Thomas Jefferson's gospel ends with Jesus in the tomb. Jefferson also omitted references to the Holy Spirit. His rendition of the Christmas story deletes the shepherds, angels, and references to the glory of God, and it does not make Jesus the Savior who is Christ the Lord. Although his scissors-and-paste Bible denies by omission the hope of life after death that God's Word assures us of, Jefferson did believe in a vague personal immortality. Perhaps that was because his wife and child had preceded him in death; at least he talked of being reunited with them.

Jefferson cut everything out of the Bible that he did not believe and pasted the rest together. We know, however, that "all scripture is given by inspiration of God" (II Tim. 3:16). Jefferson's shortened gospels show us that we cannot expect the natural man—then or now—to receive the things of the Spirit of Christ, "for they are foolishness unto him" (I Cor. 2:14). In all Jefferson's dealings with Scripture he ignored Revelation 22:19—"If any man shall take away from the words of the book of this prophecy, God shall take away his part out of the book of life."

When the *Chesapeake* left harbor on June 1, 1807, the British were on the lookout for her. The British ship H.M.S. *Leopard* ordered the frigate to stop to be searched. The captain refused. The *Leopard* then fired three broadsides (all the guns on one side of the ship firing together) at the *Chesapeake,* leaving three dead, eighteen wounded, and a nation incensed. Ratford and three other deserters were forcibly removed.

The ***Chesapeake* affair** stirred a desire for war, but Jefferson, like Adams, took a more moderate course. Since Jefferson had just disarmed the navy and the army to reduce his budget, he really had few options. He chose an economic option, believing that if the United States withheld goods and closed her ports to trade, Britain and France would soon be begging for American goods.

The Embargo Act of 1807—Jefferson asked Congress to place an **embargo,** a stop on all exports from the United States, and to forbid imports from Europe to be carried on American ships. Since foreign ships could not carry any exports, there was little reason for them to come. Domestic coastal trade was still allowed. Clever shippers found loopholes and turned to smuggling, but when the Giles Enforcement Act of 1809 closed some of the loopholes, American trade ceased.

Although the people had complained about impressment and ship seizures, the lack of any trade at all angered them more. Farmers who sold foodstuffs and raw materials to Europe saw prices plunge because there were no buyers for their goods. Merchants and those dependent on them were hurt too. Sympathy toward Britain grew, especially in Federalist New England, the area most affected. The Embargo Act did little to hurt Britain but its effect on America was great.

The law came under attack from both parties, and just before leaving office in March 1809, Jefferson signed a new act. The Non-

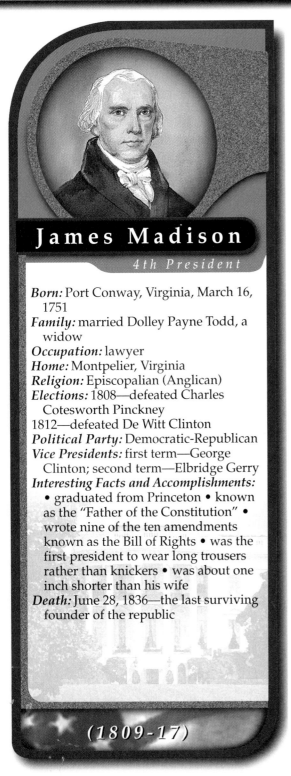

James Madison

4th President

Born: Port Conway, Virginia, March 16, 1751

Family: married Dolley Payne Todd, a widow

Occupation: lawyer

Home: Montpelier, Virginia

Religion: Episcopalian (Anglican)

Elections: 1808—defeated Charles Cotesworth Pinckney
1812—defeated De Witt Clinton

Political Party: Democratic-Republican

Vice Presidents: first term—George Clinton; second term—Elbridge Gerry

Interesting Facts and Accomplishments:
• graduated from Princeton • known as the "Father of the Constitution" • wrote nine of the ten amendments known as the Bill of Rights • was the first president to wear long trousers rather than knickers • was about one inch shorter than his wife

Death: June 28, 1836—the last surviving founder of the republic

(1809-17)

Intercourse Act lifted the embargo somewhat and permitted trade with foreign nations except France and Britain.

James Madison Meets More Difficulties

Thomas Jefferson declined a third term. His secretary of state, James Madison, ran for the Republicans in 1808 and defeated Federalist C. C. Pinckney. Madison had secured his place in history before becoming president. He brought a wealth of experience to his office and was one of America's most intelligent presidents. His two terms in office, however, proved both difficult and frustrating. He was indecisive in both peace and war, and when he finally did act, he always seemed to do the wrong thing.

Since the Non-Intercourse Act put too much strain on trade, Congress replaced it with Macon's Bill Number 2. This act offered to open trade with Britain and France if those countries ceased to attack American ships.

Napoleon's foreign minister responded by saying that the Berlin and Milan Decrees had been lifted. But the same day that he "repealed" the decrees, he signed a new order confiscating American ships in French ports. Nevertheless, America began trading again with the French. Naturally, England was upset.

Indian Stirrings

By the spring of 1810, there were sporadic Indian attacks on settlements in the western Indiana Territory. Settlers blamed the English or the Canadians for inciting the Indian raids. But the truth was that America was now reaping the consequences of unfair treaties that had robbed the Indians of millions of acres of choice land.

The Indians were now unwilling to give up any more land and united their forces in an Indian confederation under a Shawnee chief, **Tecumseh** (tih KUM suh). In late 1811 General **William Henry Harrison** marched on Prophetstown, Tecumseh's Indian capital beside the Tippecanoe River. Although he failed to capture Tecumseh, who was elsewhere, Harrison burned the village and became "the hero of Tippecanoe." Tecumseh joined the British cause in Canada and died in 1812 in the battle of the Thames (TEMZ) River.

Montpelier in Orange County, Virginia, the home of President Madison.

SECTION REVIEW

1. When the war between England and France reached a stalemate, how did each country plan to defeat the other?

2. What did Britain and France do to prevent each other from receiving goods? Why did American ships continue to sail under these conditions?

3. Why did the British fire on the U.S.S. *Chesapeake?*

4. Who was the leader of the Indian Confederation in the West? Why did the Indians unite their forces?

 Explain the Embargo Act of 1807. What effect did it have on Americans?

The War of 1812

Work of the War Hawks

Although the battle of Tippecanoe had somewhat lessened their fears, westerners did not believe they could be really safe until the British were out of Canada. Besides, they blamed the British for the surplus of grain that Americans in the West could not sell. In Congress a group of forty western and southern representatives, united by their strong

An artist's romantic view of the battle between Chief Tecumseh and William Henry Harrison

nationalism and desire to be free of English influence, formed a **coalition** (a temporary alliance of groups) under the leadership of Kentucky's **Henry Clay.** Called the **War Hawks,** these men successfully elected Clay as Speaker of the House and placed their supporters on important congressional committees. From such positions they denounced Britain and pushed for a stronger defense.

War Is Declared

Relations with Great Britain worsened throughout 1811 and early 1812. The British, angered by the embargo, now blockaded the American coast more than ever, and they continued to stop American ships to remove suspected British deserters. Madison asked the British to suspend their Orders in Council in April of 1812. When they refused, Congress gave the president the power to activate state militias for six months.

Weakened by the loss of trade, Britain was soon ready to suspend the Orders in Council and did so on June 16, 1812. But since there were no quick means of communicating across the Atlantic, word did not reach the United States until after the United States had declared war on June 18. The resulting war with Britain lasted two and a half years, and it is known as the **War of 1812.**

American Handicaps

The United States was unprepared for the war it faced. The army had only 6,700 men, most of whom were in western forts. Although Congress allowed an increase in the size of the army and allowed for calling out a militia of 100,000, some states, especially those in New England, had not wanted war and refused to commit their troops. In addition, the navy was small—it had only sixteen vessels. But Britain had two hundred frigates, and most had twice the number of mounted guns as the seven seaworthy American ships.

Financing was a problem too. In 1811 Congress had voted against rechartering the National Bank. Now there was no bank to borrow from or to transfer funds to pay for war supplies. In addition, reduced trade had cut tariff income, curtailing funds even more. The public, divided over the war, refused to buy war bonds to support it.

Poor communications and transportation systems also troubled the American cause. Few roads had been built to the West. With the coast blockaded and the West isolated, it was hard to move men and supplies to the places where they were needed. Sometimes the president had little idea where his armies really were.

America's generals also handicapped the war effort. Most of the generals Madison chose were older men who had not fought actively since the War for Independence. The first year of fighting was a disaster.

Fighting the War in the North: The War in 1812

The war plan was to attack Canada since it was nearby and sparsely populated. Also, since some Canadians were French and therefore were lukewarm to British rule, Americans believed that they might have some support there.

In August of 1812, Major General William Hull, on his way to attack the British at Ontario, surrendered in disgrace to General Isaac Brock at Detroit. William Henry Harrison's attempt to regain Detroit failed, resulting in the loss of much of the Northwest. Fort Dearborn (modern Chicago) also fell to the British.

In October an American force moved to take the Niagara peninsula. But the Americans attacking Queenstown, New York, were thrown back, as was an attack on Fort Niagara. A second attack on Fort Niagara met defeat because the New York militia refused to co-

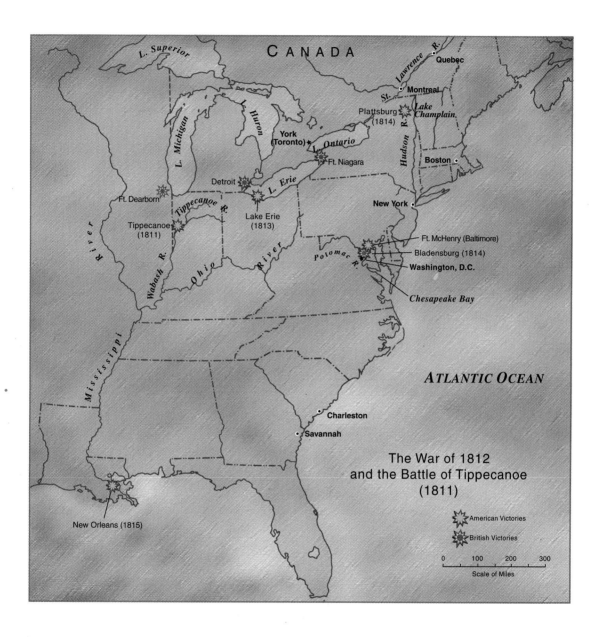

The War of 1812
and the Battle of Tippecanoe
(1811)

★ American Victories

★ British Victories

| 0 | 100 | 200 | 300 |
Scale of Miles

operate and move across the border. Instead they stood by and watched the British defeat the American regulars. In the first year of the war, the only American successes were at sea. The American frigate *Constitution* defeated the *Guerrière* (GEHR ih EHR), and the *United States* victoriously battled the *Macedonian* (MAS ih DOH nee un).

In November 1812 Madison won reelection. Despite the war disasters, most electors stuck with Madison rather than change leaders in the middle of a crisis.

Fighting for the Great Lakes: The War in 1813

The second year of the war did not go much better. Harrison and his lesser commanders lost land battles around the Great Lakes. Finally the Americans realized that the British were probably winning because they controlled the Great Lakes. **Oliver Hazard Perry,** a twenty-seven-year-old dynamo, spent almost a year preparing to win control of Lake Erie. This was no easy task. Perry built a naval base on Erie's south shore by bringing artillery

The U.S.S. Constitution earned the name "Old Ironsides" by surviving the War of 1812 and winning more battles than any other early American warship. Today it is moored in Boston, manned by sailors dressed in the style of 1812.

and ammunition hundreds of miles over rough roads and unbridged streams. He instilled pride into local militias, entrusting them with the job of keeping local outposts and shipyards from falling into British hands. He built two new frigates, the *Lawrence* and the *Niagara,* especially for use on the Great Lakes. In September of 1813, Perry's new ships were ready to meet the British. The *Lawrence,* Perry's flagship, was heavily damaged early in the attack. Perry, in a small boat, crossed to the *Niagara* and refused to surrender. An hour later the tables turned. Perry wrote General Harrison: "We have met the enemy and they are ours!" The British abandoned Fort Detroit and their interest in the Northwest. They then decided to launch a three-pronged attack on the Northeast, the Chesapeake Bay, and the Mississippi Valley.

Invasions in the East: The War in 1814

The defeat of the French in Europe freed the British to fight much harder against America. They massed troops at Montreal and then moved southward using Lake Champlain as a gateway. Their goal was to take New York City and to cut off New England, but they were defeated on September 11 at Plattsburg, New York.

A second British prong shoved into Chesapeake Bay, a hideaway of American privateers. They easily routed an inexperienced American militia at Bladensburg, Maryland, on August 23. This left the capital open to attack the next day. Congress fled across the Potomac to Virginia, as did the president, whom the British were hoping to make their prisoner.

The president told his wife, Dolley, to leave too. She had crammed two trunks full of papers belonging to her husband and cabinet members and had packed much of the silver. These things were sent to Virginia in the only wagon she could commandeer at the time. The last thing Dolley paused to take was a full-length portrait of George Washington done by Gilbert Stuart. It was screwed to the wall, and her servant French John could not get it down. Dolley then told him to cut out the canvas and roll up the portrait. The portrait she saved hangs today in the East Room of the White House.

At six o'clock the same evening, the British marched into Washington. First Admiral Cockburn and his army went up Capitol Hill to the House chamber. He stood in the Speaker's chair, rapped the gavel for order, and asked his men if the Capitol should be burned. "Aye! Aye!" they cheered. Heaping furniture, files, and the books from the Library of Congress in the middle of the floor, they soon set the building afire.

By 9:00 P.M. Admiral Cockburn had made his way to the president's house on

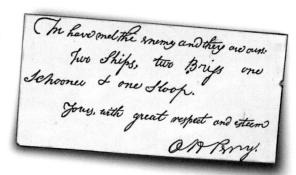

Pennsylvania Avenue. He bowed in front of the mirror in the drawing room and took a pillow and one of Madison's hats for souvenirs. His soldiers roamed the building seeking objects for keepsakes. They again piled up the furniture, using it as kindling to torch the building. They burned all the government buildings except the Patent Office.

A gentle summer rain began to fall about midnight. It soon turned into a heavy downpour that put out the flames and kept the buildings from heavier damage. The Capitol and the president's house could be rebuilt because the outside walls were in good condition. However, the sandstone on the president's house was so darkened by smoke that the house was repainted white. Over a period of years, people started to call it the White House.

Because the capture of Washington had been so easy, the British now decided to launch a joint land-sea attack on Baltimore, Maryland, the nation's third largest city. American troops, however, kept the British army out. The British navy opened its guns on Fort McHenry, the harbor fortress, but Fort McHenry stood and the British soon retreated.

The third prong of the British attack came at New Orleans. **Andrew Jackson** had rushed south from Baton Rouge to attempt to save the city. The British attacked twice in January

Fort McHenry at Baltimore

would have tried to take the Louisiana Territory. Oddly, though neither force knew it, the battle of New Orleans was fought after the war had officially ended.

The Treaty of Ghent

In February of 1815, Americans got word that the **Treaty of Ghent** (GENT), ending the war, had been signed on December 24, 1814. Sometimes called "the Treaty of Christmas Eve," the treaty took its name from the city of Ghent in neutral Belgium, where it had been signed. John Quincy Adams, son of an earlier president, headed the American delegation. The treaty failed to settle the key issue over which the war had been fought—neutral rights at sea. However, it did provide for special commissions, or groups of men, to settle disputes in later years.

of 1815, but Jackson's men threw them back, killing more than two thousand.

The **battle of New Orleans** was the biggest American victory of the war. Had the Americans lost, it is possible that the British

---

"And the Flag Was Still There"

Almost everyone knows the story of Francis Scott Key, but few know the story of the flag that "was still there." The flag had been made by a widow named Mary Young Pickersgill. She had sewn it the year before when Fort McHenry was being renovated. The flag was gigantic; four hundred yards of cloth were needed to make the thirty- by forty-two-foot flag. Each of the fifteen stars was twenty-six inches across; the fifteen stripes were all two feet wide. The flag was visible from several miles away on a clear day. Major Armistead, the man in charge of the fort, clipped part of it to give away after the thrilling victory. Today the original flag hangs in the Smithsonian's Museum of History and Technology, protected from temperature and humidity by special controls.

If better communication had existed, the battle of New Orleans may never have happened.

Results of the War of 1812

Although the Treaty of Ghent made some Americans unhappy, and no territory was gained, the War of 1812 did have important results. First, the United States gained respect in the eyes of other nations. They saw that the United States was ready to fight for what she believed was right—freedom of the seas—and to protect her honor. Second, the war inspired a greater sense of **nationalism.** People were proud to be Americans and had a strong love for their country. They saw that they could compete and win. This gave them more national confidence. Third, new heroes emerged from its fields of battle. Americans were willing to follow Andrew Jackson and William Henry Harrison and would later elect them as presidents.

Fourth, Americans developed much of their own industry during the war. Because they could not get goods from England and France, they had to make their own. After the war the need to rely on foreign countries almost disappeared. Americans continued to increase their output to keep pace with the needs of a growing country. Fifth, Napoleon's defeat in Europe and Britain's rebuff in North America ended the long struggle between France and Britain for colonies in North America and for supremacy in Europe. The war brought America nearly a century of freedom from European conflicts. It enabled Americans to focus on their own affairs. Instead of fighting wars, they fought and tamed the vast American wilderness. Sixth, the War of 1812 affected both political parties. The Federalist Party, already declining, was ruined beyond all hope of recovery because of its opposition to the war. The Republican Party changed its stand slightly on some issues. It had opposed efforts to strengthen and centralize the federal government. Now its leaders began to favor it at times.

SECTION REVIEW

1. What sections of the country did the "War Hawks" represent? Who was their leader in Congress?

2. List several ways the United States was unprepared for war with Britain.

3. List the three regions the British planned to invade in 1814. Where were they defeated in each attempted invasion?

4. What treaty ended the war? What was unusual about the battle of New Orleans?

5. List six results of the War of 1812.

 Why were the Great Lakes so important to the war?

SUMMARY

The early 1800s was a time of growth for the United States. Not only did the young nation add the vast area of the Louisiana Purchase to its territory, but it also added to its stature among the countries of the world by its actions in the Tripolitan War and the War of 1812. Thomas Jefferson continued to extend the powers of the government, but the Supreme Court under John Marshall kept presidential power in check. New leaders in Congress and in the military began to arise to take charge of the continued development of the nation. The United States was beginning to mature.

Chapter Review

People, Places, and Things to Remember

Tripolitan War
Louisiana Purchase
Meriwether Lewis
William Clark
Zebulon Pike
Orders in Council
Berlin and Milan Decrees

Chesapeake affair
embargo
Tecumseh
William Henry Harrison
coalition
Henry Clay
War Hawks

War of 1812
Oliver Hazard Perry
Andrew Jackson
Battle of New Orleans
Treaty of Ghent
nationalism

Review Questions

Complete each of these statements about Thomas Jefferson.

1. The political party to which Thomas Jefferson belonged as president was the _?_ .

2. Jefferson refused to pay tribute to the _?_ .

3. Jefferson bought from France the large western area called the _?_ .

4. To explore the source of the Missouri River, Jefferson sent out _?_ .

5. Despite the *Chesapeake* affair, Jefferson avoided a war with _?_ .

Match each of the following terms to their definition or significance.

6. embargo
7. coalition
8. War Hawks
9. Treaty of Ghent
10. nationalism

   a. made peace with Britain

   b. a temporary alliance of groups

   c. one's pride in and support for his country.

   d. forbidding trade with a foreign country

   e. congressmen who wanted to take action against Britain

Who was the man who did each of the following things?

11. He was victorious on Lake Erie in the War of 1812.

12. He won the battle of Tippecanoe.

13. He won the battle of New Orleans.

14. He was a Shawnee chief who fought against the Americans.

15. He explored Colorado, followed the Rio Grande, and was captured by the Spanish.

Questions for Discussion

16. Why should people not accept only parts of the Bible as the Word of God as Thomas Jefferson did?

17. What can you learn from the life of Aaron Burr?

Location

The Midwest region includes the states of Ohio, Indiana, Michigan, Illinois, Wisconsin, Missouri, Iowa, Minnesota, Kansas, Nebraska, North Dakota, and South Dakota. Its northern border is formed by four of the five Great Lakes and the Canadian border. The Ohio River borders the region on the east. It is the only region discussed in this text that does not touch an ocean.

Climate

The climate in the Midwest is humid continental. Temperatures vary based on latitude, but generally the region has hot summers and cold winters. With adequate water, the growing season is long. The Midwest has several states that are included in "Tornado Alley." This area of frequent tornadoes runs from northern Texas to Nebraska through Oklahoma, Arkansas, Missouri, and Kansas. When the cool, dry air moving down from the north meets the warm, moist air coming up from the Gulf of Mexico, conditions are right for violent storms. In January 1999 alone, fifty-two tornadoes were recorded in the region.

Topography

The Mississippi River system that drains the region includes great rivers such as the Ohio, Missouri, and Illinois. Each of these rivers has been altered in some way to help barge traffic move down the river. Goods transported on these rivers reach nearly all the big cities in the region. The St. Lawrence Seaway (the Great Lakes and St. Lawrence River) makes it possible for ocean-going vessels to move from the Atlantic Ocean all the way to Chicago. With the exception of the Black Hills of the Dakotas, the Ozarks of southern Missouri, and the hills around Lake Superior, the entire region is plains, from the Central Plains to the Great Plains.

Natural Resources

The greatest resource of the region is its soil. Corn and wheat are produced in great abundance; however, very little of the corn produced is eaten as a vegetable by families. Families consume corn in the form of cereal, flour, oil, and syrup, but the greatest portion is used for livestock feed. Most Americans also eat wheat in some form every day, but Midwestern farms produce so much wheat that America is able to export more wheat than any other country in the world. The less fertile soil of Minnesota, Wisconsin, and Michigan is used as pastureland for herds of dairy cattle. Products from the Dairy Belt are found in markets around the country. Coal and low-grade iron, called taconite, are abundant in the Ohio River valley. The availability of these two resources has fueled industry across the region.

Geography and Culture

Sometimes called America's Heartland, the majority of the Midwest embodies the small town and farm life that were once the lifeblood of America. The Midwest's central location has made it a crossroads for goods being transported across the nation, and its fertile fields have made it the nation's breadbasket. Settled by common people, the region is proud that its children have risen to positions of leadership in the nation. Midwesterners such as Abraham Lincoln proved early that America was a land of freedom where even a person from humble beginnings could become president.

However, the region is not all small towns and farms. Predominant in its eastern portion are much more urban and industrial areas. Detroit, Michigan; Gary, Indiana; and Akron, Ohio, are all known for their industry. Iron and coal mining, as well as the nearby river transportation, have greatly benefited industrial endeavors there.

The Midwest has gone through many changes in the past few decades. Its industries have declined, and its family farms are in crisis, but these problems give the region the opportunity to show once again its American spirit.

11

The Era of Good Feelings

hen President James Monroe visited Boston in 1817, a local paper reported the event in an article and spoke of an "Era of Good Feelings" that the nation was enjoying during the Monroe presidency. It was true that the United States was experiencing a brief period of relative harmony. Political rivalries were not intense. The North, the South, and the West all had their particular needs, desires, and opinions, but sectional differences were in a temporary calm. No great national crisis, such as the War of 1812, was arising, and the great trials that were to come over slavery and its related issues were as yet only smoldering.

"Good feelings," whether between men or nations, are often hard to maintain, and Monroe and his successor, John Quincy Adams, soon saw the harmony begin to break up. The problems of national government began to loom again as the United States recognized its position in world affairs and also as it began to deal with its own expansion.

Monroe Begins the Era

Madison's secretary of state during the War of 1812 had been **James Monroe**. By the summer of 1816, the governors of twelve states and the senators and congressmen from fourteen had signed a petition asking Monroe to run for president. Madison also urged him to run. Monroe was hesitant, but he agreed to accept the nomination on two conditions. First, he would not be tied to a single political party. Second, he would not wage an active campaign. He would run on his own record, as he had for an earlier seat in Congress and for governor of Virginia.

Winning the Election

While his opponent, Rufus King, toured the country making speeches, Monroe stayed in Washington performing his duties in the state department. "If they want me, they'll vote for me if I don't make a single speech or open a single county fair," he said. The voters sensed Monroe's sincerity, and he won the election.

Although the major political parties did not clash nationally during the **"Era of Good Feelings"** (Monroe's two terms in office), some rivalries still existed on the state level. Voter turnouts were small, however, because people had little influence in choosing the national and state candidates. Most candidates were picked by party **caucus**, a closed meeting of party leaders. For president, the parties usually nominated the **incumbent**, the current officeholder, to run again. If he had served his two terms, they chose the secretary of state. The position of secretary of state thus seemed to be the stepping stone to the presidency. Things were so cut-and-dried that the voters lost interest for a while.

Monroe in Charge

Monroe was the fourth Virginian to become president. He broke precedent by not

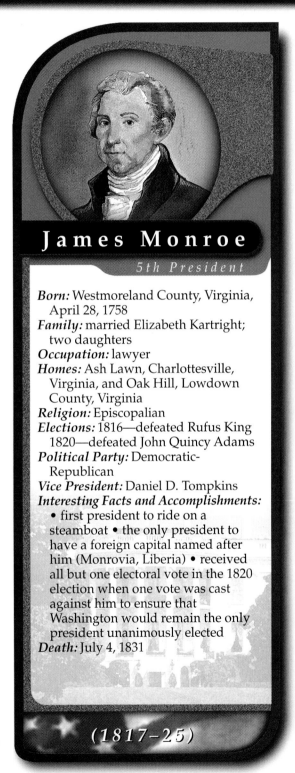

James Monroe
5th President

Born: Westmoreland County, Virginia, April 28, 1758
Family: married Elizabeth Kartright; two daughters
Occupation: lawyer
Homes: Ash Lawn, Charlottesville, Virginia, and Oak Hill, Lowdown County, Virginia
Religion: Episcopalian
Elections: 1816—defeated Rufus King 1820—defeated John Quincy Adams
Political Party: Democratic-Republican
Vice President: Daniel D. Tompkins
Interesting Facts and Accomplishments:
• first president to ride on a steamboat • the only president to have a foreign capital named after him (Monrovia, Liberia) • received all but one electoral vote in the 1820 election when one vote was cast against him to ensure that Washington would remain the only president unanimously elected
Death: July 4, 1831

(1817–25)

giving an inaugural address. After his oath he simply said: "I will do my best."

Monroe was basically a Democratic-Republican, but he was also sympathetic to some of the ideas of the Federalist Party, which was now dying out. In addition, he was ready to hear the varied views that were developing within the Democratic-Republican party. Monroe's ideal of not being tied to a single party was reflected in his cabinet. He said, "I want the best men in the country working with me regardless of their party beliefs." He chose such men as **John Quincy Adams** (who would later run against him in 1820 as an Independent Republican) as his secretary of state and South Carolina's young war hawk, **John C. Calhoun**, as his secretary of war.

SECTION REVIEW

1. On what two conditions did Monroe agree to accept the presidential nomination?

2. Why had many voters lost interest in the election process?

3. How did Monroe choose members of his cabinet?

 Was the "Era of Good Feelings" an appropriate name for this period? Give reasons for your answer.

International Concerns

Although Monroe did not totally neglect affairs at home during his terms, he is most noted for championing American interests abroad. With the war over, the United States now faced different challenges that centered on Latin America. These lands south of the border were so named because the languages brought there by Portuguese and Spanish colonizers had come from Latin.

The Florida Purchase

Florida was the first challenge. Over the years Spain's power had been weakening, and she had nearly lost control of Florida. For example, in 1810 Americans in West Florida, the part of Florida extending to the Mississippi River, had revolted against Spanish rule and had asked to become a part of the United States. Spain did nothing to stop them. Then in 1814 Creek Indians who had gone on the warpath from their base in West Florida were defeated by Andrew Jackson in the battle of Horseshoe Bend in Alabama. Because the Indian menace was lessened and Spain was doing little to develop the area, Americans, particularly cotton farmers, moved into the Deep South region. By 1817 Mississippi had enough people to apply for statehood, and by 1819 so did Alabama.

Trouble Along the Border—In 1817 trouble developed in East Florida and the small part of West Florida still under Spanish rule.

James Monroe was born in this humble home in Westmoreland County, Virginia.

Southern slaves fled to Florida by the hundreds if not by the thousands. Some runaways fled to the Seminole Indian settlements while others started farms, plantations, or ranches. The Indians and their runaway slave allies frequently crossed over the border and attacked unprotected American settlements. Then they would retreat to Florida, defying the few soldiers along the frontier to go after them. Moreover, Florida had also become a haven for smugglers of European goods.

Andrew Jackson Invades Florida—Secretary of State Adams complained to Spanish leaders and warned them that if they could not control their own territory, the United States would take action. When the Spanish did nothing, Secretary of War Calhoun gave General Andrew Jackson control of the Tennessee and Georgia militias. Jackson was to go to the border and stop the smugglers. Jackson chose to interpret his order liberally rather than literally and invaded Florida. His actions surprised the Indians and enabled him to defeat them, capture towns, and even depose the Spanish governor.

Spain soon demanded money for damages and asked for the punishment of Jackson. Monroe refused both demands and even allowed Jackson to stay in Florida until Spain sent enough men to end the abuses. Lacking funds and troops, Spain soon decided it would be better off selling Florida. In 1819 the United States made a treaty with Spain, purchasing East Florida for $5 million and keeping American ownership of the lands already taken in West Florida. The Spanish boundary west of the Mississippi was also defined. Spain kept control of Texas and her other western lands.

Revolutions in Latin America

Spain's inability to control its other Latin American colonies resulted in their loss as well. In these colonies Spanish-born settlers

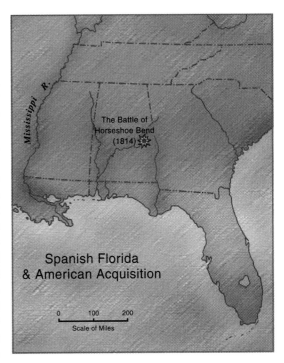

The Battle of Horseshoe Bend (1814)

Spanish Florida & American Acquisition

0   100   200
Scale of Miles

had the most political power and social status. The Creoles, those born in Latin America but of European descent, were thought inferior. But because they were men of wealth and education, they had the means and leadership ability to take action. Of course, mestizos (those who were half-Indian and half-European), Indians, and blacks, regarded even lower on the Spanish social scale, did not object. The Creoles resented Spanish control of their economy. Spain got profits that the colonists believed they should be enjoying. Furthermore, the colonists felt no loyalty to their new king, who was not Spanish but French. (In 1808 Napoleon had named one of his brothers, Joseph Bonaparte, king of Spain.)

Mexico tried to overthrow Spanish rule as early as 1810 and in 1821 finally gained her independence. Mexico's success encouraged the other countries of Central America to revolt. Then South America followed, led by two inspiring Creoles, **Jose de San Martín** (ho-ZAY day san mahr-TEEN) in the southern areas, and **Simón Bolívar** (see MOHN BOH-luh-vahr) in the northern areas. Most of the new republics modeled their constitutions after that of the United States. But the poor economic conditions, the high illiteracy, the tradition of **autocracy** (government by one powerful ruler), and the power of the Roman Catholic Church weakened these new republics. Strong military leaders easily took control, and foreign powers were also tempted to intervene.

Secretary of State John Quincy Adams wrote the statement known as the Monroe Doctrine.

President Monroe feared the latter. He and his fellow Americans were sympathetic to the new republics; so with the approval of Congress, Monroe established diplomatic outposts in those countries. Britain recognized the new lands, too, but some of the other European rulers did not. Austria, France, Prussia, and Russia planned to resist revolutions and republican forms of government wherever they emerged. Although Britain at first cooperated with these countries in an alliance, it later voiced objections to their plans.

Other Foreign Threats

Monroe also had reason to eye Russia closely. The Russians owned Alaska, where they had developed a profitable fur trade. They began to move down the coast seeking greater profits. By 1812 they had built a fort only a short distance north of San Francisco. By 1821 they had laid claim to Pacific lands on what is now the west coast of Canada. Some of this land lay within the lands that the British and the United States had already jointly claimed.

Then in early 1823 the president learned that the French were preparing to send shiploads of troops to Latin America. In August of 1823, Lord George Canning, the British Foreign Secretary, contacted John Quincy Adams. He suggested that the United States and Britain issue a joint declaration to warn the other European nations to stay out of the New World.

Since Monroe did not want to make a mistake that would have long-range consequences, he waited. He asked Jefferson, Madison, and John Quincy Adams to come to the capital to advise him. Although few realized it at the time, it was a historic occasion. Four men—past, present, and future presidents—met together to discuss the matter.

Several weeks later Monroe told Adams: "When a weak nation accepts partnership with a stronger, she places herself at the mercy of her ally." By fall, Monroe decided to issue a declaration separate from any made by Britain. John Quincy Adams wrote the statement, and President Monroe included it in his annual message to Congress on December 2, 1823. This statement has been called the **Monroe Doctrine**.

The Monroe Doctrine

The Monroe Doctrine added three new basic principles to America's foreign policy. First, "the American continents . . . [were] not to be considered as subjects for future colonization by any European powers." In other words, European nations could not set up new colonies in the Americas. Second, the United States would not interfere in European affairs or wars unless its rights were "invaded or seriously menaced," when it would then "make preparations for [its] defense." Third, the United States "should consider any attempt . . . to extend their system to any portion of our hemisphere as dangerous to [its] space and safety" and to be an unfriendly act. The Monroe Doctrine simply told the Europeans not to meddle with Western Hemisphere countries while it promised that the United States would not get involved unnecessarily in European affairs.

The Monroe Doctrine did stop the immediate threat of European intervention in the Americas. Some believe this was because European powers feared the British navy, not because they feared the United States. In future years, however, the importance of the Monroe Doctrine increased. In fact, it became a foundational element of American foreign policy.

SECTION REVIEW

1. What two groups of people were using Florida as a haven to avoid capture and possible punishment?

2. When Spain did not solve Florida's problems, what American was given authority to take action?

3. Why did many people in Spain's Latin American colonies resent Spanish control?

4. What two Creoles led revolutions in South America?

5. What two countries approved and recognized the new republics in Latin America?

 What basic guideline was established by the Monroe Doctrine?

Internal Affairs Under Monroe

Although the nation avoided foreign problems during the Era of Good Feelings, it could not avoid some problems at home.

The Economic Crisis of 1819

The War of 1812, by creating greater demands for raw materials, caused an economic boom. Because farmers were getting higher prices for their crops, more and more people went west and bought farmland. In addition, Europe was again producing her own agricultural products. Soon, because so many farms were producing crops, there was a surplus in America, and prices of farm products began to drop.

The charter of the National Bank, although allowed to lapse briefly, had been reissued. Meanwhile, state banks had grown in number. They had begun to issue their own bank notes even when they lacked silver and gold to back them up. When the new National Bank called in loans from western banks, the state banks could not pay them, and the economy collapsed. The collapse was especially hard on southern and western farmers. They called this crisis **"The Panic of '19."**

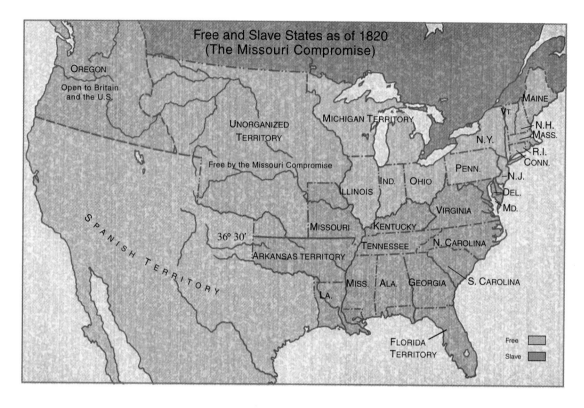

Free and Slave States as of 1820
(The Missouri Compromise)

OREGON
Open to Britain
and the U.S.

SPANISH TERRITORY

UNORGANIZED
TERRITORY

Free by the Missouri Compromise

36° 30'

ARKANSAS TERRITORY

MICHIGAN TERRITORY

MISSOURI   KENTUCKY
TENNESSEE   N. CAROLINA

MISS. ALA. GEORGIA   S. CAROLINA
LA.

ILLINOIS   IND. OHIO
VIRGINIA
N.Y.   PENN.
N.J.
DEL.
MD.

MAINE
VT.
N.H.
MASS.
R.I.
CONN.

FLORIDA
TERRITORY

Free
Slave

The Marshall Court's Nationalist Decisions

The panic led to a major Supreme Court decision. Since the states tended to dislike national banks, some states began to tax their national branches, hoping that the increased costs would make people less likely to use them. When Maryland required the Baltimore branch to issue bank notes on paper bought from the state, the bank would not do it. Maryland then sued the federal cashier, James McCulloch. The case soon reached the Supreme Court. This was one of several cases in which Chief Justice John Marshall asserted the national government's power over that of the states. In *McCulloch v. Maryland,* the court ruled that a state could not tax the federal government because the "power to tax includes the power to destroy." Marshall based his decision on the supremacy clause of the Constitution. He asserted that when the national government performed a function permitted by the Constitution, it could not be threatened by the states.

In other cases Marshall declared certain state laws to be unconstitutional. Thus the Supreme Court and the federal government were given definite authority over state governments. Another case settled by the Supreme Court gave the federal government power to regulate **interstate commerce** (selling and transporting of goods from one state to another).

Slavery and the Missouri Compromise

The original northern states had already abolished or were in the process of abolishing slavery. The newer states formed out of the Northwest Territory had never had it. Of course, slavery was still allowed in the southern states. By 1819 there were twenty-two states in the Union. Eleven were free; eleven were slave states. There was almost a straight line between the two sets of states.

Although slavery had not yet become a moral issue, it now produced an economic and political squabble. The nation had continued to grow, especially in a westward direction, and in 1819 Missouri asked to join the union as a slave state. Northerners could see that if Missouri came in as a slave state, the balance between slave and free would be upset. James Tallmadge of New York added an amendment to Missouri's statehood bill saying that no more slaves could be brought into Missouri and that all children born to slave parents would be freed when they reached the age of twenty-five. Southerners protested loudly. The House passed the bill, but the Senate refused it.

The possibility of a compromise arose in late 1819 when Maine, earlier a part of Massachusetts, applied for statehood. If Maine came in free and Missouri came in slave, then the balance would be maintained. This seemed fine on the surface, but it did not settle the problem of what would be done in the future. Would slavery be permitted in the rest of the Louisiana Purchase? When Florida grew in population and applied for statehood, would it be a slave state? If Texas gained its independence from Mexico, what would its status be? If more slaveholders moved into northern states such as Indiana and Illinois, could they change the free status of those states? If the Supreme Court could rule on the legality of a national bank, could it also abolish slavery? The debates over these questions were long and heated.

The deadlock was finally broken when Henry Clay of Kentucky, a border state, worked out the **Missouri Compromise.** Maine's admission would be tied to Missouri's, keeping a balance of slave and free

states. Slavery would be forbidden north of 36° 30′ north latitude, Missouri's southern boundary. Slavery would be permitted, although not necessarily protected, south of the invisible line. The bill passed by a slim margin. Monroe said he would veto it but was talked out of it at the last minute. The emotion involved in discussing slavery made it obvious that feelings on the subject ran deep. John Quincy Adams wrote, "I take it for granted that the present question is a mere preamble— a title page to a great tragic volume." Former President Jefferson called it "a firebell in the night . . . which awakened and filled me with terror. I considered it at once as the knell of the Union."

SECTION REVIEW

1. Why did many western banks collapse in 1819?

2. Why did states tax branches of the national bank?

3. What issue was brought up by Missouri's request to join the Union?

4. What were the terms of the Missouri Compromise?

 What was the significance of *McCulloch v. Maryland*?

A Disappearance of Good Feelings

There had been few major problems for the nation during the Monroe administration. But as these years passed, new challenges were ready to surface.

A Candidate Collection

In 1824 the Democratic-Republican Party defied tradition. Rather than choosing the current secretary of state as their candidate, the Republicans chose William Crawford, who drew most of his support from the southern states. His thinking was close to Thomas

Jefferson's. He disliked protective tariffs, which would increase the price of goods for southern planters and western farmers. He opposed federal support of internal improvements because they would have to be paid for by taxes. Crawford, however, lacked national support. Furthermore, he had been briefly paralyzed by a stroke in 1823, and some thought he might not be able to face the rigors of office.

The remaining candidates were selected by state legislatures. Massachusetts chose John Quincy Adams, a career diplomat. Kentucky nominated Henry Clay, the Speaker of the House, believing he would be elected because the new western states backed him. The views of Clay and Adams were close on many issues. For example, both were strong nationalists, favoring a strong central government. Neither feared the federal government's playing an active role in the nation's economy. Hence, they favored the rechartering of the National Bank and a high tariff. They believed tariff monies could pay for internal improvements such as roads, canals, and harbors. Such projects, in their opinion, would help the nation to grow and would benefit their sections of the country—New England and the West.

Tennessee's candidate, Andrew Jackson, had been a lawyer and United States senator, but his fame had been gained as the hero of New Orleans, and as an Indian fighter in Spanish Florida. Jackson's slogan became "Old Hickory, the Nation's Hero, and the People's Friend."

The Election Goes to the House

Jackson won more votes than anyone else in both the electoral college and the popular vote. He surprised many with his national following by carrying some states from each section. Adams came in second. Crawford was a distant third with Clay just behind him. But with so many candidates, no man won a majority of the electoral vote (131 votes in 1824). This meant that the election went to the House of Representatives. The Twelfth Amendment had given each state one vote and said that the states must choose from among the top three candidates.

Jackson's followers believed that the House had a moral responsibility to pick the man with the largest vote. The most important factor in the House's decision, however, turned out to be Henry Clay, who had to drop out of the race. Whomever Clay chose to support with his votes would be the winner. Since his views were close to Adams's and he disliked Jackson, Clay chose to support John Quincy Adams. Clay also believed that he stood a better chance of following Adams into the White House.

When John Quincy Adams became president, he kept most of Monroe's cabinet because he believed they were qualified. He replaced only three men. One position he had to replace was his own, secretary of state. Although Monroe told him that making Henry Clay secretary of state might be an unwise political move, Adams picked Clay because of his qualifications and experience. This decision did prove to be a downfall for Adams.

Jackson's followers angrily charged that Adams and Clay had made a "corrupt bargain." They thought that Clay had made a deal with Adams in which Clay supported Adams for president in return for the high political appointment. John Quincy Adams was both hurt and horrified. His strong moral conscience and devotion to duty would never have allowed it. An angry Andrew Jackson resigned his Senate seat and set out for Tennessee. But before he left, Jackson allowed his supporters to start organizing for the 1828 election. They plotted Adams's political demise and made his presidency the most miserable experience of his life.

The Presidency of John Quincy Adams

John Quincy Adams, the son of John Adams, had been in public service thirty-six years before becoming president. He had served in the Department of State during every presidential administration. Probably the best-educated man of his day, he had an enviable record. But in an era when other politicians used their personalities to draw support, John Quincy Adams appeared cold, aloof, plain, and unexciting. While other politicians awarded jobs to those who would follow them, Adams refused to do so. He did his best work behind the scenes. Although he would have appreciated praise and honor from others, he would not seek either.

Ideas and Opponents—Adams's single term of office turned into a series of unending disasters. For one thing, his talents did not make him sensitive to either opinions or trends. In addition, his program was highly nationalistic, designed to improve the national economy at a time when people were trying to protect the interests of their own sections of the country. Henry Clay suggested an American system, a high tariff package rewarding all sections of the nation with projects paid for out of the monies collected. Adams endorsed it. After the public debt was repaid, the monies left from the tariff and the sale of public lands could be used to build roads and canals to aid the communication "between distant regions and multitudes of men." He also wanted to build lighthouses along the coast to aid shipping, a national university to improve the minds of Americans, and an observatory to view the skies. His critics made fun of his "lighthouses in the sky" as well as his suggestion that Congress promote art, literature, and science. His ideas were not well accepted, and in the 1826 elections he lost most of his support in Congress.

The moderate tariff that he had favored was revised upward (had its rates raised).

John Quincy Adams

6th President

Born: Braintree, Massachusetts, July 11, 1767
Family: married Louisa Catherine Johnston; three sons, one daughter
Occupation: lawyer
Home: Quincy, Massachusetts
Religion: Congregationalist
Election: 1824—by the House of Representatives following an election with no candidate receiving a majority; defeated Andrew Jackson, William Crawford, and Henry Clay
Political Party: no major party affiliation
Vice President: John C. Calhoun
Interesting Facts and Accomplishments:
• served as secretary to his father when his father was foreign minister in Russia and France • graduated from Harvard University • wrote the Monroe Doctrine • helped establish the Smithsonian Institution • kept a diary for over sixty years • first president to be photographed (after he left office)
Death: February 23, 1848, from a stroke while in the House of Representatives

(1825-29)

The home of John Quincy Adams in Quincy, Massachusetts is preserved as a museum.

Southerners called the tariff of 1828 **"the tariff of abominations"** and threatened to leave the Union. Yet Adams signed the bill. He further angered those who promoted states' rights by standing up for the Indians, threatening to use federal troops to protect the Creeks and Cherokees from invasions by Georgians.

Adams Deals with Latin America— Even in foreign affairs where Adams had vast experience, he made little headway. Simón Bolívar called a Pan-

---

Old Man Eloquent: The President Who Never Retired

John Quincy Adams's career continued after he left the White House. In 1830 he was persuaded to run for Congress for his home district in Massachusetts. He had the attitude of a servant. The position did not matter nor did the pay. (He received $8.00 a day for his services.) Serving the people, however, did matter. He wrote, "No person could be degraded by serving the people. . . . If the people elected me town selectman, I would consider it an honor."

In Congress he was highly respected for his many accomplishments. His speech-making was so skilled he was soon nicknamed "old man eloquent." In 1832 he led the fight to revise the tariff downward (lower the rates). The new tariff has sometimes been called "the Adams tariff."

A lifelong foe of slavery, he forced the House to repeal the Gag Rule, which had forbidden antislave petitions to be submitted to the House. He predicted correctly that wars would be fought if the issue of slavery was not settled. He introduced a constitutional amendment to abolish slavery in 1839. His antislavery speeches were not just idle talk. When a freed slave named Nathan Jones saw his family sold into slavery, Adams gave him money and the names of friends to contact to raise the funds needed to secure their freedom.

He helped establish the United States Naval Academy at Severn, Maryland, and led an eleven-year drive to found a national museum, the Smithsonian. James Smithson, a British chemist, had willed one-half million dollars to the United States for such a purpose, but Congress wanted to divert the money to other causes.

In 1846 a tall, slim, Whig congressman from Illinois was elected to the House. In his initial meeting with Adams, Abraham Lincoln praised the veteran congressman for what he had done to repeal the Gag Rule and help slaves. The old patriarch looked at Lincoln and slowly said, "There is much yet to be done."

On February 21, 1848, when Adams rose for a roll call vote in Congress, he collapsed from a stroke. He was carried into the cloak-room. Too sick to be moved, he died there two days later. Abraham Lincoln represented the House and rode the funeral train back to Massachusetts. John C. Calhoun, who often opposed Adams, served as a pallbearer. Daniel Webster wrote his epitaph. Adams had devoted fifty-eight years of his life to serving his nation directly. He has been called "the president who never retired."

American Conference. Adams was wary of it, but Clay convinced him to take part. The names of two delegates were sent to the Senate, but their approval was delayed. Some senators believed the United States should stay out of foreign affairs. Southern senators withheld support after hearing a rumor that the conference would try to abolish slavery. Finally the delegates left for Panama. One died en route; the other arrived after the meeting had ended. Even though it suffered this failure, the administration did make some commercial treaties with the major nations of Europe and Latin America. Adams also enlarged the American navy and pushed for a naval academy.

The Election of 1828

By the end of Adams's term, two political parties existed once again. John Quincy Adams and his running mate, Richard Rush, were selected by a party called the National Republican party. Jackson and his running mate, John C. Calhoun, were named by the Tennessee legislature and then placed on the ballot by supporters in state legislatures in other states. Jackson's group, composed largely of former Democratic-Republicans, was called the **Democratic Party.**

The election of 1828 was unique for other reasons too. For the first time, many techniques of mass campaigning appeared. Broadsides (posters), banners, editorials, testimonials, barbecues, banquets, and torchlight parades were all used to win voter support.

Such techniques brought out more voters than ever before, as did changes in voting requirements. Some states had already lifted the requirement that voters own property. Most new western states had constitutions that allowed white manhood suffrage or at least gave the vote to male taxpayers, which was almost the same thing. This expansion of suf-

John C. Calhoun of South Carolina, Andrew Jackson's vice president.

frage in some states plus the addition of new states into the Union caused the number of voters to more than double between 1824 and 1828. By 1840 virtually all adult white males could vote. Moreover, three-quarters of those eligible did so, a much higher percentage than in elections today.

The election of 1828 was also one of the worst in terms of **mudslinging** (making malicious statements about opponents). The Democrats claimed that John Quincy Adams was a snob who displayed fancy foreign manners. Because he had a billiard table in the White House, he was charged with being a gambler. He was even accused falsely of immorality.

Honorable Murder

Duels—fights to the death to preserve one's honor—unfortunately were not uncommon during the early history of the United States. Thousands of them were fought in the name of honor. This was particularly true in the West and South, although America's most famous duel (the one between Hamilton and Burr) took place in Weehawken, New Jersey. Duels were fought even during the Civil War between officers on the same side.

There were rules to be followed when one was involved in a duel. The person being challenged chose what weapons would be used. The seconds, or alternates, usually decided the manner in which a duel was to be fought. It was also their duty to try to negotiate a peaceful settlement of the argument in order to avoid actual combat. The first thing that had to be decided—after the choice of weapons—was how far apart the two combatants were to stand. Then a decision had to be made on who would give the command to fire. Also a time limit had to be set unless the two parties involved agreed not to have a time limit at all. Usually the duelists would face each other at the arranged distance with the pistols pointed down or straight up. On command the duelists would commence firing. If there was a time limit, the command would be spoken very fast: "Fire! One, two, three!" If someone had not fired by then, it was too late. One shot was normally all the duelist was allowed, although in the last recorded duel, one of the men shot six times—and missed. Misses or slight wounds were common because the weapons were of poor quality. In one duel involving two women—over a man—both women missed. The man, however, who was standing in the crowd watching, was shot in the head and killed.

Of the two most famous duels in American history, that of Burr and Hamilton has been a source of controversy among historians for years. Some suggest from Hamilton's last letter and dying words that he had no intention of shooting at Burr at all. Witnesses at the scene, however, describe Hamilton's actions as giving every indication that he did mean to shoot at his opponent. The bullet from Hamilton's gun lodged in a tree limb some twenty feet or so above the ground—too high but not straight up. There was some argument among the three witnesses concerning who fired first. Burr and his second claimed that Hamilton did. Hamilton's second claimed Burr did. Either way, Burr killed Hamilton and although all the rules of dueling had been observed, Hamilton became a martyr, and Burr a scoundrel.

The other famous duel involved Andrew Jackson and a man named John Dickinson. This duel nearly cost "Old Hickory" his political career. Allegedly, Jackson's duel was fought because Dickinson had insulted Mrs. Jackson. Dickinson was the favorite to win the duel because he was an expert marksman. Supposedly he could hit a string with a bullet at a distance of twenty-five feet or even farther. Jackson, however, showed up at the duel in a heavy overcoat and twisted his body as much as he could beneath it. He resolved to let Dickinson shoot first and then to shoot him. Because of Jackson's contortions, Dickinson's shot barely missed "Old Hickory's" heart. Jackson then aimed and—after one misfire— gave his opponent a mortal wound. The public considered it a cold-blooded execution. Jackson, who could have regained his honor by simply wounding Dickinson, should not have fired again when the first shot misfired. Only Jackson's crushing victory over the British at the battle of New Orleans during the War of 1812 restored him to public favor.

Eventually dueling became unacceptable to the public. Some men in the eighteenth and nineteenth centuries valued their honor or the honor of someone dear to them more than they valued life itself. For others, dueling indicated faulty reasoning. They dueled in an effort to seek revenge. Although dueling was (and is) illegal, many people exhaust countless hours trying to express their hatred toward others in more subtle ways. They succeed only in wasting time and embittering themselves. They do not realize that "whosoever hateth his brother is a murderer" (I John 3:15).

Adams's followers fought back. They claimed Jackson was a murderer since he had killed at least one man in a duel and had sentenced others to death while in the military. They also accused him of adultery. Jackson had married Rachel Donelson Robards, believing her divorce was final. Later he discovered it was not and had another marriage ceremony. Jackson loved his wife and defended her honor. Unfortunately, Rachel, suffering from an illness, died on December 22, 1828, after reading a pamphlet that slandered her. Jackson took office a few weeks later, and for the rest of his life he blamed the National Republicans for causing Rachel's death. Although the candidates themselves were not directly involved in the mudslinging, they did not use their authority to stop it. They allowed the evil to continue when they could have used their leadership to prohibit it.

SECTION REVIEW

1. Why did Jackson not win the election of 1824 even though he had the largest number of votes?

2. Why did Adams choose Clay to be his secretary of state, and how did Jackson's followers interpret this action?

3. What did southerners call the tariff of 1828? What had Adams hoped to accomplish with the monies from a tariff?

4. Name two aspects of the election of 1828 that made it different from other elections.

5. For what two reasons did the number of voters more than double between 1824 and 1828?

 Why was there more mudslinging in the election of 1828 than in previous ones?

SUMMARY

America enjoyed an "Era of Good Feelings" after the War of 1812 ended. Relations with foreign nations were peaceful, and problems within the nation were minimal. Yet the troubles of the years to come were developing—especially the sectional rivalry between regions of the country. These differences grew during the presidency of John Quincy Adams, and his main opponent, Andrew Jackson, played on these sectional differences to promote his own popularity.

Chapter Review

People, Places, and Things to Remember

James Monroe
Era of Good Feelings
caucus
incumbent
John Quincy Adams
John C. Calhoun
Jose de San Martín

Simón Bolívar
autocracy
Monroe Doctrine
The Panic of '19
McCulloch v. Maryland
interstate commerce
Missouri Compromise

the tariff of abominations
Democratic party
mudslinging

Review Questions

Write the correct answer for each blank.

James Monroe's presidency has often been called the (1) . During that time the United States purchased (2) . It also issued a warning to European nations interested in American lands. This warning, called the (3) , was written largely by (4) , who followed Monroe into the presidency. The nation faced a major decision when the number of free and slave states might have lost their balance, but Henry Clay worked out the (5) to settle the issue for that time and allow the entrance of two new states to the union.

Answer these who, what, or when questions.

6. What is a meeting of political party leaders who choose a candidate called?

7. Who defeated the Indians at the battle of Horseshoe Bend?

8. Who were the two men who led much of South America to independence?

9. When did the United States buy Florida?

10. What court case was used to strengthen the federal government's power over that of the states?

11. Who was said to have made a "corrupt bargain" with John Quincy Adams?

12. What was Andrew Jackson's political party?

13. Who was the incumbent presidential candidate in 1828?

14. What state came into the union as a free state as a result of the Missouri Compromise?

Questions for Discussion

15. Do you think a candidate with Monroe's attitude toward campaigning could win a presidential election today? Why or why not?

16. What effect does mudslinging have on a political election?

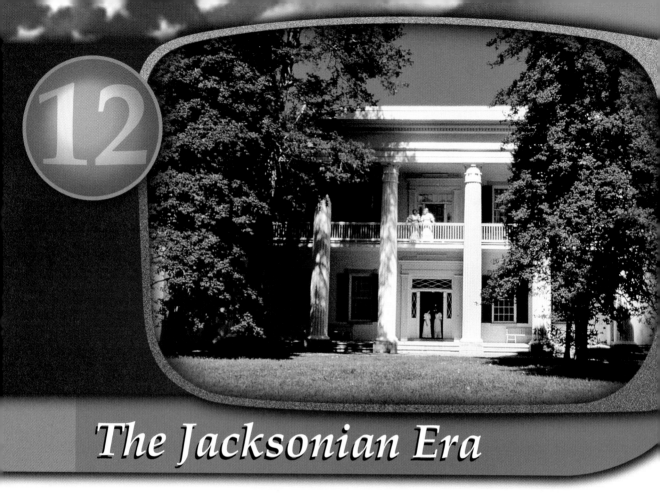

The Jacksonian Era

Outside Nashville, Tennessee, stands a stately southern mansion called the Hermitage. This beautiful home of Andrew Jackson is a far cry from the log cabin in which the president was born. The self-taught lawyer and Indian fighter who lived there became an inspiration to many Americans who wished for a similar chance to better themselves.

Jackson's log cabin birthplace was in South Carolina. His parents had been linen weavers in Ireland before coming to America. His father died shortly before Jackson's birth. Then his mother and brother died of smallpox when he was fifteen, leaving him totally on his own. Made bitter by these early experiences, he lived a wild life for a time. Eventually, however, he studied law and moved to Tennessee. There he became a lawyer, judge, land speculator, politician, Indian fighter, and planter. The battle of New Orleans brought him national fame.

Jackson was the first president elected from a state west of the original thirteen states and the first president from a poor family. His was a new formula for political success: log cabin to the White House. However, this did not mean he was a crude frontiersman at the time of his election (although his political enemies worked hard to portray him so). He owned over a hundred slaves and much land, and he was one of the richest planters in Tennessee. Yet he made his causes those of the common people.

Coming into office at a time of great advantages for a president, Jackson became the symbol of the age. More and more western lands were opening, and new states were joining the union. Industry and agriculture were expanding at a rapid pace with the introduction of many inventions and ideas of the Industrial Revolution. In addition, immigration was helping the population grow at an amazing rate, and more people had the vote than ever before.

Jacksonian Democracy for Some

Andrew Jackson came to office in 1829 as a champion of the common man—particularly the western farmer and the eastern worker. His rise from humble beginnings to wealth, influence, and the presidency gave Americans an example of the possibilities of achievement in their land. The common man elected Jackson, and he intended to represent their interests by molding his form of democracy for the country.

After Jackson took office, he boldly made changes that he believed the people wanted. He was a strong president who used the powers of the presidency more than they had ever been used before. Jackson made friends—and enemies—easily. He also translated his thoughts into actions so swiftly that he sometimes appeared reckless and unthinking. He had a short temper, which he never really learned to control. As a result his actions did not always benefit the nation.

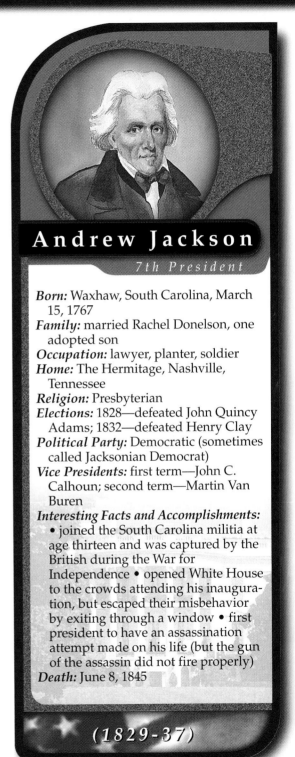

Andrew Jackson

7th President

Born: Waxhaw, South Carolina, March 15, 1767
Family: married Rachel Donelson, one adopted son
Occupation: lawyer, planter, soldier
Home: The Hermitage, Nashville, Tennessee
Religion: Presbyterian
Elections: 1828—defeated John Quincy Adams; 1832—defeated Henry Clay
Political Party: Democratic (sometimes called Jacksonian Democrat)
Vice Presidents: first term—John C. Calhoun; second term—Martin Van Buren
Interesting Facts and Accomplishments:
• joined the South Carolina militia at age thirteen and was captured by the British during the War for Independence • opened White House to the crowds attending his inauguration, but escaped their misbehavior by exiting through a window • first president to have an assassination attempt made on his life (but the gun of the assassin did not fire properly)
Death: June 8, 1845

(1829-37)

Jackson and the Spoils System

At the beginning of his administration, Jackson replaced hundreds of capable government workers with his followers. This method of handing out government jobs to loyal followers is known as the **"spoils system."** The spoils system for jobs was not new. It had been used on both national and state levels earlier, but Jackson used it on a wider scale.

Jackson and his followers defended the spoils system, claiming that workers of already proven loyalty would do a better job than uncaring holdovers. The spoils system was a way to get rid of officials who might not go along with the desires of the new administration. Jackson also held that giving new people jobs gave the government fresh vigor and gave the people a chance to see how government really worked. This, he argued, would make them more useful citizens. In reality, the spoils system gave the party in power more political muscle.

The spoils system also had disadvantages. It did not encourage efficiency or the hiring of highly qualified workers. In later years it sometimes even caused corruption because people paid bribes to get high-paying jobs. It also aided the growth of **political machines,** organized groups of politicians who sought to control government. These political machines used their power to keep themselves in office and to gain profits from public funds. Such politicians often joined parties not for what they could give but for what they could get.

Since many of the government jobs in the Jacksonian era did not require special skills or a high level of training, the effects of the spoils systems were only slight. Many of the common people to whom Jackson gave offices had the good qualities nurtured on the frontier: determination, honesty, hard work, and common sense. But though less than twenty percent of the workers were replaced, Jackson's actions set an unwise precedent. Other presidents extended the system until Congress stopped it in 1883 by adopting a civil service system.

Jackson's Kitchen Cabinet

Jackson appointed men to cabinet posts as he did to other government jobs. He used the positions as rewards for party loyalty. Although Jackson had a formally appointed cabinet, he rarely consulted it as a group. Instead he consulted informally with another group of men who were his close friends. These men were known as Jackson's **"Kitchen Cabinet."** The kitchen cabinet members were really the idea men. Jackson asked for their ideas and also discussed his own ideas with them.

Jackson and the Indians

Jackson sought to involve the common man in government, and the new emphasis of his administration brought some attention to the needs of others. Active crusades to free the slaves and give women more rights were launched—although real changes were not to come for many years. The Indians, however, received nothing but mistreatment during the Jackson years and gained no benefit from Jacksonian Democracy.

Attitudes and Policies—Jackson's policies toward the Indians were harsh, but they reflected the thinking of many people in that era. They did not see Indians as real people, as individuals. They did not understand Indians because the Indians did not live or think as they did. White men wanted the Indians to become civilized and to live as the white man did. They also believed that because they had purchased Indian lands through treaties, the Indians should leave and let them use what was now the white man's private property.

The Indians, on the other hand, believed that most white men were greedy, always wanting more goods, money, and land. The Indians did not own land as private property in the sense that the white man did, and they often did not understand that they were giving up all rights to the land by signing treaties. Because some whites had victimized the Indians and lied to them in the past, many Indians resisted any further advance by the white man. The mistreatment of the Indians by some encouraged many of the Indians to react with hostility. Unfortunately, the misunderstandings between white men and Indians led to many confrontations as the frontier was settled.

Jackson believed that the Indians were "subjects of the United States, inhabiting its territory and acknowledging its sovereignty." Yet almost one hundred treaties were signed with Indians under Jackson. These actions clearly showed that the United States treated the Indian tribes as foreign nations. As a result the Indians had an uncertain status within the United States.

Trouble in Georgia—In 1827 the Creeks ceded their lands in Georgia to the government, but the **Cherokees** refused to give up their lands. The Cherokees were highly civilized Indians. They had copied both the white man's political and agricultural systems. They wrote a constitution declaring that they were an independent nation. They did not want their lands to be taken by the United States, but in 1828 gold was discovered at Dahlonega, Georgia, bringing miners who coveted the Cherokee lands. The Georgia legislature then passed laws making any whites in Cherokee areas subject to Georgia's laws rather than Cherokee laws. They also made all Cherokee laws void after 1830.

In 1831 a white missionary, Samuel A. Worcester, was con-

victed for his refusal to take an oath of allegiance to the state of Georgia. He held that Georgia had no authority over Cherokee lands. The next year the Supreme Court agreed with him. Chief Justice John Marshall in *Worcester v. Georgia* ordered Georgia to release the missionary and told the president to send troops into Georgia to remove white men from Cherokee lands. Both Georgia and Jackson, assuming a states' rights position, ignored the court. Jackson said, "John Marshall has made his decision. Now let him enforce it." The Cherokees, under their elected chief, John Ross, held out, but by 1838 they were worn down from dealing with the government. Those that had not gone West to Indian Territory (now Oklahoma) were moved forcibly by the U.S. Army. Ironically it was the Cherokees who had taken Jackson's side and fought with him against other Indian tribes in the battle of Horseshoe Bend. Yet they received no help from Jackson as they tried to keep their own lands.

One of the greatest injustices to the Indian people was the forced march of the Cherokees to Oklahoma in what has been called the Trail of Tears.

Sequoyah: Cherokee Scholar

One Indian who made a name for himself in history is not known for fighting battles. Sequoyah earned such a reputation as a Cherokee scholar that the California redwoods were given his name. (The tree name, *sequoia,* is the Latin feminine form of his name.)

Sequoyah, whose father was a white man, was recognized among his Cherokee tribesmen as an excellent silversmith. His work excelled that of most of the silversmiths in the area, both white and Indian. A hunting accident left him crippled, but he did not waste his mental powers in feeling sorry for himself. Instead he decided to develop a Cherokee alphabet.

Despite opposition from some of his own people, Sequoyah completed the work, and it was an unqualified success. Using his alphabet, he taught many of the Cherokees, not only in the East but also in the Indian Territory, how to read. No doubt due partly to his teachings, the Cherokee became leaders among the Indian nations. Eventually they published a weekly newspaper in Oklahoma and even printed the Bible.

In his later years Sequoyah served as an envoy to Washington. He also studied the languages of other tribes and tried to come up with a single Indian language. In addition, he attempted to trace the history of his own people, the Cherokees. Sequoyah was a man with a host of discouraging circumstances surrounding him, who, nevertheless, used the gift he had—a ready mind—to accomplish great things.

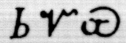

= si kwo yah

By the middle of the 1830s the best lands in the Mississippi Valley had been taken by the white men, and the Indians had been moved to supposedly permanent homes across the Great River, the Mississippi. In 1837 John Quincy Adams judged the Indian policy and found it wanting. "We have done more harm to the Indians since our Revolution than had ever been done to them by the French and English nations before. . . . These are," he said, "crying sins for which we are answerable before a higher jurisdiction."

The Black Hawk War—Although the Indians lacked the power to resist the advancement of the white settlers, they tried. One Indian who fought against the Americans was **Black Hawk,** an Indian leader among the Sauk and Fox tribes. Black Hawk had fought with the British in the War of 1812 and was a friend of Tecumseh. Forced off their land by a treaty with the United States, Black Hawk and his followers found themselves facing starvation. Consequently, in 1832 Black Hawk and about four hundred Indians returned to their lands to try to find food. The settlers in the area panicked and viewed the return as an act of war. The army was called out, and a force of militiamen organized to battle Black Hawk's band.

After battling with those who assembled against him, Black Hawk fled with his band to the swamps of Wisconsin. The army and the militia pursued. Trapped once at the battle of Wisconsin Heights, Black Hawk retreated across a river to safety. Finally, the militia cornered him again and attacked. Almost all of his followers were killed at the Bad Axe Massacre. Black Hawk escaped but surrendered himself to a band of Winnebago Indians who turned him over to the authorities.

SECTION REVIEW

1. What was the spoils system?
2. What name was given to Jackson's informal group of advisors?
3. What was the view of many whites toward Indians?
4. How did Indians typically view whites?
5. What Indian leader lost most of his followers at the Bad Axe Massacre?

 What factors contributed to making Andrew Jackson a symbol of his age?

The Nullification Controversy

One of the most important issues that arose during the Jackson presidency concerned the states and their rights in relation to the power of the federal government. This **states' rights** issue sprang to the forefront as Congress considered the imposition of tariffs.

Tariff Troubles

The idea of a tariff, a tax on goods coming into the country, was not new. Congress had passed a **revenue tariff**—a tariff designed to raise money—during Washington's administration. But by Jackson's time, different sections of the country sharply disagreed on the value of tariffs.

Reasons for Tariffs—One reason for this disagreement stemmed from the fact that the purpose of tariffs had changed. Initially, tariffs were used simply to raise money. Later they were also used to limit the importation of foreign goods. The latter type of tariff, called a **protective tariff,** protected businesses and manufacturers from foreign competition, but it also raised the price of foreign goods.

American industries had developed rapidly in the years just before the War of 1812. The Embargo Act of 1807 and other acts that limited trade from Europe had forced people to buy American goods. Then the British blockades during the War of 1812 required Americans to build their own factories to make needed products. Most of these factories were in New England or in the Middle Atlantic States of New York, Pennsylvania, and New Jersey. These areas had ample waterpower and capital (money) available for investment. They also had plenty of manpower to work in the factories. The South, on the other hand, attracted few factories since much of its money was tied up in slaves and cotton. Also, few immigrants went to the South because slaves provided much of the labor.

The Tariff

Cost of British hat before tariff: $3.00

Cost of British hat with 8% revenue tariff: $3.24

Cost of British hat with 28% protective tariff: $3.84

Cost of American hat: $3.50

Effects of revenue tariff: Revenue tariffs add money to the federal treasury. Since the British hat maker can still undersell his American competitor, he will bring his hats to America. The government will make money. The American hat maker, however, is in trouble. He can't compete unless he becomes smarter and uses more efficient methods or new technology so that he can sell his product for a lower price.

Advantage: British manufacturer and federal treasury

Effects of protective tariff: Now the British manufacturer cannot compete. He will probably quit sending hats to America. The American hat maker will have the market to himself. But the federal treasury will not collect as much money. The American manufacturer may also become more complacent, less competitive, and not as open to improvements.

Advantage: American manufacturer

Despite rapid industrial growth in the North, most new American industries—often called infant industries—wanted protection from foreign competition. They wanted a protective tariff.

The Tariff of Abominations—In 1816 Congress responded to the demands of protectionists and levied a higher tariff. In 1824 the tariff was revised upward and more products were put on the tariff list. Four years later in 1828 the tariff was raised again. Some Americans had objected to the earlier tariffs, but the 1828 tariff drew wide protest. Most of the protests came from areas and states that had little industry. They believed this "tariff of abominations" raised the price on almost everything they bought or manufactured.

Because the South had remained agricultural, it needed to buy most of its manufactured goods either from the North or from foreign countries. The Southerners depended on the profits they made from their crops to pay for those goods. Because the high tariff forced the South to buy American-made products, it increased their costs and decreased their trade with foreign countries. Selling cotton became more difficult as the trade decreased, and cotton prices fell. In addition, increased competition from new cotton states in the Southwest complicated the problem. In hopes of selling more cotton, Southerners were farming more acres. This meant they needed more slaves—and slave prices went up steadily. Thus, while the price for cotton fell, production costs rose. Southern planters began to blame their troubles on the high tariff.

John C. Calhoun, Defender of States' Rights

These economic troubles, along with worry over the slavery questions, increased political tensions. The troubles also brought a stronger defense of states' rights.

South Carolina's John C. Calhoun, Jackson's vice president, became the leading defender of the idea of states' rights. The South Carolina legislature had formed a committee to study the tariff problem and had asked Calhoun to write the final report. The report said that the people of South Carolina—or anyone else in the minority—could protect themselves from tariffs or any other laws that might hurt them by nullifying them. According to this theory of nullification, a state could declare a federal law harmful and thus unconstitutional and not enforceable in the state. Calhoun thought that nullification would satisfy the South by allowing it to protect itself from the ever-growing North while not limiting his appeal in the North and West. He hoped that this would help him gain the presidency after Jackson and protect the outnumbered Southerners. (Remember that nullification had been proposed earlier by Thomas Jefferson in the Virginia and Kentucky Resolutions, p. 188.)

Webster vs. Hayne

When Jackson did not pursue tariff reform, the South decided to seek it by bargaining with the West. They pushed the West to support a lower tariff in return for southern support of a free land policy. (Westerners wanted more western lands opened to settlement without cost, but Northerners opposed the idea because they feared that their workers would move away to the free lands.) In the Senate debate that followed, Calhoun's doctrine of nullification came under attack.

In an 1830 speech, South Carolina Senator **Robert Y. Hayne** defended nullification and state sovereignty. Hayne noted that the states had voluntarily joined the union and that the Constitution protected their authority by granting them their reserved powers. Hayne argued that the Constitution did not give the national government the power to pass laws hurting one group of people while helping another. Since such laws violated the Constitution, the state had the right to nullify and refuse to obey them.

Senator **Daniel Webster** of Massachusetts attacked nullification point by point, carefully defending the Constitution and the federal union. Webster argued that the people, rather than the states, had established the Union, making the Constitution and the Union superior to state governments. He said that nullification would lead to the end of the Union. Webster argued that if anyone believed that a law was unconstitutional, he should take his case to the Supreme Court. But a state, he said, did not have the right to disobey federal law. He closed his speech pleading, "Liberty and Union, now and forever, one and inseparable!"

Daniel Webster was one of America's greatest statesmen.

Calhoun and Jackson Clash

Jackson had not taken sides. He had a deep respect for states' rights and believed the South was justified in its complaint about the tariff. But to Jackson, nullification was out of the question.

On April 13, 1830, the Democrats gathered for a dinner in honor of the birthday of their party's founder, Thomas Jefferson. A series of toasts—speeches in honor of someone—was a regular part of such gatherings. When the president rose to make his toast, he looked squarely at John C. Calhoun and in a clear voice said only, "Our Federal Union: it must and shall be preserved!" After all had sat back down, John C. Calhoun responded, "The Union! Next to our liberty most dear!"

This incident was but one of many in a growing rift that eventually led John C. Calhoun to resign the vice-presidency. Calhoun then went to the Senate, where he led the fight for states' rights.

A Time of Crisis

The issue of states' rights simmered dangerously for another two years until it boiled over in 1832. Congress passed a new tariff. The tariff of 1832 gained some support in the South and West because it was a bit lower than the 1828 tariff. But it retained high tariffs on textiles and iron. Nullifiers saw that Congress was still protariff; therefore, they felt the tariff of 1832 was a direct challenge. When Jackson signed the tariff, they believed all hope was gone.

South Carolina legislators called a state convention late in November and declared both the tariff of 1828 and 1832 "null, void, and no law, nor binding upon the State; its officers or citizens." Their Ordinance of Nullification forbade state and federal officers from collecting tariffs after February 1, 1833. If there was any federal attempt to use force in South Carolina, the state would

Andrew Jackson, toward the end of his life

issue an order of **secession**—it would leave the Union.

Jackson met the crisis head on. He sent a warship and a revenue cutter (a federal boat that collected tariffs in ports) to Charleston, said he would personally take the field if it came to an armed clash, and threatened to hang John C. Calhoun. In December 1832 he told the people of South Carolina that he understood their plight but that nullifying a federal law defied both the spirit and letter of the Constitution. He also told them that they could not leave the Union. "The dictates of a high duty oblige me solemnly to announce that you cannot secede. The laws of the United States must be executed. . . . My duty is emphatically pronounced in the Constitution."

Congress supported Jackson by passing a Force Bill allowing the president to use the army and navy to enforce the laws. Meanwhile, South Carolina looked for allies. The state called a national convention to support nullification. To its surprise, not one state responded.

The Compromise of 1833

Henry Clay, who always seemed to find a compromise that would settle disputes, believed South Carolina might want a way of escape. He also knew Jackson wanted to avoid violence. Clay talked with Calhoun and worked out the details for a compromise tariff. This tariff lowered duties gradually. By 1842 no tariff was to be over twenty percent. This plan gave the infant industries in the North time to grow stronger before they lost their protection. Congress adopted this **Compromise of 1833** on March 1 of that year. Two weeks later South Carolina withdrew its nullification of the tariff. But it still held the Force Bill null and void. Jackson, however, ignored this action. Although Jackson and Clay had managed to keep the Union together, the question of states' rights remained unsettled. Many Southerners still believed they could leave the Union if they wanted to.

SECTION REVIEW

1. What are the two basic types of tariffs? What is the purpose of each?

2. What area of the country received the most benefit from tariffs? Why?

3. Who became the South's spokesman and leading defender of states' rights?

4. What senator attacked nullification, and what did he fear would happen to the Union if nullification were carried out?

5. How did President Jackson respond to the threat of secession by South Carolina?

 How did the Compromise of 1833 temporarily quiet the issue of nullification?

242

Jackson and the National Bank

The election of 1832 differed from the 1828 election. There was no mudslinging, and there was an issue—the future of the National Bank. The bank had been rechartered for twenty more years in 1816. Thus it would cease to exist after 1836 unless Congress renewed its charter and the president endorsed the action.

Banker Nicholas Biddle

Nicholas Biddle, a talented, wealthy Philadelphian, had handled the bank skillfully. Its twenty-nine branches regulated the nation's finances and had helped the country tremendously. It was powerful because it controlled one-fifth of all bank notes and one-third of bank deposits and coins. Since four-fifths of its stock was held by private parties, most of whom were rich Easterners, the bank was responsible to them. The bank did earn a profit. Biddle courted Jackson's favor by making loans to Jackson supporters and suggesting that the national debt be repaid on the anniversary of Jackson's victory at New Orleans.

Although such a goal was dear to Jackson's heart, Jackson was not won over. He made it known that he disliked banks—not just Biddle's but all banks. But Jackson vented his dislike only on the National Bank. Moreover, Jackson thought the bank unconstitutional. Although the Supreme Court had already upheld the bank, Jackson was not impressed. "I have read the opinion of John Marshall," he said, "and could not agree with him." Although Jackson's supporters pursued wealth and economic power as eagerly as Eastern merchant and factory owners, they made it sound as if the Easterners were interested only in special privilege and maintaining a monopoly.

Jackson also had the support of state bankers. He led them to believe that Biddle would destroy state banks by calling in their notes. Although Biddle had never used the bank's power to this end, he did hold this threat over them. The threat had forced the state banks to be more careful in their lending. In addition, New York bankers, whose wealth was growing from the Erie Canal trade, joined

This political cartoon shows the conflict between Biddle's banks and President Jackson.

The Bank of the United States in Philadelphia

the antibank group out of jealous resentment. If Biddle's bank was not rechartered, New Yorkers thought the business might be thrown their way.

The Election of 1832

Aware of the feelings of Jackson and others, Biddle could have played a waiting game. But in 1832 Henry Clay thought he saw a way to win the presidency for himself and save the National Bank at the same time by making the bank the central campaign issue. Although Biddle hesitated, Clay introduced the bill for the bank's recharter in 1832, four years ahead of its scheduled renewal. Congress passed the bill with strong support from Jackson's own party, but Jackson angrily vetoed it. More of the voters supported Jackson's view in the presidential election that year, and he won 219 electoral votes to Clay's 39. Congress did not override Jackson's decision.

Jackson and His "Pet Banks"

Jackson's veto meant that there would be no National Bank after 1836. But to Jackson that was not enough. He was now out to kill the bank and ruin his enemy Biddle. Jackson ordered the secretary of the treasury to quit depositing government money in Biddle's bank. Instead, the government revenues from taxes and land sales would go into newly opened accounts in eighty-nine different state banks. These soon became known as Jackson's **"pet banks."** Fearing an economic panic, the secretary refused to follow Jackson's orders, and Jackson fired him. Jackson then went through three secretaries before he found one willing to do his bidding. Since the law required current bills to be paid out of national bank deposits, the balance dropped $17 million in a year's time. Lacking funds, Biddle was forced to call in loans owed by state banks. Unfortunately, that recall caused hundreds of state banks to fail, and the savings of thousands of Americans were wiped out. What Jackson had feared would happen was now a reality—and the president was partly to blame for it.

Biddle soon responded to pressure from bankers and businessmen. Rather than calling money in, he lent it out in an effort to save more banks from failure. In the West this sudden influx of money led to a new problem: speculation in western lands. Money became freely available to almost anyone who wanted it.

Congress, with Jackson's approval, added to the instability of western banks. It passed a Distribution Bill providing state governments with $37 million to be spent for internal improvements. In response, with more money being spent in the states, more state banks were founded hoping to profit from such windfall spending. Between 1830 and 1837, the number of state banks increased from 330 to about 800.

The Specie Circular

The rising inflation alarmed Jackson—especially the great rise in prices for western lands. Since he would not use the bank to settle prices down, Jackson requested the Treasury Department to issue a **Specie Circular**. This act required anyone who bought government lands to pay for them in **specie** (gold or silver coins) rather than paper money.

The Circular did cut down on bank loans issued. But at the same time, it meant that borrowers, including speculators, could no longer pay back their debts. Soon people did not trust paper money at all. More banks failed, and more farmers lost their lands. With no money for people to spend and no banks to borrow from, businesses failed. The economic crisis grew worse. By the time Jackson's hand-picked successor took office, the nation was suffering from an economic depression that was to last five years.

SECTION REVIEW

1. In what political contest was the National Bank the major issue?

2. Who was the head of the National Bank?

3. How did Jackson view the bank?

4. Where did Jackson order federal monies to be placed?

5. Losing funds from the federal government forced the National Bank to do what?

 How did the Specie Circular affect the economy?

Effects of the Jackson Administration

Although Jackson left office in 1837, his strong imprint remained. He had greatly increased the powers of the executive branch. When challenged by advocates of states' rights on the tariff, he had staunchly defended the Union. But when Indian policy was the issue, he had favored the states and deprived the Indians of their lands. He claimed to follow the Constitution strictly yet refused to enforce Supreme Court decisions. He said he believed in free enterprise; yet he caused an economic panic by undermining a bank that was largely privately owned. He promised to return the government to that "simple machine which the Constitution created." But by cutting the government's role, he also created many problems for the national government to deal with in later years.

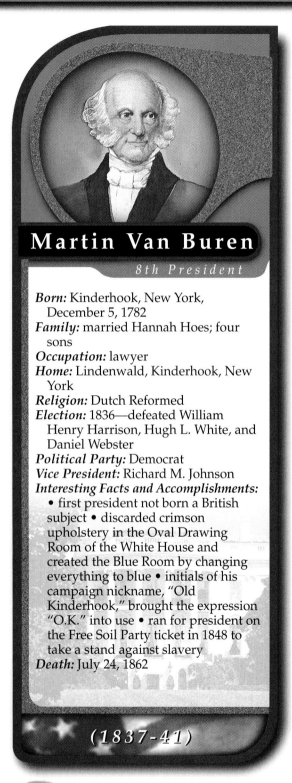

Martin Van Buren

8th President

Born: Kinderhook, New York, December 5, 1782
Family: married Hannah Hoes; four sons
Occupation: lawyer
Home: Lindenwald, Kinderhook, New York
Religion: Dutch Reformed
Election: 1836—defeated William Henry Harrison, Hugh L. White, and Daniel Webster
Political Party: Democrat
Vice President: Richard M. Johnson
Interesting Facts and Accomplishments:
• first president not born a British subject • discarded crimson upholstery in the Oval Drawing Room of the White House and created the Blue Room by changing everything to blue • initials of his campaign nickname, "Old Kinderhook," brought the expression "O.K." into use • ran for president on the Free Soil Party ticket in 1848 to take a stand against slavery
Death: July 24, 1862

(1837-41)

The Election of 1836

Martin Van Buren, who had served as Andrew Jackson's vice president since 1832, was Jackson's hand-picked choice for the Democratic candidacy in 1836. The new opposing party, the **Whigs,** was eager to restore the proper constitutional balance of power. They unified several diverse groups into one party, and the biggest element uniting the groups was opposition to Jackson. The Whigs wanted the national government to promote a strong economy by restoring the national bank and sponsoring a protective tariff as well as internal improvements.

Also, the ideals of Democrats and Whigs seemed to differ. The Democrats did not make as many statements as the Whigs about religion and morals. The Whigs applauded Sunday closing laws, and some wanted to outlaw alcohol. The Democrats held that such matters were more personal than they were public. The northern Whigs saw slavery as sinful. The Democrats said slavery was not the North's concern because Northerners could not solve the problem. As a result of the issues, evangelical Protestants tended to favor the Whigs. The hands-off approach of Democrats attracted more Catholics, Episcopalians, and free thinkers. Since many of the newer immigrants, especially the Irish, were Catholic, they joined with the Jacksonian Democrats, giving Democrats an added advantage in upcoming elections.

The Whig strategy was to try to throw the election into the House by running strong sectional candidates. In Tennessee they ran Hugh L. White, who had broken with Jackson. In the mid-Atlantic and western states, General William Henry Harrison carried the Whig banner. In Massachusetts Daniel Webster was the choice. The Whig strategy backfired. Fifty-one percent of the popular vote went to Van Buren, and his margin of victory in the electoral college was comfortable.

The Van Buren Years

Van Buren was the first president not to have been born a British subject. His family was Dutch and never gained prominence in society. Denied the education acquired by other national politicians, he mastered the practical: he learned how to unite men, motives, and issues into a plan of action. Although not always right, Van Buren learned from his mistakes. He was a masterful politician who retained personal principles.

The first problem that Van Buren faced was an economic depression that began in 1837. British trade and investments dropped off sharply. Cotton prices went down to six cents a pound from an earlier high of fifteen cents. With no money, the canal and road building stopped, throwing thousands of men out of work. Van Buren called Congress into special session to deal with the crisis. He suggested that government end all contact with banks, both central and pet banks. "The less government interferes with private pursuits, the better for the general prosperity," he said. In Massachusetts and Pennsylvania, state legislatures took over the building of roads and canals. But nine other states **defaulted** (did not repay the money they owed) on their bonds.

Van Buren proposed an **independent treasury** system that would consist of a number of separate federal vaults and depositories. The treasury could collect and spend from these subtreasuries without using any banks. Gold and silver would be the medium for all federal business. Congress adopted Van Buren's plan in 1840.

Chief Justice John Marshall had died in 1835, allowing Jackson to appoint **Roger B. Taney** (TAW nee) to his position. Jackson had appointed four new associate justices in his term as well. Van Buren was also able to appoint two justices when vacancies occurred in 1837. With all these new appointments,

Taney now had control of a new court. Whigs were panic-stricken. They feared that the Democratic court would reverse all Marshall's nationalist decisions. As it turned out, Marshall's decisions stood, and few dramatic changes occurred, but the court did move to protect states' rights in business, banking, and commerce. The court's greatest impact came in the late 1850s when it moved strongly for states' rights as the Civil War approached.

William Henry Harrison

When the election of 1840 came, Van Buren was again the Democratic choice. Convinced that Clay would not attract Eastern voters, the Whigs turned to William Henry Harrison, a man not closely identified with either party. Harrison, however, was a Southerner by birth and could attract Democratic votes in the South. He was a military hero too, known for his victory at Tippecanoe and his efforts in the War of 1812. Since his political views were not known, they could not hurt him. A careless comment by a Democrat—that if Harrison were given a log cabin and a barrel of hard cider, he would retire on a pension—played directly into Whig hands. They soon pictured Harrison, who was really wealthy, as a simple man of common tastes, and they labeled Van Buren as a snobbish aristocrat.

The Whigs campaigned with gusto. Dressed as Indians, they played up "Tippecanoe's" victory over Tecumseh. They served gallons of cider to voters and put on parades complete with bands, banners, and flags. Voter turnout increased sixty percent over 1836. This, when added to his war fame, helped Harrison and his running mate, **John Tyler,** to win nineteen of the twenty-six states and fifty-three percent of the popular vote. With campaign slogans such as "Tippecanoe and Tyler Too!" "Van, Van, Van is a used-up man!" and

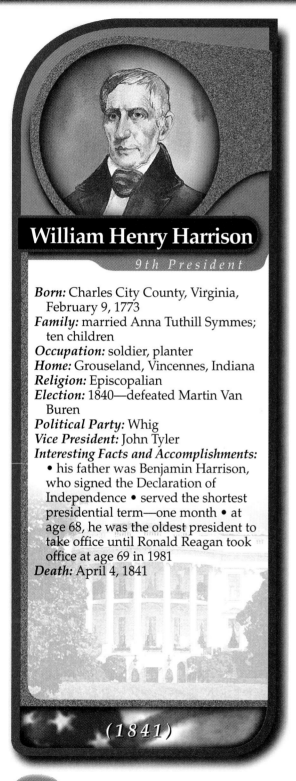

William Henry Harrison

9th President

Born: Charles City County, Virginia, February 9, 1773
Family: married Anna Tuthill Symmes; ten children
Occupation: soldier, planter
Home: Grouseland, Vincennes, Indiana
Religion: Episcopalian
Election: 1840—defeated Martin Van Buren
Political Party: Whig
Vice President: John Tyler
Interesting Facts and Accomplishments:
• his father was Benjamin Harrison, who signed the Declaration of Independence • served the shortest presidential term—one month • at age 68, he was the oldest president to take office until Ronald Reagan took office at age 69 in 1981
Death: April 4, 1841

(1841)

"To guide the ship, we'll try old Tip!" the Whig ticket put Van Buren out of office.

No sooner had the sixty-eight year-old Harrison taken office than disaster struck. While making the longest inaugural address in the nation's history (an hour and forty minutes), Harrison caught cold. Before Congress could even convene, Harrison's cold turned into pneumonia. Just four weeks after he took office, he died, the first president to do so while in office.

Tyler Too

John Tyler, the first vice president to reach office through the death of a president, was a Virginian. He was a Whig because he disagreed with Jackson on nullification and the removal of bank deposits. Clay told Tyler that since he had not really been elected as president, Tyler should let a congressional committee of Whigs make crucial decisions. Clay, of course, intended to head the committee. Tyler, however, had a mind of his own, and he knew what the Constitution said. He was unquestionably the rightful president.

Man Without a Party—The Whig program went before Congress with Henry Clay in charge. It abolished the independent treasury system. Clay also pushed through a new land act. The Preemption Act of 1841 allowed **squatters**—settlers on western lands without titles to the land—to buy those lands when they came up for public sale. Moreover, the act allowed them to buy the land at a low price—$1.25 an acre for a minimum of 160 acres. This "log cabin" bill also said that monies from the sale of lands could be distributed to the states as long as the tariff stayed under 20 percent. This would help the states out of debt. Tyler had little say over this program.

When the national debt increased, Tyler was forced to sign a bill to raise the tariff back to its 1832 level. Clay then submitted a bill establishing a new national bank. Tyler vetoed it, holding it to be unconstitutional and of greater benefit to the Northeast than to the rest of the nation. The Whigs, who were already calling Tyler "his accidency" because of how he had gained office, now turned on the president and expelled him from the party. All the Whigs in Tyler's cabinet resigned except Daniel Webster. Tyler became "a man without a party."

The Webster-Ashburton Treaty—In foreign affairs the Tyler administration faced problems with Britain, primarily as a result of the vaguely drawn northeastern border with Canada. Daniel Webster and Lord Ashburton, the British minister, met to resolve matters. The resulting treaty, the **Webster-Ashburton Treaty** of 1842, was a compromise. The United States gave a portion of Maine to Canada. The United States gained additional land in northern New York and Vermont as well as lands on Lake Superior in northeastern Minnesota. The undefined portion of the boundary line between the United States and Canada was drawn from Lake of the Woods east to the Atlantic. As soon as the Senate had ratified the treaty, Webster resigned, joining the other Whig leaders in their protest against President Tyler.

The End of Tyler's Term—When Tyler's cabinet resigned, he created a power base of his own by placing southern Whigs in the vacant cabinet seats. Tyler worked to add Texas to the Union partly because he believed Texas would aid his reelection. His early efforts failed. Texas remained outside the Union, and **James K. Polk** won the election of 1844. In the time that remained between the election and his leaving office, Tyler kept pushing his ideas. (A president during the time between election and leaving office is called a **lame duck** because he does not have as much support and political power as the president-elect, who has just won the election.)

John Tyler

10th President

Born: Charles City County, Virginia, March 29, 1790
Family: married Letitia Christian and, after her death, Julia Gardiner; fifteen children
Occupation: lawyer
Home: Sherwood Forest, Charles City County, Virginia
Religion: Episcopalian
Election: 1840—as vice president, succeeded to the presidency upon the death of Harrison
Political Party: Whig
Vice President: none
Interesting Facts and Accomplishments:
• almost killed in two accidents while he was president—when a cannon exploded on a ship, and when a horse ran wild at the funeral for those who were killed in the previous accident • first wife died in 1842; became the first president to marry while in office when he married his second wife • had the most children of any president—fifteen • was elected to the Confederate Congress, but died before he could take office
Death: January 14, 1862

(1841-45)

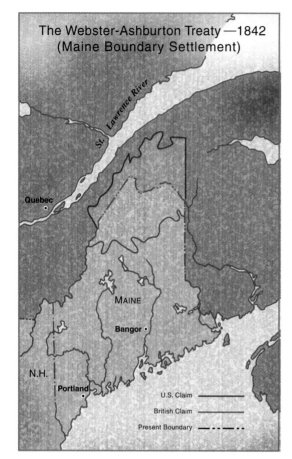

The Webster-Ashburton Treaty —1842
(Maine Boundary Settlement)

St. Lawrence River

Quebec

MAINE

Bangor

N.H.

Portland

U.S. Claim ——————
British Claim ——————
Present Boundary —— ·· —— ··

When the Senate refused to ratify a treaty by the required two-thirds vote to annex Texas, Tyler proposed Texas be admitted by a joint resolution. The resolution, requiring only a simple majority vote, passed.

Harrison had been elected in 1840 because of the popular opinion against Jackson's policies and those of Van Buren, his successor. By the end of Tyler's administration, however, many Americans were clamoring for another strong leader like Jackson.

SECTION REVIEW

1. What was the Whig strategy in the election of 1836?

2. What did Van Buren substitute for the regular banking system?

3. How did John Tyler become the president?

4. How did members of the Whig party treat President Tyler?

5. The Webster-Ashburton Treaty of 1842 settled what vaguely-drawn American border?

 How did Whigs and Democrats differ on the proper role of government in matters of religion and morality?

SUMMARY

As the first "log cabin" president, Andrew Jackson did much to change the influences on the national government. The "common man," especially the poor western farmer, gained as great a voice in government as that of the eastern industrialist or the southern planter. Jackson's policies helped to open land for the farmers and to create business opportunities for those outside of the industrial Northeast. Although he was committed to the preservation of the Union, some of his actions were rash and harmful to the country. Financial problems resulted in the Van Buren administration that followed, and other presidents faced the growing sectional and political differences without the help of permanent solutions.

Chapter Review

People, Places, and Things to Remember

spoils system	Daniel Webster	defaulted
political machines	secession	independent treasury
Kitchen Cabinet	Compromise of 1833	Roger B. Taney
Cherokees	Nicholas Biddle	John Tyler
Black Hawk	pet banks	squatters
states' rights	Specie Circular	Webster-Ashburton Treaty
revenue tariff	specie	James K. Polk
protective tariff	Martin Van Buren	lame duck
Robert Y. Hayne	Whigs	

Review Questions

Match each of the following items or descriptions with the man or men with whom they are most closely related. Answers may be used more than once, and questions may have more than one answer.

1. helped make the Compromise of 1833
2. most prominent defender of states' rights
3. had "pet banks"
4. first president to die while in office
5. participated in a debate over nullification
6. helped make a treaty with Britain
7. Bad Axe Massacre
8. Chief Justice
9. National Bank president
10. vice president under Jackson
11. became a hero as a soldier
12. formed a "Kitchen Cabinet"
13. first Whig president
14. wanted to form an independent treasury
15. first vice president to become president at the death of his predecessor

a. Andrew Jackson
b. Black Hawk
c. Robert Y. Hayne
d. Daniel Webster
e. John C. Calhoun
f. Henry Clay
g. Nicholas Biddle
h. Martin Van Buren
i. William Henry Harrison
j. Roger B. Taney
k. John Tyler
l. James K. Polk

Questions for Discussion

16. Do you think the hostilities between the Indians and the white man could have been avoided? Explain your answer.
17. Is states' rights an issue in government today? Why or why not?

The march of invention has clothed mankind with powers of which a century ago the boldest imagination could not have dreamt.
— Henry George

The twentieth century has been a century of change. Technology that we often take for granted today has made busy lives far easier, but the technology of today had roots in innovations of the past.

From Telegraph to Satellite

The Telegraph

After Samuel Morse's successful exhibit of the telegraph in 1837, businesses, news agencies, and even the government began thinking of connecting Europe and North America by cable. Although Morse successfully laid a submarine cable across New York Harbor in 1842, laying a cable across the Atlantic would be much more difficult.

Cyrus Fields, a retired paper merchant with little knowledge of the telegraph, directed the project. He raised money and made the first transatlantic cable attempt in 1857. Two American and two British ships met near Ireland, where the cable line would begin. The 2,500 tons of cable was divided between the two lead boats. After a promising start the cable snapped, costing the project half a million dollars.

The next summer Fields made another, seemingly successful, attempt. Celebrations began on both continents. People believed the telegraph would improve communication and even bring world peace. Queen Victoria sent President Buchanan a short message. To everyone's disappointment, the transmission went dead soon after. A sensitive waterproofing substance used on the cable had failed.

Fields was unable to try again until 1865 at the close of the Civil War. This time the cable broke again and could not be retrieved. Undaunted, Fields tried again the next year. The cable held, and transmission was successful. Still dissatisfied, he located the cable lost the previous year, pulled it up, and spliced it to a new cable. Fields returned to Newfoundland with two transatlantic cables in service.

The Satellite

Almost one hundred years after the transatlantic cable was laid, the United States was again trying to send messages across the ocean, this time through the sky. With the development of more powerful rockets, scientists began to see the possibility of placing satellites in earth's orbit. Positioned correctly, the satellite could receive high-frequency microwaves and bounce them back to earth.

Americans were shocked when the Soviets successfully launched the first manmade satellite, *Sputnik,* on October 4, 1957. Many Americans feared that Soviet technology was far better than their own. American researchers worked tirelessly to launch their own successful satellite. The goal was achieved when *Explorer I* soared into orbit on January 31, 1958. Manmade satellites were a reality but were not yet tools of communication.

A few years later the United States launched *Echo I,* which made the first telephone and television transmissions using radio waves. However, *Echo I* lacked an electronic transmitter to relay messages rapidly.

When *Telstar I* was launched by AT&T in 1962, it carried a microwave receiver and transmitter. With these features it successfully transmitted live television programs and telephone conversations. Unfortunately, *Telstar I* was damaged from the fallout of a high altitude atomic bomb test. However, before transmission ended, *Telstar* relayed live messages across the Atlantic. A new age had begun.

From Elevators to Skyscrapers

The Safety Elevator

Since ancient times people have been using elevators. The Greek mathematician Archimedes invented a simple one in 230 B.C. The Romans put a simple combination of ropes and pulleys to practical use lifting heavy construction materials. However, not until the twentieth century were people commonly passengers on elevators, and for good reason. The ropes used to lift early elevator cars often broke, sending the car on a quick trip down.

Using elevators to transport people depended on the invention of a safe elevator. An American inventor named Elisha G. Otis worked at this problem. He framed the elevator car with guide rails. If the rope holding the car broke, the loss of tension would cause clamps to snap out from the rails, catching the car.

Otis demonstrated his invention in 1853 in New York City. In dramatic fashion Otis stood on the elevator platform as the rope above his head was cut. The rope snapped, the crowd gasped, and Otis rested safely in the safety elevator.

In 1861 Otis died, not knowing just how important his invention would be. The safety elevator made tall buildings practical.

The Skyscraper

Before the safety elevator was designed, buildings were built only as high as people were willing to climb stairs. Otis's invention soon changed this. Higher buildings began to spring up in major cities throughout the United States.

By the 1920s and 1930s, buildings were towering over 1,000 feet and 100 floors. New York City's Chrysler Building (1929-30) reached 1,046 feet, and the Empire State Building reached 1,250 feet. In August of 1970 construction began on a new skyscraper in Chicago, Illinois.

Sears, Roebuck and Company commissioned Bruce Graham and Fazlur Khan to build what would be known as the Sears Tower. The architects began by laying the foundation in a hole one hundred feet deep. From the foundation a steel frame was built at a rate of two floors per week. The building is actually nine separate towers connected like a ticktacktoe board. Two of the towers end at the fiftieth floor, two at the sixtieth, three at the ninetieth, and the last two at the 110th floor. The tallest towers use the shorter ones for support.

The Sears Tower took about two and a half years to build. It includes 4.5 million square feet of office and commercial space. A total of 103 cab elevators and 24 freight elevators are inside. The two express elevators can reach the 1,353-foot skydeck in one minute.

When first built, the Sears Tower was meant to house the corporate headquarters of Sears. Since then the company has moved out for financial reasons and other companies have struggled to keep the tower occupied. Otis' elevator allowed man to reach higher floors, but it never guaranteed they would stay there.

Although Mr. Smith was able to successfully launch over 30 monkeys across Wood County, his idea never caught on as a popular means of tranportation.

Means of Transportation and Communication

ost of America's early settlements were located along the coast because water made transportation easy. Over the years, however, the nation acquired vast areas of new land. Explorers and traders told of the value of these western lands, and some Americans wanted to go settle there. They faced a serious problem, however. The distances were great, and there were no good roads to the West. Because of poor transportation and communication, people who left for the frontier knew that they might never see or hear from their friends and relatives in the East again.

Roads in the Early 1800s

Colonial America had few roads and most of those were in the East and few were no more than dirt paths or muddy ruts. Many of them were initially paths that animals and Indians had used to get to streams or clearings. Settlers later cut back the bushes and trees a few feet to widen the roads.

A few roads linked major cities. The Boston Post Road between Boston and New York was usually passable year-round. It took three days to travel the ninety miles between New York and Philadelphia in a covered

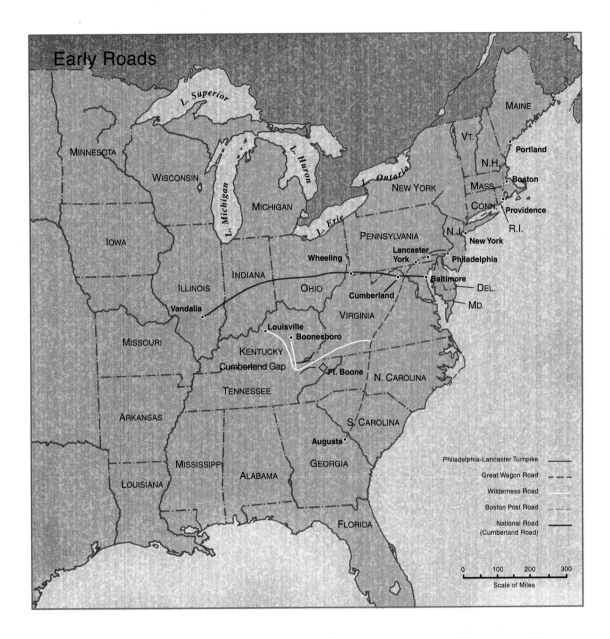

Early Roads

Philadelphia-Lancaster Turnpike	——
Great Wagon Road	– – –
Wilderness Road	——
Boston Post Road	– – –
National Road (Cumberland Road)	——

0   100   200   300

Scale of Miles

wagon. By 1766 "flying machines"—stage-coaches—cut the time by a day (when the weather was good). Because the South had a fairly good water transportation system, few roads were built there.

New Roads Improve Transportation

Three major roads provided transportation routes for thousands of intrepid early Americans, their stock, and their products. These roads stretched into the frontier to help open new areas of settlement.

Transportation and Communication Timeline

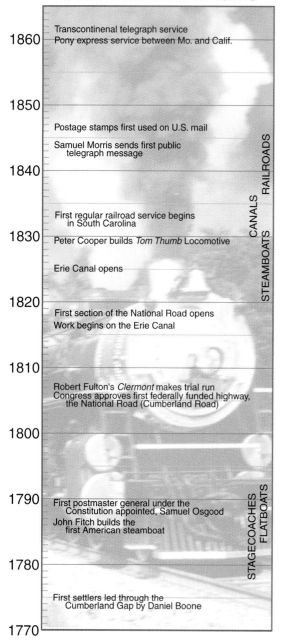

Year	Event	Mode

1860 — Transcontinenal telegraph service
Pony express service between Mo. and Calif.

1850

Postage stamps first used on U.S. mail

Samuel Morris sends first public
   telegraph message

1840

First regular railroad service begins
   in South Carolina

1830 — Peter Cooper builds *Tom Thumb* Locomotive

Erie Canal opens

1820

First section of the National Road opens
Work begins on the Erie Canal

1810

Robert Fulton's *Clermont* makes trial run
Congress approves first federally funded highway,
   the National Road (Cumberland Road)

1800

1790 — First postmaster general under the
   Constitution appointed, Samuel Osgood
John Fitch builds the
   first American steamboat

1780

First settlers led through the
   Cumberland Gap by Daniel Boone

1770

RAILROADS
CANALS
STEAMBOATS
STAGECOACHES
FLATBOATS

The Wilderness Road winds through the Cumberland Gap.

The Great Wagon Road—The Five Nations of the Iroquois, all eastern woodland tribes, had traveled through the Appalachian Mountains long before the white man. These Indians used a road called the Great Warrior's Path, which ran north and south along the western slope of the mountains. In 1744 the English took control of the Warrior's Path through a treaty. Freed of Indian dangers, hardy Germans and Scots-Irish farmers from Pennsylvania followed the road southward to settle less crowded lands. They went from Philadelphia to Lancaster and York. Then they crossed the Potomac to Virginia and eventually moved south across the Carolinas to Augusta, Georgia. Thousands of settlers used this route, which came to be known as the **Great Wagon Road.**

The Wilderness Road—In 1775 a land speculator, Richard Henderson, purchased twenty million acres of Kentucky and western Virginia from the Cherokee Indians for $44,500. Henderson summoned woodsman **Daniel Boone** to handle final details with the Indians and to cut a road into Kentucky. This road was a westward extension of the Great Wagon Road. Boone and his thirty axe men started in March 1775. Their route took them through the **Cumberland Gap,** a natural passage through the mountain barrier. Thomas Walker had discovered the gap in 1750. Their **Wilderness Road** finally reached Boonesboro in east central Kentucky—over two hundred miles from their starting point.

The National Road—Despite opposition to using government funds, Congress approved the first federally funded highway in 1806. Construction began in 1811 at Cumberland, Maryland. The first section of the road, reaching to Wheeling (now in West Virginia), was opened in August 1818. Because of the need for drainage, the road was raised with ten-foot shoulders and ditches sloping from each side. The twenty-foot roadbed was dug into the ground a foot deep on the sides and a foot and a half in the middle. All stones for the bottom layer were to be passed through a seven-inch ring while those for the surface had to go through a three-inch ring. The original **National Road,** or Cumberland Road as it was sometimes called, cost $1.7 million or about $13,000 a mile. Later the road extended westward to Vandalia, Illinois.

Road Construction: How Roads Were Built

By our standards the tools used for road building were primitive—carts, picks, shovels, and crude blasting tools. In 1831 a "sulky scraper," a simple horse-drawn board device, was used to scrape dirt from the ditch to the center of the road. In 1843 a horsedrawn roller system was introduced to pack road surfaces.

One type of road—a stone railroad— used stone slabs for wheel tracks and cobblestone in the center. From 1845 to 1855, plank roads became popular. Workers laid two parallel rows of stringers or log pieces; space between was covered with earth. The builders then nailed a plank floor eight to twelve feet wide to the stringers. This type of road was a great improvement and the smoothest surface available until blacktop and concrete were introduced. But the toll companies found that at $2,000 a mile the plank roads were expensive to build and maintain.

In other areas logs were laid side by side to form a rough road surface. These "corduroy roads" provided a bumpy ride, but they could be hastily constructed to help travelers avoid being stuck in mud holes. They were also used in swampy areas.

From England came the idea of macadamized roads of crushed stone placed in a pre-dug road bed. These roads multiplied when in 1858 an American, Eli Whitney Blake, invented a stone crusher operated by a belt from a steam engine.

Few of America's early roads were designed by engineers. Road building was considered nonprofessional and highly dangerous work. Engineers were called on only for bridge construction. Irish immigrants were often hired for the other jobs. Eager for work and used to poverty, these newcomers were willing to take the low-wage, high-risk jobs of building roads.

Turnpikes

Additional roads called **turnpikes** were built by private companies hoping to make a profit. Their name came from the sharp sticks guarding the entrances to the road. On payment of the toll or charge to use the road, the sticks were turned down into a grate. While up, the fence-like pikes kept animals from wandering onto the roads. The Philadelphia-Lancaster Pike, built of stone in 1792, was the nation's longest pike. Turnpikes became a business rage in the early 1800s. In Connecticut in the 1830s, fifty turnpike companies were incorporated. Pennsylvania ranked first in mileage; Maryland was second. Unfortunately, builders did not make the profits they had planned on, and some projects were phased out. Generally, individual states then inherited the responsibility of keeping up the roads.

SECTION REVIEW

1. Why had there been little inland settlement up to this time?

2. What three major roads provided routes to the frontier?

3. Who cut a westward extension of the road that led into Kentucky, and what natural passage through a mountain barrier did this road use to its advantage?

4. What was the first federally funded highway called?

5. Who built turnpikes? Why were they built?

 For what reasons did roads tend to develop where they did?

Water Transportation

While colonial America had built up a valuable coastal trade and sailing ships crossed the Atlantic and later the Gulf of Mexico to New Orleans, there had been little development of inland waterways.

Upstream Without a Paddle

The early river craft included canoes of all sizes, flatboats, keelboats, and barges. Moving downstream with these vessels was relatively easy because they could float with the current. Moving upstream, however, required extra effort. Paddling a canoe upstream was not too difficult, but paddles could not propel the larger craft against river currents. Winds would sometimes push boats with sails, but winds were unreliable. Some keelboats and barges could be poled upstream if the water was not too deep and the current not too strong. Animals along the shore could also tow boats upstream with a rope. Because of the difficulties and expenses involved, many boats never returned upstream. Instead they were dismantled and used for lumber or firewood.

Passenger and freight rates were high; it cost $160 in 1800 to take a flatboat down the Ohio and Mississippi Rivers from Pittsburgh to New Orleans. Freight shipments cost $6.75 per hundred pounds.

Steamboats Furnish a Vital Link

Steamboats, which could easily paddle upstream, quickly became a vital part of America's transportation system. Although early experiments with them took place on the Atlantic seaboard, the greatest possibility for their use came later on western inland waters. In the East they made the Hudson, Potomac, and Delaware Rivers busy waterways. Steamboats helped settlement along western rivers like the Ohio and the Mississippi. By 1839 tonnage on the western rivers was two times that of all Atlantic ports. Major cities—such as New Orleans, St. Louis, Cincinnati, and Pittsburgh—grew up along steamboat routes.

Steamboats made going west to settle much easier. Settlers within reach of steamboats no longer faced isolation. Letters, newspapers, and books, as well as manufactured goods, flowed west. Trade between the East and the West also became more profitable. The West was full of opportunities for the immigrants who were swelling eastern cities, and steamboats were ready to transport new settlers to those lands.

Robert Fulton is credited with building the first commercially successful steamboat in 1807. But as early as 1790 five other steamboat pioneers had built and operated steam-driven vessels. Very little attention was paid to their trial runs. Shore-bound spectators laughed at their efforts to race against currents. Probably the best known of this group of disappointed inventors is John Fitch.

John Fitch Experiments with Steamboats—John Fitch's life was problem-plagued from his early years. His father was a tyrant; his wife was a nag; and his great idea—for which he thought he should be remembered forever—was twenty years ahead of its time. Fitch had been a clock maker and a silver-

smith, but during an attack of rheumatism in his knee he had the idea to make a "steam carriage" to help him get around. However, he soon abandoned the steam carriage as impractical and drew a plan for a steamboat.

Fitch brought his idea to Philadelphia and asked prominent statesmen to finance the craft. But even Benjamin Franklin had doubts that Fitch's craft would work. Fitch did not give up. He met a watchmaker, Henry Voight, who had the mechanical knowledge that Fitch lacked. Their first boat wallowed in the Delaware River while boatmen laughed. His second craft was a partial success. It went three to four miles per hour against the current. Then he built the *Perseverance,* a seven-ton boat with twelve paddles. Fitch demonstrated it for some delegates to the Philadelphia Convention of 1787, but they were too skeptical to help.

In 1790 Fitch built a boat that could go eight miles an hour. By fall Fitch's boat had

Even early versions of the steamboat revolutionized transportation on the water.

Robert Fulton made the steamboat a success.

logged three thousand miles and had carried over a thousand passengers. Fitch claimed that he and Voight "reigned as Lord High Admirals of the Delaware, and no boat in the River could hold its way with [them]." But his boat could carry only seven passengers per trip because the engine took up so much space. Although the boat ride was more comfortable than being bounced in a stagecoach, it also took longer. Speed seemed more important to the public than comfort; the company lost money. Then the *Perseverance* was destroyed by a storm. In 1798 a dejected Fitch took an overdose of opium and ended his life.

Robert Fulton and his Clermont—About the same time Fitch was making trial runs on the Delaware, a young artist-turned-engineer named Robert Fulton entered the contest. He had just built a submarine, the *Nautilus,* which he thought the French Navy could use to blow up British vessels in the English Channel. In Paris Fulton met Robert Livingston, American minister to France. Fulton told Livingston of another idea he had—a steamboat. Livingston had the money, the right to navigate the Hudson, and the political clout to help Fulton's idea become a reality.

Fulton got his steam engine from England. Because the British did not want other countries to outdo them, they tried to keep any inventions from leaving the country. But Fulton was not to be denied. A suave diplomat, he convinced Boulton and Watt, the inventors of the engine, to sell him one for $2,600. Returning to America with it, he built a vessel, installed his engine, and named the vessel the *Clermont* after Livingston's home on the Hudson. On August 17, 1807, the boat made its first public trial. The lone newspaper to cover the event said the boat was "invented with view to the navigation of the Mississippi upward." The steamboat line paid off and paid well. Fulton and Livingston made $16,000 their first year. By 1825 steamship travel was so common that no one could even remember scoffing at it. Fulton became a national hero.

Canals

Although Europe had been building useful canals for years, America's great canal age began in 1817, with the construction of the Erie Canal, and lasted until about 1840. A **canal** is a shallow, manmade water highway that connects two bodies of water. Most canals were thirty-six to forty feet wide at the top, twenty-four to twenty-eight feet wide at the bottom, and four feet deep. Canals used a system of **locks** (water compartments that can be opened and shut) and dams to keep a constant water level. Most of the brightly colored canal boats and barges on the canals were privately owned. Their owners paid tolls to the construction companies to use the canals. The most famous canal, the **Erie Canal,** opened in 1825. It connected Albany, New York, on the Hudson River with Lake Erie. Boats could

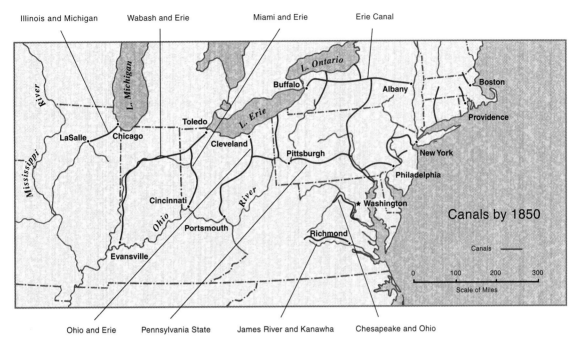

Illinois and Michigan   Wabash and Erie   Miami and Erie   Erie Canal

Canals by 1850

Canals ——

0   100   200   300

Scale of Miles

Ohio and Erie   Pennsylvania State   James River and Kanawha   Chesapeake and Ohio

enter the Hudson River at New York City and sail to Albany to reach the canal. This made water transportation possible between the Atlantic Ocean and the Great Lakes.

Other states, quick to follow New York's example, built their own canals to compete. In Ohio, the Ohio and Erie Canal linked the Ohio River to Lake Erie. The Miami and Erie Canal connected the Miami and Ohio Rivers with Lake Erie. Indiana's Wabash and Erie Canal tied Indiana to the trade system. The Chesapeake and Ohio brought trade to Washington, D.C., and the James River and Kanawha Canal linked Richmond to interior Virginia.

When the Illinois and Michigan Canal, connecting Chicago on Lake Michigan and LaSalle on the Illinois River, was completed in 1848, a system of water travel was complete that made it possible to travel by inland waterway from New York City to New Orleans. Farmers in the Mississippi Valley could now market their livestock and grain in the East.

They, as well as railroad builders, could get from the Northeast the lumber they needed to build on treeless western prairies.

Not all the canals that were built turned out to be so useful. Pennsylvania's canal system was much harder to build than those in flat areas. Because the terrain was much hillier, a horse-drawn railroad was used to carry loads over the highest points between canals. Although ingenious, the Penn State Canal proved both costly and impractical.

At its height in the 1840s, the canal craze produced a water highway network of 3,326 miles. But because canals were expensive to build and to keep up and because they were closed in the winter due to freezes, the canal era soon drew to a close. The greatest problem for canals, however, was competition from the new railroads. Nevertheless, for a time the canals reduced freight rates, opened new areas to settlement, and helped America to expand its activities. A few continued to give useful service.

The Big Ditch

"You must have heard of it," wrote Herman Melville, referring to the Erie Canal in 1851 in *Moby Dick.* The Erie Canal became so famous that most foreign tourists wanted to see it. Called "the eighth wonder of the world," the Erie Canal became the perfect example of Yankee ingenuity.

The drive to build a state-financed canal linking New York City with the Great Lakes was led by Governor DeWitt Clinton. He believed that a canal would make New York the nation's leading port by diverting traffic from a then more prosperous New Orleans. The water connection would also give New York City an edge over Philadelphia and Baltimore in the race for western trade.

The 363-mile-long Erie Canal connected Albany on the Hudson River with Lake Erie and cost $7 million to build. The finished canal had a series of eighty-three lift locks and eighteen aqueducts. Locks were used to raise and lower the water level. Each lock was just long enough to hold a canal boat. Giant gates at both ends of the lock opened and closed to let the water in or out. When a canal boat entered a lock on the lower end of an upward slope, gates closed behind it. Water poured into the lock from the canal above until the boat floated at a higher level, a level even with that part of the canal. The canal gates at the far end then opened and the boat continued upstream. When boats came from the opposite direction, the locks were gradually drained to lower the levels.

SECTION REVIEW

1. How were river vessels propelled upstream before the steamboat?

2. Where did steamboats prove to be most valuable in their use?

3. Who built the first commercially successful steamboat?

4. What canal became most famous, and what two points did it join?

5. For what two reasons was the canal era short-lived?

 Why was John Fitch never a financial success?

Railroads

Steam engines that could run on tracks were in use in Britain shortly after 1800. The first American locomotive on a railroad track was one built in 1825 by John Stevens in Hoboken, New Jersey. Another locomotive was used briefly by a Pennsylvania canal company in 1829, but the first major trial of a railroad was that made by **Peter Cooper** in 1830.

Railroad developments such as the iron rail, the flanged or rimmed wheel, and the steam locomotive helped Cooper's invention to be a success. In the next twenty years railroads added a new dimension to American travel. The railroad was a faster and cheaper

The canal was the brainchild of three men, James Geddes, Benjamin Wright, and Charles Broadhead, all self-made engineers. The canal became their school of practical civil engineering. They had to dig their canal through all types of terrain: mosquito-infested marshes, river valleys, and rock walls. Sometimes solid rock had to be blasted away with gunpowder.

Travel along the canal was slow. Speeds ranged from one and a half to three miles per hour. Mules or horses walking on narrow tow paths beside the canal dragged the freight barges or passenger canal boats. If a boat did not offer sleeping quarters or food, the charge for a passenger was only one cent per mile—far less than the fares for stagecoaches, which ran as high as ten cents a mile. Larger packet boats with bunks and food charged only five cents a mile.

The canal's completion on October 25, 1825, was marked by huge celebrations. The Erie Canal paid for itself through tolls within seven years, and the cost of shipping a ton of freight dropped by ninety-five percent from one hundred dollars a ton to about five dollars. New York City, where boats bound for the canal entered the Hudson River, soon became the nation's busiest port and most prosperous city.

type of transportation than the canal. Moreover, railroads were not much affected by weather. Winter ice, spring floods, and summer drought did not keep railroads from operating as they did canals. Since railroads were not dependent on water, they could go into areas where canal construction would have been impractical.

The first regularly scheduled service in the United States began in 1831. It was the largest railroad in the world at the time—136 miles—and it ran from Charleston to Hamburg, South Carolina. The railroad's locomotive, called *Best Friend,* was the first to pull a train of cars in regular service, and although it was successful, the South was slow to build more track. Ten years later there was no new track in South Carolina, and by 1850, track miles had only doubled.

Northeasterners were quick to see the potential value of railroads for moving their manufactured goods and raw materials. In the New England states the 1840s brought a five-fold increase in railroads. Also, better technology made the locomotives safer and more powerful. "Railroad fever" swept the nation. Many railroads were financed by private investors, who bought stocks and bonds from railroad companies. State governments and local communities also furnished money, and the federal government underwrote some of the costs with land grants.

More than two-thirds of the total mileage was in the North and West. This tended to unite the economic interests of those regions, a factor that would be of great importance when the nation was later torn by the Civil War.

SECTION REVIEW

1. What four advantages did railroads have over other forms of transportation?

2. When did regular rail service begin?

 What sections of the country built the most railroads, and why?

Communications

In early colonial times news generally spread by word of mouth. Colonists often gathered in local businesses to hear the latest news brought by travelers. Sometimes special messengers were sent to take important news to someone, but that type of communication was reserved mostly for the wealthy.

Postal Service

Ships arriving at a port in America might carry written messages from people in Europe

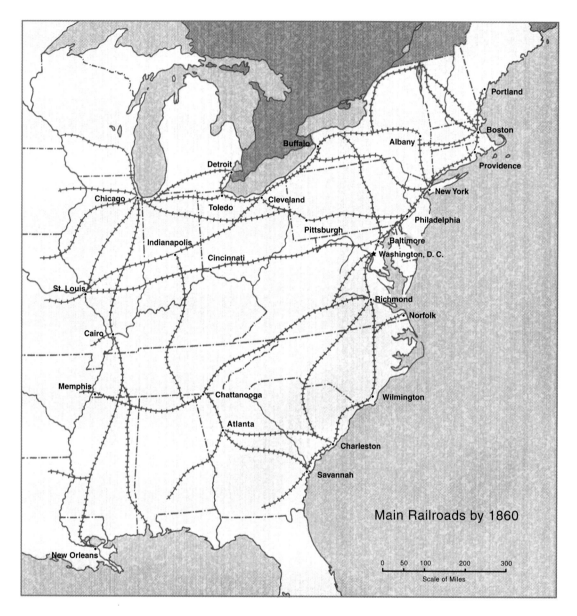

Main Railroads by 1860

0 50 100   200   300
Scale of Miles

or other American ports. These letters might be delivered by friends and neighbors, but there was no real postal service. Then in 1639 Massachusetts Bay Colony gave Richard Fairbanks permission to use his home in Boston as a post office. Mail for people in the area would be brought from the ships to his house for distribution, and people could leave letters with him to be sent by ship to other places. Similar situations developed in other colonial areas, but service was irregular and unreliable. The king authorized a colonial postal system in 1692, but the colonists disliked it. A high postage rate was charged, and letters could be opened if the authorities wished to check for disloyalty to the king.

Benjamin Franklin became the first postmaster general of the United States, serving under the Continental Congress. He helped organize a working postal service for the new nation. The Continental Congress helped make this service more useful to Americans by prohibiting postal authorities from opening or delaying private letters. Some roads were built or improved as "post roads," roads necessary for the delivery of the mail.

When the government was organized under the Constitution in 1789, Samuel Osgood became the postmaster general. The young country had fewer than seventy-five post offices at that time, but the postal system grew. Ships, stagecoaches, and later railroad trains carried the mail from place to place. As settlement spread westward, the service expanded with it.

Perhaps the most exciting activity for the nation's postal service was the operation of the **pony express.** Beginning on April 3, 1860, riders carried mail on horseback from St. Joseph, Missouri, to Sacramento, California. The trip took eight to ten days as young riders rode about seventy-five miles before turning the mail over to another rider. They changed horses at relay stations every ten to fifteen miles along the route. Although the pony express was successful, it ended on October 24, 1861, after only a year and a half of service.

The Little Engine That Couldn't

Peter Cooper, a New York glue maker and part-time inventor, thought he could build a steam locomotive—and he did. Cooper's engine, named the *Tom Thumb* because of its small size, was more often called "a tea kettle on a track" by passersby. Cooper himself ran the locomotive on its first round trip from Baltimore to Endicott, Maryland, and back. The train reached the unheard-of speed of eighteen miles per hour. Cooper's triumph, however, turned to shame on the return trip. A stagecoach company challenged the *Tom Thumb* to race the last eight miles back to Baltimore. The train gained the lead, but a pulley slipped off the train's drum, causing the engine to lose power. Cooper cut his hands trying to tug it back on, but the horse-drawn stagecoach won. The victory for the stagecoach was short-lived. Soon even presidents took the train; Andrew Jackson was the first in 1833.

Tom Thumb

Postal covers such as these allowed mail to be successfully transported across the country.

The reason for its end was the success of another system of communication—the telegraph.

The Telegraph

The telegraph was invented to meet a serious need that railroads had. Lack of communication presented a difficulty in running trains and, later, steamships. There was a simple system for communicating on the train itself: bell cords were installed for the workers to pull. Different rings carried different meanings to the engineer in the cab. Signal lanterns were also used along the tracks and by trainmen. However, early railroads did not have two sets of tracks—one for trains going each direction. There were sidings or pull-offs at specific spots for trains to stop to let others pass, but head-on collisions were always a danger. What the railroads really needed was a dependable way for the train stations to communicate with each other and keep track of the moving trains.

An American artist, **Samuel F. B. Morse,** solved the communication problem by inventing the telegraph. By stopping and starting electrical impulses, he could send messages over long distances in just a few seconds through a wire. In 1837 Morse applied for government funds to develop his idea, but Congress did not grant the money until 1843. Morse was down to thirty-seven cents when he got the news. The grant—$30,000—was to be used to build a telegraph line from Washington, D.C., to Baltimore, Maryland. In fourteen hectic months, forty miles of copper wire was strung between trees and poles. Broken bottle necks served as insulators. On May 24, 1844, Morse was at a telegraph key in the Supreme Court room of the Capitol. A crowd of judges, senators, and congressmen stood by. Morse's first message, part of a Bible verse, was "What hath God wrought!" The next day news of James K. Polk's nomination for president was sent from the Democratic Convention in Baltimore using the telegraph.

Soon telegraph poles were placed alongside railroad tracks. Cities and towns were linked by a giant network of telegraph communication. Railroad stations could relay information that could keep the trains operating more safely and on schedule. The Western Union Telegraph Company combined many of the independent telegraph companies that had come into existence and formed a more unified service for the country in 1856. By October 24, 1861, telegraph wires had been strung all across the continent. California sent the first telegraph message across the continent on that day in 1861. It notified Abraham Lincoln that California would be loyal to the Union. Because California could receive communication almost instantly by wire, there was little need for the pony express.

SECTION REVIEW

1. Who was the first postmaster general of the United States?

2. What was the pony express?

3. Who invented the telegraph?

4. Between what two cities was the first telegraph message sent?

5. When did telegraph communication first stretch across North America?

 How did the telegraph change communication in the United States?

Within fifteen years of its creation, Samuel Morse's telegraph made instant transcontinental communication possible.

SUMMARY

Traveling and communicating across colonial America had been very difficult because of the lack of roads and technical abilities. In the early 1800s, however, transportation and communication changed rapidly as new inventions and better methods of doing things came into use. New roads and canals opened up some regions of the nation to better transportation, and railroads and steamships became important new carriers of people and goods. Communications also improved through better-organized postal services, and telegraph wires eventually linked all the regions of the nation with immediate service.

Chapter Review

People, Places, and Things to Remember

Great Wagon Road	turnpikes	Erie Canal
Daniel Boone	steamboats	Peter Cooper
Cumberland Gap	Robert Fulton	pony express
Wilderness Road	canal	Samuel F. B. Morse
National Road	locks	

Review Questions

Tell whether each of the following men or items was most closely associated with roads, water transportation, or railroads in the early 1800s.

1. locks
2. Robert Fulton
3. John Fitch
4. turnpikes
5. Daniel Boone
6. canal
7. Peter Cooper
8. Cumberland Gap

Match each of these transportation routes with its description.

9. Great Wagon Road
10. Wilderness Road
11. National Road
12. Erie Canal

a. provided a route across New York State
b. also known as the Cumberland Road
c. the Great Warrior's Path made by the Iroquois
d. built through the Cumberland Gap

Questions for Discussion

13. How did transportation and communication improvements in the early 1800s help the United States to grow?
14. Why do you suppose the Erie Canal helped New York City to grow?

14

Changing American Life

The changing means of transportation and communication helped to bring many more changes to American life. New ideas and inventions spread quickly around the country as businessmen saw opportunities to make a profit from these advances. Farming, manufacturing, and trade benefited from the innovations as America experienced its own Industrial Revolution.

American Agriculture

In 1800 most Americans were still farmers who owned and worked their own lands with the help of large families. By using simple tools and by working hard, the farmer raised enough food for his own family. He sold or traded any surplus for items that could not be grown or made on the family farm.

Between 1815 and 1860 the Industrial Revolution profoundly affected not only the American factory worker but also the American farmer. The use of new farm machinery enabled the farmer to improve his methods and lower his costs, thereby increasing his profits. Since fewer farmers were needed to produce the same amount of food, some farmers were free to join the growing urban work force in factories, shipyards, banks, and other businesses.

Farming Before 1800

Before new labor-saving machines were invented, American farmers used tools similar to those used centuries before. They still plowed with oxen as Elisha had done (I Kings 19:19). If there were hard lumps left after the plowing, farmers used a harrow, a device with teeth, or later disks, to break up the soil. Sometimes they simply used a hoe. At harvest time the farmers used a scythe or a sickle to gather the grain, just as in the time of Moses (Deut. 23:25) and Christ (Mark 4:26-29). After the grain had been dried by the sun, it was picked up for threshing. Sometimes wealthy farmers hired a crew of reapers to harvest their crops, as Boaz did (Ruth 2). When grain was threshed, it was beaten with a flail (stick) until the kernels fell out of the husks. Then the farmers hauled their grain to a mill, where it was crushed between rotating stones to produce meal. All the farmers' toil usually produced only a meager amount of food to feed their families.

When most crops ripen and are ready for harvest, they must be gathered in quickly or they will rot in the fields. For this reason farmers had to be careful not to plant more than they could harvest successfully. In many areas plantings were limited or staggered to avoid harvesting problems. But as new farm machines were developed, the farmers found it easier to plow and plant more acres and to harvest their crops more quickly and efficiently. In addition, new machines made some farm products easier to process. As a result America's farm production increased rapidly.

Agricultural Advances

The new farm implements produced by inventors during the Industrial Revolution greatly improved the life of the farmers. With all the new equipment and the demand for food in eastern cities, farmers could increase their production, meet the needs of their own families, and still make a profit by selling the extra grain in eastern markets. American grain even became an important export to Europe after crop failures and political disputes there created food shortages and a demand for American grain. Three particular inventors and inventions played important roles as America developed its agricultural production.

John Deere's Plow—By 1838 a young blacksmith named **John Deere** realized that the common iron plow needed improvement. One great problem with the iron plow was that

Agriculture Time Line

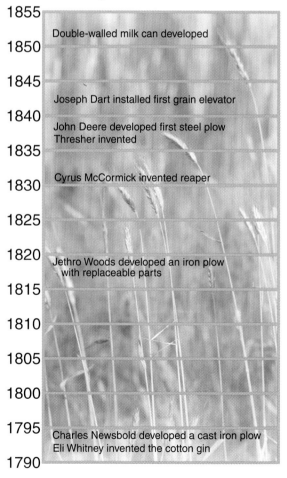

1855

1850 — Double-walled milk can developed

1845

Joseph Dart installed first grain elevator

1840

John Deere developed first steel plow
Thresher invented

1835

Cyrus McCormick invented reaper

1830

1825

1820 — Jethro Woods developed an iron plow with replaceable parts

1815

1810

1805

1800

1795 — Charles Newsbold developed a cast iron plow
Eli Whitney invented the cotton gin

1790

the soil stuck to the blade. While visiting a saw mill, Deere noted that a steel blade shone when it had been polished by friction. He thought that steel might clean itself, too, when cutting earth. Using an old circular steel blade, he made a plow. He cut twelve smooth, straight furrows nonstop while a group of Illinois farmers looked on in amazement.

Deere began to build plows for sale, and his first plows sold for ten dollars each. Seeing the possibilities of his product, Deere built a plow factory in Moline, Illinois. He went into commercial plow production using high-grade steel from Pittsburgh. His plows made a humming sound and were popularly called "singing plows." Almost every wagon going west carried a John Deere plow. The steel plow was important in opening and conquering the prairies of the West.

Cyrus McCormick's Reaper—Planting more grain, however, was of little value if it could not be harvested quickly enough. In the 1820s **Cyrus McCormick,** son of a Virginia blacksmith, started work on a **reaper,** a machine for cutting or harvesting grain. By 1831 he had invented a reaper that could cut six acres of oats in one day. Pulled by four horses, this reaper could do the work of six men. In 1841 McCormick sold two reapers, and the next year he sold seven more.

By 1844 he was ready to turn his back on the East and go west to the heartland with sixty dollars in his pocket. Since his reaper could cut twenty acres of wheat per day, he knew that sales would flourish when the vast prairies were plowed into wheat fields. He picked Chicago for his headquarters, where in 1851 he built and sold a thousand reapers. He then entered his reaper in the London Exposition, where it won first prize and made him an instant celebrity. By 1857 his profits were $1.25 million.

Eli Whitney's Cotton Gin—Tobacco had been a profitable crop for the South since colonial days, but the appeal of that product was limited. Since the English were using new machines to make cloth, selling them raw cotton seemed like a good activity for the South. But cotton was not a profitable crop except on the Sea Islands off the coast of South Carolina and Georgia. Sea Island cotton, which would not grow on the mainland, had seeds that could easily be removed from its long fibers. Upland cotton, grown on the mainland, had shorter staples (fibers), and the seeds were difficult to remove. If a workman cleaned seeds from this short-staple cotton for an entire day, his yield would be just one pound of cleaned cotton. Even when slaves were put to the task of cleaning the fibers, farming upland cotton just did not pay until **Eli Whitney** appeared on the scene.

The cotton gin made cotton production more profitable.

Eli Whitney's **cotton gin** could clean the short-staple cotton quickly and efficiently. It suddenly made growing cotton more profitable. In 1793, the year he invented the gin, 138,328 pounds of cotton were exported.

Within one year, exports reached 6,276,000 pounds. By 1825, 176 million pounds of cotton were exported to Britain, and 100 million more pounds were sent to northern mills. By 1850 cotton made up seven-eighths of all American exports. It was little wonder that Southerners believed that cotton might be king, not only in the South, but throughout America.

Southern Agriculture and Slavery

Both cotton and tobacco could be grown profitably only on large plantations worked by gangs of unskilled laborers. Because the many workers could be supervised by one man and the tasks involved were simple, plantation owners believed that slaves were the ideal laborers for them. Slavery, a practice that many Americans had thought would die out, was now a growing, profitable way of life in the South, thanks to the cotton gin.

Although slavery became important to the South during the early 1800s, it did not become common for most Southerners to own slaves. Only about one-fourth of all southern families owned slaves before the Civil War. The majority of those slaveholding families owned fewer than ten slaves, and probably only a little over five thousand planters in the entire South had fifty or more slaves. Yet the cotton and other crops produced on plantations by slave labor were an important part of the South's economy. Lacking other industries, the South increasingly depended on the money earned from its cotton exports.

The *Amistad*

In 1806 Britain became the first country to abolish slavery. In 1808 the American Congress followed with a law that forbade American vessels from taking on slaves. Unfortunately, because profits were high—more than $100,000 per load—and because men are evil, the law was not strictly enforced. As late as 1847 the United States Navy had seven ships patrolling Africa's Guinea Coast and the British had twelve. They did little to slow the vicious traffic.

Because there was a shortage of slaves for sugar plantations in Cuba, American ships carried slaves there. In 1839 thirty slaves from Liberia were held captive on the *Amistad,* bound for Cuba. Several Africans managed to cut their chains. Under the leadership of Singbé Piéh, called Cinq by the Spaniards, the slaves killed the ship's captain and cook but spared two Cubans to navigate them back to Africa. By day the Cubans sailed east, but by night they doubled back and edged north, reaching Long Island, New York. The Coast Guard stumbled on a landing party of four blacks wandering on shore near Sag's Harbor, Long Island.

Since the slaves were from Mendi in northern Liberia and spoke no English, there were problems. A linguist at Yale helped identify their language so that someone could decide what would be done with them. Under American law slavery was still legal, and so the slaves would have been returned to Cuba to be sold. It was then that former president John Quincy Adams took on their case and cause. He saw the case through the Supreme Court. On March 9, 1841, the court declared the Mendi captives free on the basis that the laws of Spain allowed such an act. With this victory, Adams was inspired to continue his fight for the repeal of the Gag Rule. In 1842 he suggested an amendment to end slavery. His suggestion was eventually adopted as the Thirteenth Amendment in 1865.

Scene in the Hold of the "Blood-Stained Gloria." Middle Passage.

The hold of a slave ship was a pit of despair for its victims.

SECTION REVIEW

1. What tools did American farmers use before 1800?

2. What were the inventions of John Deere, Cyrus McCormick, and Eli Whitney?

3. What were the two major crops grown by southern farmers?

 Why did slavery not die out in the South?

American Industry

While the ideal place to build mills for weaving cotton into cloth would have been near southern cotton fields, few mills were built in the South. There were several reasons the southern textile industry failed to develop at this time. First, the South lacked an adequate power supply. It had few fast-flowing rivers for turning water wheels. Also, since

Southerners knew that they could make money easily through agriculture, they were not eager to work in factories. It seemed illogical to waste capital and energy on factories when plenty of money could be made growing cotton. As a result, industrial growth bypassed the South and took hold in other areas of the country, especially New England.

The Factory System

With the Industrial Revolution came the factory system. Before machines became available, most work was done in homes. Other items were made in craftsmen's shops. The **factory system,** however, collected many workers in one place, where many like items could be turned out in one day. Schedules rarely varied, and the workers did not come and go as they wished. Usually they performed only one step of a many-staged process. In other words, there was a division of labor. One person, a group of men, or numerous investors owned the building, the machinery, and the tools. The workers received a fixed salary, with the owners receiving the profits.

The idea of the factory system came from England. Some Americans had tried to start factories in the 1780s, but they had failed because the machinery was not adequate and because most Americans still preferred British imports. Some states were so eager to have factories that they offered rewards to get them started. They even advertised in British newspapers to get men to come. The British feared that if the United States gained access to their men and machines, they would soon lose their industrial advantage. To protect the textile industry, the British forbade the export of their machinery and the emigration of the men who could build and operate it.

Samuel Slater's Factory

An English mechanic named **Samuel Slater** saw one of the American advertisements. He had been an apprentice to the partner of Richard Arkwright, father of the English factory system and inventor of the water frame, a waterpowered textile machine. Knowing the risks he was taking by leaving the country illegally, Slater did not even tell his own family he was going. He had no plans for machinery on paper, but he had learned how to use and repair every machine in the Arkwright system.

Once in the United States he was told about Moses Brown, a famous Quaker merchant who had just built a textile mill in Rhode Island. Brown was seeking a manager; so Slater wrote him a letter telling of his experience and applying for the position. Brown offered Slater the job and all the profits once

A waterwheel provides the power to run the machinery in a mill.

the cost and interest on the machinery were subtracted. Slater had applied for a job by letter and got an entire plant by return mail!

Slater went to the factory in Pawtucket. Seeing the machines, he wrote, "These will not do. They are good for nothing in their present condition." Slater then built a whole series of machines from memory. The yarn plant got off to a slow start, but ten years later Brown and Slater were ready to open a second factory.

Slater ran his factory using children as young as seven years old, as was done in England. He broke with British tradition by giving the children meals and more humane treatment. Since American children on farms went to work when they were very young, using such young laborers was not considered improper, and most people rated his factory highly. Parents were happy to have their children in such a place. Slater's factory with its simple machines was ideally suited to a young country that would have a shortage of skilled labor for the next seventy-five years. Although it was not perfect, the system provided work that helped to feed and clothe people and to give them more than they had ever had before.

Further Development of Industry

Other developments of machinery and methods of production helped to boost American industries in the early 1800s.

The Sewing Machine—Another invention, the **sewing machine,** aided the growth of the factory system. The sewing machine allowed seamstresses to cut drastically the time needed to sew garments and other textile products. Thus the textiles flowing from the new yarn and weaving machinery could quickly become clothing and other products for consumers at home and abroad. Sewing factories soon sprang up, with hundreds of sewing machines humming as the operators turned out the products.

Although Walter Hunt had invented a sewing machine in 1838, he never sought a patent for it. Because it was believed that machinery took jobs away from the laboring class, especially women, Hunt withdrew his invention. Little did anyone know that during the Civil War the sewing machine would permit women to enter the work force in ever-increasing numbers.

The credit for inventing the sewing machine has gone to **Elias Howe,** who patented it in 1846. Like many inventors, Howe made little money while trying to perfect his invention. His family suffered terribly; Howe had to borrow from his father to get to the bedside of his dying wife. He fared little better in England while promoting his machine because he was cheated out of his royalties.

In 1851 a third inventor, **Isaac Singer,** also patented a sewing machine. Differing from Howe's, Singer's machine used a foot treadle rather than a hand crank so that the operator's hands were left free. The needle operated vertically rather than horizontally and could sew a curved seam. However, like Howe's, it did use an eyepointed needle, and Singer was charged with violating Howe's patent.

Howe won the case, and Singer was forced to pay damages for every machine that had infringed Howe's rights. Heeding the adage "if you can't beat them, join them," Singer suggested combining ideas. The result was the first patent pool in American history, uniting seven sewing machine companies into one. Singer was above all a genius at promoting his idea. His was the first company to spend a million dollars a year on advertising. Believing that every American home would want a sewing machine if the price were within range, he sold machines on the installment, or time-payment, plan.

Eli Whitney's Influence on the Factory System—Besides inventing the cotton gin, Eli

Eli Whitney revolutionized the factory system with the development of interchangeable parts.

Whitney also played an important role in improving the factory system through the development of **interchangeable parts.** He and other men used the idea of assembling products, guns in particular, by producing large numbers of each part. In the past each gun had been assembled individually from parts made specifically for that gun by skilled craftsmen. Whitney instead made molds that could form large numbers of each part. The interchangeable parts could then be assembled quickly by less skilled workers to make large quantities of guns. This idea led to the **mass production** of many other products.

New England Industry—The factory system grew quickly in New England, where fast-moving streams provided needed power for turning the water wheels. When steam power superseded waterpower, New England was still in the running because her vast forests could be cut down to provide fuel. Since New England soil was too poor for most heavy agriculture, New Englanders willingly tried other ways to make their livings.

New England's banking system also financed new industry. Even when the Bank of the United States went out of existence, state banks offered loans to build mills. Some of their state governments also underwrote internal improvements, fostering transportation to aid new industries.

New England was also an ideal place for factories because a labor force was readily available. Her cold climate allowed only a short growing season and left long winters without work, and subsistence farmers often could not support larger families. Therefore, the youth of New England were attracted to factory work. Although sometimes families and single men went west or to other cities seeking better opportunities, young women were often available for employment. **Francis Cabot Lowell,** a New England cloth maker, organized a mill town for girls in Waltham, Massachusetts. The factory provided their room and board and strict supervision, and the girls received one to two dollars a week for long hours of labor in the mill. Of course, a dollar was a lot of money in those days.

Results of the Rise of Industry

Industrialization influenced the lives of many Americans. The new inventions made work easier for many. Money enabled some to enjoy a higher living standard. People moved from farms to cities, where new jobs were available. Factories were placed near sources of waterpower, and towns and cities grew up near these sites. The factories also gave many immigrants the opportunity for a new life in America.

Although the factory system contributed much that was positive, there were some aspects that would be hard for us to accept today. For example, workers labored six days, seventy-five hours a week. Most had only half an hour for lunch, and wages were low. Thus it was necessary for several people in a family, including children, to work just to provide enough money to live. In 1818 a factory in Paterson, New Jersey, reported the following weekly wages: men, $5.00; women $2.37; children, $1.37. By the early 1850s, pay for some common laborers and factory workers reached a new high of $6.00 a week.

Often both working and living conditions were miserable. Factories were stuffy, cramped, and noisy. Machines were not equipped with safety devices, and injuries resulted. Besides the fear of injury, workers feared losing their jobs to new machines that were brought in. Factory towns were usually crowded and drab. Working families were squeezed into one-room tenements as the urban population more than doubled between 1820 and 1860. Because many children worked, few children could attend school, even free public schools. To combat these problems, some workers joined labor organizations.

The Rise of Labor Unions

In 1827 the first **labor union** was organized. Called the Mechanics' Union of Trade Associations, the group united skilled craftsmen in Philadelphia. In 1828 the Workingmen's Party, a labor party, began. This party started the country's first labor newspaper, *The Mechanics' Free Press,* to promote labor goals.

The labor groups concentrated on broad reforms, not just specific changes. Among their goals were free public education, the end of imprisonment or seizure of tools for failure to pay debts, a ten-hour work day, and the end of child labor.

Although the federal government did give the workers a ten-hour day in 1840 and more

towns started schools, the unions' successes were limited. When the nation prospered, so did unions. When depressions came, the unions failed. Workers were willing to accept wage cuts and feared being fired in hard times. Many Americans believed that if they applied the work ethic and used their God-given talents and abilities, they could succeed without unions. Where they could not, they could leave and try to seek a new life somewhere else in the country.

Immigration also worked against the unions. Most newcomers were eager to work and knew they were better off than they had been in Europe. Many of them held factory jobs for only a few years. As soon as they had learned the language and could go elsewhere, they did.

SECTION REVIEW

1. List two reasons for the slow development of the South's textile industry.

2. What system brought workers together in one place to produce many like items?

3. What Englishman made significant contributions to the rise of this system through his knowledge of machinery?

4. Who received the first patent for a sewing machine? Who received a patent a few years later and eventually joined forces with the first man?

5. List some of the negative effects of the rise of industry.

 How did Eli Whitney contribute to the development of mass production?

Expanding Sea Trade

The Industrial Revolution also affected overseas trade. Americans had been involved in shipping and trade since colonial times. After the War for Independence Americans sought new markets overseas. Trade with European countries expanded. France, Prussia

(Germany), the Netherlands, and countries with Baltic and Mediterranean ports all traded with the United States. Americans traded their surplus goods, like cotton, tobacco, and lumber, for things unavailable or scarce in America, such as hemp, raisins, olive oil, and iron.

New Asian Markets

Americans also surveyed markets in Asia. Americans had heard of Europeans gaining riches by trade in China and did not want to be left out. In 1784, only a year after the War for Independence had ended, a ship was refitted for a trading expedition to China. New York merchants hired John Green, assisted by Major Samuel Shaw, to captain the *Empress of China.*

China had shown little interest in foreign products and had insisted that goods be paid for in gold and silver coin. But there was one product the Chinese wanted to buy: a root called ginseng. The Chinese believed that ginseng had some medicinal qualities. The *Empress of China* carried thirty tons of ginseng.

The *Empress* sailed across the Atlantic to Africa, around the Cape of Good Hope, and across the Indian Ocean. A French vessel, the *Triton,* helped guide it across the reef-filled South China Sea. The ship finally reached Whampoa, the Chinese port fourteen miles below Canton, where foreigners were allowed to drop anchor.

The Chinese welcomed the Americans, and the *Empress* brought home tea, spices, silk, chinaware, and stories of its profitable trip. Upon Shaw's return, he was named as the consul, a special trade minister, to China. By 1786 Shaw had opened America's first trading company in Canton itself.

The Chinese also liked furs. The first American to engage in the new fur trade was Captain **Robert Gray,** whose trinket-laden ship sailed around South America to what is now Oregon to buy furs from the Indians. There they learned that the Indians now desired iron and copper tools and weapons more than trinkets. Aboard ship for the winter, the crewmen made chisels that were worth eight otter skins.

After trading for the furs, Gray's ship, the *Columbia,* headed for Hawaii and became the first American ship to visit those islands. After taking on fresh fruits, hogs, and water, the ship crossed the Pacific to China. The homeward trip took Gray west through the Indian Ocean, around Africa, and across the Atlantic. Gray and his crew returned to Boston in the summer of 1790. His profits were disappointing, but Gray had made Americans proud by becoming the first American to circumnavigate the earth. He had also established an American claim to Oregon territory by going up the Columbia

Captain Robert Gray became the first American to circumnavigate the world.

River and had set up a three-corner trade route that skippers, the so-called "lords of the China trade," followed. Hardware from the East Coast was carried to the Pacific Coast and traded for furs. Once the Pacific crossing was made, the furs were exchanged for Chinese tea, dishes, and silk.

On these voyages the Americans also found the source of the Dutch pepper trade in Sumatra. They soon cornered that trade for themselves. Touching on the coast of Brazil, they brought back coffee, which soon became a favorite beverage. Americans began—and continue—to drink more coffee than the people of any other country.

The most important new Asian market for America was Japan. For centuries the Japanese had rejected any kind of contact with the outside world. In 1852, however, President Fillmore ordered Commodore Matthew Perry to take several warships to Japan and attempt to secure a trade treaty. Perry arrived in 1853 and told the Japanese of his mission. He then went to China to give the Japanese government time to consider his offer. When Perry returned in 1854, the Japanese agreed to allow the United States to begin trading with their nation.

Fishing and Whaling

Fishing had been an important way of making a living from America's earliest years. Cod were harvested from Newfoundland's Grand Banks, and herring and lobster were caught off the Atlantic coast. Whaling cruises to the Bering Sea, though long and treacherous, attracted other venturers. There were profits to be made from whale oil burned to give light. Sailors spent the long hours aboard ship on the way home carving on whalebone or whale ivory, producing a new and exquisite art called scrimshaw.

The Age of the Yankee Clipper

Over the years the United States had developed a highly productive shipbuilding industry. Shipyards dotted the eastern coast. American shipbuilders were not afraid to try new things, and in the 1840s they developed a new type of sailing vessel designed for increased speeds. The **clipper** was invented by John W. Griffiths, but Donald McKay surpassed him in both fame and design with his clipper ships. In contrast to earlier ocean-going vessels, the clipper had a much sharper point on her bow that could "clip" into the waves. The bow or front portion of the ship curved inward. But what caught the eye and excited people the most were the sails. Some clippers had as many as thirty-five sails; the area of the canvas sails was one and a half acres, equal to one and a half football fields.

Clippers reached their heyday after 1848 when gold was discovered in California. They carried the many gold seekers west. (Sometimes, though, they had problems coming back; the crews deserted to go to the gold fields.) The clipper ship era lasted only about fifteen years. It came to an end by the mid-1850s, when new advances such as railroads and steamships outdated the clipper ships.

SECTION REVIEW

1. What was the first American ship to make a trading expedition to China? Who were its captains?

2. Who was the first American to circumnavigate the earth? What was the three-corner trade route that he helped to establish?

3. What military leader opened up American trade with Japan?

4. What is scrimshaw?

5. What eventually made clipper ships obsolete?

 Why did the Americans want to open trade with the Chinese?

Off to the Races

Clippers often raced each other carrying cargoes from New York to San Francisco or New York to Canton, China. The first great race to San Francisco, in 1850, pitted seven clippers against each other and was won by Donald McKay's *Sea Witch*. His *Flying Cloud* soon set a record, making the run from New York to San Francisco in 89 days and 2 hours, a record that has never been bettered by any ship. The record for a day's run, 495 miles, was set by the *Sovereign of the Seas,* Another clipper, *Lightning,* set a record of thirteen and a half days from New York to Liverpool.

America's Spiritual Life

America experienced many changes during the early decades of its independence. New inventions and techniques brought advancements in agriculture, industry, and trade. And the nation's government was growing stronger and adapting to the new needs of Americans. Religious ideas were also changing. Nevertheless, the spiritual needs of the people remained the same.

American religious life in the early 1800s was marked by two contrasting movements.

On the one hand was a tremendous revival known as the **Second Great Awakening.** On the other was Unitarianism, a movement that denied many truths of the Christian faith.

The Second Great Awakening

After the War for Independence, American churches entered a period of spiritual deadness. John Marshall, chief justice of the Supreme Court, declared sadly that the church was "too far gone ever to be revived." At this low point in America's spiritual life, God sent a sweeping revival to the young nation. Called the Second Great Awakening, this revival transformed the lives of cold church members and saw thousands won to Christ who had never before professed any interest in religion.

The revivals in the East centered in the colleges and individual churches. Although most American colleges had been founded by godly men, the schools had grown increasingly non-Christian. At Yale, for example, the students debated over whether Christianity was true, and they delighted in calling each other by the names of famous infidels.

Into this appalling situation came minister **Timothy Dwight,** who became president of Yale in 1795. Dwight dealt directly with this unbelief. He debated students on questions such as "Is the Bible the Word of God?", and he won. Dwight also began preaching a series of sermons on the true biblical faith. After seven years of his lecturing and preaching, Yale experienced a revival in which one-third of the students professed faith in Christ. This was the first of several Yale revivals. Other colleges experienced similar revivals.

In the churches in the East, members were stirred to new life through the preaching of faithful men like evangelist Asahel Nettleton. Fearful of the excessive emotionalism of some earlier revivals, Nettleton always insisted on calm, orderly services. When inquirers came to him under conviction of sin, Nettleton would talk and pray with them at great length. Such evangelists wanted to be sure that converts knew what they were professing and were not being pressured into quick decisions. On the frontier the revival took a different form. "Out West," which at this time meant areas like Kentucky and Tennessee, revivals usually came in the form of **"camp meetings."** Hundreds or even thousands of people would gather in some central location to listen to preachers and to sing camp meeting songs such as "Brethren, We Have Met to Worship."

The most famous camp meeting was held in 1801 at Cane Ridge, Kentucky, not far from the city of Lexington. The crowd numbered at least ten thousand people and may have been as large as twenty-five thousand. The camp meetings seemed to have a positive effect on frontier life.

Timothy Dwight led the first of a series of revivals at Yale University.

Unitarianism: The Unbelieving Religion

While these revivals were sweeping across America, Unitarianism was also making an impact on the country, especially in New England. (We discussed the teachings of Unitarianism in Chapter 4. See page 62.) The first church in America to become Unitarian was King's Chapel (formerly an Anglican church) in Boston in 1785. The movement became much stronger in the 1800s, especially when Harvard became Unitarian. The movement did not found churches itself. Instead it took over churches that had formerly believed the Bible.

The Unitarians were usually intellectual men, and the movement provided many political and educational leaders. Probably the most famous Unitarian minister was **William Ellery Channing,** a persuasive preacher and writer in Boston. His sermons, books, and articles promoted Unitarianism throughout the East. Orthodox, Bible-believing men opposed the movement, however, and founded new churches and schools to replace the ones the Unitarians had taken over. Nevertheless, the faith of many Americans was being eroded by unbelieving preachers, even in that day. As the years passed, more and more people followed the teachings of such men instead of supporting the preachers who continued to stand for the truth of God's Word.

SECTION REVIEW

1. What two contrasting religious movements marked the early 1800s?

2. Name two men influential in the revival of the early nineteenth century.

3. What was the first Unitarian church in America?

4. Name one famous Unitarian leader.

 Why was Unitarianism such an influential movement?

SUMMARY

While means of transportation and communication were changing during the early 1800s, so too were agriculture, industry, and trade. New inventions and methods of production helped America's farms and factories to produce much more than they had in colonial days. American traders were ready to ship the nation's products for sale abroad. While these changes affected the way Americans made their living, their religious ideas affected the way they lived. Some people were influenced by the Second Great Awakening and its emphasis on the Scriptures. Other Americans allowed Unitarianism to destroy their faith in Jesus Christ and God's Word.

Chapter Review

People, Places, and Things to Remember

John Deere
Cyrus McCormick
reaper
Eli Whitney
cotton gin
factory system
Samuel Slater

sewing machine
Elias Howe
Isaac Singer
interchangeable parts
mass production
Francis Cabot Lowell
labor union

Robert Gray
clipper
Second Great Awakening
Timothy Dwight
camp meetings
William Ellery Channing

Review Questions

Match each man with his invention or accomplishment.

1. William Ellery Channing
2. Timothy Dwight
3. John Deere
4. Robert Gray
5. Elias Howe
6. Francis Cabot Lowell
7. Cyrus McCormick
8. Isaac Singer
9. Samuel Slater
10. Eli Whitney

a. the steel plow
b. the reaper
c. leader of Second Great Awakening at Yale
d. credited with inventing the sewing machine
e. cotton gin and interchangeable parts
f. set up a textile mill in Pawtucket, R.I.
g. formed a large, sewing machine company
h. leading Unitarian
i. circumnavigated the earth
j. organized factory work for girls in Massachusetts

Explain the significance of each of the following inventions or accomplishments.

11. steel plow
12. reaper
13. cotton gin
14. factory system
15. interchangeable parts

Questions for Discussion

16. How do you suppose American history would have been different if the cotton gin had not been invented?

17. Why was Asahel Nettleton's method of evangelism wise?

The Era of Manifest Destiny

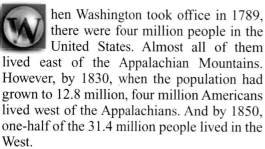 hen Washington took office in 1789, there were four million people in the United States. Almost all of them lived east of the Appalachian Mountains. However, by 1830, when the population had grown to 12.8 million, four million Americans lived west of the Appalachians. And by 1850, one-half of the 31.4 million people lived in the West.

Westward Movement

For over a hundred years, moving west was an almost constant process in America's development. Over the Appalachians into Kentucky, Tennessee, and the old Northwest Territory, and on past the Mississippi River, Americans moved to begin their new lives and to expand their nation. By the 1840s many Americans believed that God intended for them to have all the western lands to the shores of the Pacific. This expansion was their **"Manifest Destiny."**

Reasons for Going West

Americans had many reasons for moving westward, and western areas had much to offer. Some settlers found good farmland; others found mineral riches. Plenty found endless toil and many hardships, but the hardy pioneers succeeded in building the American West.

The Mood of the Day—The mood of the day encouraged people to go west. Americans believed that the West was theirs to claim. Many saw neighbors and relatives pack up and head west with great optimism. It was easy to catch the excitement and the dreams of others. The leaders of the day, especially President James K. Polk, encouraged expansion, and the people willingly followed.

The Lure of the Land—The West had a nearly irresistible attraction for American farmers. Planters whose soils had been worn out felt certain that the rich acreage near the Mississippi River could restore their prosperity. Poor farmers who could not compete with large plantation owners, but could afford the cheap new western lands, thought they could improve their lives by moving west. The land could also become a refuge for thousands of immigrants seeking to escape the troubles of other countries. Political disturbances, low wages, high taxes, lack of economic opportunity, religious persecution, and famine encouraged immigrants from Ireland, Germany, and later the Scandinavian countries to come to the American West.

Desire for Wealth—Riches were available in the West in many forms. With the discovery of gold in California in 1848 and silver in Colorado and Nevada, many men went west seeking their fortunes. A few did become rich by mining, but others sought wealth in land. Land speculators took the risk of buying land at low prices from the government. They hoped that they could then develop settlements and resell the lands at a profit. Some lost money; others broke even; a few made fortunes. Real wealth out west was also made by those who built new businesses and made large profits by taking risks in business ventures such as railroads and supply companies.

Adventure and a New Start—Some restless Americans moved west seeking adventure. Such challenges as taming the land, facing hostile Indians, and starting new local and state governments rarely disappointed them. Some people went west because they wanted a new start, a chance to put the past behind them. A few left bills, jail sentences, wives, or criminal records behind them—but no forwarding addresses.

Religious Reasons—The desire to spread the gospel to both Indians and new settlers caused a few Easterners to go west as missionaries. In 1833 the *Christian Advocate and Journal* printed a letter about the arrival of four Indians in St. Louis who had come seeking the "white man's Book of Heaven."

When some Methodist and Presbyterian groups read of the request, they rallied to the challenge. Some Indians, especially the Nez Perce (nez purs) and Flatheads, reasoned that the white man's power centered in his religion. Because they wanted a share of the power, they concluded that they needed to learn about Christianity. The new religion might bring them enough guns and goods to defeat their enemies. Missionaries grieved over these so-called converts whose responses to the gospel were self-centered and short-lived. However, because of the power of the Word of God and the faithfulness of the missionaries, some Indians were genuinely saved.

One religious group called the **Mormons** saw the West as a refuge from the persecution they were experiencing in the East. Their movement to Utah was responsible for much of the settlement in the Great Basin area.

Trails to the West

Once American pioneers moved west of the Mississippi, they temporarily bypassed the vast Great Plains region. As yet, its dryness and its Indians discouraged settlements. The riches of western trade, California gold, and Oregon farms tempted many to make long journeys to reach their western goals. Finding

The Mormons

The Mormons started out in Palmyra, New York. There **Joseph Smith,** the cult's founder, supposedly received tablets containing the *Book of Mormon.* This book and another called *Pearl of Great Price* contain additions to God's Word and are the basis for some of Mormonism's false doctrines. The Mormons believed they were to gather the elect together and build their Zion. The first attempt to build Zion, in Kirtland, Ohio, failed because of a shortage of funds. Next they moved to Missouri, where they were forced from two sites by unfriendly neighbors. In 1838-39 attitudes became so hostile that a Mormon War broke out and forty lives were lost. The next city of refuge was Nauvoo, Illinois. There the Mormon practice of polygamy, having more than one wife, angered the local population. Smith and his brother were murdered while being held in jail in nearby Carthage.

The Mormons were forced to leave Illinois in February in subzero temperatures. A new leader, **Brigham Young,** emerged. After reorganizing at a temporary winter headquarters near Omaha, Nebraska, the

ways to get to the far West proved to be a challenge. But over a period of years, several major westward routes were established.

The Santa Fe Trail—The first American route west of the Missouri River was the **Santa Fe** (SAN-tuh fay) **Trail.** This route was primarily a trade route and was used less by settlers than other trails. When explorer Zebulon Pike, who had made it to Spanish-held Santa Fe, returned, he told Americans of the high prices that goods were bringing there. The only problem was that Spain wanted to keep the trade profits to herself. Consequently, the members of an 1812 American expedition to Santa Fe were captured and held in a lice-infested jail for eight years. But when Mexico broke free of Spain in 1821, changes came.

Mormons again trekked west. Two days after sighting the valley of the Great Salt Lake in Utah, Young declared, "It is enough. This is the right place!" By the time Young died in 1877, about 140,000 had made their way to Utah on what came to be called the Mormon Trail.

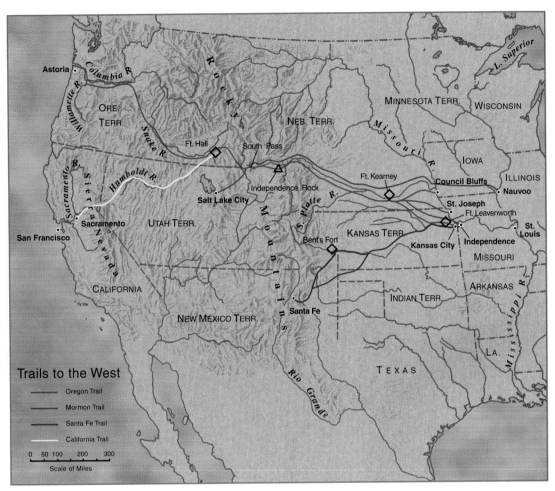

Astoria

Columbia R.

Willamette R.

ORE. TERR.

Snake R.

Ft. Hall

South Pass

NEB. TERR.

Missouri R.

MINNESOTA TERR.

WISCONSIN

L. Superior

Rocky

Sacramento R.

Sierra

Humboldt R.

Independence Rock

Salt Lake City

Ft. Kearney

Council Bluffs

IOWA

ILLINOIS

Nauvoo

San Francisco

Sacramento

Nevada

UTAH TERR.

Mountains

S. Platte R.

Bent's Fort

KANSAS TERR.

Kansas City

St. Joseph

Ft. Leavenworth

Independence

St. Louis

CALIFORNIA

NEW MEXICO TERR.

Santa Fe

INDIAN TERR.

MISSOURI

ARKANSAS

Mississippi R.

Rio Grande

TEXAS

LA.

Trails to the West

—— Oregon Trail
—— Mormon Trail
—— Santa Fe Trail
—— California Trail

0 50 100   200   300

Scale of Miles

Trade was permitted, but the Mexican government imposed high taxes, sixty percent, on imported goods. Still, $35,000 worth of goods—cotton, wool, tools, and needles—could be sold for $185,000 once the ten- to twelve-week journey on the Santa Fe Trail was completed.

To insure safety on the trail and to ward off Indian attacks, the traders gathered at one spot, usually Independence, Missouri, and made a single annual caravan from there. All the men in the caravan, including hired hands, voted for a captain to lead them. Other positions included wagon boss, pack train boss, chief scout, lieutenants for divisions, and

wranglers for the loose livestock being taken along. The caravan traveled in three to four parallel columns to aid in defense. The heavily laden wagons formed a square at night. Horses and mules were tethered in the middle since one of the favorite and most deadly Indian strategies was to stampede the animals and scatter them. Without any animals for travel and with water frequently miles away, the traders could not last long.

William and Charles Bent, two brothers who used the Santa Fe Trail and later founded a trading outpost called Bent's Fort, discovered that oxen could out-travel mules and were safer from Indian raids. The Bents also took a

thousand miles. Sticking closer to the Arkansas River, it went to Bent's Fort. The route then turned more sharply south through steep mountain terrain and Raton Pass.

With the start of the Mexican War in 1846, the Santa Fe Trail took on more importance. It was used to move both troops and supplies to Mexico and California. But in later years, as parts of the Atchison, Topeka, and Santa Fe Railroad were finished, the trail shrank in both length and importance. When the last miles of track opened on February 14, 1880, a Santa Fe

Covered wagons carried so many travelers along the Oregon Trail that wagon ruts are still visible.

cannon on the trail. The Indians, familiar by now with musket and rifle fire, had little fear of either. Cannon fire was another matter, however. Because the Indians tended to treat anything unknown as supernatural, cannon fire usually scattered them.

In 1827, with the establishment of Fort Leavenworth, Kansas, the military began patrolling the Santa Fe and later the Oregon Trail. The Santa Fe Trail had two branches: one, the Cimarron Cutoff, though shorter by one hundred miles, exposed the travelers to acute danger from hostile Indians and took them far from reliable water sources. The other route stretched more than a

newspaper headline told the final story: "The Old Santa Fe Trail Passes into Oblivion."

The Oregon Trail—The **Oregon Trail** was first traced by a mountain man, a representative of a fur company sent out to deal with the Indians. Robert Stuart led fur trappers from Astoria, Oregon, to Missouri by way of the South Pass in 1812-13. But the trail was

Horses and oxen were used to pull the wagons along the trail.

largely forgotten until 1824, when **Jedediah Smith** rediscovered it. The Oregon Trail became an important route for settlers and missionaries going west. Because the trail had several starting points—St. Joseph, Missouri; Independence, Missouri; Fort Leavenworth; and Council Bluffs—as well as several ending spots, depending on one's destination in Oregon, one writer has described the trail "like rope twisted hard in the middle and raveled at both ends."

In the spring, settlers wanting to follow its two-thousand-mile route gathered at the starting points. Organized much the same way as the trade caravans on the Santa Fe Trail, the wagons traveled twelve abreast across the expanse of the Great Plains. This enabled the captain to keep more wagons going if one wagon broke down. Others could continue and time would not be lost. Since the Oregon Trail crossed America farther north than did the Santa Fe, time was always a factor. If the wag-

ons did not reach Independence Rock by July 4, they ran the risk of being caught in the mountains by early snow and cold. One observer at Fort Kearny reported that all the traffic passed in a fifteen-day period. The Great Emigration of 1843 left Kansas on May 22 and arrived at Oregon City on October 27, more than twenty-two weeks later.

In 1841 fewer than one hundred settlers set out for Oregon, an area claimed jointly by both the United States and Great Britain at that time. But soon the trail traffic increased. As every new wagon with settlers started for Oregon, British efforts to hold Oregon became less certain. In 1844, fifteen hundred emigrants made the trip—some walked most of the way because of the jolts and ruts—and the next year more than three thousand people used the trail. In 1847 emigration swelled to four thousand. The settlers on the trail faced many hardships. Missionary Narcissa Whitman rejoiced at being able to wash clothes near Parma, Idaho. It was only the third time she had been able to do so in fifteen hundred miles of travel. Diaries tell of travelers with cracked lips and dry nostrils in the dry lands. Near or just west of the 100th meridian of longitude, the turf changed to bunch grasses, and the colors shifted from greens to browns and tans. Even the animals were different. Bison (buffalo), jack rabbits, prairie dogs, and horny toads surprised the travelers. Rattlesnakes struck at both livestock and humans. Their venom was fatal to animals although it did not always kill people. Bolts of lightning zigzagged across the sky and touched the earth as late-afternoon thundershowers struck. Sleepy children fell off wagons and were run over by iron-shod wagon wheels. Rolled into almost every mile on the trail are little-known stories of self-reliance, determination, courage, and answered prayers.

The California Trail—The **California Trail,** a branch of the Oregon Trail, extended south and west. Blazed by mountain men in 1846, it gained importance as a route for gold seekers and settlers. This trail followed the Oregon Trail for twelve hundred miles. When it cut south from Fort Hall, few travelers had any idea of what lay ahead over the next eight hundred miles. The wagons faced the challenge of the rugged Rockies, weeks of wading in loose, warm desert sand, and days with only the water that could be carried in barrels hanging on hoops on the backs of wagons. A four-hundred-mile stretch along the Humboldt River provided the wagon trains with needed grass and water before they faced the forty-mile desert or a murderous ascent through the Sierra Nevada (see-EHR-uh nuh-VAH-duh). Despite the horrors of the trail, 165,000 pioneers risked their lives to reach California between 1846 and 1858.

Growth of Towns

Usually the first men to arrive in a new western area were trappers and traders. After they had worked in an area for a while, pioneer farmers would begin to arrive. When they cleared the land, the number of game and fur-bearing animals decreased. As this happened, the trappers and traders moved on.

As more and more settlers came into an area, it became more civilized. Settlers established county governments. Often a church was the first nonresidential building to be built in an area. As in colonial days, the church met both the spiritual and social needs of a community. Circuit-riding preachers served some of the churches. Until a store was built in the area, itinerant or traveling peddlers brought goods to sell. Their horses and wagons carried pots, pans, tools, cloth, thread, and other goods to meet the needs of pioneer families. Eventually settlers built stores and other businesses such as forges and mills. The resulting towns were usually located on transportation arteries or near power sources. Most western towns grew slowly.

SECTION REVIEW

1. Define the term "Manifest Destiny."

2. List four reasons for westward expansion.

3. What group settled in Utah and why?

4. Name the first trail route west of the Missouri.

5. What other famous trail branched off from the Oregon Trail?

 On which trail was weather the greatest concern? Why?

Acquiring Texas and the Southwest

The Spanish had explored Texas and the Southwest in the 1500s and 1600s. Spain later tried to cement its claim by setting up missions in these areas. Because the Indians were hostile, however, this system did not work well in Texas. Thus by 1800 there were only three prominent Spanish settlements in Texas: San Antonio, Goliad (GO lee ad), and Nacogdoches (nak uh DOH chiz). Unrest in Spanish Mexico spread over the border into Texas after 1810. When Mexico gained its freedom from Spain, Texas and the Southwest came under Mexican control.

American Settlement of Texas

The Mexicans then decided to allow a limited number of Americans to enter Texas. In 1821 a Missouri promoter named Moses Austin secured a permit to bring three hundred families to Texas. When he died, his son Stephen took over the project. Each family received at least 640 acres at low cost along with six years of freedom from taxation, the right to have slaves, and protection from suits to collect any debts they owed back in the States. In return the settlers had to pledge allegiance to Mexico and become Roman Catholics. Because of the great opportunity offered and the expectation that Mexico would not enforce its religious policies, the settlers willingly agreed to come.

Although the American colonists helped Texas to prosper and to control the Indians, they were not absorbed into the Spanish population as Mexico had hoped. By the end of the 1820s, more than thirty thousand Americans had poured into Texas. Although they became Mexican citizens, some of the new settlers were hot-tempered firebrands who stirred up trouble and pushed the weak Mexican government to the limit. Consequently, in 1830 Mexico reversed its policy, closed its borders to immigrants, and restricted its trade. The few

Mexican soldiers who patrolled the borders, however, could not control the flood of incoming Americans. When **Stephen Austin** went to Mexico City in 1833, he asked the Mexican officials to let the American-settled area become a separate Mexican state. He also advised his colonists to become a state even if his mission failed. As a result, he spent eighteen months in jail on charges of treason.

Meanwhile, Mexico's president, **Antonio López de Santa Anna,** decided to use force against Texas and sent troops there under the command of his brother-in-law, General Martin Cos. Texans grabbed their rifles and muskets and manned cannons on town plazas. Although the United States government sent no official aid, some southern states sent help secretly. Three hundred volunteers from Georgia and two companies from New Orleans joined the Texan forces. The thought of thirty thousand Texan colonists facing the might of a nation with seven million subjects inspired Americans.

Texas Battles for Independence

The Texans were tough and determined. On October 2, 1835, a Mexican military detachment arrived at Gonzalez and demanded surrender of the town's brass cannon. The cannon fired a shot, the Mexican forces retreated, and the skirmish became "the Lexington of the Texas Revolution."

The Texans declared that they were fighting to gain the republican rights that the Mexican constitution promised. Texans easily took Goliad, a Mexican supply base, and then took control of San Antonio. Some of the American volunteers believed the war was over, but **Jim Bowie** and **Sam Houston,** two of the American commanders, knew otherwise. They correctly believed that Santa Anna would try a winter invasion.

Houston believed that the Americans stood a chance of winning if they fought in the

"Remember the Alamo!" became a rallying cry for Texas independence.

field. They knew the terrain, and American rifles were more accurate than Mexican muskets. The last place Houston wanted to fight a battle was at San Antonio's huge abandoned mission, **the Alamo.** Since it was never meant to be a fort, it would be difficult to defend. He ordered the Texans to abandon the mission before the Mexicans arrived.

"Remember the Alamo!"—But when Houston's order to abandon the fortress came, Jim Bowie decided against it. In his opinion, the Alamo kept Mexico from invading all of Texas. Although the resources at hand were limited, the men used them well. They secured the three-acre mission as well as possible with wood and earthen barricades, and they positioned cannons for their defense.

When Lieutenant Colonel William Travis arrived, he assumed command. He vowed to hold the mission and to fight until "victory or death." Davy Crockett arrived from Tennessee, carrying his country fiddle and a long rifle named Betsy. The defenders fully expected more help. But no more came. Only 183 men were left to defend a quarter mile of makeshift walls.

Santa Anna crossed the Rio Grande and moved toward San Antonio. Once there, he sent the Alamo a demand for unconditional surrender. He said that every man would be "put to the sword in case of refusal." The defenders answered with a cannon shot, and on February 23, the historic siege by more than four thousand Mexican troops began.

As the siege dragged on, the supply of powder and cannonballs dwindled. On March 3, Travis told the defenders to expect no aid. He drew a line on the ground with his sword and asked all who would stand by him to cross it. Every man crossed. Jim Bowie lay on a cot, too ill to move, suffering from tuberculosis and typhoid-pneumonia, but he asked his comrades to lift him across the line.

On the thirteenth day of the siege, Santa Anna, aided by fresh reinforcements, attacked. His gun batteries opened two holes in the walls, and his men placed ladders at other points. The fighting became hand to hand as Texans clubbed any attackers who made it over the walls. But the enemy burst through the holes, opening up an attack from both sides.

Travis was slumped over a cannon, shot through the forehead. Davy Crockett's right arm was broken by a bullet. He fired with his left until the stock of his rifle was shattered. He went down only when a knife was buried in his chest. Five Texan prisoners were paraded before the victorious army before being cruelly bayoneted.

Oil was poured over the mound of bodies, and they were burned. The only American survivors were Susannah Dickinson, wife of a soldier, her daughter Angelina, and a black slave sent along to escort her as she carried back the gruesome news to the Texan forces.

To Santa Anna the battle was "but a small affair." But to Americans and Texans, it had tremendous impact. To Texans the only alternative now was freedom; enraged, they wanted revenge.

Goliad and San Jacinto—The feelings of rage deepened when a group of soldiers under James Fannin surrendered to the Mexicans near Goliad. They believed they would be treated as prisoners of war, but when they arrived at Goliad, the Mexicans killed over three hundred of the prisoners, all of them unarmed.

Texas's last hope was Sam Houston with his army of eight hundred men. Houston planned carefully for one last battle on the

Sam Houston was the leader of the Texan army and became the first president of the Lone Star Republic.

plain where the San Jacinto (san juh-SIN-toh) River ran into Galveston Bay. The forces made a surprise attack on Santa Anna, yelling, "Remember the Alamo!" as they charged. In twenty minutes the **battle of San Jacinto** was history. Almost the entire Mexican Army of fourteen hundred was either killed or captured. Houston kept the Texans from murdering Santa Anna, choosing rather to hold Santa Anna hostage to prevent further attacks on Texas.

The Lone Star Republic

Houston recrossed the river and returned to Texas. Only a few days before the fall of the Alamo, Texans had met in a convention, issuing a declaration of independence and writing a constitution. Sam Houston was elected the first president of their provisional government by a landslide. Texas first applied for admission into the Union in 1836 but was refused because Mexico threatened war with the United States if action were taken on statehood. Hence, Texas stood alone for nine years as the **"Lone Star Republic."**

Other attempts at **annexation** (the formal process of being added to the Union) were refused, not only because of fear of war with Mexico but also because of slavery. Rumors that supporters of slavery were planning to carve five or six states from Texas brought strong protest from opponents of slavery.

Texas Gains Statehood

By 1844, a presidential election year, the dispute between Britain and the United States over Oregon had resurfaced. The Whig candi-

Flag of Texas, "The Lone Star State"

date, Henry Clay, vowed to keep Texas out of the Union, as did Martin Van Buren, the Democratic front-runner. Ex-president Jackson astutely read public opinion. He told "Young Hickory," **James K. Polk,** a fellow Tennessean, that he could win both the nomination and the presidency by promising "All of Oregon, All of Texas." This pledge lured both Northerners and Southerners into the Democrats' fold, made James K. Polk, the Democrat dark horse (little-known candidate), president, and led to statehood for Texas in 1845.

Before it became a state, Texas was an independent republic with its own flag and currency.

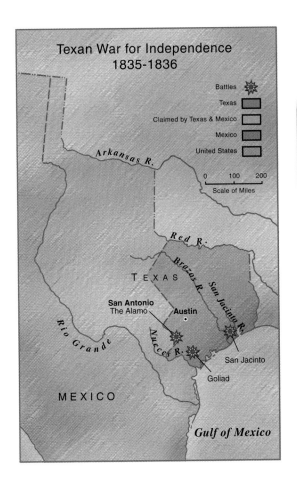

Texan War for Independence
1835-1836

Battles
Texas
Claimed by Texas & Mexico
Mexico
United States

0   100   200
Scale of Miles

Arkansas R.

Red R.

Brazos R.

San Jacinto R.

TEXAS

San Antonio
The Alamo
Austin

Rio Grande

Nueces R.

San Jacinto

Goliad

MEXICO

Gulf of Mexico

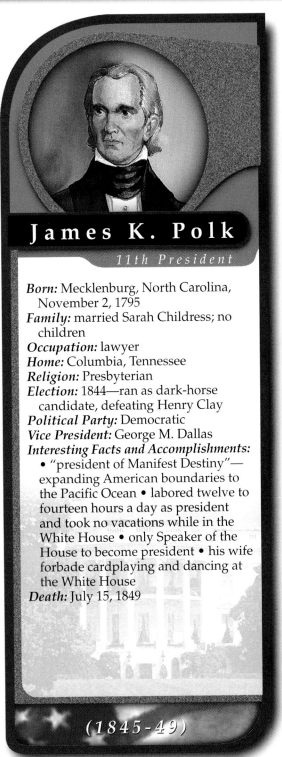

James K. Polk

11th President

Born: Mecklenburg, North Carolina,
November 2, 1795
Family: married Sarah Childress; no
children
Occupation: lawyer
Home: Columbia, Tennessee
Religion: Presbyterian
Election: 1844—ran as dark-horse
candidate, defeating Henry Clay
Political Party: Democratic
Vice President: George M. Dallas
Interesting Facts and Accomplishments:
  • "president of Manifest Destiny"—
  expanding American boundaries to
  the Pacific Ocean • labored twelve to
  fourteen hours a day as president
  and took no vacations while in the
  White House • only Speaker of the
  House to become president • his wife
  forbade cardplaying and dancing at
  the White House
Death: July 15, 1849

(1845-49)

The Mexican War

Just three weeks after Polk took office,
Mexico broke off relations with the United
States. President Polk sent General **Zachary
Taylor** and fourteen hundred troops across the
Gulf of Mexico to land at Corpus Christi in
case war broke out. While he expected war, he
also sought a peaceful settlement. He sent
John Slidell to Mexico City, Mexico's capital,
to offer to buy California and New Mexico,
but the Mexicans refused to meet with Slidell.

Mexico held that the southern border of
Texas was the Nueces (noo AY sis) River.
Therefore, Mexico held that the presence of
American troops south of that river was an act
of war. Polk and Taylor chose to believe that

the Rio Grande was the border and cared little about what Mexico thought. For two weeks the two armies taunted each other across the river.

On May 8, 1846, the Mexican general Mariano Arista slipped across the border and launched a surprise attack on Taylor at Palo Alto. After staunch American resistance, the Mexicans withdrew to a dry, thorny riverbed called Resaca de la Palma. American sharpshooters routed them. Happy Americans celebrated with torchlight parades and even talked of making Zachary Taylor the new president.

War Is Declared—When Taylor's reports reached Washington, President Polk asked Congress to declare war on Mexico. The declaration was signed May 13, 1846, and Congress authorized the president to call fifty thousand volunteers. More volunteers came forward than were needed; in some places they drew lots to see who would get to go to war.

The **Mexican War,** however, was not universally popular. Many New Englanders believed the war was a well-planned attempt by Southerners to grasp more land to create new slave states. The war was especially unpopular in the American intellectual community. For example, an American writer, Henry David Thoreau (thuh ROH), went to jail rather than pay a poll tax, part of which might go to support a war that he believed unjust.

Nonetheless the war was fought with patriotic fervor. A press corps followed the armies; using Samuel Morse's new telegraph, reporters wired back descriptions of American bravery to an eager public. For the first time Americans had a chance to follow a war closely.

Old Rough and Ready—Taylor's volunteer army was shaped into seasoned regulars through training and hardships. Their camp at Corpus Christi contributed its share of hardships. The area was infested with rattlesnakes and malarial mosquitoes, and the water caused

dysentery. The rations were almost inedible: the bacon was spoiled, the hardtack was wormy, and the flour was maggot-laden.

Although Taylor was not a brilliant strategist, he was a brave soldier. He had no love for military pomp; his field uniform included a wide-brimmed straw hat, a soiled white linen

"Old Rough and Ready" Zachary Taylor

jacket, and baggy trousers. His nickname, earned in the Seminole War, was "Old Rough and Ready." His men loved him.

By September, Taylor had marched his troops into Mexico toward Monterrey. Mexican resistance in Monterrey was stronger than expected, but the city was captured by house-to-house fighting.

Taylor then faced a period of inactivity. Polk believed that Taylor's popularity had increased enough to make him a presidential competitor. To take the focus off Taylor, Polk appointed several Democrats as brigadier generals, hoping that one would outshine Taylor. In the meantime, the Americans grew careless and did not send out patrols. Santa Anna's army captured a half-dozen outposts, then wheeled into position to take Taylor's army from the rear. Taylor retreated to a sheep ranch called Buena Vista (BWAY-nuh VEE-stuh). He had to burn tons of supplies to keep them from capture.

Twice the American troops were pushed back. A severe thunderstorm halted the Mexicans, allowing the Americans to stiffen their line and prepare for a counterattack. Taylor was outnumbered three to one, but he still won the battle for Buena Vista.

The Santa Fe and California Campaigns—While the Mexican War progressed, Polk saw opportunity for the dream of Manifest Destiny to be fulfilled. The Mexican provinces of California and New Mexico were tempting prizes that soon became a war objective. Polk made plans to seize both territories, and Americans already in those areas were ready to show the American government that they were loyal.

The scheme to conquer California was shrewd. Captain **John Charles Frémont,** called "the Pathfinder" because of his western explorations, came to California with sixty soldiers clad in buckskin. He said they were making a geographic survey. Frémont's secret orders, however, were to help the United States Pacific Squadron if war came. Commodore John Sloat had brought several warships to California to guard the American interests. Sloat proclaimed California American territory and turned the command

John C. Frémont's victory in the Bear Flag Revolution brought California under American control.

over to Commodore Robert Stockton, who headed south with a land force. Learning of the war with Mexico, Frémont led his band and some American settlers in what was called the **"Bear Flag Revolution."** California fell easily into American hands.

In the meantime, Colonel Stephen Kearny was leading an army to California from Fort Leavenworth, Kansas. The first leg of Kearny's trek to San Diego took him to Santa Fe. But the Mexicans in Santa Fe fled their positions, allowing Kearny to take the town without firing a shot. He left Colonel Alexander Doniphan (DON ih fun) and nine hundred men to complete the conquest of New Mexico and to seize Chihuahua (chee WAH wah), a province in northern Mexico.

The Battles of Veracruz and Mexico City—General **Winfield Scott** was placed in command of the Veracruz operation, the closing campaign of the war. Scott was just about everything Zachary Taylor was not. Scott was a handsome, six-foot-four-inch man who had a taste for dress uniforms and who expected his men and others to adhere to military regulations. His liking for discipline and pomp had won him the nickname "Old Fuss and Feathers," but he was a skilled soldier. Scott and his troops left New Orleans, traveled to Veracruz by steamer, and took the city.

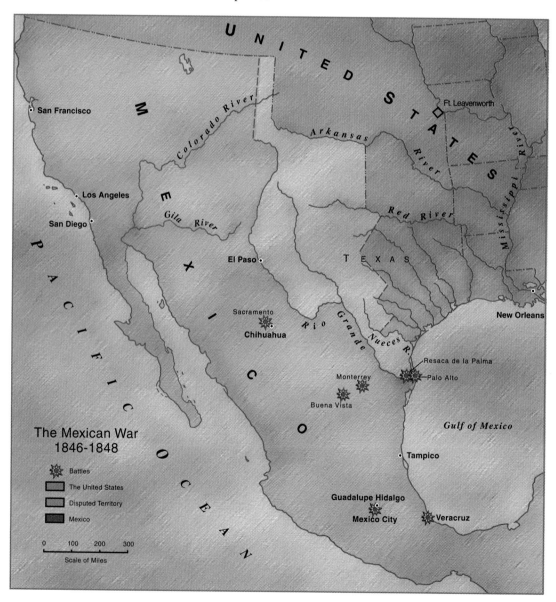

The Mexican War
1846-1848

✦ Battles
☐ The United States
☐ Disputed Territory
■ Mexico

0   100   200   300
Scale of Miles

Despite the losses at Buena Vista and Veracruz, Santa Anna did not concede defeat. He reorganized his army for a last stand, but Scott found a route through the mountains and attacked him from the side. Santa Anna's army panicked and fled to Mexico City. Four more minor battles were fought before Mexico City finally surrendered in September of 1847.

The Treaty of Guadalupe Hidalgo—By the terms of the **Treaty of Guadalupe Hidalgo** (GWAHD-ul-oop hih-DAL-go), the fighting was ended. The Rio Grande became the boundary of Texas. The **Mexican Cession,**

Winfield Scott got the nickname "Old Fuss and Feathers" because of his love for discipline and pomp.

consisting of California, Nevada, and Utah plus parts of Wyoming, Colorado, Arizona, and New Mexico, became part of the United States. The United States agreed to pay Mexico $15 million for the land and canceled all debts Mexico owed to the United States.

Results of the Mexican War

The Mexican War made the expansionists' dream of "Manifest Destiny" a reality. It also made a hero of Zachary Taylor, soon putting him into the White House.

But the Mexican War reopened the old controversy over slavery. Would the new lands of the Mexican Cession be slave or free? The South wanted the new cession to be open to slavery; the North wanted it to be free. "The United States will conquer Mexico," author Ralph Waldo Emerson wrote, "but it will be as the man who swallows the arsenic which brings him down in turn. Mexico will poison us."

The Mexican War served as a training ground for the Civil War, which was to come thirteen years later. Many of the men who became famous leaders in the Civil War gained valued experience in this earlier conflict. Jefferson Davis, Robert E. Lee, Ulysses S. Grant, Thomas "Stonewall" Jackson, George G. Meade, and George McClellan were among the many army officers who fought in Mexico.

The lands gained in the Mexican War proved to be valuable. Already in 1848 Americans realized the value of California's fine harbors. These could be used to aid Pacific trade. As the war ended, gold was discovered in California, and in later years major sources of silver and uranium were also found in these lands. Although much of the land was desert or at least semiarid, through the use of irrigation some of the lands became valuable even for farming.

The Gadsden Purchase

Just five years after the war ended, the United States realized its need for another section of Mexican land on the border of New Mexico and Arizona. The United States wanted this narrow strip of land as a possible southern transcontinental railroad route. Mexico agreed to sell the land, and diplomat

James Gadsden arranged the American purchase for $10 million. This **Gadsden Purchase** completed the acquisition of territory for the forty-eight contiguous United States.

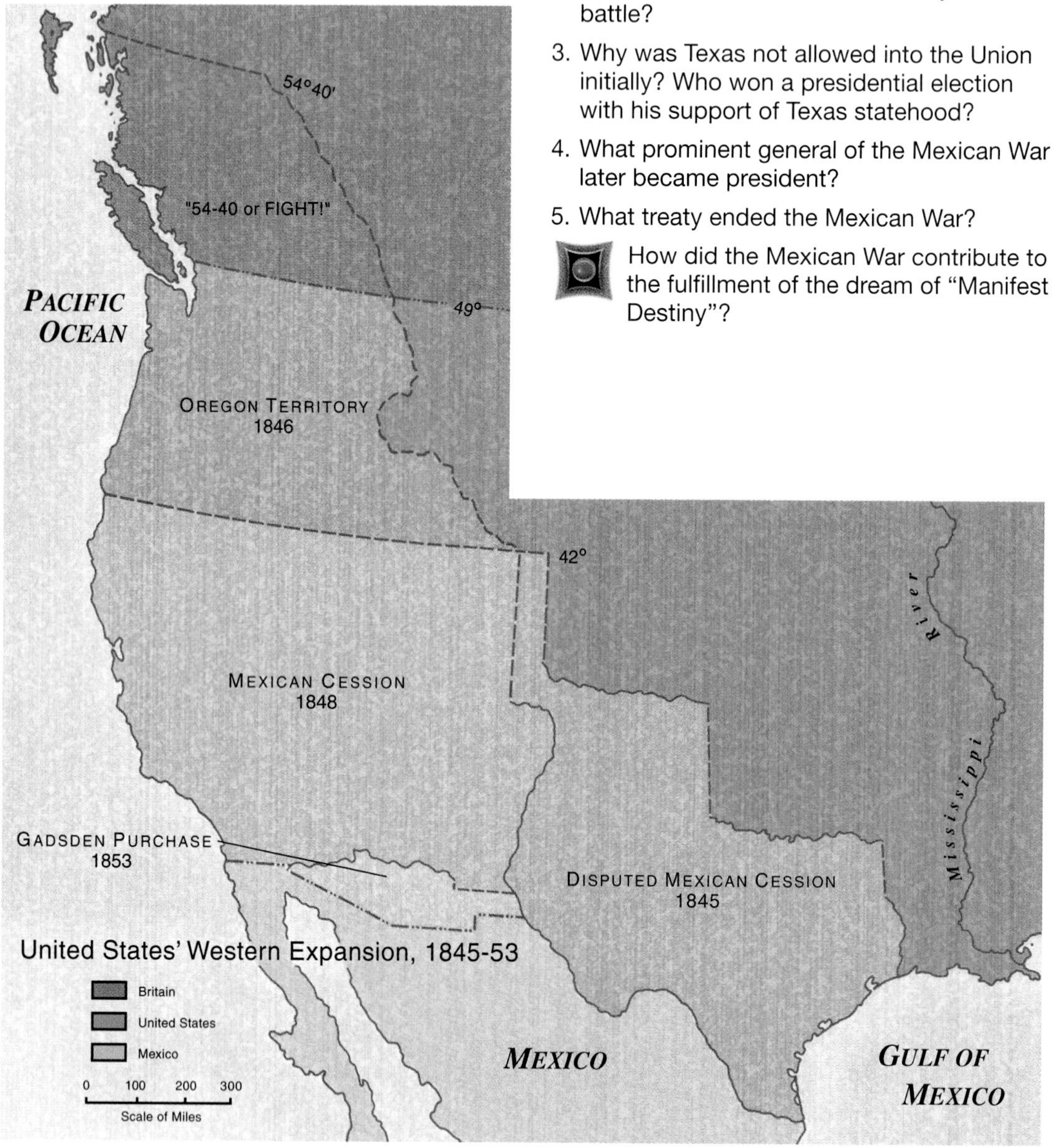

1. What disastrous defeat pushed the Texans to fight for their independence?

2. At what short battle did the Texans defeat the Mexicans? Who led each army in that battle?

3. Why was Texas not allowed into the Union initially? Who won a presidential election with his support of Texas statehood?

4. What prominent general of the Mexican War later became president?

5. What treaty ended the Mexican War?

How did the Mexican War contribute to the fulfillment of the dream of "Manifest Destiny"?

PACIFIC OCEAN

54°40'

"54-40 or FIGHT!"

49°

OREGON TERRITORY 1846

42°

MEXICAN CESSION 1848

GADSDEN PURCHASE 1853

DISPUTED MEXICAN CESSION 1845

Mississippi River

United States' Western Expansion, 1845-53

Britain

United States

Mexico

0   100   200   300

Scale of Miles

MEXICO

GULF OF MEXICO

The Settling of Oregon and California

The far western lands of Oregon and California held many treasures for Americans, and the 1840s and 1850s saw the great rush of settlers and miners to these areas.

Opening Oregon

Great Britain and the United States both claimed Oregon, and in 1818 they agreed to a joint occupation of the area. This was extended indefinitely after 1827. The first lure to Oregon Territory was furs. After trapping first on the coast, the traders turned eastward to the Rocky Mountains. More fur trading companies became involved in the area, joining the Hudson Bay Company, a company that had been active since its founding in 1670 and still exists today. John Jacob Astor, a German immigrant, set up the American Fur Company in 1808. The Rocky Mountain Fur Company, directed by three trappers—Thomas Fitzpatrick, James Bridger, and Milton Sublette—also entered the region.

Each year beginning in the early 1820s, the fur companies in the area hired parties to go west from St. Louis to meet the **mountain men.** About six hundred in number, these men lived in the Rockies and trapped furs themselves or bought pelts from the Indians. Each summer all the mountain men, many Indians, and several company agents gathered in one place. They usually met at Green River Flats, Wyoming, near Fort Laramie (LAHR uh mee). There the trappers traded their furs for goods and caught up on the year's events. The rendezvous (RAHN day voo), or coming together, also brought out some of the worst in the mountain men; gambling, drinking, and fighting were commonplace.

The mountain men did provide valuable services, however. They marked the best routes, explored the courses of the rivers, and found major passes through the mountains.

The most useful pass, South Pass, was located by Jedediah Smith, whose Christian life made him notable among the mountain men. South Pass greatly aided western caravans and enabled missionaries to bring the gospel to the West. Mountain men like Joe Meek and Kit Carson also served as guides for the wagon trains.

The first Americans to seek permanent homes in Oregon were Methodist missionaries. Although their primary purpose had been to bring the gospel to the Indians, their work was soon frustrated by the arrival of great numbers of whites who got "Oregon fever." Reports of cheap fertile land in the Willamette (wuh LAM it) Valley drew thousands west. Every American settler helped to reinforce the United States' claim to the territory. Although Polk's use of "54° 40′ or fight" during his presidential campaign had made that slogan a battle cry, the British were willing to

John Astor's fur company joined other fur companies in the Oregon Territory.

compromise. (54° 40′ was the extreme northern boundary of the disputed Oregon Territory.) Since most of the furs had been trapped in the region near to and south of the Columbia River, and since more Americans were in that region, the British base was moved north to Vancouver (van KOO vur) Island. Therefore, in 1846 the boundary line was set at the 49th parallel, stretching from Minnesota's Northwest Angle west to Puget (PYOO jit) Sound.

California

When the Spanish explorer Cabrillo (kah BREE yoh) claimed California in 1540, the Spanish shared it with the "digger Indians." Those Indians lived by seed gathering or digging for shellfish along the Pacific Coastal Plain. Franciscan missionary priests moved into the area, but it was only after 1769, when the British and Russians threatened to move into the area as well, that the Spanish settled there in earnest. Gaspar de Portolá (por toh LAH) established a settlement at Monterrey in 1770, and Junípero Serra (HOO-nih-peh-roh SEHR-ah) set up a mission system along the coast. After Mexico declared its independence from Spain, Californians declared allegiance to Mexico. Trading opportunities and the Frémont expeditions west stimulated the

Mountain Man of Faith

As a group the mountain men were rough, profane, ungodly men, determined to make their fortune as trappers and traders in the unsettled West. Their yearly rendezvous was a time of gambling, violence, and drunkenness.

Yet perhaps the greatest of these trappers, Jedediah Smith, stands in stark contrast to the common image of a mountain man. Smith rediscovered the Oregon Trail and thus paved the way for the host of pioneers who settled in that territory. He was the first white man to travel by land to California. He was the first to cross the Sierra Nevada range from the west and the first to cross the arid Great Basin. In the history of America, Jedediah Smith takes his place among the greatest of the explorers.

His personal courage is also unquestioned. Fearlessly he explored lands unknown to white men. Often he battled Indians; once only he and three companions escaped a massacre at the hands of the Umpqua. Early in his explorations he was almost killed by a grizzly bear. The bear had bitten him on the head, and as Smith lay on the ground bleeding, he calmly supervised a friend who sewed up his wounds. Such courage soon established Jedediah Smith as a leader of men.

But as a man of faith, Jedediah Smith excelled all of the other mountain men. He never drank, smoked, or swore. Along with his trapper's gear he carried his Bible, a hymnbook, a set of Matthew Henry's commentaries, and other theological texts. When a fellow trapper died, Jedediah insisted on having a service and reading from his Bible. As fellow trapper, William Waldo, testified, "No one who knew him well doubted the sincerity of his piety." He had been raised in a Christian home, and despite the hostile environment of the mountains and the ungodly influences of the other men, Jedediah Smith never turned back from service for His Lord. His own testimony was, "How often ought we on our bended knees to offer God our grateful acknowledgments for the gift of His dear Son."

At the age of 32, while scouting for a group of pioneers, Jedediah Smith was attacked and killed by a party of Comanches. The testimony of his Christian character, however, lives on today.

American interest in California. The area became an American possession following the Mexican War and the Treaty of Guadalupe Hidalgo.

Discovery of Gold—On January 24, 1848, just ten days before the signing of the treaty, an event that would drastically shape the history of California occurred at Sutter's Fort. **John Sutter,** a Swiss immigrant who had left his wife and family in Europe, secured a fifty-thousand-acre grant from the Spanish. On this land he had set up his own community called Sutter's Fort. Sutter had hired a mechanic, **James W. Marshall,** to build and operate a sawmill. The site Marshall chose for the mill was by the American River, forty miles

The gold rush of 1849 began after John Sutter found gold particles in his mill channel.

upstream from the fort, in a valley that the Indians called the Columa, meaning "Beautiful Vale." Marshall tried to deepen the river channel and divert the channel to form a fast-running millrace to drive the mill's water wheel.

While making his daily inspection of the lower part of the channel in January of 1848, Marshall saw a sparkling object in the mud and sand. Using a tin plate, Marshall washed out the dirt, leaving yellow particles "about as

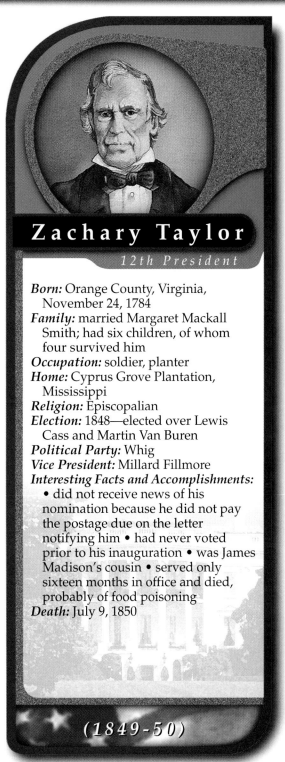

Zachary Taylor
12th President

Born: Orange County, Virginia, November 24, 1784
Family: married Margaret Mackall Smith; had six children, of whom four survived him
Occupation: soldier, planter
Home: Cyprus Grove Plantation, Mississippi
Religion: Episcopalian
Election: 1848—elected over Lewis Cass and Martin Van Buren
Political Party: Whig
Vice President: Millard Fillmore
Interesting Facts and Accomplishments:
  • did not receive news of his nomination because he did not pay the postage due on the letter notifying him • had never voted prior to his inauguration • was James Madison's cousin • served only sixteen months in office and died, probably of food poisoning
Death: July 9, 1850

(1849-50)

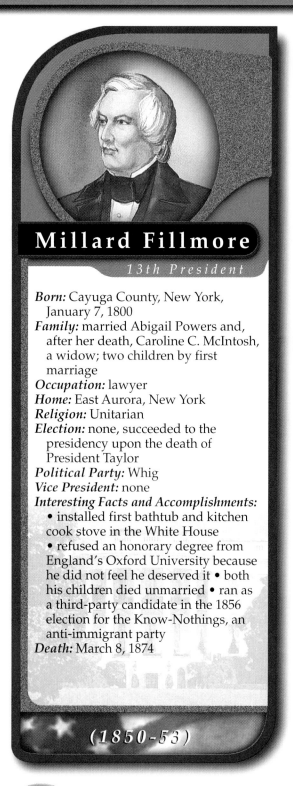

Millard Fillmore

13th President

Born: Cayuga County, New York, January 7, 1800

Family: married Abigail Powers and, after her death, Caroline C. McIntosh, a widow; two children by first marriage

Occupation: lawyer

Home: East Aurora, New York

Religion: Unitarian

Election: none, succeeded to the presidency upon the death of President Taylor

Political Party: Whig

Vice President: none

Interesting Facts and Accomplishments:
• installed first bathtub and kitchen cook stove in the White House
• refused an honorary degree from England's Oxford University because he did not feel he deserved it • both his children died unmarried • ran as a third-party candidate in the 1856 election for the Know-Nothings, an anti-immigrant party

Death: March 8, 1874

(1850-53)

much as would cover a dime." He found more metal the next morning. Since no one was sure whether it was real gold, he performed several tests. Marshall returned to Sutter's Fort to share the news with his employer. Sutter also tested the metal and was convinced that it was gold. It was impossible to keep the news secret. When one of Marshall's workmen tried to pay off a bill in gold bits, the creditor asked for confirmation. The word was out, and the **California gold rush** was on.

The Forty-Niners—The argonauts, as the men who searched for gold called themselves, were hard-working men who set out for California full of hope and energy. In 1849 alone, over eighty thousand men came to California, and they came to be called **"forty-niners."** Thirty-nine thousand came by sea on the four- to five-month journey around Cape Horn. Some sailed to Panama, crossed the isthmus by foot or horseback, and got on a ship on the other side. More than forty thousand made the trip by land using trails.

Hard physical labor in the gold fields was the key to wealth. Since all the men worked with their hands, there was little snobbery. Most of the miners dressed alike, wearing colorful shirts, broad-brimmed hats, and trousers stuffed into high boots. Mining camps grew up wherever gold was being found. Pans, rockers, troughs, and sluice boxes were used to separate the gold from the dirt. As miners accumulated their wealth, crime became rampant in many of the camps. Claim disputes, robberies, and murders were common.

About half of the would-be miners chose to pursue wealth another way. They became farmers, ranchers, and storekeepers and provided the miners with needed goods and services.

By the fall of 1849, Californians had written a state constitution. Since its writers voted to prohibit slavery in California, Congress delayed California's request for statehood.

California became a state on September 9, 1850, because of a compromise made in Congress.

SECTION REVIEW

1. What two countries agreed in 1818 to occupy Oregon jointly?

2. What drew men to the Oregon Territory at the beginning? Who were the first Americans to seek permanent homes there?

3. The Americans took possession of California during what war?

 How did the California gold rush shape the settlement of the state?

Sectional Rivalry Increases

With the acquisition of the new western lands, the slavery issue boiled. The South wanted to keep the lands open to slavery while most Northerners wished to ban slavery from these territories. When California sought admission to the union as a free state, debate raged for months.

The Compromise of 1850

The year 1848 was an election year. Zachary Taylor, the hero of Buena Vista, was elected president over Michigan's Lewis Cass. Although Taylor was a Southerner and a slave owner, he had taken little interest in politics before 1848, and Northerners did not think he was a strong supporter of slavery. Taylor stunned Southerners by encouraging Californians to apply directly for statehood as a free state.

Henry Clay and other leaders in congress proposed a compromise. In the **Compromise of 1850** Northerners got what they wanted with California admitted as a free state. To please Southerners, the rest of the land gained through the Mexican Cession was divided into New Mexico and Utah territories. In both territories the people were allowed to decide

Franklin Pierce

14th President

Born: Hillshore, New Hampshire, November 23, 1804
Family: married Jane Means Appleton; three sons who died in childhood
Occupation: lawyer
Home: Pierce Homestead, Hillshore Upper Village, New Hampshire
Religion: Episcopalian
Election: 1852—defeated Winfield Scott
Political Party: Democratic
Vice President: William Rufus King (who died one month after his inauguration)
Interesting Facts and Accomplishments:
• a college classmate of Nathaniel Hawthorne at Bowdoin College • served as a brigadier general in the Mexican War • lost his sons and claimed that his personal tragedies were God's punishments for sin
Death: October 8, 1869

(1853-57)

whether they wanted to have slavery. This was called **popular sovereignty.** In addition, a stricter Fugitive Slave Law required all federal government officials to help return runaway slaves, and slave trade was outlawed in the District of Columbia. Finally, Texas was paid for giving up some of its land.

Because California statehood was linked to the other legislation, Taylor refused to back the whole bill.

He believed that the Texans should not be paid. However, after only sixteen months in office, Taylor died in 1850.

Taylor's vice president, **Millard Fillmore,** who was a Whig and a supporter of the compromise, took the office of president. By splitting Clay's measures into five separate bills that could individually gather enough support to be passed, **Stephen Douglas** got the compromise through. Fillmore approved the compromise even though it proved to be political suicide because the Whig Party strongly opposed the Fugitive Slave Law.

Doughfaces

By 1850 Congress and the nation were changing. The Great Compromisers—Clay, Calhoun, Webster, and Thomas Hart Benton—were passing from the scene. New, younger leaders were of a different frame of mind.

Charles Sumner of Massachusetts, William H. Seward of New York, Thaddeus Stevens of Pennsylvania, and Salmon P. Chase of Ohio bitterly fought against slavery in Congress while Southerners fought to protect it. The only ones willing to compromise on the problems of the 1850s were Stephen Douglas and a group of Northern Democrats called **Doughfaces.** The Doughfaces seemed more moderate because they did not oppose the pro-slavery position. They were willing to concentrate on other political issues and let the South handle its own affairs.

War hero Winfield Scott was the Whig nominee for president in 1852. Because he lost votes to Democrats in the South and Free Soilers in the North, Scott lost the election to **Franklin Pierce,** a Doughface Democrat.

SECTION REVIEW

1. What were the terms of the Compromise of 1850?

2. What president was elected in 1848 and died after sixteen months in office?

3. What was a Doughface?

 Why was it harder to get a compromise passed in this time than it had been earlier?

SUMMARY

The United States expanded to fulfill its "Manifest Destiny" before the Civil War. Trails west carried traders and settlers who sought new opportunities in Oregon, California, Utah, and the Southwest. Texas, heavily settled by Americans, won its independence from Mexico and later joined the Union. The resulting Mexican War gave the United States opportunities to gain California and the rest of the Southwest for its own. These acquisitions, along with settled boundaries for the Oregon Territory, made the United States a land that stretched from coast to coast.

Chapter Review

People, Places, and Things to Remember

Manifest Destiny
Mormons
Joseph Smith
Brigham Young
Santa Fe Trail
Oregon Trail
Jedediah Smith
California Trail
Stephen Austin
Antonio López de Santa
   Anna
Jim Bowie
Sam Houston

the Alamo
battle of San Jacinto
Lone Star Republic
annexation
James K. Polk
Zachary Taylor
Mexican War
John Charles Frémont
Bear Flag Revolution
Winfield Scott
Treaty of Guadalupe
   Hidalgo
Mexican Cession

Gadsden Purchase
mountain men
John Sutter
James W. Marshall
California gold rush
forty-niners
Compromise of 1850
popular sovereignty
Millard Fillmore
Stephen Douglas
Doughfaces
Franklin Pierce

Review Questions

What were these people often called?

1. miners who rushed to California

2. followers of Joseph Smith

3. moderate northern Democrats who did not fight against slavery

4. fur trappers and traders who blazed trails in the West

Who am I?

5. James W. Marshall

6. Zachary Taylor

7. Stephen Douglas

8. Jim Bowie

9. Brigham Young

10. Jedediah Smith

11. Stephen Austin

12. John Charles Frémont

a. I was called "the Pathfinder."

b. I led the Mormons to Utah.

c. I discovered gold in California.

d. I led American settlers to Texas.

e. I supported the Compromise of 1850.

f. I fought at the Alamo.

g. I rediscovered the Oregon Trail.

h. I was a Mexican War hero and a president.

Questions for Discussion

13. Why was the skirmish at Gonzalez called the "Lexington of the Texas Revolution"?

14. Is it necessary for Congress to make compromises on some political issues? Why or why not?

Facing a Crisis

1860: Abraham Lincoln came to the presidency during one of the most divisive periods of American history and led the nation boldly yet compassionately through its time of crisis.

1865: After four years of bloody civil war, Confederate general Robert E. Lee surrendered his troops to Ulysses S. Grant in the McLean House at Appomattox Courthouse, Virginia.

1861-65: There were over one million casualties in the Civil War, including Confederate private Edwin Francis Jemison, who died on July 1, 1863, at Malvern Hill.

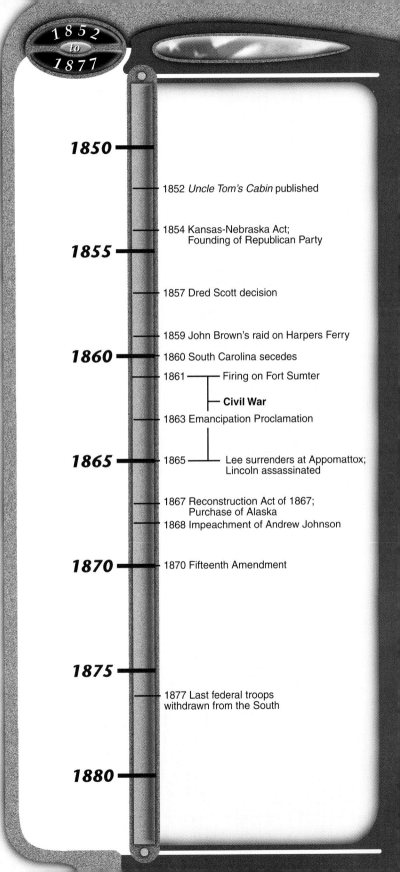

1852
to
1877

1850

1852 *Uncle Tom's Cabin* published

1854 Kansas-Nebraska Act; Founding of Republican Party

1855

1857 Dred Scott decision

1859 John Brown's raid on Harpers Ferry

1860 1860 South Carolina secedes

1861 — Firing on Fort Sumter

— **Civil War**

1863 Emancipation Proclamation

1865 1865 — Lee surrenders at Appomattox; Lincoln assassinated

1867 Reconstruction Act of 1867; Purchase of Alaska

1868 Impeachment of Andrew Johnson

1870 1870 Fifteenth Amendment

1875

1877 Last federal troops withdrawn from the South

1880

Unit IV: Facing a Crisis

Stowe's Account of the Publication of *Uncle Tom's Cabin*

Harriet Beecher Stowe gave the story behind the writing of *Uncle Tom's Cabin,* the most influential book in American history. Read this excerpt and the questions below. Then write the first five words of the sentence in the text that answers each question.

With astonishment and distress Mrs. Stowe heard on all sides, from humane and Christian people, that the slavery of the blacks was a guaranteed constitutional right, and that all opposition to it endangered the national Union. With this conviction she saw that even earnest and tenderhearted Christians seemed to feel it a duty to close their eyes, ears, and hearts to the harrowing details of slavery, to put down all discussion of the subject, and even to assist slave owners to recover fugitives in Northern States. She said to herself, These people can not know what slavery is: they do not see what they are defending; and hence arose a purpose to write some sketches which would show to the world of slavery as she had herself seen it. . . .

In shaping her material, the author had but one purpose, to show the institution of slavery truly, just as it existed. She had visited Kentucky, had formed the acquaintance of people who were just, upright, and generous, and yet slave holders. She had heard their views and appreciated their situation. She felt that justice required that their difficulties should be recognized and their virtues acknowledged. It was her object to show that the evils of slavery were the inherent evils of a bad system, and not always the fault of those who had become involved in it and were its actual administrators. . . .

Uncle Tom's Cabin was published March 20, 1852. The despondency of the author as to the question whether anybody would read or attend to her appeal was soon dispelled. Ten thousand copies were sold in a few days, and over 300,000 within a year; and eight power presses, running day and night, were barely able to keep pace with the demand for it. It was read everywhere, apparently, and by everyone; and she soon began to hear echoes of sympathy all over the land. The indignation, the pity, the distress that had long weighed upon her soul, seemed to pass off from her and into the readers of the book.

In one respect, Mrs. Stowe's expectations were strikingly different from fact. She had painted slaveholders as amiable, generous, and just. She had shown examples among them of the noblest and most beautiful traits of character, had admitted fully their temptations, their perplexities, so that a friend of hers who had many relatives in the South wrote to her in exultation, "Your book is going to be the great pacificator: it will unite both North and South." Her expectation was that the professed Abolitionists would denounce it as altogether too mild in its dealings with slaveholders. To her astonishment, it was the extreme Abolitionists who received it, and the entire South who rose up against it.

1. According to Stowe, why did Northerners shut their eyes to slavery?

2. Stowe did not write her novel simply to entertain her readers. What did she want to "pass into them"?

3. Did Stowe write her novel to help the cause of extreme abolitionism?

4. Did Stowe expect the Southerners to ban her novel?

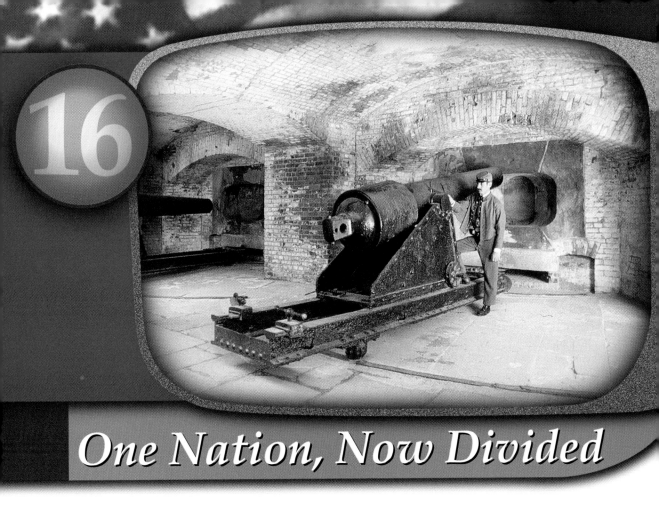

16

One Nation, Now Divided

I n the 1850s, the United States experienced new growth and, except for a brief financial panic in 1857, prosperity. The population reached thirty-one million, a thirty-five percent increase in just ten years. Production of foodstuffs and manufactured goods reached new heights. The resources that God had given the United States, acres of unoccupied land, a network of navigable rivers, and huge amounts of timber, would allow the country to sustain progress. But this economic boom was only part of the picture of the United States at that time. Greater problems were about to rend the nation in two.

Differences Between the North and the South

There were several key issues that led to a division between the North and the South. Although the issues were not new, more people were beginning to see the issues as matters of right and wrong instead of as mere regional preferences. There was no longer much room for compromise between the two regions of the country.

Differing Economies and Lifestyles

There were major economic differences between the North and the South. The South was agricultural. Towns and villages were few—cities, scarcer yet. Furthermore, nearly all of the South's cities, such as Charleston, Richmond, and Savannah, were relatively small, having populations under 40,000. Only New Orleans, with its population of 150,000, compared to northern cities in size and diversity. Instead of factories, the South had plantations and farms that raised cotton and other crops for sale. Much of the business of southern cities revolved around the trade of agricultural materials and crops.

In the South, the upper class, one percent of the population, was made up of planters owning large plantations and many slaves. This top one percent was the ruling class politically, socially, and economically. Other white farmers owned only a few slaves (generally fewer than ten). A much larger part of the southern white population, however, owned no slaves at all. (Owners of small farms and other Southerners without slaves made up three-quarters of the white population.) Yet the way of life of all Southerners was greatly influenced by the needs and desires of the slaveholders.

This photograph taken in South Carolina in 1862 shows a slave family that was fortunate enough to have several generations living on one plantation.

In contrast to the agricultural, slaveholding South, the North was industrialized and had few slaves. Its many cities were crowded and noisy. Some grew so quickly that it was hard for them to handle the growth. New York City's population soared to over 800,000. When Chicago became incorporated in 1837, it had only 4,170 people. In 1860 the census takers counted 112,000 Chicago residents.

One reason for the great population increase in the North was immigration. More than 2.8 million immigrants had come to America, and seven out of eight settled in the North or West. Initially many were forced to live in filth and misery in the cities while laboring long hours for low wages. The working and living conditions of some northern workers were so poor that Southerners called them "wage slaves." But soon many foreigners adopted American ways and raised their standards of living. Many held political offices. In Boston, New York, and Philadelphia, Irish voters were influential, and in St. Louis, Cincinnati, and Milwaukee anyone running for office had to consider the wishes of the German residents.

In the North owners of small farms, merchants, and increasing numbers of factory workers made up most of the population. Four-fifths of the nation's factories were in the North. Although most people were still farmers, mechanized agriculture helped them to produce food for nearby towns. Railroads carried food to the ever-growing cities and returned to rural areas carrying manufactured goods. Owners of factories, railroads, and other businesses and industries became the wealthy and influential people in northern society.

Differing Political Views

The differing economies and lifestyles produced differing political views as well. Generally the North favored a strong central government. Northerners tended to be more willing to pay higher taxes to provide local and state goods and services. The North also had more wage earners to help pay for such costs.

Many Southerners feared a strong central government. They still believed in Jefferson's ideal that the best government was local and state government. Little money was spent on local services because few of the Southerners lived in cities and towns where services such as police protection or city building projects were needed. Since education was considered a private matter, there were few public schools in the South at this time. Neither did most southern taxpayers wish to pay large amounts of taxes to the federal government for spending on improvements and benefits that often chiefly aided the more populous areas in the North.

The two sections also sharply disagreed about what level of government (federal or state) should possess more authority. Most Northerners believed that the Constitution was the nation's highest law under God and that the Constitution and federal law overruled any conflicting state and local laws. They based their view on Article VI of the Constitution.

Many Southerners disagreed, arguing that the federal government could not overrule the rights of the states. They emphasized the idea that government was an agreement between a ruling body and those ruled. When those rulers exceeded the power given to them by the people, the people had the right to nullify unacceptable laws. In this way states' rights could be upheld over national sovereignty or authority.

The South feared being in the minority, and every time a new state applied to join the Union, the South's fears resurfaced. Every new free state in the Union meant more votes against the southern views. If the North gained too large a majority, it might force the South into submission.

Another political issue dividing the North and South was the tariff. The North generally favored a high protective tariff to protect its industries from foreign imports. The South opposed it because it had little industry of its own and also because it needed foreign imports and trade to support its livelihood. The South was, in effect, being forced to pay the tariff to support northern industry.

In addition to the other differences, the issue of slavery was widening the rift between the North and the South.

SECTION REVIEW

1. What was the main economic focus of the South? the North?

2. What groups of people were most influential in northern and southern society?

 How and why did Northerners and Southerners differ in their views of government?

Slavery: America's Great Debate

In Chapter 3 we learned about how slaves first came to America and how slavery developed there (see pp. 42-43). Although slavery is nearly as old as the human race, slavery in the United States was different from other instances of slavery in history in three ways. It was limited to the black race; it was usually a permanent condition for the slave; and slave traders seeking profits promoted it.

Slavery came about largely because of the need for labor, especially in the South. In that region many laborers were needed to produce the profitable crops of the region—tobacco, indigo, rice, cotton, and sugar cane. Few whites sought low-paying, hard field jobs on southern plantations when they could easily acquire land to farm for themselves. White landowners saw the forced labor of black slaves as a solution. In northern and western areas, farms were smaller, and large money crops had not developed. Not needing large numbers of field hands, and with immigrants to supply labor for many factories, the North did not use slaves, for the most part. Slavery was a terrible injustice, but it developed with little protest under the disguise of a "needed" and "acceptable" institution in early America.

By the 1830s, however, many Americans realized that slavery was not just another system of labor. The question of whether it was morally right or wrong became a great debate. Whites who depended on slavery defended the institution. Some justified slavery on religious grounds. They said that bringing the uncivilized slave to the New World helped him to be Christianized. Some praised it as "a positive good," as had a college professor, Thomas R. Dew, in 1832. He wrote that instead of being an evil, slavery was a positive good when compared to other labor systems. Dew used religious, historical, cultural, racial, and sociological arguments to support his "positive good" theory. John C. Calhoun and other Southerners used these arguments to defend slavery against rising attacks. Nonetheless, opposition to slavery increased as whites and free blacks exposed its wrongs.

How Slaves Were Acquired

Most slaves came from the nations on Africa's western coast. Some slaves were captured in raids and sold to traders. Some were prisoners of war captured by warring African tribes. These tribes were sometimes guilty of selling their enemies into slavery for personal profit. Men, women, and children were captured, chained together, and marched to the seacoast, where slave traders bought them with liquor and various utensils and trinkets. In early colonial days Europeans and New Englanders provided most of the slave ships that then carried the captives to the New World.

Slaves were treated inhumanly from the moment of capture, but perhaps the slave's worst experience was crossing the Atlantic to America. This crossing was called the **"middle passage."** (The first passage took the slave to the coast of Africa; the third passage involved the final sale to slave owners in America.)

Since slave traders knew that even under the best conditions many captives would die, they tried to pack their ships with as many people as possible. Crowded into shelflike decks, the Africans were then chained and shackled wrist-to-wrist and ankle-to-ankle. Poorly fed, these people usually received gruel and water twice a day. Disease spread quickly because of poor sanitation. Some captives broke down under the stress of the voyage and killed themselves and others. There is no way to estimate the number of Africans who died on the middle passage—it was at least one in seven or eight, but it may have been as high as one in four.

Slave auctions had no regard for a slave's family relations. If the highest bid split a family, few dealers cared.

In 1808 the United States became the last major western nation to ban foreign slave trade. (See Article I, Section 9 of the Constitution.) Some slave smuggling did continue, but most new slaves after this time were the children of men and women already living in the United States. Most of the northern states had abolished slavery by the end of the War for Independence.

Some Southerners, moved by the ideals of American independence, spoke out against slavery. As early as the 1820s, a few Quaker-sponsored **emancipation** (ih man suh PAY shun) societies campaigned for gradual emancipation, or freeing of the slaves. Some also pushed for an overseas colony for freed American blacks. Low tobacco prices and worn-out soil caused some to predict that slavery was a dying institution. But the invention of the cotton gin and the opening of new fertile lands in the West revived the plantation economy and made slavery profitable again. When the first American census of the population was made in 1790, there were about 750,000 slaves in the United States. By 1860 the slave population had reached three and a half million; one out of every three Southerners was a slave.

The Northern Viewpoint

Since there was little slavery in the North, the practice had little direct effect on the region. Most Northerners in the early 1800s were not concerned with its existence in the South, either. The prospect that brought the issue of slavery to the attention of the North was its possible spread to new areas in the West. The North did not want more western states to gain the same interests and political views as the South.

Northern feelings also began to change with the growth of **abolitionism** (ab uh LISH uh niz um), a movement to do away with slavery completely. Abolitionists supported emancipation, either gradually or immediately. Some favored **compensated emancipation**, whereby the slave owner would be paid for the loss of his slave. One of the most vocal and militant abolitionists, **William Lloyd Garrison,** began a newspaper in Boston called the *Liberator.* Garrison strongly advocated immediate abolition of slavery without compensation.

While most Northerners embraced antislavery views, they were not willing to give blacks an equal place in society. Few northern states allowed free blacks to vote or offered them public education. Northerners also restricted blacks from many occupations and public offices, and they assigned them separate areas in many churches and other establishments. Some of the western states would not even let blacks settle within their borders!

The Southern Viewpoint

The more abolitionists attacked slavery, the more white Southerners rallied to defend it. Even those who were not slave owners supported it; some hoped one day to own slaves themselves. Because many of the South's businesses relied on cotton produced by slave labor, the prosperity of the entire region seemed to be dependent on the institution. Some whites might have been opposed to slavery, but they saw it as a necessary evil for keeping the cotton culture going.

On the other hand, struggling white farmers on the fringes of the Appalachians in western Virginia and North Carolina and some farmers in eastern Kentucky and Tennessee opposed slavery. Ownership of slaves gave the large plantation owners most of the influence

Bond Slave of Jesus Christ

John Jasper was the youngest of twenty-four children. He was born on a plantation in 1812 to parents who were both slaves. His mother was the main spiritual influence in his life. After his salvation, Jasper said of his mother, "She gave me to God before I was born, prayed me into glory when I was a wild, reckless boy. Prayed me into preaching the Gospel."

Jasper was saved on July 4, 1839, seven months after he learned to read by studying with a fellow slave. For Jasper that day became not only a day to celebrate the nation's independence but also a day to celebrate his own independence from the bonds of sin.

When Jasper's master heard the news of his salvation, he said, "John, your Savior is mine, and we are brothers in the Lord." Jasper was given the day off to "go and tell it." Jasper did just that. For forty years, God used John Jasper to preach the gospel, first as a slave and later as a free man.

As a free black preacher, Jasper started a church in Richmond, Virginia, with nine people meeting in a stable. Soon, however, this handful became a thriving church of over a thousand members. When white people came to hear him preach, they usually sat in a separate section in the balcony. Jasper would joke, "Now, look'a here, you all white people, you keep over in your section. Don't get in the places of the regular customers."

Freed from slavery and freed from sin, John Jasper became a bond slave for Christ. One of Jasper's church members said of him, "He always thought of hisself as the servant of King Jesus. That was a slavery that he liked and never wished to get free from it."

in state government. Many people from these highlands would later side with the North on the issue of slavery.

Treatment of Slaves

Slaves were treated differently from plantation to plantation. Since slaves were an economic investment, keeping them fit and treating them well made sense. They were generally assured of receiving food, clothing, and shelter, and care in childhood and old age was expected. The slave's food was plain like that of poor white Southerners. Cornmeal mush or cornbread, fatback (fat pork from the back of a hog), beans or field peas, and vegetables from the slaves' own gardens composed their staple diet. Slaves who did their work well were occasionally rewarded with an extra day off, better food, or even a little cash. Owners also used the promise of a bigger Christmas celebration or a marriage to someone on a nearby plantation to motivate the slaves. Some slaves became almost like members of the master's family. As a rule, house slaves were treated better than field slaves, and the smaller the plantation, the closer the slaves were to their master. Nonetheless, they were still a people with no basic rights other than those granted by their masters.

Slaves had no legal assistance in cases of mistreatment, and there is no question that some of them were badly treated. Some white masters treated their slaves little better than farm animals. Public whippings for laziness and disobedience sometimes took place. Slaves who were continual troublemakers might be sold to another plantation. Such a sale meant a forced parting with friends and loved ones. The typical slave was sold at least once in a lifetime. Especially dreadful was being "sold down river" (down the Mississippi) to sugar plantations. Cutting sugar cane was extremely hard work; some people were actually worked to death.

Black Responses to Conditions on Plantations

Obviously slaves were not slaves by choice. Strict slave codes in every southern state kept blacks in bondage. In some states even if a slave gained his freedom, he was not allowed to stay in the state.

The Underground Railroad—Hundreds of slaves ran away from their masters to find freedom. The **"Underground Railroad"** offered blacks who could reach the border states a reasonably good chance to escape. This "railroad" was actually a network of people who aided runaway slaves. These "conductors" hid the slaves by day from captors. Then they aided their night travels to the next stop, where others on the escape route helped the runaways move farther north. When the Fugitive Slave Law of 1850 required northern states to return runaways, the "railroad" extended its route. Ontario, Canada, became the final destination for many people seeking freedom.

Slave Rebellions—Some slaves, such as Nat Turner in Virginia and Denmark Vesey (VEE zee) in South Carolina, led revolts. All of them failed, and the blacks involved were hanged. While the hangings made other slaves less likely to rebel, the revolts panicked the whites. They slept with guns and enacted even stricter laws to control the blacks. Several southern states even made it illegal to teach slaves to read and write. They feared that ideas of revolt would spread uncontrollably if blacks possessed these skills.

Black Leaders Against Slavery—Among the blacks who worked against slavery in the troubled years before the Civil War were **Frederick Douglass** and **Harriet Tubman.** Douglass, the leading black abolitionist, escaped from slavery in 1838. A talented speaker, he lectured against slavery in the North and in Britain. Douglass used money that he made from speaking engagements to

Former slave Frederick Douglass used money raised from speaking engagements to help escaped slaves.

1. What three characteristics distinguished American slavery?
2. Describe the "middle passage."
3. Contrast the northern and southern viewpoints on slavery.
4. What was the "positive good" theory concerning slavery?

 How did those who opposed slavery show their dissatisfaction?

Final Eruptions of the Slavery Issue

The nation had attempted to deal with the spread of slavery at different times. However, attempts such as the Missouri Compromise and the Compromise of 1850 never really solved the problem. All they did was postpone facing the problem.

help other escaped slaves. He also wrote an influential autobiography entitled *The Narrative of the Life of Frederick Douglass.* Douglass risked his freedom because the book told the name of his former master. To escape possible reenslavement, Douglass fled to England where sympathetic people bought his freedom from his master. When Douglass returned to the United States, he published an antislavery newspaper. His newspaper, the *North Star,* also supported women's rights.

After much abuse at the hands of her master, Harriet Tubman escaped from slavery in Maryland in 1849. Aided by Quaker friends, she returned to slave territory nearly twenty times to help runaway slaves. During these ventures she guided about three hundred blacks, including her own parents, whom she freed in 1857, along the Underground Railroad northward. Through a book about her life, Harriet Tubman became known as the "Moses" of her people.

Harriet Tubman

Uncle Tom's Cabin

The plight of slave families and runaways was brought to public attention in a unique way in 1852. **Harriet Beecher Stowe,** a preacher's daughter from Connecticut, lost a young son to cholera in 1849. Believing she now understood how slave mothers felt when their children were taken from them, she vowed to do something on their behalf.

Since the Stowe family had lived for a while in Cincinnati, Ohio, across the Ohio River from the slave state of Kentucky, Mrs.

Concerned women like Harriet Beecher Stowe and Harriet Tubman (opposite) helped lead the fight against slavery.

Stowe had glimpsed something of slavery and the plight of fugitive slaves. From 1850 to 1851 she submitted a novel in installments to the *National Era,* an antislavery paper. When the novel was released in book form, as *Life Among the Lowly, or Uncle Tom's Cabin,* 300,000 copies sold within a year. Although the book seems emotional and artificial by today's standards, ***Uncle Tom's Cabin*** became one of the most influential pieces of literature ever written. The story reached an even wider audience when performing troupes of actors toured the country enacting it. Soon the tragic sufferings of Little Eva and of the slaves Uncle Tom and Eliza were tugging at the heartstrings of readers and audiences. The novel rallied antislavery opinion in the North, but its implication that southern society was evil angered Southerners. The book was banned in the South.

The Kansas-Nebraska Act

When Kansas and Nebraska sought acceptance as new territories, the government again faced the slavery issue. Senator Stephen Douglas applied the idea of popular sovereignty to these territories in 1854. The Illinois senator designed a compromise that would allow the settlers in western lands to decide for or against slavery for themselves. Feelings ran so deep, however, that the bill produced rifts in the existing political parties. As soon as the **Kansas-Nebraska Act** passed, both proslavery and antislavery groups urged their supporters to go west. Naturally the two sides clashed, especially in Kansas, where open fighting took place between those supporting each side. The territory soon earned the nickname Bleeding Kansas. The bloodshed there was a foretaste of what was to happen nationwide.

The Founding of the Republican Party

By 1852 the Whig Party had split into two factions over the slavery issue—the Cotton Whigs and the Conscience Whigs. After the passage of the Kansas-Nebraska Act, the Cotton Whigs joined with southern Democrats because of their stand for slavery. The Conscience Whigs and northern Democrats, angered by the Kansas-Nebraska Act, now joined with Free Soilers, those against the spread of slavery to new lands. In 1854 these antislavery groups formed a new political

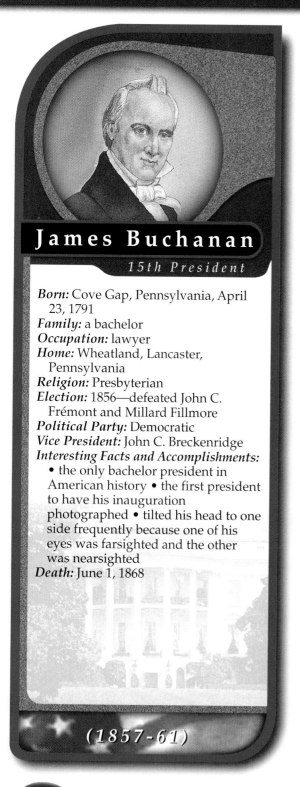

James Buchanan

15th President

Born: Cove Gap, Pennsylvania, April 23, 1791
Family: a bachelor
Occupation: lawyer
Home: Wheatland, Lancaster, Pennsylvania
Religion: Presbyterian
Election: 1856—defeated John C. Frémont and Millard Fillmore
Political Party: Democratic
Vice President: John C. Breckenridge
Interesting Facts and Accomplishments:
• the only bachelor president in American history • the first president to have his inauguration photographed • tilted his head to one side frequently because one of his eyes was farsighted and the other was nearsighted
Death: June 1, 1868

(1857-61)

party, the **Republican Party**. The party grew with startling speed, electing Congressmen its first year. In 1856 John C. Frémont became the first Republican to run for president. He was defeated, however, by the Democratic candidate, **James Buchanan.**

The Dred Scott Decision

For three years after the Kansas crisis, the nation experienced a relative calm. But two days after President Buchanan took office in 1857, the quiet ended when the question of the legal status of slavery in the territories came before the Supreme Court.

At stake was the freedom of an elderly black man, **Dred Scott.** Scott, born a slave, was owned by an army doctor, John Emerson of Missouri. Emerson took Scott with him to military posts in the state of Illinois and to the Wisconsin territory, where slavery was outlawed. In 1838 Scott returned with Emerson to Missouri. After Emerson's death, local anti-slavery lawyers helped Scott sue Emerson's heirs for his freedom on the grounds that living on free soil had made him free. Finally the case reached the Supreme Court, where the chief justice at that time was Roger B. Taney, a Southerner.

The majority of the court ruled against Scott, and Taney stated that since Scott was a slave and black, he was not a citizen. Hence, he had no right to sue in the nation's courts. Further, Taney ruled that Scott was not free as a result of having lived on free soil. Taney reasoned that the Fifth Amendment forbade the government from depriving a person of life, liberty, or property without due process of law. He ruled that the Missouri Compromise had deprived citizens north of 36° 30' of property, their slaves, and was thus invalid.

The consequences of the **Dred Scott decision** were serious. The South temporarily rejoiced in the fact that slavery had been upheld and could lawfully expand into new

Dred Scott became the focus of attention when the Supreme Court handed down a proslavery decision.

territories. The Supreme Court, however, had made the national conflict more serious. Politically the decision wrecked any chance for future political compromise. The Republican stand against the spread of slavery into new territories had suffered a setback, but antislavery forces were not to be quieted. Now the question of slavery expansion lay in the hands of the new settlers who would vote on it. No one knew whether the North or the South would be willing to abide by the outcome in the West.

Loss of the Compromisers

Compromise to solve problems became even less likely after the men who had accomplished it in earlier years died. Henry Clay, John C. Calhoun, and Daniel Webster, giants of the first half of the century, were all dead by 1852. Most of their successors had less experi-

ence, less wisdom, and less patience. Men such as Millard Fillmore, Franklin Pierce, Stephen Douglas, and James Buchanan were not strong enough leaders to provide needed and acceptable solutions to the nation's problems.

John Brown: Slavery's Avenger

One settler who set out for Kansas to aid antislavery forces was **John Brown**. Although Brown's mental state has been questioned, his hatred for slavery cannot be denied. While most abolitionists sought peaceful means to end slavery, Brown saw violence as the only effective method for dealing with the issue. He wanted to do great harm to slaveholders, to "smite them for God." Brown used Scripture wrongly to justify his acts. He often quoted Hebrews 9:22—"Without shedding of blood is no remission"—implying that the verse meant that slaveholders would pay for the sin of slavery with their blood. In spite of the violence of his message, Brown won a following. "Wherever he spoke, his words commanded earnest attention," said Frederick Douglass. "His arguments seemed to convince all; his appeals touched all, and his will impressed all." Brown's bearing and dignity seemed to wash away all questions about his purposes.

Brown's first effort in his war against slavery was waged at Pottawatomie (paht uh WAHT uh mee), the center for proslavery efforts in Kansas in 1856. For no apparent reason, Brown and four of his seven sons murdered five proslavery men in one night of terror, adding to the turmoil of "Bleeding Kansas."

Then in the late 1850s, Brown began planning his most daring move against slavery. For several months he tried to stir up backing for his efforts, but rumors of the nature of his plans caused several abolitionists to withdraw their support. In the summer of 1859, Brown armed a small band, including four of his own sons and two slaves he had freed. His plans were to raid a federal arsenal, or storage place for weapons, at Harpers Ferry, Virginia. On October 16, 1859, Brown and his twenty-one-man army rode into Harpers Ferry. They caught the watchman at the arsenal by surprise and took prominent local slave owners as hostages. Brown thought this action would stir slaves into rebellion. He hoped that thousands of slaves would revolt and rally to him; no such revolt occurred.

Brown allowed word of his takeover at Harpers Ferry to leak out. Soon local militia had blocked all the escape routes from the town. Colonel **Robert E. Lee** and J.E.B. Stuart arrived with federal troops the following day.

Brown refused to surrender. In the military action that followed, Brown was injured and two of his sons were killed. Only ten days after his capture, Brown faced trial. Before and during the trial he won many admirers. The Virginia jury, however, convicted him of murder, and he was hanged. Southern whites now feared a slave revolt more than ever. Although the revolt Brown hoped for never came, his actions did have a profound and far-reaching effect. Brown's trial and death made him a martyr for the antislavery cause. Soon Yankee soldiers marched off to war singing "John Brown's body lies a-mouldering in the grave, . . . His soul goes marching on."

SECTION REVIEW

1. What famous novel prompted a wave of sympathy for the abolitionist cause? Who wrote the novel?

2. The clash over slavery in Kansas led to what nickname for that territory?

3. What issue united the groups that formed the Republican Party?

4. Where did John Brown direct his attack to end slavery?

 What was the significance of the Dred Scott decision?

The Election of 1860 and Secession

The Election of 1860 was to have great consequence on the nation. The turmoil was displayed in the disruption of traditional ties in the political parties. The new regional bonds that formed were to remain for decades to come.

A Republican Victory

The South was clearly worried about the election of 1860. Southern extremists, called **fire-eaters,** threatened **secession,** to leave the Union, if the Republicans won. The views of the Republicans on almost all issues were in opposition to the interests of the South. Not only views on slavery but also positions on states' rights and the tariff were placing the Republicans at odds with most Southerners.

The best chance for defeating the Republicans lay in the Democrats' picking a moderate candidate acceptable to both the South and the North. Illinois Senator Stephen Douglas was such a moderate. But in 1860 fire-eaters, who had undue influence, thought him their enemy. Rather than uniting to stand behind Douglas, the southern Democrats left the nominating convention. Their split foreshadowed the Civil War. The divided party led to a divided nation. The Democrats no longer accepted "compromise" presidents like Pierce or Buchanan. While the northern Democrats nominated Douglas, the Southerners chose **John C. Breckinridge** of Kentucky. Their **platform** (statement of what they stood for politically), based on the Dred Scott decision, called for Congress to enact a federal slave code to protect slavery in all the territories.

A campaign banner from the election of 1860.

With the Democrats divided, the Republicans had real hopes for victory. In an effort to keep the Union intact, they chose a moderate rather than an abolitionist or Free Soiler. Their choice was an Illinois lawyer, **Abraham Lincoln.**

In the Illinois senate election in 1858, Lincoln had challenged Stephen Douglas, the Democratic candidate, to a series of seven debates. Although Douglas won the election, the debates gave Lincoln and his views public exposure. Although Lincoln was not an abolitionist and was not opposed to slavery where it already existed, he was against the spread of slavery to new territories. This stand, however, was not acceptable to the southern fire-eaters.

The Whigs from the border states of Delaware, Maryland, Virginia, and Kentucky were not eager to leave the Union. They decided to pick an alternate candidate, **John Bell** of Tennessee, who stood for staying in the Union. Their party was called the Constitutional Union Party. They were trying to buy time, hoping that the fire-eaters would see there was no real future in their position.

Southerners believed that a Lincoln victory would put southern states at a disadvantage in Washington and might spark more raids like John Brown's. They said that if Lincoln were elected, they would leave the Union and form their own nation. President Buchanan did nothing to discourage them.

Lincoln carried the northern and western states, enabling him to win more popular votes than any other candidate. Douglas came in second in popular votes, followed by Breckinridge and Bell. Lincoln's victory, however, was far from overwhelming. Douglas and Bell's vote total exceeded that of Lincoln's, and combined with the Breckinridge vote, these candidates won over sixty percent of the vote. In addition, Lincoln had failed to carry a single southern state or border state. The circumstances of the election put Lincoln at a disadvantage. No one knew what side the border states would take in the secession controversy. If Lincoln had been able to take office right away, however, he might have been able to save the Union.

The Confederacy Takes Shape

Fearing that its rights as a state could not be maintained, South Carolina voted to leave the Union on December 20. The nation waited for President Buchanan to react. Although he believed secession was illegal, he was unwilling

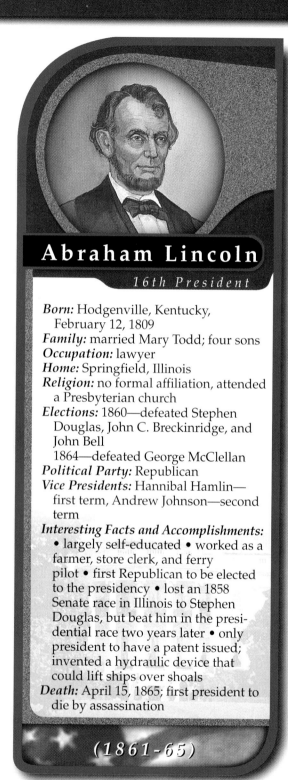

Abraham Lincoln

16th President

Born: Hodgenville, Kentucky, February 12, 1809
Family: married Mary Todd; four sons
Occupation: lawyer
Home: Springfield, Illinois
Religion: no formal affiliation, attended a Presbyterian church
Elections: 1860—defeated Stephen Douglas, John C. Breckinridge, and John Bell
1864—defeated George McClellan
Political Party: Republican
Vice Presidents: Hannibal Hamlin—first term, Andrew Johnson—second term
Interesting Facts and Accomplishments:
• largely self-educated • worked as a farmer, store clerk, and ferry pilot • first Republican to be elected to the presidency • lost an 1858 Senate race in Illinois to Stephen Douglas, but beat him in the presidential race two years later • only president to have a patent issued; invented a hydraulic device that could lift ships over shoals
Death: April 15, 1865; first president to die by assassination

(1861-65)

to use his influence or force to halt it. Instead he left the problem for Lincoln to face.

But before Lincoln could take office, other southern states called conventions.

Mississippi, Florida, Alabama, Georgia, Louisiana, and Texas all followed South Carolina's example. South Carolina summoned the other slaveholding states to a convention held in Montgomery, Alabama, on February 1, 1861.

Delegates from these seven states formed the **Confederate States of America.** They wrote their own constitution. It was like the American Constitution, except that it recognized the "sovereign and independent character" of the states and guaranteed states' rights. It also promised that no law against slavery could ever be passed, allowed cabinet members to take part in legislative debates, and gave the president a single six-year term.

Next, the Confederacy had to choose its leaders. Fire-eaters chose moderates, hoping to win the support of Southerners who were still unsure about splitting from the Union. **Jefferson Davis** from Mississippi became president. Alexander Stephens, a Georgian who had firmly opposed secession, took the vice-presidency.

The Confederacy sent out commissioners seeking to increase the size of the Confederacy. But the border and upper southern states took a "wait-and-see" position.

SECTION REVIEW

1. Name the four presidential candidates in 1860 and their parties.

2. What was Lincoln's attitude toward slavery?

3. Which state was the first to leave the Union?

4. Who became president of the Confederacy?

 What generally was the political position of the men chosen for leadership in the Confederacy? Why were they chosen?

Fort Sumter, Charleston Harbor, April 1865;
Inset: Fort Sumter today

Fort Sumter and War

The South, realizing that the Union had been formed as a voluntary organization of the states, believed that it could withdraw its membership in the Union by secession to form the Confederacy. Lincoln believed that secession was not possible—the Union was permanent, and no state could pull out once it had joined. The Civil War resulted to determine whether the South's view or President Lincoln's view of the Union would prevail.

On March 4, 1861, Abraham Lincoln took office. In his inaugural address he appealed to the people, "In your hands, my dissatisfied fellow-countrymen, and not in mine, is the momentous issue of civil war." Lincoln held that the Union was still whole; it was, he held, indivisible and indissoluble (not able to be dissolved or split up). He hoped to reconcile the sections, but he would fight, if he had to, to preserve the Constitution and the Union. He stated that he would use the power of government "to hold, occupy, and possess the property and places belonging to the government."

By property Lincoln meant the two federal forts in the South where the Stars and Stripes still flew: Fort Pickens at Pensacola, Florida, and Fort Sumter in South Carolina's Charleston harbor. To retain control of these forts, however, it would be necessary to send them supplies.

Firing on Fort Sumter

In January South Carolina had already shown it was unlikely to allow the government to land supplies at the fort. When a merchant ship, *The Star of the West*, approached **Fort Sumter** with supplies and troops, it was fired on and was turned away.

Lincoln reasoned that if he let the Confederates have Fort Sumter, he would have to invade the South to preserve the Union, and an invasion would probably drive the border states into the Confederate fold. The South might react to the Union's keeping its hold on

Fort Sumter in one of two ways: either by rejoining the Union or by shelling the fort. If the Confederates shelled Sumter, they would be the ones who started the war. Then if Lincoln had to call for federal troops to quell the rebelling Confederates, his action could be defended.

Lincoln sent a note to F. W. Pickens, the governor of South Carolina, telling him that a supply ship but no troops would be coming to Sumter. (Lincoln chose to write Pickens, the lawful governor of the state, rather than Jefferson Davis. He held that writing Davis meant recognizing the Confederacy.) Pickens contacted Davis, who gave orders to prevent all efforts to resupply Fort Sumter. When the federal supply ship came to Charleston harbor on April 12, 1861, the batteries (rows of guns) in Charleston harbor fired on the fort. After enduring a forty-hour Confederate bombardment, the Union troops surrendered the fort.

Across the Confederacy church bells rang and people celebrated. A pastor in Charleston confidently told his flock, "Providence is fast uniting the whole South in a common brotherhood of sympathy and action, and our first essay in arms has been crowned with perfect success."

The Call for Troops

Lincoln, meanwhile, sent out a call for 75,000 troops. Any reluctant border or southern states now had to take sides. Davis was especially eager to have Virginia join the Confederacy because it was the South's richest and most populous state. Virginia joined, as did Arkansas and Tennessee, although neither was especially eager to do so. Since North Carolina was now encircled by Confederate states, it was forced to join the Confederacy.

The people in fifty counties of western Virginia had long resented the tidewater area's greater influence in their state. This was their chance to strike back. They boldly set up their own state government and sought statehood. Since Virginia had left the Union, they held that they hardly needed her permission to become a state. In 1863 West Virginia came into the Union.

Lincoln took action to keep the four border slave states (Kentucky, Missouri, Delaware, and Maryland) in the Union. People in these states were divided in their loyalties. Some favored secession while others wanted to stay in the Union.

If Kentucky had become Confederate (and it did have a Confederate governor for a time), the North's access to the Ohio River would have been threatened. Its population, lukewarm to the Confederacy, was kept in the Union through persuasion and force. In Missouri, Union troops moved to key areas, preventing secession there. Missourians against the Union were carefully isolated and ignored, except when ruffian bands carried on warfare within the state.

There was little concern about Delaware, whose culture and location aligned her with other Middle Atlantic States more than with the South. But Maryland presented a real problem. If it joined the Confederate camp, Washington, D.C., could end up there too. Lincoln sent federal troops to Maryland and then closed bridges to keep others out. Potential Confederate leaders were held against their will. Lincoln justified his actions, the use of martial or military law, since a grave emergency existed. Maryland had little choice but to stay in the Union.

Northern Advantages

Looking at the resources available to the North and the South, it's obvious that the North had a great advantage. The North had both the means and the manpower to industrialize. This tremendous industrial capacity was the Union's most significant advantage, even more so as the war wore on.

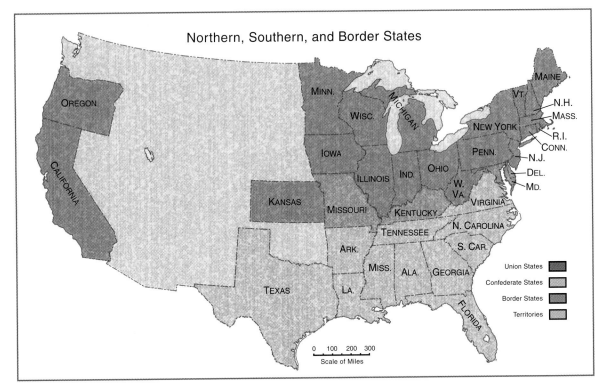

Northern, Southern, and Border States

The South produced only ten percent of the nation's manufactured goods and had only 110,000 industrial workers. The North, meanwhile, had 120,000 factories. Consequently, the South had to buy overseas what it could not produce at home. Only at the outset of the war would she have the capital and the freedom to do this. The lack of southern sea power to maintain its trade routes would soon greatly hinder its war effort. In addition, the North was adding 300,000 immigrants a year to its population, almost as many as the total number of northern troops killed in the entire war.

Why the South Stood a Chance

With so many disadvantages, why did the South believe it could win? First, the southern goal was a simple one: to set up and to maintain a separate independent nation, the Confederate States of America. To do this, the South did not need to conquer the North; it had only to defend its own territory. Also, the

South was immense. The North would need long supply lines to attack and hold so vast an area.

Second, the average Southerner was more deeply involved in the war than was the average Northerner. The Southerner was fighting for his home and way of life. The Northerner, perhaps an immigrant, was supposedly "fighting for the Union." The North would lose if its people lost the desire to stay on the offensive. It could win only when it destroyed the Confederate desire and ability to fight.

Third, the Confederacy believed it would get foreign help. Since it was the source of much of Britain's cotton, the Confederacy believed that the British would be at least sympathetic, if not supportive.

Fourth, the South had an almost endless coastline. Even though the Confederacy had no real navy at the start, the North would need thousands of ships to block the entire coast from supply ships.

327

General Robert E. Lee

Robert E. Lee, the son of Lighthorse Harry Lee, a hero in the War for Independence, went to West Point. There Lee's behavior and academic excellence soon placed him at the top of his class. During the Mexican War Lee distinguished himself for bravery and leadership. After the Mexican War, Lee continued in the service, and while home in Virginia on leave, the army called on him to lead the small force that recaptured Harpers Ferry from John Brown and his group of fanatics.

When the Civil War broke out, Lee had a choice to make. His stand on slavery was well documented: "Slavery as an institution is a moral and political evil in any country." Yet he was a loyal Virginian. His dilemma was increased when he was offered the position of commander-in-chief of the Union army. Torn between loyalties, Lee decided for Virginia and was appointed commander of the Army of Northern Virginia. His methods were unconventional but brilliant. Constantly outnumbered, he managed time and again to defeat the northern armies. Only the tenacity of U. S. Grant and the Union's numerical supremacy in men and equipment eventually defeated Lee.

After the war Lee accepted the presidency of Washington College—now Washington and Lee. His presidency was an enormous success as the college grew and prospered. He was buried at a site on the university campus. The South greatly loved and honored him; the North also highly esteemed him. He is, perhaps, history's most admired losing general.

In 1960 as Dwight D. Eisenhower's second term neared its end, the president received a critical letter from a citizen. The citizen was upset that a picture of Robert E. Lee, a Confederate, was included among the Eisenhower mementos in the White House. Eisenhower had gained an interest in Lee as a fellow graduate of West Point. This was Eisenhower's reply to the citizen.

The White House
Washington, DC
August 18, 1960

Dear Dr. Scott:

General Robert E. Lee was, in my estimation, one of the supremely gifted men produced by our nation. He believed unswervingly in the constitutional validity of his cause, which until 1865 was still an arguable question in America; he was a poised and inspiring leader, true to the high trust reposed in him by millions of his fellow citizens. . . .

From deep conviction, I simply say this: A nation of men of Lee's calibre would be unconquerable in spirit and soul. Indeed, to the degree that present-day American youth will strive to emulate his painstaking efforts to help heal the nation's wounds once the bitter struggle was over, we, in our time of danger in a divided world, will be strengthened and our love of freedom sustained.

Such are the reasons I proudly display the picture of the great American on my office wall.

Dwight D. Eisenhower

Fifth, the Confederacy believed its soldiers were better. Confederates had little respect for Yankees as fighting men, and the South did have better commanders, at least in the beginning. Most of the Confederate officers were well trained; many were West Point graduates. And no one argued about Robert E. Lee's abilities. Lee had been Lincoln's first choice to be commander-in-chief of the Union armies. But because he believed that his duty was to his native state of Virginia, Lee declined. President Lincoln, on the other hand, had to go through seven different commanders before finding the one who could win the war, Ulysses S. Grant.

SECTION REVIEW

1. What state in particular did Jefferson Davis want to join the Confederacy?

2. What were the four key border states?

3. What was the Union's most significant advantage?

4. What factors gave the South a fighting chance despite the North's advantages?

 Why did Lincoln feel he must hold on to Fort Sumter?

SUMMARY

Political issues of the early 1800s came to a boil in the 1850s. The North's and South's differing views on states' rights, the tariff, slavery, and other topics led to great controversy. When Abraham Lincoln won the 1860 election for the Republicans, the South lost hope for a continued federal government tolerant of its views. The South then broke its ties with the Union by seceding. Whether the South could secede from the Union was the issue that would pull the nation into the Civil War. With the firing on Fort Sumter in April of 1861, the war had begun.

Chapter Review

People, Places, and Things to Remember

middle passage	*Uncle Tom's Cabin*	secession
emancipation	Kansas-Nebraska Act	John C. Breckinridge
abolitionism	Republican Party	platform
compensated emancipation	James Buchanan	Abraham Lincoln
William Lloyd Garrison	Dred Scott	John Bell
Underground Railroad	Dred Scott decision	Confederate States of
Frederick Douglass	John Brown	America
Harriet Tubman	Robert E. Lee	Jefferson Davis
Harriet Beecher Stowe	fire-eaters	Fort Sumter

Review Questions

Choose the correct name or term for each blank in the paragraph below. Not all will be used.

Middle Passage	John Brown
emancipation	Frederick Douglass
abolitionists	William Lloyd Garrison
compensated emancipation	Dred Scott
Underground Railroad	Harriet Beecher Stowe
Uncle Tom's Cabin	Harriet Tubman

As the problem of slavery troubled America, (1) began to work to put an end to slavery. They wanted (2) for the slaves, although some supported the idea of (3), reimbursing the slaveholders for their loss. (4) was a vocal supporter of abolitionism in Boston where he published a paper called the *Liberator*. Other abolitionists helped runaway slaves follow the (5) to freedom in the North or in Canada. (6) was an escaped slave who helped many other slaves follow that route. Another influence against slavery was the book (7), written by (8). (9), a black abolitionist, also spoke out against slavery in speeches and publications. The most daring antislavery action was probably that taken by (10), who tried to spark a slave rebellion by capturing a federal arsenal.

Make two columns on your paper: the United States of America and the Confederate States of America. Then answer these questions for each.

11. Who became its president in 1861?

12. Who was its leading general?

13. What advantages did it have as the war began?

14. What disadvantages did it have as the war began?

Questions for Discussion

15. Why was slavery a difficult problem for Americans to deal with?

16. What do you suppose would have happened if southern Democrats had supported Stephen Douglas in the 1860 election? Why?

History Skills

Facts and Speculation

History books give many facts (what actually occurred). They also offer speculations (guesses about what might have happened under different circumstances). Read each statement below. Decide whether it is a fact or a speculation.

1. Slavery would have died out in the South if the cotton gin had never been invented.

2. Southern professor Thomas R. Dew argued that slavery was "a positive good" compared to other labor systems.

3. By 1860 one out of every three Southerners was a slave.

4. The United States was the last major western nation to ban foreign slave trade.

5. Gradual emancipation would have been a workable solution to the slavery issue.

6. The great compromisers Clay, Calhoun, and Webster would have been able to prevent the Civil War had they lived.

7. After the Dred Scott decision, no peaceful solutions to the slavery issue were possible.

8. John Brown made a mistake when he expected thousands of slaves to rally to him at Harper's Ferry.

9. During the presidential election of 1860, Southern Democrats voted for John C. Breckinridge.

10. If Lincoln had been able to take office right away in 1860, he would have been able to avoid a civil war.

11. Lincoln refused to write to Jefferson Davis because he did not want to recognize him as the president of the Confederacy.

12. If the North had fired the first shots of the Civil War, the border states would have joined the Confederacy.

13. North Carolina was forced to join the Confederacy because it was surrounded by Confederate states.

14. West Virginia held that it did not need Virginia's permission to become a state because Virginia had left the Union.

15. Robert E. Lee became a commander in the Confederate army even though he considered slavery an evil institution.

Regions of American Geography
The South

Location

The South includes Alabama, Arkansas, Florida, Georgia, Kentucky, Louisiana, Mississippi, North Carolina, Oklahoma, South Carolina, Tennessee, Texas, Virginia, and West Virginia. With the exception of Kentucky, Virginia, and West Virginia, the entire region lies below the 34th parallel (latitude). All but five states border either the Gulf of Mexico or the Atlantic Ocean. The Rio Grande separates the region from Mexico in the West, while the remaining western border is shared with the state of New Mexico.

Climate

A humid subtropical climate dominates the region. Hot, humid summers end in mild winters, except at the southern tip of Florida, where the tropical climate keeps the weather warm all year round. Sufficient rainfall and warm temperatures give the region an extended growing season. In the late summers, hurricanes that start over the Atlantic Ocean or Gulf of Mexico sometimes blow over the region, causing extensive damage.

Topography

The Atlantic and Gulf Coastal Plains run along the entire coastline and join the Interior Plain along the Mississippi River valley. West of the Atlantic Coastal Plain, the Piedmont rises to meet some of the highest mountains of the Appalachian Range. In northwestern Arkansas, Oklahoma, and the western two-thirds of Texas the elevation rises. It increases first in Arkansas, where the Arkansas River splits the Ozark Mountains and the Ouachita Mountains, and again farther west into the Great Plains and Rocky Mountains.

Natural Resources

Variety is the word that best describes the South. With wide, fertile plains and a mild climate, the region has had great success in large agricultural efforts. The type of agriculture varies greatly. Kentucky, North Carolina, and Virginia are the leading states in the tobacco industry. South Carolina, Georgia, and Alabama turned to the production of peanuts, soybeans, and peaches (as well as other fruits) after cotton and rice had leached many nutrients from the soil. Once known for its swamps, Florida has become a tropical oasis complete with year-round vegetable farms and citrus groves. Across Mississippi, Louisiana, Arkansas, Oklahoma, and much of Texas, small farmers send their cotton, soybean, and vegetable harvests to factories that process and then send the crops to the busy ports along the Mississippi River. Along the Gulf of Mexico, oil and natural gas fields have boosted the economies of Texas and Louisiana. Where the terrain changes to dry plateaus in Texas, cattle roam on rangelands that remind visitors of the Wild West and a time past.

Geography and Culture

Religion is an important part of Southern culture. Many black churches became meeting places in the 1960s for blacks who fought for civil rights. The region has made great strides in equal rights issues over the past several decades, but old wounds are sometimes hard to heal. Prejudiced beliefs sometimes take generations to pass away. The entire South generally shares a conservative political outlook. Conservative views probably go back to the pre–Civil War years with the rejection of central government control and intervention in state matters. Such views also come from the small-town focus of the region. Family connections are important, and cousins, aunts, uncles, and grandparents may all live in the same community. The lack of large cities in much of the region makes Southerners less worried about some of the social issues confronted by the people of the Northeast.

Eloquence and education are marks of southern gentility. Elegant homes and gardens, refined accents, and polished etiquette go hand in hand with the "Y'all come back now" hospitality for which the region is best known.

Map of the southeastern United States showing state boundaries, cities, rivers, and physical features.

States and labels:

COLORADO · KANSAS · MISSOURI · ILLINOIS · INDIANA · OHIO · PENNSYLVANIA · N.J. · MD. · DEL. · NEW MEXICO · OKLAHOMA · ARKANSAS · TENNESSEE · KENTUCKY · WEST VIRGINIA · VIRGINIA · NORTH CAROLINA · TEXAS · LOUISIANA · MISSISSIPPI · ALABAMA · GEORGIA · SOUTH CAROLINA · FLORIDA · MEXICO

Physical features:

GREAT PLAINS · LLANO ESTACADO · EDWARDS PLATEAU · OZARK PLATEAU · OUACHITA MTS. · CUMBERLAND PLATEAU · GREAT SMOKY MTS. · BLUE RIDGE MTS. · APPALACHIAN MOUNTAINS · ATLANTIC COASTAL PLAIN · COASTAL PLAIN · GULF · Gulf of Mexico · ATLANTIC OCEAN · CAPE HATTERAS · CAPE CANAVERAL · CAPE SABLE · FLORIDA KEYS · Straits of Florida · Okefenokee Swamp · Lake Okeechobee

Rivers:

Canadian R. · Arkansas R. · Red R. · Colorado R. · Rio Grande · Nueces R. · Brazos R. · Trinity R. · Sabine R. · Pearl R. · Tennessee R. · Ohio R. · Cumberland R. · Potomac R. · Roanoke R.

Cities:

Amarillo · Lubbock · El Paso · Midland · Wichita Falls · Fort Worth · Dallas · Longview · Killeen · Austin · San Antonio · Laredo · Corpus Christi · Brownsville · Houston · Beaumont · Tulsa · Oklahoma City · Little Rock · Hot Springs · Shreveport · Baton Rouge · New Orleans · Memphis · Tupelo · Vicksburg · Jackson · Biloxi · Mobile · Pensacola · Birmingham · Tuscaloosa · Montgomery · Columbus · Nashville · Knoxville · Chattanooga · Huntsville · Atlanta · Macon · Columbia · Augusta · Savannah · Tallahassee · Jacksonville · Gainesville · Daytona Beach · Orlando · Tampa · St. Petersburg · Sarasota · Fort Myers · West Palm Beach · Fort Lauderdale · Miami · Key West · Louisville · Frankfort · Lexington · Charleston · Huntington · Charlottesville · Alexandria · Richmond · Norfolk · Greensboro · Winston-Salem · Raleigh · Charlotte · Spartanburg · Greenville · Wilmington · Myrtle Beach · Charleston

Scale:

0 · 150 · 300 Miles
0 · 150 · 300 Kilometers

20°N · 100°W · 90°W · 80°W · 30°N

17

The Civil War

As war loomed ahead after the election of Lincoln in 1860, Senator John Crittenden of Kentucky led one last vain attempt to preserve the Union peacefully. Despite his passionate pleas and stirring speeches, Crittenden's compromise plan failed to win enough support to pass the Senate. The defeat became doubly bitter for Crittenden when his own family divided over the issue of secession. His son George became a major general in the Confederate army, while his son Thomas became a major general in the Union army. After George took his stand with the South, a newspaper editor who opposed Crittenden roundly criticized the senator for his son's action. The editor must have been embarrassed a short while later, however, when his own son went south to join the Confederacy.

All through the country families split over the war. Brother sometimes fought against brother and father against son in the four years of bloody conflict. In his plea for the Union, Lincoln echoed Jesus' words in Matthew 12:25—A "house divided against itself shall not stand." When families fought against each other, what hope could there be for the nation?

Gearing Up for War

The firing on Fort Sumter in April of 1861 ignited the flame of civil war between North and South. Billy Yank and Johnny Reb were soon to struggle through the triumphs and tragedies of four years of bitter conflict. Not only the soldiers but also many civilian Americans came to know the hardships and the death and destruction that were part of this war to save the Union.

Turning Men into Soldiers

Thousands of young recruits, responding to the patriotic fervor, joined the armies. Union recruits poured into Washington, D.C., or newly built camps in the West. At the same time southern patriots were gathering in Confederate camps.

Life in the camps, however, was far from exciting. A soldier spent sixty-five percent of his time in camp, thirty percent marching or bivouacking (BIV wak ing; camping temporarily in the open air), and only five percent of his time fighting. Some soldiers assigned to forts never fired a shot.

At the beginning of the war, both sides relied totally on volunteers. But soon volunteers became too scarce to supply the needed troops, and thus both Lincoln and Davis resorted to drafting men to fill their armies.

Raising Northern Forces—President Lincoln's Fourth of July message in 1861 called for 500,000 volunteers to enlist for three years. The next year Congress called "all able-bodied male citizens between the ages of eighteen and forty-five" into state militias. At this point drafting soldiers was a state function. Most of the states also offered a large sum of money, a bounty, for those who joined.

In March of 1863 Congress passed a law for drafting a national army. The North had a harder time motivating the people to join its forces. While the South could appeal to the men to protect their own land and honor, the North's cause of fighting to preserve a nation was not so personal. This lack of personal concern for the northern cause led many northern men to join the army halfheartedly.

All men between the ages of twenty and forty-five were subject to regular army service. Those who were physically or mentally unfit were exempted, as were certain officeholders. A draftee was also allowed to hire a substitute or to pay $300 for an exemption. (Recent immigrants, who were not subject to the draft, often served as substitutes to earn money.) The system did not work well. At first over twice as many men bought substitutes as actually entered the army. Others ran away from service. Furthermore, the law caused ill will. Believing that the new draft law was unfair, penniless Irish immigrants, already harmed by runaway wartime inflation, rioted for four days in New York City. The rioters' hatred was vented on local blacks. The mob resented that they were being drafted to free the blacks while blacks stayed home. Most of the 128 people killed in the riot were black.

Raising Southern Forces—The South had more of a fighting spirit than the North. Furthermore, some of West Point's best students joined the Confederate command, providing able leadership for that army.

At the outset the South had no problem getting enough men to fight. In fact, there were more volunteers than the South could equip and train. But such enthusiasm was short-lived. When the first one-year enlistments were up and no special benefits were offered, the number of recruits declined. In April 1862, the South had to resort to drafting all men aged eighteen to thirty-five. Later the upper limit was extended to fifty, and men up to sixty-five could be placed in a home guard.

The southern system was not foolproof either. There were so many ways to get out of war duty that a War Department clerk joked: "Our Bureau of Conscription ought to be called the Bureau of Exemptions." The most disputed feature of the law was the so-called "Twenty-Negro Law," which exempted any planter or overseer with more than twenty slaves. Its supporters claimed that these men were needed at home to keep the blacks from rioting. But poor Southerners who were drafted resented this exemption for the rich. Understandably, when the southern army began losing, getting recruits became even more difficult.

Blacks in the War—As early as 1861, Indiana blacks offered to serve the Union. Since blacks were fighting for freedom for their own people and being captured would mean almost certain enslavement, they had good reason to fight hard, harder perhaps than some whites. Yet it wasn't until after the Emancipation Proclamation was issued and the number of northern recruits dwindled that blacks were allowed to join the army.

Black soldiers, however, were not treated the same as white soldiers. Until 1864 black soldiers served at lower wages than white soldiers. Blacks also had medical care far below the norm. As a result the death toll for blacks ran thirty-seven percent higher than that of the whites. Blacks were also given the most mundane tasks. Because Northerners were unsure of how well blacks could lead, no blacks were appointed as officers. Instead, black regiments had white officers.

In the South blacks served in the army in noncombatant (nonfighting) positions such as

Many escaped slaves joined the Union Army to help fight for the freedom of all slaves.

cooks, wagon drivers, laborers, and personal servants to officers. By March of 1865, however, when there was an extremely severe manpower shortage, the Confederate Congress passed a bill to draft 300,000 blacks. The first two black companies astounded southern whites with their skill at arms. But no blacks fought for the Confederacy; the southern war effort ended before blacks could take the field.

Civilian Preparations

The Civil War was a total war; it involved both the military and civilians. Hardly anyone escaped at least some of its effects.

In the North—The North had begun to widen its industrial base even before the war. The North drew its workers from among women, who were new to the work force, and from a pool of 800,000 immigrants who came to America between 1861 and 1865. When war came, uniforms, boots, shoes, hats, blankets, tents, rifles, swords, cannon, revolvers, ammunition, wagons, canned foods, lumber, shovels, steamboats, and surgical instruments all went from northern factories into the war effort.

Industrialism also had a positive effect on farm production. Even though thousands of men left their farms to fight in the war, farm production did not decline. Instead, as the demand for food products increased, farmers began to mechanize. As many harvesters, reapers, and mowers were bought in one year as had been bought in the previous decade. In addition to feeding the Union army, these farms began to feed Europeans. For example, forty percent of England's wheat and flour now came from the North.

The war also made private volunteer groups stronger. Private groups, sometimes called commissions, helped to purchase medicines and to supply Bibles and other reading materials. These commissions sent money home to a soldier's family and even secured food, shelter, and clothing for slaves who had fled from behind Confederate lines.

In the South—In the first months of the war, life changed little for most Southerners. Confident of their cause, they believed they would win and win quickly. Early victories at Fort Sumter and Bull Run seemed to confirm that belief. As the war continued, however, life began to change. The Union navy kept many needed imports from arriving in the South, and the small number of southern factories could not produce enough materials to supply the South and its armies. Soon there were severe shortages of some goods. Southerners also had to pay high prices for what goods they could get. Coffee, tea, sugar, butter, lard, flour, and fresh fruits became expensive. Then such things disappeared altogether, along with household items such as candles and oil.

Substitutions became common. Okra seeds, rye, sweet potatoes, and even peanuts were used to make coffee. As the need for medicines grew, the woods became the South's medicine chest. For example, Southerners could no longer import quinine to treat malaria, a disease that was a problem in swampy areas; so a less effective mixture of red pepper, table salt, and tea took its place.

Since cotton could be neither sold nor eaten, Jefferson Davis waged a crusade to get planters and farmers to grow corn. One Georgia newspaper said: "Plant corn and be

Young men such as Private Edwin Francis Jemison sacrificed their lives in the Civil War.

free, or plant cotton and be whipped!" *Corn* and *patriotism* became synonyms.

Farmers and planters often struggled more than others. The Confederate government took livestock, mules, horses, and carriages as well as tools and buckets for the war effort. Southerners had to use what they had available or do without. The longer the war lasted, the greater was the sacrifice required.

As real and counterfeit currency flooded the South, inflation occurred. Prices soared. By 1864 bacon sold at twenty dollars a pound and flour for one hundred dollars a barrel. Some people used a barter system, trading goods for food. To fight inflation and provide needed war materials, the South used **taxes in kind.** Such taxes required the producers to send one-tenth of their products—hogs, corn, or whatever—directly to the Confederacy.

Southern farmers did produce enough food. But hampered by a poor transportation system, they could not always get it to those who needed it.

Military Methods

Because of the development of industry and technology and because of improved weapons, tactics, and strategies, the Civil War was really the first modern war.

Modern Warfare—For the first time the army was able to use the railroad to move goods and soldiers from place to place. In addition, the government could use the telegraph for its communications. Almost every evening before President Lincoln went to bed, he walked over to the War Department to read the war dispatches from the front lines. The telegraph helped him to make military decisions and to stay in close contact with his generals.

Mines, trench warfare, wire barricades, and other methods of fighting or hindering the enemy were put to use. Rifled guns and cannon were also used. These weapons spin the bullet or shell as it is fired to give it a straighter path, thus making it more accurate in hitting its intended target.

Tactics of the war progressed on land, in the sea, and also in the air. Much use was made of cavalry (mounted troops) for reconnaissance, or information gathering. On the sea, ironclad ships proved their superiority in warfare. The fight between the **Monitor,** a Union ironclad, and the **Merrimac,** a Confederate ironclad, was decisive in the future of fighting vessels. Balloons were first used in the Civil War for observing troop movements. In that way aerial reconnaissance began even before the invention of the airplane.

Images of the Civil War, its death and destruction, linger with us today because of another innovation of that time—photography. Photography had developed twenty years before, but its use had been limited. Only a few photographs were taken of wars in the 1840s and '50s. In addition, the complicated processes and the large expenses involved in early photography prohibited its common use.

By the time of the Civil War, however, photography was becoming less expensive

Union soldiers sit on the deck of the "victorious Union gunboat, Monitor."

and more common. Many soldiers had their pictures taken for their families or sweethearts. Photographers also followed the troops and captured images of war. One of these photographers was **Mathew Brady,** who kept his darkroom with him in a horsedrawn wagon. His many scenes of the war continue to offer revealing glimpses of that time of conflict.

Northern and Southern Strategy—As the South faced the task of making the North accept its independence, the North proceeded to show the South that the Union would not be dissolved. As each side approached its objective, it developed a strategy for winning the war that consisted of a few basic goals. Whichever side could accomplish its goals would emerge as the victor.

Mathew Brady specialized in taking Civil War photographs such as this one he titled "Between Decks."

Confederate Strategy

1. Break the blockade.

2. Gain recognition from Britain and France. Cut off cotton shipments to Britain so that it would recognize its dependence on the South.

3. Fight a defensive battle.

Union Strategy

1. Impose a naval blockade to shut off southern ports from foreign trade and thus strangle the Confederate economy.

2. Take control of the Mississippi River, splitting the Confederacy in two and cutting off the states west of the Mississippi from their sister states.

3. Take Richmond, the new Confederate capital.

4. Protect Washington, D.C.

Northern War Strategy

DEFEND WASHINGTON, D.C.

SEIZE RICHMOND

CUT OFF FROM WEST

NAVAL BLOCKADE

NAVAL BLOCKADE

SECTION REVIEW

1. Why was the draft initiated?

2. What are "taxes in kind"? Why did the South go to this system?

3. List several factors that made the Civil War the first "modern war."

 Compare and contrast the northern and southern war strategies.

Marching into Battle

The fervor for war was on. After the attack on Fort Sumter, Northerners were eager for something to happen. But the Union Army, under seventy-five-year-old Winfield Scott, was made up of rough, untried recruits. Since many Northerners believed they had a decided edge and could win the war and be home before harvest, the pressure to attack Richmond grew greater. Richmond, the Confederate capital, lay only about one hundred miles away from Washington, D.C. The press cried "On to Richmond!" so loudly and so often that Congress soon joined the refrain.

Confederate soldiers ride to the battle of Petersburg, Virginia, in this reenactment.

First Battle of Bull Run

In July 1861, the Union army moved south, now led by General **Irvin McDowell,** a good strategist from West Point. A Confederate force was encamped twenty miles to the south of Washington, D.C., at Manassas, Virginia, and McDowell planned to capture it. Congressmen, their wives, and northern journalists followed McDowell's forces down the Centreville Turnpike to admire "the greatest army in the world."

The Confederates learned of this advance, and Jefferson Davis ordered General Joseph E. Johnston to leave the Shenandoah Valley and come to aid the troops at Bull Run Creek.

At the outset Union troops fought well. The Confederate Army gave ground and appeared to be retreating. But the brigade under the command of **Thomas Jackson** stood fast against the attack. (This action won Jackson the nickname "Stonewall.") Newly arriving Confederate troops then staged a southern counterattack, which forced the Union to retreat. The orderly retreat turned into a rout when a small Confederate force attacked some troops on the turnpike and they panicked. Instead of having supper in Richmond, the Union soldiers threw down their guns and canteens and ran for Washington. Dazed Congressmen and reporters joined the exodus. In the resulting chaos, Washington was left unprotected, but the Confederate forces were just as disorganized as the Union troops, and they could not follow up their great victory.

Results of the First Battle

The **battle of Bull Run** (also called Manassas) affected both sides. The North realized that its troops were not yet ready to fight.

George B. McClellan was called to the White House, where Lincoln placed him in charge of all federal troops protecting Washington and told him to forge a new army to take Richmond. McClellan soon turned the army into a well-drilled machine. The troops sang, "For McClellan's our leader, he is gallant and strong! For God and our country, we are marching along." Meanwhile, the South had won so easily, just as Southerners had expected, that Bull Run made them overconfident.

Hesitation and Loss for the North

The North's goal of taking Richmond proved to be difficult. Slow progress in this "War in the East" frustrated Lincoln and most of the Union. Although McClellan claimed he needed more men and more time, Lincoln decided that McClellan had had enough time to ready the army.

McClellan finally tried a new approach. His army sailed down the Potomac River around the Virginia peninsula and debarked between the James and York Rivers. Since the Confederacy had spent less time fortifying that area, McClellan chose to attack there.

Joseph E. Johnston, the Confederate commander, was caught totally off guard. That should have been to McClellan's advantage, but McClellan, believing he needed more men to win, stalled.

McClellan's troubles were only beginning. Because the Confederate commander, Johnston, was wounded in an indecisive battle at Fair Oaks, the Confederacy got a new commander for the Army of Northern Virginia, Robert E. Lee. Although his troops were outnumbered, Lee knew his men, his resources, and the area. In seven days (hence the name Seven Days' Battle), Lee attacked McClellan in six different places and drove the Union army back. McClellan had been nine miles from Richmond on June 25. Seven days later he was back again where he had started, at the tip of the peninsula.

Back to Bull Run

Lincoln quickly changed Union commanders and ordered McClellan back to Washington to join John Pope in a new land attack. But Lee decided the Confederacy could beat Pope before he gained strength.

Lee left half his force in Richmond and sent the other half north to keep John Pope busy. Meanwhile, J.E.B. Stuart, a dashing cav-

A portrait of Confederate generals Thomas J. "Stonewall" Jackson, Joseph E. Johnston, and Robert E. Lee

alry officer, raided Pope's headquarters while Pope was gone. Seeking revenge because his favorite hat had been lost to Yankees in a skirmish several days before, Stuart collected Pope's war chest of $300,000, his dress coat, and the dispatch book that told where Union forces would be going. Of course, this gave Lee the offensive advantage he needed.

As the armies of the North and South converged, they took their stand once more on the battlegrounds of Bull Run. Stonewall Jackson's foot soldiers raced to aid Lee,

General George B. McClellan (fifth from the left) and his staff

covering sixty-two miles in less than forty-eight hours. The two-day fight, the **second battle of Bull Run** (Manassas Junction), ended with the Union troops back in Washington. Jackson said that the day had been won "by nothing but the blessing and protection of Providence." A disgraced Pope was sent off to Minnesota to fight Indians, and he was replaced by McClellan, who was now given a second chance.

This was probably the high tide of the Confederacy. Lee had defeated the army that faced him and the relief army that had come to aid them and had successfully switched the locale of fighting from Richmond back to Washington where it would do more damage to the Union than to the Confederacy.

SECTION REVIEW

1. What key city was the Union army striving to conquer?

2. What Confederate commander kept his men from retreating at the first battle of Bull Run?

3. How did each side respond to that Confederate victory?

4. What exceptional Confederate leader overcame McClellan in the Seven Days' Battle?

5. What battle was probably the high tide of the Confederacy?

 What proved to be a major flaw in McClellan's leadership?

Controlling the Waters

Two goals of the Union forces involved shutting off the South's major water transportation links. The North achieved these objectives with a minimum of delay and a better demonstration of leadership.

The Union Blockade

On April 17, 1861, only a few days after the fall of Fort Sumter, the Confederacy permitted privately owned ships to be outfitted to capture Union vessels. Two days later Lincoln issued orders for a naval **blockade** of the southern coast from South Carolina around to the Mexican border. Later he extended it northward to the Potomac River. Because of the shortage of ships, however, it was difficult at first for the Union to maintain a successful blockade. But the Secretary of the Navy began a giant ship-buying program, leasing or purchasing just about anything big enough to be armed. Once ready, the North concentrated the blockade on ten major southern ports, each of which had inland connections by rail or river.

The South tried to overcome the blockade with **blockade runners.** Because the runners had shallow drafts (little of the ship extended below the water line), they could dart into shallow inlets for cover. Since the Union ships needed deeper water to operate, they could not follow them. Runner ships had low profiles and were usually painted dull gray to blend with the seas. Most of them were steam-powered, and some could do eighteen knots (27 m.p.h.), enabling them to outrun any Union vessel. Their powerful engines burned hard coal because its smoke was less noticeable. The easiest ports for blockade runners were those with more than one outlet, such as Wilmington, North Carolina. From these ports the outbound runners, loaded with cotton, usually headed south to British-held islands; Bermuda and the Bahama Islands were only about three days away. The goods were then shifted to ocean-going freighters that flew the flags of neutral countries. To overcome their ship and manpower shortage, the Confederates hired British ships and young captains from the Royal Navy. The chance for wealth made it worth the risks; a captain could make $5,000 in gold for one round trip, and the lowest crewman, $250. The Confederates made more than 8,500 successful trips through the blockade. Even in the closing months of the war, there was an even chance of evading the blockade.

In 1861 the chances of slipping through the blockade were high. Nine of every ten southern ships got through. But as the months went by, the Union increased its efforts. As various ports fell into Yankee hands, the blockade had more land bases to make it even more successful. In the spring of 1865, thirty-five fully laden runners carrying $15 million worth of goods sat in Nassau harbor with no ports of call open on the southern coast. Their provisions would never reach the starving South.

Although its effective rate at the war's end was only fifty percent, the blockade took a huge toll on the Confederacy. In three years the South went from exporting ten million bales of cotton a year to shipping only one million bales. Drained of income, the South had to issue money backed only by faith in its cause. Its credit was undermined, and the foreign products it desperately needed became nearly unattainable, its foreign trade decreasing by two-thirds. While the outcome of the war was not decided on the blockade line but on the battlefield, it would have been a far different war if the Union navy had not guarded the southern coast.

Taking the Mississippi

The "War in the West" centered on the North's goal of gaining control of the Mississippi River. With control of the river, the North could separate Texas, Arkansas, Louisiana, and their resources from the rest of the Confederacy. They could also eliminate southern use of the important riverway and take advantage of its transportation opportunities for the Union. Instrumental in achieving

Ulysses S. Grant helped lead the Union Army to gain control of the Mississippi River.

this goal was the leadership of a Union officer named **Ulysses S. Grant.**

Gaining the Upper Mississippi—Grant, who had given up soldiering earlier and had since failed at farming and business, rejoined the army in Illinois. He believed that the key to success west of the Appalachians was control of the Tennessee and Cumberland Rivers. (These rivers emptied into the Ohio River, which in turn flowed to the Mississippi.) Leaving Cairo, Illinois, he and his troops moved down to the Tennessee border and captured two forts, Fort Henry and Fort Donelson. These forts defended the key waterways, and their fall, followed by the capture of Corinth and the battle of Shiloh in April 1862, meant that the Union had control of the upper Mississippi and access to points south. The capture of these forts also made Grant a hero.

Gaining the Lower Mississippi—Next on the Union war agenda was gaining control of the lower Mississippi to prevent Confederate use of it. Two Confederate forts on a peninsula guarded the river. The Confederacy had also

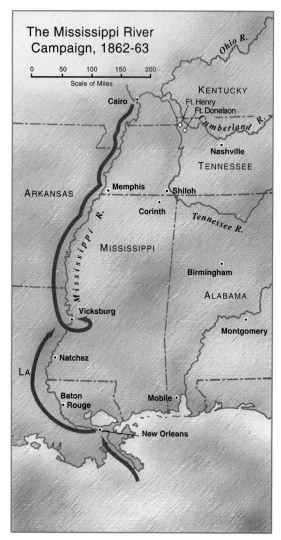

The Mississippi River Campaign, 1862-63

0   50   100   150   200
Scale of Miles

Ohio R.

Cairo

KENTUCKY
Ft. Henry
Ft. Donelson

Cumberland R.

Nashville

TENNESSEE

ARKANSAS

Memphis

Shiloh

Corinth

Tennessee R.

Mississippi R.

MISSISSIPPI

Birmingham

ALABAMA

Vicksburg

Montgomery

Natchez

LA

Baton
Rouge

Mobile

New Orleans

chains, and Farragut's fleet slipped past the forts despite heavy fire from the Confederates. Once past the forts, he scattered and disabled the Confederate fleet. New Orleans fell two days later. Butler's troops remained there to keep it under Federal control.

The Union navy then began moving up river, occupying first Baton Rouge, Louisiana, and then Natchez, Mississippi. By July of 1863 the Federals had won control of the entire Mississippi River, except for a small area around Vicksburg, Mississippi, a prime Union target.

Vicksburg—Control of the Mississippi eluded the North because the Confederacy held **Vicksburg,** built high on the bluffs overlooking the river. Six times Confederate General John C. Pemberton had repelled Union attacks on Vicksburg, each time inflicting heavy Union casualties.

Grant sought a new angle of attack. He designed a strategy that broke his army away from its own supply line. Grant announced his forces would "carry what rations of hard bread, coffee, and sort we can, and make the country furnish the balance." In a move that shocked Pemberton, Grant moved east to cut Confederate rail access to Vicksburg. Pemberton moved to cut off Grant's supply line only to find Grant had none. When Pemberton returned to Vicksburg, he was caught in a trap without an escape route. Now Grant could starve out Pemberton in the city. For six weeks, around the clock, the Union shelled Vicksburg. Short of goods, the people resorted to eating mules, rats, and even their own pets. Finally, with no food and no hope of relief, the Confederates surrendered Vicksburg. The date was July 4, 1863. It had taken Grant eighteen months to capture the Mississippi. A rising Union commander, William T. Sherman, had called it the "spinal column of America."

stretched two huge link chains across the Mississippi. The chains would be lifted to permit Confederate vessels to pass by and then lowered to snag any others that might try.

David Glasgow Farragut, a naval officer, devised a plan that with the aid of a land force, led by General Benjamin Butler, would take New Orleans. Farragut decided to bypass the forts and head for New Orleans. Under cover of night, an advance party unhooked the

SECTION REVIEW

1. Why was it initially difficult for the Union to maintain a successful naval blockade?

2. What did Grant believe to be the key to military success west of the Appalachians?

3. What Union naval officer was responsible for breaking through the Confederate chain in the lower Mississippi?

4. What was the last Confederate stronghold on the Mississippi River? On what date did it fall to Union troops?

 Why did the North want to shut off the South's water links?

The War in the East

While Grant found quick success in the West, the Union forces slowly moved from defeat to victory in the East. In September of 1862, Lee decided to take the offensive and move into Maryland, hoping to free it from Union control. Since it was early fall, the move would also free farmers in the rich granary of the Confederacy to harvest their crops. Moreover, Lee had reason to believe that a successful southern offensive would bring Britain in on the Confederate side.

Antietam

Lee divided his army, sending Jackson into the Shenandoah Valley. J.E.B. Stuart's cavalry was left behind to halt any Union attempts at pursuit. McClellan would have had little idea where Lee had planned to attack had it not been for an amazing discovery.

When McClellan was moving across an area recently vacated by Confederates, a Union corporal and a sergeant picked up three cigars. Wrapped around the cigars was a dispatch from Lee that a courier had lost, giving Lee's location and making it obvious that his army was divided. Using the information, McClellan moved to force Lee into a battle before Jackson could reach him. Lee found

out about the lost dispatch less than twenty-four hours later and planned to pull back across the Potomac and change his strategy. But on September 17, 1862, McClellan's forces made massive attacks on Lee's lines. In one long, ghastly day, three battles were fought. Just before dusk, though, Lee's reinforcements arrived. With one more attack McClellan might have defeated Lee, but the attack never came, only a stalemate. Rather than renewing the attack at daybreak, McClellan waited, permitting Lee to engineer an orderly retreat across the Potomac back into the safety of northern Virginia.

Since the Confederacy did not win at **Antietam** (an TEE tum), Britain stayed out of the war. Since the Union did not lose, Lincoln used the occasion to issue the Emancipation Proclamation.

Fredericksburg

Ambrose Burnside, the dashing officer Lincoln picked to replace McClellan, had no better success than his predecessor. On December 13, 1862, Burnside drove his refitted army across the Rappahanock to attack Confederates entrenched at Fredericksburg. Wave after wave of men failed to dislodge the Confederate forces, and the Union lost twice as many men as the Confederacy. Union morale dipped to the lowest point of the war. In twenty months the North had organized a grand army; yet no general seemed to be able to win with it. Lincoln now sent for "Fighting Joe" Hooker.

Chancellorsville

Hooker, with 130,000 men, now decided to strike Lee's army of 60,000 by going west to **Chancellorsville.** The Union forces had an overwhelming advantage not only in numbers of men but also in supplies. An overconfident Hooker boasted, "May God have mercy on General Lee, for I will have none." Since the isolated crossroads was within easy reach of

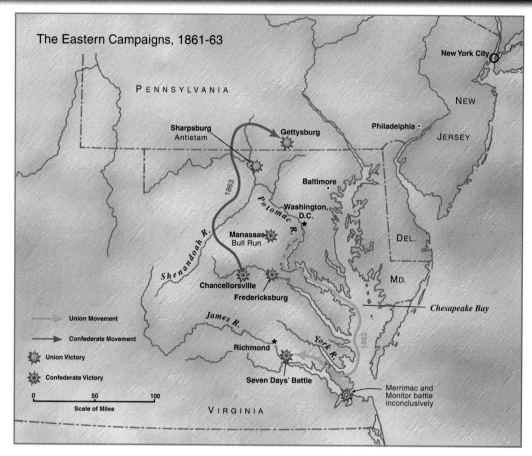

The Eastern Campaigns, 1861-63

PENNSYLVANIA

New York City

NEW

JERSEY

Philadelphia

Sharpsburg
Antietam

Gettysburg

1863

Baltimore

Potomac R.

Washington, D.C.

Manassas
Bull Run

Shenandoah R.

DEL.

MD.

Chancellorsville

Fredericksburg

Chesapeake Bay

James R.

Richmond

York R.

1862

Seven Days' Battle

Merrimac and
Monitor battle
inconclusively

Union Movement

Confederate Movement

Union Victory

Confederate Victory

0   50   100

Scale of Miles

VIRGINIA

Richmond, Lee risked a bold initiative. He split his army again and caught the Union by surprise. The battle, considered by many to be Lee's finest, raged for five days, and the fifth Union offensive for Richmond then failed.

Although the Confederate victory was probably the finest of the war, it cost the South dearly. The evening after the first day of battle, Stonewall Jackson was mortally wounded by some Confederate guards. In the darkness they failed to recognize Jackson, who was out scouting for information. When Lee heard of Jackson's wounds and the necessary amputation of his left arm, Lee sent word for Jackson to "make haste and get well, and come back to me as soon as he can. He has lost his left arm, but I have lost my right." However, Jackson died within the week. It was a loss that Lee

Confederate soldiers lie dead behind the "terrible stone wall," where they withstood wave after wave of Union assaults during the battle of Fredricksburg.

and the Confederacy felt keenly. Because of his skill and unselfish cooperation, Jackson had been worth as much as many regiments to the Confederate cause.

Gettysburg

Buoyed by victory, Lee decided on a bold advance into Pennsylvania. This was his second and last invasion of the North. Lee believed that northern support for the war would be lost if he captured a northern city like Harrisburg or Baltimore. He also thought that it would make Lincoln pull some troops out of the campaign along the Mississippi River and lessen pressure there. Lee also hoped his famished army could be resupplied as they passed through lush Pennsylvania farmlands.

Lee's Hopeful Advance—Lee started north early in June, going up the Shenandoah Valley, across the Potomac, across western Maryland, and then into Pennsylvania. Even with ninety thousand men, Hooker was unable to stop Lee. In desperation, on June 28, Lincoln gave the army its fifth commander that year, George Gordon Meade. Although shy and scholarly, Meade was well qualified.

On July 1, Lee's advance troops came to a small town called **Gettysburg,** where they stopped to buy some badly needed shoes. There they unexpectedly met a Union scouting party. Both armies quickly pulled up to fight from two ridges. The Confederates were on Seminary Ridge; the Union forces stood on Cemetery Ridge about one mile away. At the southern end of Cemetery Ridge were two rocky points called Round Top and Little Round Top.

On the first day of the three-day battle, Lee's troops forced the Union lines back but did not break them. The next day, July 2, Lee attacked on the left end of the Union line near the Round Tops but was beaten back. That night Lee planned an attack on the Union center.

A Bitter Defeat for the South—The attack on July 3 began with the heaviest bombardment the South could deliver. Between one and two o'clock in the afternoon, fifteen thousand Confederate troops under General George Pickett gave the bloodcurdling "rebel yell" and charged across an open, mile-wide wheat field. Union firepower was murderous, and thousands of Pickett's men were killed in the courageous effort. "Pickett's charge" failed to break the Union lines.

Lee waited on July 4, poised for a counterattack that never came. Meade chose not to send his tired men across that open field. Thus he missed a golden opportunity to capture Lee and his forces. The next day Lee and his tattered troops rode back into Virginia in a torrential downpour. The Confederates and their baggage train were spread out over seventeen miles but returned without the slightest harassment from the Union army.

With Lee back in Virginia, the Union had no choice but to attack there. Since Meade showed no desire to follow through, Lincoln promoted a new general above him. On March 2, 1864, Lincoln brought Ulysses S. Grant from the West and made Grant his supreme commander. **William T. Sherman** took Grant's place in the West.

SECTION REVIEW

1. What discovery prevented Lee from winning at Antietam?

2. What valuable Confederate leader was mortally wounded during the battle of Chancellorsville?

3. Who led the famous Confederate charge at Gettysburg?

4. Who became supreme leader of the Union forces following the battle of Gettysburg?

 What would have been the benefit to the South of opening conflict in northern territory?

The War of Attrition and Destruction

Many Northerners, tiring of the war, wanted a negotiated peace. Lincoln and his cabinet planned definite steps to bring the war to a victorious end. They believed that freeing the slaves, destroying southern property, and winning the presidential election of 1864 might all help end the war.

Freeing the Slaves: The Emancipation Proclamation

President Lincoln had brought the nation into a war to preserve the Union, not to free the slaves. However, as the war continued, it became obvious that ending slavery was necessary. The war-weary North needed a new cause to revive its fighting spirit, and so the proclamation was an important political move for Lincoln. In 1862 Congress had abolished slavery in Washington and in the new territories. Then in September 1862 Lincoln issued his **Emancipation Proclamation,** not to take effect until January 1, 1863. Even then it would free slaves only in Confederate-held areas, not in the border states or any other areas then under federal control. Also, if any Confederate states quit fighting before January 1, they could keep their slaves. Not one state, however, quit.

The Gettysburg Address

The battle at Gettysburg left thousands of dead soldiers who could not be returned to their homes for burial. Instead they were laid to rest on the battlefield at Gettysburg, where they had fought and died. President Lincoln came to dedicate the new cemetery there and delivered one of the shortest but most memorable speeches of all time:

Four score and seven years ago our fathers brought forth on this continent, a new nation, conceived in Liberty, and dedicated to the proposition that all men are created equal.

Now we are engaged in a great civil war, testing whether that nation, or any nation so conceived and so dedicated, can long endure. We are met on a great battlefield of that war. We have come to dedicate a portion of that field, as a final resting place for those who here gave their lives that that nation might live. It is altogether fitting and proper that we should do this.

But, in a larger sense, we cannot dedicate—we cannot consecrate—we cannot hallow—this ground. The brave men, living and dead, who struggled here, have consecrated it, far above our poor power to add or detract. The world will little note, nor long remember what we say here, but it can never forget what they did here. It is for us the living, rather, to be dedicated here to the unfinished work which they who fought here have thus far so nobly advanced. It is rather for us to be here dedicated to the great task remaining before us—that from these honored dead we take increased devotion to that cause for which they gave the last full measure of devotion—that we here highly resolve that these dead shall not have died in vain—that this nation, under God, shall have a new birth of freedom—and that government of the people, by the people, for the people, shall not perish from the earth.

Lincoln reads the Emancipation Proclamation before his cabinet.

Encouraging the Confederacy to give up was but one reason for issuing the proclamation. It also gave the Union a positive, measurable goal. Instead of merely fighting for the Union, Northerners were now waging war "to make men free," in the words of Julia Ward Howe's new "Battle Hymn of the Republic." Third, since they would be fighting to end slavery, blacks were now given a real reason for joining the fight. More than 190,000 blacks fought on the Union side. Fourth, the proclamation hurt the South's war efforts because many slaves left their masters. As the word spread that slaves who reached northern lines would be freed, thousands deserted. Moreover, the proclamation paved the way for public acceptance of the total end of slavery, which came with the Thirteenth Amendment. Finally, it helped prevent Britain from entering the war on the South's side, because most of the British people opposed slavery.

Destroying the South

A war of attrition meant wearing down the South until it was too poor, too tired, and too hungry to fight. While the blockade cut off foreign supplies from the Confederacy, and Union control of the Mississippi prevented further aid from the West, Union armies now began to destroy provisions in the very heart of the Confederacy.

***Sheridan in the Shenandoah Valley*—**Since Lee was aware of northern war weariness, he sent Jubal Early and his cavalry north. Although Lee did not expect Early to win any major battles, he hoped to create some anxiety. From his base in the Shenandoah Valley, Early's men raided Maryland farms, stealing livestock. In July 1864, Early and his men rode to the outskirts of Washington. This action did keep some of Grant's troops in Washington for protection and out of the fight against Lee.

But Early's raid led Grant to make a decision that had a grave effect on the South. Grant decided to send **Philip Sheridan** to close down the Shenandoah Valley once and for all. Grant told Sheridan, "Leave nothing to invite the enemy to return. Destroy whatever cannot be consumed. Let that valley be left so that crows flying over it will have to carry their own rations."

Sheridan complied with grim efficiency. He not only defeated Jubal Early's outnumbered army three times but also laid waste to the valley that had fed Lee's army for three years. Sheridan's men rode out of nowhere, killing farm livestock and striking terror. They burned houses, barns, and crops. More than any one single battle, Sheridan's destruction marked the end of Lee's army. Now Lee's men lacked not only weapons but also food.

***Taking Tennessee*—**Before Grant had been called to take control of the Union army, he had led his men from the Mississippi River eastward toward Chattanooga (chat uh NOO guh). There the Union general William S. Rosecrans had taken control of the city.

The Confederate forces, however, had moved south to Chickamauga (chik uh MAH guh), Cherokee for "river of death." Lee sent eleven thousand men to assist the Confederate commander, Braxton Bragg. Lee had no intention of letting the heartland go without a fight. On September 19, 1863, Bragg launched a hard counterattack that forced the Union forces to retreat to Chattanooga. Things looked grim for the northern army while they were isolated there.

Then Grant and Sherman arrived. Union forces opened up the Tennessee River to get food in. On November 23 Grant gave the orders to attack. Sherman struck the Confederate right flank on Missionary Ridge while another force attacked Lookout Mountain. The combined Union armies dislodged the Confederates and regained Chattanooga. Their efforts cleared Tennessee of Confederate forces, sending Braxton Bragg south into Georgia.

Sherman's March to the Sea—Confederate troops lodged in north Georgia hoped to ride west into Alabama and slide back into Tennessee to attack Sherman again. Grant, leaving the western command to Sherman, told him to go after the Confederate army, to "break it up, and to get into the interior of the enemy's country as far as you can, inflicting all the damage you can." And that Sherman did.

Moving southeast into Georgia, Sherman met staunch resistance from General Joseph Johnston. In a series of brilliant moves, Sherman attacked the flanks, or edges, of Johnston's troops. Every time Johnston was ready to take a stand, Sherman threatened to sweep around him, forcing Johnston to retreat still farther. Finally, however, Johnston took his stand at Kennesaw (KEN ih saw) Mountain, and the Union troops could not assault his defenses. Sherman then threatened the rear, forcing a retreat.

When Jefferson Davis became impatient with Johnston's slowness, he foolishly replaced him with the less able John Bell Hood. Hood lost heavily in Atlanta and by September 1 realized he could save his army only by evacuating the city. Sherman was more than willing to have Atlanta, a major railroad center whose loss devastated the southern cause.

Sherman saw, however, that keeping Atlanta might not be to his advantage. After all, he was now in the heart of the Confederacy and had moved far away from his supply base in Tennessee. His supplies were coming in by rail on a one-hundred-mile line that could easily be cut, placing his own men in grave danger.

Sherman, though, saw a way to change danger into triumph. Although Hood had already destroyed the supplies in Atlanta, Sherman got Grant's permission to destroy the city and leave only ruins behind. The civilians were told to leave, the city was torched, and Sherman cut the railroad back to Chattanooga. Thus he kept the Confederates from using it to counterattack him.

On November 10, 1864, Sherman's army moved out of Atlanta quickly to avoid fighting another major battle. Sherman divided his army into four groups and sent them toward Savannah on four roads across a sixty-mile-wide band of Georgia. They carried maps that carefully marked every village, path, and plantation. Their orders were "to forage liberally on the country during the march," keeping a ten-day supply on hand at all times. What was not needed was to be destroyed.

In the years since, many have wondered why Sherman was so destructive. Simply put, Sherman destroyed what was left to make it impossible for the Confederate army, now back under Johnston's command, to chase him. Second, this area of the Confederacy had yet to be physically affected by the war. By destroying the spirit and resources of this area, Sherman hoped to press Davis and the Confederates into surrendering more quickly. Finally, Sherman was under orders from Grant to destroy the area.

Sherman's orders stated, "Soldiers must not enter the dwellings of any inhabitant or

Mathew Brady's photo of Chattanooga in 1864 shows army tents in the foreground.

"commit any trespass" unless local bushwhackers molested them. Since the locals almost always did, wholesale destruction resulted. Confederate and Union deserters, called **bummers,** added to the problem, following the army and pillaging. Sherman did not attempt to stop them. As a result, Sherman's **March to the Sea** did cause a great deal of bitterness. To generations of Americans not accustomed to war, this was war at its worst.

By December 10 Sherman's men had reached the port city of Savannah. The city fell easily; now supplies could not come by sea. Sherman presented Savannah to Lincoln as a

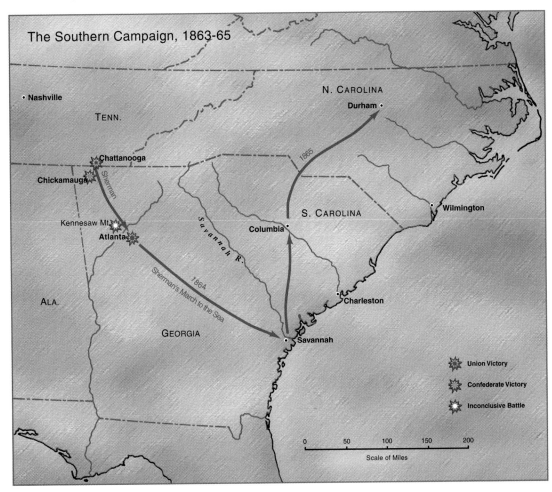

The Southern Campaign, 1863-65

Nashville

TENN.

Chattanooga

Chickamauga

Kennesaw Mt.

Atlanta

ALA.

GEORGIA

Sherman's March to the Sea
1864

Savannah R.

Columbia

S. CAROLINA

Charleston

Savannah

N. CAROLINA

Durham

1865

Wilmington

Union Victory

Confederate Victory

Inconclusive Battle

0   50   100   150   200

Scale of Miles

Christmas present. Six weeks later he turned north to march across the Carolinas. His men devastated this area also. Sherman hoped to be able to join Grant in the final effort to defeat Lee.

The Election of 1864

Lincoln faced reelection in the fall of 1864. On August 23, 1864, Lincoln told his cabinet that he did not believe he would be reelected. Journalist Horace Greeley wrote that nine-tenths of all Americans were "anxious for peace, peace on almost any terms." The former Union general George McClellan,

Mathew Brady took this photograph of President Lincoln in February 1864.

who was running on a peace ticket, was Lincoln's opponent in the race.

Radical Republicans believed Lincoln was being too generous with the South, and northern Democrats criticized him at every turn. Yet they really could not see anyone else who could do better. Although he had not yet been able to end the war, he could not be faulted for lack of political skill. Lincoln used government jobs to increase his support; he picked cabinet members to appeal to different parts of the country and differing factions. He even picked a new running mate, a Southerner from Tennessee named **Andrew Johnson,** who, he believed, could help him bring the South back into the Union more easily. Lincoln's experience also had taught him how to win political fights without making personal enemies of those he defeated. He was a man of force, ability, and vision.

The American public sensed this more than did the politicians. Lincoln also had some men who helped to turn the tide for him. Their names were Sherman, Sheridan, and Farragut. Their victories in the fall of 1864 increased Lincoln's popularity and ensured his win over McClellan.

SECTION REVIEW

1. What were the provisions of the Emancipation Proclamation?

2. Near what Tennessee city did Union forces attack and send Confederate troops south into Georgia?

3. Who ran on the "peace ticket" in the 1864 election?

4. Why did Lincoln choose Andrew Johnson as his running mate?

 What was the general strategy behind Philip Sheridan's Shenandoah Valley campaign and William Sherman's March to the Sea?

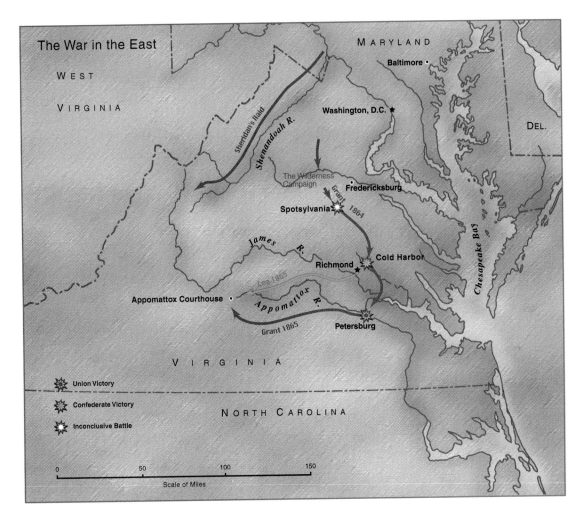

The War in the East

WEST VIRGINIA

MARYLAND

Baltimore

Washington, D.C. ★

DEL.

Sheridan's Raid

Shenandoah R.

The Wilderness Campaign

Fredericksburg

Spotsylvania

Grant 1864

James R.

Lee 1865

Richmond

Cold Harbor

Appomattox Courthouse

Appomattox R.

Grant 1865

Petersburg

Chesapeake Bay

VIRGINIA

Union Victory

Confederate Victory

Inconclusive Battle

NORTH CAROLINA

Scale of Miles

0   50   100   150

Appomattox and Aftermath

By May of 1864, Grant was ready to open a new Virginia campaign. His army moved into a heavily wooded area west of Fredericksburg called "The Wilderness." There Grant hurled a force of 100,000 men against Lee's smaller army. Although Grant suffered heavy losses, he knew he could replace his men while Lee could not. Grant believed that if he pressed Lee's army long enough and prevented Lee from maneuvering to fight him, he could wear Lee down and win.

The Road to Richmond

Despite his losses, Grant rebounded, moving east and then south. Lee marched all night to head him off and caught him at Spotsylvania Courthouse. But Grant moved south again, and Lee had to throw himself and his troops between the Union army and Richmond. Grant lost more men at Cold Harbor (the dead covered five acres of ground), but his advance continued. By now Yankee newspaper editors were calling the North's leading general "the butcher." In one month he had lost more than 50,000 men. But Grant was wearing Lee down. He had no thought of changing his plans: "I intend to fight it out on this line if it takes all summer." Lincoln told his cabinet, "I cannot spare this man. He wins."

In June 1864, Grant crossed the James River, planning to attack Richmond from the south. To do this, the Federals needed to take Petersburg. Lee came to Petersburg's rescue. Grant settled in for a siege that did not end until April 1865. Eighteen trainloads of supplies came daily to Grant's aid while Lee's troops had less and less. The battle for Petersburg went on, and the South lost four thousand men but did not retreat. Lincoln told Grant, "Hold on with a bulldog grip and chew and choke as much as possible."

By March 1865 Lee realized he could not hold out much longer. On April 2 Lee moved the 54,000 men left in his army away from Petersburg. He hoped to lure Grant into open country and to neutralize Union numbers with superior tactics. But, outnumbered more than two to one, Lee had to fall back.

Surrender at Appomattox

Lee feared having his army trapped in Richmond. He decided to destroy Richmond and bolt west. Johnston's army was in upper North Carolina, and Lee's last hope was to link with it for one last stand, but Sheridan blocked Lee's retreat to the Blue Ridge Mountains. On April 9, 1865, near Appomattox (ap uh MAT uks) Courthouse, the Confederacy made one final hopeless attack on Grant's line, hoping to buy time. When it failed, Lee asked for terms of surrender.

Only half of Lee's men had arms to stack when they laid down their weapons at **Appomattox.** Some were barefoot, and most were hungry. With a nation to be reunited, Grant had been told to offer Lee generous terms. Officers could keep their revolvers and swords. Because horses were needed for farm work, the men were allowed to keep them. A local printer stayed up all night to print parole certificates. No prisoners would be kept. As soon as the soldiers signed a pledge not to take

A modern reenactment of the battle of Petersburg looks green and bright compared to the reality of an artillery stockpile outside of Richmond, Virginia, in 1865.

Grant accepted Lee's surrender at the McLean House at Appomattox Courthouse.

up arms again, they would be given enough provisions from Union supplies and captured Confederate supplies to get them home.

Since Lee's army was the keystone of the Confederate army, it was only a matter of time until the more scattered units surrendered. On April 18 Joseph Johnston surrendered to Sherman at the Bennett House in Durham, North Carolina. The last group of Confederates to receive the news, in Texas, gave up early in May.

Counting the Casualties

The Civil War was the most destructive war America has ever experienced. About one-third of the approximately two million men who served in it were killed, injured, or captured. Practically every family lost at least one member or close friend in the war. In the South one-fourth of all manpower of military draft age never returned from war. By contrast, in World War II only one in sixteen was lost.

There had been great destruction of personal property, especially in the South. Unlike any other war since then, the Civil War was fought on America's own soil. Ruined homes, roads, businesses, and farmland were some of the material losses.

In addition, the war left deep bitterness. Mutual distrust and even hatred lingered between the North and South for decades, because each blamed the other for losses or problems.

Lincoln's Assassination

There was still one casualty to come. It affected both sides, the South perhaps more than the North. On Good Friday, April 14, 1865, President and Mrs. Lincoln went to

A Letter of Consolation

The Civil War took a terrible toll on the lives of America's young men. One powerful example of the suffering endured by the mothers of soldiers was a poignant letter of condolence written by President Lincoln to a bereaved mother in Massachusetts.

Dear Madam,

I have been shown in the files of the War Department a statement of the Adjutant General of Massachusetts, that you are the mother of five sons who have died gloriously on the field of battle.

I feel how weak and fruitless must be any word of mine which should attempt to beguile you from the grief of a loss so overwhelming. But I cannot refrain from tendering to you the consolation that may be found in the thanks of the Republic they died to save.

I pray that our Heavenly Father may assuage the anguish of your bereavement, and leave you only the cherished memory of the loved and lost, and the solemn pride that must be yours to have laid so costly a sacrifice upon the altar of Freedom.

Yours very sincerely
and respectfully
A. Lincoln

Mrs Bixby
Boston Massachusetts

and his stated terms for reentry of the Southern states were quite generous. One writer said that Booth's "trigger finger had done the South more harm than all the lawless bummers in Sherman's Army."

Lincoln's funeral train retraced the route that had taken him to Washington only a little more than four years earlier. He was buried in his hometown of Springfield, Illinois, on May 4, 1865. After the nation laid a president to rest, it soon awakened to problems it had never faced before. These problems would challenge our nation for a century.

SECTION REVIEW

1. What was Grant's reason for continuing his pursuit of Lee despite the heavy losses Grant was suffering?

2. What strategic city did the Union soldiers need to take before attacking Richmond?

3. Where did Lee and his men lay down their weapons?

4. Who assassinated President Lincoln?

 Why is the Civil War called the most "destructive war Americans ever experienced"?

Ford's Theater to attend a play. An actor who was also a fanatical Confederate sympathizer slipped into the president's box while the guard was away. **John Wilkes Booth** then shot Lincoln in the back of the head, and President Lincoln died the next morning. Booth was later trapped in a barn in Virginia. The barn was burned, and Booth either took his own life or was shot by one of his pursuers.

No one really knows what would have happened in the postwar years had Lincoln lived. However, Lincoln's second inaugural address had stressed "malice toward none,"

Arlington National Cemetery

Across the Potomac River from Washington, D.C., stands a stately columned mansion on a hilltop. That mansion is the Arlington House, once called the Custis-Lee Mansion. Today the mansion is more often associated with Arlington National Cemetery, the site it overlooks, than with the families who once lived there.

In 1669 Governor Berkeley of Virginia deeded six thousand acres of land to a ship's captain. This was his pay for bringing over a shipload of colonists. Later the land was purchased by John Parke Custis, a son of Martha Washington by her first marriage. His granddaughter, Mary Ann Randolph Custis, married Robert E. Lee at the family mansion in 1831. In time Mary inherited the mansion and the surrounding lands.

When Mrs. Lee and her four children fled Arlington in 1861, the mansion fell into federal hands. Because of delinquent taxes, United States commissioners purchased the land in 1864. (Mrs. Lee had tried to pay the $92.00 due plus a fifty percent penalty, but her emissary was sent back with the message that she would have to pay the taxes in person. As a result the government took the mansion.)

Washington's many hospitals had become crowded with wounded men. Because of poor medical conditions, many died. Some place was needed to bury them. Quartermaster Montgomery C. Meigs suggested that the grounds around Arlington be dedicated as a

national cemetery so as to prevent Lee from ever returning to his family's home. Meigs even came up personally to ensure that the graves were placed as close to the house as possible. The burials were made throughout the war.

In 1866 the bones of 2,111 unknown Union soldiers were gathered from the battlefields of

northern Virginia, brought to Arlington, and buried in a single mass grave right beside Lee's rose garden.

After the war Robert E. Lee's eldest son sued to regain his estate, and the Supreme Court ruled that it should be restored. But because thousands of soldiers were now buried on the estate, he settled quickly with the government for $150,000. Arlington National Cemetery was left to become America's most prestigious military cemetery.

SUMMARY

The Civil War began in 1861 between the North and the South. Although greatly outnumbered and lacking in materials, the Confederate armies successfully kept the Union armies from victory for four years. Eventually, however, the northern forces wore down the South's ability to fight until Lee finally surrendered to Grant in 1865. Four years of devastating struggle left much of the South in ruins and the nation in need of healing.

Chapter Review

People, Places, and Things to Remember

taxes in kind
Monitor
Merrimac
Mathew Brady
Irvin McDowell
Thomas Jackson
battle of Bull Run
George B. McClellan
second battle of Bull Run

blockade
blockade runners
Ulysses S. Grant
David Glasgow Farragut
Vicksburg
Antietam
Chancellorsville
Gettysburg
William T. Sherman

Emancipation
    Proclamation
Philip Sheridan
bummers
March to the Sea
Andrew Johnson
Appomattox
John Wilkes Booth

Review Questions

Identify the following.

1. The fall of this city in the West gave the Union control of the Mississippi.
2. This is the name given to Sherman's devastating trip through the South.
3. This one location was the site of two early battles won by the South.
4. These two ironclad ships fought a major naval battle during the Civil War.
5. Lee surrendered at this site.
6. This man shot Lincoln.
7. Lincoln hoped to make Union soldiers more willing to fight by issuing this document to free the slaves.
8. This man was a famous Civil War photographer.
9. This Pennsylvania battle was an important Union victory.

Identify each of the following men as Union or Confederate leaders, and then write a statement describing each man's role in the war.

10. Philip Sheridan
11. Thomas Jackson
12. Ulysses S. Grant
13. George B. McClellan
14. Robert E. Lee
15. William T. Sherman

Questions for Discussion

16. How did the first battle of Bull Run show that the people misunderstood what the war would be like?
17. Why did the North win the war?

History Skills

Geography in War

Answer these questions with the help of the text and the maps on pages 327, 339, 343, 346, 351, 353, and 646-45.

1. What mountain range separated the armies in the East and the West?

2. What river divided the Confederacy? How many states in the West were cut off when the Union captured this river?

3. What two important rivers run past Fort Henry, Grant's first objective in the West?

4. Rivers were important in supplying armies. After looking closely at the geography of Tennessee, guess why most of the fighting in the West took place there.

5. What geographic feature protected Vicksburg from Union attacks? (Because other cities on the Mississippi lacked this advantage, they were easily captured.)

6. What river, emptying into Chesapeake Bay, protected Washington from direct attack?

7. Based on the map scale, how many miles separate Washington and Richmond? In what state did most of the fighting in the East take place? Why?

8. What valley did Lee move through in 1863 and Sheridan in 1864?

9. The states of Alabama and Florida did not see as much action as other Confederate states. Look at their location. Why do you think they avoided major campaigns?

Think About It

There was more fighting in Missouri than almost any other state. Yet neither side paid much attention to it. Why? (Examine its location and the strategies listed in the text on page 339.)

18

Reconstruction

J ust weeks before the end of the weary conflict and his own tragic death, Lincoln had given his second inaugural address. Expressing his desire for the future of the United States, he said, "With malice toward none; with charity for all; with firmness in the right, as God gives us to see the right, let us strive on to finish the work we are in; to bind up the nation's wounds; to care for him who shall have borne the battle, and for his widow, and his orphan—to do all which may achieve and cherish a just, and a lasting peace, among ourselves, and with all nations."

But as the Civil War ended and time progressed, more malice and less charity appeared than Lincoln would have liked. The wounds of the war were deep, and it would take years, even decades, before they would begin to heal. Some scars would linger for over a century.

Reconstruction and the South

The time following the Civil War is called **Reconstruction.** This was the time of reuniting the nation and attempting to solve the South's postwar problems.

The South's Need for Reconstruction

For many Northerners, life following the war changed little from life before the war. The North had lost thousands of men, and it felt that wound deeply, but industry had progressed. Immigration continued to add to the northern population. Only a minor amount of northern property had been damaged in the war, so returning soldiers could go back to their farms or jobs with little hindrance.

The situation in the postwar South, however, was entirely different. Not only had it lost many of its young men, but it also had lost its slaves. Thus its labor force was entirely disrupted, and no great wave of immigrants came to add to the working population.

In addition to lost lives, the South had suffered severe property damage. Many of its major cities—Atlanta, Columbia, and Richmond—lay in ruins. Many of the South's fields had been stripped bare, and its livestock confiscated or destroyed. Homes, businesses, and railroads had been demolished. After the war little remained with which the South could rebuild.

Not only was the South's plantation system dead, but also the money that remained was worthless. The South had almost no U.S. currency, and the paper Confederate money had no value. The South was bankrupt, and its accustomed means of making its living had been destroyed.

The freed slaves, or **freedmen,** were another problem for the South. No longer controlled under slavery, over four million blacks were free to live in the South. They needed jobs for support, but white Southerners had no money to pay them. Neither were the freedmen particularly eager to return to the same work they had done as slaves. Slaves had been vital to the South's economy before the war, but the freedmen lacked an important role in the postwar South. Yet they were there, and they had to be given a place in southern society.

The South not only suffered great loss of property but also was unable to pay for rebuilding with the worthless Confederate money (top).

In addition to these problems was the need for the South to reestablish its state governments. Those governments in control during the Confederacy had been thrown out by the Union's victory. New governments had to be formed, and they in turn would have to deal with the conditions in the South.

All these problems of the postwar South were a major concern of the federal government. Presidents, Congress, and the states themselves would argue over their powers to control the methods of solving these problems of Reconstruction.

Phases of Reconstruction

Reconstruction is usually considered to be the twelve-year period from 1865 to 1877. During that time the federal government directly supervised the rebuilding of the South. In a larger sense, however, Reconstruction continued at least until the turn of the century as southern state governments continued to deal with the special problems of their region. According to the influences guiding Reconstruction policies, this larger period divides into three phases:

Phase 1 (1865-67):	Presidential Reconstruction or Self-Reconstruction
Phase 2 (1867-76):	Congressional Reconstruction or Radical Reconstruction
Phase 3 (1877-1900):	Bourbon Reconstruction or Redeemers' Reconstruction

---

SECTION REVIEW

1. What was the postwar era called?
2. What was the purpose of this era?
3. What were its three phases?

 How was the economic situation after the war different in the South from what it was in the North?

Presidential Reconstruction

For just a short time, Presidents Lincoln and Johnson directed the process of Reconstruction; this was the time of **Presidential Reconstruction.** Even before the war had ended, President Lincoln had developed a plan for bringing the seceded states back into the Union. Lincoln believed that the southern states, by illegally trying to secede, had committed an act of rebellion and had started an insurrection. As the commander in chief, his duty had been to quell their insurrection. Once this was done, he had the power given him under the Constitution to pardon their wrongdoing.

Lincoln's Ten Percent Plan and Congress's Reactions

In December 1863, Lincoln announced his **Ten Percent Plan** to reconstruct the areas of the South that had already come under Union control. This plan offered pardons to former Confederates who would swear an oath to support the Constitution and the Union. When ten percent of the registered voters in 1860 in any state had taken the oath, the state could form a new government and be restored to the Union. They could even get seats back in Congress and elect senators and representatives. By the spring of 1864 three occupied states (Tennessee, Louisiana, and Arkansas) had met these "easy" terms and were ready to reenter the Union.

Radical Republicans Object—Lincoln's plan, however, met resistance from a group of Republicans known as **Radical Republicans.** They believed that the plan treated the South too kindly. They wished the South to be treated as a conquered foreign nation, not as erring brethren. They were not ready to forgive the South for the war. According to these Radical Republicans, the South should be punished severely or all the sacrifices of war would be worthless. They also believed that if Southerners were let off too easily, they would try to regain the influence they had possessed before the war. Although a minority, the Radicals won moderate Republicans to their side. Because the Radicals and moderates did not wish to see Confederates back in Congress before the war ended, they refused to let the three states back into the Union under the president's plan.

The Radicals also reacted to Lincoln's use of executive (presidential) powers during the war. Since war created many emergencies, the president had made decisions without asking Congress. The Emancipation Proclamation, for example, had not received the approval of Congress. The Radicals believed that Lincoln had gone beyond his powers as president.

The Wade-Davis Bill—In 1864 Congress responded with its own Reconstruction plan, the **Wade-Davis Bill.** Under this plan a state could reenter the Union when fifty percent of the state's registered voters in 1860 had taken the oath of allegiance. In addition, those who wished to vote or help govern their states had to swear that they had never supported the Confederacy voluntarily. The states also had to abolish slavery and repudiate (rih PYOO dee ATE; refuse to pay or acknowledge) their debts and their acts of secession.

The Wade-Davis Bill passed both houses. Congress was letting the president know that it alone, not the president, would be the judge for state readmissions and reseating members of the legislative branch. In turn, Lincoln let Congress know he disagreed. Rather than

vetoing the bill by sending a formal message to Congress listing his objections, Lincoln killed the Wade-Davis Bill by pocket veto (See page 141.)

The conflict between Congress and Lincoln had not yet been resolved when Lincoln was shot. Andrew Johnson was left to battle with Congress for control of Reconstruction.

Andrew Johnson Takes Over

Vice President Andrew Johnson had been born in poverty in North Carolina. His wife, who was a teacher, had taught him to read and write. After moving to Tennessee, Johnson held his first political office. He moved up the local and state ladders to become a congressman and a senator. When Tennessee seceded in 1861, Johnson opposed its action and was the only southern senator who did not resign his Senate seat. President Lincoln named him military governor of Union-held areas of Tennessee and later chose him as his running mate. Johnson's outspokenness (he once said that Jefferson Davis and other leading Confederates should be hanged) won him the support of Radical Republicans.

When Johnson took over the presidency, Congress was out of session. Since he did not reconvene Congress, he had from April through December to state his ideals and to put them into effect without its interference. Johnson shared Lincoln's belief that it was impossible for a state to secede. Thus, Confederate states were still in the Union. Even so, Johnson believed individuals in the states had left the

Andrew Johnson faced the incredible task of trying to rebuild the nation.

363

Union, and they, rather than the states, deserved to be punished.

Johnson's Plan—Johnson began by offering **amnesty,** or group pardon, to Southerners who willingly took a loyalty oath to the Union. However, he excluded those whose taxable property was over $20,000. These people, mostly former planters, had to apply to him for a pardon. Unpardoned Southerners were unable to vote, hold office, or get back any property seized by the federal government.

Next, Johnson's plan provided for presidential appointment of provisional state governors to hold state conventions. Such state bodies would draft new state constitutions that repudiated Confederate debts and ratified the **Thirteenth Amendment,** the recent Constitutional amendment that had abolished slavery. When a state had taken this action and fifty percent of its voters had sworn loyalty, Johnson assumed Congress would readmit it.

By winter all of the former Confederate states except Texas had met most of Johnson's terms. But South Carolina refused to repudiate its war debt, Mississippi did not ratify the Thirteenth Amendment, and not one southern state offered voting rights to blacks. When Congress convened, it refused to seat southern representatives. Instead, moderate and Radical Republicans in the House and Senate formed their own Joint Committee on Reconstruction. They would determine whether the southern states were really reconstructed. Unsurprisingly, they decided they were not.

Republicans React to the "Johnson Governments"—Several things offended northern Republicans. First, when southern states held their state and local elections, they voted former Confederates into office. Second, many Radicals and others believed that the government should take southern lands and divide them among the newly freed slaves, but this was not done.

Third, because most of the South's representatives and senators were Democrats, Republicans realized that seating them might cost them their power. The Republicans would be in the minority if northern Democrats sided with the Southerners to outvote them.

Fourth, some believed that the cost of the war could be justified only if black Americans received full rights of citizens. "We must," one said, "see to it that the man made free in the Constitution . . . is a free man indeed . . . and that he walks the earth proud and erect in the conscious dignity of a free man." When the Joint Committee held hearings early in 1866, it found out that instead of being granted more rights, the former slaves were being denied them through **black codes.**

Black Codes—The black codes established after the war in the South were much like the old slave laws, although they did allow a few new basic rights. Black codes allowed blacks to sue, to be sued, and to testify in courts. They were also entitled to legalize their marriages and to marry within their own race. They could now buy, own, and transfer property. But in trying to control the large population of freed blacks, the codes were very restrictive. They placed blacks in an inferior position to whites, making them, in essence, second-class citizens. The codes were in some ways a replacement for slavery.

In some states, for example, blacks were allowed to work only as domestic servants or farmers. Some codes forbade blacks to live in towns or cities. Hence it seemed that the codes condemned many blacks to do the same field work they had done in slave days. Blacks who wanted to practice trades or do anything besides farming had to be apprenticed and often had to get licenses. Since few blacks had money, this closed trade doors to them. Blacks not usefully employed could be arrested for vagrancy (wandering around with no job). Blacks who could not pay fines for vagrancy or other crimes could be hired out to anyone who would pay their fines. Southern states forbade blacks to carry arms, and some codes told them where they could or could not own property. Southerners held that the black codes prevented the chaos that could have come from freeing four million slaves at once.

***Johnson's Response to the Radicals*—** Although Johnson had worked hard to overcome poverty and a lack of formal education, he did not have the ability to be a strong but sensitive leader for the nation at that time. He was firm in his positions on Reconstruction, and when his policies were defied, he stubbornly refused to change and lashed back at those who opposed him. His stubbornness often forced his foes into harsher positions. Because Johnson refused to give any ground, his inflexibility disheartened moderates and drove them into the Radical camp. Soon, with the majority of Congress united against Johnson, Presidential Reconstruction was coming to an end.

SECTION REVIEW

1. How could Confederate states be restored to the Union under Lincoln's Ten Percent Plan?

2. How did Congress's plan differ from Lincoln's?

3. Who assumed the presidency after Lincoln's assassination?

4. The black codes might be said to have replaced what former southern institution?

 How could Johnson have improved his handling of Reconstruction?

Radical Republicans Take Over Reconstruction

Radical Republicans in the House were led by **Thaddeus Stevens** of Pennsylvania and Senate Radicals by **Charles Sumner** of Massachusetts. After refusing Southerners

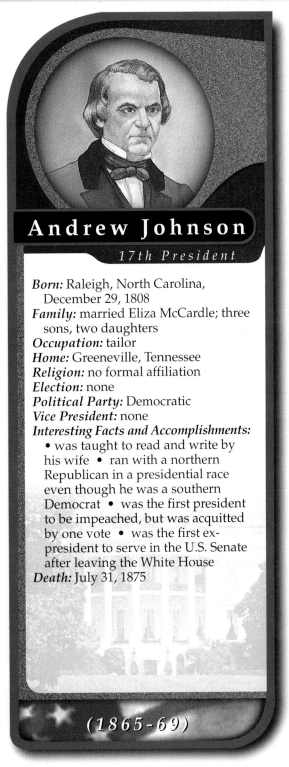

Andrew Johnson
17th President

Born: Raleigh, North Carolina, December 29, 1808
Family: married Eliza McCardle; three sons, two daughters
Occupation: tailor
Home: Greeneville, Tennessee
Religion: no formal affiliation
Election: none
Political Party: Democratic
Vice President: none
Interesting Facts and Accomplishments:
• was taught to read and write by his wife • ran with a northern Republican in a presidential race even though he was a southern Democrat • was the first president to be impeached, but was acquitted by one vote • was the first ex-president to serve in the U.S. Senate after leaving the White House
Death: July 31, 1875

(1865-69)

Charles Sumner and Thaddeus Stevens led the Radical Republicans against President Johnson.

entrance into the House, they then took action to ensure that the legislative branch, and not the executive, would control Reconstruction. However, President Johnson could and did use his power to veto their acts. The president retained his power until February of 1866, when the Radicals gained control of two-thirds of both houses of Congress and could override his vetoes.

Radical Republican Legislation

While Radical Republican strength grew in Congress, several pieces of legislation were brought forward to fight against the black codes and to aid the freedmen in the South.

The Freedmen's Bureau—In March of 1865 Congress had passed laws to set up a short-term agency to provide aid for refugees. The **Freedmen's Bureau** was the first federal relief agency ever established. It issued rations of surplus army food and clothing to freed slaves and to poverty-stricken whites. It also sent agents into the South to establish schools and hospitals for blacks of all ages. The bureau tried to locate jobs for the freedmen and to prevent employers from exploiting them. Because Congress assumed that state governments would soon be able to provide relief services, the bureau was to be federally funded for only one year. Since Congress refused to recognize the new state governments, it voted to keep the bureau going and even to extend its powers. President Johnson vetoed two versions of the bill, but the Republicans united to override his veto the second time. The Freedmen's Bureau then continued its work.

The Fourteenth Amendment—Next, Congress voted to give blacks legal citizenship through the Civil Rights Act of 1866. Because Johnson believed that the Constitution gave the states power over citizenship, he vetoed the act, but Congress passed it over his veto. However, Congress still feared that it would be declared unconstitutional. In June of that year Congress solved the problem of granting blacks citizenship by proposing the Fourteenth Amendment. The longest amendment to date, the **Fourteenth Amendment** was, and still is, significant.

First, the amendment made all persons citizens of both the United States and of the states where they resided. It also prohibited

The Plight of Robert E. Lee

Robert E. Lee, who had served as commander in chief of the Confederate army, was one of many Confederate soldiers and leaders affected by the government's policies for Reconstruction. Since he had served in the Confederacy, Lee had lost his American citizenship.

After the surrender Lee applied for pardon and restoration of his citizenship. General Grant endorsed his request and sent it on to President Andrew Johnson. Although Lee was not aware of it, he was also to have taken an oath of allegiance. On October 2, 1865, when he was sworn in as president of Washington College, Lee took that oath. Proof of the oath-taking was then sent to Washington. President Johnson had the power to issue pardons and restore citizenship until 1868. Either Johnson never received the oath or he chose not to sign it (perhaps because Grant, whom he saw as a political rival, had made the request).

In 1868 the Fourteenth Amendment changed the system. Congress was allowed to pardon Confederates who had lost their citizenship by a two-thirds vote of each house.

Treason charges against Lee, his sons, and fourteen other Confederates were dropped in 1869. Yet he died in 1870 without regaining his citizenship.

In 1971 a historian rediscovered Lee's petition among some Civil War papers in the National Archives. The Virginia State Senate asked Congress to pass a resolution restoring Lee's citizenship posthumously (POSS chuh mus lee; after his death). In April 1974 the Senate approved his request and by June the House had concurred. One-hundred ten years after he had lost his citizenship, Lee's status as a man without a country ended.

any state from depriving a person of his life, liberty, or property without due process of law (a proper trial). Moreover, a state could not deny equal protection of its laws to any person under its jurisdiction.

Second, a state's representation in Congress would be based on its whole population. This provision meant that blacks were no longer to be counted as three-fifths of a person. States that denied voting rights to blacks could have the number of representatives they had in Congress reduced.

Third, those who had engaged in insurrection or rebellion against the United States would be barred from voting or holding office unless Congress specifically pardoned them by a two-thirds vote. Finally, Congress refused to assume Confederate debts or accept claims for any costs of freeing the slaves.

When ratified, the amendment would cancel black codes in the southern states as well as laws against blacks in some midwestern states. President Johnson urged southern states to vote against it. He held the amendment to be an invasion of states' rights. He traveled in the North and Midwest to give speeches against Radical Republicans running for the 1866 Congressional elections. Johnson's tour cost him support. His audiences rudely heckled him. Instead of ignoring them, Johnson lost his temper. Some people had rejected his plan for Reconstruction already because they feared it would put former Confederates back into power. Now many more were skeptical of his leadership.

When Congress convened in 1867, Reconstruction was wholly in Radical hands, and the phase of **Radical Reconstruction** had begun. By 1868 enough states had ratified the Fourteenth Amendment to put it into effect.

Further Radical Reconstruction Rule

Beginning in 1867 the Radical Republicans in Congress put their program into effect with great speed and little resistance. When the president vetoed their legislation, Congress quickly overrode his vetoes.

Reconstruction Act of 1867—The **Reconstruction Act of 1867** went far beyond the controls Lincoln and Johnson had wished to place on the South. This radical legislation put the area under military rule or "martial law," thus sending in the army to make sure that the South complied with the wishes of Congress. Naturally, Southerners resented this military occupation.

First, the act cut the South into five military districts, each ruled by a Union general. Second, it gave blacks the right to vote and hold office. At the same time the act denied voting rights to those who had served in the Confederacy. Third, southern states wanting to reenter the Union were to hold open conventions with both black and white voting delegates. These conventions were to draw up new state constitutions using the guidelines given by Congress. The act also required the states to submit their documents to Congress for approval. Finally, to return to the fold, states would be required to ratify the Fourteenth Amendment. When these requirements were met, the troops would be withdrawn.

Scalawags and Carpetbaggers in the South—Few former southern leaders were eligible to hold public offices, because they had lost their citizenship by serving the Confederacy. And since Congress had opened politics to blacks by its Reconstruction acts, southern politics now underwent great change. New groups now took command of the South.

Northerners who came south to assist in Radical Reconstruction were called **carpetbaggers.** (They were supposed to have come south carrying their possessions in small suitcases made from pieces of carpet.) Most car-

During Reconstruction some politicians used posters such as the one above to play upon the white voter's fears about blacks.

petbaggers were opportunists who came south seeking financial or political gain. Of course, Southerners resented them. A few carpetbaggers, however, were sincere men who came because they wanted to help the freedmen change the South. Some were Union soldiers who liked what they had seen of the South and decided to stay. Carpetbaggers took control of Southern politics for a while, but they also brought needed investment capital to a ravaged South.

White Southerners who supported Radical Reconstruction received the derisive name of **scalawag.** Some had been Unionists during the war and had no reason to change after. Others endorsed Radical Reconstruction because they honestly believed it was in the

South's best interest. Some scalawags were prewar Whigs seeking a new party since theirs had collapsed. However, there were scalawags who did deserve their bad name. Many were those who saw a chance to get ahead with the help of Radical Republican support and military protection. Most Southerners looked upon scalawags as traitors.

Although they did not control the government in any state, black freedmen did gain office in every southern state. Unfortunately, since blacks had no earlier political experience, they were sometimes more susceptible to improper influence.

The House impeachment council that brought charges against President Johnson

Radical Republicans often used the black officeholders as puppets for their purposes. Some of the blacks were bribed to promote the interests of carpetbaggers and scalawags. Since southern whites already resented their former slaves, they were especially critical of any black corruption. Most of the blacks who held national political offices—for example,

Mississippi senators Hiram H. Revels and Blanche K. Bruce, and South Carolina's Robert Smalls—were well educated. Many blacks elected to offices served with dignity.

Congress Impeaches Johnson

Although the Congress passed its Radical legislation over Johnson's veto, he still enforced the laws that were passed. He carried out the laws because this was his constitutional duty. The Radical Republicans, however, were still unhappy with him and sought ways to limit what power he had. One executive power is to appoint officials. The Radicals feared that Johnson would remove those officials sympathetic to their views and replace them with his own men. Therefore, they passed the **Tenure of Office Act** in 1867. This act made it illegal to remove any presidential appointments approved by the Senate unless the Senate also approved their dismissal.

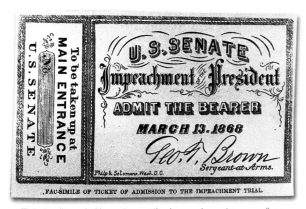

Tickets allowed citizens to see the impeachment proceedings.

Johnson tested the law by removing from office **Edwin Stanton,** Lincoln's holdover secretary of war. (Stanton had never upheld Johnson's views and now openly sided with the Radicals.) Stanton refused to leave. He barricaded himself behind his office doors, accepted food through the windows, and cooked for himself. He even slept in his office. Congress now believed it had grounds for impeaching, or bringing charges against, Johnson so that they could remove him from office. (See page 149.) In presidential impeachments the Constitution says that the House of Representatives is to file the charges; the Senate then serves as the trial court, and the chief justice of the Supreme Court presides as the judge. A two-thirds vote is required to remove the president. The basis for removal is "conviction of treason, bribery, or other high crimes and misdemeanors." A congressional committee did not believe President Johnson was guilty of such crimes, but the Radicals pressed on.

On February 24, 1868, the House voted to impeach Johnson. The president's trial under Justice Salmon P. Chase began March 13 and lasted until May 26. Johnson himself never attended the trial. He believed he had done nothing wrong and that his attendance would lend credence to his accusers' cause. Senators sold tickets to the affair, and at times the trial rivaled a theater performance.

Senators could not agree on whether the Tenure of Office Act was constitutional. Even if it had been, they did not know whether the act applied in Stanton's case. Stanton, after all, had been Lincoln's appointee before the Tenure of Office Act had been passed. The real issue was that Radicals were trying to get rid of the president because they disagreed with him politically, not because he was guilty of a crime. Removing a president for political reasons would have set a dangerous precedent.

Some senators saw this danger, and others knew that if Johnson were removed, Ben Wade, an extreme radical, would be named the next president. Wade's views on public finance, labor, women's suffrage, and blacks were too shocking for most Americans to accept at that time.

When the final vote was taken, thirty-five Senators voted to convict the president; nineteen voted against. This was one vote short of the total needed to remove Johnson. Johnson finished his term; the presidency was preserved. But Johnson's reputation was never the same. Years later, however, the Supreme Court completely cleared Johnson of any blame by declaring the Tenure of Office Act to be unconstitutional.

Johnson's Achievements in Foreign Affairs

Although Congress had kept Johnson's policies at home from working well, his

Secretary of State William Seward's "foolish" purchase of Alaska proved to be a great bargain.

achievements in foreign affairs were noteworthy. **William Seward,** his talented secretary of state, ably directed his foreign policy.

In 1864 Napoleon III, the emperor of France, had violated the Monroe Doctrine by setting up Austrian Archduke Maximilian (mak suh MIL yun) as the puppet emperor of Mexico. Since the Civil War occupied America's attention at the time, Lincoln and Seward only reprimanded the French for their actions, but they could not send troops to evict Maximilian. In 1866, however, President Johnson moved against the French. He sent fifty thousand veteran troops to the border, and their presence forced the withdrawal of French troops.

Seward was also an expansionist. He signed a treaty of friendship and commerce with China in 1868. In 1867 he secretly negotiated a treaty with Russia to purchase Alaska for $7 million. When President Johnson sought Senate approval, cries of "Seward's Folly," "Johnson's Polar Bear Garden," and "Frigidia" flooded the press. But within ten days the treaty went through by a thirty-seven to two vote. Years later this purchase would prove to be a great bargain for the United States.

President U.S. Grant

By 1868 Andrew Johnson had lost almost all influence in the Republican Party. For their presidential candidate in the election, the Republicans chose Ulysses S. Grant. The Democrats were still hampered by their ties to the old Civil War issues and by the Radical Republican takeover of the South, the party's former stronghold.

Even so, Grant only narrowly defeated the Democratic candidate, New York's governor Horatio Seymour. The support of a half-million new black voters helped bring about the Republican victory.

An 1868 campaign banner for the Republicans

The Fifteenth Amendment—Once in office Grant disappointed the Radicals. He did reward black support, however, by calling for the passage of the **Fifteenth Amendment.** This amendment kept states from denying the vote to any person "on account of race, color, or previous condition of servitude." (See

371

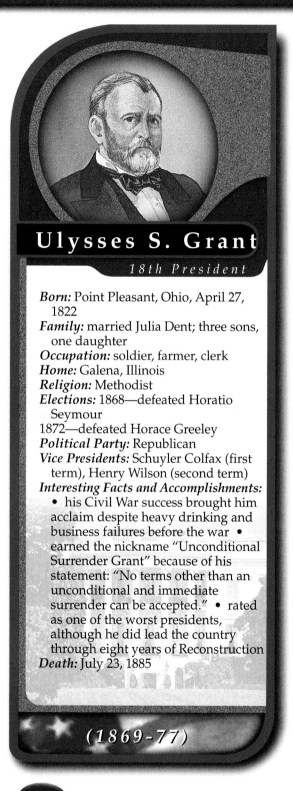

Ulysses S. Grant

18th President

Born: Point Pleasant, Ohio, April 27, 1822

Family: married Julia Dent; three sons, one daughter

Occupation: soldier, farmer, clerk

Home: Galena, Illinois

Religion: Methodist

Elections: 1868—defeated Horatio Seymour

1872—defeated Horace Greeley

Political Party: Republican

Vice Presidents: Schuyler Colfax (first term), Henry Wilson (second term)

Interesting Facts and Accomplishments:
• his Civil War success brought him acclaim despite heavy drinking and business failures before the war • earned the nickname "Unconditional Surrender Grant" because of his statement: "No terms other than an unconditional and immediate surrender can be accepted." • rated as one of the worst presidents, although he did lead the country through eight years of Reconstruction

Death: July 23, 1885

(1869-77)

pages 160-61.) Passage of the amendment kept Republicans in power by giving them more votes in northern states that still had antiblack laws. Since the southern states still had Republican governments that favored the blacks, the Fifteenth Amendment was ratified in less than a year. It took effect in 1870.

Grant was sympathetic to the plight of the South, and he limited the number of federal troops there. Six states—Alabama, Arkansas, Florida, South Carolina, North Carolina, and Louisiana—had been readmitted to the Union by the summer of 1868. (Tennessee had been readmitted in 1866.) Four remaining states—Georgia, Mississippi, Texas, and Virginia—held out until 1870. By the time they sought readmission, they were also required to ratify the Fifteenth Amendment.

The Grant Scandals—Ulysses S. Grant served two terms as president. Unfortunately he showed that a good general does not always make a good president. Both of Grant's terms in office were marked by political corruption. The corruption, largely the result of greed, was not the president's doing and existed on national, state, and local levels. But when the corruption was uncovered, the president allowed the dishonest to resign rather than face prosecution. He believed that prosecution would only divide the nation further. To distract the voters from the scandals, the party appealed to people to unite against the ex-rebels. Reviving these ill feelings, however, was not what the country wanted. The Radical Republicans, with their fierce hatred for the South, were losing power.

SECTION REVIEW

1. What was the first federal relief agency? What groups did it assist?

2. The basic purpose of the Fourteenth Amendment was to provide what for blacks?

3. What type of system did the Reconstruction Act of 1867 establish to enforce Congress's will in the South?

4. Who were the scalawags, the carpetbaggers, and the freedmen?

5. The conflict between Johnson and the Radical Republicans came to a climax when Johnson attempted to remove whom from office? His action was said to be a violation of what law?

6. What significant contributions did Johnson make in foreign affairs?

7. Who won the election of 1868?

 What potential danger did Johnson's impeachment trial pose for our system of government?

Bourbon Reconstruction Begins

Even while Grant was still in office, views toward Reconstruction were changing. Many Republican supporters were beginning to think that abandoning blacks and Southerners might be better than losing the whole country to the turmoil of Radical Reconstruction. They believed that peace in the South would certainly be better for business. The country was sick of bitter controversy and scandal. These attitudes paved the way for **Bourbon Reconstruction,** reconstruction led by conservative Southerners, or "Redeemers."

Liberal Republicans in 1872 persuaded Congress to pardon the remaining former Confederate leaders. A General Amnesty Act in 1872 pardoned all but a few hundred Confederate leaders. Those who had held federal offices at the time of secession were

An 1876 campaign banner for the Democrats

among those excluded. This action would allow many former southern leaders to regain their influence in government.

Although the blacks had gained rights on paper, the white Southerners did not find it easy to accept the changes that made blacks their legal equals. While blacks and Radicals were able to hang on to offices for a while, they soon found they could not match the organization and experience of Southerners who now sought to "redeem the South" from black rule. Southern states began the process of turning out blacks and Republicans and replacing them with southern Democrats. It was only in areas still occupied by Federal forces that Republican governments held on a bit longer. Grant, meanwhile, became more and more reluctant to send troops into the South to keep Republicans in power.

The Disputed Election of 1876

Since the Grant administration had been marred by one scandal after another and since corruption existed in some state and local governments as well, both political parties chose honest reformers as presidential candidates in 1876. When the results came in, Democrat **Samuel J. Tilden** of New York won the popular vote. He also had an electoral college vote of 184, compared to 165 for **Rutherford B. Hayes,** his opponent. But the votes of three southern states occupied by Federal troops— Florida, Louisiana, and South Carolina—were disputed. If the Democratic votes from those states were counted, Tilden would win easily. But if the Republican votes were accepted, Hayes would win, 185 to 184.

This was an unusual situation. Whose electoral votes should be counted? Finally Congress appointed a special electoral commission. Five senators, five representatives, and five Supreme Court justices were picked for the commission. Seven of the commissioners were Republicans; seven were Democrats. Justice David Stevens was an independent. But he resigned rather than cast the deciding vote. His replacement, a Republican, voted to accept the Republican ballots, making Hayes the president.

The Hayes Presidency

Even though the Republicans won in 1876, the election was the final blow to the harsh Reconstruction of the Radicals. Rutherford B. Hayes had sought the support of southern whites, who favored his economic

Lemonade Lucy

Lucy Ware Webb Hayes was popular throughout her life for her moral uprightness and charity. When Lucy was only two, her father died while on a trip to Kentucky to arrange for the freeing of his slaves. Lucy's mother was a woman of strong convictions, and she shared them with her two sons and daughter. Lucy was trained in religious schools along with her two older brothers; she later attended Wesleyan Women's College (the first chartered college for women in the United States) at age sixteen and graduated with honors. Her commencement essay, entitled "The Influence of Christianity on National Prosperity," was read at her graduation.

The young lawyer Rutherford B. Hayes was attracted by Lucy's beauty as well as by her reputation for religious devotion and intelligence. One year after her graduation, the two were engaged; and on December 30, 1852, they were married. She encouraged him as he defended fugitive slaves in court. In 1856 he first made a public stand against slavery by joining the new Republican Party. With the coming of the Civil War, he believed it was his duty to join the Union army. Lucy did not discourage him, and when he was wounded in September of 1862, she joined him at the battlefront to nurse him back to health. Whenever she visited the Twenty-third Ohio Regiment, which he commanded, she spent much time encouraging the sick, writing for them, and tending to their needs. The grateful soldiers affectionately called her "Mother Lucy."

While still serving in the army, Hayes was elected to Congress. He served there from 1864 until he was elected the governor of Ohio in 1867. During his three terms in the Governor's Mansion, Lucy proved to be a perfect hostess and tremendous support to her husband. She was especially active in community services, and by her labors the Home for Soldiers' Orphans was started at Xenia, Ohio, in 1869. She and her husband remained aloof from the scandals and waste of the Grant administration. When Hayes was elected president in 1877, he brought with him a wife who was well prepared for her role as First Lady.

From the day of the inauguration, Lucy set a new trend of modesty and dignity in Washington. As the first First Lady with a college degree, she was hailed as a "new woman" in a new period of American history. The couple continued to have receptions and balls, but they were much more modest than the extravagant ones of the previous administration. The Hayes family was wholesome and God-fearing. The daily routine included after-dinner family gatherings in the Red Room to sing popular ballads and hymns. Afterward they retired to the Blue Room for family devotions and prayer.

The most noted trait of Lucy's stay in the White House was her insistence on abstinence from all gambling and liquor and from most dances. She was labeled as "Lemonade Lucy" and was criticized when she would not allow alcoholic beverages in the White House. But she was so gracious about her views that she gained the respect and good-humored support of the Washington officials. Her popularity did much to improve the popularity of her husband.

Two events during Hayes's administration are popular stories from White House lore. On Sunday, December 30, 1877, the couple held their twenty-fifth wedding anniversary in the Blue Room. Lucy dressed up in her original satin gown, many of the original guests were present, and the original minister led them in a renewal of their wedding vows. After the ceremony the two youngest children were baptized. The other event came on the following Easter, when Lucy came to the rescue of some children who were egg-rolling on Capitol grounds. When some Congressmen told them to leave, Lucy invited the children to the White House lawn. A similar invitation for Easter egg rolling has been given every year since.

Rutherford B. Hayes

19th President

Born: Delaware, Ohio, October 4, 1822
Family: married Lucy Ware Webb; seven sons, one daughter
Occupation: lawyer
Home: Spiegel Grove, Fremont, Ohio
Religion: no formal affiliation
Election: 1876—elected by an electoral commission over Samuel J. Tilden in a disputed election
Political Party: Republican
Vice President: William A. Wheeler
Interesting Facts and Accomplishments:
• took oath of office privately and had no inaugural parade or ball because of national turmoil over his disputed election • first president to visit the Pacific Coast (1880) • had the first telephone installed in the White House • his wife was the first president's wife who was a college graduate; she received the nickname "Lemonade Lucy" because she served lemonade instead of liquor at White House receptions
Death: January 17, 1893

(1877-81)

policies. To gain their support, he embraced policies that were to their liking. Undoubtedly southern Democrats chose not to dispute his election because he had promised the South the freedoms it wanted. However, Hayes soon found that he had bargained away most of his presidential power. By the time he saw the real picture, it was too late to change his position.

Once in office Hayes pleased the Democrats more than he did his own party. In April of 1877, a month after taking office, Hayes withdrew the last federal troops from South Carolina and Louisiana. With troops no longer supervising elections, Democratic governors soon replaced the Republicans in power. With the military gone and with white southern Democrats back in control in the southern states, Reconstruction now followed the dictates of these state leaders.

SECTION REVIEW

1. What did the General Amnesty Act do?

2. What action did President Hayes take to please Southerners?

 What was unusual about the 1876 election?

Recovery in the South

While government tried to deal with the South's problems during the phases of Reconstruction, many unusual features developed in southern life. The South's people, economy, and political organization were molded by the pressures of Reconstruction.

Economic Aspects of Reconstruction

Because the Civil War had destroyed the South's plantation system, the freedmen were at once without jobs. Some hoped that the government would take over the old plantations and from them give every freed slave forty acres and a mule. Although some politi-

cians supported such a plan, it never came to pass. While southern farmland needed laborers to grow its crops once again, there was no money to pay hired hands. To meet the needs of southern agriculture under such conditions, **sharecropping** became common.

Sharecropping—Blacks and poor whites became involved in this new economic system. Sharecroppers farmed small plots owned by planters and paid their annual rent for the use of the land with a part, or share, of their crop. Since sharecroppers had little money, especially at the beginning of the season, they borrowed for seed and provisions. Often the landlord was their creditor and owned the local store. When the harvest came in, the sharecropper squared up. If the sharecropper broke even, he was fortunate. He often started the next season in debt, however. The average sharecropper showed a profit only two years out of twenty-five. As a result the sharecropper was locked into a cycle of debt and poverty. The chances of breaking out of it were small indeed. Under such conditions, having the right to vote meant little. Most sharecroppers were more concerned about putting food on the family table.

Industry—During Reconstruction the Industrial Revolution finally reached the South. The Southerners had little money for industry, but many Northerners had capital and were eager to make profitable investments. These men saw the South as a place of opportunity. Consequently railroads, steelmaking, and the textile industry all expanded widely. As the need for laborers increased, Southerners moved from rural areas to factory towns and cities. The South's economy began to boom. By 1890 Southerners and Northerners spoke hopefully of a "New South" that would rival the North as an economic force.

One feature of southern industry was the **mill town.** Mill towns had some of the same features as plantations. The owner or investors built the housing, usually identical rows of houses near the factory site. The mill owners often built towns with churches and other community needs such as stores and doctors' offices. Often the workers bought needed items like food and clothing from company stores. Generally, employers in the textile industry hired whole families. Manufacturers of machines lowered the heights of their looms so that children could work them.

Political Trends

The prosperity of the nation through most of the era helped the Republicans control the presidency and usually Congress during most of the Reconstruction years. Stirring up war hatreds, or "waving the bloody shirt," also helped them stay in power, because Republicans were associated with winning the war and with freeing the slaves. The Republicans made inroads right after the war as the vote was given to blacks for the first time and ex-Confederate whites were barred from the polls. But when southern "Redeemers" got their power back, the Republican Party declined dramatically in the South.

Because Southerners generally blamed the war and the hardships of Reconstruction on the Republicans, the South aligned itself with the Democratic Party. For a century the South voted solidly for Democratic candidates almost without exception. Sometimes when people referred to the South's strong support of the Democratic Party, they called it the Solid South.

In 1866 a secret organization, the **Ku Klux Klan,** was founded to frighten blacks and whites sympathetic to black interests in order to keep blacks away from the polls. Their least offensive tactic was to boycott businesses and force them to close. More unsavory were Klansmen dressed as white-hooded ghosts who rode through black communities at night, erecting burning crosses and even beating or killing blacks who tried to exercise their civil rights.

The Ku Klux Klan tried to prevent blacks from exercising their political rights.

Southern moderates and many Northerners were upset by the Klan's activities. Congress passed two acts in 1870 and 1871, the Force Act and the Ku Klux Klan Act, to deal with Klan abuses. The acts outlawed the use of force to prevent people from voting and gave President Grant the power to place federal troops in polling places to ensure everyone's voting rights. The Klan was officially disbanded, but in reality it went underground.

Civil Rights

Congress passed two acts to give blacks citizenship and all of its privileges or civil rights. The Civil Rights Act of 1866, noted earlier, had granted freedmen the same rights and legal protection as whites regardless of local laws. A second act, the Civil Rights Act of 1875, guaranteed equal accommodations in public places, such as inns and theaters. It also said blacks could serve on juries. However, the bill did not provide any means of enforcing its provisions. The Supreme Court further weakened the legislation when in 1883 it declared the social provisions of the bill to be unconstitutional.

As the years passed, concern for the rights of the blacks lessened. The Civil Rights Acts were no longer enforced, although they did serve as precedents for the civil rights acts passed in the twentieth century. In the meantime blacks found little political equality.

Reforms in the South

Before the war the South had collected few taxes for public purposes. After the war both taxes and spending increased. Many people were critical of the high spending of southern governments, but in many instances the spending was justified. For the first time southern states began providing free public education. Prison systems were improved. Care for mentally and physically handicapped

people developed, and imprisonment for debt was abolished.

Reconstruction Evaluated

Reconstruction was generally not a happy time for anyone. Northerners were not satisfied with its processes or results, and many Southerners remained bitter. The Civil War and Reconstruction had caused the South to change economically and socially. However, not all the changes were ushered in smoothly. While many social advances were later lost, a foundation for future change had been laid in the postwar years.

Some critics believe that Reconstruction was unduly hard on the South. Radical Republicans had gone the furthest treating the South more as a foreign nation than a part of the United States. However, any attempt to rebuild the South would have been difficult considering the political, economic, and social devastation of the region.

Other critics believe Reconstruction did not go far enough. While on paper it ensured civil rights for blacks, those rights did not become permanently established during Reconstruction. The granting of such rights was a major step, but few whites even in the North were willing for blacks to gain significant social and political power. Reconstruction left many social, political, and economic problems for future generations to solve, but it also began the legislation and set an example for present Americans to follow or improve.

Reconstruction's chances for success were limited still further by great changes that America was undergoing at the same time. America was industrializing, and the industrial age brought a whole new set of problems. In both Reconstruction and the industrial era, people tried to solve these problems in new ways. Sometimes the solutions proposed were merely experiments. When they did not work, they should have been discarded.

Unfortunately, when the people of a country fail to assume their responsibility, government moves in. Some of the problems of Reconstruction should have been solved first by individuals willing to follow biblical precepts on how to treat others. Some problems could have been solved by churches or private groups. But when they were not solved these ways, the federal government moved in. And life for Americans was really never the same again, as federal government powers began to increase.

SECTION REVIEW

1. How did sharecropping get its name?

2. In what kind of community did southern factory workers sometimes live?

3. What was the purpose of the Ku Klux Klan?

4. Why did civil rights legislation of the late 1800s bring little real change for blacks?

 What answer could be made to the charge that Reconstruction went either too far or not far enough?

SUMMARY

At the end of the Civil War the South's government, economy, and society were in disarray. Because of its condition, the South needed a time of reconstruction. The Reconstruction did not come easily or smoothly, however, because of conflicting policies and desires in the nation. Presidents Lincoln and Johnson tried to restore the South quickly and with little punishment. Radical Republicans in Congress opposed these lenient policies and determined to make Reconstruction follow their strict guidelines. Eventually the Radicals lost their control, and Southerners were able to finish Reconstruction on their own terms.

Chapter Review

People, Places, and Things to Remember

Reconstruction
freedmen
Presidential
  Reconstruction
Ten Percent Plan
Radical Republicans
Wade-Davis Bill
amnesty
Thirteenth Amendment
black codes

Thaddeus Stevens
Charles Sumner
Freedmen's Bureau
Fourteenth Amendment
Radical Reconstruction
Reconstruction Act of
  1867
carpetbaggers
scalawag
Tenure of Office Act

Edwin Stanton
Fifteenth Amendment
William Seward
Bourbon Reconstruction
Samuel J. Tilden
Rutherford B. Hayes
sharecropping
mill town
Ku Klux Klan

Review Questions

Match each item with the corresponding man.

1. Ten Percent Plan
2. impeached president
3. secretary of war
4. Alaska purchase
5. presidential scandals
6. withdrew the last federal troops from the South

  a. Ulysses S. Grant
  b. Rutherford B. Hayes
  c. Andrew Johnson
  d. Abraham Lincoln
  e. William Seward
  f. Edwin Stanton

Unscramble these letters to find the names of groups involved in Reconstruction.

7. TARGEBACSPREG (Northerners in the South)
8. DEFEMERN (slaves no longer)
9. PRORRASHECEPS (poor farmers)
10. GACLASAWS (despised Southerners)

Match the following legislation and amendments with their effects.

11. Thirteenth Amendment
12. Fourteenth Amendment
13. Reconstruction Act of 1867
14. Tenure of Office Act
15. Fifteenth Amendment

  a. made all persons citizens
  b. used to impeach Johnson
  c. abolished slavery
  d. gave blacks the vote
  e. put the South under military rule

Questions for Discussion

16. Why is Reconstruction a good name for the time following the Civil War?
17. How might Reconstruction have been different if Lincoln had lived?

History Skills

Writing a History Paper

Writing an essay for a history class will be much easier if you follow some basic procedures. The first step is to break the topic down into logical parts. Let's go through an example together. Suppose the essay topic is "The United States had difficulty trying to solve the South's problems following the Civil War." How can you break down this topic? A good approach is to discuss each major problem separately. A possible outline appears below.

I. The South needed to raise money to meet basic needs for food, services, and industry.

II. The South needed to give freedmen a new place in a changed society.

III. The South needed to establish new state governments.

After you choose a basic outline, you need to decide what things to discuss under each main point. Northerners and Southerners had completely different ideas about how to solve each problem. Perhaps under each point you could discuss (A) the solutions adopted by the federal government and Northerners, and (B) the solutions later adopted by Southerners. Your discussion under each main point would look something like this:

I. The South needed to raise money to meet basic needs for food, services, and industry.
   A. Northern ideas
   B. Southern ideas

Now all that is left for you is to fill in the details! Look for key terms and concepts. Below is a list of the key terms under each main point in the outline:

I. The South needed to raise money to meet basic needs for food, services, and industry.
   A. Northern ideas: the Freedmen's Bureau
   B. Southern ideas: mill towns

II. The South needed to give freedmen a new place in a changed society.
   A. Northern ideas: constitutional amendments, civil rights acts
   B. Southern ideas: black codes, the Ku Klux Klan, sharecropping

III. The South needed to establish new state governments.
   A. Northern ideas: the Reconstruction Act of 1867, carpetbaggers
   B. Southern ideas: scalawags, Redeemers, and the Solid South

Write a short paragraph on each of the main ideas above (three paragraphs). To complete your essay, write a brief introductory paragraph stating your topic. Then write a brief concluding paragraph. Ask your teacher for help if you do not know how to write an introduction and conclusion.

Nearly one hundred years after the Civil Rights Act of 1866 was passed, civil rights gained national attention again. Various groups within the nation pressed for legislation that would provide for actual social changes. The following people represent several of these movements. As you read about them, consider the issues they fought for and the methods they used. Were they fighting for good causes? Did they use methods that would be acceptable to Christians? How should Christians respond to these issues?

Hispanic Rights: Cesar Chavez (1927-93)

Cesar Chavez was born near Yuma, Arizona, and grew up migrating across the Southwest with his family. Like other Hispanic migrant workers, he made less than minimum wage and had to endure life in pitiful work camps. After serving in World War II, Chavez began working in an apricot field near San Jose. It was there that he became involved with an organization called the Community Service Organization (CSO). Chavez eventually became its general director and dreamed of uniting farm workers and helping them fight against poor work conditions. He later resigned and formed his own National Farm Worker's Organization. In 1966 he merged his organization with another union to form the United Farm Workers (UFW).

To fight for higher pay, family health coverage, and pension benefits, Chavez used the same nonviolent tactics of Gandhi and Martin Luther King Jr. One of his most successful methods was the boycott—refusing to buy from, sell to, or deal with a company. In 1965 he organized a boycott against grape growers around Delano, California. By 1970 most growers had signed contracts with the UFW. Another method he used was the fast. Chavez held a thirty-six-day fast in 1988 to protest the use of poisonous pesticides where grape workers worked. Despite his death in 1993, the UFW has continued Chavez's fight for Hispanic workers' rights in America.

Native American Rights: Russell Means (1939-)

Born in 1939, Russell Means grew up on the Pine Ridge Indian Reservation near the Black Hills of South Dakota. In 1969 he joined an Indian rights group in Minnesota called the American Indian Movement (AIM). He soon became its first national director. In February 1973 Means led two hundred members of AIM to declare their own nation at Wounded Knee, South Dakota. Federal marshals arrived, and an armed standoff began. By its end on May 3, two Indians had been killed and one marshal seriously injured. Means and the other protesters surrendered after the government promised to discuss the Indians' grievances.

The Wounded Knee standoff marked a high point in Means's career. He continued working with AIM, ran for United States president in 1987, and launched a successful Hollywood career in the 1990s. However, some members of AIM sought to separate the organization from Means. They believed he was portraying Indians falsely in the movies. The differences between AIM and Means became greater when he was charged with battery against his father-in-law. Respecting one's elders is highly valued in the Indian community, and Means had gone too far. AIM continued without him.

Women's Rights: Betty Friedan (1921-)

Betty Friedan was born in Peoria, Illinois, and grew up in a Jewish family. She attended Smith College, majored in psychology, and edited a campus magazine covering social issues. Although offered a scholarship to get a Ph.D. at Berkley, she turned it down believing that if she accepted it, she wouldn't have time to get married and start a family. Instead, she became a reporter for the Worker's Press in New York. While working there she began to notice discrimination against women in the workplace.

Friedan married in 1947 and started a family. After she requested time off to have her second baby, the newspaper fired her. Friedan became a housewife, but she was never content. She surveyed some of her college friends and found that many of them were dissatisfied as well. They wanted to have families but also have careers outside the home. Friedan expressed her ideas in a book called *The Feminine Mystique*. The book was an instant success among liberals, and Friedan soon became a leading spokesperson for women's rights. In 1966 she helped found the National Organization for Women (NOW) and was named its first president.

Friedan fought for changes such as equal pay for women in the work force and legalized abortions. Not all women in NOW supported Friedan though. Some believed she was going too far. Others thought she was not going far enough. Friedan divorced in 1969 and retired from NOW's presidency the following year. She continued to focus on political reform and became an active member in the women's liberation movement.

Black Rights: Malcolm X (1925-65)

Malcolm Little was reared in Omaha, Nebraska, in an environment of social turmoil. His home was burned by members of the Ku Klux Klan, and his father, a black Baptist minister, was killed by racists when Malcolm was six. At fifteen he dropped out of school and got involved in crime. In 1946 he was convicted of a petty burglary and sent to prison. While there he joined the Black Muslim faith (Nation of Islam). Upon his release he dedicated himself to his faith and became one of its leading spokespersons. He also changed his last name to "X," rejecting "Little" because the name was given to his ancestors by their slave masters.

Malcolm skillfully described the racial conditions of the United States and denounced the white man. Although it appeared he would become the Nation of Islam's second leader, disagreements with the leader, Elijah Muhammad, led Malcolm to form his own religious organization—the Muslim Mosque. After a pilgrimage to Mecca in 1964, he publicly denounced racism and envisioned world brotherhood. However, he still promoted the use of violence. Other groups soon made Malcolm the target of their attacks. While preparing for a speech in New York, Malcolm X was assassinated by three Black Muslims. Since his death, he has continued to be a powerful symbol of the black civil rights movement.

Henrietta's plans for a passive resistance demonstration were quickly foiled.

UNIT

5

Growing to Meet Challenges

CHAPTERS IN THIS UNIT:

1876: Relationships between Indians and frontier settlers were often tense, requiring frequent intervention by the United States Cavalry. The most famous Indian battle was at Little Big Horn, where Colonel George A. Custer and his men were all killed.

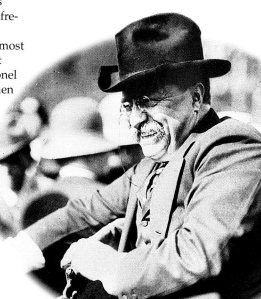

1912: Theodore Roosevelt, a strong supporter of progressive reforms, chose to run for president from the new Progressive Party.

1800s: Rescue missions reached out to "rescue" the people of the inner cities from their sin.

1869: The Union Pacific and Central Pacific railroads met at Promontory Point near Ogden, Utah, on May 10. The transcontinental railroad moved settlement of the West forward at a rapid pace.

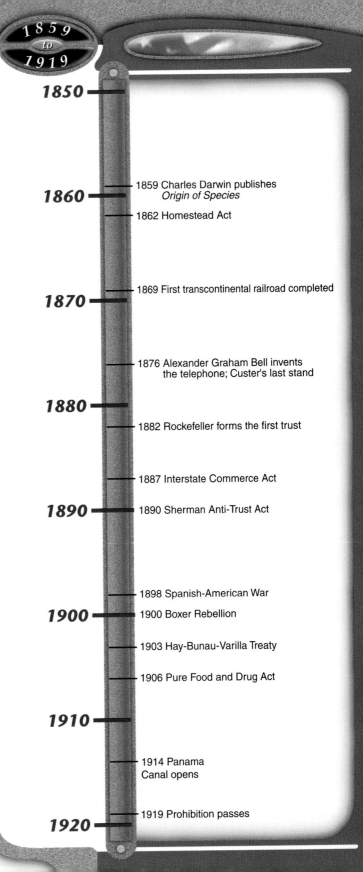

1859 to 1919

1850

1859 Charles Darwin publishes *Origin of Species*

1862 Homestead Act

1860

1869 First transcontinental railroad completed

1870

1876 Alexander Graham Bell invents the telephone; Custer's last stand

1880

1882 Rockefeller forms the first trust

1887 Interstate Commerce Act

1890 Sherman Anti-Trust Act

1890

1898 Spanish-American War

1900 Boxer Rebellion

1900

1903 Hay-Bunau-Varilla Treaty

1906 Pure Food and Drug Act

1910

1914 Panama Canal opens

1919 Prohibition passes

1920

Unit V: Growing to Meet Challenges

The Death of Rodriguez

Yellow journalism in Hearst's New York Journal created sympathy for the Cuban rebellion. On January 19, 1897, Richard Harding Davis, America's most popular war correspondent, watched the predawn execution of a twenty-year-old Cuban rebel, Adolpho Rodriguez.

He had a handsome, gentle face of the peasant type, a light, pointed beard, great wistful eyes, and a mass of curly black hair. He was shockingly young for such a sacrifice. . . .

The officer of the firing squad hastily whipped up his sword, the men . . . leveled their rifles, the sword rose, dropped, and the men fired. At the report the Cuban's head snapped back almost between his shoulders, but his body fell slowly, as though someone had pushed him gently forward from behind and he had stumbled. . . .

He sank on his side in the wet grass without a struggle or sound, and did not move again. . . .

At that moment the sun, which had shown some promise of its coming in the glow above the hills, shot up suddenly from behind them in all the splendor of the tropics, a fierce red disk of heat, and filled the air with warmth and light. . . .

The whole world of Santa Clara seemed to stir and stretch itself and to wake to welcome the day just begun.

But as I fell in at the rear of the procession and looked back, the figure of the young Cuban, who was no longer part of the world of Santa Clara, was asleep in the wet grass, with his motionless arms still tightly bound behind him, with the scapular twisted awry across his face, and the blood from his breast sinking into the soil he had tried to free.

1. In the first paragraph, what word does the report use for execution? Does the report's description of the peasant create sympathy for him?

2. In the second paragraph, how does the officer perform his duty? Does this description create sympathy for him?

3. Do the two paragraphs about the sun and the town tell anything about the execution? Why does the report include these details?

4. What do the last seven words imply about the reason for the peasant's execution?

19

Industrialism

When the United States entered the nineteenth century, it was a quiet land with family farms, small villages, and a few small cities on the Atlantic coastline. By the end of the century, however, crowded cities, busy factories, and mechanized farms stretched across the country. At the dawn of the twentieth century, the United States was on its way to becoming the greatest industrial nation in the world. Capitalism, America's economic system, along with new industrial techniques and American ingenuity, was providing people with a host of products that made life easier. At the same time, America's population was swelling. The population in 1800 was less than 5.5 million. The 1870 census counted 40 million, and by 1910 the population had reached 92 million. Immigration was the biggest single reason for that growth, though the birthrate was high as well. Not only the population but also the size of the country increased. In 1800 there were only sixteen states in the Union, but a hundred years later there were forty-five.

The late nineteenth century was a time of growth for the nation, especially for its industries. The land and its people were uniquely suited for its large industrial building projects.

Mining towns rose up overnight only to be deserted when the mine played out.

Materials and People

The United States was able to undergo such rapid changes for a variety of reasons. No single factor could have produced such change by itself. Two of the resources that helped the United States to produce goods for itself and the world were its supplies of raw materials and its labor force.

Natural Resources

One key to American industrial growth was its abundant natural resources. God endowed the nation with fertile soil and almost all the raw materials needed for important industries. After the purchase of Alaska in 1867, little geographic growth occurred. Hawaii, Puerto Rico, and a few other areas were added. Yet the resources grew as new minerals were discovered and previously inaccessible regions were opened by new means of transportation.

Great lodes of gold, silver, and copper were found in the Rocky Mountains, the Far West, and Alaska. After the Civil War, thousands of miners and businessmen streamed into the sparsely settled West. Towns with exotic or unusual names like Eureka, Paradise, Coarsegold, Sloughouse, Dinkey Creek, and Whiskeytown flourished briefly near the rich ore veins. When the ore was gone, most miners moved on, leaving behind some ghost towns. But some stayed in the West and found new ways to earn their living.

The rich iron ore deposits of northern Minnesota, the Mesabi (muh SAH bee) and Cayuna (kuh YOO nuh) ranges, provided raw materials for the growing iron and steel industries. Discovery of petroleum fuel resources added to America's wealth of natural resources. Tremendous coal deposits also provided an important fuel. And another source of energy, water power, would soon help the nation to produce electricity.

Another important American resource was its timber. Vast forests covering the Northwest and other areas of the country supplied timber for lumber, pulp, and other uses.

Immigration Provides Labor

Developing industries need workers. Most of the American population was hard at work in the 1800s. Yet, for the country to expand its industrial production, it needed even more. The growing tide of immigrants met America's need for laborers.

Immigrants Come to America— Before 1880 most of the immigrants came from northwestern European countries like Britain, Ireland, Germany, or the Scandinavian countries, and they were largely Protestant. Although immigrants continued to come from those countries, a greater proportion now came from eastern and southern European countries, and they were often Roman Catholics. Italians, Turks, Greeks, Slavs, Hungarians, and Rumanians all flocked to America. From northern Russia came Russians, Poles (Poland was then part of Russia), Finns, and Jews. Other immigrants came from Russia's Baltic States—Estonia, Latvia, and Lithuania. Between 1890 and 1914, the largest single group of immigrants was the Italians.

Most Europeans crossed the Atlantic by the shortest and cheapest routes. Many traveled first to Liverpool, England, or to Bremen or Hamburg, Germany, where the major steamship companies were located. Steamship companies often used freighters to carry passengers over to the United States and then carried raw materials or manufactured goods back to Europe. The cheapest tickets gave travelers space in steerage, the noisiest, most crowded part of the ship, located underneath the deck and near the engine and rudder.

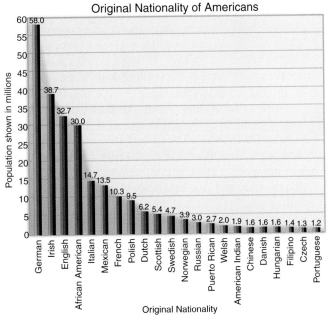

Original Nationality of Americans

Passengers brought their food with them in their bundles. Seasickness or disease often made the voyage a miserable experience, and some immigrants lost their lives. People from different walks of life were thrown together under strange conditions. In addition, many came from different countries and spoke different languages.

Some immigrants had been recruited in their homelands by agents of various American companies in need of laborers. It was common for companies to make contracts with immigrants. The companies agreed to pay their fares if the immigrants would agree to work a specified length of time for the employer. Other immigrants used most of their life's savings to come to America. Still others had their trans-Atlantic tickets and even their rail tickets from the port where they landed paid for by relatives who had come earlier.

Employers eagerly hired immigrants. Because the recent immigrants were usually happy just to have a job, they were generally willing to work for cheaper wages than other

Americans. Moreover, immigrants who complained risked losing their jobs. There were always newcomers waiting to be hired. Employers also liked hiring immigrants because most were hard working and reluctant to join the labor unions.

Ellis Island and Ports of Entry—The largest number of European immigrants came to America by way of New York harbor. Many were registered there at **Ellis Island.** It served as a temporary stopover for incoming immigrants who used its beautifully designed great hall, dining room, and hospital. Those who looked healthy enough to hold a job and who could prove they had the means to reach distant destinations usually took the ferry to New Jersey and rode a train inland. Others entered New York City totally bewildered. Public Health Service doctors assisted the immigrants who were ill. If they could be cured, they were treated and sent on their way as soon as possible. The immigrant center at Ellis Island operated from 1894 to 1943 and handled the entry of more than seventeen million immigrants. Often immigrants feared being turned back at Ellis Island, but of the millions who came, the total number rejected was under two percent.

Some immigrants landed in Montreal; others, especially the Irish, came to Boston. New Orleans was a port of entry for many immigrants planning to go to the Midwest or the Far West.

Immigrants often settled in neighborhoods of cities where others of their nationality lived. Some of these neighborhoods came to be known by such names as "Chinatown" or "Little Italy." In later years, after immigrants learned the language and saved enough money, many moved on to other areas of the city or suburbs and left the inner city to be occupied by newer immigrants.

Immigrants Work to Build America— While immigrants came from many lands,

Ellis Island was the first stop for immigrants coming into America by way of New York City.

Ireland provided a large share in the 1800s. In the 1840s a potato blight spread slowly across Europe. The plant disease devastated Ireland, where the potato was the major farm crop and food. One-eighth of Ireland's population starved to death or died from diseases caused by malnutrition. Another three-eighths of the people, three million in all, left Ireland. Many of them came to the United States, primarily to Boston and New York City.

The Irish played important roles in the construction of America's canal and railroad systems. An early group of Irish immigrants provided the muscle to build the Erie Canal. Crews of Irishmen were also responsible for laying the track for western railroads. The Irish took these jobs despite a high risk of injury because they saw them as a means to escape their poverty.

Some Irishmen sought altogether different work. Because of previously unstable circumstances, they sought more stable jobs in civic service. Men became police or firemen, and Irish women became schoolmarms and domestic servants.

China also provided many immigrants for America. Because American ships were involved in the China trade, news of the discovery of gold in California soon reached China. Since China was overpopulated and her people faced flood and famine, the Chinese were easily attracted to America. Opportunities of the California gold rush brought them in great numbers. As was frequently the case with immigrants, the men came first. Once they had attained their riches, they hoped to return to China and find wives. Instead of mining for gold themselves, many of the Chinese founded businesses such as restaurants and laundries, providing needed services for others. Later, Chinese workers were hired to build western sections of the transcontinental railroad.

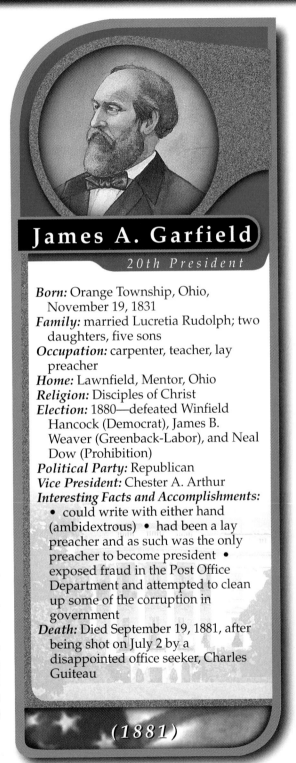

James A. Garfield

20th President

Born: Orange Township, Ohio, November 19, 1831
Family: married Lucretia Rudolph; two daughters, five sons
Occupation: carpenter, teacher, lay preacher
Home: Lawnfield, Mentor, Ohio
Religion: Disciples of Christ
Election: 1880—defeated Winfield Hancock (Democrat), James B. Weaver (Greenback-Labor), and Neal Dow (Prohibition)
Political Party: Republican
Vice President: Chester A. Arthur
Interesting Facts and Accomplishments:
• could write with either hand (ambidextrous) • had been a lay preacher and as such was the only preacher to become president • exposed fraud in the Post Office Department and attempted to clean up some of the corruption in government
Death: Died September 19, 1881, after being shot on July 2 by a disappointed office seeker, Charles Guiteau

(1881)

Chinese immigrants continued to come, and as long as jobs were available, Americans did not object too much to their arrival. But when financial panics came, hostility grew. Californians claimed that the Chinese, who were willing to work for lower wages, were getting the jobs that whites deserved. They soon influenced politicians to pass the **Exclusion Act of 1882,** which cut off all legal Chinese immigration except for a few hundred per year. This act was passed over the veto of President Chester Arthur, who had assumed office after the assassination of James Garfield in 1881.

Northern Europe also sent many of its people to America. Political and religious unrest swept the German states during the 1840s. When the revolutions failed, people left that land. Many of these people had been landowners in Europe, so they had enough money to buy land in the United States when they arrived. They often settled in the farming areas of America's heartland, such as in Wisconsin. Others found work as lumberjacks in the northern woods, and then they bought farmland soon after.

Scandinavians—Norwegians, Swedes, and Finns—also came to America. They tended to settle whole towns or counties in Iowa, Minnesota, Wisconsin, and the Dakotas. They had their own newspapers and started their own colleges. Most were Lutheran and had come to America in protest of the policies of their churches back home. Some Swedes, Norwegians, and Finns worked in logging camps; others worked in the iron mines of northern Minnesota and the copper mines of Michigan.

The people of these and other ethnic groups contributed greatly to the American way of life. Inventions, works of literature and music, designs, and customs came with the immigrants. America would not be what it is today without the contributions these citizens made to the developing culture of the nation.

SECTION REVIEW

1. What was the biggest single reason for the growth of the American population in the nineteenth century?

2. What were two of the factors that helped the industries of the United States to grow?

3. After 1880 many immigrants came from what regions of Europe?

4. Where did many European immigrants go first to be registered?

5. What piece of legislation attempted to limit Chinese immigration?

 Why did established Americans sometimes object to immigrants?

Transportation and Technology

Two more American resources that helped the land's industries grow were its transportation networks and its technological developments. Promoting the development of these features became an important goal for the country.

Transportation and the Railroads

While steamships were improving transportation for trade with foreign countries, the railroads made it possible for America to conquer its immense territory. Railroads also moved America's raw materials to distant factories and distributed the manufactured goods to ready markets.

By 1860 there were 30,626 miles of track, but almost all of it was in the East. There were still no railroad bridges across the Hudson, Ohio, or Mississippi Rivers. In addition, since different companies built the railroads, they failed to use a uniform gauge (width) of track. Different gauges kept lines from connecting, prohibiting transportation from area to area unless goods were transferred from one line to another. Such problems made it difficult to travel by rail or to send freight long distances. Chicago and New York had rails between them, but passengers and cargo had to change cars six times en route. The Civil War made the problems obvious and stimulated the building of more track and the development of more efficient and economical systems.

Consolidation Helps the Railroads—One means of making railroads more efficient and more economical was **consolidation,** combining small lines. Sometimes this was done through the friendly purchase of one company by another, but more often it was the result of ruthless pressure. Several men sought to gain control of large railroad networks. **Cornelius Vanderbilt** had the vision of connecting the Great Lake states to New York City by rail. He forced all his competition to sell out and gained a railroad empire. J. Edgar Thompson secretly bought up small lines in Pennsylvania and Ohio. Once he had a base, he cut his rates and drove his rivals out of business. Then he raised his rates.

Other men tried to make fortunes as they built railroad empires. Although small railroads were often hurt by the consolidation, the process did help the nation acquire an efficient railroad transportation network.

Government Policy Aids Railroad Building—A second factor leading to the development of a railroad system was government policy. Lincoln and the Republican Party supported the idea of a transcontinental railroad. The outbreak of the war caused Congress to agree, and it chartered the **Union Pacific** and **Central Pacific** railroads in 1864. These two lines—the Union Pacific building westward using Irish workers and war veterans, and the Central Pacific building eastward using Chinese laborers—were linked on May 10, 1869. The official wedding of the rails took place at Promontory Point near Ogden, Utah,

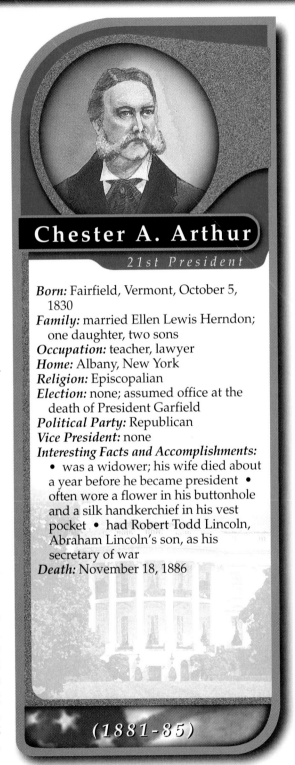

Chester A. Arthur
21st President

Born: Fairfield, Vermont, October 5, 1830
Family: married Ellen Lewis Herndon; one daughter, two sons
Occupation: teacher, lawyer
Home: Albany, New York
Religion: Episcopalian
Election: none; assumed office at the death of President Garfield
Political Party: Republican
Vice President: none
Interesting Facts and Accomplishments:
• was a widower; his wife died about a year before he became president •
often wore a flower in his buttonhole and a silk handkerchief in his vest pocket • had Robert Todd Lincoln, Abraham Lincoln's son, as his secretary of war
Death: November 18, 1886

(1881-85)

The celebration at Promontory Point marked the completion of the first transcontinental railroad.

a short distance from the Great Salt Lake. The Central Pacific had faced the trial of crossing the steep Sierra Nevada range. The Union Pacific gang had its problems, too. Because of a lack of wood, most of their ties had to be shipped long distances. A lack of water and the danger of attacks from fierce plains Indian tribes also hindered their work.

The federal government not only gave financial aid to the railroad builders but also provided the builders with land. In 1862 and 1864 Congress developed a new land grant system. Each railroad got a strip of land

four hundred feet wide for the right of way for its tracks. It also received two sections of land on alternating sides of the tracks. The railroad could do whatever it wanted with the 1,280 acres of land it was given for each mile of track it laid. The railroads held on to some lands. More often than not, they sold the lands next to their tracks to eager settlers. The money from the sales helped pay for building the railroad.

The government's Homestead Act of 1862 also helped railroads. The alternate sections of land owned by the federal government were sold at low prices or made

The Union Pacific offered passage from Omaha to San Francisco in four days.

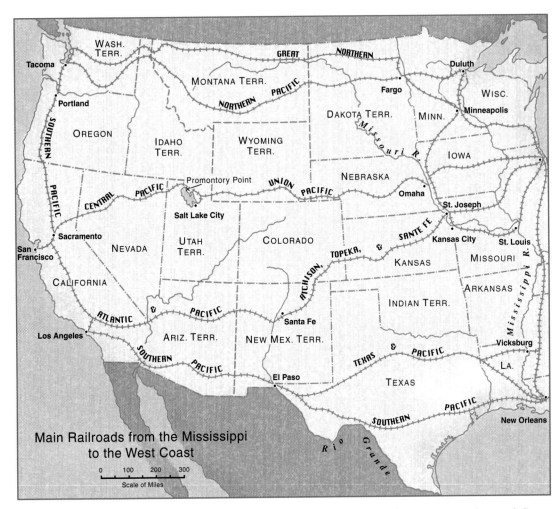

Main Railroads from the Mississippi to the West Coast

0   100   200   300

Scale of Miles

available free under the Homestead Act. Thus even more settlers and land speculators came into the region by means of the new railroad lines.

Building Other Lines—Because the men investing in railroads were accumulating enormous wealth, other people soon sought railroad land grants of their own. In 1864 Congress approved generous land grants for building a railroad linking Lake Superior and the Pacific Ocean. The Northern Pacific line, finished in 1883, joined Duluth, Minnesota, to Portland, Oregon, and also to Spokane and Tacoma, Washington.

In 1884 the Atchison, Topeka, and Santa Fe Railroad provided a more southerly route. The Texas Pacific Railroad built across Texas linked to the Southern Pacific at El Paso, Texas. When this route was finished, New Orleans was linked by rail with Los Angeles and San Francisco. Another transcontinental line was built with private funds by **James J. Hill.** His **Great Northern Railroad** included extensions into Canada to help provide transportation for farmers there.

Technology

Another important ingredient in American industrialization was technology—scientific inventions and improved methods for industry. The Yankee ingenuity at the dawn of the nineteenth century had, by the century's end, turned into a remarkable ability to innovate. Some inventions, like **Alexander Graham Bell**'s telephone, led to whole new industries and big changes in American life. Other simple inventions—rivets for points of stress in Levi Strauss's blue jeans, for example—although minor, remain useful even today. The number of patents issued by the patent office shot up, averaging more than 21,000 a year through the 1880s and 1890s.

The increased use of electricity was especially beneficial to the advancement of both industry and technology. **Thomas Edison** promoted the generation of electricity for practical uses and also invented many electrical appliances. His incandescent light (light bulb) was among the most important. Hundreds of other inventors also made important contributions to American industry.

SECTION REVIEW

1. Give three reasons for the difficulty of traveling long distances by rail.

2. What regions of the country did Cornelius Vanderbilt connect with his railroad empire?

3. What did the federal government give railroad companies to aid their building?

4. Name two key inventors of the period and the inventions for which they are best known.

 What could be the potential danger(s) of railroad empires?

New Ways of Doing Business

America's industries grew in size and produced more and more during the late 1800s. Competition, new technology, and better management helped to bring about this industrial growth. Companies were constantly looking

for ways to improve their production, but improvements often required investment money or **capital.** To meet this financial need and other legal needs, businesses began to find new ways to organize and obtain capital.

Corporations for Increased Capital

In America's early years most businesses were either **sole proprietorships** or **partnerships.** Sole proprietorships were businesses owned by one person, while partnerships were owned by two or more people. Both worked well for small-scale operations. Proprietorships had the advantages of catering to individual needs. The owner got all the profit, but he also absorbed all the losses and often lacked the funds to expand his business.

Partnerships had the distinct advantage of increasing capital in a business and of sharing the losses of the business. **Andrew Carnegie** built a huge steel empire with the help of multiple partners. They provided him with expertise in areas about which he knew little. He suggested that the epitaph on his tombstone should read: "Here lies a man who was able to surround himself with others far wiser than he." However, a big disadvantage of sharing the responsibility for all losses in a partnership was that those losses must be shared even when they resulted from the faults or failures of just one partner. It could lead to the financial ruin of all the partners unless protective measures were taken. Other disadvantages were that all the partners had to participate in the business's legal dealings, and if one partner died or pulled out, the partnership ended.

Another way to organize a business is to incorporate, a method that became very popular in the late 1800s. A **corporation** is formed when a business gains a legal charter and sells stock to many individual investors. Although the stockholders are essentially the owners, they can lose only the amount they invested in the stock if the corporation fails. If the business makes a profit, the stockholders receive dividends, or payments from that profit. Moreover, a corporation is considered a "person" in the eyes of the law, and it can carry on legal dealings without all of its stockholders being present. Nor is its existence ended by the death of a manager or single stockholder.

Andrew Carnegie built a huge empire based on steel production.

Because of advantages like these, more and more executives sought to incorporate in the years after the Civil War. Steel, petroleum, and chemical manufacturers are but a few of the many who used the corporate form of business.

Sources of Corporate Money

Company executives realized that they needed large amounts of capital to finance the growth of their ventures. Some people with savings or other wealth became stockholders, buying stock with money that provided the corporation with capital. More capital, however, was raised in larger amounts from other sources.

The nation's banking system also helped provide industry with capital. As more Americans entered the work force and the number of businesses grew, the number of bank deposits increased. Banks invested their money in corporations to make more money and also offered credit to such corporations to cover the expansion of industry. Another large-scale source of capital came from life insurance companies that invested the premiums paid by policy holders.

Corporations Find New Ways to Organize

As the corporations grew larger, they needed better internal organization. America's early factories had employed few executives, usually just managers and bookkeepers. Most new large-scale operations, however, required more management. Thus, separate departments to handle each major phase of operations became normal. There were department heads for such responsibilities as purchasing, marketing, accounting, financing, and development. These specialized executives often helped to manage businesses more efficiently and profitably.

In 1882 oilman **John D. Rockefeller** and his associates formed the first **trust.** A trust combined several separate companies into one super-size corporation, such as Rockefeller's Standard Oil. The executives of the trust then had power to organize and manage all the companies involved as they wished. Other

John D. Rockefeller and his associates combined several companies to form the Standard Oil Company.

industries followed Rockefeller's example and set up trusts of their own in the 1880s.

SECTION REVIEW

1. What is the difference between a proprietorship and a partnership?

2. Who built a huge steel empire by means of a partnership?

3. Name two sources of capital for corporations besides individuals.

4. What is a trust? Who formed the first business trust?

 What problems of a proprietorship or partnership does a corporation avoid? How?

Effects of Industrial Expansion

The growth of industries brought many changes to the way Americans lived and to the government's attention to industry.

Changing American Life

First, America's trade increased greatly. American foodstuffs and factory products found their way to distant parts of the world. This trade also helped to make many more products available to Americans.

Second, urbanization occurred. Immigrants swelled city populations. In addition, as farming mechanized and farm production increased, fewer farmers were needed. Farmers—or at least several of their children—often moved to towns and cities where work was available.

Industrialization emphasized urban problems. Pollution of air or water, overcrowding, and crime all became more obvious when concentrated in a single area.

Industrialism also meant that Americans began to have more leisure time. Machines freed people from some work, while other machines, labor-saving devices, made work easier. Americans soon found new ways to use the extra time. New spectator sports captured the public fancy. Others participated in already existing sports or tried the newly invented or popularized ones, such as bicycling, tennis, or basketball.

In addition, industrialism affected American family life. Some women had gone to work outside the home during the Civil War. A few continued to work after the war. Some were recruited to work in expanding industries. And because inventions made housekeeping easier, some women were finding time to take other jobs. The number of women in the work force would continue to grow in the years that followed, changing the lifestyle of more and more families.

Americans Focus on Capitalism

The United States had been founded with a capitalistic economy. **Capitalism** is an economy in which people are free to invest in businesses and make profits on their investments. Businesses are owned by private citizens instead of the government, and anyone is allowed to go into business, competing with others. Generally, capitalism works well because it recognizes man's natural selfish desires. In competing for personal gain, businesses usually strive to sell good products or services so that the business can continue and grow. Poor products or services drive customers away. The competition among businesses, created by a capitalistic system, helped to bring Americans a high standard of living.

Nonetheless, industrialization revealed some weaknesses in the capitalistic system. The capitalistic system is not perfect, and man's evil nature caused some industrialists to run roughshod over their competitors. In some industries, workers labored long hours doing dangerous work at low pay while company owners became millionaires. The biblical idea that "the labourer is worthy of his hire" (Luke 10:7) was sometimes ignored.

At that time of rapid industrial growth, a philosophy that justified harsh actions became popular. Charles Darwin's theory of evolution was used to defend piling up wealth by any means one wanted. Darwin's theory said that there was a constant struggle in nature. Only the fittest members of the species would survive. Applied to society, this thinking was called **social Darwinism**. Social Darwinists showed little mercy and no recognition of human weaknesses. In industry, social Darwinists held that driving weaker competitors out of business was just a part of the struggle for survival. Making a profit, according to their philosophy, should be accomplished by any means possible, even if others were hurt.

The ageless principles of God's Word shed light on this thinking. God's Word does not justify taking advantage of the weaknesses of others, even our enemies, for personal gain. The Bible reminds us often of the need to show mercy and love. Some industrialists gained wealth but ignored the principles of God's Word. "He that oppresseth the poor to increase his riches . . . shall surely come to want" (Prov. 22:16).

Closely tied to capitalism was the idea of *laissez-faire* economics. Most Americans believed that the best way for a capitalistic economy to develop was without any government interference or regulation. Those who supported *laissez-faire* policies argued that government regulation would disturb the fine balance between supply of products and the public's demand for those products; the economy might be ruined. Yet because individual men and some companies did not take on the responsibility to make changes, to right wrongs, and to correct imperfections in the system, people put more and more pressure on the government to do so. Americans were growing fearful that large corporations were going to control the nation. They generally preferred that their elected representative in Congress would take that control instead.

America's Government Begins to Regulate Business

Thus another result of industrialism was governmental regulation of business. Although the regulation at the time was probably meant to be experimental and was not as extensive as today's, a precedent was set. Government regulation of business and industry grew ever after.

A monopoly is the total control of a certain business or industry so that free trade is discouraged. A trust or a holding company, for example, creates a monopoly. This 1881 political cartoon depicts a monopoly as a snake threatening America's liberty.

The Interstate Commerce Act of 1887— Because the ruthless competition among railroads had hurt small shippers and western farmers, government first demanded regulation of railroad rates. The first law regulating industry, the **Interstate Commerce Act** of 1887, was a reaction to the unjust practices of the railroads.

Initially, states set up commissions to regulate the rates railroads could charge. Midwestern states like Illinois and Iowa provided strong enforcement, but in other states, like Massachusetts and Alabama, commissions gave only advisory opinions. Disputes grew as the rulings of some states affected railroad transportation in other states.

When the Supreme Court ruled that states could regulate railroads only within their own state boundaries and not those crossing state lines, Congress felt pressure to act. In 1887 the Interstate Commerce Act was passed. It directed railroads to set "reasonable and just rates." It also prevented railroads from charging more for short runs that involved little competition than for long runs involving stiff competion. An Interstate Commerce Commission was formed to examine complaints and take offenders to court.

But when the offenders came to court, the judges usually decided in favor of the railroads. Thus the ICC lost nearly every case filed from 1887 to 1906. Yet the act had an impact. It set a precedent for the government to organize other independent regulatory agencies. And in later years as the Supreme Court judges changed and reflected public opinion toward business practices more closely, court cases made more regulation effective.

The Sherman Anti-Trust Act of 1890—The public viewed trusts with suspicion. They felt that their size and power gave them an unfair edge that harmed free enterprise. Large trusts such as Rockefeller's had driven small companies out of business by lowering prices. Once the competition was gone, prices reached new highs. By 1880 both political parties promised to regulate trusts.

In 1890 under Benjamin Harrison's presidency, Congress passed the **Sherman Anti-Trust Act.** The act said, "Every contract, combination in the form of trust or otherwise . . . in restraint of trade or commerce . . . is declared to be illegal." But since "restraint of trade" was not defined and the courts still favored big business, the act had little effect at first. Its effects were also weakened when trusts devised ways to get around it. A new form of business consolidation, the **holding company,** came into being. The holding company gained control of companies by buying stock. While member companies retained their names, the holding company made decisions for them in the interest of the entire group, as if it were one giant corporation. The holding companies controlled the businesses as efficiently as the trusts had before them.

Abuses of Workers Lead to Labor Unions

The industrial era aided the rapid rise of labor unions. The abuses in some factories opened the door to unofficial and organized protests by the workers. Many began to organize in large groups or unions that could stand up against the management and ask for desired wages and working conditions. Although unions showed spurts of growth in this era, growth was often uneven. Competition for jobs among war veterans and immigrants plus economic depressions in 1873, 1882, and 1893 hindered their growth.

The Knights of Labor—The **Knights of Labor** began in 1869 under the leadership of Uriah P. Stephens. Its goal was the formation of one big union for all workers, skilled and unskilled, men and women. It sought equal pay for men and women, an eight-hour day for workers, safety features, and compensation (payment for loss) for injuries occurring on the job. In the year 1879 Terence V. Powderly took over the union's leadership. He was against strikes and believed that the union should not take sides politically. The membership rose from 9,000 in 1879 to 115,000 by 1884. By 1886 the Knights had a membership of 700,000.

Unfortunately for the future of the union, 1886 was a bad year. In Chicago about 80,000 workers, mostly Knights, struck for an eight-hour day. The police killed several workers when things appeared to get out of hand. Some anarchists (people who refused to obey the laws) staged a protest rally soon after. The police moved in to break up the meeting and someone threw a bomb into the crowd, killing a policeman and six spectators. A riot ensued, in which eleven more people were killed. The Haymarket Square Riot, as it was called, hurt the unions because people then linked the union with violence. Membership dropped to just 100,000 in four years.

The American Federation of Labor—A second union, the **American Federation of Labor,** began in 1881. Its first president was a British-born cigar maker, **Samuel Gompers.** Gompers saw the problem in the structure of the Knights of Labor and set up his union on different lines. Only skilled workers could join; dues were high; women were not allowed. Workers joined local craft unions with those of the same skills. Local unions then affiliated or associated with state and national groups. Each local union, however, made its own decisions and handled its own funds. The national group provided guidelines. This union also pushed for an eight-hour day and for **collective bargaining** (the right of unions to represent workers in negotiations with owners and managers). This union did use strikes, and its high dues were spent supporting the workers during strike times. A violent strike over a wage cut at Carnegie Steel's Homestead Plant in 1892 greatly hurt this union's attempt to organize in other industries.

Responses to Unions—Employers were often unsympathetic to unions and their demands. They wanted the right to bargain with workers individually and deplored strikes because they hurt production. Courts did not favor unions either and often issued **injunctions,** official court orders, to stop strikes. The local press usually sided with employers too. Since most of the papers made their money from local advertising, they could ill afford to anger their advertisers. The general public reacted negatively to unions because they associated labor aims, like the distribution of wealth and agitation by lower classes, with socialism. Some also opposed collective bargaining because it could deprive an individual of his own worth.

In 1893 a group of employers joined together to form the National Association of Manufacturers. Its aim was to counteract unionism. In 1900 the National Civic Federation was formed. Its leaders, Frank Easley and Marcus Hanna, believed that labor unions were here to stay. The choice then became what kind of union employers would work with. They discouraged anticapitalistic, socialistic, revolutionary unions and encouraged contact with conservative procapitalistic unions.

The Johnstown Flood: The Nightmare of 1889

One of the great disasters in American history occurred in Pennsylvania in 1889. The victims were inhabitants of the mining town of Johnstown and inhabitants of some smaller towns to its north. Over two thousand people died. The killer was a flood resulting from the breaking of an old, neglected earthen dam. To some, however, the killer was actually the negligence of a group of millionaires who owned the dam and refused to make repairs they knew were necessary. These wealthy families were too busy enjoying the lake resort and the hunting and fishing spot created by the formation of Lake Conemaugh (KAHN uh MAW), at the time the largest artificial lake in the world.

The lake was three miles long, one mile wide, and in places one hundred feet deep. It contained twenty million tons of water. The earthen dam, located fourteen miles from Johnstown and at an elevation four hundred feet higher than the town, was thirty-seven years old. It stretched three hundred yards wide and seventy-two feet deep. It was wide enough at the top for a two-lane dirt road. To keep the fish in the lake, the spillways had been closed off. The overflow valves had clogged because of neglect. The few repairs that had been made on the dam had been done by stuffing tree stumps, leaves, and straw into the numerous leaks that had developed since the dam's construction. Several engineers had warned the owners of the dam's deteriorated condition. One company had even offered to pay half the cost of repairing the structure. Yet nothing had been done.

The people in the towns below had become indifferent as well. They had heard so many times that the dam was breaking that they had lost all concern. No one could convince them that the dam would someday actually break. And if it did break, they did not believe that the result would be disastrous.

At 3:10 P.M. on May 31, 1889, it happened. After a number of heavy storms, the dam burst. In thirty-five minutes, all twenty million tons of Lake Conemaugh came rushing down the valley in a wave forty feet high and traveling at forty miles an hour. At times it met an obstruction and the water piled higher, once up to ninety feet, and then it burst through again to rush down on the towns below. Along the way it picked up debris that became as deadly as the wall of water itself: twenty-nine locomotives weighing up to eighty tons each, other railroad cars, boiling hot water from the iron works, hundreds of miles of barbed wire from a factory, the bricks and lumber from crushed houses and businesses, along with trees and animals. Because of the debris, the water at the top of the flood wave moved faster than the water at the bottom. Engineers estimated that the crushing force caused by that difference in speeds was as great as the power behind the water flowing over Niagara Falls. Nothing could stand in its way.

Had it not been for the heroic efforts of many of the townspeople, many more lives would have been lost than actually were. Those who managed to escape the flood stood on the edge and hauled other people out. Some in buildings on the edge of the waters pulled others through windows to the safety of the buildings. Some people even leaped into the rushing waters to make rescues.

Every town along the flood's path was flattened. Finally, the waters were stopped at a bridge in Johnstown, where the debris piled up thirty feet high and covered sixty acres. Behind the debris, Johnstown had become a twenty-foot-deep lake. Then, to make matters worse, the debris caught fire. Some that had escaped drowning but were pinned in the rubble were

The Dangers of Materialism

Another obvious result of industrialism was an increase in wealth, both nationally and individually. By the year 1900 the nation counted four hundred millionaires. The buying power of the average worker had increased by fifty percent over forty years. God's Word

Cornelius Vanderbilt's home displayed the extravagant luxury of the wealthy.

killed by the fire. Nearly one thousand people were never found.

America and the world came to the rescue of the survivors. Clara Barton and her newly formed Red Cross reacted magnificently to its first major disaster. People from all over the world donated money and food to aid the needy. The millionaires who owned the lake did little except go into hiding to avoid the press.

In a remarkably short time, Johnstown was rebuilt and again became a thriving iron and steel town. A coroner's investigation held the dam's owners responsible for the flood, but few people sued and no one won a suit against the millionaires. The total damages, staggering in 1889, came to seventeen million dollars. None of the survivors would ever forget the tragic day when neglect and indifference brought a rushing wall of death into unprepared Johnstown, Pennsylvania.

does not denounce wealth or money; instead, it denounces the love of money, its unwise use, and the envy and greed it can encourage. Christians are told to give God the first fruits of their labor. Sadly, in the industrial era as well as today, many Americans who had wealth were never satisfied. They wanted and sought more. Some of the rich competed with one another in showing off their wealth. **Materialism,** putting a higher value on money and possessions than Scripture and common sense dictate, surfaced as an American problem. It was a problem that would appear repeatedly throughout the twentieth century.

SECTION REVIEW

1. List five major changes in America that resulted from industrial growth.

2. What is capitalism?

3. How was social Darwinism applied to industry?

4. What industry was regulated by the Interstate Commerce Act of 1887?

5. Why did labor unions emerge? Name two of the earliest ones.

 How did holding companies allow businesses to get around the legislation against trusts?

SUMMARY

The late 1800s was a time of great industrial expansion for the United States. Growing industries used the nation's resources, its labor supply, railroad networks, and developing technology to produce more and more. Businesses also used forms of organization such as incorporation, trusts, and holding companies to increase capital and grow more powerful. While industrial expansion was generally good for the country, it did allow some men to take advantage of others while amassing large personal fortunes. Fear of ruthless business practices aided the growth of labor unions and eventually prompted the beginnings of government regulation of industry.

Chapter Review

People, Places, and Things to Remember

Ellis Island
Exclusion Act of 1882
consolidation
Cornelius Vanderbilt
Union Pacific
Central Pacific
James J. Hill
Great Northern Railroad
Alexander Graham Bell
Thomas Edison

capital
sole proprietorships
partnerships
Andrew Carnegie
corporation
John D. Rockefeller
trust
capitalism
social Darwinism
Interstate Commerce Act

Sherman Anti-Trust Act
holding company
Knights of Labor
American Federation of
   Labor
Samuel Gompers
collective bargaining
injunctions
materialism

Review Questions

Write the word that best completes each sentence.

1. A business owned by just one person is called a ___.

2. Businesses need large amounts of money or ___ to finance their operations.

3. The Interstate Commerce Act was intended to regulate some of the abuses in the ___ industry.

4. Union members wanted ___ so that the union could negotiate with owners and management.

5. Many of America's turn-of-the-century immigrants landed first at ___.

6. A ___ is an advantageous business organization assembled under a charter by individual stockholders.

7. A theory of ___ was used to support the idea that the biggest and best businesses would survive while others would fall.

8. Uriah P. Stephens first led an early labor union called the ___.

9. The ___ was legislation intended to break up the unfair advantages of trusts.

Match these men with their achievements.

10. Alexander Graham Bell   a. invented the incandescent light

11. Andrew Carnegie   b. formed a trust in the oil industry

12. Thomas Edison   c. consolidated railroads in the Northeast

13. Samuel Gompers   d. invented the telephone

14. John D. Rockefeller   e. built a huge steel empire

15. Cornelius Vanderbilt   f. president of the American Federation of Labor

Questions for Discussion

16. Should government place controls on industries? Explain your answer.

17. Can Christians be wealthy without being materialistic? Can Christians be materialistic without being wealthy? Explain your answers.

History Skills

What God Says About the Problems of an Industrial Society

As they adapted to the industrial age, Americans tended to ignore the Bible. Use your Bible to find what God says about (1) selfish employers, (2) angry employees, (3) government regulations, and (4) materialism.

A. Social Darwinists believed it was the duty of the strong to take advantage of the weak.

   1. What does God say employers owe employees (Luke 10:7)?

   2. How does God respond to those who oppress the poor (Prov. 22:16)?

   3. Who was told not to abuse their power to collect money (Luke 3:12-13)?

B. Gompers's AFL supported strikes, even though strikes sometimes became violent.

   4. What should be our attitude towards our wages (Luke 3:14)?

   5. Why should Christians honor their masters (I Tim. 6:1)?

   6. How should servants respond to cruel masters (I Pet. 2:18)?

C. The American public asked the government to solve their problems with industry.

   7. Where should men look for help (Jer. 17:5, 7)?

   8. What are the responsibilities of a ruler (Rom. 13:3-4)?

   9. What abuses are rulers prone to commit (Ezek. 45:9-10)?

D. Rich Americans replaced the true gospel with a false "gospel of wealth."

   10. What is the purpose of riches (Eph. 4:28)?

   11. What is the ultimate value of riches (Matt. 16:26)?

   12. How much wealth should we seek (Prov. 30:8-9)?

The Last Frontier

The term *frontier* refers to the outer fringe of settlement. America's frontier had moved west gradually. First men, moved across the Appalachians and then on to the Mississippi River. The next frontier, however, had been the far West. The discovery of gold and rich lands on the West Coast had lured numbers of settlers west. At the same time, much of the land from the Mississippi River to the Great Plains and beyond the Rocky Mountains to the Great Basin was bypassed and remained unsettled until after the Civil War.

Western explorers and wagon trains crossing the plains and deserts believed that the hard soil was not fertile. The climate seemed unsuitable too. The winters were cold, and the summers almost unbearably hot. Even worse, rainfall was scarce. Many areas received less than twenty inches annually. The area could have made up for its lack of rainfall had a good water supply been available. But the flow of most of the rivers and the underground water supply rose and fell with the amount of precipitation. A further hindrance to settlement was the lack of trees on the plains. Not only would it be hard for settlers to get used to the glaring sun, but they also could not build the log cabins and wooden houses that had been their homes in the East.

As if the geography of the vast region were not enough to deter settlement, the Indians added to the risk. The land west of the ninety-fifth meridian of longitude (roughly west of the first tier of states west of the Mississippi) was occupied by the Plains Indian tribes, and the Plains Indians were very warlike. Their lands had been invaded by eastern Woodland tribes who had been forced west by previous white settlement. The Plains Indians knew enough American history to realize that the eastern Indians had been cheated out of their land. These Plains Indians knew that white settlement meant being uprooted, and they were not about to give up the plains lands without a fight.

Despite these many discouragements to pioneers, the West would be settled. The building of the transcontinental railroad brought change to the Great Plains. With this new form of transportation, people and agricultural products could easily move across the grasslands. As the railroads crisscrossed the prairies, the vast herds of buffalo on which the

nomadic Indians depended declined. Railroad crews shot buffalo for meat, to prevent the buffalo from damaging the tracks, and for the sheer sport. This activity took away the Plains Indian's source of food, shelter, and clothing and made him a less formidable enemy.

New inventions and pioneer flexibility also aided the plains settler in his quest to conquer and adapt to the prairie environment. Although earlier writers had predicted it would take seventy-five to a hundred years to settle the remaining lands, by 1890 the frontier was closed. There were no more large tracts of land that had enough water available to make them useful for settlement. The frontier had been conquered largely by three groups of Americans who had sought its wealth and opportunity. They were the miners, the cattlemen, and the settled farmers.

Gold and Silver Miners

In 1848 the discovery of gold had drawn thousands to California. When the California gold fields had no more to offer, prospectors turned to other jobs or moved elsewhere to seek their fortunes. Some wandered into the mountain areas of the West that had known few explorers, and many were not disappointed by what they found. For about a generation these lands yielded new riches.

Riches in the West

There were several great strikes of gold and silver that brought miners into the West. The first was near Pikes Peak in Colorado. (Colorado was then part of the Kansas Territory.) Many prospectors raced across the prairie with "Pikes Peak or bust!" written on their wagons. This strike made few men rich, but it brought attention to the region.

A richer strike was made in northern Nevada. There James Finney and Henry Comstock mined gold. At ground level they made $5.00 a day. Two feet down, their take

Pioneers saw great herds of buffalo roaming the West.

rose to $20.00 a day. At a depth of four feet, they hit heavy blue-black sand. It had gold in it, but the gold did not seem as pure because it was being affected by a blue substance. They did not know what the blue mineral was, nor did they know that they had found the northern end of a rich lode, or deposit, of precious metal. Several weeks later someone else found out that the "blue stuff" was silver, nearly pure. Over the next thirty years the **Comstock Lode** yielded more than $400 million worth of

metal. (Fifty-five percent of the wealth from the lode was from silver; forty-five percent from gold.)

Farther north the Fraser and Columbia River valleys also yielded rich finds. Strikes in Idaho and Montana along the Bitterroot and Salmon Rivers attracted thousands of miners. Gold was discovered in Helena, Montana, in 1864 and also in Butte. In the 1880s copper mines were developed in Butte as well. The city is built over a vein one mile deep.

In 1876 two soldiers with prospecting experience discovered gold in the Black Hills of South Dakota, an area that was supposed to belong to the Indians. Fortune seekers soon invaded the area. Although the army had been sent to keep the whites out, it did not. When the government tried to buy back the land from the Sioux—land they had just given them in 1868—the Indians went on a rampage. Nevertheless, the miners got their claim, and the resulting **Homestake Mine** became the world's richest single gold mine.

Mining Camps and Boom Towns

Some miners came west alone, but for safety and for economy in buying supplies, mining guidebooks suggested four-man companies. Miners gathered into makeshift mining camps, living in tents or hastily constructed brush arbors. They staked claims quickly. To keep a claim, a miner had to work it one day out of every three. If a miner did not show up after ten days, someone else could take the claim. Of course the mining claims were not really official, since the miners did not own the land. They depended on claim societies that they had organized to protect their interests.

As more people came, businesses came with them. Supply stores and saloons were usually first. Soon after, a meeting would be called to plan a town. Streets were drawn out and a town name picked. Lots were drawn for

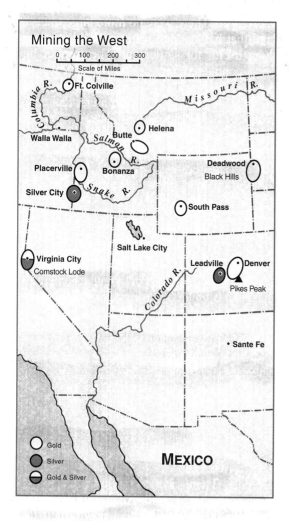

Mining the West

home sites. A church, a school, a miner's union hall, and processing mills for ore soon dotted the town's horizon. Where services were lacking, enterprising people could just about name their own fees. For example, one woman made $18,000 in one year just baking pies for the miners.

A few people made fortunes in mining. Many more made only a living. If the ore ran out or prices dropped, the mines closed down. Often miners, storekeepers, hotel owners, newsmen, and their families left when a mine closed. If everyone left, the empty buildings became weather-beaten over the years and were known as ghost towns. In addition to the mining towns, other ghost towns resulted from abandoned railroad towns, cow towns, lumber towns, and even farm towns across the West.

Silver and the Currency System

The mining of silver and gold aided the growth of the nation's economy. From before the Civil War until 1873, the government had minted both gold and silver coins. These coins were the nation's money during that time, along with greenbacks (paper money) printed during the war. When both the greenbacks and the silver coins were phased out, however, the money supply rested on its gold. The country was on the "gold standard."

Naturally, the price of silver plunged sharply once the government quit buying it for coins. Miners were disappointed by this action, and so were many other Westerners. The public began to pressure Congress for legislation that would put money backed by silver into circulation along with that backed by gold. They wanted more money (which would cause inflation) because they believed it would be easier for them to buy goods and to pay off old debts.

Finally in 1878 Congress passed the **Bland-Allison Act.** It set the price of silver at a 16:1 ratio (sixteen ounces of silver would be

equal to one ounce of gold) and also required the secretary of the treasury to buy $2 to $4 million a month in silver at the market price. This silver was coined but only into token silver dollars that were still backed by gold in the treasury's vaults. Farmers, silver miners, and mine owners were not satisfied. When six new states having agricultural and mining interests came into the Union, supporters of the free coinage of silver had more leverage. They were able to force the issue, and by 1896 the Democratic Party supported free silver in its party platform.

SECTION REVIEW

1. List at least four reasons people were hesitant to settle the frontier.

2. What system of transportation encouraged the settlement of the frontier?

3. The discovery of what two metals drew thousands into the Great Plains territories?

4. Why did ghost towns emerge?

 Why did Westerners object to a "gold standard" for the nation's money supply?

The Cowboys

Cattlemen played an important role in developing the American West. Acre for acre, they were responsible for taming more of the new frontier than the miners or pioneer farmers, and they did so with a relish and a romance that have appealed to people ever since.

The era of the cattle frontier was short. Although the animals had roamed the Southwest since the Spanish explorers brought the first cattle to the New World, a large cattle industry did not boom until after the Civil War. The peak of cowboy activity came in the 1880s, and by the early 1890s most of the cowboy legend had passed into history,

The Outlaws: Men Who Reaped What They Sowed

Jesse and Frank James: Both had been Confederate raiders with a rebel leader named Quantrill. After the war they took up a career of robbing banks, trains, and stagecoaches in Missouri and other nearby states. Their gang included the four Younger brothers. They claimed that the Northerners drove them to their life of crime, and they gained many sympathizers who regarded them as modern "Robin Hoods" instead of the thieves that they were. Jesse, whom his friends called Dingus, was shot in the back by a "friend" who wanted the reward. He was thirty-four. Frank surrendered, was tried, and was acquitted because of a great deal of political pressure.

Billy the Kid: At the age of seventeen he became involved in the Lincoln County, New Mexico, cattle wars. He fought for an English gentleman, John H. Tunstall, who became a father-image to the young boy. When a crooked sheriff and his posse murdered Tunstall, Billy swore to get revenge, and he did. By the time he was eighteen, Billy was charged with twelve murders.

Frank James

Captured by a former friend, Pat Garrett, Billy murdered his two guards and escaped again. Garrett eventually found him again and killed him. He was only twenty-one years old.

Black Bart: He was called "the gentleman bandit." Primarily a stagecoach robber, he wore a flour sack with eyeholes as a mask, treated everyone with the best of manners, and left a poem at the scene of each crime. Bart was captured when a handkerchief he dropped at one job was traced to him, and his real name was discovered to be Charles Bolton. After his release from prison, Bolton disappeared.

The Dalton Gang: Most of their crime spree took place over an eighteen-month period. All the gangmen were in their twenties. While attempting to rob a bank at Coffeyville, Kansas, all except one were killed. The survivor, Emmett, had eighteen wounds. After spending fourteen years in prison, he married the girl who had waited for him. They moved to Los Angeles, where Emmett worked as a building contractor, a real estate man, and a movie writer. Outspoken in his condemnation of outlaws, Emmett died in 1937, a respected businessman.

Jesse James

Harry Tracy: Tracy was the subject of one of the greatest manhunts in the nation's history. Being pursued throughout the state of Oregon, he could have escaped back to the hideouts in the West but seemed to relish the hunt. He stole a boat and sailed around Puget Sound, stole a train, had lunch with farmers and their families, joined the posses looking for him, called sheriffs on the telephone to tell them he was in town, and even helped do some of the work on the farms he visited. Eventually cornered by a group of farmers, Tracy killed himself.

leaving the dress and song to be copied and idealized by twentieth-century Americans. In the twenty-five short years that the cattle trade flourished, forty thousand men drove ten million head of cattle over a network of trails, most of which led north from Texas.

The term *cowboy* was a fitting one. Photographs of the era, and there are many, and artwork by such cowboy artists as Charles M. Russell, Frederic Remington, and Olaf Seltzer show faces of young men. Booking and arrest records from cowboy towns show that most were under twenty. Young cowboys spent a few years riding the range or trail and then usually married, settling down as farmers or ranchers.

A Wealth of Cattle

Following the Civil War, Texans began to realize that the growing herds of longhorn cattle on their lands would bring large prices at market. The Easterners were hungry for beef, and they had the money to buy the cattle. Since there were no railroads reaching to Texas, the only way to get the cattle to market was to walk them there.

The Cattle Trails—Cattle could be sold at a much higher price in the East than in the West. Steers cost $5.00 when fed on the open range on free public lands. It cost about one cent per mile to drive them north. There they could be sold for between $25 and $50 a head. To take advantage of such profits, cattlemen began to move herds across the Red River in 1866.

The closest railroad at that time reached to Sedalia, Missouri. But cowboys moving north on the Sedalia Trail did not find a warm welcome. For one thing, the cowboys had trouble driving the cattle through the forests and brush of eastern Oklahoma and southern Missouri. For another, cattle ticks clung to the Texas longhorns for hundreds of miles. The insects then fell off and attached themselves to stock in Oklahoma and Missouri. Those cattle lacked the immunity of the longhorns, and many animals died from outbreaks of Texas fever. Some laws were passed to prohibit the passage of Texas herds, but some people took matters into their own hands. They set up "shotgun quarantines" to keep the longhorns from passing through their lands.

In 1867 Joseph G. McCoy, a shrewd cattle broker from Illinois, built large corrals in Abilene (AB uh leen), Kansas. Using the railroad, which had just reached Abilene, he shipped cattle to the Chicago stockyards. This cut the distance of the long drives and freed the cattlemen from the dangers of armed farmers farther east. It also made the **Chisholm** (CHIZ um) **Trail** the busiest trail north.

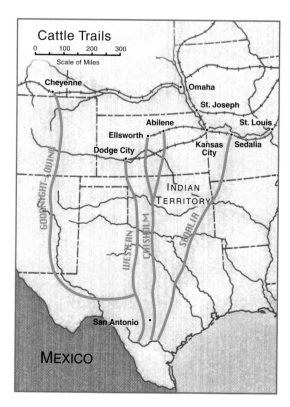

Cattle Trails

Huge herds of longhorn steers were driven along trails and then taken by train to Chicago stockyards.

The Chisholm Trail took its name from an Indian trader, Jesse Chisholm, who used the 225-mile trail not to move cattle, but to take supplies to Indian Territory (modern Oklahoma). Although cattle drives became common, they continued to meet difficulties. The trail ran through Indian Territory, and the Chickasaw Indians began levying a grazing tax of up to fifty cents a head on all the cattle driven through. Also, farmers near the trails began putting up fences to keep the cattle out. This meant less open range and fewer water holes for moving stock. Thus, the cowboys began to swing farther west before heading north. They connected with new railroad lines at Ellsworth and Dodge City, Kansas. The Ellsworth route was a cutoff from the Chisholm Trail. The trail to Dodge City was named the Western Trail.

Two New Mexico ranchers looked for a southeasterly route that would allow them to drive their cattle to the Pecos River and then up the Pecos to the markets in Colorado. Many people thought such a trail to be impossible, primarily because of one stretch of eighty miles that had no water. Nonetheless, Charles Goodnight and Oliver Loving hired eighteen well-armed men, rounded up two thousand head of cattle, and set out for the Pecos in 1866. On the first trip they lost nearly four hundred cattle, but on their second trip they lost no cattle at all. By 1895 ten thousand head of cattle had taken the **Goodnight-Loving Trail** to western markets. The greatest danger along the route became Comanche Indians, who were on the lookout for free steak on the hoof. In fact, Loving, who had also opened the Shawnee Trail, was killed in an Indian raid on one of his drives.

The Cattle Drive—The heart of the cattle industry and the most important part of a cowboy's job was the trail drive. Getting ready for the drive took careful planning. A rancher or cattle buyer set out to gather a herd in the early spring. The ideal size for a herd was two thousand head of four-year-olds.

The **trail boss,** who was paid around $125 a month, was in charge of the men, equipment, and animals. It was his responsibility to get the herd to market safely. About eight cowboys were hired to work the herd at salaries ranging from $25 to $40 a month. Two were "point" men who rode in the lead. Two "swing" men and two "flank" men rode beside the herd and kept the stock from wandering off. Two "drag" men brought up the rear. Riding in choking dust, they had to keep any weak and tired stragglers moving along. The outfit was accompanied by a cook. He hauled the chuck wagon a mile or two ahead of the herd. Thus he could stop to have food ready for a tired crew. The cook's day could start as early as 3:00 A.M. and sometimes lasted until

The Lawmen: The Guys in the White Hats

Tom Smith: He served as the sheriff of Abilene, Kansas, before Wild Bill Hickock. Smith was actually the man who cleaned up Abilene, and he did it with his fists more than with his guns. He was widely respected by the citizens. He was killed when trying to arrest a homesteader.

Wyatt Earp: Wherever he was sheriff, Earp was not well liked. He and a brother and some friends killed three cowboys in the famous gunfight at the O.K. Corral in Tombstone, Arizona. Considered murderers by the townspeople, Earp and his group left town shortly thereafter. Earp died in 1927 at the age of seventy-one.

Bat Masterson: His first love was gambling, but he also served as a rider for the railroads. As sheriff of Tombstone, Arizona, for two years, he did an excellent job of maintaining the peace. Later he became a sportswriter in New York. Teddy Roosevelt made him a deputy U.S. marshal.

The Pinkertons: This detective agency hunted down and captured many criminals. They also established the first Rogues Gallery for identifying known outlaws. The Pinkertons also became known as strikebreakers and union infiltrators as well.

Bill Tilghman: Like Tom Smith, Tilghman used his guns only when he had to. He served as the U.S. marshal in Perry, Oklahoma, for thirty-five years. Tilghman was so well respected by even the outlaws and their gangs that one famous thief refused to let a henchman shoot Tilghman in the back because he was "too good a man." Tilghman was killed when he grabbed a gunman and asked a bystander to take the man's gun. The bystander did, and then he shot Tilghman.

midnight. A **wrangler** was usually the youngest of the hands and paid the least. He took care of the horses and the riding equipment.

The drive started at daylight and went until dusk or even later—if the trail boss couldn't find good grass and water. After dinner, a cowboy's work was still not done. At night there were four two-hour watches. Pairs of riders circled the herd, riding in opposite directions, on guard for any signs of trouble. Night riding was not only hated for its loneliness but feared because of its dangers. Almost all stampedes, the most frightening experience faced by a cowboy, started at night. The snap of a twig, the bolt of a jack rabbit, a strange smell, or a streak of lightning could set off a dreaded stampede. If a stampede could not be stopped quickly, the cowboys faced several days of gathering the scattered herd. Even worse, cowboys often died if their horses stumbled and they fell in the dust to be trampled by the herd.

The Development of the Meatpacking Industry

The continued success of the open-range cattle industry was assured for a time by the development of a new industry, meatpacking. Two men, **Philip Armour** and **Gustavus Swift,** led the way in making the meatpacking industry successful. Their success came because they were willing to try new ideas and ways of doing things.

Philip Armour left his Massachusetts home to build sluices (long boxes for separating ore) for California forty-niners. Becoming bored upon his return east, he went to Milwaukee, Wisconsin, where he became his brother's partner in a firm dealing in wholesale grains and provisions. Armour's business boomed when he contracted to sell barrels of meat to the Union armies. Before and during the Civil War, meat was usually slaughtered locally because the only ways to preserve it for transport were by salting, drying, or pickling. Armour's meat packing operation during the war was a success, and after the war he realized that there would be a large market in the eastern cities for meat if it were shipped there in large quantities. The trail drives helped supply the cattle his business needed, and the railroads provided the transportation to the packing plants. Because the cattle were transported quickly and slaughtered almost immediately, they lost little weight during their journey and yielded large amounts of beef.

In 1875 Armour moved to Chicago and opened a packing plant. Hogs and steers moved down narrow wooden chutes to the slaughterhouse. On entrance, they were stunned by a hammer blow on the head. Slung up by the hind legs from a moving overhead belt, they moved past men who cut their throats, took out their organs, peeled off their hides and bristles, and cut up the meat.

A meat market in the late 1800s looks quite different from a modern supermarket.

Armour also saw the possible value of using **by-products**—bones, hide, and other parts of the animal not generally used for meat. Since his company handled many thousands of cattle and hogs a day, it would be better to turn the by-products into something profitable than to discard them. Consequently, he hired chemists to find uses for them. The fat was used to make soap; bones to make glue, buttons, and fertilizer; and hides to make shoes and gloves. It was said that the meatpackers used "every part of a pig but the squeal."

Gustavus Swift believed there was a market for more fresh meat in his native Massachusetts. In 1875 he also set up a meatpacking company in Chicago, and he began shipping fresh meat across the country a few years later. The meatpackers knew that chilled meat, whether frozen in winter or chilled on ice in summer, stayed fresh as long as a month. With this knowledge, beef had been put on ice in a railroad car and sent to Boston in 1877. But since the meat had lain directly on the ice, it had discolored. Soon after, specially designed refrigerator cars with separate ice bins came into common use. Their ability to carry fresh meat long distances from the meatpacking plants boosted the industry.

The End of the Open Range

By the 1890s the open-range cattle industry was declining. The last long drive was in 1896. Many factors combined to cause this decline. One problem was a drop in meat prices. With the efficiency of production and the amount of meat produced, meat prices plummeted. Thus it became less profitable to raise livestock.

Overgrazing was also a problem. When more and more people became involved in the cattle industry, grazing grasses became shorter and more scarce. Overgrazing was a greater problem as the season wore on, partic-

ularly if there had been little rain. In the summer of 1885, especially dry ranges with short grasses left the herds in poor condition. With overgrazing, pure clear springs became stinking mudholes. Harmful weeds took the place of lush prairie grasses. Erosion turned cattle trails into ravines.

Even water could prove a danger to the cattle. Sometimes steers broke for water holes or rivers, and as they charged in on top of each other, some drowned. Some died while crossing rain-swollen rivers like the Colorado, the Brazos, the Red, the Washita (WOSH ih TAW), or the Arkansas. Deadly flash floods were frequent because the sun-baked prairie ground simply could not absorb all of the run-off from sudden thunderstorms.

Droughts and blizzards threatened the cattle as well. When water could not be found, both the cowboys and the cattle suffered terribly. Dehydration made the cattle unmanageable; some even went blind. Winter's cold could freeze the livestock to death if they were stranded in a blizzard without food or shelter.

The summer of 1884 brought severe drought; the winter that followed was the most severe of the century. A raging December blizzard laid a thick coat of ice and sleet over the thin grasses. Cattle drifted south until they reached a 170-mile-long fence that stockmen had built to end earlier feuding with farmers. There thousands of cattle starved or froze to death. More than 10,000 dead cows were found along the fence. Over fifty percent of the stock had died that winter, and the cattle that survived faced another severe drought the following summer. The cycle of drought and blizzard was repeated again in 1886-87. The weather in those years dealt the extensive cattle operations in the West a blow from which they did not quickly recover. President Grover Cleveland, although sympathetic with the plight of the cattlemen, wisely did not offer government aid. This forced American agri-

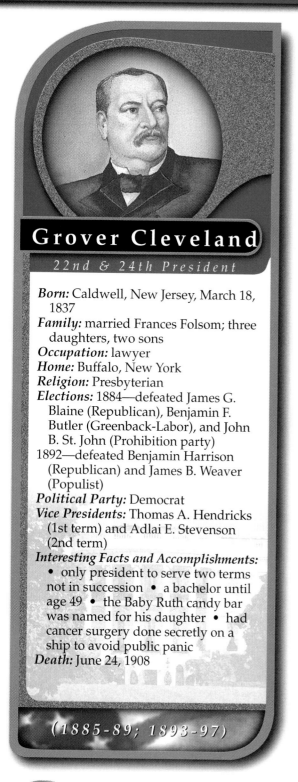

Grover Cleveland

22nd & 24th President

Born: Caldwell, New Jersey, March 18, 1837
Family: married Frances Folsom; three daughters, two sons
Occupation: lawyer
Home: Buffalo, New York
Religion: Presbyterian
Elections: 1884—defeated James G. Blaine (Republican), Benjamin F. Butler (Greenback-Labor), and John B. St. John (Prohibition party)
1892—defeated Benjamin Harrison (Republican) and James B. Weaver (Populist)
Political Party: Democrat
Vice Presidents: Thomas A. Hendricks (1st term) and Adlai E. Stevenson (2nd term)
Interesting Facts and Accomplishments:
• only president to serve two terms not in succession • a bachelor until age 49 • the Baby Ruth candy bar was named for his daughter • had cancer surgery done secretly on a ship to avoid public panic
Death: June 24, 1908

(1885-89; 1893-97)

culture to face its own problems and adjust to the needs of the market at that time instead of letting the government give it immediate help.

Indians and horse thieves also plagued the cowboy trails. Indians often demanded a toll of beef or horses. If the cowboys refused to pay the toll, the Indians would set off a stampede. Horse thieves and cattle rustlers hid along the trail. Stockgrowers' associations tried to rid the plains of such thieves by hanging or shooting them.

Sheep on the Range

One more problem for the cattlemen was the sheepherders. The vast vacant grasslands of the plains were as attractive to sheep owners as they were to cattlemen. In 1880 there were about 200,000 sheep in the northern mountain states and territories. By 1890 there were 1.5 million and by 1900, 15 million.

Cattlemen had reached the grasslands first. Now they eyed the "woollyback" invasion with anger. To the already overstocked ranges, sheep meant disaster. Cattlemen said that sheep ate grass down to the roots and then trampled what little grass was left behind, stripped the ground so that no new growth appeared until the next spring's rain, and fouled water holes, leaving a smell that made cattle refuse to drink.

As grass ran out and tempers grew short, the more numerous cowboys resorted to bullying, intimidating, and even attacking sheepmen and their flocks. Clubbing, shooting, torching, stampeding, and rim-rocking (driving sheep over cliffs) were all effective means of destroying herds. The murder of sheepherders was common too.

A combination of events lessened disputes: the winter of 1886-87 reduced the number of cattle that needed to be grazed; fencing began to divide range lands; some found that it was possible for sheep and cattle to share some of the same range lands.

The Candlish Movable Home on the Range

Until the late nineteenth century, sheepherders slept on the ground on blankets. Home on the range was very bumpy and cold. But finally a Wyoming blacksmith came to the rescue. His name was James Candlish. In 1884 he took an old wagon and converted it into the first home on wheels. Open in the front, the wagon had a canvas flap to block the wind. In 1892 a hardware company came out with an improved model that had a stove with an oven, a window, and Dutch doors among other "conveniences." Soon most sheepherders, especially on the northern plains, were owners of their own home on wheels.

There, of course, were some diehards who thought the manufacturers were just trying to pull the wool over their eyes. Some sheep ranchers wouldn't even hire herders who used a wagon. The most legitimate complaint was that to return to his wagon each night the sheepherder had to herd his sheep back over land already grazed.

Nevertheless, for a vast majority of the sheepherders "home, home, on the range" came with wheels in what was the forerunner of the mobile home.

SECTION REVIEW

1. Where did most cattle trails start? How long did the cattle trade flourish?

2. List two trails that were used to herd longhorns from the South to the North.

3. List four reasons for the decline of the cattle industry.

 How was the cattle industry benefited by the meatpacking industry?

The Homesteaders

Rich lands and the promise of a better lifestyle lured people steadily west. Easterners who had farmed worn-out soil left for the West. They were joined by immigrants and Civil War veterans who were looking for a place to settle down. Even a few thousand freed slaves joined these other pioneers on the plains.

Conflict with the Cattlemen

As more and more farmers went west to stake claims on western public lands (the public domain), the acreage left for open-range grazing decreased. Because these homesteaders did not appreciate having their crops overrun by marauding livestock, they put up fences. Since wood for fencing was practically nonexistent, the invention of barbed wire gave farmers the fencing material they needed.

For a time cattlemen fought the homesteaders, cutting the fences and threatening the farmers. There were even some range wars. The cattlemen eventually changed their style. Rather than grazing their cattle on the public domain, they took up ranching on their own lands or land that they leased from the government or other owners.

Farmers on the Plains

The **Homestead Act** of 1862 opened western lands for free settlement. Although the 160 acres allowed to a homesteader was hardly enough to sustain a family in these areas, no one seemed to mind. A settler was supposed to build a 12' by 12' house with windows, have a well, improve the land, and live on the homestead for five years. If he met these terms, the land became his. To cheat on the homesteading terms, some built 12" by 12" houses or had a house on wheels with a

Homesteaders faced great obstacles to claim their land.

bucket of water on it rolled onto (and off) the land. Some lived on the land seasonally. This last practice was a legal option, however.

Settlers could also increase land holdings legally by outright purchase of as much as an extra quarter-section (a section was 640 acres) at $1.25 per acre. The smallest amount someone could purchase was forty acres. That would have cost the princely sum of $50.00, a large amount in those days. If a pioneer filed a timber claim and planted ten acres in trees, another quarter-section could be added to his holdings. In the first six months after the Homestead Act was passed, settlers gobbled up 224,550 acres of land in Kansas and Nebraska alone.

The railroads sold farmland too, at $2.50 an acre. They sent agents to Europe with millions of pamphlets and posters. Thus the news of cheap American lands circulated in Norway, Denmark, Germany, England, and Wales. The Nebraska and Dakota territorial legislatures also paid immigration bureaus to attract settlers.

The Morrill Land Grant Act of 1862 gave states thirty thousand acres of federal land for every representative and senator they had. Most of the states sold the land to speculators. They in turn sold it to lumber companies, mining companies, and farmers.

The Oklahoma Land Rush

You have read how the government moved the Cherokee and other eastern Indian tribes west in the 1830s. Five tribes from the Southwest, all farming tribes, also were moved to **Indian Territory** (Oklahoma). By the 1880s most of the desirable farmland in the West had been claimed. Then the white man began to look greedily at this Indian Territory.

The railroads, land-hungry white settlers, and speculators saw the opportunity to make some money and pressured the federal government to open up Oklahoma to white settlers.

In 1885 the government bought lands in the territory. President Benjamin Harrison announced that some of these lands would be opened to settlers at noon on April 22, 1889. The U.S. Army was on hand to keep the settlers out until the given hour. More than twenty thousand pioneers were poised on the border that day. At the sound of cannons, they raced across the border to claim their land. Those who made their way into the area in this land boom were called "Boomers." (Some had "jumped the gun" illegally and made their claim ahead of time. These people were called **Sooners**.) Some 1.9 million acres of land were claimed in a few hours. In the year 1893 another part of Oklahoma, the Cherokee Strip, was opened to settlement. Oklahoma gained territorial status in 1890, and in 1907 President Theodore Roosevelt welcomed the

"Sooner State" as the forty-sixth state in the Union.

Overcoming the Obstacles to Settlement

As the farmers settled on the plains in the later 1800s, they faced some of the same obstacles that cowboys and ranchers had faced. They faced some additional problems besides. The ways that the homesteaders overcame these difficulties are a tribute to their faith in God, their perseverance, and their ingenuity.

A Lack of Some Resources—Since trees were rare on the plains, wood had to be brought from other places. This made the log cabin both expensive and impractical. Some settlers began by living in sod dugouts braced by a few purchased boards. These dreary homes were little more than ditches dug into a hillside and covered with a roof of sod (grass and soil). The **sod house,** however, was a little more pleasant, and it became the classic dwelling on the prairie.

A sod house was drier, sturdier, and more comfortable than a dugout. The sod strips used to build it were twelve to eighteen inches wide, three inches deep, and two or three feet long. The sod blocks were staggered like bricks, grass side down, to form the thick walls of the house. Soddies, as such shelters were called, were warm in winter and cool in summer. Usually a lattice of willow branches was woven and covered with clay from a nearby creek bed for the base of the roof. Then sod shingles were laid over it. In heavy rains, however, such roofs leaked water like oversoaked sponges. Debris often fell from the roof, but pioneer wives hung cheesecloth below the rafters to catch the mud and bugs. Inside walls were whitewashed with a mixture of lime and sand. Tight construction was crucial, not just to keep out the cold but also to make snakes

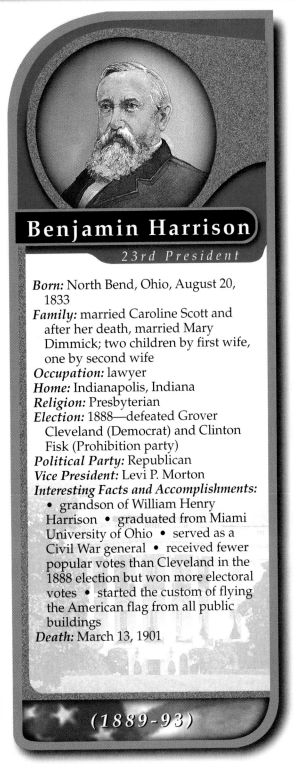

Benjamin Harrison
23rd President

Born: North Bend, Ohio, August 20, 1833
Family: married Caroline Scott and after her death, married Mary Dimmick; two children by first wife, one by second wife
Occupation: lawyer
Home: Indianapolis, Indiana
Religion: Presbyterian
Election: 1888—defeated Grover Cleveland (Democrat) and Clinton Fisk (Prohibition party)
Political Party: Republican
Vice President: Levi P. Morton
Interesting Facts and Accomplishments:
• grandson of William Henry Harrison • graduated from Miami University of Ohio • served as a Civil War general • received fewer popular votes than Cleveland in the 1888 election but won more electoral votes • started the custom of flying the American flag from all public buildings
Death: March 13, 1901

(1889-93)

Sod houses were common on the plains, but when wood was available, settlers sometimes built a sod-roofed house like this one.

and field mice unwelcome. Some sod houses were real works of art; a few, combined with some lumber, were two stories high.

The lack of wood also gave the farmers a couple of other obstacles to overcome. One was scarcity of fuel for fires. Until the railroads brought coal to heat prairie homes, corncobs, hay, and even manure served as fuel. Another problem was the lack of wood for the split rail fences commonly used back east. Although prairie farmers were generally glad their lands were not rocky, they did lack stones to be used for building purposes. There was no practical material for constructing fences until barbed wire was invented.

A sodbuster had to have an adequate water supply. Some settlers set out rain barrels or cisterns to collect rain. Some homesteaded near creeks. Most found water by digging wells, but wells had to be exceptionally deep to reach water in many areas of the dry plains. Even with wells, the farmers could not pump enough water by hand to water their stock and irrigate their crop land. The invention of the **windmill**, however, put the strong breezes of the region to this use.

Even wells or rivers could not necessarily irrigate many crops. Other means of overcoming this lack of water included raising crops that required less water or using dry-farming techniques, such as the use of mulch to protect what little moisture there was in the ground.

Help for the Prairie Farmers—The late 1800s brought many new and helpful developments for western settlers. One was barbed wire. Without wood and rocks, fences could not be built. And with cattle grazing contentedly in his corn and wheat, a farmer could not hope to prosper. Plain wire fences were tried, but they failed to hold up when herds pressed on them. Some farmers started thorn hedges, but it was often years before the hedges were high enough to do any good. In 1874 an Illinois farmer, **Joseph Glidden,** designed the first practical barbed wire. He used part of a coffee grinder to cut and coil small lengths of wire and then strung the barbs on by hand. Soon a machine was invented to do the work. Within a decade 120 million pounds of wire were being sold per year.

A Connecticut mechanic, David Halladay, perfected a windmill that helped farmers get water they needed for their family and stock. His device pivoted to face the wind and used centrifugal force to adjust the pitch of its wooden vanes. This feature allowed the windmill to withstand the pressure of high prairie winds. A crankshaft transferred the mill's rotary motion to force the pump to go up and down.

Railroads helped alleviate some of the transportation problems on the vast plains. Many lines built spurs (extensions) to the scattered towns to bring in needed goods and to carry out the farmers' harvests. The lines also made trips to other cities or regions easier.

American ingenuity helped the prairie farmer too. Heavier steel plows were designed to cut through the matted sod, and mechanical grain drills planted seeds of grain at the proper depth. The crops were harvested using a binder, an improvement on the reaper. Steam engines provided power for the larger inventions, and threshing crews often traveled through areas with this equipment for harvesting the crops of many farmers. The steam-driven tractor also appeared later in the century to aid the farmer.

Hardships of the Prairie Settler—Not only did the homesteaders have to overcome the lack of some needed resources; they also had to deal with many hazards of prairie life. One of these problems arose as more and more western lands were plowed. Especially in dry years, the wind blew tons of topsoil across the dry ground. It was impossible to keep a house clean since the dust settled everywhere. Outside the dust was blinding. Sadly, in addition to the inconvenience, the erosion of precious topsoil left much land infertile. In their eagerness to cultivate more land, settlers plowed up soil that God in His wisdom had given a protective layer of grasses. The grasses had prevented erosion and helped hold the moisture in the ground.

The prairie fire was another danger for the sodbuster. What little rain there was came in spring and early summer. As the season wore on, the grasses became dry. The smallest spark from a campfire or chimney or a stroke of lightning could turn the prairie into an inferno. When the flames were fanned by winds, the settler was powerless to stop the spreading fire. Damp clothing and blankets were used to beat out small fires. Sometimes farmers used the carcasses of slaughtered livestock, dragging them over the flaming grass. Backfires were lit to slow the progress of the flames. More often the only thing to do was to go inside the dugouts or soddies and pray. The heavy sod of the house and wet sheets over openings might protect people; but it could not keep the crops from going up in smoke.

Hailstorms did as much damage as fires. Crops were flattened, and little could be salvaged for harvest. Sometimes the settlers themselves were battered. Another one of nature's assaults on the prairie was the tornado. These small intense whirlwinds formed by severe thunderstorms destroyed everything in their paths. There were so many tornadoes on the plains that the region was called "tornado alley." For protection against such storms the sodbusters often dug root cellars. These cellars could be used for storing food, and they doubled as storm shelters when tornadoes threatened.

Large swarms of locusts and grasshoppers were an additional scourge. Swarming across the prairies in the 1870s, they devoured everything that grew. "Their fluttering wings," wrote the editor of the *Wichita City Eagle*, "looked like a sweeping snowstorm in the heavens, until their dark bodies covered everything green upon the earth." Accounts say the locusts covered the ground in a wiggling layer up to six inches deep. They ate crops, grasses, leaves, tree bark, leather boots, harness straps, and even fence posts and door frames. No one knew what caused the swarms to drop from the skies or what caused them to leave, but everyone feared them. Their arrival usually meant a two-year crop loss, because the locusts laid eggs that hatched the next year.

Barbed wire made it possible for prairie farmers to keep out hungry cattle roaming on the plains.

Homesteads were often miles from a settlement. Because neighbors were few and the distances between homesteads great, loneliness was a problem. Of course, efforts were made to deal with loneliness. For example, pioneers made great efforts to go long distances to churches built in towns. Another link to the outside world was mail. After pressure by farmers, the post office began **rural free delivery** (RFD), making it cost no more to send a letter to a soddie than to send one across New York City. Mail-order catalog houses also began. The first, Montgomery Ward and Company, began in Chicago in 1872, and soon afterward, Sears Roebuck and Company started. These businesses offered settlers a wide array of products to be ordered from their catalogs. Most could be delivered to the door; some were shipped by rail to the nearest town for pickup. Farmers also formed their own social groups. The **Grange**, founded in 1867 by Oliver H. Kelley, a Minnesotan, began as a social organization. Later it became a political tool to promote the interests of farmers. It may even have encouraged the rise of the Populists, a political party that sought to help relieve farmers from some of their problems.

 How did the federal government encourage the settlement of the frontier?

A romanticized lithograph of Custer's Last Stand reminds viewers of the hostility between the U.S. Army and Indians.

The Indians

The Indians who fought against the miners and cowboys fought against the settlers too. Frustrated and desperate over the loss of their lands and the destruction of the buffalo, some of the Indians were quick to fight back.

Indian attacks and uprisings were common during the latter part of the nineteenth century. The United States Cavalry often defended settlers and traders. Probably the best-known Indian battle of these Indian wars was at Little Big Horn in 1876. There Colonel **George Armstrong Custer** misjudged the strength and ferocity of a group of Sioux warriors. His defeat at Little Big Horn ("Custer's Last Stand") was led by **Crazy Horse** and Gall. **Sitting Bull,** who stayed behind the lines, was the medicine man who inspired the attack.

SECTION REVIEW

1. How did the homesteaders react to the cattle drives?

2. What major territory was the last to open to homesteaders?

3. What two important resources did homesteaders often lack?

4. What contributions did Joseph Glidden and David Halladay make to the improvement of prairie farming?

5. List at least five hardships faced by plains settlers.

Sioux chief and medicine man, Sitting Bull

Indians Surrender

Plains Indian resistance ended as much from defeat in war as from the destruction of the buffalo herds on which they depended. Although the frontiersmen had little sympathy for the Indians, for many Easterners, who lived far from the conflict, the mistreatment of the Indians was inexcusable. In 1877 President Rutherford B. Hayes made a statement about this issue in his yearly national address. "Many, if not most, of our Indian Wars have had their origin in broken promises and acts of injustice on our part."

But recognition of the problem by Easterners did little to change reality for the Indians. The same year that President Hayes made his speech, the peaceful Nez Perce tribe of Idaho made a desperate attempt to avoid captivity on a reservation by fleeing to

Canada. The United States Cavalry caught up with the tribe forty miles from the border. Their leader, **Chief Joseph,** had little choice but to surrender to American troops.

By 1885 all but a few scattered groups of Indians had been forced onto **reservations,** tracts of land set aside for them. One such group was a rebel band of Apache Indians. Their leader Geronimo, who had been captured and then escaped from reservations several times, finally gave up in 1886.

In 1890, as final defeat for the Indian seemed apparent, the Dakota Sioux gathered for a Ghost Dance. The ritual celebrated a time when the Indians envisioned the earth would die and be reborn. The white men would go to

Apache warrior, Geronimo

Sioux warrior, Gall

another world; the Indians would then get their lands back. These strange ceremonies stirred fears among whites. On December 29, 1890, army troops sent to disarm the Indians panicked, and mowed down almost two hundred Sioux at Wounded Knee, South Dakota. This action proved to be the last of many Indian battles—the Indians were conquered.

Those Indians who had not resisted were made **wards** of the federal government. The government supported them with an annual payment system and placed them under federal protection. Missionaries often proved to be the Indian's best friends during this time of transition. They offered not only help for the physical needs of the Indian but also the gospel to meet his spiritual need. Un-

fortunately, the greed and malice of some other whites caused many Indians to reject the aid of the missionaries.

The Dawes Act

By 1887 pro-Indian sentiment was strong enough to force Congress to do something for the Indians. The **Dawes Act** of 1887 assumed that the Indian way of life would no longer work. Hence the Indian should be Americanized and assimilated (absorbed culturally) into the mainstream of American life. Under this act tribal unions were to be dissolved, and individual Indians were to receive lands and become self-supporting. Each head of a household was assigned 160 acres.

The reformers, mostly Easterners, did not understand the Indian's needs, however. First, most western Indians who were given lands had been hunters and traders, not farmers. Second, the lands the Indians had been allotted were very dry. Whites had given them to the Indians because they were undesirable for their own use. Such small plots of arid land could not sustain a family. Third, Indians were not used to the idea of private ownership of land, so the land deeds meant little to them. Also, their basic social units were the tribe and extended family (several generations of a family, including grandparents, aunts, uncles, and cousins). When these two units were broken down on the reservations, the Indian way of life suffered even more.

Defeated militarily, economically, and psychologically, the Indians became idle and often turned to alcohol. All too eager to make money, some greedy whites offered to buy Indian lands. Since Indians now owned the land personally, they had the option to sell it and often did. Not used to a money economy, however, the Indians were easily cheated. When oil was found on Indian lands, speculators bought up even more Indian land.

The Indian Today

By the late 1960s, Indian problems regained federal attention when Indian groups pressed for rights for Indians. Not all of the pressure has been peaceful, nor have all the motives involved been for the good of the Indians.

In 1970 the Nixon administration set up a policy of Indian self-determination. This allowed Indians to set up their own tribal systems on reservations. The federal government would assist them by providing housing and vocational training as well as money for economic development. The Department of the Interior also set up a new official to coordinate these programs for the Indians: the Assistant Secretary of the Interior for Indian Affairs.

During the 1980s Indian tribes that gave up land under questionable treaties in earlier centuries sued the federal government for the value of those lands. Although not much can be done to restore lands now owned by others, the Indians have called attention to their plight.

SECTION REVIEW

1. How did the Indians react to white settlers taking over their land?

2. What was probably the most famous Indian battle? Who was defeated during this battle?

3. Name four ways in which the Dawes Act failed to meet the needs of the Indians.

 What issues continue to concern Indians today? Why?

SUMMARY

Settlement had moved across the continent to the Pacific Coast before the Civil War, but the vast areas of the Great Plains and Rocky Mountains had been passed by. The dry climate, fierce Indians, and rugged terrain had discouraged early settlement. After the war, however, settlement in these regions began. Gold and silver brought miners, especially to mountain regions of the West. The demand for beef in the East prompted cattlemen on the plains to expand their herds and drive them to the railheads where they could be shipped to market. Farmers joined the cattlemen on the plains, attempting to raise their crops in the prairie soil. Although settlement was not dense on the plains or in the mountains, the advances of the miners, cattlemen, and farmers pushed the Indians off the land and onto reservations.

Chapter Review

People, Places, and Things to Remember

Comstock Lode
Homestake Mine
Bland-Allison Act
Chisholm Trail
Goodnight-Loving Trail
trail boss
wrangler
Philip Armour
Gustavus Swift

by-products
Homestead Act
Indian Territory
Sooners
sod house
windmill
Joseph Glidden
rural free delivery
Grange

George Armstrong
   Custer
Crazy Horse
Sitting Bull
reservations
Chief Joseph
wards
Dawes Act

Review Questions

Indicate whether each of the following would be most closely associated with the miners, the cattlemen, the homesteaders, or the Indians.

1. windmills

2. Chisholm Trail

3. Comstock Lode

4. wrangler

5. Ghost Dance

6. Dawes Act

7. "Pikes Peak or bust!"

8. Sooners

Who Am I?

9. I am the colonel killed at the battle of Little Big Horn.

10. I am the Nez Perce chief who sought refuge in Canada.

11. I am the Sioux medicine man.

12. I am the businessman who sold meat to the Union army.

Which term in each set does not belong with the others?

13. Chisholm, Comstock, Goodnight-Loving

14. ghost town, sod house, windmill

15. by-products, refrigerator car, wrangler

Questions for Discussion

16. Why can homesteaders, rather than miners and cowboys, be given more credit for actually settling the frontier?

17. How could the Indians have been treated differently during the settlement of the West?

History Skills

Analysis: Find the Related Words

In each row, decide which words are related to the first term and list them on a piece of paper. The number of related terms will vary from one to four. (The first answers are underlined for you.)

1.	*chief*	<u>Crazy Horse</u>	Custer	<u>Joseph</u>	<u>Sitting Bull</u>
2.	*cowboy*	Armour	Swift	Goodnight	Loving
3.	*outlaw*	Jesse James	Black Bart	Tom Smith	Emmett Dalton
4.	*lawman*	Joe Glidden	Wyatt Earp	Oliver Kelley	Jesse Chisholm
5.	*meat-packer*	Armour	Glidden	Halladay	Swift
6.	*inventor*	Glidden	Halladay	Chisholm	Custer
7.	*mining town*	Helena	Butte	Dodge City	Chicago
8.	*cow town*	Bonanza	St. Louis	Ellsworth	Abilene
9.	*cattle trail*	Western	Sedalia	Chisholm	Goodnight-Loving
10.	*mine*	Cheyenne	Grange	Comstock	Homestake

In each row below, decide the word that is least related to the other words. (The first answer is underlined for you.)

11.	cook	wrangler	trail boss	<u>ward</u>
12.	bones	hide	wagon	fat
13.	sheep	fire	tornado	hailstorm
14.	tractor	railroad	by-product	barbed wire
15.	silver	wheat	gold	copper
16.	drought	blizzard	overgrazing	reservation
17.	Iroquois	Apache	Sioux	Nez Perce
18.	Pecos	Pikes Peak	Bitterfoot	Black Hills
19.	cowboy	miner	president	homesteader
20.	steer	hog	windmill	sheep

Location

The West includes the states of Montana, Wyoming, Colorado, New Mexico, Arizona, Utah, Nevada, Idaho, Washington, Oregon, and California. It extends the entire length of the country, bordered by Canada to the north and Mexico to the south. To the east are the Great Plains, and to the west is the Pacific Ocean.

Climate

The interior of the West is generally dry. To the south is desert. Farther north the land, though still dry, receives enough rainfall to support grass. Climate in the mountains varies according to altitude; the higher the elevation, the thinner and cooler the air. Even in the middle of a warm summer, the peaks of tall mountains might be snow-covered. Washington, Oregon, and northern California have marine west coast climates. Temperatures are generally mild throughout the year with cloudy, rainy winters and warm, sunny summers. Central and southern California enjoy mediterranean climates. Summers are warm and dry, while winters are mild.

Topography

Mountains dominate the landscape of the West. The Rocky Mountains are the largest range on the entire continent. Extending from northern New Mexico through northern Alaska, the Rockies are sometimes called the Backbone of North America. They serve as the Continental Divide, separating waters that flow into the Atlantic from those that flow into the Pacific. The Pacific Coast states have the Coast Ranges along the ocean and the Sierra Nevada (in California) and Cascades (in Oregon and Washington) farther inland. Between the mountain ranges on the coast is fertile farmland: the Central Valley in California, the Willamette Valley in Oregon, and the Puget Sound Lowland in Washington. Dry lands prevail between the coast and the Rocky Mountains. The Colorado Plateau extends into the desert southwest, and the Columbia Plateau dominates in the temperate northwest. These two plateaus are separated by the Great Basin, a bowl of low, rugged land. The Basin includes Utah's Great Salt Lake and California's Death Valley, the lowest (282 feet below sea level), hottest (often over 120° F), and driest (less than 2" of rain annually) spot in North America. The West ends in the edges of the Great Plains.

Natural Resources

Promise of great mineral wealth drew many settlers to the West in the 1800s. Though some veins of gold and silver have run out, the land still holds minerals. For example, Utah, Montana, and New Mexico are leading producers of copper. Oil has been found on the western slopes of the Rockies and off the coast of California. Forests and fish are major resources of the Northwest. Agriculture is abundant in the fertile valleys of California, Washington, and Oregon and in the irrigated plateau east of the Cascade Mountains. Because it is scarce, fresh water is one of the most precious resources in the West. The Colorado River in the south and the Columbia River in the north are crucial sources.

Geography & Culture

The West has always intrigued Americans and continues to do so today. The land offers spectacular scenery and exciting activities. Skiing, snowboarding, hiking, biking, climbing, and white-water rafting lure the adventure lover. Warm weather also brings many to the West. The film industry settled in southern California in the early 1900s to take advantage of the mild temperatures, sunny weather, and variety of scenery. Young people and retirees alike enjoy the relaxed atmosphere that comes with a year-round summer playground. Finally, the West reflects the independent spirit of the American pioneer. That spirit has led to the position of the West Coast as trendsetter. The West is an important part of America and is likely to become even more important as the region continues to grow.

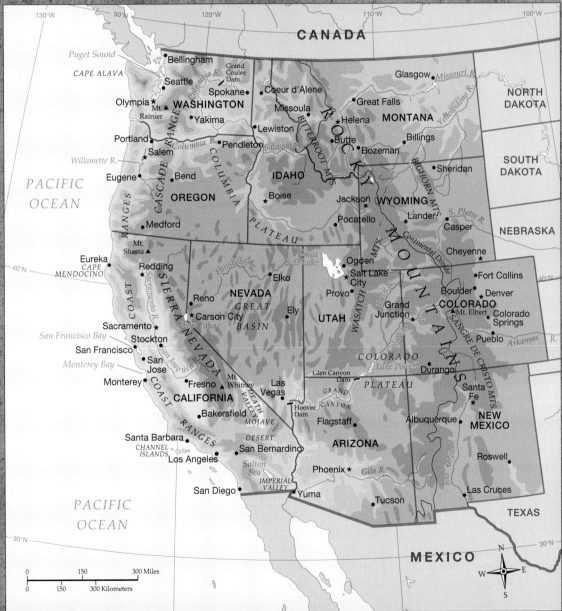

130°W   50°N   120°W   110°W   100°W

CANADA

Puget Sound
Bellingham
CAPE ALAVA
Seattle
Grand Coulee Dam
Spokane   **Coeur d'Alene**   **Glasgow**   *Missouri R.*
Columbia R.
Olympia   **WASHINGTON**   **Missoula**   **Great Falls**   **NORTH DAKOTA**
Mt. Rainier
Yakima   **Helena**   **MONTANA**
Portland   **Lewiston**   **Butte**   **Billings**   **SOUTH DAKOTA**
Columbia R.   **Pendleton**   **Bozeman**
Salem
Willamette R.
Eugene   **Bend**   **IDAHO**   **Jackson**   **WYOMING**   **Sheridan**
OREGON   **Boise**   *BIGHORN MTS.*   **NEBRASKA**
COLUMBIA   **Pocatello**   **Lander**   *S. Platte R.*
PACIFIC OCEAN   *PLATEAU*   **Casper**
Mt. Shasta   *Great Salt Lake*   **Ogden**   **Cheyenne**   40°N
40°N   *CAPE MENDOCINO*   **Eureka**   **Redding**   **Elko**   **Salt Lake City**   **Fort Collins**
Humboldt R.   **Boulder**   **Denver**
NEVADA   **Provo**   **Grand Junction**   **COLORADO**   Mt. Elbert   Colorado Springs
Reno   *GREAT BASIN*   **UTAH**   *SANGRE DE CRISTO MTS.*   **Pueblo**
Carson City   **Ely**   *Arkansas R.*
Sacramento   *SIERRA NEVADA*   *COLORADO*   **Durango**
San Francisco Bay   **Stockton**   *PLATEAU*
San Francisco   **San Jose**   Glen Canyon Dam   *Lake Powell*
Monterey Bay   Mt. Whitney   **Las Vegas**   *GRAND CANYON*   **Santa Fe**
Monterey   **Fresno**   *DEATH VALLEY*   **NEW MEXICO**
CALIFORNIA   Hoover Dam   **Flagstaff**   **Albuquerque**
Bakersfield   *MOJAVE*
Santa Barbara   *DESERT*   **San Bernardino**   *ARIZONA*   **Roswell**
CHANNEL ISLANDS   *COAST RANGES*   **Los Angeles**   *Salton Sea*   **Phoenix**   *Gila R.*   **Las Cruces**
San Diego   *IMPERIAL VALLEY*   **Yuma**   **Tucson**   **TEXAS**

PACIFIC OCEAN   30°N   30°N

MEXICO   N W E S

0   150   300 Miles
0   150   300 Kilometers

America and the World

Throughout the nineteenth century America increased its population, built its industries, and expanded its settlement across the continent. As it grew, the United States had extended its influence and developed its strength. By the turn of the century, much of the world began to recognize that America was an impressive, new world power.

Imperialism in the Late Nineteenth Century

The Civil War and Reconstruction, the settlement of the frontier, and the development of new businesses had kept the attention of America through much of the 1800s. The United States showed little concern for foreign affairs that did not affect its borders or its people. This attitude of minding the country's own business and staying out of world politics is known as **isolationism.**

During the late 1800s, however, the United States saw that other countries were building world empires. Britain, France, Germany, and a few other nations were taking control of foreign lands. This **imperialism,** the extension of one's way of life over another people, brought many of these controlling countries greater wealth and power. Soon Americans began to wonder if their own country would end its isolationism and join these imperialist powers by building its own overseas empire.

Reasons for Imperialism

Aside from the prestige of building a large world empire, imperialist countries had several reasons for extending their control in other areas of the world. One reason concerned military strength. Because taking control of foreign lands often required military force, an imperialist power could naturally be proud of its strong army. Empire building required a large and well-trained army ready to handle the needs of the empire and to defend against enemies. The military also gained important naval bases and army bases around the world in the lands it controlled. These bases increased the nation's strength as a world power.

Another major reason for imperialism was wealth. An imperialist country could regulate the trade and the development of natural resources in its colonies. The country could send its own businessmen to oversee the industries of the colony. It could hire the natives for very low wages and send the profits back to the mother country. The mother country could benefit from the products of the mines and plantations, and it could also make sure that the colony bought all its imported items from the mother country. Thus the imperialist country held every economic advantage over the colony. Sometimes the imperialist country took extreme advantage of the native people and their poverty and ignorance to keep them working for the benefit of the mother country. Such practices are called exploitation.

The final major reason for imperialist activity in the late 1800s was a desire to help the unlearned and poor peoples in undeveloped lands. Some people in the imperialist countries wished to teach the "uncivilized" peoples of the world how to read and write, especially in European languages. They wanted to extend the benefits of education and Western art and science to the natives of their colonies so that the natives could learn to live like Europeans.

Many imperialists wished to extend not only education but also food and health care to the hungry and sick. Helping poorer peoples who need food, medicine, education, or other assistance is called **humanitarianism.** British writer Rudyard Kipling spoke of the task of aiding the needy people of the world as the "white man's burden." This burden, or responsibility, motivated many western Europeans and Americans to take humanitarian aid and Christianity to lands in Asia, Africa, and the Pacific. Thousands of missionaries were recruited, and many sincerely spread the gospel of Jesus Christ. Others, lacking a personal knowledge of Christ as Saviour themselves, spread a "social gospel" which stressed the good works of humanitarian aid rather than salvation through Jesus Christ.

America's desire to evangelize foreign fields is exemplified by the work of the evangelist **Dwight L. Moody.** He had a profound influence on both American and British missions through his preaching and recruiting at many universities. Missions-minded American students were invited to a summer session at Moody's school in Northfield, Massachusetts, in 1886. In one month, one hundred students pledged themselves to be foreign missionaries. By the next summer session there were twenty-one hundred young men and women in attendance. In 1888 the Student Volunteer Movement was set up with the goal of "the evangelization of the world in this generation." Although it did not attain its lofty goal, its missionaries fanned out across India, Africa, China, and Japan. Sadly, within forty years even this group had strayed from preaching the Bible as God's truth and preached instead a social gospel.

The Student Volunteer Movement was established as a result of Dwight L. Moody's faithful evangelism.

Arguments About American Imperialism

The United States saw the economic benefits and other advantages of empire building. By 1880 Americans were producing far more food and goods than could be sold at home. They were also looking for new supplies of raw materials, and some people wanted a stronger army and navy. As a result, Americans began to think about imperialism as an aid to their own country.

Some Americans were opposed to the nation's expansion. Since the United States was large and lacked few natural resources, it really did not need to acquire the raw materials of lands overseas as smaller countries did. Moreover, Americans opposed imperialism because it contradicted their ideals. Americans had fought for their own liberty. Could they now take away the liberty of foreign people? Some people were also concerned because exploitation of other peoples violates God's Word.

Other Americans favored expansion. First, some believed that the United States would become a second-rate nation if it did not build an empire. Second, America's supply of raw materials was not inexhaustible. New sources of raw materials might be needed. Third, new markets for America's manufactured products would be needed if the market at home became saturated. Fourth, the nation needed Pacific islands so that American ships traveling west could refuel. Fifth, the United States needed to extend its military power and position to protect itself from other countries.

America Acquires New Territory

The United States practiced imperialism when it purchased Alaska from Russia in 1867. Unlike all the land acquired before that time, Alaska was not connected to the other land areas of the United States. It was a "distant land" bought for America's benefit. As it turned out, Alaska proved to be very beneficial.

A gold rush in 1897 brought a flood of miners to the area around the Yukon River. The rush also boosted the economy of the United States. Later, silver, copper, and oil were found in Alaska to add to the nation's resources. Fishing became important to Alaska's economy; salmon fishing produced far more wealth for the area than gold ever did. In later years Alaska also became important for national defense. And, of course, Alaska did become the forty-ninth state when it joined the union in 1959. Yet when Alaska was purchased in 1867, no one realized that was the beginning of American imperialism.

Another advance toward America's world empire also took place in 1867 with a far smaller acquisition than Alaska. American seamen had discovered Midway Island, located to the northwest of Hawaii, in 1859. Midway, however, remained a little-known Pacific outpost until it became the focus of a major battle for control of the Pacific Ocean in World War II.

Alaska and Midway aside, the first intentional imperial gain for the United States did not come until early in 1898, when Congress annexed the islands of Hawaii. American missionaries and businessmen had gone to the islands in the early 1800s. The large pineapple and sugarcane plantations built by the businessmen had taken advantage of the native Hawaiian workers. The Americans had also gained influence in the Hawaiian government. In 1893, they forced Hawaii's queen, Liliuokalani (lee LEE oo oh kah LAH nee), out of power, declared a republic, and asked the United States for annexation. President Cleveland, however, refused to purchase the islands because the queen had been removed from power illegally. But in 1898 President McKinley agreed to the purchase, and Hawaii became the first in a series of imperial gains for the nation.

SECTION REVIEW

1. Define *imperialism.*

2. What were the three major reasons for imperialism?

3. List at least three reasons for opposition to American expansion in the early 1900s.

4. What 1898 American acquisition in the Pacific started the country on its quest for an overseas empire?

 What shift in focus was manifested by some missionaries of this period?

The Spanish-American War

Along with adding Hawaii to its territories in 1898, America also entered a war that would greatly expand its overseas empire. Although a short and inexpensive war (as wars go), the **Spanish-American War** was an action of great consequence for American imperialism.

The island of Cuba, lying less than one hundred miles off the coast of Florida in the Caribbean Sea, was the source of America's quarrel with Spain. Although four centuries had passed since Cuba's discovery and the beginning of Spanish rule, this island nation had experienced only about a dozen years of well-run, peaceful, productive existence. Spain had allowed this colony to suffer from exploitation and poor government. The United States and other nations had tried to help the Cubans and had encouraged Spain to improve the situation, but little change occurred.

Causes of the War

As Americans watched the plight of their Cuban neighbors, conditions developed that encouraged them to do something to help.

Cuban Dissatisfaction—The Cubans had long been dissatisfied with conditions in their land. Many of the people suffered from poverty and cruel treatment. Several rebellions had erupted in the land, and in 1895 revolution again came to Cuba. The revolutionaries had three goals: terrorizing Cuba, destroying its livelihood (the sugar industry), and drawing the United States into the conflict. While fighting in Cuba, the revolutionary forces were smart enough to have agents in the United States who helped to raise money for the revolution and to feed the American press a steady diet of overblown incidents, all blamed on Spain.

The Yellow Press—The news that the revolutionaries wanted the Americans to hear was funneled to key newspapers. Many of these newspapers were themselves locked in deadly warfare to sell subscriptions. One way to increase sales was to subject the reading public to a steady diet of sensational stories. They manipulated news stories, trying to make each one more exciting and attention-getting than the others, a technique called **yellow journalism.** Two powerful newspapermen facing off in this struggle were **William Randolph Hearst** (HURST), owner of the *New York Journal,* and **Joseph Pulitzer** (POOL it sur) with the *New York World.* Unfortunately, some of what they reported was either inaccurate or greatly exaggerated. They knew that if they wrote about extremely poor conditions in Cuba and about Spain insulting the United States, they could stir up great interest in a growing conflict. Their reporting intentionally drove America toward war.

United States Sympathies—The humanitarian sympathies stirred by the news reports caused Americans to want to help. Many believed that the Cubans were oppressed by Spain. They wished that Cuba could obtain the freedoms and advantages that Americans enjoyed. Influenced by the press, most Americans favored helping the Cubans rid themselves of Spanish oppression.

American Investment—Another reason for United States interest in Cuba was that American businessmen had invested in Cuban sugar plantations and refineries. These investors feared that if the government stayed unstable and the terrorist acts continued, they might lose their money. The investors frantically pressured President **William McKinley** to protect their financial interests.

Immediate Causes—As tensions rose concerning the Cuban situation, two impor-

tant events took place that spurred the United States into action.

In February 1898 Hearst's *New York Journal* published a letter written by **Dupuy de Lôme,** the Spanish minister to the United States. The letter, to a personal friend of the minister, was never meant for publication, but it was stolen by Cuban rebels who gave it to the Hearst press. The letter described President McKinley as "weak and a bidder for the admiration of the crowd, besides being a common politician." At this time Americans held the presidency in such high esteem that they considered any criticism of the person holding the office as a national insult. The press demanded Spain be punished. De Lôme resigned, but the furor did not diminish.

Less than a week after the de Lôme letter, a second incident occurred. On February 15, 1898, an American warship, the **U.S.S.** *Maine,* anchored in Havana, Cuba, for an indefinite stay. The navy called it a goodwill mission, and Spain reacted appropriately. However, on February 15 at 9:40 P.M. the *Maine* mysteriously blew up. Two officers and 250 enlisted men died in the initial blast. Of course, the conclusion drawn by the yellow press was that Spain was responsible. There were other possible explanations, but Americans wished to blame Spain. The public yelled, "Remember the *Maine*!" and cried for action.

The president and Congress stalled briefly, but they issued a resolution that approved the use of force to end hostilities in Cuba and set up a stable government there. They

American journalist Joseph Pulitzer established an endowment to fund annual awards for excellence in journalism, literature, and music.

The Press, Public Opinion, and Comic Strips Too

Joseph Pulitzer, a Hungarian immigrant, had refined his journalistic trade in St. Louis with his powerful paper, the *St. Louis Post-Dispatch*. In 1883 he invaded New York City and bought out the dying *New York World*. Alert reporting, sensational stunts, and vivid pictures helped the *World* make a profit. Pulitzer was a crusader. No matter what the cause, he was able to drum up excitement and inspiration much as a bandmaster does with a band.

Editors across America studied his techniques and imitated them. His most successful imitator, William Randolph Hearst, copied him so well that Hearst soon became Pulitzer's chief competitor. Hearst had been given the *San Francisco Examiner* by his father. When he later inherited his father's millions, he enlarged his base and bought the *New York Journal.* He used some of his fortune to hire writers away from Pulitzer. When news was lacking, Hearst made his own news. He turned reporters into detectives to pursue criminals and made crime columns more exciting. He hired preachers to furnish religious material that would fire editorial controversy.

In 1897 Hearst challenged Pulitzer to a duel for subscribers. The battleground became events leading to the Spanish-American War. In 1897 artist-reporter Frederic Remington was ready to leave Cuba, believing that there was nothing of importance to report. Pulitzer is said to have cabled him: "Please remain. You furnish the pictures and I'll furnish the war." Hearst entered the journalistic battleground claiming that he was just doing his patriotic duty.

Smaller newspapers copied the style of Hearst and Pulitzer; their pages were filled with the same jingoism (extreme nationalism). Some thoughtful citizens were troubled when they realized that these journalists were not just reporting public opinion, but creating and controlling it. And the issue involved, entry into a war, was deadly serious. This was not the first time the American press had created rather than reflected opinion. But it had never happened before on such a wide scale.

Once this round with Hearst was over, Pulitzer quit the fight and decided to compete on a higher level. He turned his paper into a responsible journal. Although liberal, it did maintain high standards of journalism. He tried to raise standards for future journalists by endowing a School of Journalism at Columbia University in 1912. Hearst meanwhile created a chain of newspapers and bought magazines. He had political ambitions, but he was widely distrusted, and his ambitions were frustrated.

The Hearst press did leave a lasting legacy to journalism: the funnies, or Sunday comics. Trying to capture working-class families as readers, Hearst's Sunday *Journal* added an eight-page colored Sunday supplement in 1896. Hearst hired the artist who drew Pulitzer's "Yellow Kid" drawings away from him. The *Journal* then published the first real comic strip. Called the "Katzenjammer Kids," it was written by a cartoonist named Rudolph Dirks. Other comics included "Mutt and Jeff" and "Krazy Kat." Editors found that the funnies were the first part of the paper most people read. The funnies became a kind of American folk art expressing what some Americans thought or felt or at least what amused them.

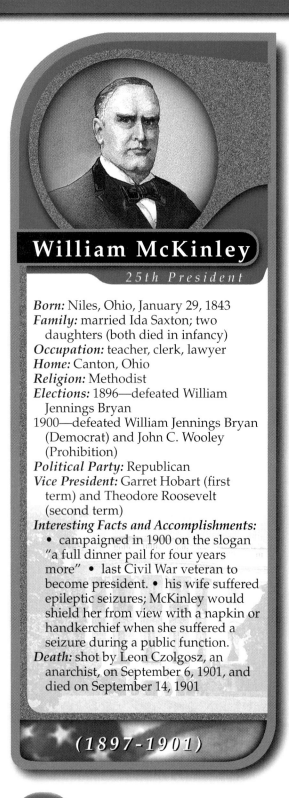

William McKinley

25th President

Born: Niles, Ohio, January 29, 1843
Family: married Ida Saxton; two daughters (both died in infancy)
Occupation: teacher, clerk, lawyer
Home: Canton, Ohio
Religion: Methodist
Elections: 1896—defeated William Jennings Bryan
1900—defeated William Jennings Bryan (Democrat) and John C. Wooley (Prohibition)
Political Party: Republican
Vice President: Garret Hobart (first term) and Theodore Roosevelt (second term)
Interesting Facts and Accomplishments:
 • campaigned in 1900 on the slogan "a full dinner pail for four years more" • last Civil War veteran to become president. • his wife suffered epileptic seizures; McKinley would shield her from view with a napkin or handkerchief when she suffered a seizure during a public function.
Death: shot by Leon Czolgosz, an anarchist, on September 6, 1901, and died on September 14, 1901

(1897–1901)

also added the **Teller amendment** to the resolution. It said that the United States had no intention of adding Cuba to its empire but desired only the independence of that land. This statement gave Americans confidence that further action would only help the Cubans, not further American imperialism.

Some believe that McKinley yielded to public pressure. McKinley believed Spain would never grant Cuba independence and that only independence would satisfy the American public. When Congress recognized Cuba's independence (even though Cuba did not have its own government at the time), Spain tried to uphold its honor by declaring war on the United States. And on April 25, 1898, the United States declared war on Spain.

Many historians today believe that United States involvement in the Spanish-American War was not justified. However, we need to remember that we are far removed from the feelings that Americans shared in 1898. It is much easier for us to pass judgment on events and motives of the past than it is to evaluate our own actions and motives honestly. As we study history, it is important that we not look at an event with only a modern, critical eye. We must also examine it in the context of the culture of that day, considering the information and attitudes we would have had if we had lived at that time.

Americans desired a better way of life for Cuba, and most honestly thought that the United States could help the Cubans achieve progress. As it turned out, however, their interest in Cuba opened the way for the expansion of American power and influence along with the problems of an empire.

Course of the War

The Spanish-American War was over in one hundred days. The United States was not really ready for a full-scale war, but the

After the destruction of the U.S.S. Maine, "Remember the Maine" became a call for action against the Spanish.

Spanish government and army were weak. The United States won every battle fought in this war.

Military Preparedness—Most of the fighting men came from the state's national guards. By late spring, troops had gathered at a military base in Tampa, Florida. Although the war would be fought in a subtropical area, many soldiers had been issued wool uniforms, and some cavalry troops lacked horses. But the invasion force sailed on June 14.

While the army fought bravely, and several regiments, such as the **Rough Riders,** gained special fame, the navy played the most important role. President Cleveland had approved a program to build a fleet of steel ships, and the ships now came in handy. More than anything, the navy's success showed that the United States had arrived as one of the world's great powers.

Battles of the Spanish-American War—Long before war was declared, Assistant

Theodore Roosevelt served as a colonel in the Spanish-American War and became a hero as the leader of the Rough Riders.

Secretary of the Navy **Theodore Roosevelt** sent secret orders to Commodore George Dewey, who was in Hong Kong with the American fleet in the Pacific. Roosevelt told Dewey to prepare for an attack on the Spanish fleet in the Philippines in case war broke out with Spain. The American force arrived in Manila on April 30 and met the Spanish fleet the next morning. By noon the **battle of Manila Bay** was over. No Americans died from wounds, though one engineer died from sunstroke. Spain lost 167 men and much of its fleet, and it was quickly defeated in the Pacific.

In the Caribbean, the American fleet was able to trap the Spanish fleet in the harbor at Santiago, which was then the capital of Cuba. American troops then came to storm their way to the city. The soldiers landed near Santiago and pushed the Spanish back to their defenses on San Juan Hill. Theodore Roosevelt's all-volunteer group, the "Rough Riders," was among the troops. Their famous charge up San Juan Hill helped defeat the Spanish on land while the Caribbean Spanish fleet lost every ship in a sea battle. On July 17 Santiago officially surrendered. The American army took Puerto Rico, another Spanish possession, without resistance on July 25.

When the war was officially over in August, fewer than four hundred American soldiers had died in battle or from combat wounds. Disease, however, took a far greater toll. Over five thousand died of typhoid, malaria, yellow fever, or other diseases.

The Treaty of Paris—The Spanish sued for peace and signed a truce on August 12, 1898. Spanish and American treaty commis-

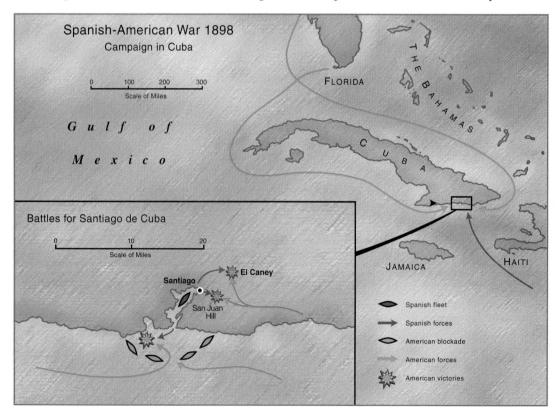

Spanish-American War 1898
Campaign in Cuba

0   100   200   300
Scale of Miles

Gulf of Mexico

THE BAHAMAS

FLORIDA

CUBA

Battles for Santiago de Cuba

0   10   20
Scale of Miles

El Caney

Santiago

San Juan Hill

JAMAICA

HAITI

Spanish fleet
Spanish forces
American blockade
American forces
American victories

sioners met in Paris on October 1, and by December 10, 1898, a treaty had been worked out. Spain agreed to give up its claim to Cuba and also to cede Guam and the Philippines in the Pacific and Puerto Rico in the Caribbean to the United States. In return the United States gave Spain $20 million.

However, a great debate soon ensued in the Senate. Influential anti-imperialists, including Charles Francis Adams, Andrew Carnegie, former presidents Cleveland and Harrison, and authors Mark Twain and William Dean Howells, opposed the treaty. They said the treaty violated the principles of the Monroe Doctrine. Only when William Jennings Bryan, the leader of the Democratic Party, supported the treaty and promised Filipino independence did the Senate ratify the treaty by a margin of two votes.

More New Territories and Responsibilities

By the terms of the peace treaty the United States, like it or not, now had an empire and all the problems that came with taking care of one.

Governing Cuba—The Teller Amendment had promised Cuba its independence. But until Cuba was ready for independence, the United States supervised the government. In 1901 Congress passed the **Platt amendment,** which gave Cuba strict regulations for its new independent government. In effect this legislation kept Cuba from alliances with countries other than the United States, allowed the United States to oversee Cuba's financial affairs, and authorized the United States to send forces to Cuba to keep order. This arrangement was not exactly "independence." In addition, the United States was permitted to establish and keep a navy base in Cuba. The U.S. Navy still uses the base at **Guantanamo Bay** today.

Despite its reluctance to give up control of Cuba after the war, the United States did a great deal to help the island. The tropical disease yellow fever was a scourge in the Caribbean. A Cuban doctor, Dr. Carlos Finlay, believed the disease was carried by a certain type of mosquito. An American army doctor, **Walter Reed,** proved that Finlay was right. Major **William Gorgas** (GOR gus) and a crew of army engineers then drained the swamps and low-lying areas and succeeded in getting rid of the water where the mosquitoes bred. The United States also provided food and clothing for the poor and built roads, schools, railroads, and hospitals.

Puerto Rico—The United States gave Puerto Rico much of the same aid that Cuba received. Puerto Rico also got special economic considerations such as duty-free trade with the United States. This trade benefitted the sugar industry. Puerto Rico was also exempted from having to contribute to the United States federal treasury. In 1917 under the Jones Act, Puerto Rico became a territory with a governor appointed by the president and a two-house legislative assembly. In 1952, at Puerto Rico's request, it became a commonwealth, a freely associated part of the United States.

Governing the Philippines—Many Americans were skeptical about taking the Philippines, a land made up of over seven thousand Pacific islands. It would be hard for the United States to provide even the most basic government to rule the people of the entire area. Since the Filipinos were largely uneducated and had almost no experience in self-government, the United States would have trouble helping them set up a republican form of government. Opponents also held that annexing the Philippines violated the American ideal of liberty and might even be unconstitutional. Some even believed that the United States's presence in the Philippines

might involve the United States in a needless foreign war.

Nonetheless, President McKinley believed that if left to itself, the Philippines might be taken over by another major power or fall into anarchy. The land would also make a good base for trade with China, and American missionaries could go to help the Filipinos. McKinley's view won, and Congress decided to take over the islands.

The Philippines had long fought against Spanish rule, under the leadership of **Emilio Aguinaldo.** When the United States won the war, Aguinaldo and his followers hoped that the Philippines would be given their independence. The news of the takeover by the United States angered the Filipinos, and Aguinaldo and his forces went to work again. The United States then had to fight the rebels for two and one-half years to suppress the insurrection. This problem cost the United States far more time, military expense, and casualties than had the entire Spanish-American War.

The United States worked to prepare the Philippines for eventual independence by establishing a public school system to train Filipinos for citizenship. Hospitals, railroads, power plants, and greatly improved communication systems were also built. The islands were ruled for a few years by American governors. In the year 1934 the islands were granted commonwealth status. World War II

New responsibilities in Cuba, Puerto Rico, the Philippines, and elsewhere forced the United States to commit troops to the defense and administration of those lands.

442

delayed Philippine independence, however, until July 4, 1946.

SECTION REVIEW

1. What were the two immediate causes of the Spanish-American War?
2. What did the Teller amendment state?
3. How long did the Spanish-American War last?
4. What were the provisions of the treaty that ended the Spanish-American War?
5. Who was Emilio Aguinaldo? Why did he cause problems for the United States?

 How did American journalists contribute to the outbreak of the Spanish-American War?

American Foreign Policy

As American interests widened in the late 1800s, United States foreign policy began to steer away from isolationism. The government was no longer careful to stay out of disputes between foreign countries if it was to America's advantage to become involved. If American trade and power could be advanced, the United States began to get involved in world affairs, especially those in Latin America and eastern Asia.

In Latin America

Ever since the Monroe Doctrine, the United States protected its American neighbors. In 1867 the United States drove French forces out of Mexico. In 1895 the U.S. forced Britain to allow American mediations of a boundary dispute between Venezuela and British Guinea. By 1900, the United States was ready to take its place as leader of the Western Hemisphere.

The Panama Canal—A first priority for the United States in Latin America was to build a canal. American naval officers had been pressing for the building of a canal across Central America. A canal would enable the few ships in the American fleet to defend both the Atlantic and Pacific coasts more easily. The Spanish-American War helped prove the point. It took two months to sail a warship from Puget Sound to the East Coast by way of the Cape Horn of South America.

The idea of a canal was not new. In 1851 the United States and England had signed a treaty to build an inter-ocean canal open to both nations. The construction of a canal, however, eventually fell to a French company headed by Ferdinand de Lesseps (LES ups), builder of the Suez Canal. The French chose a route across the Isthmus of Panama. But when the project took much longer than expected, the company went bankrupt. The United States then stepped in to take over the project.

Although the United States had considered an alternate route across Nicaragua, it decided to pursue the Panama canal. Since Panama was legally a part of Colombia, the United States now took steps to obtain the land from Colombia. The United States offered Colombia $10 million for the right to build the canal and an annual rental fee of $250,000. Colombia refused, holding out for $25 million.

Meanwhile, leaders in Panama wanted independence. America realized that if there were a revolt against Colombia, and Panama gained its independence, the new Panamanian government would gladly sell the United States rights for a canal. No time was wasted. Several American warships moved into positions off the coast on November 2, 1903. The next day Panamanians rioted and declared their independence from Colombia. When Colombia tried to send troops, American ships conveniently blocked the harbors. Then the rebels overcame the Colombian opposition within the country. On November 6, President Roosevelt used his presidential power to

extend diplomatic recognition to the new nation of Panama.

On November 18, 1903, the United States signed the **Hay-Bunau-Varilla Treaty** with Panama. Negotiated by Secretary of State **John Hay** and Panama's new foreign minister, Philippe Bunau-Varilla (byoo-NOH va-REE-ya), the terms were generous. The United States received perpetual use of a ten-mile-wide strip of land. This "canal zone" would be controlled and fortified by the United States, and the canal built on it would be open to all nations on equal terms through payment of tolls. Eleven years later, the **Panama Canal** opened.

Theodore Roosevelt and the Big Stick— Theodore Roosevelt operated his foreign policy in Latin America with the same zest he showed in his charge up San Juan Hill. He summarized his policy by saying:, "I have always been fond of the West African proverb, 'Speak softly and carry a big stick, and you will go far!'" Roosevelt believed that the United States was the most important nation in the Western Hemisphere; in fact, he believed that this hemisphere was actually an American sphere of influence and that the Caribbean was an American lake. Roosevelt's foreign policy relied on America's military strength to persuade foreign nations to act properly, and this became known as the **"big stick" policy.**

In 1902, Britain, Germany, and Italy sent warships to blockade Venezuelan ports to collect unpaid loans. Venezuela asked the United States to intervene, and Great Britain asked Roosevelt to mediate. He eagerly obliged, but he saw the incident as a warning that European interests in Latin America were growing. This European presence was perhaps a possible violation of the Monroe Doctrine of 1823. Hence he made a new policy to clear up any misunderstanding: the **Roosevelt Corollary** to the Monroe Doctrine. In this statement the United States asserted the right to be an "international police power" in the Western Hemisphere. Whenever a country was guilty of long-term wrongdoing, the United States reserved the right to intervene.

Digging the Big Ditch

Building the Panama Canal was no easy task. The United States first attacked the problem of disease in the isthmus. Colonel William Gorgas and his workers made war on the mosquitoes that spread yellow fever and malaria and on the rats that carried the dreaded bubonic plague. By 1906 swamps had been drained and brush and grassy marshes eliminated.

An army engineer, Colonel George W. Goethals, supervised construction of the canal itself. Sixty-eight huge steam shovels hacked away. For seven years Goethals supervised 43,000 workers, 5,000 of whom were Americans. The final cost came to $400 million.

On August 5, 1914, the *Ancon* became the first ship to pass through the completed canal, saving almost seven thousand of travel. The formal opening of the canal, under President Woodrow Wilson, came on July 12, 1915. Most of the credit for completing the canal was claimed by Theodore Roosevelt. "If I had followed traditional, conservative methods," he said in 1911, "the debates on it would have been going on yet; but I took the Canal Zone and let Congress debate: and while the debate goes on, the Canal does also."

One of Teddy Roosevelt's hobbies was big-game hunting. This room at Sagamore Hill displays some of his trophies.

Because of Roosevelt's policy, the United States would send forces to Cuba, Venezuela, the Dominican Republic, Haiti, Nicaragua, Guatemala, and Mexico throughout the next sixty years. Although the policy kept European powers out of Latin America and made Americans happy by protecting their financial interests, some Latin Americans began to regard the United States as an unwelcome powerful neighbor, "the colossus of the North."

Dollar Diplomacy and Moral Diplomacy—Roosevelt's successors modified his policy slightly. **William Howard Taft** substituted dollars for bullets, a policy known as **"dollar diplomacy."** American investments in Latin America helped those countries develop their industries and improve the lives of their peoples. If the Latin American countries did not follow the wishes of the United States, investments could be withdrawn.

Woodrow Wilson and his secretary of state, William Jennings Bryan, turned the policy into **"moral diplomacy."** They wanted to use negotiation in international affairs. Not wanting to pressure countries into decisions, Wilson wished to talk these countries into following the example of the United States. He believed that "the force of America is the force of moral principle." Wilson tried to promote democratic principles and secure American interests overseas while maintaining peace on all fronts. Wilson's policy proved overly idealistic, and before he left office the president had been forced to send troops into the Dominican Republic, Haiti, and Mexico.

In Asia

In the late 1800s China was becoming one of the most profitable trading spots in the world. Britain, France, Germany, Russia, and Japan had divided China into **"spheres of influence."** Each of these countries controlled all the trading operations within its "sphere," or division of the country. The United States, however, had missed out in this arrangement and was now ready to seek some trading opportunities of its own.

China and the Open Door Policy—Some of the foreign powers in China wanted more than control of trade—they wanted land. Some European nations as well as Japan began to seize land, literally creating their own colonies. The United States objected to such European and Asian colonization in China. Americans wanted all of China to be open to everyone.

In 1899 Secretary of State John Hay sent a series of circular letters to those countries involved in China. These memos formally stated an **Open Door Policy.** No nation would have its own sphere any longer: all of China would be open to all nations on equal terms. No more Chinese land was to be seized. Germany and Japan were not at all eager to follow this policy, but to go against it, they would have to risk the wrath of two major powers, America and Britain. Consequently, Germany and Japan agreed. Since Chinese territories were not united and no army existed to protect them, China had no choice but to tolerate the invasion of foreign traders. Even so, some Chinese took action. They formed a secret group called the Society of Righteous and Harmonious Fists. Foreigners called them the Boxers because one of their rituals was shadowboxing.

The Boxers decided to force all foreigners to leave China. The uprising began in rural areas and then moved to Peking (now Beijing), the capital of China. The Boxers surrounded the sections of the city where foreigners lived and terrorized the foreigners. Some foreigners were murdered. Boxers also attacked and killed many Chinese Christians. The foreigners and Chinese Christians took refuge together and tried to hold out until help could arrive.

The United States acted to protect the lives of its citizens. The first relief expedition on June 10, 1900, was forced back. By August, John Hay had played European powers against each other enough to engineer an international force of twenty thousand men. These soldiers marched from Tientsin (TIN tsin) to Peking and freed the hostages.

Some of the eleven countries involved thought they should get land. But under the Boxer Protocol, signed September 7, 1901, none of them did. Ten high Chinese officials responsible for the **Boxer Rebellion** were executed and twenty-five Chinese forts destroyed. Giving up, China had to make damage payments totaling $333 million over the next forty years.

The United States government put most of its share into a fund for educating Chinese students in America. Schools and colleges in China were also built with this money. In addition, American churches and mission boards sent personnel and money to China. Because of such efforts, the Chinese response to the United States was friendlier than to other imperialist powers. The United States and China remained friends until the Communists took over that land in 1949.

The United States and Japan—After Commodore Matthew Perry and the United States Navy opened Japan to trade with the outside world in 1853, Japan quickly grew to be a powerful Asian country. In less than forty years Japan transformed itself into a modern industrial nation. Japan also gained the technical know-how that allowed it to become a modern military power. It became a militaristic nation by building up a strong army and navy.

Being a militaristic nation is a short step from being an imperialistic one. Japan had demanded a sphere of influence from China, and in 1894 and 95 the Japanese easily defeated the Chinese and took the land they wanted. The Japanese also joined the international force that defeated the Boxers, and in 1905 they defeated Russia in the Russo-Japanese War.

John Hay and President Roosevelt sought to use American power in Asia to maintain a **balance of power.** President Roosevelt could see that Japan would soon be one of the great powers and might be a threat to the rest of the world. He believed that the power of the United States could be used to offset Japan's power and that the United States should command the respect of the world. In 1905 President Roosevelt persuaded representatives from Russia and Japan to meet him at Portsmouth, New Hampshire. There he helped negotiate a treaty that maintained a balance of power in Asia while upholding Chinese independence. For his efforts he became the first American president to win a Nobel Prize for Peace.

In 1907 Roosevelt made a dramatic show of American military strength. He sent the entire U.S. battle fleet on a world cruise. While Congress protested the expense, the Great White Fleet, as the American ships were called, sailed on. The fleet visited the Japanese ports and so impressed the Japanese that their imperialistic designs were curbed for the time being.

SECTION REVIEW

1. Why did American naval officers want the United States to build the Panama Canal?
2. What were the terms of the Hay-Bunau-Varilla Treaty?
3. What famous quotation summarizes Theodore Roosevelt's foreign policy?
4. Who was John Hay? What policy did he propose for relations with China?
5. Who were the "Boxers"?
6. Why did Roosevelt send the U.S. battle fleet on a world cruise?

Contrast the diplomatic philosophies of Theodore Roosevelt, William Howard Taft, and Woodrow Wilson.

SUMMARY

As imperialism became a common practice among the world's nations in the late 1800s, the United States began to break away from its traditional isolationist stance. After acquiring Alaska, Hawaii, and Midway Island peacefully, it entered the Spanish-American War in 1898. Although the United States intended only to aid Cuba, the war also resulted in adding new territories to the United States. The United States also began to boldly assert its strong position in world affairs after the turn of the century. American strength brought about the building of the Panama Canal, the opening of China to more foreign trade, and the establishment of the leadership of the United States in the Western Hemisphere.

Chapter Review

People, Places, and Things to Remember

isolationism	Teller amendment	Panama Canal
imperialism	Rough Riders	big stick policy
humanitarianism	Theodore Roosevelt	Roosevelt Corollary
Dwight L. Moody	battle of Manila Bay	William Howard Taft
Spanish-American War	Platt amendment	dollar diplomacy
yellow journalism	Guantanamo Bay	Woodrow Wilson
William Randolph Hearst	Walter Reed	moral diplomacy
Joseph Pulitzer	William Gorgas	spheres of influence
William McKinley	Emilio Aguinaldo	Open Door Policy
Dupuy de Lôme	Hay-Bunau-Varilla Treaty	Boxer Rebellion
U.S.S. *Maine*	John Hay	balance of power

Review Questions

Match these terms with their descriptions.

1. exploitation
2. humanitarianism
3. imperialism
4. isolationism
5. yellow journalism

a. meeting the physical needs of poor people
b. distorting the news to make it more exciting
c. taking advantage of a people's weakness
d. not getting involved in world affairs
e. taking control of foreign lands

Match each of the items below with the president with whom it is most closely associated.

6. moral diplomacy
7. de Lôme Letter
8. dollar diplomacy
9. "big stick" policy

a. William McKinley
b. Theodore Roosevelt
c. William Howard Taft
d. Woodrow Wilson

Fill in the blanks.

10. The sinking of the __ helped to trigger the Spanish-American War.

11. The __ assured Americans that action against Spain was intended to secure Cuban independence and not to build an American empire.

12. __ was a leader in the Philippines who wanted independence for his land.

13. Secretary of State __ negotiated a treaty with Panama and helped establish the Open Door Policy with China.

14. Several countries gained trading privileges in areas called __ in China.

15. The __ staged a rebellion in China because of their dislike for foreigners.

Questions for Discussion

16. Is humanitarianism good or bad? Explain your answer.

17. Does the news media still use yellow journalism today? Explain your answer.

History Skills

Sensationalism, Jingoism, and Impartiality

After the newspaper war of 1898, Pulitzer encouraged impartiality in his paper and tried to avoid sensationalism and jingoism. *Impartiality* means "not favoring one side of an issue." *Sensationalism* is "the use of exaggeration or shocking details to arouse curiosity." *Jingoism* is "loud support for aggressive action toward other countries." Decide whether each statement below shows *sensationalism, jingoism,* or *impartiality.*

1. The Cubans have rebelled because they believe their Spanish rulers have grossly mistreated them.

2. The Spanish devils have painted the town squares red with the blood of Cubans fighting for freedom.

3. American honor demands swift action against Spain because de Lôme dared to insult our president.

4. Clara Barton was one of the many nurses who rushed to the Havana harbor to care for the wounded American sailors.

5. The American army in Cuba has been almost wiped out by the dreaded yellow fever. Everywhere you look you can see dead bodies and feverish soldiers waiting to die.

6. Unless Congress ratifies the Treaty of Paris and takes its share of new territories, America is doomed to become a second-rate nation.

7. Dr. Walter Reed has proved that mosquitoes carry the deadly yellow fever.

8. If pip-squeak Colombia thinks it can blackmail America for $25 million, we'll show them who calls the shots around here!

9. The day before Panama declared its independence, American warships moved into position off the coast.

10. Before Gorgas went to work clearing the swamps, the rats were so thick that you couldn't take a step without touching one, and the mosquitoes were so thick they blocked the sun.

Extra! Extra! On another sheet of paper, rewrite the sentences that contain sensationalism or jingoism so that they are impartial.

Bring me your tired, your poor,
Your huddled masses yearning to breathe free,
The retched refuse of your teaming shore.
Send these, the homeless, tempest-tossed to me.
I lift my lamp beside the golden door.

(Engraved at the base of the Statue of Liberty)

For Americans the question "What nationality are you?" is sometimes hard to answer. Unlike people in many other countries, few Americans can trace their roots to the earliest inhabitants of this country. Many Americans have a long list of nationalities attached to their family history.

There have been several major waves of immigration. The first came in the early 1700s. At that time Pennsylvanian colonists began to worry about German and Scotch-Irish immigrants flooding into the colony. At least the Scotch-Irish spoke English, but the Germans? Colonists were sure that the Germans would change the whole colony, but they did not. The Pennsylvania Dutch (from the German word *Deutsch,* meaning "German") established a profitable farming region and became established members of early American society.

The next two waves of immigration occurred from the early nineteenth century to the early twentieth century. More than thirty million Europeans flooded into the United States. At first the immigrants came from Western Europe, but by the close of the century, most of the immigrants came from Eastern European countries. Many Jews facing persecution in Europe came to the United States in the early 1900s.

Another wave of immigration arrived in the 1980s and 1990s as Hispanic and Asian immigrants came into the nation. Refugees from Haiti and Cuba established large communities in New York City and Miami. Mexican immigrants crossed the border into America legally and illegally. Many went to Southern California to work on truck farms as migrant workers. (Truck farms are vegetable farms located within easy trucking distance to distribution centers.) Southeast Asians came into America fleeing poverty and government oppression.

Since the first colonist made landfall in North America, immigration has been a source of benefit and trouble. Each group that establishes dominance in a region feels threatened when newcomers enter that area. But newcomers often fill an important place in society. They bring new skills or are willing to work at important but low-paying jobs. By becoming productive citizens, they encourage growth in the economy. Why is it then that people are sometimes so resistant to new immigrants?

Three fears have dominated America's reaction to immigration. American's biggest fear has been that the new people will take jobs away from American citizens. In the early years when most Americans were farmers, there was plenty of land for all, and immigrants seemed less threatening to the economy. But as the country's economy focused on industry and people moved into the cities, citizens felt more threatened. In the late 1870s this fear was caused by the influx of Chinese immigrants, whose backbreaking labor made the Union Pacific Railroad possible. The Chinese immigrants were willing to do the hardest labor for long hours and low pay. Plus, they were willing to live without many of the special foods and other comforts that many Californians felt were essential. In reality, the Chinese did not take American jobs; Americans gave them up. When the railroad was finished, the Chinese created new jobs for themselves. However, when economic depression and crop failure hit California, politicians easily stirred opinions of worried Californians against immigrants. Emotions were so inflamed that in 1882 the Chinese Exclusion Act, which banned most Chinese from immigration, was passed. The ban remained in effect until World War II.

Another fear about immigration has been that American tax dollars will have to pay to take care of unemployed foreign-born citizens. However, statistics show that, except in isolated areas and in the case of illegal immigrants, the incomes of foreign-born citizens are the same as or higher than those of their American-born counterparts. Just like the Chinese in the 1800s, many new immigrants are quick to work long hours for less pay and to do without things that American-born citizens think are essential. They also often combine family incomes to increase their standard of living.

As the trend in twentieth-century immigration has moved from Europe to South America, Asia, and underdeveloped countries, Americans are especially afraid that immigrants will change the nation. Immigrants do change America. From the beginning of our nation, every new group that has entered the Land of Opportunity has brought with it new ideas and new ways of doing things. These changes have brought challenges. Americans struggle with incorporating the newcomers into society, providing them with jobs, educating their children, and understanding their cultures.

In *Letters from an American Farmer,* written in 1782, J. Hector St. John Crévecoeur expressed his thoughts about this new nation filled with immigrants: "Here individuals of all nations are melted into a new race of men, whose labors and posterity will one day cause great changes in the world."

Melt they did, not by losing their original heritage and culture but by incorporating it with a shared American culture. Most people who have been here since their birth say, "I am an American," even if their parents are natives of a different country halfway around the world. And Americans did change the world. The United States' influence has mixed into the big cities around the world until travelers find the same language, hotels, fast-food restaurants, music, and entertainment available wherever they go.

For the Christian, the challenge is great. As the United States leaves its original standard of biblical morality, government is more accepting of other religions and cultures that do not honor God. But the challenge to Christians is not to fight against immigration and different cultures but to spread the gospel. God in His providence has brought all nations to America. In the United States, faithful Christians can present the gospel to all nations by simply walking across the street and telling their neighbors.

"Er . . . I can't spell that . . . From now on you will be known as Mr. Bobo Clown."

22

Progressivism

he last few years of the nineteenth century and the first few years of the twentieth century were exciting for America. These years contained good prospects for growth as a world power and as a prosperous nation. Cities and industries were expanding while technology was making more and more conveniences available to the American people. Yet while life in the United States had so much to offer, it also held many problems. Sins such as greed, dishonesty, and immorality afflicted the nation then as they afflict all nations. In recognition of the evils of society, many Americans began to try to right the wrongs and cure the ills in hopes of achieving social progress. Making life in America even better through reform was the goal of these "progressives," and their movement was called **progressivism.**

Changing American Life

Life was changing in the United States. New living and working conditions, new opportunities, new possessions, and new attitudes resulted from the changes and also brought more changes. Americans soon found that while some of these changes were pleasant, others were full of problems.

More People

The population of the United States at the turn of the century was seventy-five million, and it was growing by over a million a year. Involved in this tremendous growth were a trend toward urbanization and the contribution of immigration.

By 1900 **urbanization** (UR bun ih ZAY shun), the movement of people to cities, had changed America. There were more cities, and the population in the cities was growing. Many young people reared in rural areas had moved to the cities seeking greater opportunities. Between 1860 and 1910 the percentage of Americans involved in agriculture decreased from sixty percent to thirty-one percent. By 1920 more than one-half of America's population lived in towns and cities. Urban areas, especially large cities such as New York, Philadelphia, Boston, and Chicago, became sprawling giants. Inner-city areas were often plagued by crowded tenements (apartments), poor sanitation, crime, and poverty.

A New York City policeman inspects the cluttered basement living room of a tenement house around 1900.

America welcomed 5.2 million immigrants in the 1880s, 3.7 million in the 1890s, and in the peak decade between 1901 and 1910, 8.8 million. Almost all these immigrants faced problems in adjusting to their new home. In fact, not all of the original immigrants would become "Americanized." That plateau would be reached, however, by most of their children. Most of them learned English quickly, although the first few months of their early education was difficult. Few schools at this time offered bilingual education. Many foreign parents opposed it because they wanted their offspring to become a part of American life as quickly as possible.

The new immigrant groups contributed a great deal to the building of America. They extracted raw materials from the land and became the work force for many of America's diverse new industries. But immigrants brought more than labor. They brought the traditions and customs of their homelands as well, including their foods, music, and literature. All these things added more diversity to America's unique culture.

More Opportunity

America's millions were able to enjoy many opportunities to improve their lives and amuse themselves.

Education—Education was becoming more widespread. Throughout much of the 1800s, public education had been available at taxpayer's expense only on the elementary level. In 1860 there were only three hundred secondary schools in America, and only one hundred of them did not charge tuition. But by 1900, six thousand free secondary schools existed and by 1915, twelve thousand.

Opportunities for higher education reflected the same trend. Throughout the Civil War era, upper-class white males were about the only people who attended colleges or universities. By 1900, however, increasing numbers of people, including blacks and women, enrolled, and those who did go to college had a wider choice of study. Many new curriculums designed to prepare students for more specific professions were introduced. For example, schools in agriculture and the mechanical arts multiplied, more elective courses became available, and more graduate schools offered advanced training.

Some of the colleges and universities were aided by millionaire businessmen who provided endowments (large sums of money) to finance specific programs or salaries. Some even founded schools. Tulane (1834), Cornell (1865), Drew (1866), Vanderbilt (1873), Johns

Hopkins (1876), and Stanford (1885) all bear the names of such educational **philanthropists** (fih LAN thruh pists; wealthy people who donate money to charitable causes). Philadelphia's Temple University (1884) was established by Russell Conway to educate young men who had talent and the desire to succeed but who lacked the money. The University of Chicago (1890) was founded with gifts made by John D. Rockefeller.

More educational opportunities also became available for women. In the Midwest and in the West women had an easier time getting university educations than elsewhere. They were admitted to most programs and attended classes with the men. But in the East women tended to be educated separately in women's colleges. It was unusual for women to attend state universities. Those who did needed to be strongly motivated in order to outlast the ridicule of male students.

Blacks were able to go to college too, but they almost always attended segregated schools founded just for them. The first black university, Lincoln University in Pennsylvania, opened its doors in 1854. Nashville's Fisk University and Howard University in Washington, D.C., were both founded in 1867.

The most famous black school was **Tuskegee** (tus KEE gee) **Institute** in Alabama, founded by **Booker T. Washington,** a self-educated former slave. The school's philosophy focused on hard work, self-worth, and self-reliance. An Iowa-educated botanist, Dr. **George Washington Carver,** aided the school's reputation and finances through his work. He found more than 300 new uses for the peanut and 118 uses for the sweet potato. He also explored ways to use pecans. His work was important because it helped the South become less dependent on its cotton crop.

A Rising Middle Class—Education and opportunities to work and advance in business

Self-educated Booker T. Washington founded Tuskegee Institute in 1881 as the first institution dedicated to the education of black Americans.

and industry helped many Americans improve their standard of living. A significant number of people who had been penniless immigrants, poor farmers, or poverty-stricken factory workers had found a way to improve their situation. Hard work and some business sense could bring financial gain. The fact that a person was born in poverty did not condemn him to stay there.

Only a few Americans became millionaires, and some never escaped poverty, but many Americans joined the ranks of the middle class. They had enough money to enjoy a comfortable home, adequate food, and some of the newly available consumer goods.

Leisure Time Activities

In the early 1800s, factories, mines, and other employers often demanded that their laborers work six days a week, often for a total of seventy hours or more. Complaints against such long hours (and the poor conditions and wages that often accompanied such labor) began to bring great changes during the era of progressivism. By 1910 the average workweek had dropped to 54.6 hours. Such a change gave many Americans some leisure time—time they could use to improve themselves or enjoy recreation and amusements.

Interest in both spectator sports and sports participation mushroomed. Baseball, basketball, and football were all relatively new sports that had developed in the United States. All three were popular, but baseball became the favorite. The first World Series took place in 1903. After baseball, boxing was America's most popular sport of the era. Watching heavyweights fight it out attracted many crowds. Rollerskating and bicycling were new crazes of the day, and many other sports, such as golf and tennis, were gaining attention.

Besides sports, amusement parks, concerts, theaters, and other attractions offered entertainment for Americans. There was a

Samuel L. Clemens is better known as Mark Twain.

surge of interest in opera and classical music, especially in areas where European immigrants had settled. Many symphony orchestra members and almost all the conductors had been born overseas. Of course immigrants packed the concert halls to listen to the music of European composers.

Although reading books was not new, literature did take on new importance in the era. Throughout the 1800s more people who became part of the middle class could read and had money for books. Reading then became more popular. Americans were especially fond of new American themes and regional settings. The most popular American writer of the day was **Samuel L. Clemens,** whose pen name was Mark Twain.

Magazines appealing to literary circles were common in the 1800s. But because they were expensive (thirty-five cents per issue), magazines like *Harper's* and the *Atlantic Monthly* never enjoyed wide circulation. The invention of better printing presses and better methods of making paper eventually lowered prices. Publisher Hermann Cyrus Curtis introduced *Ladies' Home Journal* for ten cents a copy and *Saturday Evening Post* for only a nickel.

Different Values

America had received a godly heritage from its early Pilgrim and Puritan fathers. Even through the 1700s and early 1800s, most of the people who came to America were from a Protestant background. While many were not true Christians, most of these earlier Americans had a respect for the Bible as the Word of God and a belief in its moral standards. The immigration of the 1800s and the changes in American society, however, greatly altered the nation's religious attitudes.

Between 1860 and 1910 almost twenty-one million immigrants entered the United States. Some German immigrants were Lutheran, some Roman Catholic, and others rationalists (those who exalted man's reason above the revelation of God's Word). Most immigrants from Ireland were strong Roman Catholics. Later groups of Scandinavian immigrants were largely Lutheran, while Italian immigrants were usually Roman Catholics. Immigrants from eastern Europe were a mixed group including Mennonites, Russian Orthodox, Catholics, and Jews.

Almost all churches increased their memberships in these years, including the well-known "mainline" denominations such as the Methodists, Presbyterians, and Baptists. When some people began to feel that mainline denominations were not meeting their needs, they formed new denominations, such as the Holiness and Pentecostal groups. Several newly organized cults that denied some biblical truths also began during this period. For example, Mary Baker Eddy founded Christian Science, which teaches that "matter and death are mental illusions," as are sin, pain, and disease. Seventh-Day Adventism grew under the leadership of Ellen G. Harmon White. Another cult, the Jehovah's Witnesses (Watchtower Society), was founded in 1872 by Charles Taze Russell. These cults offered attractive ideas to religious Americans who lacked knowledge of Bible doctrines. The cults won great followings, but they also blinded people to the truths of God's Word.

As German rationalists and some theologians cast doubts on the truth of Scripture, their ideas began to break down the standards of many religious groups in America. Some people began to accept the notion that the Bible was just a good book written by man. Men began to think that they had the right to examine Scripture and to say what parts were right and what parts were in error. This "liberalism" led ministers to emphasize a social

During the time of increased immigration, church membership across the nation grew.

This temperance banner shows a table filled with the other vices associated with drinking.

lished. Written by **Charles Darwin,** *Origin of Species* proposed a theory of evolution. While most Americans did not readily accept evolution at that time, the theory began to influence both science and religious thought. In 1874 **Charles Hodge,** a leading conservative theologian, made what was probably the most successful attack on evolution. He attacked the evolutionary idea of natural selection, showing that it contradicted the existence of an all-powerful, all-knowing Creator.

While religious liberalism and other common philosophies prompted men to humanitarianism, they also hardened many Americans in their sin. But many Bible-believing pastors and evangelists were still preaching salvation through Christ. The existence of both liberal religion and true Christianity in American culture led to a mixture of religious goals in the progressive era. Some endeavors sincerely sought to reach souls for Christ. Others aimed at improving morals or living conditions, and some tried to do both.

Temperance Groups—The heavy use of alcohol had become a big problem in many areas of the country. Some immigrant groups were particularly heavy drinkers, and their actions were offensive to many others. Wherever alcoholism occurred, abuse of family members, increased poverty, and crime often followed.

Many religious Americans saw the need to correct the problem and formed **temperance societies** to fight against the evils of liquor. Most of them were associated with the Women's Christian Temperance Union (1874) or the Anti-Saloon League (1893). The efforts of these societies, combined with the efforts of evangelists who preached against the sin of drunkenness, led to the prohibition movement.

Interdenominational Organizations—Laymen founded interdenominational organizations that crossed church boundary lines.

gospel because doing good to mankind was obviously right. Many quit preaching the true gospel—repentance from sin and faith in Jesus Christ, who alone can give salvation—because they wished to think that man could solve his own problems. The focus of many American churches was quickly changing from God's provision for man's eternal need to man's abilities to solve temporal needs.

Some men, called **agnostics,** even scoffed at the existence of God, saying that man cannot know whether there is a God. The most famous agnostic, **Robert Ingersoll,** traveled the country giving lectures. People paid to hear him mock true faith, though many attended his lectures more out of curiosity than agreement.

In 1859 in England, one of the influential works of the nineteenth century was pub-

"Rescue the Perishing"

As American cities grew in the 1800s, so did their problems. Sections of large cities such as New York became slum areas,—places where the poor, usually immigrants, lived close together in dirty, noisy tenements. The main "entertainment" in the slums was often found in saloons, where drinking, gambling, and other vices took much of the little money that the people had. Churches tended to move away from the slums, locating where more prosperous and "respectable" people could support them.

Some Christians did try to reach the people in the slums. They held services in rented halls, passed out tracts, and attempted to witness to the people. One man, Jerry McAuley, wanted to do more. Born in Ireland in 1837, he came to New York City at the age of thirteen. McAuley soon became a thief; at the age of nineteen he was arrested for robbery and sent to prison.

In prison McAuley was converted through the testimony of a former convict. After getting out, McAuley thought that Christians were not doing enough to help the real "down-and-outs"—the drunks, prostitutes, and others who dwelt in the worst parts of the city. He decided to start a "rescue mission," a work located in the slums and designed to "rescue" people from sin. His Water Street Mission in New York City is usually considered the first rescue mission in the United States.

Probably the most famous rescue mission is the Pacific Garden Mission in Chicago. This mission was started in 1877 by Colonel George Clark and his wife, Sarah Dunn. D. L. Moody helped to name it. Thousands of people were reached for Christ through the Pacific Garden Mission. In 1886 a half-drunk baseball player named Billy Sunday heard a group of mission workers singing on a street corner. He followed them back to the Garden, where he was converted. Later, of course, he became a well-known evangelist.

Other people started rescue missions in other cities. Mel Trotter, for example, began a successful work in Grand Rapids, Michigan, and later helped found missions in other cities. Trotter loved the mission work because he had been saved in a mission. In 1897 he had stumbled into the Pacific Garden Mission. Although it was January, he was barefoot because he had sold his shoes to buy a drink. Converted, Trotter dedicated his life to reaching people like himself who had reached the bottom physically, mentally, and spiritually.

Rescue mission work varied in operation from city to city. Usually missions were open day and night to minister to anyone who came in. Services normally consisted of the singing of gospel songs, testimonies of converted sinners from the slums, and simple salvation sermons. The missions also tried to provide hot meals and a place to stay, at least for a night or two. Some more ambitious missions tried to provide work for their people. In these missions the people repaired clothing, made brooms, or did some other kind of work to help pay for their room and board.

Poor children such as these in Washington, D.C., were reached by gospel missions.

The Young Men's Christian Association (YMCA), which had originated in England, came to America. The "Y," as it was called, stressed four areas of growth: physical, educational, social, and religious. Another group of British origin was the Salvation Army. It provided relief for the poor and set up rescue missions to convert and rebuild the lives of those people who knew only defeat. Various other groups began rescue missions to work with such people. Probably the most famous rescue mission is Chicago's Pacific Garden Mission, founded in 1877. Other groups set up missions to work with specific immigrant groups.

Foreign Missions and Evangelistic Efforts—Americans were also concerned about taking the gospel to others. America sent out more missionary workers than any other country. The evangelistic and cultural impact of Christianity was so great at the end of the nineteenth century that some historians have called it the "Great Century of Christian Missions."

Important throughout the era was the work of evangelists and revival leaders. Camp meetings were held, but tents and brush arbors were abandoned for woodframe tabernacles. Some groups even held meetings at modern campgrounds with cabins for the visitors to stay in.

SECTION REVIEW

1. What is urbanization?

2. Who founded Tuskegee Institute?

3. List at least three ways in which the American laborer used his newly acquired leisure time.

4. What was one reason for the increased diversity of religious groups from 1860 to 1910?

5. List at least three cults that began during this time.

6. What does an agnostic believe?

7. What was the purpose of the temperance groups?

 How did German rationalism lead religion towards the social gospel?

The Progressive Era

Besides its growing spiritual needs, America's growing and changing society was beset with many other problems. Some of the problems were very big—too big for individuals to solve alone. The progressives began to look for help in solving America's problems. More and more they looked to government for the answers.

Progressive Aims

Progressives sought to abolish corruption and unfair practices in government, industry, labor, and even society. They were able to make permanent changes in the way the cities, the states, and the nation were governed, although social reforms were harder to accomplish.

A second progressive aim was to give people more say in governing. Some progressives believed that the evils of government could be cured by making government more democratic (giving individual citizens more power over laws and government officials). Some governmental practices thought commonplace today, such as primary elections and voting by secret ballot, were started by progressives.

Third, progressives believed that the quality of life in America could be improved by government. Many thought that government should improve society, that government was to be a minister of good. Some of the progressive ideals were definitely moral in tone. Combating crime in cities, establishing prohibition, and eliminating prostitution were among such moral aims.

Uncovering Corruption

Progressives sought to correct widespread corruption through reform. Corruption existed on all levels of government: city, state, and national. In New York City, for example, William Marcy **"Boss" Tweed** milked the city of millions of dollars by using city funds to give himself and his friends large profits on city contracts. One example of corruption on the state level was the bribing of officials to give special favors to certain industries. In Pennsylvania, Standard Oil had been accused of doing everything to the state legislature except refine it. On the national level, the presidency of U. S. Grant had produced so many scandals that the term *grantism* became a synonym for illegal dealings in public office.

The spoils system used by Andrew Jackson and other presidents who followed him had allowed much corruption in the appointment of government employees. This was curbed in the late 1800s by the implementation of several civil service reforms that made merit, or ability, the standard by which jobs were awarded instead of loyalty to the political party in power. Even the reforms in the civil service system, however, were not enough to prevent some politicians from finding ways to abuse the policies.

Corruption was also rampant in industry. The public, especially western farmers, had been victimized by corrupt and unfair practices of the railroads. The railroads had been guilty of overcharging some customers while offering rebates to petroleum shippers. In states where timber was being harvested, some lumber companies stripped public lands for their own profit.

A cartoon from an 1871 issue of Harper's Weekly *attacks the political corruption of Boss Tweed and his gang by asking, "Who stole the people's money?"*

Some industrialists were not only dishonest in their business dealings but also unfair and even cruel to their workers. The workers often labored under terrible and unsafe conditions. Perhaps the worst disaster was the Triangle Shirtwaist Company fire in New York City in March 1911. Nearly 150 people, mostly girls and women, perished because doors had been locked to keep the workers on the job until the end of the shift. Because filtering systems in southern textile plants were rare, textile workers inhaled cotton lint dust. Some then contracted "brown lung" disease and later died from it. Long hours at low pay were normal. Since almost all jobs had the same hours and since employers exchanged lists of employees who caused trouble or went on strike, it did little good to try to change jobs. Women and children were also victimized by industry. Early efforts to protect women from some occupations and to forbid the employment of children under fourteen years of age failed.

Muckrakers: Journalists Who Exposed the Worst

If it had not been for muckraking journalists, it is possible that progressivism would have died; certainly it would have been less influential. **Muckrakers,** journalists who exposed society's ills, were given their name by Teddy Roosevelt. But the term was not original with him. It is the name of a character in John Bunyan's *Pilgrim's Progress* who was always looking down and could not look up even when offered a heavenly crown.

Muckraker journalists and authors named specific financiers, industrialists, and congressmen who undermined public interests. Muckraker **Lincoln Steffens** revealed city problems in articles for *McClure's*. Later they were put into a book, *The Shame of the Cities*. Steffens charged Philadelphia politicians with using the votes of "dead dogs, children, and nonexistent persons" to keep themselves in power.

Ida M. Tarbell was a Pennsylvania school teacher turned author. She had grown up near Titusville, Pennsylvania, at the height of Standard Oil's attempt to squeeze out its competitors. She later wrote a series of articles on the company's ruthless tactics. In 1903 the articles were printed in a two-volume work, *History of the Standard Oil Company.* Her book led to the court case requiring the company to break down its holdings.

John Spargo wrote of the ills of child labor and of the poverty that sent many children to school hungry each day. His work *The Bitter Cry of Children* (1906) aided the passage of child labor laws. Ray Stannard Baker attacked lynching, execution without trial, of blacks in southern states. **Upton Sinclair** used his novel *The Jungle* to show that Chicago meatpackers killed diseased cattle and used chemicals and dyes to cover up bad meat. His descriptions were effective enough to spark the final drive for the Pure Food and Drug Act.

The political and religious views of many of the muckraking writers were not sound, but their work did force some hidden problems to the attention of the American public and the government.

Revealing Society's Ills

Living conditions were worst in crowded cities. Rents were high and housing was limited, so the poor huddled together. Small, often one-room, apartments were common for entire families, who sometimes even kept boarders. More than 400,000 residents of New York City lived in windowless tenements. Twenty thousand more lived in damp cellar apartments where their rooms often flooded with water.

Epidemics were common. Diphtheria, smallpox, cholera, typhus, scarlet fever, and tuberculosis took many lives. Even "childhood" diseases such as measles, mumps, and chicken pox became dangerous under such conditions. Garbage created a terrible stench and became a breeding ground for insects, germs, and disease. Even where sanitation departments existed, they could not keep pace.

Insufficient water supply and inadequate plumbing were other urban problems. Many tenements did not have running water or indoor bathrooms. People got water from street wells. Because run-off water flowed into them, the water was impure. Fire hydrants were opened at certain times for bathing or other uses. Where indoor plumbing existed, it was usually shared by many people and was undependable.

While housing conditions for the poor were bad, those for people confined in prisons, mental hospitals, and other institutions were even worse. Filth and cruel treatment were commonplace.

Reforms

During this era many city officials had little ability, limited knowledge, and weak character. To overcome these problems, new methods of running city governments were tried. Rather than electing a mayor, some cities hired a trained expert called a city manager. Since his position did not depend on his popularity, the manager was under less pressure to bow to special interest groups. Other cities tried a commission form of government. Several commissioners were selected, and each was put in charge of a specific area of government. This system made it much easier to detect corruption.

Two states, Oregon and Wisconsin, were leaders in progressive reforms. Oregon reformed so many parts of its government that the package of ideas they tried was called the Oregon System. One new democratic practice was the **recall** of elected officials. If citizens became unhappy with the actions of an elected official, they could get a required number of signatures on a petition and force the official either to resign or to stand for special election, even if his term of office had not yet expired.

Two other government reforms enacted in many states were the initiative and referendum. An **initiative** allowed voters to propose their own legislation. First, a set number of voters' signatures had to be collected on a petition. Next, the proposed law would go on a ballot allowing voters to accept or reject it. **Referendums,** on the other hand, allowed voters to pass judgment on acts already passed by their state legislatures. A similar petition and voting system was used.

One other major government reform was the direct election of senators, brought about in 1913 by Amendment Seventeen. Up to that time senators had been elected by state legislatures. The progressives believed that responsibility belonged to the people. They also believed that such an approach would put elections out of the reach of corrupt manipulators in state government. However, they failed to recognize that senators elected directly by the people would be more likely to follow the immediate desires of the public rather than stand for what was right for the nation in the long run. Thus a practical part of America's republican government was lost.

Many attempts were made to cure some of the problems of the cities. Individuals responded to the terrible conditions in tenements by founding settlement houses. The first settlement house, Toynbee Hall, was in Whitehall, a London slum. Americans modeled theirs after it. Besides providing food, clothing, and child care, the settlement houses offered recreation and classes to slum area women. America's first settlement house, called Neighborhood Guild, was founded in 1886 in New York City. Probably the most famous was Chicago's Hull House. **Jane Addams,** an avowed socialist, founded the work in 1889. She was assisted by Florence Kelly, who later channeled her energies into law. Her efforts led to the passage of child labor laws in several states.

Other citizens and social groups worked for improving prisons and mental institutions and for aiding people in other distressed conditions. While government stayed out of most of these social programs, it did begin to press regulations on industries' abuses of employees and consumers.

SECTION REVIEW

1. List three of the progressives' aims.

2. Who was "Boss Tweed"?

3. List three government reform ideas that gave more control to individual citizens.

4. What was the purpose of Toynbee Hall and Hull House?

 How did new methods of government help check corruption in cities?

Roosevelt Brings Progressivism to the White House

During the years when these issues of corruption, reform, and government regulation and aid were chief concerns for the country, Americans elected three presidents with progressive goals: Theodore Roosevelt, William Howard Taft, and Woodrow Wilson.

Theodore Roosevelt had been governor of New York when Tom Platt, the state political boss, discovered he could not control him. He then urged Republicans to nominate Roosevelt for the vice-presidency of the United States. Since the vice-presidency was thought to be a political graveyard, Platt hoped that it would shut Roosevelt up and keep him out of the public eye. However, when President McKinley was assassinated, Theodore Roosevelt became president. Although he believed it was "a dreadful thing" to gain the presidency that way, few people have enjoyed the office as much as Roosevelt did.

Roosevelt had some critics, but he gained a large popular following. He was wealthy and well educated, but his adventures as a cowboy and a soldier had given him an ability to identify with the people and endeared him to the public. A candy store owner even named a new toy, the Teddy bear, for him. A graduate of Harvard, Roosevelt spoke several languages and had written at least a dozen books before becoming president. Roosevelt was also a skilled politician with many progressive goals. Unlike many Republican leaders of the day, he wanted change and improvement for the nation's government.

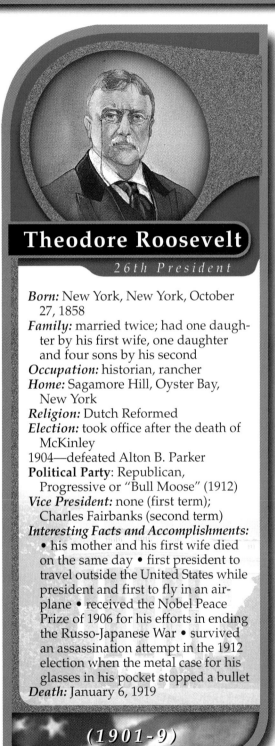

Theodore Roosevelt

26th President

Born: New York, New York, October 27, 1858
Family: married twice; had one daughter by his first wife, one daughter and four sons by his second
Occupation: historian, rancher
Home: Sagamore Hill, Oyster Bay, New York
Religion: Dutch Reformed
Election: took office after the death of McKinley
1904—defeated Alton B. Parker
Political Party: Republican, Progressive or "Bull Moose" (1912)
Vice President: none (first term); Charles Fairbanks (second term)
Interesting Facts and Accomplishments:
• his mother and his first wife died on the same day • first president to travel outside the United States while president and first to fly in an airplane • received the Nobel Peace Prize of 1906 for his efforts in ending the Russo-Japanese War • survived an assassination attempt in the 1912 election when the metal case for his glasses in his pocket stopped a bullet
Death: January 6, 1919

(1901-9)

Theodore Roosevelt's Square Deal

Roosevelt believed that the government should control big business and promote competition. Government should also promote better working conditions and job safety. Roosevelt's views and his efforts to put big business under the government's thumb won over other progressives.

Like other progressives, Roosevelt believed that workers should receive just and fair treatment. Roosevelt's labor policy was shown in his handling of the United Mine Workers' strike in 1902. Workers demanded a shorter workday, raises, and recognition for their union. The strike dragged on for months as management refused to negotiate, and coal shortages caused public discomfort. Instead of siding with the owners and forcing the workers back to the mines, Roosevelt warned that he might use troops to run the coal mines. He also formed a special commission to help settle the dispute. This was the first time that the federal government had become a third party in settling a dispute between labor and management. Roosevelt claimed that he wanted to give both labor and management "a square deal." The question of whether such intervention is a proper use of federal powers remains. Nevertheless, a compromise reduced the working day for the miners to nine hours and raised pay by ten percent.

Protecting People and Resources

Upton Sinclair's *The Jungle* had exposed corruption in the meatpacking industry. In 1906 Congress passed the **Pure Food and Drug Act.** Federal inspectors gained the right to inspect all slaughterhouses and meat companies that shipped across state lines. Provisions forbade the use of harmful additives, even if they were designed to stop spoilage.

Many contemporary patent medicines, widely advertised and available over the counter or by mail, contained opium derivatives or a high percentage of alcohol. Although these medicines were often useful, they were also addictive. The Pure Food and Drug Act regulated the use of narcotics and required a list of contents on product labels. It also made it illegal to make unverifiable claims about medicines.

Another issue very dear to Roosevelt's heart was conservation. An outdoorsman, he readily responded to demands that the government protect lands for future generations to enjoy. America's first national park, Yellowstone, had become federal property in 1872. By 1901 there were three more national parks: Sequoia (sih KWOY uh; 1890), Yosemite (yoh SEM ih tee; 1890), and Mount Rainier (ray NEER; 1891). When Roosevelt left office in 1909, he had more than doubled the number of national parks, adding Wind Cave (1901), Crater Lake (1902), Mesa Verde (MAY-suh VURD; 1906), the Petrified Forest (1906), and Platt (1906).

To protect forest lands from loggers, Congress had started a forest reserve system in 1891. While Presidents Harrison, Cleveland, and McKinley had all added to the forest acreage, Theodore Roosevelt more than doubled the acreage in reserve. Theodore Roosevelt's close personal friend and a professionally trained forester, **Gifford Pinchot** (PIN SHOW), was appointed chief forester. Pinchot not only helped to preserve America's forest resources but also set up a program to conserve its grasslands.

In 1902 Congress passed the New Lands Act, which permitted the sale of federal lands in arid areas. The money gained through such a sale was to pay for irrigation projects to make arid lands usable.

Roosevelt Steps Down

Although Theodore Roosevelt could have run again in 1908, he chose instead to hand-pick the next Republican presidential candidate. This was the first time since Andrew Jackson that a president in power had enough backing to do so. Theodore Roosevelt picked William Howard Taft, who had given him loyal service.

SECTION REVIEW

1. How did Roosevelt gain the presidency?

2. What was Theodore Roosevelt's attitude toward big business?

3. Whom did Roosevelt wish to be his successor?

 How did the power of the federal government increase during the progressive era?

The Taft Administration

William Howard Taft was a lawyer who had spent most of his career in the federal court system. Although Roosevelt had named him civil governor of the Philippines and later secretary of war, Taft preferred the courts. His lifelong dream was to be chief justice of the Supreme Court. However, he set aside that dream temporarily at the urging of Roosevelt. (In 1921, nine years after Taft left the presidency, he was appointed to the Supreme Court as chief justice by President Harding.)

Taft agreed with Roosevelt that government should control big business. However, when Taft won the 1908 election over Democrat William Jennings Bryan, the course he took as president was somewhat different from Roosevelt's. He followed the advice of Republican leaders more readily, and he did not publicly push progressive reforms. Although his methods and personality made him appear to be more easygoing than Roosevelt, Taft actually initiated eighty-nine antitrust suits, compared to Roosevelt's forty-three. But Taft was unable to dramatize his successes as Roosevelt had done. People saw only Taft's mistakes, and he left office a failure in the eyes of many Americans.

Taft's Term in Office

Nevertheless, Taft could claim many progressive actions. He helped to give the Interstate Commerce Commission more power to control the railroads, and he put telegraph and telephone companies under federal control. Taft backed reforms in the post office, created the Department of Labor to protect workers, and organized the Children's Bureau to end child labor. Also during Taft's administration the Sixteenth and Seventeenth Amendments to the Constitution were ratified. The income tax amendment (Sixteenth) gave government a source of revenues that would allow it to expand its activities greatly in later years. The Seventeenth Amendment required the direct election of senators.

The Republican Party Splits

Taft's political future was endangered by fighting within the Republican Party. Disputes over the passage of the Payne-Aldrich Tariff in 1909 made some Republicans think Taft had sold out Roosevelt's ideas. A bitter dispute between two of Taft's cabinet members over some western forest lands was the final straw. When Taft wanted Gifford Pinchot dismissed from his cabinet, Theodore Roosevelt came home from an African safari convinced that Taft had sold out progressive Republican principles.

The Election of 1912

Theodore Roosevelt had been home less than two months when he hit the campaign trail. He said that he was out to persuade voters to elect progressive Republicans to the House and Senate. But he was really widening the rift within the Republican Party and building his own support for the 1912 convention. By February 1912, Theodore Roosevelt "gave in" to the urging of progressive Republicans

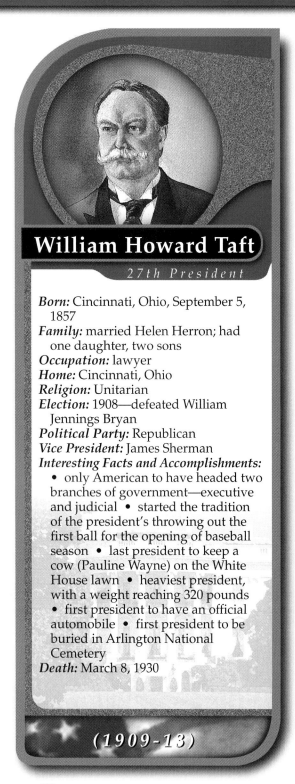

William Howard Taft

27th President

Born: Cincinnati, Ohio, September 5, 1857
Family: married Helen Herron; had one daughter, two sons
Occupation: lawyer
Home: Cincinnati, Ohio
Religion: Unitarian
Election: 1908—defeated William Jennings Bryan
Political Party: Republican
Vice President: James Sherman
Interesting Facts and Accomplishments:
• only American to have headed two branches of government—executive and judicial • started the tradition of the president's throwing out the first ball for the opening of baseball season • last president to keep a cow (Pauline Wayne) on the White House lawn • heaviest president, with a weight reaching 320 pounds • first president to have an official automobile • first president to be buried in Arlington National Cemetery
Death: March 8, 1930

(1909-13)

and announced, "My hat is in the ring. I will accept the nomination for president if it is tendered to me."

But Taft and his followers had the support of most of the Republican Party leaders. They helped him win the Republican nomination on the first ballot. Theodore Roosevelt declared that Taft Republican conservatives had stolen the nomination from him. Thus the new Progressive Party was launched, with Theodore Roosevelt as its candidate. When Roosevelt announced that he felt "as fit as a Bull Moose," his party became known as the **Bull Moose Party.** Theodore Roosevelt's political ideals were known as "The New Nationalism" and would have involved the federal government in still more areas had he won.

The Democratic candidate was New Jersey's progressive Democratic governor, Woodrow Wilson. His campaign catchwords spoke of the "New Freedom." He wanted strict government regulation to restore business competition. Although Roosevelt and Taft together got more votes than Wilson, Wilson won because of the split Republican vote.

Teddy Roosevelt flashes his famous grin.

SECTION REVIEW

1. During his career, Taft headed what other branch of government besides the executive branch?

2. What were the provisions of the Sixteenth and Seventeenth Amendments?

3. The Republican split enabled what Democrat to win the 1912 election?

 Why was the Bull Moose party created?

Progressivism with a Democrat

Woodrow Wilson, son of a Presbyterian pastor, grew up in the South. His ideas reflected his background. He believed that there were two sides to every issue, "a right side and a wrong side," and he stubbornly hung on to principles, refusing to compromise. He had confidence in his judgment perhaps because he believed God had led him. He viewed men idealistically, sincerely believing that most people learned from experience and desired to do right. Politically, this view meant that he often underestimated his opposition, whether at home or abroad.

Wilson and Business

At first Wilson favored less government regulation of business than either Roosevelt or Taft. But rather than try to regulate large trusts, he believed that the government should break them up into smaller companies. He believed small companies would be less monopolistic and more likely to operate in the public interest. To deal with big business and get around the courts, which usually decided in favor of big business, Wilson took two steps. First, he set up the **Federal Trade Commission.** This independent regulatory agency had the power to get data from corporations and to issue orders to stop abuses. Second, Congress passed the **Clayton Anti-Trust Act** of 1914. This act closed some loop-

Woodrow Wilson and his wife, Edith, at his inauguration.

holes of the earlier Sherman Anti-Trust Act. It defined the unfair acts for which corporations could be fined or their executives jailed. The act also exempted both labor unions and farmers' cooperatives from antitrust laws so that these groups could lawfully protest unfair practices.

The Tariff and Income Tax

One of Wilson's major accomplishments concerned the tariff. Since the Democrats had gained majorities in both the House and Senate, Wilson had the support for the reforms he had proposed in his 1912 campaign. Wilson believed that a high protective tariff encouraged monopolies and led to higher charges for consumers. Lowering the tariff would force American businesses to compete with rivals and become more efficient. The **Underwood Tariff of 1913** gave the first major tariff decrease since the Civil War. The tariff rate on

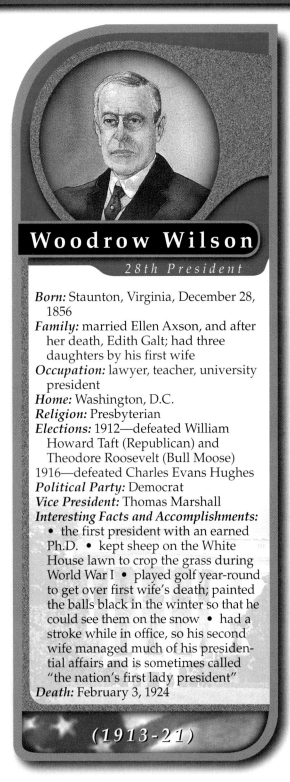

Woodrow Wilson

28th President

Born: Staunton, Virginia, December 28, 1856
Family: married Ellen Axson, and after her death, Edith Galt; had three daughters by his first wife
Occupation: lawyer, teacher, university president
Home: Washington, D.C.
Religion: Presbyterian
Elections: 1912—defeated William Howard Taft (Republican) and Theodore Roosevelt (Bull Moose) 1916—defeated Charles Evans Hughes
Political Party: Democrat
Vice President: Thomas Marshall
Interesting Facts and Accomplishments:
• the first president with an earned Ph.D. • kept sheep on the White House lawn to crop the grass during World War I • played golf year-round to get over first wife's death; painted the balls black in the winter so that he could see them on the snow • had a stroke while in office, so his second wife managed much of his presidential affairs and is sometimes called "the nation's first lady president"
Death: February 3, 1924

(1913-21)

imports went down from forty pecent to less than thirty percent.

Since the Sixteenth Amendment had legalized the income tax, Congress used it to make up for the loss of tariff revenue. Incomes under $4,000 were not taxed. Annual incomes between $4,000 and $20,000 were taxed one percent. The income tax was a graduated tax: the more a person made, the higher percentage of his income he had to pay. The top bracket was six percent on incomes over $500,000. This beginning of income taxes paved the way for higher taxes and more government spending in the future.

Another financial reform accomplished during the Wilson presidency was the establishment of the **Federal Reserve System.** It set up twelve district banks under a national Federal Reserve Board. The Federal Reserve Banks served as bankers' banks. The district reserve banks could increase or decrease the amount of money in circulation. The Board could use its power to control many banking operations throughout the country and thus try to manage the nation's economy.

The Election of 1916

As the nation approached the 1916 election, Wilson was more and more preoccupied with events in war-torn Europe. Seeking to avoid American involvement in the conflict, his campaign slogan became: "He kept us out of war."

When Teddy Roosevelt refused to run as a progressive candidate, the Bull Moose Party dissolved. Progressive followers then had to decide whom to follow. Some backed Wilson because of his reforms, while others returned to the Republican fold.

The election of 1916 was a very close one. Wilson narrowly defeated Republican Charles Evans Hughes. Hughes was a former governor of New York and a Supreme Court justice. The key state in the election proved to be

A New York City women's suffrage parade in 1913 calls for women to receive the right to vote.

entry of the United States into World War I. In addition to problems in Europe, Wilson faced problems in Latin America, where he tried to implement his moral diplomacy. With all this attention on actions in other lands, progressive politics began to fall by the wayside. Two major issues that were resolved, however, were the questions of prohibition and women's suffrage. To the delight of prohibitionists, the Eighteenth Amendment, banning the manufacture and sale of alcoholic beverages, passed in 1919. One year later, when the Nineteenth Amendment was passed, the suffragettes won their right to vote. However, the progressive era in American history was over.

California. Election returns from that state were late to arrive, and Hughes went to bed believing he was the next president. The next morning he found out that Wilson had been reelected.

Wilson's Second Term

During his second term Wilson was forced to focus on foreign affairs and the eventual

SECTION REVIEW

1. What system set up district banks to manage the nation's economy?

2. What gained most of the national government's attention during Wilson's second term?

3. What two major progressive issues were passed during Wilson's second term?

 How did the reduction of the tariff make the passage of the Sixteenth Amendment more important?

SUMMARY

Americans generally enjoyed great prosperity at the turn of the century, but they also realized that there were many problems in their nation. Greed, poverty, alcoholism, corruption in government, and other evils troubled many people in the United States, so Americans began to pressure government leaders to do something about these conditions. Progressive politicians campaigned for government reforms as well as regulations for industry. Although a few of the accomplishments of progressivism did prove helpful, their basic effect was to increase the government's activity and power in a search for solutions. Most people failed to realize that government could never solve the underlying problems of sin.

Chapter Review

People, Places, and Things to Remember

progressivism
urbanization
philanthropists
Tuskegee Institute
Booker T. Washington
George Washington
　Carver
Samuel L. Clemens
agnostics
Robert Ingersoll

Charles Darwin
Charles Hodge
temperance societies
"Boss" Tweed
muckrakers
Lincoln Steffens
Ida M. Tarbell
Upton Sinclair
recall
initiative

referendums
Jane Addams
Pure Food and Drug Act
Gifford Pinchot
Bull Moose Party
Federal Trade
　Commission
Clayton Anti-Trust Act
Underwood Tariff of 1913
Federal Reserve System

Review Questions

Match each of the following terms with its description.

1. agnostic
2. initiative
3. muckraker
4. recall
5. referendum
6. temperance society
7. urbanization

a. movement to the cities
b. says no one can know whether God exists
c. worked to prohibit alcohol use and abuse
d. one who reported poor conditions in society
e. voters' attempt to remove elected officials
f. voters propose legislation themselves
g. voters' reaction to a law already passed by their legislature

Answer the following questions.

8. What was the famous black school founded by Booker T. Washington?
9. What scientist helped to give that school a good reputation?
10. Name three religious cults that became popular around the turn of the century.
11. Who were the three progressive presidents?
12. What legislation helped to combat corruption in meatpacking companies and the abuse of patent medicines?
13. What was Roosevelt's party called in 1912?
14. What did the Sixteenth and Seventeenth Amendments do?
15. What is the term for the group of twelve banks and their board that regulate the nation's money system?

Questions for Discussion

16. In what ways was progressivism helpful to the country, and in what ways was it harmful?
17. How did America's government change during the progressive era?

History Skills

Types of Graphs

Graphs are a useful tool to display complex information in a simple format. The three basic types are line graphs, which show changes over time; bar graphs, which compare similar quantities to each other; and pie graphs, which compare individual quantities to the total.

Below are two graphs about changes in American life between 1860 and 1920. They are based on information supplied by the U.S. Census Bureau. Look at the graphs carefully and answer the questions that follow.

1. Which decade had the highest number of immigrants? How many came in that decade?

2. Approximately how many Americans lived in urban areas in 1860?

3. In what year did the number of urbanized Americans surpass the number of rural Americans?

Think About It—If you needed to create a chart showing the number of American cities whose population exceeded 100,000 from 1860 to 1920, which type of graph would you use: bar, line, or pie graph?

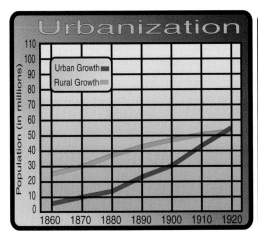

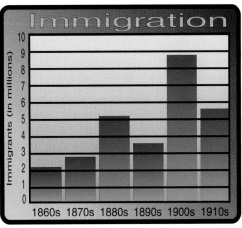

UNIT 6

Taking the Lead

1914-17: The tank was a significant invention of World War I. Its ability to advance over rugged terrain was critical for trench warfare.

1920s: Home run hitter Babe Ruth was a great hero to the excitement-loving Americans of the Roaring Twenties.

1930s: Economic troubles of the 1930s forced many men out of work. Soup kitchens provided warm meals for those in need.

1941: The crippling Japanese attack on the naval base at Pearl Harbor launched the United States into World War II.

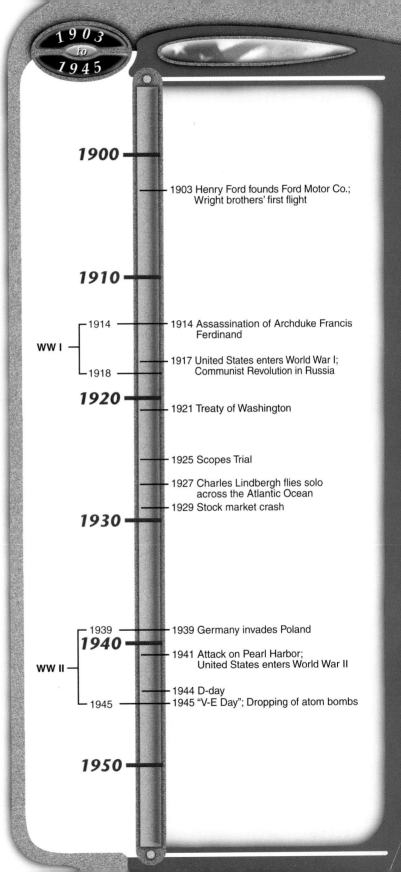

1900

— 1903 Henry Ford founds Ford Motor Co.; Wright brothers' first flight

1910

WW I
1914 — — 1914 Assassination of Archduke Francis Ferdinand
1918 — — 1917 United States enters World War I; Communist Revolution in Russia

1920 — 1921 Treaty of Washington

— 1925 Scopes Trial

— 1927 Charles Lindbergh flies solo across the Atlantic Ocean

— 1929 Stock market crash

1930

WW II
1939 — — 1939 Germany invades Poland
1940
— 1941 Attack on Pearl Harbor; United States enters World War II
— 1944 D-day
1945 — — 1945 "V-E Day"; Dropping of atom bombs

1950

Unit VI: Taking the Lead

Roosevelt's "Nothing to Fear" Speech

Roosevelt's first inaugural speech set the tone for his forceful administration, which revolutionized American government. Read this excerpt. Then write the first five words of the sentence in the text that answers each question.

First of all, let me assert my firm belief that the only thing we have to fear is fear itself—nameless, unreasoning, unjustified terror which paralyzes needed efforts to convert retreat into advance. . . . Plenty is at our doorstep, but a generous use of it languishes in the very sight of the supply. Primarily this is because rulers of the exchange of mankind's goods have failed through their own stubbornness and their own incompetence. . . .

This nation asks for action, and action now.

Our greatest primary task is to put people to work. This is no unsolvable problem if we face it wisely and courageously. It can be accomplished in part by direct recruiting by the government itself, treating the task as we would treat the emergency of a war. . . .

We must frankly recognize the overbalance of population in our industrial centers and, by engaging on a national scale in a redistribution, endeavor to provide a better use of the land for those best fitted for the land. The task can be helped by definite efforts to raise the values of agricultural products and with this the power to purchase the output of our cities. . . . It can be helped by national planning for and supervision of all forms of transportation and of communications and other utilities which have a definitely public character. There are many ways in which it can be helped, but it can never be helped merely by talking about it. We must act and act quickly.

Finally, in our progress toward a resumption of work we require two safeguards against a return of the evils of the old order: there must be a strict supervision of all banking and credits and investments, so that there will be an end to speculation with other people's money; and there must be provision for an adequate but sound currency. . . .

If we are to go forward, we must move as a trained and loyal army willing to sacrifice for the good of a common discipline, because without such discipline no progress is made, no leadership becomes effective. We are, I know, ready and willing to submit our lives and property to such discipline. . . . I assume unhesitatingly the leadership of this great army of our people dedicated to a disciplined attack upon our common problems. . . .

It is hoped that the normal balance of executive and legislative authority may be wholly adequate to meet the unprecedented task before us. But . . . in the event that the national emergency is still critical, I shall not evade the clear course of duty that will then confront me. I shall ask the Congress for the one remaining instrument to meet the crisis—broad executive power to wage war against the emergency, as great as the power that would be given to me if we were in fact invaded by a foreign foe.

1. Whom did Roosevelt blame for America's hardships in the midst of plenty?
2. According to Roosevelt, how could the government help put people back to work?
3. What radical redistribution plan did Roosevelt propose (but never enact)?
4. How would Roosevelt respond to Hoover's emphasis on "rugged individualism"?

World War I

On June 29, 1914, Americans read in their newspapers of the assassination the previous day in Sarajevo (SAH RAH yeh voh), Bosnia, of Archduke Francis Ferdinand, heir to the Austro-Hungarian throne. Most Americans probably asked, "Where is Sarajevo, Bosnia?" Little did they realize how soon all their lives would be drastically affected by that political assassination in a little town on the Balkan Peninsula that few Americans had heard of. World War I would soon follow.

World War I shocked Americans. For three years—1914 through 1916—the United States looked on as "the Great War" ravaged Europe, destroying more property and life than any other war in history up to that time. Most Americans believed that the war was Europe's affair. They agreed with President Wilson that Americans needed to be neutral in word and deed. They hoped that having the Atlantic Ocean between them and the conflict would keep America out of the war. In 1916 Americans had reelected Wilson because "he kept them out of war." But on April 6, 1917, hopes for staying at peace were dashed. The United States entered World War I.

The War As America Watched

The United States tried to mind its own business as the war began, but it could not help seeing the trouble that was brewing in Europe.

Reasons for War

There were several reasons for Europe's turmoil, and one was extreme nationalism. A devotion to and a pride in one's own nation is a natural and proper feeling, but some countries had been building a distorted nationalism in their people in the years before the war. Some nations, like Germany, began to believe they had the right to build up and expand their country no matter what the effect might be on others.

Imperialism and militarism were two more reasons for the growing tensions in Europe. Several countries had or wanted large empires, and some were willing to fight each other to gain control of colonies or nearby territories. Several nations had built large armies to further imperial goals or protect possessions. Large and powerful military forces, however, were a threat to weaker neighbors and caused rivals to increase their forces as well.

Another major reason for the eruption of World War I was the alliances of European nations. In their effort to insure security against aggression, European nations had formed alliances, agreements to support one another militarily. The **Triple Alliance** included Germany, Austria-Hungary, and Italy, nations united by common imperialistic goals. The **Triple Entente** (on TONT; *entente* is a French word for "agreement") included Britain, France, and Russia, nations united by a common fear of Germany. Because these two opposing alliances involved all the major powers of Europe, once any of these powers entered a conflict, all the others were likely to be drawn in.

The Spark and Spread of War

The assassination of the Austrian archduke was the spark that ignited the conflict. Russia quickly came to the aid of Serbia, the little Balkan country that Austria-Hungary

Troops of both the Allies and the Central Powers spent much of the war locked in uncomfortable trench warfare.

Tanks such as this one became important weapons in World War I.

blamed for the deed. Thus Russia and Austria-Hungary were soon at war with each other, and the allies of both joined in the conflict.

On August 1, Germany declared war on Russia, and France joined with Russia against Germany and Austria-Hungary two days later. When German armies marched across the neutral country of Belgium to attack France, Britain quickly stepped into the war. A few other nations also took sides. Ahead was a long and bloody war between the **Central Powers**—Germany, Austria-Hungary, Bulgaria, and Turkey—and the **Allied Powers**—Britain, France, Russia, Italy, and later the United States. (Italy switched to the Allied side in 1915.)

Action in the War

Since the United States was not involved in the European alliances and rivalries, it had no reason in the beginning to enter the war with the other powers. It simply watched in horror as soldiers slaughtered each other across Europe in their bitter fight.

Germany led the first major assault of the war by pressing its armies through Belgium to northern France. British troops came to France's aid before the Germans could take the country, however, and the two sides settled into trenches from the English Channel to the Rhine River. At the same time, the Russian armies began to attack Germany and Austria-Hungary from the east with little success.

The war dragged on with neither the Central Powers nor the Allies making large gains. However, both sides did introduce new weapons and equipment that made warfare more efficient and sometimes more brutal.

The British developed the tank, an armored vehicle that could fire shells while moving on caterpillar tracks. It was capable of almost continuous advance over rugged terrain. Soon the other powers developed their own tanks.

On April 22, 1915, at the second battle of Ypres, the Germans unleashed a new deadly weapon: poison gas. Made from chlorine, the gas harmed the nose, throat, and lungs. Poison gases made whole armies temporarily helpless in the face of enemy attacks. Mustard gas, as it was called, soon became the most feared and common gas on the battlefield. About two percent of those who came into contact with it died. As a result, the gas mask was developed and became standard equipment in some war areas.

Fighting also took to the air. For a while the Germans used zeppelins, large aircraft similar to blimps, to bomb Britain. But because zeppelins were slow moving, they were soon replaced by the airplane. This new flying machine could be used for aerial reconnaissance, bombing, and "dogfighting." Dogfighting, shooting between enemy planes, became possible after machine guns were synchronized with the airplane's propellers. (Before that development in 1915, pilots could not fire their guns forward without shooting their own propellers.) Fighter pilots who shot down five or more planes became special heroes called "flying aces." Manfred von Richthofen, "the Red Baron," was Germany's top ace. Britain's flying hero was Mick Mannock, and when the United States entered the war, Eddie Rickenbacker became the most famous American ace.

Trucks and automobiles aided the transportation of military goods and personnel. Rifles, cannon, grenades, mines, and other weapons were improved or invented for effective fighting. And for battling on the sea, the Germans perfected the submarine. These "U-boats" (underwater boats) could remain unseen while launching a surprise torpedo attack against enemy ships.

The Wild Blue Yonder

America's air force had its beginnings in France during World War I. Actually, the first American air squadron was in the French armed forces. Since the United States did not have an air corps of its own at that time, many young Americans went to Europe to fly for France. At first these adventurers could join only the French Foreign Legion. They were forbidden by French law from enlisting in the regular French forces. Soon the law changed, though, and a group of young and wealthy Americans joined the French Air Corps. (The rich became pilots simply because before the war they were the only ones who had the money to buy planes and to learn to fly.)

Soon a group of these American pilots began petitioning the French government to form an all-American French squadron. Finally permission was granted, and in April 1916 the *Escadrille Américaine* (ES-kuh-DRIL uh-mehr-ih-CAN) was begun. When President Wilson complained that the name violated America's official neutral position, the squadron changed its name to the *Lafayette Escadrille.* The young men claimed that they were repaying France for the help that the Frenchman Lafayette had given the United States during the War for Independence.

The *Lafayette Escadrille* began with seven pilots and a lion cub for a mascot. During the war a total of thirty-eight men served as pilots for the group, and many of them died in their cockpits. When the United States entered World War I, the *Lafayette Escadrille* switched over to become the first American air squadron.

SECTION REVIEW

1. What event sparked the start of World War I?

2. List four of the causes of the war's outbreak.

3. What countries comprised the Allies? the Central Powers?

4. Which country made the first major assault?

5. What country developed the tank? poison gas?

 How did airplanes contribute to a nation's defenses?

Effects of the European War on America

Although the United States was not participating in the war, it was not totally isolated from the warring nations either. Transportation, trade, and diplomatic relationships with Europe were all affected by the war, and these matters concerned Americans.

Reasons for American Interest

Although President Wilson had stated that Americans should remain neutral, maintaining neutrality proved difficult for several reasons.

First, American sentiment favored the Allied cause. Although there were eleven million Americans who had some tie to Germany, there were substantially more who had British ties. America's background, its legal system, part of its form of government, and even its language were English. Americans also recalled that another ally, France, had come to America's aid during the War for Independence. Moreover, Americans had been upset by the German invasion of neutral Belgium.

A second factor was economic. Although American businessmen sold goods and lent money to both the Allied and Central Powers, more traded with Allied countries, especially Britain. Consequently, Americans were more sympathetic to Allied interests just to protect American investments.

Gradually the United States began aiding the Allies. Right after the outbreak of war, British and French agents had come to place orders with American firms. They contracted for shipments of grain, cotton, and other needed supplies. At first these countries had paid cash for their items and carried them home on their own ships. But when their cash ran low, they asked for and received loans. By early 1917 the United States had lent Britain over $1 billion and France over $300 million. The Germans protested that this violated neutrality because American-made shells and guns were killing Germans. Wilson, however, chose not to restrict these business deals. He believed that restricting them would help the Central Powers.

Another factor was Allied propaganda. Britain and France controlled the trans-Atlantic cables that brought the news to American newspapers. The Germans had to rely on the still imperfect radio to transmit messages to the United States. In addition, the Germans, with the few messages they did get through, did not project a good image to Americans. Because they emphasized hate and destruction, more anger than sympathy was aroused. The Allies easily won the Americans over just by reprinting German hate propaganda word for word. Germany's deeds were also harmful to its relationship with America. When it invaded Belgium, a violation of an earlier treaty, the German government explained away the betrayal by calling the treaty "a scrap of paper." About five thousand Belgian civilians who had resisted the Germans were executed. British propagandists were quick to let Americans know of this and other atrocities, including a few that never happened.

Violations of America's Neutral Rights

The biggest difficulty in maintaining neutrality revolved around Britain's and

Germany's violations of America's neutral rights at sea. Since Britain was a small island nation, it was almost totally dependent on overseas trade for raw materials. Over the years Britain had developed the best and largest navy and merchant marine (trading) fleet. The United States had benefited greatly from trade with Britain, and it did not wish to lose that trade during the war. The United States wished to continue trade with Germany as well, but all sea trade with Europe was put in jeopardy by the naval strategies of Britain and Germany.

Early in the war Britain had put mines in the entrances to the North Sea. This was done to prevent nations from trading with Germany. However, instead of trading directly with Germany, some countries, including the United States, sent their goods to the Germans through neutral countries like the Netherlands, Denmark, or Sweden, who all resold them. Such actions angered the British, and they began to stop American shipping bound for neutral nations.

The British were ready to seize anything that could be useful to Germany. American ships were stopped at sea and ordered to British ports for searches. The time wasted pushed up the cost of goods. Sometimes foodstuffs spoiled before they could be delivered. The British claimed this action was necessary because of the danger of attack by German submarines. British firms also made "blacklists" of American firms that they suspected of trading with Germany through neutral nations. These actions angered Americans because they were a violation of the rights of a neutral country.

Britain did not receive all of America's anger, however. Realizing that Britain was dependent on foreign trade, too, Germany sought to cut British imports. Rather than using just a blockade, Germany chose to use **unrestricted submarine warfare.** They fired on all ships in a designated war zone around Britain. Attacking neutral ships without giving them a warning and a chance to remove their passengers was a violation of international law. Therefore the United States protested Germany's policy as inhumane. Americans also said it violated the concept of freedom of the seas. Germans, however, argued that submarines were at a disadvantage. If they surfaced to give a warning, it was easy for even a merchant ship armed with guns to sink them.

Although the German Embassy put ads in newspapers warning Americans not to travel on British vessels, the warnings were ignored. In May 1915 a British liner, the *Lusitania,* was sunk without warning off the coast of Ireland. Among the 1,198 who perished were 128 Americans. President Wilson demanded that the Germans apologize and renounce this strategy. He later threatened to withdraw diplomatic recognition if another passenger ship was attacked. Germany cooperated for a while.

Growing American Fears

When the German offensives in France slowed, however, Germany decided that the only way to win the war was to cut Britain's supply lines and force her surrender. It could accomplish this by using its large fleet of U-boats. After the German announcement in February 1917 that it was going to resume its unrestricted submarine warfare, the United States broke off diplomatic relations with Germany.

Added to the submarine tension was the discovery of a German plot. Early in March the German foreign minister, Arthur Zimmermann, sent a telegram to the German minister in Mexico. In it he said that if war broke out between Germany and the United States, Mexico would be rewarded for entering the war against the Americans. Its reward

When the S.S. Lusitania *left harbor, no one expected that its first voyage would also be its last.*

would be the return to Mexico of Texas, New Mexico, and Arizona.

British intelligence intercepted the telegram. The next day President Wilson asked Congress to arm American merchant ships, and he released the Zimmermann telegram to the public. The nation was outraged. When three more American merchant ships were sunk, the pressure increased. Finally, on April 2, 1917, a solemn president appeared before both houses of Congress asking for a declaration of war. Four days later, on April 6, 1917, the approval was given. The United States was joining the fight in Europe.

SECTION REVIEW

1. List at least three reasons for the difficulty of American neutrality.

2. How did some American ships attempt to get around Britain's blockade of German ports? What was Britain's response?

3. What German naval policy greatly angered Americans?

 What was the significance of the Zimmermann telegram?

The United States at War

By the time the United States entered the war, the Allies were in a desperate condition. At one time, because of the success of Germany's unrestricted submarine warfare, the British people were down to a three-week supply of food.

The United States responded with huge shipments of supplies to Europe. To insure safe arrival, American ships traveled in groups

President Wilson stands before the Congress on April 2, 1917, asking the nation to join the fight in Europe.

called *convoys*. Naval destroyers with antisubmarine guns escorted them. With such protection, shipping losses were cut. The **convoy system** worked so well that not one of the two million American soldiers bound for Europe was lost at sea. Although American manpower gave a boost to Allied morale, the biggest contribution was in needed war materials. Food, clothing, munitions, ships, and vehicles poured into Europe. The Central

Powers were unable to match this production themselves and soon fell behind. To provide these needs for the Allied cause, America faced the challenge of gearing up for war. The peacetime economy and production needed to be channeled into a great effort for victory.

Military Preparedness

Since Americans feared having a strong standing army, its military force had purposely been kept small, consisting of only 200,000 men. Allied losses had already exceeded the size of the whole American army. The United States had only four hundred heavy guns and enough ammunition for a nine-hour bombardment. It had no tanks, and it lacked an air force. Now, suddenly, the United States had to train men, make equipment, and build ships to carry everything to Europe.

For the first time since the Civil War, the nation resorted to a draft. Under the Selective Service Act, local draft boards under civilian leadership supplied the men. The system worked well, and there was far less opposition to the draft than there had been during the Civil War. About four million men went into the service. The recruits were trained at thirty-two training camps across the nation.

Producing for the War

As America sent its soldiers off to battle, the entire nation had to adjust to the necessities of war. As a result the government had to begin many programs and agencies that could

All segments of the armed services joined together in the war effort.

coordinate the war effort. Everything the American forces needed had to be obtained or manufactured and transported in a hurry.

The **War Industries Board** organized the industrial production needed. Factories were transformed to produce needed war materials—uniforms, guns, ammunition, vehicles, medical supplies. The board set criteria to standardize thousands of needed items and set economic priorities for the nation.

To insure that the railroads operated efficiently to carry the extra freight and passengers, the United States Railroad Administration took control of all railroads. It organized regional units, set rates and schedules, and set shipping priorities to insure that munitions (weapons, ammunition, and other war material) reached ports even if nonessential goods had to be held up.

The Fuel Administration had the job of conserving and directing the use of the nation's fuel. It asked the people to walk more and added "gasless days" to weekly calendars. Auto owners were asked to save gasoline so that trucks could run to carry war goods. The actions of these federal agencies designed to aid the war effort coordinated the activities of the nation in a remarkable way. They could do so because the national emergency had lessened the public's resistance to government power and restrictions. With Allied armies facing starvation, increasing America's food production received top priority. Herbert Hoover, who had already gained fame as organizer of a massive food relief program to Belgium, headed the Food Administration. Rather than force the public to conserve food, the administration set up a voluntary program. Americans were asked to make Mondays wheatless, Tuesdays meatless, and Thursdays porkless. Americans also raised their own vegetables in "Victory Gardens" so that more food would be available for the soldiers. With these efforts huge savings were made. Moreover, the people felt they were a part of the great war effort. Just before the war began the average annual amount of food shipped to Europe was 7 million tons. By 1919 it had reached 18.6 million tons.

The war also brought changes in the normal American work force. Since four million men were drafted, the normal work force was depleted. Because of the urgent need, many women now worked outside their homes for the first time. Some gratefully returned home when the war ended; others stayed on the job.

Volunteer groups were formed to support the "boys" in France. Memberships in the American Red Cross multiplied as women in local chapters met to roll bandages, knit sweaters or socks, and prepare packages to be sent abroad. Men who could not serve in the military also offered their time to support volunteer efforts.

Because the war caused a labor shortage, wages shot up and more jobs were available. Even with high taxes, loan drives, and

A Little Bird Named Enza

There was a little bird,
    Its name was Enza.
I opened the window,
    And in-flu-enza.

In 1918 this was the favorite poem of America's children. But the "little bird Enza" was no laughing matter. The deadly virus struck many American soldiers either while they were still in training or after they had arrived in Europe. In four months influenza killed twenty-one million people worldwide, more people than the war killed in four years. At the height of the epidemic, the last week in October 1917, twenty-seven hundred American soldiers died in Europe; twenty-one thousand American citizens died of the flu back home. But the flu was completely impartial: close to a quarter of a million Germans died as well.

The flu epidemic left as suddenly and mysteriously as it had come. By the middle of November 1918, it was over. Ironically, about the same time, so was the war. Some estimate that over forty million of the world's people died in the four years of World War I, and at least half of those were victims of the "little bird Enza."

A war bond rally in Atlanta encourages citizens to support the war effort.

increased prices for most goods, Americans were earning more than they ever had. Of course, prices went up for what the government bought too, raising the cost of fighting the war. To keep costs and wages under control, however, the government created the **War Labor Policies Board** to regulate laborers. While unions were allowed to organize and even showed significant gains in membership during the war years, the board stepped in to help settle disputes between labor and management. The board also set an eight-hour working day, stressed fair wages, and set standards for employing women and children.

The shortage of workers and the drop in immigration opened the doors of opportunity to black laborers. There was a movement of more than one-half million blacks to northern cities during the war. When the war ended, many blacks kept their jobs and remained in the North. This migration permanently changed the ethnic makeup of many northern cities.

Public Information

President Wilson did not want to leave anything to chance. He wanted Americans to know that their cause was just. To unite them behind the war effort, a Committee on Public Information was formed. Headed by journalist George Creel, 150,000 people became involved in a giant propaganda crusade to "advertise America." Talented artists designed war recruitment posters and ads. An army of lecturers appeared at local assemblies and even at silent movies. Called "four-minute men," they gave short talks on any number of patriotic topics and moved crowds to cheers or tears.

On the other hand the attitude toward the Central Powers or even things distantly related to them became negative. All things German were hated. Even though they had been in America for years and had proved their loyalty, some German Americans were sorely persecuted. Schools stopped teaching German, and school orchestras refused to play pieces by German composers such as

485

Bach and Wagner. Sauerkraut became "Liberty Cabbage," hamburgers became "Liberty Burgers," and dachshunds were renamed "Liberty Pups." If you had caught the German measles, your mother would have been careful to tell the neighbors you had "patriotic spots" or "patriotic measles."

Paying for the War

The cost of the war was enormous. The United States spent about $24 billion, and the Allies borrowed $8 billion. About one-fourth of the money came from the new income and corporate taxes. The rest came from bank loans and loan drives.

Four times during the war the government went to the American people for money, raising more than $18 billion. "Liberty" and "Victory" loan drives were held in every community. Loan chairmen went door to door asking their neighbors to buy bonds. Workers also bought bonds at their places of employment. Buyers received "Liberty Buttons" for their lapels. Goals were set, and there were great celebrations when the drives went "over the top."

Even children became involved. They sold produce to earn money to finance the war, and they bought thrift stamps each week on "stamp day." A filled thrift card could be swapped for a $5 savings stamp; ten stamps on a card were proudly exchanged for a $50 bond.

SECTION REVIEW

1. What did the Selective Service Act do?

2. What was the purpose of the War Industries Board?

3. Name some of the changes made by the War Labor Policies Board.

4. How did America finance the war?

 How did the government attempt to unite Americans behind the war?

A young "doughboy"

Newly-arriving American "Doughboys" brought fresh enthusiasm to the tired Allied troops.

The American Forces "Over There"

The chief role of the navy was to get troops and supplies safely to Europe. Congress had voted for money to enlarge the navy before war broke out. During the war it tried to build or buy more ships to carry men and supplies to the troops fighting in Europe. It was on the battlefields, particularly those in northern France, that America's soldiers were needed.

The American Expeditionary Force

The American troops who joined the European fighting force were called the **American Expeditionary Force.** Although the United States declared war in April 1917, the first American troops did not arrive in Europe until the fall of 1917. The minimum training time was three months. Often the troops were called **"doughboys."** Most combat troops did not reach Europe until the spring of 1918 because of the period of training and other delays. The American Expeditionary Force (AEF) was commanded by General **John Pershing.** Pershing worked under Marshal **Ferdinand Foch** (FOSH), a Frenchman who served as Supreme Allied Commander. The British and French troops were weary and discouraged from three years of war, and the arrival of the "Yanks," as they called the Americans, was a welcome relief. The Allies wanted to place American doughboys in already existing armies and use them to replace British and French losses, but Pershing disagreed. Fearing that American

General John J. Pershing was called away from the conflict in Mexico to command the American forces.

moved to the western front to fight France, Britain, and the United States.

The Central Powers launched an all-out offensive on the western front during the spring of 1918. The Germans hoped to reach the English Channel and also to take Paris. By June 3, 1918, they had reached the Marne River and were only about fifty miles from the French capital.

The combined American and French forces launched a counter-offensive and pushed the Germans back at a place on the Marne River called Château-Thierry (shah-TOH tyeh-REE). Next the Americans moved up to a hunting preserve called Belleau Wood (BEL oh) and stopped the Germans from making a run on Paris from that point. By the beginning of July, Paris was out of danger and the German advance was falling apart. Foch planned and carried off a massive assault at Amiens on August 8. The German general Ludendorff was to call it "the black day of the German army." Despite heavy German losses, Amiens was not the end of the war.

morale would suffer, he requested that the American troops fight as a separate force. American units were then assigned their own segments of the front to defend.

Doughboys in Action

By the time the Americans arrived, the Germans had accomplished a major goal—getting Russia out of the fight. The Germans had aided the return of **Vladimir Lenin** to Russia in 1917 after the Russians had already overthrown their czar. Weary of war, the Russians followed Lenin in the Communist Revolution. Lenin had promised peace to the Russians, and he also had promised the Germans that he would pull Russia out of the war. When he gained power, he called Russian troops home and ended support for the Allied cause. Thus Germany had one less enemy to fight. The German armies that had been fighting the Russians could now be

Shells stripped trees and leveled forests, leaving little protection for soldiers engaged in battle.

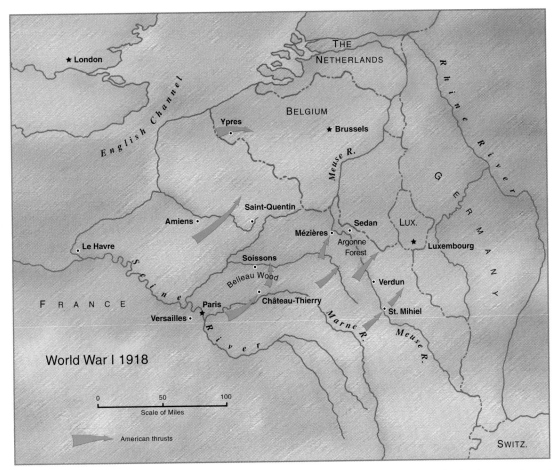

World War I 1918

0   50   100
Scale of Miles

American thrusts

With more than 250,000 American soldiers arriving monthly, Allied morale climbed. Pershing got permission to apply the separate strength of the U.S. Army as part of the larger counter-offensive. The place was St. Mihiel (SAHN mee-YEL), just south of Verdun. More than half a million doughboys came. An air corps of fifteen hundred planes was poised for takeoff, and thirty-two hundred French and American guns roared in protest against the German army. In forty-eight hours the battle was over.

Two weeks later the American forces launched an offensive into the Argonne (AHR gon) Forest. Foch had assigned the American troops the worst possible spot. American forces faced a maze of barbed wire, steel, and concrete. The hills and ridges offered almost perfect terrain for a German defensive. Historians have called this "the meat grinder offensive" because of the heavy losses.

By August 8 the British had broken through the German line. Having destroyed German resistance, the Allied troops moved swiftly across France, regaining lost lands for the Allies. The last major American activity took place in late October at Mézières, a link to the main German railway. By the end of September, however, the German commander, General Paul von Hindenburg, knew that all was lost.

489

At 11:00 A.M. on November 11, 1918, the slaughter stopped. Germany signed an armistice, or agreement to stop fighting. This day became an American national holiday called **Armistice Day.** (After World War II and the Korean War, the name was changed to Veterans' Day, honoring all veterans.)

The war had taken the lives of over eight million people and had left nearly twenty million wounded. The United States had lost 115,000 of its men in its year and a half of activity in the war. Over 200,000 Americans came home wounded. Although these casualties were light in comparison to those of the other major powers, Americans had known the heartache of war. Yet they hoped that this had been the "War to End All Wars" and the "War to Make the World Safe for Democracy." They believed they had fought for noble goals.

American soldiers and sailors in Paris.

SECTION REVIEW

1. What nickname was given to American troops?
2. Who was commander of the American Expeditionary Force?
3. Who was Marshal Foch?
4. When did the war officially end?

 Why did the Germans support Vladimir Lenin in his Communist Revolution?

Peace Comes to Europe

The end of the war brought many questions for the participants. How would Germany and the other defeated countries be treated? Would the victors claim conquered territories and possessions? Could peace be maintained in Europe?

Wilson's Fourteen Points

Even before the war ended, Woodrow Wilson had proposed a set of guidelines to help rebuild European peace. His **Fourteen Points** had been announced in January 1918. Most of the points of his program centered on establishing a just peace and building a postwar world in which war would be less likely. The crucial point to Wilson was Point 14, providing for a **League of Nations.** He idealistically believed that an organization of cooperating nations could talk over problems and settle them peacefully, preventing future wars. Freedom of the seas, a ban against secret agreements, and general disarmament were some of the other key points.

President Wilson spoke of "peace without victory," urging generous terms that would preserve the German nation. He rejected territorial gains for the winners and **reparations,** or payment for damages by the losers. He said that weak nations should have the right of self-determination—that is, they could choose to be independent.

American soldiers rest and recuperate in Paris, France.

The Paris Peace Conference

The Allied leaders met at the Palace of Versailles outside Paris on January 18, 1919, to shape the peace. President Wilson traveled to Europe to represent the United States at the conference himself. He believed that his presence would insure the victors' acceptance of a just and lasting peace. About two million people welcomed Wilson to Paris, regarding him almost as the savior of Europe. His reception strengthened his resolve to push for a treaty based on his Fourteen Points.

But the representatives from the other nations were equally determined. **Georges Clemenceau** (ZHORZH KLEM-un-SOH), the French premier, knew that his country had suffered at German hands in both the Franco-Prussian War and World War I. He wanted to ensure that Germany would never again be strong enough to hurt France. **David Lloyd George** represented Britain and **Vittorio Orlando,** Italy. These men plus Wilson were sometimes called

the Big Four. The nations that had lost and Russia were not included at the peace table. Thus the treaty has sometimes been called "a victors' peace." Leaving out the losers caused them to be resentful and to reject the treaty's provisions. Germany was forced to sign the **Treaty of Versailles** anyway on June 28, 1919. The other defeated countries signed other individual treaties. The 264-page Treaty of Versailles with Germany was very detailed. Against Wilson's wishes, it placed all the blame for the war on Germany and forced Germany to pay for its actions. Germany had to give up its overseas empire and some of its own land and resources. It had to allow foreign troops to remain on its land. Germany was also forced to pay huge reparations to Britain and France. While Wilson was disappointed about these and some of the other details of the treaty, he did convince the other leaders to provide for the formation of the League of Nations. Wilson believed that all the weaknesses of the

German and Allied leaders meet to sign the treaty to end the war in the Hall of Mirrors in the Palace of Versailles.

peace could be worked out through further negotiations in the league.

American Responses to the Treaty

When Wilson returned to the United States, he took the treaty directly to the Senate, whose approval is required for all treaties. Although most Americans probably supported the treaty, many senators were not pleased with it. Wilson had unwisely ignored the Republican leaders in the Senate while he helped formulate the treaty, and now those senators refused to ratify it without some changes. Wilson refused their changes, and the situation became deadlocked. Time passed, and the United States never did ratify the treaty. It simply declared the war to be over. Wilson was further disappointed that the United States did not join the League of Nations.

SECTION REVIEW

1. Who were the "Big Four" at the Paris Peace Conference, and what country did each represent?

2. What treaty stated the conditions for peace with Germany?

3. What key point did Wilson succeed in placing in the treaty?

4. How did the U.S. Senate respond to the treaty?

 What details of the peace process and treaty laid a foundation for German bitterness against the Allies?

SUMMARY

America had grown to be a powerful industrial nation by the beginning of the twentieth century. Although it attempted to remain aloof from the conflict that grew in Europe, its culture and interests made keeping a neutral position difficult. Eventually the nation abandoned neutrality and entered World War I in 1917. The United States made a gigantic effort to supply the faltering Allies with men and materials for the war effort. With this American aid the Allies defeated the Central Powers. President Wilson tried to persuade the delegates at the peace conference to follow his Fourteen Point program for establishing a lasting peace, but he found little support at the conference or in the United States.

Chapter Review

People, Places, and Things to Remember

Triple Alliance
Triple Entente
Central Powers
Allied Powers
unrestricted submarine
  warfare
Lusitania
convoy system

War Industries Board
War Labor Policies Board
American Expeditionary
  Force
doughboys
John Pershing
Ferdinand Foch
Vladimir Lenin

Armistice Day
Fourteen Points
League of Nations
reparations
Georges Clemenceau
David Lloyd George
Vittorio Orlando
Treaty of Versailles

Review Questions

What significant event happened on each of the following dates?

1. June 28, 1914

2. April 6, 1917

3. November 11, 1918

Who was he?

4. Who was president of the United States during World War I?

5. Who commanded the American Expeditionary Force?

6. Who was commander of all the Allied forces?

7. Who were "the Big Four," and what country did each represent?

Write the appropriate term for each blank below.

When World War I broke out in 1914, Germany, Austria-Hungary, and the nations that sided with them were called the (8) , and Britain, France, and the nations that sided with them were called the (9) .

Germany's policy of (10) greatly angered Americans. It brought about the sinking of the *Lusitania* and eventually helped to prompt America to enter the war. The American soldiers who arrived in Europe were commonly called (11). They helped the Allies win the war. Fighting stopped on (12) Day.

Allied leaders met at Versailles to draw up a treaty. President Wilson's plan for peace consisted of (13), but most of his plan was rejected, except for the formation of a (14) to help settle international problems. Britain and France especially wanted Germany to pay reparations for the damages caused by the war. The resulting treaty with Germany, called the (15), was never signed by the United States.

Questions for Discussion

16. What were the advantages of the United States's remaining neutral during the early years of the war?

17. Should America have joined the League of Nations? Why or why not?

24

The 1920s: Decade of Change

With the end of World War I, most Americans looked forward to better times. Some thought that they could return to the ideals and ways of earlier days. Instead the 1920s, sometimes called the "Roaring Twenties," became a decade of startling changes.

In prewar years progressive Americans had united to check big industry and to gain reforms. Then they had united to wage a war that would make the world safe for democracy. In the twenties diversity replaced that unity. After sacrificing for a war, many Americans now wanted a good life for themselves. They wanted all the goods big industries could supply, and they were not as interested in righting society's wrongs. Since some of the restraints that they sought to throw off were biblical ones, the 1920s was an era when sin was practiced more openly than in earlier periods of American history.

While many Americans were prosperous enough to enjoy "a chicken in every pot and a car in every garage," as the Republicans promised in 1928, others struggled to put food on the table. Serious economic problems lurked below the surface prosperity of the era, and these problems led to calamity for many Americans as the decade closed.

Postwar Problems

America emerged from the war with some attitudes and problems that would set the stage for the decade to come. First was a desire to stay out of any other foreign conflicts that might come along.

Isolationism and Peace

President Wilson had diligently sought American approval of the Treaty of Versailles with its provision for a new League of Nations. Because of his battle with the Senate, he decided to travel across the country and present his views to the people. While on his tour he had a stroke that left him unable to carry on his duties for a few weeks. In the remaining months of his presidency he never regained full strength; yet he continued to plead for the United States to ratify the treaty and join the league. The Senate and many Americans, however, feared that the obligations of the League of Nations would draw America into future wars. This fear and a general lack of concern for foreign affairs now that the war was over made most Americans ready to isolate themselves from problems outside the United States.

When the 1920 election came, the attitude of wanting to get back to business and forget about foreign problems resulted in a strong win for the Republican candidate, **Warren G. Harding.** His campaign, stressing a "return to normalcy," was victorious over that of James Cox, the Democrat. Ideas of signing the treaty and joining the league were soon forgotten.

Throughout the 1920s the United States remained true to its isolationist goals in that it stayed out of most foreign affairs. Wishing to cut expenses and to avoid temptation for future war, the government sought a way to trim down its navy. Harding's secretary of state, Charles Evans Hughes, and others believed that one cause of the war had been an arms race. Hence he suggested that the five major powers limit naval shipbuilding. This was done through the **Treaty of Washington** in 1921. Britain, the United States, Japan, France, and Italy scaled down their navies. For every five British or American ships built, Japan would be allowed three, and France and Italy one and three-quarters. The treaty, which allowed the United States to cut its budget, delighted Republicans, who were seeking bigger cuts in spending. Japan, however, considered the treaty unfair and turned its resentment against the United States in later years. In reality the treaty had little impact because the powers continued to increase their defenses by building smaller ships and submarines that were not limited under the agreement.

Another attempt to keep America free from the threat of future war was the **Kellogg-Briand Peace Pact.** Coolidge's secretary of state, Frank B. Kellogg, optimistically signed a treaty with sixty-two other nations in 1928. The countries agreed to outlaw war as a means of settling international disputes. As with most peace agreements, only some nations took it seriously. Men cannot establish peace on their own, and World War II would soon prove how futile their agreement was. It would also prove that the United States could not remain isolated from the world.

Depression

Following the war came a time of economic depression for the United States. The big demand for war products had kept industries and farms busy, but when the war was over, the demand dropped. Because many of the war products were no longer needed, factories had to change over to peace-time industry. It took time to build these new businesses. American farms had sent millions of tons of food to Europe during the war, but now Europe could start feeding itself again. There was no market for the great surplus of food.

In reaction to World War I, Warren Harding kept America true to its isolationist goals.

Unemployment became a problem in the cities. Soldiers returning home from the war found few jobs available. War industries were closing down, and many jobs that were available had been taken by blacks and immigrants. For a while the blacks and immigrants were resented by white Americans who were without jobs. Unfortunately, violence eventually erupted from the frustration of the unemployed. Race riots occurred in both the North and the South. A new Ku Klux Klan arose in the South and Midwest to terrorize not only blacks but also Roman Catholics and Jews. New immigration laws were passed that set quotas (fixed numbers) of immigrants who could enter the United States. These laws were intended to stop the heavy flow of immigrants, especially those from the Roman Catholic countries of southern and eastern Europe.

Although the nation's economy picked up quickly and unemployment ceased to be a problem, veterans continued to pressure the government until they received a bonus of a $1,000 life insurance policy. The farmers' problems continued through the 1920s as high production and low prices continued. Although representatives of the farming states moved for government aid and regulation, President Harding and his successor, **Calvin Coolidge,** believed that the federal government should not interfere by regulating the farm economy.

Fear of Communism

Although Americans had read of events in Russia leading up to and including the Communist Revolution in 1917, few really were aware of the Communist presence until it involved them directly. Americans had heard reports of massacres in Communist Russia. A fear of communism began to grow, especially when Americans learned that the Communists intended to spread their rule. Leaders of the Soviet Union, as the Russian nation now

During the 1920s the Ku Klux Klan's focus included not only blacks but also Roman Catholics and Jews. Here Klan members parade in Washington, D.C. in 1928.

called itself and the surrounding nations it controlled, had organized the Third International. This agency for world revolution would export communism anywhere, using any method. It was already making gains in Germany and Hungary.

The Communists had two political parties working in America by 1919. One of their aims was to create a struggle between common workers and the property-owning capitalists. During this time Americans began to think of any sign of worker discontent, and strikes in particular, as part of the Communist plot. In April 1919 there was also a wave of terrorist bombings. The post office intercepted letter bombs addressed to thirty-eight prominent businessmen or government officials, including John D. Rockefeller, Justice Oliver Wendell Holmes, and both the postmaster general and the U.S. attorney general. In June there were direct bombings. One bomb exploded in front of Attorney General A. Mitchell Palmer's home. In September a terrorist planted a bomb in front of the New York Stock Exchange, killing thirty-eight people.

Some have sarcastically called this period the "Red Scare," for some Americans did overreact to the Communist threat. However, we should remember that the threat itself was real. Believing that Communists were involved in the attacks, Attorney General Palmer crusaded for increased government investigation and arrests in these cases. Government agents raided offices of radical organizations and arrested 250 members of the Union of Russian Workers. In December the Labor Department sent 249 aliens, some of whom were Communists, back to Russia. Eventually the scare died down, but Americans maintained a fear of communism and its infiltration into the United States for most of the decade.

The fear of the Communists added to the resentment toward immigrants, many of whom were from southern and eastern Europe, where radical political ideas were spreading. Ill feeling toward both Communists and immigrants combined in a noted court case in 1921. Two Italian anarchists, Nicola Sacco and Bartolomeo Vanzetti, were arrested and tried for murdering two shoe company employees in a payroll robbery. They were found guilty and were sentenced to death. Protests led to the reopening of the case. Some charged that the two men had been sentenced to death because they were foreigners who held unpopular political views and not because they had committed a crime. The case dragged on for six years. Sacco and Vanzetti were convicted, and in 1927 the two were executed. Many, however, tried to make the case an example of injustice in American society.

SECTION REVIEW

1. What did Warren G. Harding stress in his presidential campaign?

2. What did the Treaty of Washington seek to limit?

3. What two groups tried to gain help from the government during the postwar depression?

4. What was the Red Scare?

 How was the Kellogg-Briand Peace Pact unrealistic?

A Desire for Prosperity

As Americans recovered from the war's effects, they developed a great desire for material prosperity. The humanitarian and reform goals of the earlier progressives were forgotten. They were replaced by desires for the possessions and the pleasures that the new decade was to offer.

Technology's Products

Inventions and improvements of industrial products greatly changed the American way of life in the 1920s. The automobile and the application of electricity to household appliances revolutionized daily life for many Americans.

The Automobile—The first successful American automobile had been built by Charles and Frank Duryea in 1893. Henry Ford had begun making cars in 1903, and many other automobile producers had also plunged into the business. Although cars had become common before the war, there were still many American families without a "horseless carriage." After the war, however, factories geared up to produce cars by the thousands. Families were eager to have their

The sleek, new Model A Ford began to roll off the assembly lines in the late 1920s.

own car, and the prices of all but the luxury models were affordable. Even if a family did not have enough money to pay for the car in full, they could buy it on the installment plan (paying for an item with weekly or monthly payments).

The great shift of transportation to the automobile had many direct effects on Americans. For example, the automobile allowed farmers to end some of the isolation of their lives in rural areas. When town was several hours away by horseback or horse and wagon, the farmer and his family ventured into town only a few times a year. With a car, however, the whole family could make the same trip in minutes, day or night. Now farm families could go to town often to shop or to attend social functions.

The automobile also changed the life of many city workers by making it possible for them to live away from the inner-city area where they worked. They could instead buy a house in the "suburbs" at the edge of the city and commute back and forth by car. With this practice came a by-product of the automobile—traffic jams.

Cars made travel easy for common Americans. As people began to drive everywhere, many other industries had to grow to meet the needs of these people and cars on the move. Service stations, motels, and drive-in restaurants, sprang up everywhere. Department stores, supermarkets, and other businesses were built where they could be easily reached by car and where they could have large parking lots for their customers.

Other results of the popularity of the automobile were the spread of paved roads, the death of many people in automobile accidents, and even fast getaways for criminals as they fled from the scenes of their crimes. The automobile certainly made the average American's way of life more mobile.

The Airplane—Although the airplane was not a major form of transportation for most Americans in the 1920s, the airplane won admiration for its capabilities. In 1903 Orville and Wilbur Wright had made what is generally accepted as the first successful powered flight. World War I boosted aviation. Soon the government provided airmail service between major cities. Budding pilots pursued their interests by putting on air circuses at county fairs and by taking people up for short rides over towns.

The biggest air sensation came in 1927, when a twenty-five-year-old aviator from Little Falls, Minnesota, won a prize for being the first to fly non-stop across the Atlantic Ocean. **Charles A. Lindbergh** (LIND BURG) flew his specially designed plane, the *Spirit of St. Louis,* from New York to Paris in thirty-three and one-half hours. When Lindbergh touched down in Paris, he became an instant hero. Called "Lucky Lindy" or "the Lone Eagle," Lindbergh came home to a ticker-tape parade in New York and an invitation to the White House. Wherever he appeared over the next few years, he was mobbed by admiring fans.

Lindbergh's transatlantic flight and the record flights of other pilots did much to encourage air transportation. The first public international passenger carrier was the Pan-American "Clipper." Regularly scheduled commercial flights soon connected all of the major American cities. They also linked America to European and South American capitals.

Charles Lindbergh captured the attention of the nation with his transatlantic flight in the Spirit of St. Louis.

Electric Wonders—Second only to cars in changing American society was electricity. By 1929 generators were producing more electricity in the United States than in the rest of the world combined. Nearly all American cities and towns had electricity by the 1920s, and some rural areas had it as well. Americans were ready not just for electric lights but also for fancy new gadgets to plug in.

Inventors added electricity to many already existing household appliances like the ice box, stove, iron, and washing machine. Housewives boasted of all-electric kitchens, complete with fan, water heater, toaster, coffee percolator, and waffle iron.

Of course, electricity was also applied to industry, where it powered large machines. When applied to the communications network, electricity further improved the quality of American life. The greatest mass communication device of the 1920s was the radio.

The basis for the invention of the radio was a sound transmitter invented by an Italian, Guglielmo Marconi (mahr COH nee), in 1895. The "wireless" could transmit messages without using the usual telegraph or telephone wires. Soon inventors began using the wireless to transmit the human voice. The resulting radio provided Americans with hours of news and entertainment. The Westinghouse Company made special home receivers and sold them in quantity during the fall of 1920. Station KDKA in Pittsburgh received its broadcasting license six days before the 1920 presidential elections. The first commercial broadcast—November 2, 1920—announced Harding's election to the presidency.

The radio soon changed the way Americans lived. News, music, entertainment, and advertising reached more than twelve million American homes by 1930. Many Americans listened to comedian Jack Benny, singer Rudy Vallee, and Will Rogers's comic impersonations of Calvin Coolidge. Broadcasts of sports events also gained large popular followings. With Americans from different areas listening to the same programs, some regional differences soon began to fade. The radio drew Americans closer to events and people that affected their lives. They could hear the voice of the president and other leaders, and they could hear broadcasts of events as they happened.

The assembly line idea, developed by Henry Ford, boosted industrial production in the 1920s.

Business Boom

After the initial depression that followed the war, America soon took off on an amazing business boom. Some workers had saved money during the war while wages were high. Others were making money on new businesses. They were all ready to spend it on automobiles, electric appliances, clothes, entertainment, and the new pleasures of the 1920s. When Americans did not have the money, they borrowed it or bought items on credit.

The demand for new industrial goods caused industries to grow. Many manufacturers used the mass production techniques devised by Henry Ford. He placed workers along a moving conveyer belt, where each performed a certain task or added a certain part to the product. By 1927 this assembly line allowed him to turn out a new car every twenty-seven seconds. Similar assembly lines turned out refrigerators, phonographs, and vacuum cleaners. Clever advertising campaigns convinced customers that they had to buy more and more of the new products.

The Man Nobody Knows

President Coolidge's pointed remark that "the business of America is business" reflected the nation's widespread enthusiasm for business—an enthusiasm that affected even religion.

Bruce Barton, a preacher's son who had become a famous advertising executive, wrote a book, *The Man Nobody Knows,* which portrayed Jesus as a model businessman. Christ, according to Barton, was "the founder of modern business. . . . He picked up twelve men from the bottom ranks of business and forged them into an organization that conquered the world." Christ, Barton said, was a "sociable man" and "the most popular dinner guest in Jerusalem." Barton claimed that Jesus practiced "modern salesmanship," persuading by asking pointed questions, and even advertising by using parables. Barton's favorite quotation from the Bible was Christ's reply to His parents in Luke 2:49: "Wist ye not that I must be about my Father's business?"

The Man Nobody Knows enjoyed great success. In the mid-twenties it was on the bestseller list for two years. Despite its popularity, however, the book revealed the author's lack of knowledge of true Christianity. In a book entitled *The Christ We Know,* conservative Bible teacher A. C. Gaebelein argued that Barton's sketch of Christ struck at the heart of Christianity by denying Christ's incarnation as the Son of God: "Can the conception of Christ as a businessman, as a leader, or advertiser or sociable man, give our conscience rest and bring us nigh unto God? No! Nothing but the blood of Jesus." Furthermore, Barton's book ended with Christ's death, not His resurrection. Clearly *The Man Nobody Knows* misinterpreted Christ's work, but it does show how religion and business were mixed in the 1920s. What Barton wanted to do was bring Christ down to the level of business rather than elevate business to the standards of Christ's teachings.

Big businesses were providing new jobs. Some Americans with money left over after paying routine expenses invested in the stock market. As stockholders were paid larger dividends, more people purchased stocks, even using credit to do so. Other people invested in real estate. Property, especially in Florida, became a tempting deal, as the land was presented as a future resort paradise. Thousands bought property and resold it for higher prices, although little development took place. Many people went into debt on these get-rich-quick land speculations.

Both public attitudes and government favored big business. While attitudes toward big business had been negative from 1880 to 1920, Americans now respected or almost worshiped business and businessmen. "The man who builds a factory builds a temple, and the man who works there worships there," said President Coolidge. Business had become the god of the age. Government rarely interfered with any of the growing business empires of the 1920s. And since the prosperity of business was most important, labor unions gained little while they appeared to be fighting against American business.

SECTION REVIEW

1. How did the automobile change life for farmers? for city workers?

2. What American pilot was a hero of the 1920s? What did he accomplish in 1927?

3. What basic mass production technique did Henry Ford introduce?

 How did the radio help to unify American culture?

Moral Decay

The new prosperity of the 1920s helped to foster not only excessive materialism but also a flagrant disregard for moral standards by many. The horrors of war had prompted some of the soldiers who returned to take a "live-for-today" attitude. They wanted to experience all the pleasure they could, regardless of the future. Other Americans were affected by the new sights and sounds of the age. The changes sometimes challenged their values, especially if those values were not firmly grounded in the truths of God's unchanging Word.

In this era changes in morals and culture were more readily expressed than they had been in earlier times. Poets and novelists freely expressed their dissatisfaction with the world, its values, its standards, and its morals. They were quick to draw attention to Christians who were hypocritical or legalistic. Such Christians indeed brought reproach on God's name. Unfortunately, those same writers and artists refused to acknowledge that there were sincere Christians. They preferred instead to reject Christianity. Nor did they offer anything to replace what they had cast aside. Men and women were left in a moral vacuum, where many did not recognize right and wrong. Thus this generation was called "the lost generation."

In Pursuit of Pleasure

The young people of "the lost generation" sought satisfaction in many pursuits. Some were new and unusual and lasted. Others were passing fancies, or "fads," that soon faded. Some were harmless; others were harmful; a few were fatal.

Alvin "Shipwreck" Kelly set a record by sitting atop a flagpole for 145 days. His food and drink were hoisted to him in a bucket. While atop the pole, Kelly met the girl who became his fiancée when she came up to interview him. Others set records in marathon dancing. Raccoon coats, crossword puzzles, and a Chinese-inspired game called mahjong (MAH-ZHONG) became popular. Silent movies were the rage through most of the decade. Movie stars became American heroes, although their lifestyles were rarely worthy of emulation. Clara Bow, Greta Garbo, Mary Pickford, Rudolf "the Sheik" Valentino, and Douglas Fairbanks soon were recognized faces throughout the nation. Comic stars Buster Keaton and Charlie Chaplin made viewers laugh.

America's young people were soon copying the dress, hairstyle, and mannerisms of the stars. "Bobbed hair," much shortened from earlier years, became popular for girls. For some, such imitations were signs of rebellion. The undisciplined lifestyle gave rise to the term "flaming youth."

Many women abandoned dress and conduct codes of the past to become **"flappers."** These rebellious girls became the symbol of the Roaring Twenties. Always restless, the flappers delighted in shocking their elders with short skirts, slang, new dances, heavy makeup, and drinking or smoking in public. The young people of the lost generation did not seem to care that the pleasures of sin are but for a season.

Pleasure-hungry people sought entertainment in the theaters of America.

Interest in sports grew too whether by actual participation, attendance at events, or listening to the radio. Women made names for themselves in sports. In 1926 Gertrude Ederle became the first woman to swim the twenty-two miles across the English Channel. Helen Wills slammed her way to glory on the tennis court.

College football drew thousands of fans. Harold "Red" Grange, the "galloping ghost" of the University of Illinois, received the longest ovation in the history of college football when he ran for four touchdowns within twelve minutes. Knute Rockne (NOOT ROKnee), a Norwegian immigrant who became head football coach at Notre Dame, unleashed his players' talents to thrill radio audiences each Saturday afternoon. The "Four Horsemen of Notre Dame," his running backs, dazzled their way to gridiron glories.

Boxer Jack Dempsey, who was described as having "a neck like a bull, a granite jaw, and fists like iron," drew in the first million-dollar gate for a sporting event. Horse and auto racing drew crowds. Some people were attracted to such sports, not for their excitement, but for a wrong reason, gambling.

Other famous names in sports included a baseball star George Herman "Babe" Ruth, a home run hitter for the New York Yankees; Bobby Jones won fame on the links as a golfer. Besides entering major car races, Barney Oldfield raced at county fairs. And a horse named Man O'War won twenty of the twenty-one races he entered.

The Roaring Twenties are memorable partly because there was a greater emphasis on the sensational. Murders and other forms of crime filled American papers. Each crime seemed more sensational than the previous

Babe Ruth began his baseball career as a talented pitcher, but he became a home run hitting hero for the New York Yankees.

one reported. Americans seemed to thrive on all the excitement they could find.

Accidents and human misfortune captured the attention of the press. A hero dog named Balto and a spelunker (spih LUNG kur; one who explores caves) named Floyd Collins were two of the big stories in 1925. Balto carried diphtheria antitoxin 655 miles across Alaska to Nome. To save lives, this lead dog covered the distance in a blinding blizzard while the temperature plunged to fifty below zero. Floyd Collins gained fame for his explorations of Mammoth Cave in Kentucky. On another cave adventure, however, a seven-ton boulder pinned him in. A thin reporter managed to wriggle down the treacherous hole to interview him. The vivid descriptions riveted the attention of the nation on Sand Cave, Kentucky, where Collins was trapped. Floyd's voice became weaker by the day. On the eighteenth day of reporting, there was no reply from the trapped man; he was dead.

Detroit police discover an illegal brewery during prohibition.

The Failure of Prohibition

Prohibition was also an important issue. In 1919 the Eighteenth Amendment had been ratified. It had established prohibition by making illegal the manufacture, sale, transportation, import, and export of intoxicating liquors as a beverage. The outlawing of liquor was supported by many Americans. Thousands had rallied to the temperance societies of the 1800s, and the progressives of the early 1900s had made prohibition a major issue.

By 1915 fifteen states had voted out "demon rum." By 1918 thirty-three states were in the prohibition column. Since the United States was selling all its surplus grain to the Allies for food, it was considered unpatriotic to make liquor. The prohibition amend- ment passed Congress and went to the states for ratification. Its widespread support at the time is evidenced by its quick approval. All the states except Rhode Island and Connecticut ratified it in just over a year. In most states prohibition won by a large majority.

Prohibition, however, proved difficult to enforce. The Volstead Act of 1919 made any beverage with more than 0.5% alcohol illegal. It also set up a Prohibition Bureau to enforce the law. But the bureau had a small budget and only three thousand agents to enforce the law. Soon the problems of prohibition appeared.

Illegal taverns called **"speakeasies"** appeared across the nation. The border with Canada, where alcohol was legal, stretched nearly three thousand miles. Officers could not effectively patrol the long border, and liquor flowed freely across it. The Atlantic seaboard also had its share of rum runners. **Bootlegging,** selling illegal liquor, became a big business and made many rich. Since it was legal to have alcohol for medicinal reasons, some people got it by doctor's prescription. Others made their own home brew in stills.

Violence often accompanied the criminals who organized bootlegging rings. "Scarface" **Al Capone,** leader of a large crime ring in Chicago, made $60 million on liquor alone in 1927. He and other ruthless criminals organized liquor networks to supply those who wanted liquor and were willing to pay any price for it. They also extended their activity to crimes such as illegal gambling and prostitution. Criminal gangs controlled these activities in certain areas, and if a rival gang tried to operate in another's territory, the gangs sometimes went to "war" with one another. Innocent people were killed in raids, and such crimes shocked the public. Although periodic crackdowns came, it proved hard to put these gangsters behind bars. Not only would the criminals refuse to testify against each other, but the gangs also threatened the lives of honest citizens called as witnesses and bought off judges and officials.

By the late 1920s it seemed apparent that prohibition was not working. More and more Americans cried out for its repeal, which finally came in 1933. Prohibition has been called the "noble experiment" because the government tried to do away with an evil in society. Liquor is certainly the source of much pain and sin, but laws cannot change the moral character of men. Only salvation through Jesus Christ can change the hearts of individuals. As long as most of society remains without Christ, it will reject restrictions on its moral actions.

Nevertheless, prohibition did bring some benefits. Less alcohol was consumed, and some people gave up drinking. There was less gambling. Alcohol-related diseases and deaths decreased, and sober workers were more efficient. When prohibition was repealed, liquor freely began to afflict Americans with its sad effects again.

Ridicule of True Christianity

Because many Americans of the 1920s wanted fortune and pleasure without moral restrictions, they attacked the authority of Scripture. They did not want to be accountable to God and the standards set forth in His Word. Instead they followed the ideas of men that gave them excuses for rejecting the truth of the Bible. The theory of evolution, popularized by Darwin, told men that God had not created them. They reasoned that if God was not their Creator, then they did not need His salvation.

They also found other ideas that they thought freed them from responsibility. The psychologist Sigmund Freud taught that man behaves the way he does because of subconscious drives. Men interpreted his writings to mean that people cannot help what they do; therefore, they should do whatever they please and not feel guilty. Even Albert Einstein, famous mathematician and scientist, added to the sense of moral freedom. His theory of relativity stated that time, space, and mass were not fixed or absolute. Although Einstein himself did not apply his theory to moral matters, many people began to think that everything was relative. These men said that there are no absolute rights and wrongs and that everyone should do what is right in his own eyes.

Of course the Bible clearly states the standard God has set for man. Men who preached about the responsibility of man to a holy God and the truth of Scripture soon found themselves scorned by the society around them. The greatest example of this scorn in the

1920s came with a trial concerning the teaching of evolution in schools.

In the 1920s Christians, angry because evolution was being taught in the public schools, pressured state legislatures to pass laws forbidding teachers to teach evolution. The Tennessee state legislature passed such a law. John Scopes, a high school biology teacher, broke the law and was brought to trial. He was convicted and fined $100.

Actually, the **Scopes Trial** had been a publicity stunt of two businessmen in Dayton, Tennessee. Eager to attract attention to their town, they asked Scopes to teach evolution with the assurance that the American Civil Liberties Union would provide legal support. The two businessmen hoped that a dramatic

William Jennings Bryan had been a prominent politician during the Progressive Era, but his participation in the Scopes Trial brought him ridicule.

J. Gresham Machen (1881-1937)

J. Gresham Machen (MAY chun) was perhaps the most scholarly spokesman for the faith during the 1920s. He studied at some of the best schools in the United States and Europe and was a professor at Princeton Seminary until its liberalism caused him to leave. During the 1920s he believed that the Presbyterian church was falling away from Scriptural truth and wrote several scholarly books defending truths such as the virgin birth, the inspiration of the Bible, the atonement, and the bodily resurrection of Christ. Machen argued that if someone held other views, he was not a Christian.

After leaving Princeton Seminary in 1929 Machen helped found Westminster Seminary in Philadelphia, where he taught until his death. He also set up a new independent mission board because of liberalism in the denominational one. Because of his stand for the truth, Machen was dismissed from the Presbyterian church, and by 1936 he and other conservatives formed the Orthodox Presbyterian Church. One of Machen's best books is *Christianity and Liberalism,* an attack on modernism.

trial would draw attention to Dayton and thus attract industry to the town.

In the summer of 1925, the trial turned into the hoped-for gigantic media event. Two hundred reporters converged on the small town of Dayton, and for the first time a trial was covered by radio. One of the prosecutors was William Jennings Bryan, three-time Democratic presidential nominee. Clarence Darrow, a famous trial lawyer and agnostic, defended Scopes. H. L. Mencken (MENG kun), a nationally known reporter who made fun of Christians, called the people of Dayton "gaping primates" and the event in Dayton the "Monkey Trial."

Bryan testified in the trial and was ridiculed by Darrow. While Bryan was a staunch defender of the faith, he did not always handle Darrow's questions well. Bryan was not a Bible scholar or a scientist. Even though Scopes was convicted for teaching evolution, the trial had made Bible-believing Christians appear ignorant and unscientific. The Scopes trial was a disappointment to true Christians, yet they knew that their faith rested in the sure Word of God. Even in such an era of open sin and ridicule of the Bible, some men still stood firm as they preached the truth of Scripture.

SECTION REVIEW

1. Why were the people of the 1920s sometimes called "the lost generation"?

2. Who were the heroes and heroines of this generation?

3. What is "bootlegging"?

4. What famous trial took place as a result of the teaching of evolution? Where did it take place?

 Why did Prohibition fail?

Political Inaction

The presidents of the 1920s reflected the attitudes and goals of the day. They promoted the unhindered growth of business and the general enjoyment of prosperity. The business and prosperity were indeed enjoyable, but some of the nation's serious problems were brushed aside at the time. Eventually the fruits of the materialism and selfishness of the era turned out to be a severe crisis for the country.

Harding's Weakness

Warren G. Harding was a likable newspaper editor from the small town of Marion,

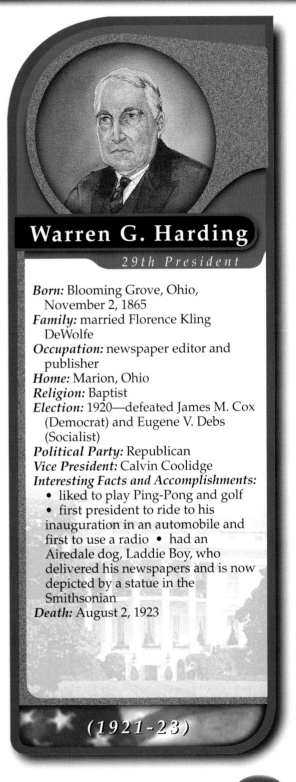

Warren G. Harding
29th President

Born: Blooming Grove, Ohio, November 2, 1865
Family: married Florence Kling DeWolfe
Occupation: newspaper editor and publisher
Home: Marion, Ohio
Religion: Baptist
Election: 1920—defeated James M. Cox (Democrat) and Eugene V. Debs (Socialist)
Political Party: Republican
Vice President: Calvin Coolidge
Interesting Facts and Accomplishments:
  • liked to play Ping-Pong and golf
  • first president to ride to his inauguration in an automobile and first to use a radio • had an Airedale dog, Laddie Boy, who delivered his newspapers and is now depicted by a statue in the Smithsonian
Death: August 2, 1923

(1921-23)

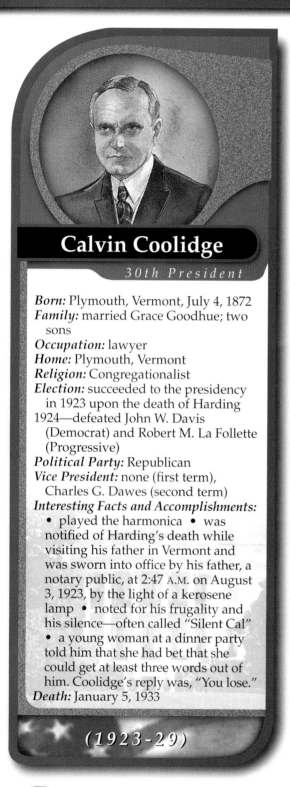

Calvin Coolidge

30th President

Born: Plymouth, Vermont, July 4, 1872
Family: married Grace Goodhue; two sons
Occupation: lawyer
Home: Plymouth, Vermont
Religion: Congregationalist
Election: succeeded to the presidency in 1923 upon the death of Harding
1924—defeated John W. Davis (Democrat) and Robert M. La Follette (Progressive)
Political Party: Republican
Vice President: none (first term), Charles G. Dawes (second term)
Interesting Facts and Accomplishments:
• played the harmonica • was notified of Harding's death while visiting his father in Vermont and was sworn into office by his father, a notary public, at 2:47 A.M. on August 3, 1923, by the light of a kerosene lamp • noted for his frugality and his silence—often called "Silent Cal"
• a young woman at a dinner party told him that she had bet that she could get at least three words out of him. Coolidge's reply was, "You lose."
Death: January 5, 1933

(1923-29)

Ohio. He had come up the political ladder through Ohio politics, eventually becoming a U.S. senator. The political leaders in the state at that time were called the "Ohio Gang," and Harding did his share of favors for these friends to achieve his political success.

Harding had promised to get the country back to normal after the war, and since that was what the country wanted, he was easily elected to the presidency. It may also be noted that the 1920 election was the first time that women could vote for a president.

Once in office, Harding supported most of the popular programs of the day, especially big business. Unfortunately, he appointed many of his political friends to important offices in which they could use the government to promote their own gain. Although Harding was basically honest, his friends turned his administration into a great scandal. The most prominent criminal was Harding's secretary of the interior, **Albert B. Fall.** Fall persuaded Harding and the secretary of the navy to transfer control of government-owned oil reserves from the Navy Department to Fall's Interior Department. He then leased the reserves at Teapot Dome, Wyoming, and Elk Hills, California, to two oil men, who paid him back with several "loans" totaling $400,000. When Fall's crime was uncovered, he went to prison, the first cabinet member in history to be imprisoned for misdeeds in office.

Although not involved in public scandal for financial gain, Harding was weak and at fault personally for allowing the law to be disobeyed within White House walls. Harding was obviously a poor leader who failed to take his executive responsibility seriously. Instead of providing firm direction, Harding allowed national affairs to simply drift along without guidance. By the summer of 1923 Harding knew something was wrong. He told journalist William Allen White, "I have no trouble with my enemies. I can take care of them all right.

But my friends, White, they're the ones that keep me walking the floor nights."

Harding took a vacation to Alaska in 1923. On the way back the president became seriously ill July 28 in his hotel room in California. He died August 2. The officially listed cause of death was ptomaine poisoning. Since no one else in the party of sixty-five got food poisoning, however, it is more likely that he died of a heart attack. The **Teapot Dome Scandal** was uncovered after his death.

Coolidge's Administration

Calvin Coolidge, born in Vermont, had studied law in Massachusetts and entered politics there. He had gained a reputation as a "law and order" man when as governor of Massachusetts he had taken a stand during a Boston police strike in 1919. He declared, "There is no right to strike against the public safety by anybody, anywhere, any time," and forced the police back to work. To a nation that was in fear of disorder and crime, this stand won him admiration.

Succeeding to the presidency on Harding's death, Coolidge was in charge when most of the Harding scandals were revealed. By firmly prosecuting the corrupt officials, Coolidge won enough support to win the presidential election of 1924. Then he carried on the same basic policies that Harding had supported. While business appeared to be successful during the Coolidge administration, ominous conditions were developing. Because of the unwise speculation of investors, prices were going higher and higher on the stock market. Buying on credit was so popular that millions of Americans were in serious debt. Farmers were still overproducing and receiving low prices for their produce. These and other features of the American economy would soon lead the nation into calamity.

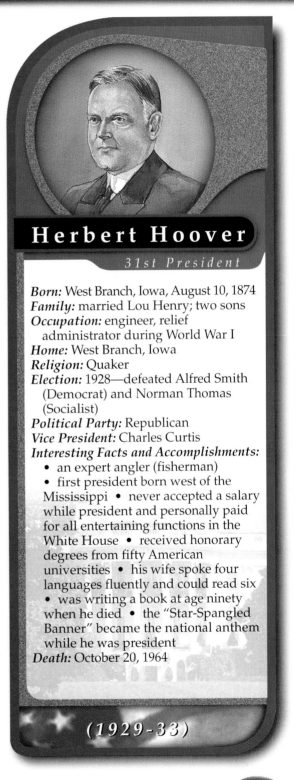

Herbert Hoover
31st President

Born: West Branch, Iowa, August 10, 1874
Family: married Lou Henry; two sons
Occupation: engineer, relief administrator during World War I
Home: West Branch, Iowa
Religion: Quaker
Election: 1928—defeated Alfred Smith (Democrat) and Norman Thomas (Socialist)
Political Party: Republican
Vice President: Charles Curtis
Interesting Facts and Accomplishments:
- an expert angler (fisherman)
- first president born west of the Mississippi • never accepted a salary while president and personally paid for all entertaining functions in the White House • received honorary degrees from fifty American universities • his wife spoke four languages fluently and could read six • was writing a book at age ninety when he died • the "Star-Spangled Banner" became the national anthem while he was president
Death: October 20, 1964

(1929-33)

Hoover's Inheritance

The nation was still enjoying prosperity, however, when the election of 1928 came. The Republican candidate, **Herbert Hoover,** was swept into office by a nation satisfied with success. Hoover, a poor, orphaned farm boy, had proved his abilities by becoming a wealthy mining engineer and then devoting his talents to public service. His Democrat opponent, Al Smith, was a Roman Catholic and was against Prohibition. The nation was not yet ready to vote a Catholic into the presidency.

Hoover was talented, but he had inherited the impending fall from prosperity. The excesses of the twenties were about to result in disaster, and Hoover would be saddled with the responsibility for the Great Depression that was to come.

SECTION REVIEW

1. Name the three Republican presidents of the 1920s.

2. What act of corruption is associated with Albert B. Fall?

 What conditions of the 1920s would help bring the nation's prosperity to an end?

SUMMARY

The Roaring Twenties was a time of prosperity for the nation, following the sacrifices of World War I. Businesses boomed, and Americans enjoyed the new consumer goods and amusements. The United States generally isolated itself from foreign problems and distrusted foreigners within the country, while it concerned itself with issues and events at home such as Prohibition, Lindbergh's flight, and the fads of the "flaming youth." The 1920s was also a time of great decline in moral character. Americans pursued material possessions, often risking their future by buying too much on credit or speculating in stock and land. They ridiculed Christianity, rebelled against moral restraints, and turned to the pleasures of sin and selfishness. Although the decade was one of general prosperity, Americans would pay for some of their excesses with the hardships of the decade to come.

Chapter Review

People, Places, and Things to Remember

Warren G. Harding
Treaty of Washington
Kellogg-Briand Peace
   Pact
Calvin Coolidge

Charles A. Lindbergh
flappers
Prohibition
speakeasies
bootlegging

Al Capone
Scopes Trial
Albert B. Fall
Teapot Dome Scandal
Herbert Hoover

Review Questions

Match each of these men with the statement or description most closely related to him.

1. Al Capone
2. Calvin Coolidge
3. Albert B. Fall
4. Warren G. Harding
5. Herbert Hoover
6. Charles Lindbergh

   a. America should "return to normalcy"
   b. flew the *Spirit of St. Louis* to Paris
   c. a Chicago gangster
   d. organizer of Teapot Dome scheme
   e. "the business of America is business"
   f. inherited the fall from prosperity

Answer the following questions about the 1920s.

7. What two international agreements did the United States sign in the 1920s?
8. What was the "Red Scare"?
9. When was the first commercial radio broadcast, and what did it announce?
10. In what fad did "Shipwreck" Kelly participate?
11. What were the shockingly fashionable young women of the 1920s called?
12. When did Prohibition begin, and when did it end?
13. What is bootlegging?
14. In what famous trial was a teacher convicted of teaching evolution but biblical Christianity ridiculed?

Questions for Discussion

15. Why is the Roaring Twenties a good name for the 1920s?
16. Are fads ever bad? Explain your answer.

Modern man expresses his beliefs every day. They are seen in politics, science, religion, education, and in many other areas. Some beliefs are expressed so frequently that they become accepted as truths—even by Christians. However, many widely accepted beliefs are far from the truths found in the Scriptures. Evolution is one of these beliefs.

Shortly after Darwin promoted the theory of evolution, philosophers began to apply it to every area of life. When William Jennings Bryan and Clarence Darrow debated evolution in 1925, they debated more than a theory of life's origin. They debated a way of thinking. According to the evolutionist, man is a well-developed animal; he was not created by God and therefore has no responsibility to Him. Any ideas of right and wrong were created by man, not by God.

Evolution's influence has been most obvious in the field of science. It is now common to hear scientists refer to the earth as "millions of years old" and life forms evolving slowly from simple to complex organisms. For instance, evolutionists look at the Grand Canyon and conclude that it formed over millions of years. A much simpler explanation might be that a catastrophic flood carved it out. Despite major gaps in evidence, scientists continue to accept evolution as a fact. They are like those mentioned in II Peter 3:5-6. ("For this they willingly are ignorant of, that by the word of God the heavens were of old, and the earth standing out of the water and in the water: Whereby the world that then was, being overflowed with water, perished.")

Once the field of science had accepted evolution, the theory moved into the field of education. Schools throughout the country receive funding each year from the National Science Foundation—an organization that also supports research on human evolution. The National Science Teacher's Association openly accepts the theory of evolution. Despite the ongoing debate between Creationism and evolution, NSTA states, "There is no longer a debate among scientists over whether evolution has taken place." When students hear that evolution is a fact and Creation is a myth, they begin to believe it.

It is not surprising that evolutionary thinking has spread to so many areas.

Evolution has also influenced economics. In the nineteenth century the German philosopher Herbert Spenser coined the evolutionary phrase "survival of the fittest," which means that life forms survive because they are strong and selfish. Ferdinand Lundberg sees a similar economic philosophy today. In his 1988 book *The Rich and the Super Rich* he states, "Standard doctrine holds that one should always pay the lowest possible wages and taxes, charge the highest possible prices and rents, and never give anything away unless the gift confers some hidden personal benefit." The doctrine might make sense if man were an animal. However, the Bible teaches that man is a unique being created in God's image. Romans 12:10 says, "Be kindly affectioned one to another with brotherly love; in honour preferring one another." Obviously the "standard doctrine" is not the doctrine of the Bible.

Evolution has had a growing influence on the American legal system as well. When laws are based on God's Word, they are unchanging, like the Bible itself. However, laws based on evolution are much different. If society is evolving, then the standards of what is right or wrong can change with it. For example, in 1993 the Hawaii Supreme Court ruled that the state could not deny same-sex couples marriage licenses without a "compelling reason." In Isaiah 5:20 and 24 God warns those who change the definition of right and wrong. "Woe unto them that call evil good, and good evil . . . their blossom shall go up as dust: because they have cast away the law of the Lord of hosts, and despised the word of the Holy One of Israel."

Effects from the theory of evolution are also very evident when it comes to social issues, such as abortion. Evolution is used to justify the killing of unborn babies because it is a natural practice among some animals. In *Science* magazine Barbara Burke writes, "Among some animal species, infant killing appears to be a natural practice. Could it be natural for humans too, a trait inherited from our ancestors?" While disabled and unwanted children may seem to serve little purpose from an evolutionary world view, Christians know that God can use these lives greatly to His glory.

No doubt many Christians see the evil influences of evolution in these areas, but they may not notice it in others.

The Bible teaches that in the family the father should be the head of the household and that children should respect his authority. Evolutionists base the family structure on animal societies and "primitive" human society, where this authority is less important.

In the area of music, true standards of beauty come from God, not man. Melody, harmony, and rhythm all demonstrate the orderliness of God's universe. When they are skillfully blended, they create beautiful music. An evolutionist who disregards these standards can claim that any music is "good" no matter how it sounds.

The same principle applies to visual art. In New York City, for example, one museum advertised its exhibition as "a deliberate rejection of all the emblems of successful art: originality, integrity of materials, coherence of form." Any effort to push ahead the "evolution" of music and art into new forms is automatically labeled as good. Evolutionary thinking has allowed subjects focusing on sin to be called good.

With all the influence evolution has had, the world can seem a scary place for Christians. We are surrounded by those who oppose what the Scriptures teach. But God has a purpose for keeping His children in this sinful environment. The root of evolutionary thinking comes from a rejection of God. The only way people can change their thinking is through a change of heart. God has given Christians the privilege of presenting people with the only one who can do that—Christ.

Charles Darwin plots with Coco, King of the Monkeys, to take over the world with his "Theory of Evolution"

25

Crash and Depression

American businesses appeared to be flourishing as stock prices rose higher and higher in 1929. Although prices reached a new high in September, conservative investors were beginning to grow cautious. Those who sold stocks found fewer buyers, and prices began to slide down. By October, orders to brokers to sell surpassed orders to buy. On Thursday, October 24, a record-breaking thirteen million shares changed hands. Prices slid so low that investors lost $9 billion on that "Black Thursday." Many investors, who lost all of their money, could not pay the stock brokers the additional money that they owed. When the investors could not pay, brokers tried desperately to sell the stock, flooding the market still more.

A panic broke out the following Tuesday, October 29, when there were orders to sell sixteen million shares on the exchange. Fortunes made over a period of years vanished in minutes. Some people became so depressed they took their lives. This **stock market crash of 1929** signaled the beginning of the **Great Depression,** a time of hardship for many Americans.

The Fall of Prosperity

In 1928 during his election campaign Herbert Hoover had declared, "We in America today are nearer to the final triumph over poverty than ever before in the history of any land," but soon millions of Americans would join the ranks of the unemployed, the homeless, and the hungry. The Roaring Twenties ended with a national financial collapse that would afflict Americans for the next decade.

Causes of the Crash

The great desires for wealth and pleasure in the 1920s had much to do with the crash that followed, but there were several specific causes for the financial crisis.

Industrial Problems—Despite the overall air of prosperity in the 1920s, many common workers had already faced economic woes. Farmers were suffering from low prices. Textile workers and coal miners were hurt by layoffs as demand for their products declined. These workers could no longer buy the industrial goods that were filling the market. Eventually, many other Americans were running out of credit to buy more. With a decreased demand for goods, industrial output slowed. Laborers worked fewer hours or were laid off, cutting incomes and causing hardships. Since industries were often interdependent, when one cut back, others were forced to do the same. As consumer spending continued to drop, industrial expansion came almost to a standstill long before the crash actually took place.

Overuse of Credit—The use of credit, especially of installment buying, had grown steadily. While credit covered some of the early symptoms of economic illness, its unwise and often unrestrained use made things worse. Before long, people were having to make such high payments on the things they had bought on credit that they could not afford to buy anything new. Auto sales and construction lagged, and workers were laid off; these people were then unable to meet their payments at all. Merchants, who had extended the credit loans, lost money, and their businesses began to falter.

Speculation—In the late twenties newspapers carried accounts of people who had profited from get-rich-quick schemes. These speculators, often motivated by greed, bought properties at a low price, hoping to sell them quickly for a much higher price. Most had speculated in land or stock.

Land prices went up in the 1920s, especially in urban areas or near recreational settings as people moved outward to the suburbs. The biggest land boom was in Florida, where the semitropical climate attracted hordes of speculators. Miami alone boasted two thousand real estate offices in 1925. Those who had speculated early and bought good land did make big profits. But others who bought land on credit found they could not make their payments. Some people were swindled into buying undesirable lands and even swamps. In 1926 hurricanes struck, helping to put an end to the desire to invest in the area. Homes were left vacant, and few sales were made thereafter. Bank failures in Florida climbed when loans were not repaid.

While risky land investments did not tempt many Americans, stock speculation did. Prices of corporate stock had risen steadily beginning in 1927. By September 1929 stock prices were 400 percent higher than they had been in 1925. People of modest means were attracted to stock purchases. The ticker-tape machine allowed purchasers across America to follow price changes almost as they happened. The number of those "playing the market" grew to about 1.5 million in 1929. But most were not buying stocks to collect quarterly dividends. Rather, they wanted to sell stocks for quick profits when the prices rose. Many investors paid scant attention to the earnings of the companies they had invested in, an indication of the actual value of the stock. They assumed stock prices would keep going up no matter what the industries did.

The problem was made even more complex because brokers allowed investors to **buy on the margin.** The investors or buyers paid only part of the purchase price in cash, usually ten percent, and borrowed the rest from the broker, using the stock as collateral. The broker borrowed money from banks and corporations to cover loans made to his investors. If the value of the stock went up, there was no

The stock market seemed to be going strong just before the crash

problem. The buyer could repay his loan with interest and gain a profit. If the stock's value went below the value of the loan, however, the buyer's margin was "called in." The speculator then had to get more cash or risk loss of the shares along with his cash investment. If the buyer could not repay his loan, the broker could take the stock.

The system satisfied many and seemed to stimulate the economy. Stock prices climbed, and in March 1928 both the volume of shares traded and their value soared. The boom lasted through the summer of 1929, although econo-

mists were baffled because both prices and business profits were falling at the same time.

International Economic Problems—In addition to economic problems such as the lack of industrial expansion, the overuse of credit, and wild speculation on land and stock, several other problems helped to bring the downfall of prosperity. Many of these involved not only the financial operations of the United States, but also those of other countries, particularly European countries.

America had lent the Allies money during World War I, and the debts and their interest amounted to over $11 billion. War-torn Europe had little cash to repay this debt. In addition, the United States had passed a high tariff on foreign goods that kept European nations from trading with America. Without profitable trade, Europe could not repay the debt. The only source of money for repayment to American creditors was the money they received from German reparations payments. Yet the Germans were also too poor to make these large payments for the war as the Treaty of Versailles had demanded. To this complex situation of international debt was added the fact that Americans began to lend Germany millions of dollars to rebuild the country, but Germany used the money to make the reparations payments. When the crash came, most of the money from these international loans was lost, and the end of American credit and prosperity threw Europe into a severe depression too.

Conditions of the Depression

Once the crash came, most Americans lost all their optimism. They saw prosperity disappear, and most had little hope that it would return very soon. Investments, money, jobs, and even homes were no longer safe.

The Run on Banks—People became increasingly afraid that the money they had deposited in banks would be lost. Some drew money out of banks to pay their brokers. Others panicked and withdrew all their money. Banks could not keep pace with the demand. In the last two weeks before Hoover left office, depositors pulled out $1 billion. Banks ran out of cash and were forced to close their doors, some permanently. Others reopened to offer depositors only a percentage of their total deposit.

Banks had unwittingly contributed to the collapse through unwise extension of credit. In September 1927 there was $1.3 billion out in loans. The same month in 1929 the total had risen to $8.5 billion. When many of these loans could not be repaid, the banks ran out of money. By 1931 about five thousand banks had closed their doors. Not all were large, but some were; the failure of the Bank of the United States in New York City affected 400,000 people.

Unemployment—Millions of Americans were thrown out of work by the depression. By 1931, thirteen million Americans, one of every four workers, were unemployed. While some workers kept their jobs, they labored only a few days a week or a few hours a day. Others who kept their jobs took wage cuts.

The loss of a man's job usually meant no steady income for his family. Even so, the family needed food. The mortgage or rent payments had to be made. Any person or business that had given credit was now beating on the

The depression caused great despair and suffering among America's poor, but conditions for families in the Dust Bowl became especially difficult.

door to receive payment. The situation seemed desperate to millions of Americans.

Wives and mothers helped out the best they could. They took in laundry and took cleaning jobs. If families had an empty room or children could double up, they took in renters. They planted gardens and canned vegetables to save on grocery bills. Clothing was patched; socks were darned. Children wore hand-me-downs. Sometimes unemployed husbands or older sons left home to search for work in another town.

Many families could not continue paying the installments on their loans. Because of

Soup kitchens provided many people their only meal of the day.

mortgage foreclosures, some eventually lost their homes. Some moved to abandoned boxcars or hastily built shacks on the edges of towns. Since these poverty dwellings were blamed on the president and his policies, they were called "Hoovervilles." Many who needed help were aided by others. Family members helped their relatives. Friends and churches also offered help. People helped each other, trading their skills and materials.

The depression forced most Americans to lower their living standards. For many the depression destroyed their sense of independence and accomplishment. It was difficult, especially for a family's primary breadwinner, to be unemployed, unable to support his own family. Some men searched for work in vain and then waited for handouts at soup kitchens or stood in bread lines. Sometimes they gleaned fields, scavenged city dumps, or searched for food in garbage cans. It was not uncommon to see once-prosperous men selling apples on the street corner. A few men tried to escape from their troubles by jumping on freight trains to ride the rails as hobos.

The depression forced some Americans to reexamine their values. They found they could live on less. For Christians the depression offered many opportunities to trust the Lord in new ways. They continually saw God's provision for His people as He supplied their needs. They saw anew the truth of Psalm 37:25: "I have been young, and now am old; yet have I not seen the righteous forsaken, nor his seed begging bread." Yet during this economic depression, there was no significant major religious revival. Many Americans, when hard

"I Remember the Drought"

The droughts of the 1930s created desperate conditions for farmers. One victim of the droughts recalled his family's situation:

"I know from experience what it means to have no rain. For three years in the thirties we had very, very little rain. There was no pasture for the cows on our dairy farm. My dad chopped down trees so the cows could eat leaves all summer. They would bellow when they heard Dad chopping. We had to make leaf haystacks, which the cows ate in the winter. The grass was so thin Mother used a hand rake and a gunnysack to pick up the hay. The winds blew every day, day after day. The grasshoppers were the only ones who were happy and multiplied easily. They skinned the thistles to live. We poisoned them at every turn. . . . To this day, I still conserve [water] and feel that it's almost a sin to use too much of it because you just don't know when it might be scarce again."

pressed, turned not to God but to the government.

Further Farm Problems—Few farmers had been prosperous, even in the booming 1920s. They produced so much grain, livestock, and other farm products that prices had stayed low. Many farmers could not make payments on farmland they had bought or on the cars, equipment, and other items that they had bought on credit. Without higher prices for their products, many were in danger of losing their farms.

Conditions for farmers became even worse, especially on the western edge of the Central Plains and on the Great Plains, where the **"Dust Bowl"** brought extreme poverty. This area, already semiarid, had first been overgrazed by cattle. Then with the increased demand for food during World War I, it had been plowed into farms. Since there had been enough rainfall then, farmers were able to make money. But in the 1930s droughts came,

Dust clouds blocked out the sun for miles

adding to the farmers' economic woes. First the crops dried up. Next the land turned to dust. Then winds whipped the rich topsoil off the dry exposed ground. By late fall of 1933, "black blizzards" blew from west to east across the country. The clouds of dust darkened skies as far away as Albany, New York. By 1934 the lands from Texas to Canada were ravaged by the dust storms. The soil drifted into banks like snow. Cars had to use their headlights in the daytime. Families put wet towels in window sills and under doors to keep out the choking dust. Livestock died of thirst. Thousands of farm families fled from their homes. Some went to areas, especially in

During the depression Herbert Hoover tried to be optomistic about the prospects for the American economy and people.

California, where farm workers were needed to tend vegetable fields and orchards.

Hoover's Plight

President Herbert Hoover tried to deal with the onset of the depression by being optimistic. The more people panicked, the more damage was done to the economy, and so he tried to encourage Americans to believe that these trials would soon pass and business would boom again. Few people seemed to listen. Stock prices continued to fall as investors tried to sell. Runs on banks continued, and industry remained inactive. Although Hoover was not responsible for the problems that beset America, he was the president, and thus he received most of the blame for everything that was going wrong.

The Veterans Demand Aid—The veterans of World War I had been promised a life insurance bonus to be paid in 1945. Although the veterans were no worse off than most other Americans in the depression, many began to ask for the government to pay them part of the face value of their insurance policies at an earlier date. In the spring of 1932, Walter Waters, an unemployed veteran from Oregon, journeyed east to the capital to pressure Congress to pay the "bonus." Soon men from all parts of the country joined him. About 20,000 veterans became a part of this "Bonus Army" and camped on a low-lying muddy area near the Potomac River. The men were there most of the summer. When the Senate defeated the Bonus Bill, many veterans left, but a few thousand remained. Hoover refused to meet with them, but he did ask Congress to advance them money from their insurance policies so they could get home. They were told that any who were left after July 28 would be evicted. At this point radicals in the group tried to start a riot. After two policemen were beaten to the ground, two Bonus marchers were killed. Hoover then opted to use troops, and the soldiers routed the veterans and set fire to their shacks. Although stern action was needed, Hoover received much criticism for treating the veterans harshly.

Hoover's Theory—The President was not insensitive to how the depression was affecting Americans. He believed first in "local responsibility. The best hearts and brains of every community could best serve their neighbors." He believed that creating government agencies to handle the problems would give the sufferers more red tape than relief. His position was that federal funds should be used only after all voluntary and local resources were exhausted.

When federal monies were used, Hoover believed they needed to be carefully regulated. They should not be given directly to people as a **dole,** or handout, such as welfare is today. Instead, they should be used for projects so that the effects of the funds would benefit more people. If cities and states, for example, were given loans to pay for public works projects, they could hire local people who would benefit from the employment.

Hoover did not believe in government regulation of big business. He saw federal control of activities as an invitation to dictatorship, corruption, waste, and inefficiency. He defended personal freedoms against government encroachment. He greatly feared socialism. He also wanted to keep the federal budget balanced, so he was reluctant to spend large amounts of money for aid programs.

Hoover's ideas were basically good, but he soon met opposition. Sound though his policies might have been, they required both time and the cooperation of the people to bring the desired results. Many Americans saw only their immediate hardships and wanted relief right away. When the president's ideas brought no quick remedy, many Americans began to complain.

Franklin Delano Roosevelt won votes with his enthusiasm and "New Deal"

Hoover did try to establish programs to help the people. He set up some government work projects to employ thousands of men and supply useful work. Public buildings were constructed, and in 1931 construction was started on what became Hoover Dam on the Colorado River. The federal government also subsidized the building of thousands of miles of roads.

In January of 1932, Congress passed Hoover's bill creating the **Reconstruction Finance Corporation.** It could lend up to $2 billion to businesses, industries, and banks to undertake projects that would employ more men. Therefore, there would be less need for direct relief. Congress also approved the president's request for twelve Federal District Home Loans Banks. These banks could lend money to loan associations, banks, and insurance companies, who in turn could aid homeowners who were having trouble making mortgage payments.

Despite these actions, Hoover continued to receive criticism. The steps he took were not dramatic enough to satisfy the many Americans who were still waiting for help.

SECTION REVIEW

1. What were four specific causes of the financial crisis?

2. What does it mean to "buy on the margin"?

3. What were "Hoovervilles"?

4. What natural disaster hit farmers on the plains?

5. Why did the "Bonus Army" travel to Washington, D.C.?

 How did Herbert Hoover want to handle the nation's financial problems?

FDR and the New Deal

While Hoover was reluctant to take dramatic action, discontent grew. Because many Americans continued to blame Hoover and the Republicans for the problems of the depression, the Democrats gained followers.

The Election of 1932

The election of 1932 was one of the most decisive in American history. The Republicans renominated Herbert Hoover. The Democrats chose New York's governor, **Franklin Delano Roosevelt,** and John Nance Garner of Texas as his running mate. Some Americans believed that the regular parties were not solving America's problems, so they turned to radical leaders. The Socialist party nominated Norman Thomas, and the Communists ran William Foster.

The President's Polio

Even though President Roosevelt had a disability, he did not let it interfere with his political aspirations. Stricken with polio in 1921 at the age of thirty-nine, Roosevelt was permanently paralyzed from the hips down. To most people that would have signaled the end of any political career. To Franklin Delano Roosevelt it was just another obstacle to push aside on his way to the highest office in the land.

It was not always easy. Roosevelt had to use metal braces just to stand. In order to minimize the effect of his disability on the public, Roosevelt refused to be seen in his wheelchair. He had to be helped to "walk" up to the podiums to give his speeches. One time the podium had not been fastened down, and it and the president went tumbling off the platform into the orchestra pit. Returning to the reset stand, Roosevelt simply picked up his speech right where he had left off. For traveling, he had a railroad car with a special elevator and a special wheelchair.

Roosevelt's condition also gave him a special burden for the similarly disabled. He was constantly visiting the hospitals and working with disabled children or soldiers. He had a car designed with hand controls, and often he would take a particularly discouraged child for a ride and talk. Always the child returned with a positive attitude and a desire to go on. Roosevelt also invested heavily in a treatment center at Warm Springs, Georgia. The springs there had a therapeutic effect on those who used them.

Whatever one's view of Roosevelt's political philosophy, his courage and perseverance in confronting his physical limitations must be admired and applauded.

Roosevelt campaigned with buoyant enthusiasm and confidence. He favored programs that were very costly, while promising to cut government spending by twenty-five percent. He promised the voters a **"New Deal,"** and many were drawn to him because he gave hope for strong actions that might bring change.

Hoover praised "rugged individualism" and encouraged voluntary efforts by industry and labor to deal with their problems. Although Hoover also pledged more government action than before, by the fall of 1932 millions of voters were convinced that Hoover's way would not work. Roosevelt carried forty-two of the forty-eight states to become the new president.

Putting the New Deal into Action

Franklin D. Roosevelt brought optimism to a depressed nation when he took office March 4, 1933. With confident voice he asserted, "This great nation will endure as it has endured, will revive and will prosper. . . . The only thing we have to fear is fear itself. . . . We do not distrust the future of essential democracy. The people of the United States have not failed. In their need they have registered a mandate that they want direct, vigorous action."

Roosevelt and his advisors, a **"Brain Trust"** of college professors (most of whom were from Columbia University), were ready to take that "vigorous action." The president began by proclaiming a **bank holiday,** closing banks temporarily, to stabilize banking. Next he called Congress into special session to deal with the crisis and to put his policies into effect. Then he went on the radio for the first of his many "fireside chats" to the nation. A good public speaker with an understanding of people, Roosevelt radiated warmth, even on the radio. He made extensive use of press conferences, seeking to make the press his allies. As allies they could sway lagging public opinion to rally support for his ideas. Soon there appeared a long line of legislation and programs that would be FDR's New Deal.

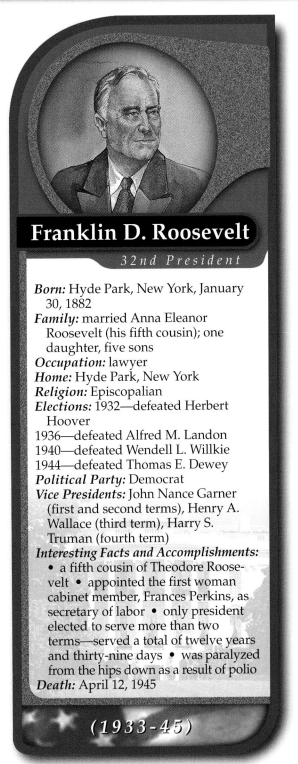

Franklin D. Roosevelt

32nd President

Born: Hyde Park, New York, January 30, 1882

Family: married Anna Eleanor Roosevelt (his fifth cousin); one daughter, five sons

Occupation: lawyer

Home: Hyde Park, New York

Religion: Episcopalian

Elections: 1932—defeated Herbert Hoover
1936—defeated Alfred M. Landon
1940—defeated Wendell L. Willkie
1944—defeated Thomas E. Dewey

Political Party: Democrat

Vice Presidents: John Nance Garner (first and second terms), Henry A. Wallace (third term), Harry S. Truman (fourth term)

Interesting Facts and Accomplishments:
• a fifth cousin of Theodore Roosevelt • appointed the first woman cabinet member, Frances Perkins, as secretary of labor • only president elected to serve more than two terms—served a total of twelve years and thirty-nine days • was paralyzed from the hips down as a result of polio

Death: April 12, 1945

(1933-45)

Early New Deal Legislation—Congress, realizing that the American people wanted the action that Roosevelt promised, became a "rubber stamp," approving almost anything the president proposed. In the first one hundred days, legislation for New Deal programs moved quickly.

As soon as Congress convened after Roosevelt's inauguration, it passed the Emergency Banking Act. This act suspended all banking activity, creating a bank holiday until banks could restabilize. The Treasury Department had the power to decide which banks were sound enough to reopen. Half of the banks, holding ninety percent of all banking resources, were back in operation by March 15. Only about one bank in twenty never reopened. When the banks reopened three weeks later, confidence returned and more than $1 billion was redeposited.

In May 1933 Congress also approved Roosevelt's creation of the Federal Emergency Relief Administration (FERA). This temporary agency (later replaced by the WPA, or Works Progress Administration) had $500 million in federal money to disburse. The agency provided funds for the states to use for relief needs. The money was to be channeled into work relief where possible so that the recipients would work for their pay. However, because the immediate need seemed so great, more of it went out as direct relief (doles) than as work relief.

Congress founded the Home Owners' Loan Corporation in June of 1933. This agency bought mortgages from holders and rewrote them on easier payment schedules. By 1936 one-fifth of all mortgaged nonfarm homes had mortgages under this agency. It was one of the most popular of the New Deal relief acts.

While the general public got relief through FERA and the Home Owners' Loan Corporation, special efforts were made to help farmers. The Farm Credit Administration (FCA) refinanced mortgages for farmers who would have lost their lands. The government also hoped to restore the farmers' purchasing power through the **Agriculture Adjustment Act** (AAA). To raise farm prices, farmers were asked to cut production. Rather than sell their products at a loss, the farmers were told to destroy crops. In 1933 they were asked to plow under between one-quarter and one-half of their crop. Milk was poured into ditches; grain was burned; cattle, sheep, and hogs were killed. Cotton and wool were stored in warehouses and held off the market until greater need would raise the prices.

Ironically, while this was being done, many Americans were hungry or in need of clothing. Yet the action seemed to offer hope to the farmers because they were being paid to cooperate with the plan. The act allowed the government to pay farmers for not producing crops. The government also bought surplus crops that it planned to store and sell when prices were higher. Farm income did go up about fifty percent over the next two years.

Despite the AAA's immediate benefits for the farmers, it was soon attacked. When the policies forced farm prices up, consumers had to pay more for their goods. Moreover, the subsidies for not producing were given to landowners. In the South, where sharecropping was used, the landowners were not the ones who actually farmed the land. The sharecropper who had labored on the land did not receive any benefits. In fact, he often lost money because he had to cut his production. Meanwhile the landlord received all the monetary gain.

In 1936 the Supreme Court nullified the AAA, but a dangerous precedent had already been set. Many farmers became dependent upon government subsidies. Farmers would

This political cartoon shows Uncle Sam's approval of the cooperation between labor and management under the NRA.

soon regain those subsidies and agricultural regulation, and they would protect them. Such policies require tremendous government expense while they artificially control the industry. Other New Deal programs would similarly hamper other industries from adjusting to the market demands.

The **National Recovery Administration** (NRA) was designed to help businesses recover from the effects of the depression. The logic behind the act was to eliminate "wasteful competition" among firms. Codes were written and given to businesses. Each company was assigned a share of the national market and given annual production quotas. The codes also set maximum hours to be worked and minimum wages. An additional provision required a company to recognize a union if the majority of the employees wished to form one. Each firm or business that complied with the NRA codes was allowed to display the NRA's Blue Eagle seal. Rather than clutching arrows in its talons as on the Great Seal, this eagle clutched lightning bolts and a gearwheel. The NRA was soon criticized as a violation of the free enterprise system. Big businesses seemed to be favored over smaller ones, and the consumer was caught in the middle when prices went up. The Supreme Court declared the NRA unconstitutional in 1935.

Another law established the **Civilian Conservation Corps.** This act gave unemployed young men jobs and at the same time conserved natural resources. In the seven years of its existence, the CCC employed two and a half million young men.

In May 1933 Congress also established permanent New Deal agencies with long-range as well as immediate goals. The **Tennessee Valley Authority** (TVA) involved seven southeastern states. The agency provided public power projects on the Tennessee River. The thirty multipurpose dams produced and sold electric power, controlled floods, eased erosion, manufactured fertilizer, and created recreation areas. Because it involved the federal government in areas where it had never been involved before and put the government in the position of competing with private companies, the act was controversial.

Further Action—Americans were generally pleased that the new president was taking firm actions to deal with the depression. When one measure did not work, Roosevelt quickly tried another one. The actions, however, were not bringing a real economic recovery to the nation, and millions were still in need. Roosevelt continued to experiment with new programs that he hoped would solve some of the problems. In 1935 he launched the Works Progress Administration (WPA). This agency put more people to work on construction projects. WPA workers built hospitals, schools, parks, playgrounds, and airports.

Eventually the WPA was extended to other areas, including the arts. Actors, actresses, and directors were employed to put on programs. Authors were hired under the Federal Writers' Project to write historical and geographical guides for the forty-eight states. Artists were hired under a Federal Art Project.

The Cees Get Passing Grades

They planted over two billion trees and spent 6.5 million man-hours fighting forest fires. They built over 420,000 dams, fixed up old parks and built new ones, and built or improved miles of trails and access roads. They made thirty dollars a week, twenty-five of which was sent home to help support their families. "They" were the *Cees,* the young men who worked for the Civilian Conservation Corps.

There were over two and one-half million jobless youths hired by the Civilian Conservation Corps. The CCC was the most popular New Deal program; even the Republicans praised it. It was the first relief agency to go into action. Some have called the Cees "The Tree Army," and others, "The Soil Soldiers." The program lasted from 1933 until World War II, when most of the young men were called into the armed forces.

The camps for the Cees were directed by army officers. Extracurricular activities were usually oriented toward sports, particularly boxing. Rising time was 5:45 A.M. and taps was at 10:00 P.M. The food had the flavor of Army meals with lots of potatoes and bologna. For most of the men, the times spent in the Cees were rewarding, and for some it was character building. Hard outdoor work kept them busy. The conservation emphasis gave meaning to their efforts. The money sent home to help their families gave them a purpose. It is easy to see why the Civilian Conservation Corps received the most praise of any of Roosevelt's programs.

They painted murals in public buildings such as post offices. The National Youth Administration (NYA) helped young people. High school and college students were hired for part-time jobs that enabled them to stay in school. Together the WPA and NYA provided jobs for almost five million Americans.

Even though Roosevelt took many daring actions, some New Deal critics believed that the president was not doing enough to relieve the poverty of many Americans. Some suggested radical plans to distribute wealth and won many supporters. One such critic was Dr. Elmer Townsend, a retired California medical doctor who designed a plan to help the elderly. His plan required the government to pay each person over sixty a $200-a-month pension. The money for the pensions would come from a national sales tax. To receive pensions, retirees would have to agree to spend every cent each month. He thought such spending would pump up the economy.

Another radical plan was proposed by Huey Long, a masterful politician from Louisiana. He suggested taxing large incomes heavily to provide a minimum income for the poor. Another popular speaker with a plan was Father Charles Coughlin, a Detroit priest who had a nationwide radio broadcast. He suggested government-stimulated inflation, government takeover of certain industries, and a guaranteed living wage for laborers. He also wanted to overhaul the currency system and abolish the Federal Reserve System for regulating the nation's banks. Most of the ideas of these critics were even more socialistic than Roosevelt's programs, and they would have led the government deeper into debt. They also would have discouraged people from working for their money.

Roosevelt countered these ideas with a government-sponsored insurance plan. It offered smaller monthly pensions by giving federal aid to the states for the elderly as well as funds for unemployment insurance, aid to dependent children, and public health programs. The old age insurance, commonly called **Social Security** today, was only a part of the program. The program was to be financed by a federal tax on wages (one percent in 1935) paid by both employer and employee.

Roosevelt supported the National Labor Relations Act of 1935, also called the Wagner Act. With it he tried to salvage some of the benefits labor had been offered under the now-outlawed NRA. This act encouraged the growth of labor unions. The largest labor union, the American Federation of Labor, now faced competition from another union, the Congress of Industrial Organizations. Formed in 1935, this union boasted a membership of 3.7 million within two years. Other regulations intended to help workers came with the Fair Labor Standards Act in 1938. It established the nation's first legal minimum wage and maximum hours for workers producing goods that crossed state lines. The wage was twenty-five cents per hour, and the workweek was to be forty-four hours. The act also forbade children under sixteen from working in most industries.

SECTION REVIEW

1. Who were the presidential candidates in 1932?

2. What New Deal provisions were made for the nation's farmers?

3. How did the Works Progress Administration and the National Youth Administration provide relief for Americans?

4. What did the old age insurance come to be called?

 How did Franklin Roosevelt seek to gain America's confidence?

Opposition to the New Deal

Although Roosevelt had gained office with a large popular vote, there were many who opposed him. Liberals and leftists opposed him because they did not think that his New Deal policies had gone far enough. They believed that the New Deal needed to be more socialistic, providing for government ownership of certain industries or providing people with income at government's expense.

Conservatives also voiced their opposition. Under Roosevelt's New Deal, the government had gained control in areas previously left to private interests. Conservatives distrusted such governmental control and feared the extension of the government's power into more areas. The New Deal was giving the federal government wide powers over industry and commerce, areas that were not government's rightful sphere. Roosevelt's agencies were replacing the free enterprises of capitalism with the government regulations of socialism. Federal powers gained during the crisis of the depression would never be curbed in the decades to come. The Supreme Court decisions in 1935 and 1936 outlawing several New Deal measures and agencies fueled the conservative opposition and reflected its thinking.

The Election of 1936

The New Deal president faced a political test in the 1936 election. A group called the American Liberty League unsuccessfully sought to block the president's renomination. The Democrats, however, chose Roosevelt on the first ballot. The party platform praised the New Deal and promised similar additional reforms.

During his first term Roosevelt had been working to change the Democratic Party's image. Until 1935 he had urged business, agriculture, bankers, and workers to settle conflicts among themselves. But in 1935 he began using the government's power to alter the bal-

ance between employees and employers, and between the rich and the middle class or poor. He tried to identify the Democratic Party with the underprivileged. Blacks, urban immigrants, and workers tended to join the Democratic Party from this time on.

Although Roosevelt had refused to support both civil rights regulations and an anti-lynching law in 1936, blacks still voted for him. The depression hit the poor especially hard. Poor blacks and whites were particularly grateful for the New Deal's financial relief. Many blacks believed that the Roosevelt's programs had saved them from starvation. The public works projects offered blacks employment at equal wages with whites (although they were not allowed to work with whites). Such policies landed FDR seventy-five percent of the black vote in 1936.

The Republicans had lost heavily in the congressional elections in 1932 and 1934. Because they lacked a leader and a program to attract voters, a 1936 win looked impossible as well. The Republicans ran Alfred M.

FDR's policies that helped blacks brought him seventy-five percent of the black vote in 1936.

President Roosevelt and his wife, Eleanor.

Declining Popularity of the New Deal

Roosevelt's strong win and congressional support encouraged him to challenge the make-up of the Supreme Court. Because it had struck down several New Deal measures, FDR became more and more critical of the court's conservative nature.

In February 1937 he presented a plan to "pack" the Supreme Court with new justices. He hoped that adding to the number of justices would protect his New Deal measures. Roosevelt requested that the number of justices be increased from nine to as many as fifteen. Each time a justice reached seventy and did not retire, FDR wanted to appoint a new justice. This court-packing plan would have allowed him to add justices who would support his programs.

For the first time, Congress defeated a Roosevelt request. They saw his action as a serious threat to the balance of power among the branches of government. Increasing the court's size in this way would have limited the independence of the judicial branch by giving the president more power to control it.

The New Deal had reached high tide in 1936. In 1937 it ebbed. Suddenly there was a **recession,** a slump in business that was supposed to be less serious than a full depression. The decline between September 1937 and June 1938 was one of the worst in American economic history. The stock market dipped and industrial production declined. In early

Landon, who had been a progressive governor in Kansas. Using the phrase "America Is in Peril," the Republicans criticized the New Deal for its overthrow of traditional ways and for betraying its promises to the people.

Although Landon campaigned hard, he carried only two states, Maine and Vermont. Roosevelt beat him by more than eleven million votes. The Congress elected in 1936 was also heavily Democratic.

1937 federal spending had dropped off. This spending cut reduced personal incomes and in turn cut the purchasing power that had been artificially sustaining industry's production.

Roosevelt had accepted the use of government spending to get the economy started up, even if it meant going into debt. But when the government reduced its spending after four years, the pumped-up economy did not stand on its own. It was becoming evident that the New Deal measures had only helped to cover the problems; they had not brought the United States recovery.

Consequences of the New Deal

The New Deal had improved conditions from their 1932 depressed state in some respects. Business profits and farm prices were up; unemployment was down. Annual per capita income had gone up from $678 in 1933 to $925 in 1939. Electricity had been extended to many rural areas, and other public works had improved buildings and parks and encouraged conservation. These benefits, however, had come at a tremendous price for the country—the growth of federal power and federal spending.

Perhaps the one positive thing that the New Deal had accomplished was the restoration of people's faith and confidence in America. Roosevelt, despite the dangers and failures of many of his programs, had offered hope and action for people who were in a panic. People trusted him to do something about their problems.

In 1939, however, after six years of Roosevelt programs, the United States had not really recovered from the depression. Prices for farm products were still low. Overall manufacturing production and corporate profits lagged far behind 1929 levels. Nine million Americans were still unemployed.

Roosevelt's money policies and excessive spending had a great effect in the following years. He had taken the United States off the gold standard in 1933. Paper money and coins were no longer convertible into gold coins. Although this action did little to aid the economy at the time, it gave the government much power over national currency for the future. And because of its high spending, the New Deal had left the country with a record debt. The national debt in 1933 was $2.6 billion. In 1939 it was $6.5 billion. Unfortunately, in future years the precedents of high government spending and unbalanced budgets continued. The public just did not want the government to cut back on what they were used to having.

Families, such as this one on their way to Oregon, traveled across the nation to wherever jobs might offer relief from the depression.

In the long run the New Deal brought other changes. The government, especially the executive branch, had greatly increased its power. Under Roosevelt both the size and scope of the federal government had been greatly increased. Unfortunately, once the government assumes the responsibility for something, it rarely gives up control. And when the people give up their personal rights and responsibilities to government, they rarely get them back.

The government had also intervened in the economy and perhaps even managed it. The economy was no longer based solely on private enterprise. Although private businesses remained the mainstay of economic activity, government had assumed a major role. The government had taken responsibility for individual and national economic welfare. It had provided special help to farmers and industrial workers. It left Americans with the idea that when there was a crisis in future years, the government would help them then, too. Some people now believed that they were entitled to public help if they became victims of any circumstances over which they had no real control.

The depression was a time of great trials for many Americans and for the nation as a whole. Those who lived through it learned many lessons about the uncertainty of money and positions in this world. Too few, however, learned to trust in God fully in the midst of their hardships. It was easier to ask the government for aid. We who are Christians must realize that men and governments may fail. The only one worthy of our trust in any crisis is our Savior, Jesus Christ. He who feeds the birds of the air and clothes the lilies of the field is certainly able to take care of His own children. "But seek ye first the kingdom of God, and his righteousness; and all these things shall be added unto you" (Matt. 6:33).

SECTION REVIEW

1. What groups of voters did the Democratic party begin to attract in 1935?

2. What Republican candidate ran against Franklin Roosevelt in the 1936 election?

3. Why did Roosevelt want to increase the number of Supreme Court justices?

4. What positive things did the New Deal accomplish?

 Why was it difficult for the government to cut back its role in society after the New Deal era?

SUMMARY

The stock market crash in 1929 signaled the end of a generally prosperous and carefree time for the nation. It also signaled the beginning of a severe economic depression that would last throughout the 1930s. Bank failures and business closings plagued the country after the crash, and millions of Americans began to experience the hardships of unemployment, the loss of their homes or farms, and even hunger. In their distress, many looked to the government to give them aid. When President Hoover's reactions did not bring them quick relief, they turned to Franklin Roosevelt for swift action. He offered one New Deal program after another in an attempt to bring recovery. The programs increased government power and federal debt, but they ultimately failed to solve the underlying problems of the depression. The American people survived the trying times of the 1930s, but in the process they learned to depend on government aid and regulation to protect them from crisis.

Chapter Review

People, Places, and Things to Remember

stock market crash of 1929
Great Depression
buy on the margin
"Dust Bowl"
dole
Reconstruction Finance Corporation

Franklin Delano Roosevelt
"New Deal"
"Brain Trust"
bank holiday
Agriculture Adjustment Act

National Recovery Administration
Civilian Conservation Corps
Tennessee Valley Authority
Social Security
recession

Review Questions

Define each of the following terms.

1. Dust Bowl

2. buying stock on the margin

3. dole

4. bank holiday

5. recession

Match each of the following terms with its description.

6. Great Depression
7. Social Security
8. New Deal
9. Brain Trust
10. Reconstruction Finance Corporation

a. Roosevelt's group of advisors
b. Hoover's aid program
c. "old age insurance"
d. the 1930s
e. Roosevelt's attempt to bring the nation relief and recovery

The New Deal contained many programs and pieces of legislation that were commonly known by their initials. For that reason they were sometimes called an "alphabet soup." What were the full names of the programs listed below, and what did each one do?

11. AAA
12. NRA
13. CCC
14. TVA

Questions for Discussion

15. Is the Social Security program, established during the New Deal, a benefit to the nation? Explain your answer.

16. How did the depression change Americans?

26

World War II

On Sunday morning, the seventh of December in 1941, the Japanese bombed Pearl Harbor in Hawaii. The attack on the American naval base resulted in the sinking or disabling of nineteen American ships, the destruction of nearly two hundred planes, the deaths of over two thousand men, and the wounding of more than one thousand more. The treacherous surprise attack prompted President Franklin D. Roosevelt to address Congress the next day with these words:

> Yesterday, December 7, 1941—a date which will live in infamy—the United States of America was suddenly and deliberately attacked by naval and air forces of the Empire of Japan.

Roosevelt then asked the Congress to declare war, and immediately America was thrown into a conflict not only with Japan but also with Germany and Italy. The United States had joined the worldwide conflict known as World War II.

Trouble Brewing

Although Americans fighting in World War I had idealistically believed that they were "fighting a war to end all wars," in less than twenty-five years Americans were back on the battlefields. The conditions leading to the conflict were many; the troubles had begun almost before the guns of World War I had cooled.

Leaders of War

Not everyone was pleased with the outcome of World War I. The peace settlements had satisfied only a few of the participants. Most countries had not gotten all they wanted from victory or had lost much more than they wanted to lose from defeat. Some of this dissatisfaction aided the rise of three strong imperialist countries in the 1930s.

Hitler Builds His Third Reich—The German nation was most upset by the Treaty of Versailles. That settlement had placed all the blame for the war on Germany and had stripped the country of some of its land, its colonial possessions, its strong army, and its self-respect. The treaty had also forced a large debt upon Germany to be paid to the Allies as reparations. Humiliated by these terms of defeat, Germany struggled through the 1920s. In the midst of the downcast German people, however, there arose a man who gave Germany a hope for future greatness.

Adolf Hitler gained Germany's attention in 1924 with the publication of his book *Mein Kampf* ("My Struggle"). In it he preached the injustice of the Treaty of Versailles, blamed the Jews for Germany's problems, and declared the superiority of the German race. Hitler also organized the National Socialist German Workers Party, or **Nazi Party,** around his leadership. He denounced communism (which the Germans greatly feared at that time), and he proposed a strong, organized Germany that would become a powerful leader of the world.

Although many Germans did not accept Hitler at first, they found Nazism to be full of excitement and pageantry, and almost no one wanted to be left out. Calling Hitler the *Führer* (leader), many joined in his support, believing that they were building a Third Reich (German empire) that would last for a thousand years. They believed that Hitler would restore Germany to its rightful place in the world. They believed the promises Hitler made in his speeches with more enthusiasm than many Christians today carry the gospel to the lost. A few people continued to mistrust him, but their influence was not strong enough to reverse his power.

As depression increased German despair in the early 1930s, Hitler and his Nazi Party swept into power. He became the German chancellor in 1933 and was given the powers of a dictator. He soon began to violate the Treaty of Versailles by sending troops into the Rhineland area near France and by organizing German men and boys into groups for military training. Hitler also set German scientists to work developing new weapons and materials that could be used in war. His power and ambition would soon threaten world peace.

Mussolini Moves to Conquer—Italy was also disappointed after World War I. It had switched to the Allied side during the war but had not received the extra territories it wanted when the war ended. Suffering from economic and political problems after the war, Italy allowed **Benito Mussolini** to seize power in 1922. Mussolini, called *Il Duce* (DOO chay; the leader), was the leader of a party that favored nationalism and opposed communism. Like Hitler, he had organized military groups across Italy. As dictator, Mussolini built efficient railroads and major highways, provided houses and lands for sixty thousand peasants, and made other improvements in Italy. Although he denied freedom to the people, he promised to give Italy back the pride of a bygone era by establishing a "Second Roman Empire." Such promises initially caused his followers to rank him with Julius Caesar.

Mussolini's first attempt to expand his empire began in 1935, when Italian soldiers crossed the Mediterranean to attack the African land of Ethiopia. Ethiopian tribesmen faced Italy's machine guns and bombers with spears and rifles. Although Europe and the United States looked on in horror, no one went to Ethiopia's aid.

Mussolini found an ally in Hitler. Both men had formed **fascist** (FASH ist) **governments,** strong dictatorships that stressed nationalism and power. They formed an alliance called the Rome-Berlin Axis. Later, Japan joined this alliance, becoming the third of the **Axis powers.**

Changes in Japan—Japan's industrial and military power had been growing since the turn of the century. A group of military leaders had gained control of Japan, and they intended to increase Japanese power in China and in other areas of Eastern Asia and the Pacific. These leaders were convinced that Japan had deserved greater recognition as a world power after World War I. They convinced the Japanese people that the United States was a threat to further growth of the Japanese Empire and that Japan should establish control of the trade and resources of Eastern Asia.

After World War I, the League of Nations had assigned Japan the responsibility of governing some Pacific islands formerly held by Germany. Fortifying these islands enabled Japan to invade China and take over the northern region called Manchuria in 1931. The United States believed that Japan's conquest of Manchuria was wrong, but the United States's request to the League of Nations to take action against Japan was ineffective, and Japan stayed in Manchuria. Since no American possessions in the Pacific were yet threatened, the United States did nothing except to slightly strengthen their defenses in the Philippines.

Roosevelt and Foreign Policy

The United States was aware that the growing powers of Hitler, Mussolini, and the Japanese military leaders were threatening the delicate balance of world peace. Even so, the isolationist attitude that had ruled in the 1920s also prevailed in the 1930s. Most Americans were more concerned that the nation take care of the problems of its own economic depression than that it get involved in foreign affairs. They hoped that the limits set for navies and the peace pacts signed by major nations in the 1920s would be enough to discourage future war. Americans did want the League of Nations to take appropriate actions against the threatening powers. Yet the League was very weak and never able to act as an effective restraint against villainous nations.

President Roosevelt was among those who wanted the United States to take a major role in foreign affairs. But without popular support little was done about the trouble that was brewing in Europe and Eastern Asia. A significant step, however, was accomplished in the United States's relationships to the countries of Latin America. President Hoover had initiated a **"Good Neighbor Policy"** in dealings with these lands, and Roosevelt continued the policy. Instead of marching into Latin American countries with a "big stick" when troubles arose, as had been done since the presidency of Theodore Roosevelt, the United States began to let these countries handle their

Benito Mussolini promised the Italians a second Roman Empire.

own affairs. The Good Neighbor Policy did much to improve relations with these countries, which had grown tired and suspicious of U.S. intervention in their lands.

SECTION REVIEW

1. What event brought the United States into World War II?

2. What two European leaders built strong military dictatorships after World War I?

3. What part of China had Japan conquered?

4. What was the general attitude of Americans toward foreign affairs in the 1930s?

5. What new policy was the United States following in its dealings with Latin America?

 How did the end of World War I prepare Germany for the start of World War II?

World War II Begins

In the late 1930s the world watched as Hitler began his conquest of European territory. His actions soon made France and Britain realize that something had to be done about this fascist leader.

German Expansion

Because other nations had not really protested Hitler's disregard of the Treaty of Versailles, Hitler chanced violating it again by uniting Austria (a German-speaking land) with Germany in 1938. In four weeks Austria came under Hitler's control. Foreign powers still did not protest too strongly against him, so he next demanded the Sudetenland, an area in Czechoslovakia. He claimed that the 3.5 million Germans who lived there "deserved to be a part of the Fatherland." However, he had secretly instructed his military to invade Czechoslovakia if he did not gain it peacefully by October 1, 1938. Hitler promised that this would be "the last territorial claim I have to make in Europe."

German soldiers stand shoulder to shoulder at a 1935 Nazi rally.

Great Britain's prime minister, Neville Chamberlain, and Hitler reached an agreement during a meeting in Munich, Germany. Chamberlain thought that if Europe would "appease" Hitler by giving in to his demand, peace would be saved. Many Europeans were relieved that war had been avoided, but they soon found that giving in to evil often causes it to resurface in an uglier form. Chamberlain returned to Britain and announced that there would be "peace in our time." **Winston Churchill,** who would soon take Chamberlain's place as prime minister, violently disagreed, saying, "You chose dishonor, and you will have war!"

Although Hitler took the Sudetenland peacefully, the **appeasement** did not work. About six months later, Hitler forcefully took over all of Czechoslovakia. Europe began to realize that Hitler intended to keep increasing his power and his empire. No European nation was safe.

By the spring of 1939, Hitler wanted Poland. This time both Britain and France warned that such action would lead to war. Hitler ignored them, saying, "Our enemies are little worms. I saw them at Munich." But Hitler was worried that the Soviet Union would also protest his actions. He realized it

Neville Chamberlain thought that his agreement with Hitler had saved Europe from war.

would be unwise to fight too much of Europe at one time. Therefore, in August he signed a nonaggression pact with **Joseph Stalin,** the dictator of the Soviet Union. They agreed not to attack each other as they both expanded their territory. Although Hitler had said that he hated the Communist Soviet Union, he would wait until later to attack that enemy. The stage was now set for the beginning of World War II.

War Envelops Europe

On September 1, 1939, Hitler unleashed his mechanized war machine on Poland. Hundreds of bombers soared over Poland while armored tanks, called *panzers,* and thousands of soldiers moved in to take control. The Soviet Union also attacked Poland from the east. Within hours Poland had lost almost all hope for avoiding conquest. A few Poles continued to resist for several weeks, but the fall of Poland was complete before the month ended. The world had seen a new type of warfare—"lightning war," or **blitzkrieg.** Nine more European countries soon would fall under Nazi control as the Germans advanced.

Britain and France, the **Allies,** knowing that Hitler had to be stopped, declared war on Germany on September 3, 1939. They rushed to prepare their armies, but little fighting took place for eight months. Then on April 9, Hitler's forces took control of Denmark and Norway. A few weeks later, on May 10, 1940, Hitler staged another blitzkrieg, sending his forces into Belgium, the Netherlands, and Luxembourg. The Belgians and the Dutch, unable to fight against his strong armies, soon became conquered states. Next, by-passing France's heavy fortifications, the Germans moved into France through the Ardennes Forest. Britain sent soldiers and equipment to help France, but the Allied army of 338,000 men was forced to retreat to northern France near the port of Dunkirk. The Germans rushed to cut off an escape across the English Channel. Having trapped the Allied army at Dunkirk, the Germans waited for their air force to finish the task. Bad weather, however, prevented German planes from bombing the fleeing forces. Meanwhile, the British and French brought every available boat to Dunkirk. Fishing boats, steamers, yachts, and even lifeboats were used to evacuate the Allied army. Fishermen, dockworkers, merchants, and farmers all helped ferry the army across the Channel to safety. The evacuation of an army, however, was hardly enough to save France. On June 14, 1940, German troops entered Paris. France had fallen to the Nazis.

While Hitler was conquering the French, Mussolini announced that Italy was joining Germany in the fight against the Allies. Mussolini had already taken control of Albania before the war began, and he intended to gain more land from an Axis conquest of Europe.

Britain Stands Alone

With the fall of France, Britain stood alone to face Hitler and Mussolini. Most believed that the Germans would cross the English Channel to invade and conquer the

Smoke rises around St. Paul's Cathedral in the aftermath of the battle of Britain.

Many believed the evacuation of Dunkirk was a miracle.

British Isles, but Hitler chose another way to try to defeat Great Britain. He ordered devastating bombing raids on English cities, including the capital, London. These bombing attacks became known as "the battle of Britain." They began in July 1940 and lasted for one year.

The Germans hoped to drive Britain's Royal Air Force (RAF) from the skies and to force a surrender by inflicting heavy damage on civilians. The RAF courageously tried to

protect Britain from the bombings. Because of a shortage of pilots, RAF pilots made as many as five flights a day to defend their homeland. Their efforts prevented the fall of Britain. The new prime minister, Winston Churchill, said of the RAF, "Never in the field of human conflict was so much owed by so many to so few." Had the attacks continued, the outcome might have been different. But the British determination to stop Hitler persuaded him to seek another approach to victory.

Hitler Turns Against the Soviet Union

Although mired in a stalemate in Great Britain, Hitler was winning elsewhere. German armies had control of Hungary and Rumania by the spring of 1941. Turkey had signed a treaty of neutrality. In early summer Hitler swept into southeastern Europe. Bulgaria, Yugoslavia, and Greece were soon Axis victims.

Hitler then made a decision that would have tremendous consequences—a decision to attack the Soviet Union. Hitler believed that the British were holding out in the hope that the Soviets would change sides and come to the aid of the Allies, so he wanted to crush the

Soviet Union before it could turn on him. He also wanted Soviet resources for German use. While the Germans were still fighting the Allies in Western Europe, Hitler's generals tried to warn him that opening up another front, or battleground, in the East would be unwise. Expanding the war into the Soviet Union late in the summer could be dangerous, but Hitler did not listen. On June 22, 1941, the blitzkrieg against the Soviet Union began. Hitler thought he could take control of the land in just eight weeks.

At first the Russian people accepted Hitler's armies as a relief from the terrors of Stalin's Communist rule. However, they soon learned that the Nazis were not friendly. Germans ravaged Soviet towns and tortured the Russians they met. The Russians began to use a "scorched earth" policy. Instead of leaving crops and livestock for Hitler to use to feed his men, the Russians, as they retreated, burned their crops and killed their animals. Thus the supplies the German army had hoped to capture were gone. With every mile conquered, the supply lines back to Germany became longer.

In mid-October German troops were only forty miles from Moscow, and they had killed over two million Russians. Even though the autumn days grew shorter and temperatures grew colder, Hitler refused to stop and wait until spring for further action. He did not want to give Stalin more time to ready his defenses. So the Germans marched on with only their summer uniforms and lightweight oil for their vehicles. Ironically, a century before, Napoleon had been in the same situation and found that the Russian winter was far more dangerous than Russian troops. But Hitler had not learned from history. On December 6, as the freezing Soviet winter closed in, the Soviet troops attacked Hitler's cold and weary forces, and they actually broke through the German lines. The Soviet army and the Russian winter

had kept Hitler from defeating the Soviet Union.

American Sympathies and Fears

Americans looked at European affairs with increased alarm. The European dictators had made it clear that they were opposed to any form of republican government. Some Americans feared that if Britain fell, Germany might try to wage war on the United States. Most Americans generally opposed Hitler and wanted the Allies to win. Yet since Congress had passed a series of neutrality acts in the 1930s, Americans were limited in what they could do to help the Allies.

In 1939 Congress had allowed the Allied powers to buy war materials from American companies if the Allies paid cash and carried the supplies on their own ships. Congress also passed a Selective Service Act in 1940. Once again young men aged twenty-one to thirty-

This 1930s political cartoon warns that America's policy of isolationism in the face of Hitler's Nazi threat was placing the United States in great danger.

five were required to register for possible military service. Some 375,000 men were drafted and started training to be ready for attack. But since the armistice in 1918, America had not been concerned with building a strong armed force; so the new soldiers had to train on old or substitute equipment until new pieces were available.

Many Americans still feared war and wanted to avoid it at all costs. The America First Committee, with such prominent members as Charles Lindbergh, and other organizations pleaded for American neutrality. Roosevelt ran for a third term as president in 1940, and he won. Because of the fear of war, however, Roosevelt had to promise that he would keep American boys out of a foreign war, a war that did not directly involve the United States.

As the battle of Britain was threatening to crush the Allies in the summer of 1941, President Roosevelt decided that Britain des-

perately needed more help. He sought a way for the Allies to obtain vital war equipment from the United States more easily. Congress complied by approving the **Lend-Lease Act.** This act permitted the president to send equipment to any nation in which the receipt of such equipment might be vital to American defense. Rather than paying with money, the countries could pay with property, services, or equipment for American use. In this way the United States received land for

Adolph Hitler salutes Nazi soldiers in a parade in Munich.

seven air bases in exchange for war supplies sent to Britain.

Americans also began to realize that the European Axis powers (Germany and Italy) might not be their only enemies. Japan had joined the Axis powers, and it was pursuing interests in Asia. Japanese forces had already entered Southeast Asia; Australia, New Zealand, or the Philippines might be Japan's next target. Most Americans did not know that Japan also intended to take control of a vast area in the Pacific. The Japanese were strengthening their position in Asia in preparation for their attack on American possessions in the area.

President Roosevelt decided to forbid almost all trade with Japan. The strain between the two nations increased as Japan continued to expand its power in defiance of American interests. In November 1941, Japanese diplomats arrived in Washington for talks. At the same time, however, Japanese aircraft carriers were sailing across the Pacific to take up positions within bombing distance of Hawaii.

The bombing of Pearl Harbor devastated the American Navy and brought America into World War II.

SECTION REVIEW

1. With what major power did Hitler make a nonaggression treaty that he later broke?

2. Hitler's invasion of what country actually triggered World War II?

3. Which countries did Hitler capture between September of 1939 and June of 1940?

4. What was the German strategy in the battle of Britain?

5. What was the Lend-Lease Act?

 Why was Hitler's decision to invade the Soviet Union unwise? Why did he do it anyway?

America Enters the War

The attack on the naval base at **Pearl Harbor** on December 7, 1941, put an end to American neutrality. When the United States declared war on Japan after the attack, Japan's allies, Germany and Italy, also declared war on the United States. The war now directly involved America in a fight against all the Axis powers.

The attack on Pearl Harbor was a great blow to the United States Navy. The damage was severe, but heavier losses were avoided

because the American carrier fleet was at sea that Sunday morning. Nonetheless, the United States had much to do to prepare itself for the long fight ahead.

Manpower for War

Following Pearl Harbor, patriotic volunteers deluged army and navy recruiting centers. Eventually about sixteen million Americans, one in eleven, wore military uniforms. Those Americans who sincerely believed that war was wrong registered as

conscientious objectors and served in the medical corps or in nonmilitary roles.

Women also became involved in the war effort in military or civilian jobs. Some served in the Women's Army Corps (WACS); others joined the Women's Naval Reserve or the WAVES (Women Accepted for Voluntary Emergency Service). The WASP (Women Airforce Service Pilots) helped to fly aircraft from the factories to air force bases. Although women were not assigned to combat roles, they did serve overseas, especially in tasks that freed men to fight.

More women also became a part of the job force, taking the places of men who were drafted. Posters picturing "Rosie the Riveter" were used to recruit women to join workforces everywhere. Some joined the Red Cross, and others worked with the USO (United Service Organizations), entertaining troops and providing other services.

As some jobs previously closed to them opened up, black Americans joined the workforce in larger numbers than ever before. Blacks also enlisted in all-black units in the armed forces.

Beginning February 1, 1943, Japanese-Americans could enlist, too. They trained as an all-Nisei (American-born Japanese) force. Because of their Japanese association, however, most were sent to fight in Europe. Some Japanese-Americans did do intelligence work in the Pacific, cracking the secret Japanese telegraph codes.

Materials for War

The United States entered the war without materials and preparation for the conflict, but Americans rose to meet the challenge. Factories were soon retooled to produce war goods, such as jeeps and tanks, rather than cars. Through teamwork and sacrifice, production doubled in less than four years. By 1945 more than 300,000 planes, 100,000

tanks and self-propelled guns, 2.5 million military trucks, 1.1 million rifles and carbines, 400,000 artillery weapons, and 50 billion rounds of ammunition had become a part of the American arsenal.

Shipbuilders set to work to increase the United States's naval fleet. Ships dubbed "Liberty Ships" were christened as quickly as every three and a half working days. Liberty Ships were employed to carry war materials to far-flung fronts. Aircraft carriers, destroyers, submarines, and other vessels also were built with amazing speed.

To meet the ever-increasing need for war goods, Americans at home had to sacrifice during the war. After 1942, automobiles were no longer made for private sale. Gasoline and

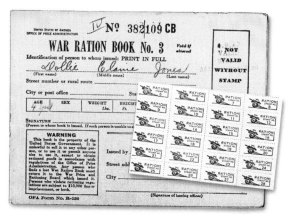

The government used ration stamps, issued to Americans in ration books, to limit purchases of goods that were in short supply during the war.

oil as well as meat, butter, sugar, coffee, most canned or frozen goods, and shoes were rationed (restricted in use) because of shortages. Americans received books of ration stamps. They could buy a rationed item only if they had an unused stamp for it. When scarce products were available in stores, there were often long lines to buy them. Little was thrown away. Drives to collect tin cans, waste paper, aluminum, and scrap iron became common.

As they had in World War I, most Americans patriotically added to their food supply with "victory gardens." These vegetable gardens popped up everywhere: in backyards, along edges of parking lots, in zoos and parks, and in window boxes. By 1943 they supplied Americans with a third of all their vegetables. These efforts ensured that there would be more food available for the boys fighting in the war. Americans also bought war bonds to help pay for the war effort.

The supply lines used to carry goods to the armed forces stretched around the globe. In addition to supplying its own men, the United States supplied much of the Allied forces. President Roosevelt called the United States "the arsenal of democracy."

Mapping the War

As commander-in-chief of all American armed forces, the president mapped the war strategy with the help of the leading military officers and advisors. Roosevelt also met with Britain's prime minister Winston Churchill. Their first meeting was held secretly aboard an American destroyer off the coast of Newfoundland in August 1941, before the United States had joined in the war on the Allied side. Later the Arcadia talks, held near Washington, D.C., made public the Allied leaders' "Hitler first" policy. This policy made Nazi Germany the first target. The United States agreed that the Germans were the biggest threat to the Allies. Once Hitler was defeated, Japan could not stand long.

Other meetings among Allied leaders allowed them to discuss their military strategy and to plan for dealing with the problems that would be faced after the war was over. At Casablanca (CAS uh BLANG kuh) in Morocco in January 1943, the Allies decided to invade

Europe through Sicily and Italy. After Hitler had turned against the Soviet Union, that country had joined the Allies. Therefore, at the next meeting in Teheran (TEH uh RAN) in Iran, Soviet dictator Joseph Stalin joined the meet-

Stalin, Roosevelt, and Churchill, the "Big Three," met at Teheran to discuss war strategy.

ings. Stalin pressed for the Allies to invade northern Europe to take pressure off his troops. With the fall of France and the end of the battle of Britain, most of the fighting was taking place in the east between the Germans and the Soviets. Stalin was promised a second European front to take the pressure off the eastern front in return for his promise that the Soviet Union would help defeat Japan once Hitler was defeated.

SECTION REVIEW

1. About how many Americans served in the armed forces during World War II?

2. Name three military organizations in which women served. How did women help the cause at home?

3. What had to be done with America's factory production?

 How were civilians able to aid the war effort?

American Efforts in Europe

Although the United States did not totally neglect events in the Pacific, it sent its major forces into the European portion of the conflict first.

Attacking North Africa

Prior to Germany's invasion of Russia, Italy had launched a major campaign in the deserts of North Africa. The British, however, defeated the Italians and threatened to drive them out of Africa altogether. In order to prop up his faltering ally, Hitler sent German troops, called the "Afrika Korps," to Africa under the brilliant command of the "Desert Fox," General Erwin Rommel (ROM ul). By clever maneuvering and swift movement, Rommel succeeded in driving back the British. He even threatened to drive into Egypt and capture the Suez Canal. The battle lines in North Africa shifted back and forth for hundreds of miles in 1941 and 1942, as first Rommel and then the British were victorious.

By the middle of the year 1942, however, American troops began to arrive. Under the skilled command of General **Dwight D. Eisenhower,** the Americans landed in western North Africa and began to push east toward Libya. The British in the meantime began to drive west from Egypt. With this "Operation Torch," as the African campaign was called, the Allies crushed the Axis forces between them. Rommel and some of his men escaped to Europe, but 240,000 Axis troops surrendered to the Allies in Tunisia in May of 1943.

The Allies Attack Italy

Although Hitler had lost in North Africa, he now fought to keep "Fortress Europe," or the lands that the Reich held in Europe. The Allies under American General George Patton launched "Operation Husky" to free Italy by invading Sicily, the island off the tip of Italy. American troops under General Mark Clark and British troops under General Bernard Montgomery then crossed to Italy. Working their way up the Italian coast, the Americans captured Naples in October 1943. But the push to take Rome was slowed by Germans who were entrenched in the mountains. It took four months for the Allies to travel through Italy's snow-clad mountains.

As they had done in World War I, the Italians decided to switch sides. They overthrew Mussolini, surrendered to the Allies, and declared war on Germany. Although the American forces freed Rome on June 4, 1944, fighting continued with German forces in Italy for another year. The Allies decided to focus their assault elsewhere in Europe. Leaving behind the fewest possible troops to hold the German force where it was in Italy, General Eisenhower worked in Britain to prepare for a bigger invasion. American generals Omar Bradley and George Patton and British general Bernard

Tanks were ideally suited for the desert terrain in the North African campaigns.

European Theater, 1943-44

Montgomery assisted Eisenhower in the planning.

The Allies began preparations for a great invasion of Germany through France, "Operation Overlord." They assembled men and equipment in southern England while they sent planes on bombing attacks in Germany. The RAF planes conducted night raids over German cities, systematically destroying two and a half cities per month. The American air force bombed by day, focusing on industrial and military sites.

Invasion at Normandy

At dawn on June 6, 1944, the largest invasion force in history moved into position in the English Channel. Twenty miles away, across the Channel, lay the German-held northwest region of France, called Normandy. Allied leaders had considered tide schedules and weather reports when they picked June 6 as **"D-day,"** the day for the operation to begin. General Eisenhower led the Allied forces in the Normandy invasion. He announced by radio, "The tide has turned. The free men of the world are marching together to victory." The D-Day invasion was the turning point of the European war.

While the Allied air forces sought to provide air protection, American soldiers landed on Normandy beaches code-named Utah and Omaha, and the British landed on other nearby beaches. German defenses were strong, and the Allied landing was challenged. Losses were heavy, but a beachhead was secured. The Allies then pushed inland yard by yard and mile by mile across some of the same ground fought over in World War I.

On August 25, after a grueling, three-month battle, the Allies liberated Paris. German resistance collapsed rapidly after Paris fell, and by October, just two months later, the Allies had advanced all the way to the Rhine River. But in mid-December the German retreat stopped. Hitler launched an immense counterattack into Belgium in an attempt to recapture the strategic port of Antwerp and divide the Allied forces. Although the Germans did not succeed in taking the port, they did succeed in pushing the Allied lines sixty miles westward at one point. This "bulge" in the lines allowed the Germans to surround an American division in the Belgian town of Bastogne. Other Allied forces rushed to the trapped forces in the resulting **battle of the Bulge.** After a month of battle, the German attack began to slow. The Allies moved in to free those in Bastogne and started pushing the Germans

back toward Germany again. Hitler's forces were faltering.

German Defeat

As the Americans and other Allies fought northward from Italy and east from the Rhine, the Soviets were fighting their way west toward Berlin. Although the American forces probably could have won the race and arrived at Berlin first, they elected not to, concentrating instead on capturing Nazi forces and liberating concentration camps.

The Soviet Union broke the promises it made at Yalta, setting the stage for the Cold War to come.

An additional factor that kept them from Berlin was the **Yalta Meeting** of FDR, Churchill, and Stalin in February 1945. There Soviet "special interests" in Eastern Europe were recognized in return for Stalin's promises of entry into the Pacific war and of holding postwar elections in any countries the Soviets liberated. The Soviet promises proved worthless, but nonetheless, Roosevelt thought these agreements necessary, and Churchill was forced to go along. Yalta would prove to be the

Berlin suffered great destruction from intense bombing near the close of the war.

last meeting of these two leaders with Stalin. Within a few months Roosevelt was dead, and Britain elected a new prime minister to replace Churchill.

Berlin fell on May 2, 1945, two days after Hitler committed suicide. On May 7, 1945, the Germans surrendered at a schoolhouse near Rheims (REEMZ). An elated America paused briefly to celebrate **"V-E Day"** ("Victory in Europe") on May 8. All efforts could be centered on forcing the Japanese to surrender in the Pacific.

SECTION REVIEW

1. Where was the first major battleground for American soldiers against the Germans in World War II?

2. What country was liberated from Axis rule under "Operation Husky"?

3. What actions did the RAF and the U.S. Air Force take against Germany so that the Allies could invade it?

4. Where and when did the largest invasion in history take place? What was this day called?

5. When did Germany finally surrender?

 How did the conference at Yalta increase the power of the Soviet Union?

The War in the Pacific

While the war in Europe was being won, events in the Pacific did not come to a standstill. America put men, ships, and planes into the Japanese conflict as it was able, but the early results were discouraging.

The Japanese Advance

The same day that Japan attacked Pearl Harbor, it also struck at other major targets in the Pacific, including the Philippines. At that time the Philippines still belonged to the United States, and the islands served as an important American base in the Pacific. On Christmas Eve, 1941, the Japanese made their second large-scale landing on the Philippines. By January they held Manila. The American-Filipino troops, under General **Douglas MacArthur,** held only the Philippine peninsula of Bataan (buh TAN) and the small, nearby island of Corregidor (kuh REHG ih DOR). But when it was realized that it would be impossible for American forces to keep the Philippines, MacArthur was ordered to leave. The United States did not want to risk the capture of a valuable general; so MacArthur escaped to safety in Australia. As he left, he promised the Filipinos, "I shall return."

With supply lines cut off, the American troops remaining in the Philippines ran low on supplies. They suffered from disease and starvation. Even in their weakened condition, they battled to defend Bataan, but it was not enough. On April 9, 1942, most troops on the Bataan peninsula had to surrender to the Japanese. The captured Allied troops were forced to march in tropical heat, without food or water, for sixty-five miles to a prison camp. Thirteen thousand of the American forces in the Philippines had escaped to Corregidor. By early May the Japanese were shelling the island constantly. Finally the remaining men

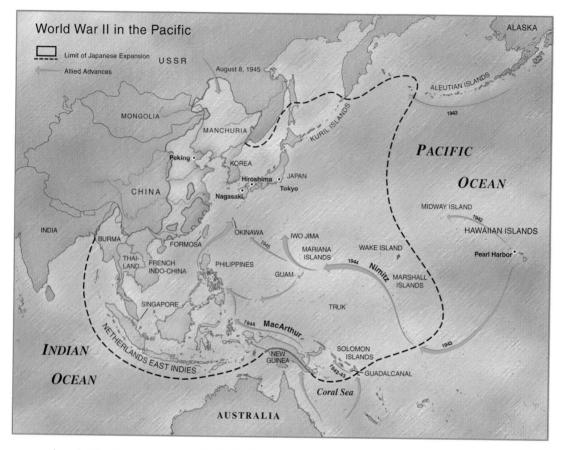

World War II in the Pacific

Limit of Japanese Expansion

Allied Advances

USSR

August 8, 1945

ALASKA

MONGOLIA

MANCHURIA

ALEUTIAN ISLANDS

1943

KURIL ISLANDS

PACIFIC

Peking

KOREA

JAPAN

Hiroshima

Tokyo

CHINA

Nagasaki

OCEAN

MIDWAY ISLAND

INDIA

BURMA

FORMOSA

OKINAWA

1945

IWO JIMA

MARIANA
ISLANDS

WAKE ISLAND

1942

HAWAIIAN ISLANDS

Pearl Harbor

THAI-
LAND

FRENCH
INDO-CHINA

PHILIPPINES

GUAM

1944

Nimitz

MARSHALL
ISLANDS

SINGAPORE

TRUK

1944 MacArthur

NETHERLANDS EAST INDIES

INDIAN

OCEAN

NEW
GUINEA

SOLOMON
ISLANDS

1943

1942-43

GUADALCANAL

Coral Sea

AUSTRALIA

surrendered. The Japanese controlled all of the Philippines.

Meanwhile, the Japanese had also captured most of Southeast Asia and many of the islands in the Pacific. In June the Japanese turned northward and even snatched two of the Aleutian Islands just off the tip of southern Alaska. To America's dismay, the Japanese seemed to control the entire region of eastern Asia and the western Pacific.

American shipyards and munitions factories were gradually making progress. They were soon able to launch and equip new aircraft carriers within fifteen months from the time their construction began. Soon, battleships, aircraft carriers, and escort vessels sailed westward to help push back the Japanese.

The Rising Sun Begins to Set

In the spring and summer of 1942, Americans saw a ray of hope in the Pacific war. On April 8, 1942, the aircraft carrier *Hornet* secretly sailed within seven hundred miles of the Japanese mainland. Sixteen B-25 bombers under the command of Jimmy Doolittle shocked the Japanese by dropping bombs on Tokyo and other Japanese cities. This successful operation was a tremendous boost to the morale of the Americans.

After the bombings, Japan changed its war strategy. The Japanese split their force of aircraft carriers. Two were sent to harass Allied naval supply lines near Australia. The other four giant carriers moved into the middle of the Pacific, acting as magnets to draw the United States into battle there. Because the

Japanese lacked the productive power to fight a long war, they gambled everything on a quick victory.

The Japanese aircraft carriers heading for Australia used the Coral Sea as an approach lane. In May of 1942 they met an American naval force led by two aircraft carriers, the *Yorktown* and the *Lexington*. The resulting three-day **battle of the Coral Sea** was unusual because it was the first sea battle in which all of the fighting was done by airplanes. The Japanese force turned back, and one of its carriers was sunk. The *Lexington* suffered such extensive damage that it had to be destroyed, but the battle successfully stopped Japanese advances toward Australia.

The other Japanese aircraft carriers had headed toward Midway Island, an American island west of Hawaii. The Japanese hoped to attack the island base and then lure American carriers into a battle. But by this time American naval intelligence had cracked the Japanese radio code and had advance warning. Planes from American carriers bombed the Japanese ships in advance, preventing the attack on Midway. The Americans sank three Japanese carriers in a few minutes, and the fourth went down the next day. The cost to America was also high. The Americans lost one aircraft carrier, and most of the planes and their pilots had been shot down. However, the huge Japanese sea offensive was stopped, and the Japanese navy had suffered a defeat.

The Americans then planned a strategy to capture the Japanese-held islands in the Pacific. Starting with the southern islands, American naval forces would work their way

The cost of the battle of Midway was high, including the loss of the U.S.S. Yorktown, but "Avenger" torpedo bombers helped win the day..

northward until they reached islands that were within bombing distance of Japan. General MacArthur would head one operation that would push northward from New Guinea to the Philippines. Admiral **Chester Nimitz** (NIM itz) would "island-hop" across the mid-Pacific, taking certain key islands in three chains: the Gilberts, the Marshalls, and the Marianas. Then both forces would converge on the Japanese mainland.

MacArthur Moves Northward

The Japanese, meanwhile, had almost finished an airfield on **Guadalcanal** (GWOD ul kuh NAL) in the Solomon Islands near New Guinea. From there they could bomb Allied convoys at will. Consequently, MacArthur began his offensive there in 1942, but it took six months to drive the Japanese out. The Japanese fought tenaciously, and American casualties were heavy. Finally, the marines dynamited the island's caves to force out the last Japanese defenders.

The American attack on New Guinea became bogged down and was saved only

General MacArthur honors his promise to return to the Philippines.

when General MacArthur airlifted fifteen thousand troops there. By October 1944 MacArthur's forces were ready to retake the Philippines, landing first at Leyte (LAY tee). Many liberty-loving Filipino fighters who had hidden in the mountains and jungles now undertook guerrilla warfare to help the Americans free the Philippines. MacArthur said, "I have returned. By the grace of Almighty God, our forces stand again on Philippine soil, soil consecrated by the blood of our two peoples." By March 1945 the forces had moved northward and had freed the Philippine capital of Manila on the island of Luzon.

Nimitz Moves West

The first target of Admiral Nimitz's Pacific operation was Tarawa, the largest atoll (a ring-like island of coral) in the Gilbert Islands. After bombing the island for a whole week and pounding it for hours with heavy gunfire, the Americans did not expect much resistance. They soon discovered how well the Japanese held out. While American losses soared, the Japanese resisted until only seventeen of more than forty-five hundred defenders remained alive.

The Americans learned lessons for future attacks. The Japanese did not surrender easily. Two months of bombing before landing troops became normal. Thousands of tons of explosives would be hurled shoreward by battleships at Japanese targets from this point on.

After launching such attacks in the Marshall Islands, the Nimitz forces recaptured Guam in the Marianas. Next, they retook the sea east of the Philippines from the Japanese. The fleet then angled northward toward **Iwo Jima** (EE-woh JEE-muh). This small island, only seven hundred miles from Tokyo, had been a station from which the Japanese could intercept American bombers headed for Japan. If the United States could capture it, Iwo Jima could serve as an emergency landing and refueling stop for American bombers. It could also provide a takeoff point for shorter-range fighter planes. But Iwo Jima proved to be the costliest chunk of rock and black sand taken by the U.S. Marine Corps in their 168-year history. Over five thousand marines died during its capture in early 1945.

As war with the Japanese intensified, the Allied seamen began to fear a new type of Japanese attack: the **kamikazes** (KAH mih KAH zeez). Kamikazes were suicide attack planes. Their pilots deliberately hurled these

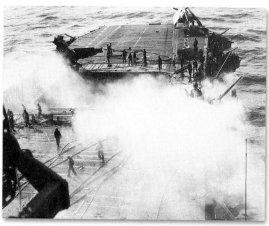
Sailors attempt to control the blaze after a kamikaze plane crashes into the U.S.S. Enterprise.

planes at an enemy target. Such attacks were a product of the Japanese belief that the highest gift one could give the emperor was one's life. Furthermore, Japan had lost both its first-rate pilots and its best planes. In kamikaze warfare out-of-date planes could be loaded with explosives and flown by inexperienced pilots who had only to dive into a ship. The results were devastating. Kamikazes sank 30 ships, damaged 368 more, and killed 11,000 sailors. In spite of the kamikaze attacks, the American forces pushed on toward Japan.

Taking **Okinawa** (OH kih NOW wah) was the last obstacle to reaching the Japanese mainland. The assault on Okinawa began in April 1945 and was completed in June. The Japanese fought hard; over 110,000 died, leaving 11,000 to surrender. But now Americans were just 325 miles from mainland Japan and were able to attack both Japan's industrial and population centers. In one ten-day bombing blitz American planes turned thirty-two square miles of factories into wasteland. Fire bombing of residential areas was especially destructive because the Japanese homes were built close together and were constructed of highly flammable materials.

SECTION REVIEW

1. What American general was forced to evacuate while attempting to hold the Philippines?

2. What two American military leaders took command of much of the action against Japan?

3. An airfield on which of the Solomon Islands took the Americans six months to capture?

4. What small island base had the Japanese used to keep American bombers from Japan? How many marines died in its capture?

5. What was the last American conquest before attacking the Japanese mainland?

 Why did the Japanese use kamikazes despite the tragic waste of human life?

The End of the War

American forces were closing in on all sides, and Japan was suffering heavily from bombing raids. The American military had learned, however, how hard the Japanese would fight. Many feared that it would take hundreds of thousands of American lives to invade and conquer Japan.

The Beginning of the Atomic Era

In 1933, as Hitler gained power and took action against the German Jews, physics professor Albert Einstein took refuge in the United States. Aware of the Nazis' efforts to develop a uranium bomb, Einstein wrote the president in July 1939 to advise him of the possibilities and dangers of such a weapon. Leaders in the United States decided to set up a secret program to make such a bomb before the Germans could.

A group of brilliant scientists joined this **"Manhattan Project."** In Los Alamos, New Mexico, the Manhattan Project engineers assembled the materials for the bomb. At dawn on July 16, 1945, the first device was successfully tested in New Mexico.

On April 12, 1945, Franklin Roosevelt, by then in his fourth term as president, died from the effects of a stroke. The day after **Harry S. Truman** stepped into the presidency, he was told of the Manhattan Project. He decided that it would be better to end the war quickly with the new weapon than to spend countless thousands of lives in an invasion of Japan. Although in later years people debated Truman's approval of dropping the bomb, Truman wrote in his *Memoirs,* "Let there be no mistake about it. I regarded the bomb as a military weapon and never had any doubt that it should be used."

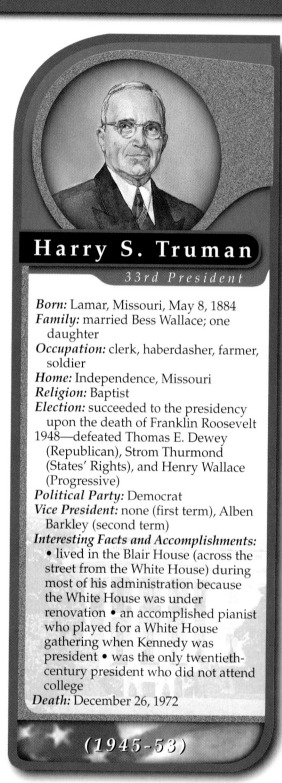

Harry S. Truman

33rd President

Born: Lamar, Missouri, May 8, 1884
Family: married Bess Wallace; one daughter
Occupation: clerk, haberdasher, farmer, soldier
Home: Independence, Missouri
Religion: Baptist
Election: succeeded to the presidency upon the death of Franklin Roosevelt
1948—defeated Thomas E. Dewey (Republican), Strom Thurmond (States' Rights), and Henry Wallace (Progressive)
Political Party: Democrat
Vice President: none (first term), Alben Barkley (second term)
Interesting Facts and Accomplishments:
• lived in the Blair House (across the street from the White House) during most of his administration because the White House was under renovation • an accomplished pianist who played for a White House gathering when Kennedy was president • was the only twentieth-century president who did not attend college
Death: December 26, 1972

(1945-53)

A "mushroom" cloud rises above Nagasaki, Japan, following the atomic explosion in 1945.

On July 26, when President Truman met at Potsdam in Germany for a conference with the major powers, he issued the **Potsdam Declaration.** It demanded that Japan surrender unconditionally or face total destruction.

Although the original military leaders in Japan's war effort were no longer in power, the new premier refused to surrender. Eleven days later, on August 6, 1945, at 8:15 A.M., an American bomber dropped a single uranium bomb on **Hiroshima** (HIR uh SHE muh). Although it was only a little more than two feet in diameter and ten feet long, the bomb's explosive power was equal to twenty thousand tons of dynamite. The blast killed eighty thousand Japanese civilians, and an equal number suffered radiation burns.

After another warning to surrender was ignored, the United States dropped a single plutonium bomb, called "Fat Boy," on **Nagasaki** (NAH guh SAH kee) on August 9. This bomb flattened the city and killed about forty thousand people.

Peace

The next day Japan sued for peace. On August 15, 1945, the Japanese people heard the voice of their emperor Hirohito. In a taped radio broadcast, the emperor told his subjects that the war was over. Americans at home ran into the streets, temporarily leaving their jobs, and hugged one another from sheer joy.

Although a few Japanese groups in distant spots continued to fight, the war was really over. On August 21 General MacArthur was in Tokyo. As he watched the same flag that had flown over the U.S. Capitol on December 7, 1941, go up over the reestablished American embassy, he said, "Let it wave in full glory as a symbol of hope for the oppressed and as a harbinger of victory."

On September 2, 1945, MacArthur accepted two of the emperor's representatives on board the battleship *Missouri* anchored in Tokyo Bay. There they signed the formal treaty of surrender.

World War II was the costliest war in history. It is estimated that over fifteen million soldiers and twenty million civilians died in the war. The United States lost nearly three hundred thousand of its military personnel,

and many more were wounded. On top of its human effort and loss, the nation spent about $300 billion on the war.

Americans returned to peacetime with great relief that the price had been paid and the war had been won. It then remained for them to take their place in the postwar world.

SECTION REVIEW

1. What was the Manhattan Project?

2. Who became president before the war ended?

3. On what two cities were the atomic bombs dropped?

4. Where, when, and by whom was the Japanese surrender accepted?

5. How many American servicemen died in the war?

 Why has there been debate over Truman's decision to drop the atomic bomb?

SUMMARY

The fascist governments that arose in Germany and Italy began to threaten Europe in the late 1930s, while Japan's militaristic government wanted more control in Asia and the Pacific. The desires of these nations led them to band together as the Axis powers and brought Britain and France into war against them in 1939. Hitler's German armies soon took control of most of Europe, including France. For over a year, Britain stood alone against the Axis powers. The United States aided the Allied cause by supplying materials but was unwilling to join the war until Japan bombed the American naval base at Pearl Harbor in December 1941.

With that attack, the United States entered the war and began to build its military strength to defeat its enemies. With Britain, the United States concentrated first on defeating Hitler and Mussolini in Europe. Campaigns were launched in North Africa, Italy, and France, and the Allied advances finally brought victory in Europe on May 8, 1945.

In the east the Japanese had taken control of much of Southeast Asia and the Pacific Islands. They had even taken control of America's Philippine Islands. But American forces began to battle back, winning control of island after island until they reached islands within bombing distance of Japan. Rather than risk a large-scale invasion, the U.S. dropped two atomic bombs on Japan. This action forced the Japanese to surrender and ended World War II in August 1945. The United States emerged from the war as leader of the free world and as a nation with many postwar problems.

Chapter Review

People, Places, and Things to Remember

Adolf Hitler
Nazi Party
Benito Mussolini
fascist governments
Axis powers
Good Neighbor Policy
Winston Churchill
appeasement
Joseph Stalin
blitzkrieg
Allies

Lend-Lease Act
Pearl Harbor
conscientious objectors
Dwight D. Eisenhower
D-Day
battle of the Bulge
Yalta Meeting
V-E Day
Douglas MacArthur
battle of the Coral Sea
Chester Nimitz

Guadalcanal
Iwo Jima
kamikazes
Okinawa
Manhattan Project
Harry S. Truman
Potsdam Declaration
Hiroshima
Nagasaki

Review Questions

What word(s) is (are) best described by each of the following phrases?

1. strong dictatorships that stressed nationalism and power

2. giving in to demands in an attempt to settle a disagreement peacefully

3. a swift attack of bombers, tanks, and troops—a "lightning war"

4. young men who were sincerely opposed to war and were thus allowed to serve in noncombat roles instead of regular military service

5. Japanese planes flown on suicide missions to destroy American ships

Match each of the following men with his country.

6. Franklin Roosevelt
7. Benito Mussolini
8. Joseph Stalin
9. Adolf Hitler
10. Winston Churchill

a. Britain
b. Germany
c. Italy
d. Soviet Union
e. United States

Match the appropriate letter on the time line with the event that occurred on that date. Also describe the significance of each event.

1939	1940	1941	1942	1943	1944	1945
A		B			C	D E

11. V-E Day
12. attack on Pearl Harbor
13. Hitler invades Poland
14. bomb dropped on Hiroshima
15. D-Day

Questions for Discussion

16. Should the United States have been better prepared for World War II? Should it be constantly prepared for war? Explain your answers.

17. How does a man like Hitler gain such popularity and power? Could such a man rise to power in the United States? Explain your answer.

History Skills

Steps to War

Although America's change from total isolationism to all-out war seemed sudden, it was provoked by a long series of events. To trace these events, use the reactions listed below to complete the chart on your own paper.

Foreign Action	American Reaction
1. Treaty of Versailles (1919)	
2. Treaty of Washington (1921)	
3. Kellogg-Briand Peace Pact (1928)	
4. Japan's conquest of Manchuria (1931)	
5. Allies' failure to pay war debts (early 1930s)	*bitterness at the Allies' ingratitude*
6. Italy's conquest of Ethiopia (1935)	
7. Germany's capture of the Rhineland (1936)	
8. Britain's appeasement (1938)	
9. Allied declaration of war (1939)	
10. fall of France (1940)	
11. Japan's entry into Southeast Asia (1941)	
12. Germany's invasion of Russia (1941)	*secret agreement with Churchill to defeat "Hitler first"*
13. Germany's sinking of U.S. convoys (1941)	
14. Japan's attack on Pearl Harbor (1941)	

American Reactions:

"lend-lease" policy
"cash-and-carry" policy
ban on most trade with Japan
disillusionment with foreign wars
declaration of war against the Axis powers
hope that naval competition would cease
horror at fascist aggression, but no action
worldwide realization of the Nazi threat to peace

hope that nations would avoid future wars to settle disputes
decision to shoot submarines on sight
no protests at the violation of the Versailles Treaty
disappointment after appealing to the League of Nations

Preparing for the Future

1963: Led by Martin Luther King Jr., 250,000 people marched on Washington, D.C. to show their support for civil rights legislation.

1969: Neil Armstrong took "one giant leap for mankind" on July 20, when he became the first person to walk on the moon.

1950s: Hula-Hoops were popular with the children of the postwar baby boom.

1974: President Richard Nixon left office in the wake of a scandal surrounding a burglary at the Democratic Party's National Campaign Headquarters and the subsequent cover-up by the White House.

1991: After five weeks of intensive bombing in the Persian Gulf War, it took ground troops just one hundred hours to force the surrender of Iraqi troops in Kuwait.

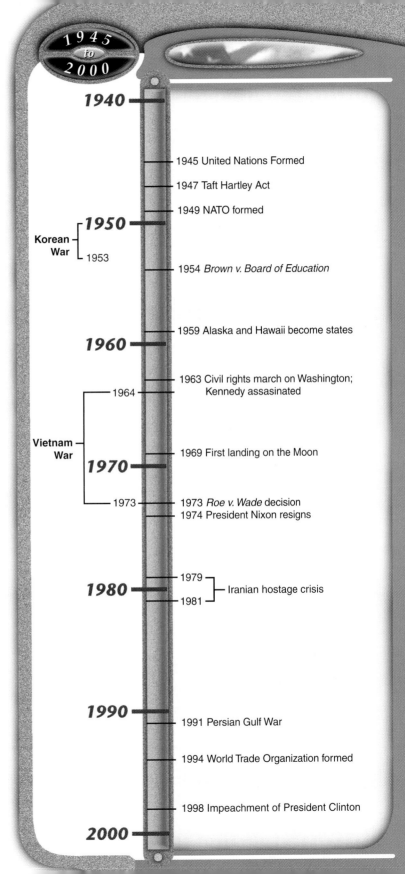

1945 to 2000

1940

1945 United Nations Formed

1947 Taft Hartley Act

1949 NATO formed

1950

Korean War — 1953

1954 *Brown v. Board of Education*

1959 Alaska and Hawaii become states

1960

1963 Civil rights march on Washington; Kennedy assasinated

1964

Vietnam War

1969 First landing on the Moon

1970

1973 — 1973 *Roe v. Wade* decision

1974 President Nixon resigns

1980 — 1979
1981 — Iranian hostage crisis

1990

1991 Persian Gulf War

1994 World Trade Organization formed

1998 Impeachment of President Clinton

2000

Unit VII: Preparing for the Future

King's "I Have a Dream" Speech

Rev. Martin Luther King used his gifts as a speaker to rally support for civil rights legislation. Read this conclusion to his powerful speech. Then answer the questions.

I say to you today, my friends, that in spite of the difficulties and frustrations of the moment, I still have a dream. It is a dream rooted in the American dream.

I have a dream that one day this nation will rise up and live out the true meaning of its creed: "We hold these truths to be self-evident, that all men are created equal."

I have a dream that one day on the red hills of Georgia the sons of former slaves and the sons of former slaveowners will be able to sit down together at the table of brotherhood.

I have a dream that one day even the state of Mississippi, a desert state sweltering with the heat of injustice and oppression, will be transformed into an oasis of freedom and justice.

I have a dream that my four little children will one day live in a nation where they will not be judged by the color of their skin but by the content of their character.

I have a dream today.

I have a dream that one day the state of Alabama, whose governor's lips are presently dripping with the words of interposition and nullification, will be transformed into a situation where little black boys and black girls will be able to join hands with little white boys and white girls and walk together as sisters and brothers.

I have a dream today.

I have a dream that one day every valley shall be exalted, every hill and mountain shall be made low, the rough places will be made plain, and the crooked places will be made straight, and the glory of the Lord shall be revealed, and all flesh shall see it together.

This is our hope. This is the faith with which I return to the South. With this faith we will be able to transform the jangling discords of our nation into a beautiful symphony of brotherhood. With this faith we will be able to work together, to pray together, to struggle together, to go to jail together, to stand up for freedom together, knowing that we will be free one day.

This will be the day when all of God's children will be able to sing with new meaning: "My country, 'tis of thee, sweet land of liberty, of thee I sing. Land where my fathers died, land of the pilgrim's pride, from every mountainside, let freedom ring."

And if America is to be a great nation, this must become true. So let freedom ring from the prodigious hilltops of New Hampshire. Let freedom ring from the mountains of New York. Let freedom ring from the heightening Alleghenies of Pennsylvania!

Let freedom ring from every hill and molehill of Mississippi! From every mountainside, let freedom ring!

When we let freedom ring, when we let it ring from every village and every hamlet, from every state and every city, we will be able to speed up that day when all of God's children, black men and white men, Jews and Gentiles, Protestants and Catholics, will be able to join hands and sing in the words of the old Negro spiritual, "Free at last! Free at last! Thank God Almighty, we are free at last!"

1. Does King appeal to any values that you support? What are some of them?

2. King appeals to equality, expressed in the Declaration of Independence. What does King believe is "the true meaning" of this creed?

3. King appeals to universal justice, prophesied by Isaiah (40:3-5) and explained in Luke 3:2-6. How does King apply this passage?

4. King appeals to freedom, promised in John 8:34-36 and expressed in the Negro spiritual "Free at last!" What does King mean when he says, "We will be free one day"?

27

Recovery, Cold War, and Coexistence

A t 7:00 P.M. (EST) on August 14, 1945, President Harry Truman announced to the nation that Japan had finally accepted the terms of surrender. Church bells rang. Whistles blew. Troop ships halfway across the Pacific turned around and headed home. World War II was over! Four years of conflict on the battlefields, on the seas, and in the air had come to a halt. The United States was at peace.

The war was over, but the United States faced new challenges that would prove to be almost as trying as the war had been. The world after the war was not the same as the one that had existed before. New problems, new threats, and new fears emerged in the postwar era. But the country would also have new opportunities and new technology that would bring a new prosperity.

Home from the War

The end of the war brought nine million men in uniform home to civilian life. It brought the retooling of industries to produce peacetime goods instead of guns and tanks. It opened the way for new inventions, new styles, and new fads to change America's way of life.

Changing Times

Many Americans feared that a depression would follow World War II as it had World War I or that the nation would return to the hardships of the Great Depression. Instead of another depression, however, Americans found plenty of jobs, and they kept businesses booming with their desire for more and more material goods. They wanted new comforts and labor-saving devices such as dishwashers, automatic washers, electric dryers, power lawn mowers, and boats. The easy availability of credit encouraged such purchasing.

Since some consumer goods had been either rationed or totally unavailable during the war, people were now ready to buy what they could not buy before. In 1944 factories had produced 100,000 planes and only 70,000 passenger cars. In 1949 only 6,000 planes were produced, but 3.7 million passenger cars rolled off assembly lines. The major problem was that so many goods were in demand, and factories could not produce enough to satisfy the public. Prices on many goods skyrocketed until the demand was met. But as more factories got in gear to produce needed items, inflation settled down, and the economy became stable.

Another aid to Americans after the war was the **GI Bill.** Fearful that soldiers returning from war would be unemployed, as many were after World War I, Congress passed a bill that helped the veterans move right into civilian life. Veterans were granted benefits in many areas, including help in finding jobs and money for education and for home purchases.

While the young men were away at war, many young couples had postponed marriage. With the war over, many newlyweds began to start families, and the resulting **"baby boom"** created tremendous new demands, which changed over the years as the children grew. A demand for housing was followed by a demand for baby goods such as baby food,

Better communication through radio and television spread fads across the nation at lightning speed. This girl enjoys the Hula-Hoop.

diapers, and strollers. When these children started school, there were acute shortages of classrooms and teachers.

With housing shortages in the early post-war years and the high cost of land in the cities, more Americans became willing to move to the suburbs. Contractors built homes cheaply and quickly, using the techniques of mass production. Bulldozers graded the lots, and work crews came to lay water, gas, sewer,

Beginning in the 1950s, the interstate highway system changed the landscape of America by allowing people in the outlying country to drive quickly to city jobs. Urban sprawl became common around major cities.

and electrical lines. They were followed by carpenters, who built row after row of identical houses. Roofers, plumbers, electricians, and painters applied their skills as well. Rolling fields turned into suburbs in a few weeks or months.

Most (about ninety-five percent) of those who moved to homes in the suburbs were younger whites. Cities were left to be occupied by the poor (mostly the elderly and racial minorities). Since cities could not collect heavy taxes from the poor, they had to function with less money. Thus cities started to decay and sought government aid for urban renewal projects.

To live in the suburbs, Americans needed more cars. Two-car families became common because the breadwinner needed a car to drive to work and the family wanted to use another.

With more cars came more automotive-related industries like service stations and car washes. Shopping centers were started in order to cut the travel distance to stores. Cities spread out so much that some described the situation as "urban sprawl."

Naturally, the traffic increased, and commuter traffic jams became more common. These problems and the desire to be able to move troops and equipment in case of war prompted the government to promote more and better highways. In 1956 a **Federal Aid Highway Act** was passed. This allowed construction of 41,000 miles of interstate highways at a cost of $28 million over thirteen years. Increased use of auto, truck, and air transportation cut back the use of railroads.

With cars, highways, and the availability of new jobs, Americans were willing to move from their hometowns and to relocate. They moved to sections of the country that offered new jobs. The West, especially California, offered the biggest attraction. The South and the Southwest also grew in population. This was the beginning of the **"sunbelt migrations,"** movements toward the areas of the country with warmer climates.

The war had produced changes in technology. Scientists had worked hard during the war to find new materials and inventions that would improve the war effort and supply substitutes for materials that were in low supply. Now that the war was over, some war inventions and materials had peacetime applications. New medicines and vaccines had been developed for diseases. Synthetic fibers, plastics, and other new materials became useful for industries. New hybrid crops, insecticides, machinery, fertilizer, and better irrigation techniques allowed American farmers to grow more crops than ever before. These changes in American agriculture have sometimes been called the **"green revolution."**

Changes in technology also affected the use of leisure time. Although the television had been made workable as early as 1927, it

President Truman holds the Chicago Tribune, which incorrectly predicted the outcome of the 1948 presidential race.

was not perfected until after World War II. In 1946 there were seven thousand television sets. By 1950 there were four million and by 1960 there were 74 million. Television had many effects on Americans. One was the lessening of regional differences as people from the North, South, East, and West all watched the same programs.

Crazes were also common in the postwar decade. More than thirty million Americans purchased Hula-Hoops, large plastic rings that could be twirled for exercise. A Walt Disney television series based on the life of a frontier hero, Davy Crockett, led to a whole series of products. Children carried Davy Crockett lunch boxes and wore coonskin caps and buckskin jackets while singing about the "King of the Wild Frontier."

The Fair Deal

Although the depression of the 1930s had ended, many people still wanted the government aid that Franklin Roosevelt's New Deal had given them. Americans wondered if the new president, Harry Truman, would continue support of similar programs. Their answer came in September 1945. The president called Congress into special session to present a twenty-one-point domestic program that he called a **"Fair Deal."** The policies were similar to those of the New Deal but established the GI Bill, provided better treatment of black Americans, increased aid to science and public education, and subsidized medical insurance. Not all of Truman's ideas were accepted by Congress, but they helped give the American people some assurance that the government would continue to come to their aid.

One of the issues that did not go Truman's way was the control of labor unions. During the days of high inflation after the war, laborers wanted higher wages without price increases. Some of the unions resorted to major strikes to get their way. Auto, steel, coal, and railroad workers went on strike for higher wages. With the growing number of strikes, some Americans thought that unions had gained too much power. Truman had difficulty controlling the labor unrest himself, but he did not like the way the Republican Congress dealt with it either.

Congress passed the **Taft-Hartley Act** of 1947 over the veto of Truman. The act limited the powers of unions by giving employees more freedom to work against unions. The bill outlawed the closed shop, a practice that forced businesses to hire only union members. It permitted states to pass laws prohibiting union shops that required workers to join the union within a certain date of their hiring. In addition, unions had to give a sixty-day notice before changing or ending work contracts. During that time they could not strike. Moreover, if a proposed strike threatened the nation's health or safety, an eighty-day **injunction,** a court order forbidding the strike, could be issued. During that time the strikers and the management were required to settle the dispute through negotiations.

In the years following the war, **civil rights** (rights guaranteed by the Constitution to every American citizen) for America's blacks became an increasingly important issue. Although Congress rejected Truman's civil rights legislation, the president did try to lessen discrimination against blacks through the influence of his position.

Both the North and the South practiced segregation. Although not required by law in the North, segregation existed in fact. Blacks generally lived in their own neighborhoods and went to black neighborhood schools and businesses. In the South **Jim Crow laws** segregated blacks from whites in schools, theaters, restaurants, and on buses.

Changes came slowly. In 1946 President Truman appointed the President's Committee on Civil Rights. In 1948, by executive order,

the president banned segregation in the armed forces. In World War II President Roosevelt had issued an executive order saying that the federal government would not contract its business to any firms that discriminated against minorities. President Truman continued the policy and also formed a committee to investigate instances of alleged discrimination.

These actions during the Truman administration advanced the civil rights movement. Other changes were made to help integrate blacks in other areas. In 1947 Jackie Robinson became the first black to play major league baseball when he joined the Brooklyn Dodgers. Higher education also began to open to blacks as the University of Oklahoma began to admit blacks to graduate school in 1948.

Truman's idea of giving a Fair Deal to the American people helped him win the presidential election of 1948. He had not been especially popular in his first few years as president. Political pollsters said his Republican opponent, Thomas E. Dewey, was a sure winner, and newspapers printed on election night declared the same. But when the ballots were counted, both the pollsters and the papers were wrong. Truman had waged an exhausting campaign, traveling across America making speeches from the end of a railroad car. The public apparently admired his fighting spirit. "I met the people face to face," he explained, "and . . . they voted for me."

SECTION REVIEW

1. How did the GI Bill help veterans?

2. What parts of the country did many Americans move to in the postwar years?

3. What was Truman's domestic plan called?

4. What act limited the powers of labor unions?

 How did the "baby boom" and suburban life affect the American economy?

Postwar Problems

The United States emerged from World War II as the most powerful nation in the world, but it now had one strong rival—the Soviet Union. These two nations had fought as allies in the war, but the differences of these two postwar world powers would create great tensions. As Europe and Eastern Asia lay in ruin after the havoc of war, they needed help for rebuilding from the superpowers. The problem was that American ideas on how they should be rebuilt often conflicted with the demands of the Soviet Union.

Postwar Germany

Because Germany's government under Hitler had been defeated, the Germans were left without a government at the war's end. To fill this power vacuum, the Allies divided Germany into four sectors, or sections. American, British, and French troops occupied the three western sectors. The Soviets occupied the fourth sector—the eastern part of Germany closest to the Russian border. The Soviet Union quickly showed that it would have its way in that sector by making sure that its economy and politics were communist-controlled. Tensions developed in Germany. These tensions later resulted in major problems between the United States and the Soviet Union.

The Allies were also concerned about dealing with Germany's former Nazi leaders. As Allied troops liberated the German-occupied areas of Europe, they discovered concentration camps. Terrible atrocities had taken place in these camps. As many as six million Jews and millions of other Europeans had been exterminated in the Nazi-driven Holocaust. The Allies decided to try the Nazi leaders publicly as war criminals. The trials began in 1945 in Nuremberg, Germany, and further unraveled the grim story of Hitler's Germany. In October 1946 the international court at the **Nuremberg trials** condemned twelve Nazi leaders to death for "crimes against peace" and "crimes against humanity." The trials of lesser Nazi officials continued over many more months, though more quietly.

Dealing with Japan

Japan had been destroyed by the war. Her cities and harbors lay in ruin. Her merchant fleet had been sunk. The United States avoided trouble with the Soviet Union over the rebuilding of Japan by taking sole responsibility for helping that country. Truman appointed General Douglas MacArthur to head a military government in postwar Japan that could supervise its recovery.

Japanese officials meet Americans on the U.S.S. Missouri to sign documents of surrender.

The United States helped the Japanese write a new constitution. The Japanese elected a legislative body and gave rights to all citizens. Women got the right to vote. As in Germany, war criminals went to trial. In an effort to help rebuild the lives of the Japanese and to instill spiritual values, General MacArthur encouraged missionaries to come to Japan. Thus the door to Japan again opened to the gospel.

The UNRRA (United Nations Relief and Recovery Administration) sent aid to the Japanese from 1945 to 1948. The United States was the chief donor to this organization, which provided food, clothing, and medicine to meet immediate needs. Japan quickly rebuilt, soon becoming a thriving industrial nation. In 1951 the United States ended its military occupation of Japan. The United States had helped Japan to rebuild, gaining her as a powerful ally for the free world.

The United States Aids Europe

Europeans, who had seen World War II fought on their own lands, had suffered more than Americans. Millions of their soldiers and civilians had been killed. Millions of the survivors were homeless, wandering from place to place seeking shelter and food. To many of these "displaced persons" life seemed hopeless. There was no one to hire them. The wartime governments of the defeated countries no longer existed, and the winners were so deeply in debt from their own war efforts that they could do little to help. Bombing and fighting had destroyed most industries. Railroads and roads were in ruin. Because they had been bombed or burned, farmlands did not produce, and near-famine conditions existed in Europe.

The United States went to work aiding Europe. First it furnished aid through the UNRRA. Immediate needs were met through shipments of tons of food, clothing, and medicine. Because communists could and did make

easy inroads among the discontented and downtrodden, the United States demonstrated a special concern for such people in an effort to keep them from ignorantly accepting communist influence.

On June 5, 1947, Secretary of State **George Marshall** proposed a vast new aid program for Europe. He asked Congress for huge sums of money to rebuild the European countries ravaged by war. The **Marshall Plan** offered aid even to Eastern European countries already subjected to Soviet control. But the Soviet Union rejected the offer. It would not allow its satellites (Soviet-dominated countries) to take advantage of the offer.

Although the Marshall Plan cost a great deal (more than $12 billion), it did aid European recovery. The Western European countries that received American help rebuilt quickly and soon surpassed their prewar production.

The Formation of the United Nations

Throughout World War II the Allies had held eleven conferences to plot strategy and deal with problems. The idea of a postwar peace-keeping organization to replace the League of Nations was voiced at the meeting in Teheran late in 1943. Because of increased tensions among the Allies, especially between free countries and the Soviet Union, the topic was raised again at Yalta in February 1945. The Big Three—the United States, Britain, and the Soviet Union—called for a meeting of nations at San Francisco to write a charter for another world peace-keeping organization.

On April 25, 1945, just thirteen days after the death of President Roosevelt, President Truman welcomed delegates from fifty nations to San Francisco. During the two months of discussion, the delegates had many arguments. Some threatened to leave the meetings because the Soviet demands were too selfish. Finally, enough concessions were

Secretary of State George Marshall meets with Nationalist China's President Chiang Kai-shek and his wife.

made to forge a charter for the new **United Nations** organization.

A permanent world headquarters for the United Nations was established in 1947 when John D. Rockefeller Jr. provided $8.5 million to construct a building. The city of New York gave land; the United States provided a generous loan of $65 million. The new headquarters opened in 1952.

The Organizational Structure of the United Nations—The three most important parts of the U.N. are the **General Assembly, the Security Council,** and the **Secretariat.** The General Assembly was to be somewhat like a legislature. Every member nation was to send a representative. By 1999 it consisted of the delegates of 185 countries. The General Assembly really has little power, however, since the nations are not forced to abide by its decisions.

The Security Council had five permanent member nations and six (now ten) nonpermanent members. The latter are elected by the General Assembly for two-year terms and are usually drawn from the smaller countries. The Security Council is the strongest part of the U.N. because it has the power to enforce U.N. policy with military action. But because any one of the five permanent members (Britain, the United States, France, China, and the Russian Federation) can exercise veto power to stop a decision, the council's power is frequently curtailed. It has acted successfully only in minor disputes or when the Big Five decided to use force. During the Cold War, the Soviet Union vetoed more than a hundred decisions of the council—more than all the other members combined. Moreover, when the seat of Free China was given to Communist China, the chance of a veto by a Communist power doubled.

The final major body of the U.N. is the Secretariat. The Secretariat is a type of executive branch, composed of U.N. agencies and administrators that handle the daily affairs of the organization. It is headed by a secretary-general elected by the General Assembly.

Weighing the Successes of the United Nations—From a Christian viewpoint it is admirable to settle disputes peacefully, as the United Nations intends. Knowing the possible consequences of today's weapons, few people want war. Yet no matter how strong and exemplary the desires for peace may be, the sinful nature of man works against them.

Although some people and nations believe that it is important to do right and keep one's word, others are mainly concerned with what will benefit them most. Sinful man will often do what he can to get ahead, even if he must disregard the rights of others to do so. Because they are led by sinful men, countries are often guilty of unjust actions. Communist countries in particular tend to honor an agreement only when it benefits them. Appealing to a higher level, that of honoring God, is fruitless because God means nothing to them. Thus, agreements made in the United Nations have little chance for success.

Moreover, the record of the U.N. shows its ineffectiveness. It has neither brought peace nor ended war. Since its founding, at least seventy-five wars have erupted in the world, and more than one-third of the world's population has come under communist domination. The member nations of the United Nations fall into three major categories—free world nations, communist nations, and the **third world.** (The third world includes the many poor nations of Africa, Asia, and Latin America.) Because the third-world nations are generally poor and politically unstable, communist influences have often swayed these countries to accept communist ideas and side with the Soviet Union in disputes at the United Nations. This communist influence creates problems for the United States in its dealings with these third-world countries. In addition, the existence of the U.N. in New York has allowed many foreign countries to spy in the United States legally, a practice contrary to the best interests of Americans.

Although the words of Isaiah 2:4—"They shall beat their swords into plowshares, and their spears into pruning hooks: nation shall not lift up sword against nation, neither shall they learn war any more"—appear in the U.N. headquarters, in God's Word the verses refer to Christ's coming kingdom. Only after Christ's return to earth will there be true peace. The United Nations cannot stop that turmoil; only God can. Yet Christians are not to be troubled over these things. The Christian's refuge is not in the organizations of man, but in the arms of the almighty God.

SECTION REVIEW

1. Which section of Germany came under communist control?

2. What changes occurred in Japan under U.S. supervision?

3. What plan was developed for giving aid to Europe after the war?

4. What are the three bodies of the United Nations? Which body is the strongest?

 Why has the United Nations been unable to achieve its goal of international peace and security?

Cold War Crises

Because the threat of Hitler and Nazism was great, the United States and the Soviet Union became allies in World War II. When the war was over, however, the United States soon learned that the Soviets were out to gain all they could in the postwar disarray. In the years after the war there developed what was called the **Cold War.** The United States and the Soviet Union did not go into a direct military conflict with each other, but they found themselves in many disputes that sprang from the tensions between them. Fear of a third world war erupting between the two countries was often present.

At Yalta Stalin had pledged to hold free elections in Poland and in other areas where the Soviets took control. But he had no intention of allowing any nation that the Soviets occupied to choose its own form of government. By organizing communist parties in the countries of Eastern Europe even before World War II, the Soviets had laid the groundwork for communist takeover. As Soviet troops moved in to occupy Eastern Europe at the war's end, they placed communists in government positions. In this way they took over the governments of Bulgaria, Yugoslavia, Albania, Rumania, Poland, Hungary, and later Czechoslovakia. To ensure that these countries remained in the communist camp, Red Army units remained in each nation, keeping pro-Soviet leaders in control despite opposition from the people.

On March 5, 1946, Britain's World War II leader, Winston Churchill, came to Fulton, Missouri, to speak at Westminster College. Churchill graphically described the problem in Eastern Europe: "From Stettin in the Baltic to Trieste in the Adriatic, an **iron curtain** has descended across the Continent." From then on countries under communist control were said to be "behind the Iron Curtain." This political and military barrier soon came to represent the differences in beliefs between the two sides. Churchill believed that the West would have to take firm action to halt future communist expansion.

The Truman Doctrine: Containing Communism

The Soviets soon proved Churchill's point by showing that they were not content to control only Eastern Europe. Their next goal was to claim the oil-rich Middle East.

Allied troops had occupied Iran during World War II to keep open its vital oil supply. When the war ended, American and British troops withdrew, but Soviet troops remained. Soviet-inspired rioting took place, and Iranian troops who sought to restore order were kept from doing so. When Iran, with American backing, complained to the U.N., the Soviet troops left.

Meanwhile, communist-led guerrillas in Greece were gaining ground in their efforts to take control. Turkey also seemed to be on the brink of tumbling into the Soviet camp. President Truman finally saw that it was

essential for the United States to "contain" communism, that is, to stop the Soviets from overtaking more governments. To carry out the **containment** policy, the president asked Congress to approve $400 million for military aid to support the pro-Western governments in Greece and Turkey. The idea of using military aid to support pro-Western, anti-communist governments soon got the name **Truman Doctrine.**

Confrontation in Germany

When Germany was divided among the Allies after the war, the country's old capital of Berlin was in the middle of Soviet-controlled East Germany. Because Berlin was such an important city, the Allies agreed to divide its control among themselves. It had four zones, one each for France, Britain, the United States, and the Soviet Union. Supplies were shipped to the French, British, and American zones of Berlin from the West by truck or train across Soviet-held lands.

When the United States, Britain, and France decided to combine their sectors of Germany, the Soviet Union responded by denying all road, rail, and river access across East Germany to Berlin, beginning June 24, 1948. This violation of the Yalta agreement left two million residents of West Berlin without food and other supplies. The Soviet Union thought that its blockade would force the Allies out of Berlin. Stalin also believed that his action would undermine the confidence of the European Allies in the United States.

President Truman responded quickly to the Soviet threat. He announced that the United States would use a massive airlift to West Berlin. For the next 321 days, more than 250,000 flights carried supplies into West Berlin. More than 2.5 million tons of supplies were airlifted to the blockaded city. The Soviets did not attack the planes, as some had predicted. When the Soviets realized that the

United States was prepared to keep the **Berlin airlift** going indefinitely, it lifted its blockade in May 1949.

Since the Soviet Union had taken such a strong grip on East Germany, attempts for unification of Germany seemed futile. In September 1949, the United States, Britain, and France allowed the sectors of Germany they held to become an independent nation. The new Federal Republic of Germany (West Germany) was formed, with Bonn as its capital.

Alliances and Aid

Because of the Soviet threat to the parts of Europe that remained free, President Truman believed that these nations needed more than financial aid. He asked Congress for military support and the formation of a joint alliance, with the United States as a member. The alliance, called the **North Atlantic Treaty Organization** (NATO), united the Western European nations of Britain, France, Italy, Portugal, the Netherlands, Denmark, Norway, Belgium, and Luxembourg, as well as the North Atlantic countries of Canada, Iceland, and the United States. In 1952 Greece and Turkey joined, and in 1959, West Germany. These nations agreed to provide money, troops, and military equipment for mutual protection. General Dwight D. Eisenhower became the first supreme commander of NATO forces. America's membership in NATO meant a change in its long-standing policy of isolationism. It was the first peacetime alliance that the United States had ever joined for the possible defense of other nations.

The Soviets, responding to the Berlin airlift and the formation of NATO, gathered representatives of their Eastern European satellites in Warsaw, Poland. The Soviets then organized their own military alliance, called the **Warsaw Pact.** The Warsaw Pact nations included Poland, Albania, East Germany, Bulgaria, Rumania, Czechoslovakia, Hungary, and the Soviet Union.

The China Question

Just as postwar Europe was undergoing change, so was the Far East. China became a special problem. China was the most populous nation in the world. The communists, led by **Mao Zedong,** were poised to gain control of the country after World War II.

China had suffered from fighting warlords and domineering foreign countries in the decades before the war. Generalissimo **Chiang Kai-shek** had emerged as leader of the strong "Nationalist" group in China. The United States had made trade agreements with

With promises of land for the poor, Mao Zedong gained control of China for the Communist Party. Chiang Kai-shek and the Nationalists fled to Taiwan.

Chiang and had aided the Chinese against Japan in World War II. Chiang's efforts to defeat the Japanese in China and to control China, however, were being sabotaged from within his own party by corruption and internal conflicts. Some American troops were sent to aid Chiang, but they were pulled out in 1947.

Almost immediately China was again engulfed in war. This conflict was between the communists, led by Mao, and the Nationalists, led by Chiang. Mao's forces were highly motivated. The communists had promised to give land to the poor. By 1949 the communists had gained control of the mainland. They forced Chiang to flee with his army to the coastal island of Taiwan, where he set up Nationalist China (also called the Republic of China or Free China). Mainland China became the communist "People's Republic of China."

The presence of communism in China posed a new threat. China and the Soviet Union signed the Sino-Soviet Pact in February 1950, confirming American suspicions that the communists might try to work together against the free world. President Truman, and several presidents who followed him, steadfastly supported Chiang and his government on Taiwan, at least in theory. Some Americans preferred, however, to recognize the communist People's Republic, which controlled the mainland, as the one legitimate government of China. Americans knew that the Chinese communists were persecuting Christians, squelching free ideas, and killing or imprisoning those who opposed Chairman Mao. Even so, in 1979 the United States reversed its policy and recognized Communist China instead of Free China.

Korea and the Korean Conflict

China was not the only communist target in Eastern Asia. The Soviet Union had begun to take a grip on part of Korea before World War II ended. As the United States was defeating Japan, the Soviet Union was pouring troops into Korea. The Yalta agreement allowed the Soviets to occupy Korea north of the 38th parallel. The Soviets again promised that at the proper time, free elections would be held. Of course, the communists established

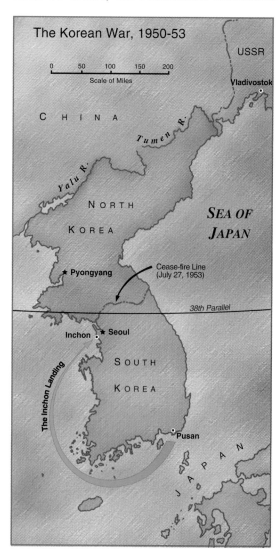

The Korean War, 1950-53

their style of government in North Korea in the meantime. South Korea held its own elections, and the Republic of Korea was formed with Seoul as capital. Korea, like Germany, was thus divided—part communist, part free.

Talks were held in hopes of unifying Korea, but they broke down. Then North Korea invaded South Korea on June 25, 1950. The U.N. Security Council quickly called an emergency session to deal with the crisis. It demanded North Korea's immediate withdrawal. When the troops were still there two days later, the Council suggested that the U.N. aid South Korea. (The Security Council was able to approve this because the Soviet Union was boycotting sessions at that time.)

That same day President Truman committed American planes and ships to support the South Koreans. On June 30 American troops were ordered to Korea. Within a week the U.N. voted to send a peacekeeping force to Korea to seek an end to the conflict. Since four-fifths of its men were American, President Truman was allowed to pick its commander. He chose General Douglas MacArthur, the most experienced American Pacific officer.

Truman hoped the troops could drive communist troops out of South Korea. But a shortage of needed equipment and American unreadiness produced a shabby start for the **Korean War.** North Korean troops, well equipped by the Soviets, continued to push their way south. By the end of August, U.N. forces held only the southeastern corner of Korea near Pusan. MacArthur then surprised the North Koreans by going behind their lines and attacking from Inchon. All the ground lost was regained in two weeks.

When the troops reached the 38th parallel, a decision was needed. Truman and the U.N. approved MacArthur's order to cross into North Korea. The U.N. hoped that MacArthur's northward push would lead to reunifying Korea. On October 26, 1950,

General MacArthur's public denunciation of President Truman for limiting the war in Korea ended his military career.

MacArthur's advance guard reached the Yalu River, the dividing line between North Korea and China. China reacted by sending more than two hundred thousand "volunteers" across the Yalu River into North Korea to stop the U.N. forces.

Fierce fighting broke out, and U.N. troops were pushed back past the 38th parallel down into South Korea. MacArthur now believed that winning a land war in Korea required the bombing of Chinese bases and supply lines in China. MacArthur declared, "There is no substitute for victory."

President Truman and his advisors, however, thought differently. They were now content simply to restore the boundary to the 38th parallel. Although MacArthur pushed for all-out war and total victory, Truman decided on a limited war with very specific aims. He did not want to risk the use of nuclear weapons in Korea. He was also afraid that the Soviet Union might fight back somewhere in Europe or Asia if the United States pushed for control of North Korea. When MacArthur publicly denounced the president's policy of limited war, Truman removed him from his command.

In July 1951 talks for a cease-fire started, but both the talks and the fighting dragged on. Following his election in 1952, President Dwight D. Eisenhower traveled to Korea to revive the stalled talks. A cease-fire was signed on July 27, 1953, restoring the 38th parallel as the boundary. There was to be a demilitarized (nonfortified) zone between communist North Korea and free South Korea.

SECTION REVIEW

1. What was the name for the barrier between communist-controlled countries and the West?

2. What idea promoted the use of military aid to carry out the United States's containment policy?

3. How did the United States keep West Berlin from falling into communist hands?

4. What military alliance was formed to halt the threat of Soviet aggression in Europe?

5. Who was the leader of Free China? Who led the communist takeover of China?

6. Whom did Truman choose to lead the U.N. forces in Korea?

 How was the Cold War a different type of war from World War I and II? Why?

The Eisenhower Era

Both the Republicans and Democrats would have been happy to have World War II hero Dwight D. Eisenhower as their candi-

date in 1952. He ran on the Republican ticket against Adlai E. Stevenson, governor of Illinois. The public decided that they "liked Ike" (as he was called), because his grandfatherly image made many Americans feel comfortable. Eisenhower won handily.

Southeast Asia

Problems with communist expansion continued during the Eisenhower era. The Southeast Asian area of Indochina (Vietnam, Cambodia, and Laos) became a target for communist control. The area had been a French colony, but after World War II French control in the land was deteriorating. **Ho Chi Minh,** a communist leader, tried to gain independence for Vietnam. His forces defeated the French at Dien Bien Phu in May 1954. The United States did not intervene with troops at this time because it did not want to risk another land war in Asia.

The conflict was referred to an international conference in Geneva, Switzerland, for settlement. As in Germany and Korea, it was decided that there would be two Vietnams. North Vietnam under Ho Chi Minh would be communist. South Vietnam would be non-communist and would receive American support. But North Vietnam was not content. Using guerrilla tactics it attacked, seeking to gain control of South Vietnam. Before long the United States discovered that the North Vietnamese were receiving Chinese and Soviet military aid.

Activities in Korea and Indochina not only had made the United States tense but also had alarmed other free countries in Southeast Asia and the southern Pacific. Therefore, in 1954 eight countries formed an alliance to contain the spread of communism there. The **Southeast Asia Treaty Organization** (SEATO) united the United States, Britain, France, Australia, New Zealand, Thailand, Pakistan, and the Philippines. The United

States agreed to aid any of these nations threatened by an aggressor. By the end of 1955, America was sending military advisors to South Vietnam to train Vietnamese forces. The United States also pledged to aid Taiwan if it was attacked by mainland China.

Soviet-American Relations

The United States had become the leading nation of the free world. America could no longer remain isolated from international affairs as it had in earlier times. Because the interests of the United States were affected by conditions abroad, it had to get involved in international problems. America's greatest international problems lay in the Cold War tensions with the Soviets. The affairs between the United States and the Soviet Union were always gaining world attention.

In July 1955 Britain, France, the Soviet Union, and the United States met in Geneva, Switzerland, to attempt to put to rest some of the Cold War tensions. About the only thing that was agreed on was that they would not resort to war to resolve differences. President Eisenhower suggested that the United States and the Soviet Union submit to air inspections of each other's military installations to see whether there were missiles present. The Soviets, however, rejected the idea.

The Soviet Union was struggling to project a new image. Stalin had died in 1953, and **Nikita Khrushchev** (KROOSH chef), his successor, claimed to be critical of the former leader's terror tactics. One time he declared that the Soviets wanted to be friends and promote peace with the United States; yet Soviet intentions had not really changed. At another time Khrushchev threatened, "We will bury you."

The United States and the Soviet Union settled into a policy of **"peaceful coexistence."** The two countries agreed to try to settle the many tension-filled situations between them without hostility. They also tried to arrange events that would promote goodwill between the two countries. Khrushchev even visited America in 1959, the first Soviet leader to do so. Unfortunately, the attitude of peaceful coexistence committed the United States to settling each issue with the Soviets peacefully even if Soviet wrongs were not stopped or punished.

European Developments

Further examples of Soviet communist oppression came in Eastern Europe. People in the Soviet satellite countries were unhappy under communist rule. In October 1956, freedom fighters in Hungary bravely led a revolt. They pleaded for help from the West on short-wave radio broadcasts, but help never came. For four days the people of Hungary had hope. Their revolt forced Soviet troops to leave their capital of Budapest. But then the Soviet army rolled back down the streets in tanks and crushed the freedom fighters. The freedom fighters were brave, but with only homemade grenades and their bare hands, they could not stop the tanks.

The Soviet invasion of Hungary was brought before the U.N. That body voted to condemn the Soviets. When the Soviets ignored the U.N. decision, the U.N. took no real action. Because the nations feared that aid to Hungary might start a third world war, the Soviets ruthlessly crushed the freedom movement with no hindrance from the free world.

Cuba

Latin America soon became another source of Cold War tensions. Communism was winning support in the region because so many of the people were poor and uneducated. Many believed the communist promises. The growth of communist activity in Latin America alarmed Americans since it brought the Soviet threat closer to home.

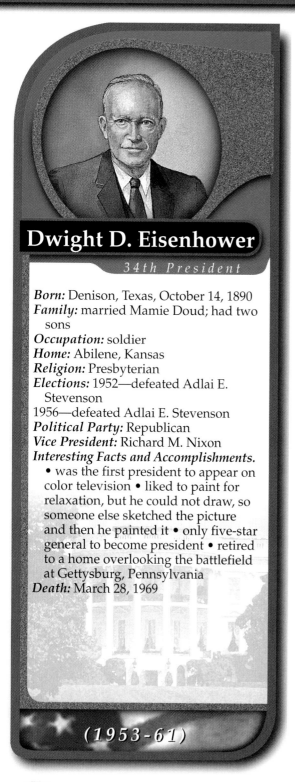

Dwight D. Eisenhower

34th President

Born: Denison, Texas, October 14, 1890
Family: married Mamie Doud; had two sons
Occupation: soldier
Home: Abilene, Kansas
Religion: Presbyterian
Elections: 1952—defeated Adlai E. Stevenson
1956—defeated Adlai E. Stevenson
Political Party: Republican
Vice President: Richard M. Nixon
Interesting Facts and Accomplishments.
• was the first president to appear on color television • liked to paint for relaxation, but he could not draw, so someone else sketched the picture and then he painted it • only five-star general to become president • retired to a home overlooking the battlefield at Gettysburg, Pennsylvania
Death: March 28, 1969

(1953-61)

The most disturbing communist gain for the Americans was that of Cuba. In 1959 Americans heard that Fulgencio Batista, a long-time dictator of Cuba, had been over-thrown by a revolutionary leader, **Fidel Castro.** Although the State Department was aware of Castro's communist leanings from the outset, the American people were not. Thus Americans idealistically believed that conditions might get better in Cuba if Castro took control.

Instead, conditions got worse. Castro, a cruel dictator, jailed thousands of his political enemies. He seized the property of Americans and American business investments in Cuba and declared himself a communist. Cuban refugees attempted to escape Castro's regime by fleeing to Florida any way they could. Some flew; more floated on rickety boats. Soon Soviet aid was on its way to Cuba. The Caribbean was no longer an American lake. Ninety miles off Florida lay a communist threat to American freedom.

Activities at Home

The United States was involved in some important activities at home during the Eisenhower era. Two of the most pleasant accomplishments were the completion of the **St. Lawrence Seaway** and the addition of two new states. In 1954 the United States and Canada had undertaken a joint project called the St. Lawrence Seaway. The two countries cooperated to deepen the St. Lawrence River and build canals and locks where necessary. The completed seaway allowed ocean-going vessels to sail from the Atlantic Ocean through the seaway to the Great Lakes. The project helped the economies of both nations and turned cities along the Great Lakes into major inland seaports. The moving water through the seaway was also used to provide electrical power.

In 1959 Congress admitted two territories to the Union. Alaska and Hawaii became the forty-ninth and fiftieth states. Alaska and Hawaii differ from the other states because they are noncontiguous, or unattached, territories away from the other forty-eight states. The states are also unique because of their populations. About one-fifth of Alaskan citizens are Indian (Eskimo, Aleut, or other tribes). One-half of Hawaii's citizens descend from Japanese, Chinese, Filipino, or Korean immigrants. The additions of Alaska and Hawaii gave the United States an even wider cultural heritage.

SECTION REVIEW

1. Who was elected president in 1952? What party did he represent?

2. What alliance was started to contain communism in Southeast Asia?

3. What Latin American country turned communist in 1959? Who became its leader?

4. How did the St. Lawrence Seaway benefit the United States and Canada?

 Was it dangerous for the United States to agree to a policy of "peaceful coexistence" with the Soviet Union?

SUMMARY

The United States emerged from World War II as the prosperous leader of the free world. Americans eagerly returned to peacetime activities, but international problems continued to concern the nation. Because of communist actions after the war, great tensions arose between the United States and the Soviet Union. The two nations avoided a direct shooting conflict, but a "Cold War" continued between the two throughout the 1950s. The ideals and demands of the United States and the communists clashed in Germany, Korea, and many other areas of the world. The new United Nations organization did little to stop regional conflicts and did not control the spread of communism. All the while, the United States continually provided protection for the free world and increased its aid to faltering free nations. The United States found its new role as world leader to be both expensive and entangling.

Chapter Review

Terms

GI Bill
baby boom
Federal Aid Highway Act
sunbelt migrations
green revolution
Fair Deal
Taft-Hartley Act
injunction
civil rights
Jim Crow laws
Nuremberg trials
George Marshall
Marshall Plan

United Nations
General Assembly
Security Council
Secretariat
third world
Cold War
iron curtain
containment
Truman Doctrine
Berlin airlift
North Atlantic Treaty
    Organization
Warsaw Pact

Mao Zedong
Chiang Kai-shek
Korean War
Ho Chi Minh
Southeast Asia Treaty
    Organization
Nikita Khrushchev
peaceful coexistence
Fidel Castro
St. Lawrence Seaway

Review Questions

Answer each of the following questions.

1. What legislation initiated the interstate highway system?

2. What did President Truman call his domestic program?

3. Who devised a plan for helping the war-torn countries of Europe?

4. What are the three important divisions of the United Nations?

5. What two states entered the Union in 1959?

Explain the meaning of each of the following terms.

6. baby boom

7. green revolution

8. Nuremberg trials

9. Cold War

10. peaceful coexistence

Match each of the following men with his country.

11. Fidel Castro   a. Communist China

12. Chiang Kai-shek   b. Free China

13. Ho Chi Minh   c. Cuba

14. Nikita Khrushchev   d. Soviet Union

15. Mao Zedong   e. Vietnam

Questions for Discussion

16. Why is the United Nations unable to maintain world peace?

17. What would have happened if the United States had taken an isolationist position after World War II?

History Skills

Using the Library: Report on the United Nations

The library is an essential resource in writing special projects for history class. Your text gives some information but not everything you need. Find a copy of a world almanac, encyclopedia, or other library resource to answer the following questions about the current status of the UN.

1. Where are UN headquarters?

2. Approximately how large is the UN staff?

3. How many nations are members of the UN?

4. What years did each of these nations become members of the UN: Australia, Germany, Japan, Egypt, Italy, Vietnam?

5. Where can you send for a copy of the UN charter?

6. How many votes does each nation get in the General Assembly?

7. What are the five permanent members of the Security Council?

8. What are the current ten nonpermanent two-year members of the Security Council?

9. How many votes are necessary to pass a measure in the Security Council?

10. Who is the current secretary general of the Secretariat?

11. How much was last year's UN budget?

12. What is the "executive branch" of the UN?

13. What is the "judicial branch" of the UN?

14. How long is each UN judge's term of office?

15. Where does the UN court meet?

28

The Sixties– Nation in Crisis

The 1960s marked the beginning of a turbulent era in American history, filled with riots, assassinations, and images of war. The nation experienced a crisis on every front, from the breakdown of morals at home to military defeats abroad. Traditional beliefs came under attack in the schools, churches, courts, homes, and legislatures. In spite of great advances in science and medicine, American civilization appeared to be in decline. The dark days continued into the 1970s when the president was forced to resign in disgrace in 1973. After over a decade of effort, the government had also failed to end poverty and racial prejudice. Meanwhile, communism continued to menace the world.

Kennedy's New Frontier

The sixties began with the bright hopes of a young senator who challenged America with a dream of conquering a "New Frontier."

The Close Election of 1960

The Republicans chose Eisenhower's vice president, Richard Nixon, as their candidate in 1960. The Democrats chose Massachusetts Senator **John F. Kennedy.** Kennedy's running mate was Texan Lyndon B. Johnson, the well-known Senate majority leader. With this ticket the party hoped to win the votes of both northern and southern Democrats. Kennedy was young, only 43, and he was a Roman Catholic. In a major change from earlier campaigns,

John F. Kennedy makes his inaugural speech with President Eisenhower and Mrs. Kennedy looking on.

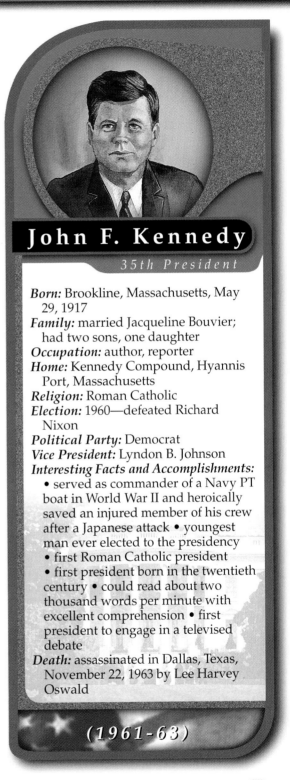

John F. Kennedy
35th President

Born: Brookline, Massachusetts, May 29, 1917

Family: married Jacqueline Bouvier; had two sons, one daughter

Occupation: author, reporter

Home: Kennedy Compound, Hyannis Port, Massachusetts

Religion: Roman Catholic

Election: 1960—defeated Richard Nixon

Political Party: Democrat

Vice President: Lyndon B. Johnson

Interesting Facts and Accomplishments:
- served as commander of a Navy PT boat in World War II and heroically saved an injured member of his crew after a Japanese attack • youngest man ever elected to the presidency
- first Roman Catholic president
- first president born in the twentieth century • could read about two thousand words per minute with excellent comprehension • first president to engage in a televised debate

Death: assassinated in Dallas, Texas, November 22, 1963 by Lee Harvey Oswald

(1961-63)

Nixon and Kennedy engaged in a series of four television debates. Kennedy entered the debates as an underdog, but he used his youthful appearance and charm to good effect. In contrast, Nixon seemed to lack energy and appeal. The election was a close one. Out of 68.3 million votes cast, Kennedy won by only 120,000. This was less than one vote per precinct (local voting place). The election highlighted the importance of individual votes even in a large country.

Kennedy's Mixed Domestic Program

Kennedy's campaign had promised a new program, the **"New Frontier."** Kennedy pressed for measures similar to those of the New Deal—economic aid to poor areas, medical insurance for the aged (called Medicare), aid for college students, and an ambitious space program. In his inaugural speech, Kennedy challenged Americans to "ask not what your country can do for you; ask what you can do for your country." Furthermore, he asked America's enemies to join the United States in a quest for lasting peace.

Since Kennedy's victory was a narrow one, and since southern Democrats often voted with House and Senate Republicans, Kennedy's "New Frontier" met opposition in Congress. Congress agreed to a few of Kennedy's goals—such as raising the minimum wage to $1.25 per hour, passing the Trade Expansion Act, and making improvements in the Social Security system. But it rejected Medicare, aid to college education, and a bill to create a department of urban affairs.

Kennedy's Mixed Foreign Program

President Kennedy had several ideas for helping needy countries and spreading peace. As he was implementing these plans, however, they were cut short by the Cold War.

Peace Corps—One popular idea, which Kennedy introduced in 1961, was a volunteer program called the Peace Corps. The "best and brightest" Americans—teachers, engineers, technicians, and businessmen—agreed to dedicate two years of their lives to help improve conditions in poverty-stricken countries. More than sixty countries received help in improving their schools, medical care, and conservation.

Many of the goals of the Peace Corps were good, but it met only a few temporal needs. It provided no permanent solutions for the world's needs. Christians should realize that although helping the poor and needy is good, people have a spiritual need that only the Lord Jesus can satisfy.

Progress in Latin America—Realizing that Cuba was training soldiers to spread communism throughout the region, Kennedy announced an **Alliance for Progress.** Under this plan almost $12 billion went to Latin American nations to provide housing, schools, and health clinics or hospitals in the 1960s. It was hoped that relieving poverty would ease some of the unrest that allowed communism to spread. Unfortunately, money cannot improve people's minds and hearts. The large expenses of the program served mainly to encourage corruption instead of benefiting the poor.

President Kennedy looks over the Berlin Wall into communist-controlled East Berlin.

The Berlin Wall—Kennedy had several dangerous confrontations with the Soviets. Thousands of East Germans—mostly professional people—were escaping into the free city of West Berlin. As a result, in 1961 the Soviet dictator, Khrushchev, ordered the construction of a concrete wall around West

Berlin. Armed guards stood waiting to shoot any who tried to cross the **Berlin Wall.**

President Kennedy responded by sending more troops to West Berlin. In 1963 he made a dramatic nighttime visit to the Berlin Wall, while thousands of Berliners lit candles to show their support of freedom. Kennedy expressed his support with these memorable words, spoken in German, "Ich bin ein Berliner." ("I am a Berliner.") Nevertheless, the wall was a blow to the free world.

On the Brink of War with Cuba—Under Communist dictator Fidel Castro, Cuba's problems were growing worse. Castro had seized all American property in Cuba and refused to pay for any of it. President Eisenhower, in reaction, had cut Cuban sugar imports and later had broken off relations completely. Castro's economic policies caused great hardships for the people. As life under Castro's regime worsened, many Cubans fled to the United States. With so many pro-democracy Cubans in Florida, the Central Intelligence Agency (CIA) devised a plan to train fifteen hundred of them to overthrow Castro. Soon after taking office, Kennedy allowed the plan to proceed. The CIA believed that when the Cubans heard about the invasion, they would rally to their cause.

Unfortunately, nothing went as planned. On April 17, 1961, the force landed at the **Bay of Pigs,** but Castro's forces easily repelled the invasion because Kennedy withheld promised air support. More than four hundred exiles died, and the rest were captured. Castro was able to use the unsuccessful invasion to embarrass the United States.

Problems with Cuba grew worse. On October 14, 1962, American U-2 spy planes flying over Cuba confirmed suspicions that the Soviet Union was shipping missiles to Cuba, missiles that could carry nuclear bombs and destroy American cities. The nation was horrified when President Kennedy announced the presence of the missiles and his decision to blockade Cuba. United States warships surrounded the island, ready to stop and search any Soviet vessels that violated the blockade. Kennedy also demanded that the Soviets remove the missiles, and he put the nation's armed forces on full alert.

Khrushchev was enraged. He blamed Kennedy for pushing mankind into nuclear war. But after a week of the tense standoff, he sent Kennedy a message on October 28 offering to remove the missiles if the United States promised never to invade Cuba. As suddenly as it had begun, the **Cuban Missile Crisis** was over. Kennedy's secretary of state, Dean Rusk, boasted, "We're eyeball to eyeball, and I think the other fellow just blinked." But he said nothing about the U.S. side of the bargain, which would have serious consequences for decades to come.

A Slight Thaw in the Cold War—In the wake of the Cuban Missile Crisis, the United States and the Soviet Union wanted to ease tensions. A "hot line," a direct telephone line between the White House and the Kremlin in

People hoped in vain that the Nuclear Test Ban Treaty was a sign that the Cold War was thawing.

Moscow, the Soviet capital, was installed in 1963. The same year at Geneva, Switzerland, the United States, Britain, and the Soviet Union signed a Limited Test Ban Treaty. They agreed that there would be no above-ground testing of nuclear weapons. Each nation was to tell the others of any underground tests and was to police itself. But France and China, who also had nuclear weapons, refused to sign the treaty.

The End of Camelot

When Kennedy came to office, the musical *Camelot* was popular on Broadway. The play retold the story of King Arthur's Round Table and his dream of creating a new England where truth, justice, and equality would reign. Seeing a parallel between King Arthur's dream and that of Kennedy, some began to refer to Kennedy's administration as "Camelot." The dreams of Camelot came to an abrupt end on November 22, 1963. While traveling down a street in Dallas, Texas, the president was shot by Lee Harvey Oswald. Kennedy was only forty-six. The reasons for the assassination remain a mystery.

After his death Kennedy became a hero. Even people who disagreed with Kennedy's politics remembered the things they liked about him—his youth, his idealism, and his vitality. Kennedy seemed to represent optimism for America's future. Congress quickly passed many of Kennedy's New Frontier programs, which had been stalled in Congress, as memorials to the late president.

LBJ's Great Society

Lyndon B. Johnson took his oath of office on the presidential airplane, Air Force One, after Kennedy's death. Since Johnson had been on Capitol Hill for thirty-two years, serving in both the House and the Senate, he knew the political system and how to work it. A powerful and persuasive man, he was able to get bills passed. Johnson called his legislative program **"The Great Society."** His program was supposed to help America bring "an end to poverty and racial injustice . . . in our time."

LBJ's Election to Four More Years—But before Johnson could achieve all his goals, he first had to win the election of 1964. His challenger was a conservative senator from Arizona named **Barry Goldwater.** He represented a small but growing branch of the Republican Party that openly denounced big government programs, wanting government "out of our pocketbooks and out of our bedrooms." Goldwater voted against the Civil Rights Act, not because he supported racial discrimination, but because he wanted citizens to be free to run their own lives. The liberal wing of the Republican Party was embar-

Shock and grief shows on the face of Jacqueline Kennedy as Lyndon Johnson is sworn into the office of President on Air Force One shortly after the assassination of President Kennedy.

rassed by Goldwater, and the press published his blunt statements about eliminating Social Security and using nuclear weapons to win the war in Vietnam, if necessary. Democratic ads frightened voters with the threat of nuclear destruction. LBJ won the contest by a landslide, receiving 61 percent of the vote.

War on Poverty—Forty million Americans did not share in the nation's rising wealth during the 1950s. This hidden minority was stuck in a "culture of poverty," according to a blockbuster book called *The Other America* (1962) by Michael Harrington. Johnson took up the cause of the poor in his Great Society, declaring a "War on Poverty." He created a Job Corps, similar to the Peace Corps but focusing on the needs at home. Other Great Society programs included aid to distressed areas of the eleven states in Appalachia, a food stamp program for poor families, and a Head Start Program for underprivileged children who needed a "head start" in education before they started regular school. Johnson also asked Congress to pass new legislation for labeling and packaging food, drugs, cosmetics, and household supplies.

In 1965 Johnson pushed through several more programs of the Great Society. Medicare and Medicaid gave qualifying Americans two months of low-cost hospital care and allowances for other medical costs. The government added two new cabinet positions—Housing and Urban Development, and Transportation.

All of these programs were expensive, costing more than the government brought in. Overspending put the nation in debt, a problem that would plague America for the next twenty years. The Great Society also made Americans more dependent on government programs and gave the federal government more power over people's lives.

Lyndon B. Johnson

36th President

Born: Stonewall, Texas, August 27, 1908
Family: married Claudia "Lady Bird" Taylor; had two daughters
Occupation: teacher, rancher
Home: LBJ Ranch, Johnson City, Texas
Religion: Disciples of Christ
Election: succeeded to the presidency upon the death of Kennedy
1964—defeated Barry Goldwater
Political Party: Democrat
Vice President: none (first term); Hubert Humphrey (second term)
Interesting Facts and Accomplishments:
• was the second tallest president at 6′3″ • his entire family had "LBJ" initials (Lyndon Baines, Lady Bird, Lynda Bird, and Luci Baines) • first president to have his oath of office administered by a woman (Judge Sarah Hughes)
Death: January 22, 1973

(1963-69)

SECTION REVIEW

1. What was the name Kennedy gave to the program for his administration?

2. What was the purpose of the Peace Corps?

3. In what city did the Soviets build a wall to stop escapes from the communist-controlled area?

4. What two situations in Cuba created problems for the United States?

5. Why did Kennedy become a hero after his death?

6. What name was given to Lyndon Johnson's legislative program?

7. What conservative senator from Arizona lost to Lyndon Johnson in the election of 1964?

 Considering the election of 1960 as well as more recent ones, do you think television has had a positive impact on the political process? Explain your answer.

The Quest for Civil Rights

Despite LBJ's skills in passing legislation, he soon came face to face with two insurmountable problems that would fill the headlines during his years in office. One was the Vietnam War. The other was civil rights.

Civil rights has stirred controversy since the Constitutional Convention. The term originally referred to the right of every citizen to receive equal treatment before the law. Despite the guarantees of the Constitution and the brave service of black soldiers in World War II, black Americans were still being denied many of their civil rights in postwar America. Their long struggle to gain equality came to be called the *civil rights movement.*

The Courts Intervene in Civil Rights

An 1896 Supreme Court case had allowed blacks to be separated from whites as long as facilities were theoretically equal. For many years the National Association for the Advancement of Colored People (NAACP) worked quietly to get judges to end inequalities. After a series of cases, black graduate students were allowed to seek an education in white universities because at the time there were no black schools on the graduate level that offered equal training.

But eventually lawyers challenged the idea of "separate but equal" facilities. In 1954 in *Brown v. Board of Education,* the Supreme Court ruled that segregation of children in public schools based solely on race violated the equal treatment that all citizens were guaranteed under the Fourteenth Amendment (see p. 159). The *Brown* case applied to schools in seventeen states. Schools were told to inte-

Influential black leader Martin Luther King Jr. leads the 1963 March on Washington where blacks and whites rallied in support of civil rights legislation.

grate "with all deliberate speed." However, some school districts did not start to integrate until 1969 or later.

President Eisenhower did not put particular pressure on the states to integrate. He hoped the states would follow the court's instructions on their own. When challenged by the government of Arkansas, however, Eisenhower put the state National Guard under his control to insure the safe enrollment of black students at Little Rock's Central High School in 1957.

President Kennedy took a stronger stand to enforce existing laws and to act on the *Brown* case. In less than three years, the Justice Department took action to integrate 183 schools. In September 1962 and June 1963, Kennedy sent federal marshals to the Universities of Mississippi and Alabama to ensure that black students could enroll.

The **Twenty-third Amendment** passed during the Kennedy administration. It gave the residents of the District of Columbia the right to vote in national elections. Since the district's population was heavily black, this was regarded as a step forward in civil rights.

Early Civil Rights Protests

Black activists did not rely on the courts alone. In 1955 Rosa Parks, a seamstress in Montgomery, Alabama, rode a city bus home after a hard day at work. Tradition and the law divided the bus into two sections, with blacks sitting in the back. But Mrs. Parks sat at the rear of the white section, in one of the few empty seats on the bus. When a white person asked her to give it up, she refused and was arrested. To show support for her action, other blacks started a bus boycott. They refused to ride city buses for over a year, depriving the buses of desperately needed money. Finally the city ended the bus law.

A small group pickets in front of an apartment complex to protest the failure of the complex to rent to minorities.

Blacks tried other forms of protest—sit-ins at white lunch counters, kneel-ins at churches, and wade-ins at schools. "Freedom riders" rode from place to place in the South, seeking to integrate the buses and to encourage blacks to register to vote. Everywhere they went, civil rights demonstrators faced angry white mobs; they were ridiculed and beaten, and some were murdered. Police employed tear gas, cattle prods, and attack dogs to stop protesters in Birmingham, Alabama, in early 1963. A bomb destroyed a black church in Birmingham, killing four girls.

The biggest single demonstration took place at the U.S. capital in August 1963. Organized by Martin Luther King Jr., its purpose was to rally support for proposed civil rights legislation. About 250,000 blacks and whites participated in the **march on Washington,** where King delivered a memorable address, repeating the phrase "I have a dream." King spoke of an ideal America where liberty and equality would be a reality for all—both black and white.

Thousands and thousands of protesters cover the green from the Washington Monument to the Capitol during the March on Washington.

Congress Passes Civil Rights Legislation

Following the march on Washington and Kennedy's assassination, Congress rallied to pass new civil rights legislation. The **Civil Rights Act of 1964** forbade racial segregation and discrimination in schools and public places, such as motels. The federal government would no longer make contracts with private companies that discriminated, and it would no longer give money to institutions that discriminated in their hiring practices.

The **Twenty-fourth Amendment** (p. 165), ratified in 1964, forbade states from levying poll taxes. This tax required voters to pay a fee before they could vote. Poll taxes were popular in the South because they kept both poor blacks and poor whites from voting.

The **Voting Rights Act of 1965** ended long-standing injustices in voting in federal elections. Although the Fifteenth Amendment (1870) kept the states from denying any one race the right to vote, southern states had gotten around the law in a variety of ways. Many required literacy tests. Often these not only tested reading knowledge but also required understanding of obscure, difficult portions of state constitutions. Blacks who sought to register had also been harassed. The new act gave the national government the power to register blacks in states where the registered black vote was significantly lower than census population. Federal officials also had the power to check any complaints of discrimination.

Divisions Among Civil Rights Leaders

The civil rights movement heard many conflicting voices. A Baptist minister, **Martin**

President Johnson signs the Voting Rights Act of 1965 ensuring black voters' rights as black leaders look on.

North. But he had many enemies, especially after a visit to Mecca in 1964 that caused him to embrace racial harmony and to denounce the "black racism" of the Nation of Islam. Gunmen killed Malcolm X at a rally in New York City the following year.

Radical young blacks were also attracted to Stokely Carmichael, who advocated "black power." No one was sure what the term meant, but its slogan—"violence is as American as cherry pie"—frightened many whites and angered conservative blacks, who feared its effects on the progress of the civil rights movement.

While the nation's attention was drawn to the segregation laws of the South, it overlooked the social prejudice that had segregated black communities in the North and on the west coast. **Urban riots** broke out in several cities. Just days after the passage of the Voting Rights Act in 1965, rioters burned a black community in Los Angeles known as Watts. Thirty-four people died, and property damage exceeded $35 million. The next year rioters burned parts of Detroit and Newark, and dozens more were killed. The looting and destruction shocked Americans. Another blow to the civil rights movement came in April 1968. A white assassin killed Martin Luther King Jr. while he was standing on a hotel balcony in Memphis, Tennessee. King's murder set off a wave of violence in black neighborhoods across America. In spite of government efforts to improve civil rights, the dream of racial harmony seemed far away.

Luther King Jr., was the first black leader to win national prominence. King founded the Southern Christian Leadership Conference. But instead of preaching the gospel, the conference spoke of liberating the poor and underprivileged through social action. King helped to organize the bus boycott in Montgomery, and he was jailed during the demonstrations at Birmingham. While in the Birmingham jail, he wrote an influential "letter" advocating nonviolent, passive resistance—also called civil disobedience—to raise public awareness of unjust laws.

Some black leaders rejected King's "soft" views, however. Among them was **Malcolm X,** a convert to the Nation of Islam (the Black Muslims), who preached black supremacy and the need to create a separate black nation to keep the black race pure. Malcolm X's preaching won a large audience, especially in the

SECTION REVIEW

1. What major court case affected civil rights? What practice did it declare to be unconstitutional?
2. What black seamstress sparked a bus boycott by her refusal to give up her seat for a white person?
3. Who was the most prominent black civil rights leader? What famous phrase did he use during the march on Washington?
4. What three pieces of civil rights legislation were passed after President Kennedy's assassination? What did each accomplish?

 What would you identify as the greatest threat to the civil rights movement? Why?

The Undeclared War in Vietnam

The biggest single issue in foreign affairs in the 1960s was the **Vietnam War.** Lyndon Johnson inherited the conflict that had been brewing in Southeast Asia for nearly a decade (pp. 572-73). During Johnson's administration, Vietnam became a raging issue as American involvement increased.

Increasing American Involvement

Although Eisenhower had pledged that he would not allow South Vietnam to fall to Communists and had supplied financial aid, Kennedy was the first president to send large numbers of Americans. By November 1963, the United States had 16,000 troops in Vietnam. Most served as "advisors," training the Vietnamese to fight their own war.

President Johnson campaigned promising not to send American boys "to do what Asian boys ought to be doing for themselves." Nevertheless, he became increasingly concerned that Southeast Asia would be conquered by the Communists as China had been in 1949.

In August 1964 Johnson found an opportunity to justify an increase in American involvement in the war. He announced on television that North Vietnamese patrol boats had attacked two American destroyers in international waters off the coast of Vietnam in the Gulf of Tonkin. The president reported this incident to Congress and requested power to act. The resulting **Gulf of Tonkin Resolution** said that the United States was now ready "to take all necessary steps, including the use of armed forces" against the North Vietnamese. The resolution was not a declaration of war, but it gave the president broad powers to increase American activity in Vietnam.

American activity in Vietnam was hotly debated in the United States. Leaders who favored increased American presence in Vietnam, or an "escalation" of the war, were called **hawks.** Those who wanted the United States to pull out completely were called **doves.** Under Johnson, the number of troops in Vietnam escalated rapidly. In May 1965

American soldiers stand back and watch as a Viet Cong base camp goes up in flames.

more than half a million Americans were on Vietnamese soil.

A Sticky Situation

The United States was committed to protecting the free government of South Vietnam. The United States effort might have had a better chance of success had Vietnamese politics been free of corruption and had the South Vietnamese people consistently backed their own government, but this was not so. During the war the United States had to fight not only the Communists from the North but also Communist supporters in the South. The **Vietcong,** Vietnamese Communists who had stayed in South Vietnam after the division of the country, carried out guerrilla warfare against Americans and the South Vietnamese troops.

The Vietnam War

America's Disadvantages in the Rice Paddies of Vietnam—The United States entered the conflict with other disadvantages. Since Congress had never officially declared war, technically the country was engaged in only a police action. The United States feared that if it declared war, many more countries would join the fight, leading even to world war. Yet thousands of Americans were dying in Vietnam for a cause that politicians were still debating. As the war dragged on, it seemed that the United States was not fighting to win anything. There seemed to be no glorious cause to rally public support.

Furthermore, although the United States had the most modern and sophisticated weapons, it could not use this advantage easily in Vietnam. In World War II the United States had defeated Germany by bombing its industrial cities. North Vietnam had no large industrial plants but rather thousands of little shops scattered across the land. The trees and terrain also made bombing difficult. American bombers found it difficult to identify targets on the **Ho Chi Minh Trail,** the route that the Vietcong forces used to move their men and goods. Even when they identified specific targets, success was not guaranteed. For example, one log bridge was destroyed at least twenty times, but the North Vietnamese kept rebuilding it in only a few days. Moreover, the North Vietnamese received a steady stream of military supplies from both China and the Soviet Union.

In addition, United States servicemen could not identify the enemy. To the servicemen, the North Vietnamese and Vietcong looked just like the loyal South Vietnamese. While those in the cities usually supported the Americans, in rural areas no one knew whom to trust. The Vietcong even employed children to lob hand grenades at American soldiers. Children killed many soldiers; yet when

U.S. Marshals bodily remove one of the protesters during a violent anti-Vietnam demonstration at the Pentagon Building.

For years, schools and liberal churches had been teaching that mankind is evolving and that there are no absolute standards of right and wrong. Young people took this teaching to heart. Hippies and other radical youths rejected their parents' vain search for happiness through hard work and acquiring wealth. The so-called **counterculture** toppled all symbols of morality and authority. They adopted standards completely different from their parents' "old-fashioned" culture, choosing long hair, brightly painted clothes, and "hip" vocabulary. They believed the world could solve its problems if everyone just started loving each other as innocent children. "All we need is love," claimed one popular rock song.

The counterculture was a logical outgrowth of Romantic philosophy taught in the schools. Romanticism argues that nature is good and that civilization is corrupt. Youths wanted to return to their natural state. Many of them indulged in drugs and sexual immorality in an effort to achieve complete freedom and happiness. They were wrong, of course. In the seventies and eighties the country reaped the bitter fruit of this foolish rebellion, as American society sank to new lows.

North Vietnam's Surprise—The Tet Offensive

By clever use of guerrilla warfare and supplies from the Soviet Union and China, the North Vietnamese, led by Ho Chi Minh, made headway against the South. If they could just prolong the war, they believed they would win because Americans would give up and pull out.

children were killed in the war, the American public was appalled.

Radical Youth on the Home Front—A greater threat than the enemy in Vietnam was the lack of unity at home. As war continued, political activists who strongly opposed the war gained increasing public attention. A **"New Left"** movement, led by Communist sympathizers, grew among disenchanted Americans and civil rights workers looking for a new cause. Many college students, who were subject to the draft, joined the protests. A few defiant ones burned their draft cards and the American flag. Some young men fled to Sweden or Canada. In October 1965 more than ninety cities had antiwar demonstrations. A left-wing organization, the Students for Democratic Society, was in the forefront. In April 1967 antiwar marches in New York and San Francisco attracted up to 300,000 people.

The antiwar movement was the most visible outpouring of a radical change in thinking and morals among American young people.

To slow the stream of supplies flowing into North Vietnam, the United States began bombing the northern port of Haiphong and the capital city, Hanoi. The bombings were extremely effective. Each time the bombings were stepped up, however, the wily Ho Chi Minh hinted that he might go to the peace table if the bombings halted. Liberal politicians convinced LBJ to slow the bombings, only to allow the Communists time to move in more troops and supplies.

In spite of the setbacks, the president and his leading general, William Westmoreland, expressed optimism in public in 1967. They expanded the air war and sent additional American soldiers into battle. Some believed the fight would be over in two to three years.

Over the Christmas holidays of 1967, the United States called another ceasefire. As usual, the Communists used the lull to their advantage. This time, however, they moved huge quantities of supplies and troops into South Vietnam. Large numbers of strangers walked or rode into South Vietnam's cities. Many more funerals were held than usual, bearing coffins stuffed with weapons, not corpses.

With their troops in position, the North Vietnamese and the Vietcong unleashed a surprise attack on January 30, 1968, the Chinese New Year (the Tet). They waited until shortly after midnight, when all the partiers were asleep. From one end of the country to the other, they fired on police stations, military bases, government buildings, radio and power stations, and foreign embassies. They captured the old imperial city of Hue (HWAY) and assaulted Saigon, the capital city.

But American forces counterattacked and regained what was captured within a few weeks. Nevertheless, the Tet Offensive was a serious blow to support for the war effort at home. Televisions, radios, magazines, and newspapers falsely reported the incident as a miserable defeat for America. Such reports, along with the growing casualty list, increased sympathy for the doves.

The Violent 1968 Election

The 1968 election arrived in the midst of the turmoil over Vietnam. Most Americans expected Lyndon Johnson to win reelection easily. But the disastrous Tet Offensive encouraged some of his opponents in the Democratic Party. The campaign of Eugene McCarthy, an antiwar senator from Minnesota, gained momentum. With the support of college students, he did extremely well in the New Hampshire primary in March 1968.

McCarthy's success led another senator from New York, **Robert Kennedy** (the brother of the late president), to try his chances in the race. Five days after the New Hampshire primary, Kennedy threw his hat into the ring. He counted on the popularity of his name, as well as

Helicopters swoop in to airlift members of the 2nd battalion.

Richard M. Nixon

37th President

Born: Yorba Linda, California, January 9, 1913
Family: married Thelma "Pat" Ryan; had two daughters
Occupation: lawyer
Home: San Clemente, California
Religion: Quaker
Elections: 1968—defeated Hubert Humphrey (Democrat) and George Wallace (American party)
1972—defeated George McGovern
Political Party: Republican
Vice Presidents: Spiro T. Agnew (resigned); Gerald R. Ford
Interesting Facts and Accomplishments:
• was named for Richard the Lionhearted, king of England • had served as Eisenhower's vice president • first president to visit all fifty states while in office • visited both the Soviet Union and Communist China while president • his youngest daughter married President Eisenhower's grandson • only president to resign (Aug. 9, 1974)
Death: April 22, 1994

(1969-74)

his support among minorities and labor unions.

Johnson's nomination was no longer a certainty. A political poll revealed that only thirty-six percent of the country supported him. On March 31 Johnson stunned the country with an announcement that he would bow out of the election. Immediately his vice president, **Hubert Humphrey,** declared his candidacy to replace Johnson.

Robert Kennedy beat the pack to become the front-runner among the Democrats. But on the night of his greatest victory in the California primaries, an Arab radical assassinated Kennedy in a Los Angeles hotel. This was a blow from which the Democrats could not recover. They held their party convention in Chicago and chose Humphrey as their candidate. But the convention was marred by a wave of antiwar riots and demonstrations.

The Republicans revived the hopes of Richard Nixon and put him on their ticket with Spiro T. Agnew of Maryland. A third party, the American Party, ran George C. Wallace, an Alabama governor noted for his opposition to integration. He shopped for votes from those who were tired of high taxes, liberal court decisions, and federal interference in the lives of citizens. The election was close between Nixon and Humphrey, but Nixon won.

Pulling Out of the War

Nixon inherited an unfinished war in Vietnam and a "no-win" war policy, as well as a huge national debt and an economy that was nearly out of control. Ignoring the advice of his Council of Economic Advisors, President Johnson hoped to fight a war, keep the Great Society programs, and still limit inflation without a tax increase. Since he was already unpopular, Johnson had no desire to raise taxes. But he did not want to cut programs, either. To escape the consequences of the difficult choices, he lied. When congressmen talked to him about a tax increase and discussed the cost of the war, Johnson gave false figures. The war was costing $100 million a day. The White House, however, reported a much lower cost.

Not wanting to repeat the failures that had ended Johnson's career, Nixon made it his priority to end American involvement in Vietnam "with dignity." Nixon intended to pull large numbers of ground troops out of Vietnam while continuing intensive bombing raids. Yet he did not want the United States to appear defeated.

Vietnamization—In the fall of 1969, Nixon announced his proposal for the **Vietnamization** of the war. This meant that the responsibility for the fighting would gradually be returned to the South Vietnamese. The United States would continue to support the South Vietnamese with supplies, air attacks, and other assistance. As Vietnamization was carried out, more American troops came home. When Nixon took office, 543,400 Americans were in Vietnam. An accelerated American pullout left 157,000 by December 1971, and only 24,000 by the end of 1972.

The success of Vietnamization depended on continued American support for the South Vietnamese and America's determination to force North Vietnam to honor its agreements. But while Americans pulled out of Vietnam, the Communist leaders built up their force of North Vietnamese soldiers and Vietcong, and they continued to stockpile supplies from Communist China and the Soviet Union.

In April of 1970 President Nixon announced a temporary expansion of the war across Vietnam's border into Cambodia, where Communist soldiers were lurking in safe hideouts. The Communists would withdraw to supply bases in Cambodia between attacks on

The Twenty-sixth Amendment

Because eighteen-year-olds were eligible to be drafted for military duty but were not able to vote, many Americans argued that the voting age should be lowered. The **Twenty-sixth Amendment** was passed in 1971 to lower the voting age from twenty-one to eighteen. Supporters said that an American who is old enough to die for his country is old enough to vote.

Americans in South Vietnam. Without bothering to seek Congress's approval, Nixon ordered the Cambodian bases bombed. In 1971 the United States also attacked Vietnamese forces in Laos.

American response to these actions, especially the move into Cambodia, was predictable. Demonstrations erupted on college campuses. At **Kent State University** in Ohio, students disobeyed the instructions of the Ohio National Guard to disperse. When the soldiers felt threatened, they panicked and fired into the crowd, killing four students. A similar riot at Jackson State University in Mississippi led to two more deaths. In a regular war, such dissent and riots would have been punishable, perhaps even defined as treason. In an undeclared war, Americans tolerated such acts, and some even cheered them on.

Paris Peace Talks—Meanwhile Nixon sought to get the North Vietnamese to the peace table. It took six weeks to get the two sides into the same room in Paris because the Communists argued about the shape of the table and the seating order. The talks broke up when the secretary of the Communist Party left in anger. Nixon responded with air strikes and heavy bombing of Hanoi and Haiphong, North Vietnamese cities. In addition, the U.S. Navy mined Haiphong's harbor. "The Christmas blitz" was heavy enough that North Vietnam came back to the peace talks and signed a ceasefire on January 24, 1973.

593

In the early 1980s the Wall was built to honor veterans of Vietnam who, despite the outcome of the war, served their country faithfully.

North Vietnam used the lull to rebuild its forces. When the Communists attacked Saigon in 1975, Nixon's successor, Gerald Ford, asked Congress to increase aid to South Vietnam, but Congress refused. The cause of South Vietnam was lost. The last American troops left Saigon in the spring of 1975. Within two weeks of the American departure, Saigon fell to the North Vietnamese. In the years following, reports of Communist massacres and inhumanity regularly found their way out of Southeast Asia.

The Cost of Vietnam—The cost of the Vietnam War was high: more than 58,000 Americans killed; 300,000 wounded; and about $140 billion spent. But the war cost far more. War veterans came back to a disillusioned country. Few were welcomed as heroes; most were ignored. Memories of past victories made it hard to understand the purpose of wasting lives in Vietnam. It was not until 1982 that a national memorial for the Vietnam dead was dedicated.

The war left several questions unanswered. To what extent should the press be allowed to report the actions of the military? How much power should the president have to wage war? Should Americans entangle themselves in foreign conflicts that might end without victory? The fate of missing soldiers troubled the nation as well. Nearly six hundred prisoners of war in Vietnam were released in 1973, but over two thousand soldiers that were listed as missing in action (MIA) are still unaccounted for.

Congress reacted to the cost of this undeclared war by limiting the president's power to fight such wars in the future. The **War Powers Act** (1973), vetoed by Nixon but overridden by Congress, defined the circumstances necessary before the president could go to war, and it required that all action be ended in thirty days unless Congress authorized action beyond that.

SECTION REVIEW

1. What action of Congress gave President Johnson the authority to increase American involvement in Vietnam?

2. What were the South Vietnamese Communists called?

3. Name three disadvantages the United States military faced in Vietnam.

4. How did American young people respond to the Vietnam War?

5. What was "Vietnamization"?

6. When did the last American troops leave Vietnam? What was the result of their departure?

 How was Vietnam different from American wars before that time? How did these differences affect public reaction?

The Fall of Richard Nixon

Richard Nixon took office at the end of the turbulent sixties. He appealed to people he called "the silent majority"—decent, law-abiding, tax-paying Americans. Although anti-war protests continued for a while, unrest seemed to be disappearing. Americans approached the next decade with hopes for an end to the turmoil. President Nixon's leadership gave the country a new confidence. But in the end, he resigned in disgrace, and his administration left the country in shambles.

Détente in Foreign Affairs

Unlike President Johnson, whose interest had been in domestic affairs, Nixon's emphasis was on foreign affairs. He dealt with the problem of Vietnam, and he gained friendlier relations with Communist China and the Soviet Union. Though Nixon had earned a reputation in the Senate as a "cold warrior" against communism, he brought in a new era of **détente,** an easing of tensions, with the Soviet Union. Nixon relied heavily on Dr. **Henry Kissinger,** a Harvard professor born in Germany who became his special advisor. In 1973 Kissinger became Nixon's secretary of state.

Treaty with the Soviets—In May 1972 President Nixon made a trip to the Soviet Union to discuss a Strategic Arms Limitations Treaty (**SALT**). Both nations agreed to restrict the types and number of nuclear warheads and missiles. They also made trade agreements and an agreement to cooperate on scientific and space projects. Conservative opponents of these agreements said they were worth little more than the paper on which they were written because of the Soviet Union's history of ignoring treaties. However, the agreements did have considerable political value at home.

Friendship with Communist China—China closed its doors to the West when the

Ping-Pong Diplomacy

"It doesn't matter whether you win or lose, but how you play the game." So the saying goes, but in April 1971 the question on everyone's mind was who was playing and where. In that year the American Ping-Pong team made a daring trip into Communist China, becoming the first American delegation to visit in twenty-two years. Henry Kissinger was already involved in secret negotiations to ease tensions with China, but the two nations needed something more to break the ice. Ping-Pong was the answer.

Under an invitation from Chinese Prime Minister Zhou Enlai, the team traveled to Beijing for a tournament. The fifteen Americans took sightseeing trips to the Great Wall and Shanghai, and they met with the prime minister himself. When it came time to play, eighteen thousand eager fans crowded into Beijing's Indoor Stadium. The Americans were not sure what to expect. Thankfully the match was "friendly." Though the Chinese were world-class champions, the Americans were able to keep the games close. The Chinese narrowly won the men's games, 5-3, and the women's, 5-4. The Chinese players had been easy on them, the visitors admitted. While the Americans lost in Ping-Pong, they won in diplomacy. The stage was set for formal talks. Three months later, Kissinger made a formal visit of his own. President Nixon's historic visit followed the next year.

The success in Beijing opened the door for "sports diplomacy" around the world. Team competition showed the common people just how much they shared with people of other lands. For example, after years of bitterness over the Iranian hostage crisis, a wrestling team helped to thaw U.S. relations with Iran in 1998. The Iranians treated the American players like kings, prompting several more wrestling teams to crisscross the ocean to compete. More recently, an American baseball team played in Cuba, where baseball is the national passion. Perhaps America's future ambassadors should wear sneakers instead of dress shoes.

Efforts at détente eased Chinese and American relations enough for President Nixon to make a visit to the Great Wall of China in 1972.

Shuttle Diplomacy in the Middle East—The Middle East was a constant source of worry. In October 1973 Egypt and Syria, armed with modern weapons from the Soviet Union, launched a surprise attack against Israel, America's ally. The first week of the Yom Kippur War devastated Israel's army, but in the second week Israel took the offensive. A brilliant thrust across the Suez Canal threatened the rear of Egypt's army. The Soviet Union prepared to send troops to assist the Arab states, but it held back after Nixon put America's nuclear forces on alert. Nixon also flew nearly two billion dollars in military hardware to strengthen Israel.

Secretary of State Henry Kissinger became the go-between to help restore peace. Over several months planes shuttled him back and forth from the United States to Damascus, Syria; to Cairo, Egypt; on to Tel Aviv, Israel; and back home again. The **shuttle diplomacy** brought an end to the bloodshed but no permanent peace agreement.

Failure to Fix the Struggling Economy

When he came to office, Richard Nixon inherited both a war debt and runaway inflation. Under the Johnson administration, the American public never sacrificed at home the way they had in other wars. Americans continued to buy all the material goods they wanted while the government spent money not only for the war but also for growing domestic programs, such as caring for the poor. The increases in government aid discouraged pri-

Communists took over in 1949. Americans feared that some day China might join forces with the Soviet Union, even though the two countries were bitter rivals. In 1971 Kissinger seized an opportunity to open relations, making a secret trip to China. There he made arrangements for a presidential visit in February 1972. Accompanied by American reporters and camera crews, Nixon toured the Great Wall, attended banquets, and met with Chinese leader Chairman Mao Zedong.

This opening of diplomatic relations with the People's Republic of China, however, hurt America's support of "Free China," its former allies during World War II who had fled to the island of Taiwan. When the United States recognized Red China, the U.N. admitted it into that organization and expelled Taiwan. The United States ended its diplomatic relationship with Taiwan on January 1, 1979, even though it is one of America's largest trade partners.

The Space Race

The Soviets dropped a "bomb" on the United States on October 4, 1957. The bomb was the news that **Sputnik I** had successfully entered orbit. After the news flashed across the country, shocked faces appeared on every street corner. How could they do it? How could the Communists be the first to develop the technology to launch a satellite into space? The United States would never be the same.

Rather than raise their hands in surrender, Americans took up the challenge and entered the space race. Americans had a long way to go. A month after the launch of Sputnik, another Soviet rocket carried a dog into space. In April 1961 yet another bomb dropped. The Soviets announced that the cosmonaut Yuri Gagarin had orbited the earth. In response, President Kennedy committed the nation to the most ambitious science project in its history: land a man on the moon by the end of the decade.

Congress established the National Aeronautics and Space Administration (**NASA**) to run the new space program, and it put aside money to promote science and math education in the classroom. Many tense years passed, but it soon became apparent the United States had pulled ahead in the race. NASA overcame the complex problems one by one. The Mercury spacecraft were the first to enter orbit, and the Gemini missions tested the technology to dock two craft in outer space. Finally, the Apollo spacecraft blasted 385,000 miles to the moon.

On July 20, 1969, word came back to NASA that "the Eagle has landed." Neil Armstrong, the commander of Apollo 11, clambered out of the Eagle lunar module and was the first to set foot on the moon. The world listened in awe as he declared, "That's one small step for man, one giant leap for mankind." President Nixon called the astronauts to congratulate them.

Apollo 14 astronaut Alan Shepard poses for a picture on the moon.

vate efforts to end poverty; the government would end it for them.

Wage and Price Controls—Nixon tried to curb inflation by slowing government spending and by increasing taxes. With less money in circulation, people would not be able to buy as much. But such action often results in an economic **recession.** (A recession is a slowdown in the economy, a time when businesses produce fewer products and must get rid of some of their workers.) This was the result of Nixon's action. To make the recession less painful to the average American—and to help his own chances of reelection—Nixon raised

government spending to create new jobs, but this action only increased the national debt.

Nixon decided to use the power of the federal government to curb inflation, despite the outcries of conservatives. In August 1971 he ordered wage and price controls. All wages, prices, and fees were frozen at August levels for ninety days. When the ninety days were up, the Cost of Living Council was organized. Under its guidelines some increases were allowed. Nixon's wage and price controls, however, did not deal with the causes of inflation—excessive government spending and national debt. They only temporarily controlled some of its symptoms. The controls artificially slowed inflation to about three percent annually. But with the end of these controls in 1973, inflation doubled. In 1974 it almost doubled again to 12.2 percent.

Arab Oil Embargo—An unexpected hardship arose when Arab nations, angry over American support of Israel, ordered an embargo (complete ban) on American oil shipments in October 1973. Since the United States imported one-quarter of its oil from Middle Eastern countries, the **oil embargo** hurt Americans. To compound the problem, the federal government's price controls prevented businesses from selling gasoline at higher prices in order to discourage buyers. Instead, gas stations were forced to close down, or they limited how much each customer could buy. Motorists had to wait in long lines at gasoline stations. When price controls were lifted, prices of gasoline, fuel oil, and petroleum-based products, such as plastics, rose dramatically. Complex government rules and regulations limited the freedom of businesses to find creative ways to adapt to the changes.

President Nixon offered no convincing solution to the problem. He asked Americans to conserve energy. Smaller cars that got more miles per gallon became popular. Car pools or "ride-sharing" became common practices in big cities. Many Americans spent vacations close to home. Congress lowered the speed limit to 55 mph, and it approved a pipeline across Alaska to mine oil reserves above the Arctic Circle. The oil embargo also encouraged Congress to spend money on new programs to develop alternate sources of energy.

The **energy crisis** eased somewhat when the Arab nations lifted their embargo in March 1974. Although OPEC (the Organization of Petroleum Exporting Countries) halted its embargo, it steadily raised crude oil prices. Some extremist Muslim countries, such as Libya and Iran, hoped to destroy America with exorbitant prices. More moderate OPEC members, such as Saudi Arabia, argued that ruining the economies of Western industrialized countries would ultimately hinder their ability to buy oil. Unable to agree on prices and production limits, OPEC countries split, and oil again flowed freely.

Failure to Restrain the Liberal Courts

Nixon's Court Appointments—President Nixon had the opportunity to appoint four justices to the Supreme Court, including a new chief justice. The Warren Court, the liberal court of the 1950s and 1960s, had grown unpopular with many Americans who believed it protected criminals and tied the hands of the police. In state after state, criminals had been freed on legal technicalities. When Chief Justice Earl Warren retired in 1969, Nixon replaced him with **Warren Burger.** He filled later vacancies by nominating Harry Blackmun, Lewis F. Powell, and William H. Rehnquist. Burger was a grave disappointment to conservatives. Although the Burger Court limited the scope of some landmark decisions of the Warren Court, it did not reverse them.

Roe v. Wade—Unfortunately, there were not enough conservatives on the court to prevent a liberal decision on abortion. In *Roe v. Wade* (1973), the court decided that a woman had the right to abort her unborn child within the first three months of pregnancy. The ruling overturned the abortion laws of all fifty states. Since then nearly 1.5 million abortions have been performed each year. This legalized murder destroys nearly one-third of all American babies each year.

Growth of Federal Powers

A growing list of issues in the 1960s, such as the environment and women's rights, led to a rapid growth of federal powers in new areas of private life.

***The Search for Clean Air and Water*—** The modern **environmentalist movement,** a concern about man's relationship to his environment, was launched by the publication of Rachel Carson's book *Silent Spring.* Published in 1962, the book alarmed Americans about the harmful impact of pesticides, such as DDT. Under LBJ, the government spent billions of dollars to clean up lakes and rivers. The first lady, Lady Bird Johnson, led a crusade for "the beautification of America." But cities and states took primary responsibility for regulating their own industries and pollution.

A nationwide protest called Earth Day on April 22, 1970, encouraged the federal government to step in. That year Congress established the Environmental Protection Agency (EPA) to oversee environmental regulations. The Clean Air Act of 1970 (amended in 1977

Phyllis Schlafly gained national attention as the outspoken opponent of the Equal Rights Amendment. Her warnings against the negative effects of the amendment helped to stop its passage.

and 1990) regulated air pollution. The Water Pollution Control Act (1972) and later the Clean Water Act (1977) regulated water pollution. Nixon also signed the Endangered Species Act in 1973, granting bureaucrats the power to decide which species are threatened and how to protect them. Environmentalists complained that the law was too weak, and conservatives complained that it was too arbitrary. Bureaucrats had a free hand to limit industry and construction, such as logging and dams, without even analyzing the costs and benefits.

***New Rights Movements*—**In the wake of the civil rights movement among blacks, many other groups began pressuring the government to give them what they believed were their rights as citizens. Among the civil rights movements was a protest among low-paid Hispanic grape pickers in California, led by César Chavez. Another protest, called the American Indian Movement (AIM), gained strength among militant Indians and won notoriety when members seized a government trading post at Wounded Knee, South Dakota, in 1973. The most prominent of the new civil rights movements was the **women's rights movement,** sparked by the publication of Betty Friedan's book *The Feminine Mystique* in 1963. Friedan mocked the lives of moms who stayed at home and raised kids in "a comfortable concentration camp."

While some joined the women's rights movement to earn equal pay, others sought far more. The radical National Organization for Women (NOW), cofounded by Friedan, pushed for legal abortions and easy divorce laws. NOW also supported the **Equal Rights Amendment (ERA).** The harmless-sounding amendment to the Constitution stated, "Equality of rights under the law shall not be denied or abridged by the United States or by any state on account of sex." Conservative women, led by Phyllis Schlafly, denounced the ERA because it would give the federal government virtually unlimited power to impose rules on daily life. She claimed that feminists would use the amendment to abolish time-honored traditions that respect the obvious differences between the sexes—everything from separate bathrooms for women to the ban on women in combat. Congress passed the ERA in 1972, but its supporters could not get enough states to ratify (confirm) the amendment, even after liberals in Congress granted extra time.

SECTION REVIEW

1. What two Communist countries did Nixon visit?

2. Who conducted shuttle diplomacy to help stop the bloodshed in the Middle East?

3. Who launched the first satellite into space? What was Neil Armstrong's historical accomplishment?

4. How did Arab countries react to American support for Israel?

5. Whom did Nixon appoint as chief justice? What landmark decision was passed under his court?

6. What group of Americans made a special push for civil rights at this time? What piece of legislation did they unsuccessfully champion?

 What happens to private citizens when government begins getting more involved in their lives?

The Watergate Scandal

Nixon won reelection in 1972 by a landslide, defeating a liberal Democrat, Senator George McGovern of South Dakota. Pleased with détente, a stable economy, and favorable developments in Vietnam, the people felt confident under Nixon's leadership. But soon cracks began to appear in the image of the Nixon administration.

Resignation of the Vice President—Nixon's running mate, Vice President **Spiro T. Agnew,** was charged with accepting bribes from construction companies while he had been governor of Maryland. He was also charged with income tax evasion, to which he pleaded no contest (similar to pleading guilty). Facing a possible prison sentence, Agnew resigned the vice-presidency on October 10, 1973. He was the first vice president to resign since 1833 and the first vice president ever to resign because of a criminal charge.

For the first time since its ratification in 1967, the Twenty-fifth Amendment was used to pick a new vice president. Following the guidelines in the amendment, Nixon selected Gerald R. Ford, a Michigan congressman. He took the oath of office on December 6, 1973.

The Watergate Cover-up—The president himself got into trouble after five men were arrested for breaking into the Democratic Party's National Campaign Headquarters and planting electronic listening devices during the election of 1972. The break-in took place in an office building in Washington, D.C., named **Watergate.** The press learned that the arrested men were members of President Nixon's committee for the reelection of the president (mockingly called CREEP). No evidence turned up that Nixon knew about the break-in, but suspicions grew that he had tried to cover up the crime after he learned about it.

The trial of the Watergate burglars and two other Nixon officials began in January 1973. One of the burglars claimed that the witnesses had committed perjury (lied in court). He also said that the men had been told to plead guilty by someone higher in the administration.

In May of 1973 the U.S. Senate began its own independent investigation of the Watergate scandal. The investigation soon discovered that the White House had secretly made tape recordings of all the president's office conversations. By listening to the tapes, the committee would be able to determine the president's role in the cover-up, if any. But when the courts ordered Nixon to turn over the tapes, the president refused. He argued that he had executive privilege and that turning them over would endanger national security.

Nixon's Resignation—The American people were outraged. They wrote angry letters to Congress asking for Nixon's impeachment. The House Judiciary Committee then began hearings on fifteen charges. The president responded by turning over the tapes to a new special prosecutor. However, some of the tapes were missing, and an eighteen-and-a-half minute section had been erased on one tape. Nixon claimed it was a secretary's error. When a court order asked for more tapes, the president refused to comply. However, he did supply a tape transcript. The transcript showed that the president had known about the efforts to cover up Watergate, although he was not necessarily the instigator.

Watergate dragged on. Believing that no man can act above the law, Republicans turned against the president. By the end of July, the House Judiciary Committee voted to impeach the president for obstructing justice, misusing his presidential powers, and refusing to comply with their requests for evidence. When the committee showed its determination to examine additional charges, the president's lawyers persuaded him to release more transcripts. These showed that the president not only had known of the burglary but also had acted to stop an FBI investigation of it. The president's position was now hopeless. Rather than face a trial before the Senate that would

lead to his removal, President Nixon resigned on August 9, 1974, the only president ever to do so.

The Watergate conspiracy troubled the public, not only because of the political corruption but also because of the president's virtually unlimited power. Actually the power of the president had been increasing steadily since the time of Franklin Roosevelt. In response, Congress acted to prevent another Watergate. It forbade the president from refus-

Seemingly unaware of his disgrace, Nixon gives his famous victory sign as he prepares to leave the White House.

ing to release budget funds set aside by Congress in order to stop a congressional program or action. It strengthened the Freedom of Information Act, allowing the public more access to government documents. A Federal Campaign Reform Act in 1974 placed a limit on the amount of money private individuals could give to candidates, hoping to limit the use of contributions to "bribe" candidates.

The American political system successfully exposed and dealt with the Watergate conspiracy rather than pushing it under a rug. It showed that the president was not above the law. The Constitution's system of checks and balances worked. Yet Nixon's corruption seriously damaged the prestige of his office, and he undermined the faith of the American people in their political leaders. Beginning in 1974, the percentage of Americans using their hard-won right to vote declined dramatically. Many wondered whether America would ever recover.

SECTION REVIEW

1. Who was Nixon's first vice president? Why did he leave office?

2. What was the crime that Nixon was accused of trying to cover up?

3. What important sources of evidence did investigators try to get from the White House?

4. What was President Nixon's response to the impeachment process?

 Was it necessary to include an impeachment clause in the Constitution? Defend your answer.

SUMMARY

The decade of the 1960s was a trying time for the United States. Divided opinions on major issues, such as civil rights and the Vietnam War, created crises that hurt all Americans. Media reports of violence stirred fears and unrest. While the Great Society attempted to regulate and improve American life, the only obvious result was a rapid increase in the national debt. The assassinations and resignations made historians wonder whether America had become a morally corrupt civilization, like the ancient Roman empire, in steady decline.

Chapter Review

People, Places, and Things to Remember

John F. Kennedy	Malcolm X	détente
New Frontier	urban riots	Henry Kissinger
Alliance for Progress	Vietnam War	SALT
Berlin Wall	Gulf of Tonkin Resolution	shuttle diplomacy
Bay of Pigs	hawks	Sputnik I
Cuban Missile Crisis	doves	NASA
Lyndon B. Johnson	Vietcong	recession
the Great Society	Ho Chi Minh Trail	oil embargo
Barry Goldwater	New Left	energy crisis
Brown v. Board of Education	counterculture	Warren Burger
	Robert Kennedy	*Roe v. Wade*
Twenty-third Amendment	Hubert Humphrey	environmentalist movement
march on Washington	Vietnamization	women's rights movement
Civil Rights Act of 1964	Kent State University	Equal Rights Amendment
Twenty-fourth Amendment	Twenty-sixth Amendment	(ERA)
Voting Rights Act of 1965	War Powers Act	Spiro T. Agnew
Martin Luther King Jr.	Richard Nixon	Watergate

Review Questions

Indicate whether each of the following items is most closely associated with (A) President Kennedy, (B) President Johnson, or (C) President Nixon.

1. Watergate
2. the Great Society
3. Vietnamization of the war
4. Gulf of Tonkin Resolution
5. the New Frontier
6. Cuban Missile Crisis

Match each of the following items with its description.

7. Berlin Wall
8. *Brown v. Board of Education*
9. Peace Corps
10. *Roe v. Wade*
11. Tet Offensive

a. Communist attack on South Vietnam
b. barrier between East and West Germany
c. legalized abortion
d. overturned "separate but equal" policy
e. sent American volunteers to needy places

Answer these questions about the 1960s.

12. Whose shuttle diplomacy temporarily ended Middle Eastern bloodshed?
13. Who was the first man to walk on the moon?
14. What black preacher led much of the civil rights activity of the 1960s?
15. What three Democrats ran for the presidential nomination in 1968?

Questions for Discussion

16. Was the civil rights movement of the 1960s necessary? Why or why not?
17. Why do you think the assassination of leaders often enhances their reputations?

29

Rise of the Right

I n many ways, the crisis of the 1960s still haunts the United States. Radical youths from the "hippie" generation eventually entered positions of leadership as writers, teachers, and politicians. From their lofty perches, these leaders proclaimed their radical ideas. Yet in the years following Watergate, Americans slowly came to see the bad consequences of big government and unrestrained morals.

Signs of a reawakening of conservative ideas appeared on every hand. On July 4, 1976, Americans of all types celebrated the **Bicentennial,** the two-hundredth anniversary of the Declaration of Independence. The event rekindled memories of the values that had made America great. A renewed drive to restore traditional values climaxed in the election of Ronald Reagan, a conservative on the "right" who promised to restore America's greatness. In just ten short years after the Bicentennial, the country was again enjoying a booming economy and new pride. That year the nation celebrated the one-hundredth birthday of the Statue of Liberty, and the next year it marked an even greater event—the bicentennial of the Constitution.

Ford, the Unelected President

The nation suffered through two weak presidents after Nixon resigned. Vice President Gerald R. Ford took the oath of office the day Nixon left. Ford's position was difficult: the public had not elected him as either vice president or president. He saw the need to restore the public's confidence in the presidential office. He promised "openness and candor" and said he was only an ordinary man who would try to do his best. Ford also promised regular news conferences so that the public would be informed of his actions. He chose as his vice president a former New York governor from the liberal wing of the Republican Party, Nelson Rockefeller. He kept Henry Kissinger, Nixon's secretary of state, and said that he would pursue a foreign policy like Nixon's.

Ford's Pardon of Nixon

One month into office Ford ignited a controversy that he never lived down. He pardoned Richard Nixon. By pardoning Nixon for any crimes he might have committed while in office, Ford angered many of his main supporters. He said that trying the former president would subject the country to added agony. Some Democrats, however, accused him of making a "buddy deal" with the president in exchange for his nomination as vice president. Many Americans were dismayed that the former president could go free while the men serving under him remained in jail for their crimes.

Ford's Failed Effort to Whip Inflation

When Gerald Ford took office, Nixon's wage and price controls had failed to check inflation. In 1974 inflation reached a record 12.2 percent.

Ford could do little directly to solve the main cause of the problem. An independent government agency that was created in 1913, called the Federal Reserve, controlled the supply of money in the country. (Too much paper money in distribution makes prices go up.) At first, Ford pushed for a voluntary anti-inflation crusade. Called WIN (Whip Inflation Now), the plan urged consumers to stop

Gerald R. Ford

38th President

Born: Omaha, Nebraska, July 14, 1913
Family: married Elizabeth "Betty" Bloomer; had three sons, one daughter
Occupation: lawyer
Home: Grand Rapids, Michigan
Religion: Episcopalian
Election: none; appointed as vice president and succeeded to the presidency upon the resignation of Nixon
Political Party: Republican
Vice President: Nelson Rockefeller (appointed)
Interesting Facts and Accomplishments:
• only president not elected to office • was born Leslie Lynch King Jr., but was adopted by his stepfather after his mother remarried; his name was changed to Gerald R. Ford Jr., and he did not know he was adopted until he was sixteen years old • MVP linebacker at the University of Michigan • offered a contract with the Green Bay Packers and Detroit Lions • two assassination attempts were made on his life during his presidency—both by women

(1974-77)

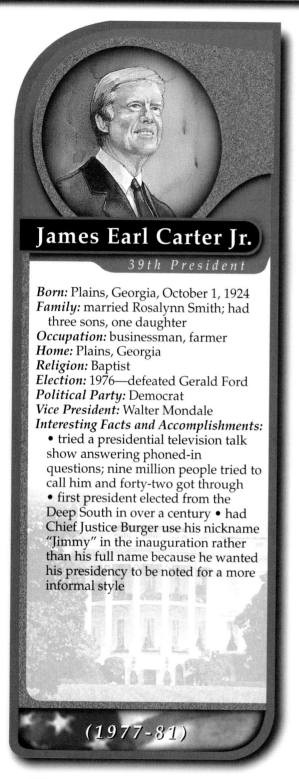

James Earl Carter Jr.

39th President

Born: Plains, Georgia, October 1, 1924
Family: married Rosalynn Smith; had three sons, one daughter
Occupation: businessman, farmer
Home: Plains, Georgia
Religion: Baptist
Election: 1976—defeated Gerald Ford
Political Party: Democrat
Vice President: Walter Mondale
Interesting Facts and Accomplishments:
• tried a presidential television talk show answering phoned-in questions; nine million people tried to call him and forty-two got through
• first president elected from the Deep South in over a century • had Chief Justice Burger use his nickname "Jimmy" in the inauguration rather than his full name because he wanted his presidency to be noted for a more informal style

(1977-81)

buying high-priced goods, and it asked workers not to seek wage increases. But since workers and businesses believed they were the victims, rather than the causes, of inflation, they ignored WIN. The economic recession grew even worse as the Federal Reserve raised interest rates (one of the tools it uses to limit the amount of money in circulation). Sales of new products fell; the number of workers out of work climbed above nine percent.

President Ford then requested a tax cut and less government spending. Liberal Democrats who controlled Congress approved the tax cut, but they spent more and more money on new programs. Ford vetoed sixty-one bills in an effort to hold down the growth of government, but inflation continued to spiral upward.

Ford's Failed Election Campaign

Ford decided to run for president in 1976. Because he had not been in office long, he had not made many of his own policies. Moreover, the Republican Party was still recovering from the shame of Watergate. Ford's inability to solve the nation's problems gave Democratic leaders assurance that "we could run an aardvark this year and win."

Out of the many candidates running for president, the Democratic Party picked little-known **Jimmy Carter,** a former one-term governor of Georgia. Carter stressed his honesty and his lack of ties to politics in Washington. Because he had taken a strong stand on civil rights in Georgia, he won black voters. He also enjoyed a following among labor unions. In spite of his natural advantages, Carter ran a lackluster campaign and defeated Ford by only a narrow margin, 51 to 48 percent.

SECTION REVIEW

1. Whom did Ford choose for his vice president?

2. What controversial step did Ford take shortly after becoming president?

3. What was Ford's plan to lower inflation? Why did it fail?

4. What was Jimmy Carter's political background?

 Do you agree with Ford's decision to pardon Nixon? Why or why not?

Carter, the Peanut Farmer

President Jimmy Carter entered office with high hopes. Democrats controlled both houses of Congress by large margins, and Americans were looking for someone to solve the pressing problems of the day. He wanted to bring new faces to Washington and to use the same simple, down-home style he had used to run his father's peanut warehouse in Georgia.

But the inexperience and idealism that helped Carter win the election greatly hindered his effectiveness in office. He failed to make the necessary effort to win support for his programs. He also got bogged down in the details of governing and failed to spell out the principles that guided his administration. Few people, even in his own party, really knew the president's long-term goals. To make matters worse, Carter did not have a solid grasp of foreign affairs.

Carter's Domestic Failures

Amnesty for Draft Dodgers—One of President Carter's first acts was to offer **amnesty,** or a group pardon, to those who had illegally dodged the draft during the Vietnam conflict. The president wanted to heal the rifts left by the war. But to Americans who had complied with the law and lost family members, the action was an insult. The number of people who took advantage of the amnesty was smaller than expected. Some draft dodgers snubbed the offer because they believed accepting it was an admission that their actions had been wrong.

Double-Digit Inflation—Economic troubles mushroomed under Carter. To escape inflation, consumers were borrowing money to get what they wanted before prices went up. With more money in circulation, inflation only increased faster. The annual inflation rates were "double-digit"—over ten percent. Workers, unable to afford the higher prices, demanded higher wages. At the same time, interest rates on loans reached some of the highest levels in years. People could not afford home mortgages, so builders found themselves out of work. Related businesses suffered, and unemployment rose.

Like Ford, Carter proposed to curb inflation by slowing the growth of federal spending and by revising the tax system. He asked people to accept voluntary wage and price controls but had little success. His tax bill was supposed to cut taxes for the poor by closing

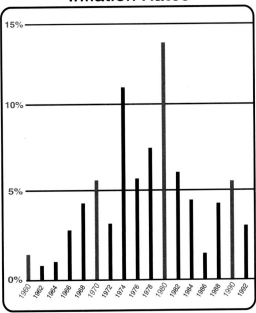

Inflation Rates

loopholes open to the rich. But by the time Congress finished with the bill, it had reduced some taxes for the wealthy, while it raised Social Security taxes on everyone.

Dependence on Foreign Energy—From 1973 to 1977, the cost of imported oil for the nation skyrocketed from $8 billion to $40 billion a year. President Carter devised a program that he believed would end dependence on foreign oil. First, he wanted nationwide conservation. Second, he created a cabinet-level Energy Department to oversee programs to help American companies to search for new oil fields and to develop alternative energy sources. Next, he proposed **deregulation,** an end to price controls, on gas and oil. He hoped

President Carter drives away from visiting Three Mile Island days after safety systems narrowly avoided a nuclear disaster.

that higher prices would encourage conservation and the search for oil at home. Carter also wanted to tax profits on oil and use this money to fund his government programs. His plans were set back when Muslim radicals took power in Iran and cut oil production in 1979, creating an energy crisis reminiscent of the 1973 oil embargo.

President Carter believed that increasing the use of nuclear power might help solve the energy crisis. But he faced opposition on all sides. Conservatives complained that nuclear

power required a massive monopoly run by the central government rather than free enterprise. Liberals complained about the hazards of nuclear waste and nuclear accidents. Their fears became reality on March 28, 1979, at the **Three Mile Island** nuclear power plant near Harrisburg, Pennsylvania. The nuclear reactor's cooling system failed. Before the reactor could be shut down, radioactive steam was released, contaminating the water in a backup stream. Although the backup system worked and the immediate crisis passed, the accident prompted antinuclear protests and hampered the building of more nuclear power plants.

Carter's Humiliation in Foreign Affairs

In his inaugural address Carter declared that human rights would be central in his foreign policy. "Because we are free, we can never be indifferent to the fact of freedom elsewhere," he said. "Thus people everywhere should have freedom to make political choices, exercise their ideas free of intimidation or persecution, and to own property." Although such ideas sound wonderful, they are hard to impose on countries where the United States has little influence.

Controversy over the Panama Canal "Surrender"— The United States had signed a ninety-nine-year lease on the Panama Canal, beginning in 1903. Panamanian nationalists were now demanding that it be put under their control immediately. Carter entered negotiations and in 1977 signed the **Panama Canal Treaty.** The United States agreed to transfer control of the canal by the year 1999. The United States, however, retained the right to intervene with military force if the canal's neutrality were ever threatened.

The Senate approved the treaty after hot debate. Those who supported the treaty believed that the United States had no right to the Canal Zone. Many Americans, however, attacked the "surrender" of a canal that

Americans had worked and died to build. They also feared that under Panamanian rule, the canal might fall into communist hands.

Camp David Accords Between Israel and Egypt—One of the few successes that Carter claimed in foreign affairs was the successful conclusion of talks begun under the previous two Republican administrations. Kissinger's shuttle diplomacy helped to persuade Egypt and Israel to end their fighting. Egypt's leader Anwar Sadat took the next step, accepting an invitation to visit Israel's prime minister Menachem Begin (BAY gin) in Tel Aviv. Carter took this opportunity to invite Sadat and Begin to Camp David, a presidential

Carter, Begin, and Sadat seem pleased at the success of the Camp David meetings.

retreat in Maryland. They reached a historic accord, or agreement, with Carter acting as mediator. In September 1978 Sadat and Begin signed the **Camp David Accords.** Israel agreed to return the Sinai Peninsula; Egypt agreed to become the first Arab nation to recognize Israel's right to exist.

Senate Rejection of SALT II—Carter continued negotiations with the Soviets for another Strategic Arms Limitations Treaty.

However, he offered the Soviets a new set of proposals. One of his aims was to guarantee equality in bombers and nuclear missiles. This slowed the talks, and the treaty called SALT II was not signed until March 1979. When Carter submitted the treaty for Senate approval, however, both the Senate and the press reacted negatively. Opposition grew when the Soviet Union invaded Afghanistan in

Jimmy Carter and Leonid Breshnev signed the SALT II Agreement, but the Senate later withheld approval.

1979, and the disappointed president withdrew the treaty.

Soviet Invasion of Afghanistan—The Soviet invasion of Afghanistan deeply angered Americans. Claiming they had been invited into Afghanistan, the Soviets executed the Afghan president soon after their paratroopers landed. Their plans to set up a puppet regime were hindered by Afghan guerillas who took to the hills. Although Carter had earlier stated his opposition to secret military operations, he let the Central Intelligence Agency (CIA) channel aid to Afghan freedom forces. Carter's punishment for the Soviets was weak, however: he stated that the United States would not take part in the 1980 Olympic Games, to be held in Moscow.

The Iranian Hostage Crisis—On November 4, 1979, America faced a new crisis. In the Middle Eastern country of Iran, a group of radical students stormed the U.S. embassy compound and took sixty-six Americans hostage. The students soon revealed their connections to Iran's new Muslim ruler, the **Ayatollah Khomeini.**

The **Iranian hostage crisis** caught most Americans by surprise, but it shouldn't have. The United States had aided the former ruler of Iran, the shah. The Iranian people were fed up with his self-serving rule and revolted. The shah was forced to flee the country, and Khomeini emerged as ruler. In a nation suffering from deep economic problems and widespread unemployment, Khomeini easily stirred up hatred toward the shah and his supporter, the United States. In October 1979

President Carter allowed the shah, ill with cancer, to enter the United States for medical treatment. Carter made his decision on humanitarian grounds, ignoring his advisors' warnings that the Iranians would retaliate.

Carter gave only a feeble response. He froze Iran's assets (investment money) in America. Then he cut off the importation of Iranian oil. Carter made one attempt to rescue the hostages by military force, but it was a fiasco. A helicopter collided with a transport plane, killing eight soldiers, and the commandos had to abort their mission hundreds of miles from their objective. This failure only added to America's feelings of frustration and humiliation. The American people were incensed that Khomeini and his country had paralyzed the United States in such a way.

The situation changed when Iran's neighbor, Iraq, invaded in September 1980. The ancient foes locked horns in a deadly war that would last eight years and send over three hundred thousand Muslims to their graves. Khomeini offered to release the American hostages on three conditions: free Iranian assets, promise never to interfere in Iranian affairs, and return the shah's wealth. Since the United States had no legal access to the shah's money, it refused. The crisis did not end until Reagan's inauguration. On January 21, 1981, after 444 days in captivity, the American hostages were set free.

SECTION REVIEW

1. What did Carter do for those who had illegally escaped service in Vietnam?

2. How high did inflation go during Carter's term of office?

3. What alternative source of energy did Carter push? What event seriously damaged support for his program?

The Ayatollah Khomeini easily stirred his nation's resentment of the United States's support of the shah of Iran into hatred against all Americans.

4. By what year was Panama to receive control of the Panama Canal according to the Panama Canal Treaty?

5. The Camp David Accords brought peace between what two Middle Eastern nations?

 Was Carter's weak leadership responsible for the Iranian hostage crisis? Explain your answer.

The Reagan Revolution

Carter faced a formidable opponent in the election of 1980, California's former governor **Ronald Reagan.** Reagan's speeches were direct, sincere, and stirring. He had run for president twice before, nearly unseating Ford in the 1976 election. Tired of the failures under Carter, Americans were ready to listen to Reagan's conservative proposals. Reagan promised to strengthen the national defense, to cut the size of the federal bureaucracy, and to get big government "off the backs of the people." He offered to restore American strength and pride, and the people were ready for a change.

On election night, Reagan carried all but six states. Riding "on the coattails" of the president, Republicans won enough seats to take control of the Senate by a small margin. Although Democrats still held a majority in the House, a group of moderate Democrats sometimes voted with the Republicans. This meant that, in his early years as president, Reagan was able to get his programs passed by Congress, especially laws dealing with the economy and with military spending.

Reagan's New Direction in Domestic Policies

Reagan's first priority was to solve the problems at home. He offered a new approach to the economy, and he promised to restrain the liberal courts.

Supply-side Economics—The causes of inflation are complicated. An easy way to

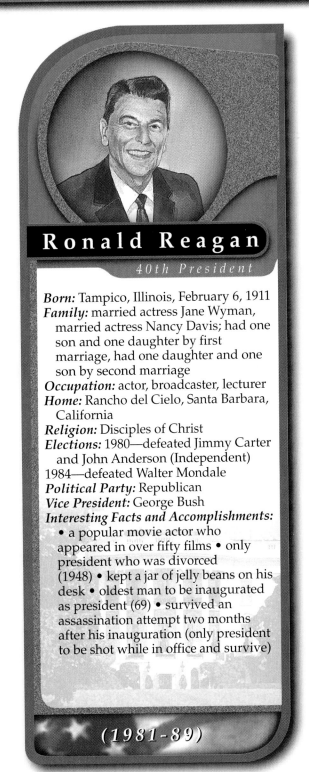

Ronald Reagan

40th President

Born: Tampico, Illinois, February 6, 1911
Family: married actress Jane Wyman, married actress Nancy Davis; had one son and one daughter by first marriage, had one daughter and one son by second marriage
Occupation: actor, broadcaster, lecturer
Home: Rancho del Cielo, Santa Barbara, California
Religion: Disciples of Christ
Elections: 1980—defeated Jimmy Carter and John Anderson (Independent) 1984—defeated Walter Mondale
Political Party: Republican
Vice President: George Bush
Interesting Facts and Accomplishments:
• a popular movie actor who appeared in over fifty films • only president who was divorced (1948) • kept a jar of jelly beans on his desk • oldest man to be inaugurated as president (69) • survived an assassination attempt two months after his inauguration (only president to be shot while in office and survive)

(1981-89)

explain it is that the supply of money is greater than the supply of products that people can buy. (Too much money is chasing too few goods.) Under these circumstances, businesses must raise prices. The government can stop businesses from raising prices in several ways. One option is to take money away from buyers through taxes and high interest rates. Reagan suggested another way. He focused on the other side of the equation: make more products available by reducing taxes and regulations on businesses and investors. Industries would then have more money to make products. Reagan called this positive approach **"supply-side economics."** He argued that tax cuts would increase the amount of tax money that the government would collect. Critics referred to his magic plan as "voodoo economics" or "Reaganomics." Both sides waited to see what would happen.

In 1981 Congress passed the first part of Reagan's plan by cutting inheritance and gift taxes, corporate taxes, and income taxes. The Economic Recovery Tax Act of 1981 included the largest income tax cut in American history—a 25 percent reduction for each taxpayer. To help balance the budget, the president also hoped to cut the size of the government bureaucracy and to slow down increases in federal spending in almost every area except the military. But the House of Representatives, which is responsible for budget bills, showed little interest in reducing federal spending. Democratic leaders in Congress accused Reagan of being hard-hearted and wanting to hurt the poor.

Before the tax reforms were passed, the country fell back into a deep recession. The president agreed to some tax increases, such as taxes on cigarettes and airline tickets, to ease worries that the government was not earning enough money, but otherwise he called on Americans to "stay the course" he had proposed. The recession lifted, and in 1983 the United States entered its longest period of continuous economic growth in history. Inflation disappeared, and jobs were abundant. As the decade wore on, Democrats watched government income from taxes almost double, just as Reagan had hoped. But Congress continued to spend money even faster than it came in. Government debts mounted to record levels, threatening America's long-term prosperity.

Reagan's Stab at a More Conservative Court—Another goal of the Reagan administration was to restore law and order. This required replacing liberal judges with more conservative ones. President Reagan's first appointment to the Supreme Court was the first woman on the Court, **Sandra Day O'Connor.** Afterward the president named Justice **William H. Rehnquist,** a conservative justice already on the court, to replace Chief Justice Warren Burger when he stepped down. Another conservative appointment, Antonin Scalia, helped to tilt the high court away from its liberal predecessor. However, O'Connor—and a later appointment Anthony Kennedy—disappointed conservatives. While they ruled in favor of strong criminal laws and police powers, these appointments refused to overturn abortion.

Chief Justice Warren Burger administers the oath to Sandra Day O'Connor, the first woman to serve on the Supreme Court.

Reelection by a Landslide—The Democratic Party nominated former Vice President Walter Mondale to face Reagan in the 1984 elections. But he surprised many by promising to raise taxes and by choosing a woman as his running mate—Geraldine Ferraro, a liberal congresswoman from New York. The Democrats attacked the high debt, the military build-up, and the limits on spending for social programs. However, Americans trusted the president, and he led in the polls the entire campaign. On election night he carried every state but Mondale's home state of Minnesota. It was one of the biggest landslides in American history.

Reagan's Foreign Triumphs

Reagan was just as successful abroad as he was at home, but it took longer for Americans to see the fruit of his labors.

Bare Knuckles Toward the "Evil Empire"—President Reagan was a vocal opponent of communism. Carter's friendly relationship with the Soviets had turned to frost—if not ice— before Reagan even took office. The Soviets had invaded Afghanistan, and Soviet-equipped Cuban troops were fighting America's ally in Angola, Africa. Moreover, the Soviets were installing long-range missiles in Eastern Europe. Tensions increased in 1983 when the Soviets shot down a Korean airliner with 61 Americans on board, including a U.S. congressman. (The Soviets claimed the plane had crossed its border and was spying.) The Soviets also backed Poland's crackdown on workers demanding greater freedom. Reagan made no attempt to melt the frost. Indeed, he boldly condemned the Soviet Union as an "evil empire."

President Reagan wanted to negotiate limits on nuclear arms, but he took a different tack from Carter. Liberal Democrats argued that the best way to make peace with the Soviets was to voluntarily reduce the U.S. military, allaying Soviet fears of American aggression. Reagan, on the other hand, believed the best way to achieve peace was a strong military. He set aside money to develop a modern bomber, called the B-1, and he asked for further research on nuclear and chemical weapons. By removing Soviet hopes

President Reagan addresses Congress.

of ever defeating the United States, he believed the Soviets would have no choice but to negotiate a better peace agreement. When the Soviets stalled during talks in 1982, Reagan daringly placed more nuclear missiles in Western Europe.

Reagan's tough stand made American allies nervous, but he stuck to his policies. A sore spot among Soviet leaders was Reagan's ambitious proposal, the Strategic Defense Initiative (SDI). SDI's aim was to develop a defense system that could knock down nuclear missiles aimed at American cities. The liberal

Forty years of Soviet domination end with the tearing down of the Berlin Wall.

press mockingly called SDI the **"Star Wars"** program. But the Soviet Union suffered a crisis of leadership, as the Soviets realized they could not keep up with America's dynamic economy and sophisticated technology. Three of the Soviet Union's old-guard leaders died within a three-year span. Finally, **Mikhail Gorbachev,** a young leader brimming with new ideas, came to power in 1985. That same year he became the first Soviet leader to meet with Reagan. A second meeting on arms limitations two years later in Reykjavik, Iceland, collapsed because Reagan refused to give up SDI. Meanwhile, discontent was growing within the Soviet Union. A desperate Gorbachev finally gave in to Reagan's demands. On December 9, 1987, the two leaders signed the historic Intermediate Nuclear Forces (INF) Treaty, which eliminated most of Europe's medium-range nuclear missiles, a first step toward further reductions.

Battling Middle-Eastern Terrorism— Early in Reagan's first term, civil war and foreign intervention in Lebanon led the U.N. to send in peace-keeping troops. American marines were stationed in Lebanon as a part of this force. But on October 23, 1983, a truck loaded with heavy explosives ran through a series of barricades and slammed into the marine headquarters on the outskirts of Beirut. The suicide attack killed over two hundred marines, and Reagan pulled the remaining force out of the country.

Elsewhere in the Middle East, Muslim terrorists led a series of attacks on Westerners. When intelligence officials in the United States learned that Libya's leader, **Muammar Qaddafi,** was behind some of the terrorism, and after Qaddafi added new threats against the United States, Reagan responded with a surprise bombing raid. The attack on March 31, 1986, was brief, but it quieted the terrorist rampage.

Reagan Doctrine in Latin America— After Castro's rise to power in Cuba, the United States made every effort to limit the spread of communism. Struggling with poverty, unequal wealth, and evil dictators, Latin America was a breeding ground for revolution. A small island in the Caribbean— Grenada—became a focus of concern after Reagan took office. An anti-American government, which had ruled Grenada since the 1970s, allowed Cuba to build a major runway which could be used to fly supplies to communist rebels throughout the region. The threat increased after rebels overthrew and executed Grenada's president in 1983.

The resulting civil war in Grenada threatened the lives of about seven hundred American students enrolled in medical school there. Fearing for their own safety, several Caribbean nations asked the United States to intervene. In a surprise attack, American paratroopers, joined by forces from five Caribbean nations, restored peace to Grenada. The United States finished the airstrip and oversaw a free election in 1984, while American troops remained in Grenada only a matter of weeks.

Another dangerous revolution had taken place before Reagan took office. With the help of Cuban advisors, the **Sandinistas** had set up a Communist government in Nicaragua. In response, the CIA had begun channeling aid to the freedom-fighting rebels, called **Contras** (short for the Spanish word for counter-revolutionary). President Reagan feared that revolution would spread to Nicaragua's neighbors. Reagan was particularly concerned about El Salvador, the most crowded nation in Central America. At first Congress went along with Reagan's plans to give aid to the Contras and to El Salvador. Eventually, however, the unstable conditions raised fears that America might be pulled into another conflict like Vietnam. Investigators also found that some Contras were guilty of violating human rights.

The Iran-Contra Affair—An incident came to light in 1987 that hampered Reagan's effectiveness in the final years of his presidency. The administration had arranged the sale of weapons to Iran in exchange for Iran's help in freeing some Americans who had been captured and were being held hostage in Lebanon. The president apparently approved this deal, contrary to his official stand against bargaining with terrorists. The situation grew worse when it was learned that some of the profits from the sale of the weapons were being sent by third parties to aid the Contras in Nicaragua.

Congress had cut all government aid to the Contras at the time of the transactions, so Reagan's enemies charged that he had violated the law. Reagan claimed he knew nothing of this diversion of funds. Many Americans believed him, but opponents made much of his apparent lack of control. Congress hired an independent counsel (lawyer) to investigate, but after he spent almost seven years and $37 million, no one was ever convicted. The counsel's report concluded, "President Reagan's conduct fell well short of criminality which could be successfully prosecuted."

SECTION REVIEW

1. How did "supply-side economics" propose to lower inflation?

2. Who was the first woman appointed to the Supreme Court?

3. Which Soviet leader agreed to come to the bargaining table with Reagan?

4. What were the Communist rulers in Nicaragua called? Who were the freedom fighters that were trying to overthrow them?

5. One of the complaints in the Iran-Contra affair was that weapons were sold to Iran. What was the other complaint?

 Do you agree with Reagan's view that the best way to achieve peace is to build a powerful military? Defend your answer.

Bush's Problem with "the Vision Thing"

The Reagan Administration marked a turning point in the history of the nation and of the world. The year Reagan left office, 1989, communism collapsed in Eastern Europe. Two years later, the Communist leader of the Soviet Union stepped down, and fifteen new countries rose out of the ashes of the former empire. The American system of government and free enterprise had proved victorious. The Cold War that had dominated the last half of the twentieth century was finally over. All eyes now turned to the president of the United States to guide the free world into the next century. Americans were ready for sweeping changes at home, now that the specter of communism had stopped haunting Europe. Who was the right man to lead the nation?

Reagan proposed that his vice president, **George Bush,** would be the best man to carry on his vision. Unlike Reagan, however, Bush was a pragmatist (a person who believes that

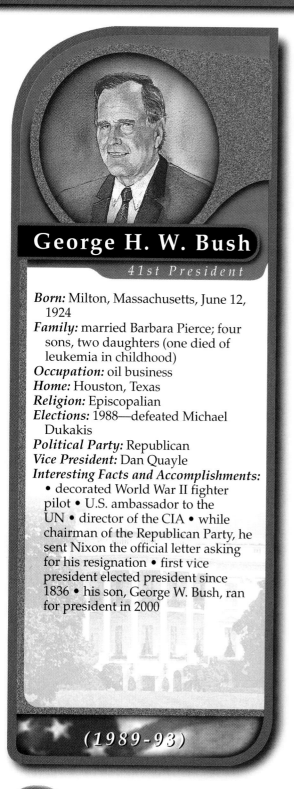

George H. W. Bush

41st President

Born: Milton, Massachusetts, June 12, 1924

Family: married Barbara Pierce; four sons, two daughters (one died of leukemia in childhood)

Occupation: oil business

Home: Houston, Texas

Religion: Episcopalian

Elections: 1988—defeated Michael Dukakis

Political Party: Republican

Vice President: Dan Quayle

Interesting Facts and Accomplishments:
• decorated World War II fighter pilot • U.S. ambassador to the UN • director of the CIA • while chairman of the Republican Party, he sent Nixon the official letter asking for his resignation • first vice president elected president since 1836 • his son, George W. Bush, ran for president in 2000

(1989–93)

whatever works best is right). This Eastern "gentleman" accepted many of the traditional values with which he was reared, yet he rarely spoke of right and wrong. Instead, he spoke of the views of "my generation" and "your generation." He voiced support for many of Reagan's policies, not based on principle but on practical concerns. He was an uninspiring speaker who once admitted that he lacked "the vision thing."

In Reagan's Shadow, Election of 1988

The election of 1988 pitted George Bush against a liberal governor from Massachusetts, Michael Dukakis. During his eight years in Reagan's shadow, Bush had remained a mystery to the American people. When Reagan picked him as a running mate in 1979, Bush was a "moderate" Republican with a lifetime of experience in public service and foreign affairs. Bush now struggled to establish a separate identity. He wanted to soften Reagan's strictly conservative message. "I want a kinder, gentler nation," Bush said in his acceptance speech at the Republican convention. He spoke of solving the nation's social ills by kindling the vast resources of the American people as "a thousand points of light."

After a shaky start, Bush rallied support largely by returning to Reagan's popular positions: American strength at home and abroad. He also vowed, "Read my lips—no new taxes." The result for Bush and his running mate, Dan Quayle, was a solid win on election day. Bush's election was in many ways a vote of approval for Ronald Reagan. Bush became the first vice president since 1836 to replace the president under whom he served. Unfortunately, like that earlier president, Martin Van Buren, Bush inherited serious troubles that demanded immediate attention.

Foreign Affairs

In foreign affairs President Bush brought the same resolve as his predecessor. His experience and skill led to major triumphs in Panama and the Persian Gulf, but he was slow to see the significance of sweeping changes in China and the Soviet Union.

Invasion of Panama—Bush faced several international crises with amazing success. His first major triumph involved Panama's drug-dealing leader, Manuel Noriega, whose criminal activities had become an embarrassment to the U.S. government. Reagan had attempted to remove Noriega peacefully, but in vain. In December 1989 Noriega went too far. His troops killed a U.S. marine and attacked an American couple, and then the general declared war on the United States. In the early morning hours of December 20, Bush launched Operation Just Cause. Within days American troops had crushed Noriega's forces and captured the general, at a cost of only twenty-three American lives. Noriega became the first foreign head of state to be captured and tried in a U.S. court. He was convicted in 1992 of drug trafficking and sentenced to forty years in prison.

Protests Break Out in China and the Soviet Union—Meanwhile rumblings were heard on the other side of the globe. The Cold War was coming to an end, but Bush was slow to see the significance of events. Chinese students led a massive protest at Beijing's Tiananmen Square in 1989, hoping to spread democracy to their Communist land. When tanks crushed the protest, killing over two thousand people, Bush refused to take any action. Indeed, when it came time to renew China's "most-favored-nation" trade status, Bush did so.

A similar series of events was taking place in the Soviet Union. As that "evil empire" began to tear apart, Bush continued to support its Communist leader, Gorbachev. Bush spoke with Gorbachev about creating a "new world order," and they negotiated a nuclear arms reduction treaty (START). Bush was slow to support the reformer Boris Yeltsin, even when it became obvious that he was the people's choice to lead Russia out of communism.

The Persian Gulf War—Bush reached a high point in his career when he negotiated an international alliance to stop Iraq's invasion of Kuwait in 1990. The dictator **Saddam Hussein** had invaded this tiny, oil-rich neighbor, hoping to win glory for himself and easy wealth for his nation. But Bush vowed, "This will not stand." A UN directive (order) told Hussein to withdraw by January 15, 1991, and it authorized the allies to use "all necessary means" to liberate Kuwait if Hussein did not comply. The U.S. Congress also approved war, if necessary. It was America's first official declaration of war since World War II.

President and Mrs. Bush meet with troops stationed in Saudi Arabia before the conflict known as the Gulf War.

The brief **Persian Gulf War** (January 16 to February 27, 1991) began with five weeks of massive, around-the-clock bombing. It was followed by a surprise ground attack in the desert. General Norman Schwarzkopf secretly ordered soldiers and tanks to move into the desert west of Kuwait. This force circled around the Iraqi army and trapped it in

The massive assault called Operation Desert Storm began five weeks of the most intensive American military effort since World War II.

Kuwait. The Iraqi army surrendered en masse. The ground war was over within one hundred hours, and Americans rejoiced that the ghosts of the Vietnam War had vanished. Yet the cream of Hussein's army, the Republican Guard, remained safe at home in Iraq. Schwarzkopf, his hands tied by UN directives, could not move north to capture Hussein.

In the wake of victory, Bush's popularity ratings soared to an unprecedented 89 percent. No leading Democrat wanted to run against him in the next election. Yet Bush's decision to place United States troops under UN directives would come back to haunt him. Hussein remained in power and continued to take actions that embarrassed the United States.

Government Scandals and Demands for Reform

The U.S. government was rocked by a series of financial scandals beginning in 1989. Many liberals said that these scandals were a sign of the greed and decadence caused by Reagan's deregulation of banking, business, insurance, and health care. Yet blame quickly spread to the Democrat-controlled Congress.

Savings and Loan Bankruptcies—The first scandals involved savings and loan (S & L) banks, which began to go bankrupt because of unsound investments and a drop in oil prices. The federal government had to spend over $300 billion to keep Franklin D. Roosevelt's promises to safeguard individuals' bank accounts. This cost the average taxpayer roughly $3,000. Efforts to sell the bankrupt S & Ls proved to be a nightmare of waste and fraud.

Other Business Scandals—Health care overcharges, insurance fraud, empty retirement funds, and similar instances of dishonesty hit the headlines during the same period. Most of the scandals had a similar theme: the government guaranteed benefits but provided insufficient regulation. Liberals argued that the government needed more regulation. Conservatives argued that the government needed to stay out of private business.

Congressional Scandals—Congress was embarrassed by its own scandals. In 1989 Congress passed the so-called "Ethics Reform Act." In exchange for giving up money for speeches (honoraria), Congress gave itself a massive pay raise and established automatic annual cost-of-living adjustments (COLAs). In 1993 alone, the COLAs gave congressmen a pay raise of $4,100, which they never had to vote for. Taxpayers were furious. States responded by ratifying the Twenty-seventh Amendment on May 7, 1992. The amendment reads, "No law, varying the compensation for the services of the Senators and Representatives, shall take effect, until an election of Representatives shall have intervened."

In 1992 news leaked that a majority of congressmen had serious House Bank overdrafts. It became clear that they were abusing the perks of office. They were allowed to overdraw on their checking accounts without penalties, while taxpayers paid the interest. The House Ethics Committee released names of 247 congressmen who had overdrafts.

A more serious scandal, involving the House Post Office, came to light. Investigators found that congressmen were abusing their privileges to pay office expenses and to buy stamps. The most infamous case involved the powerful chairman of the Ways and Means Committee, Dan Rostenkowski. He was eventually sent to jail for pocketing over ten thousand dollars worth in money for stamps, hiring employees who were paid for work they never did, and using his congressional staff for private work (at a total cost of half a million dollars to taxpayers).

Many Americans decided that wealthy incumbents (officeholders) had lost touch with the people who elected them. Support grew for **term limits**—restrictions on the number of years that a congressman can stay in office. During the 1992 elections, fourteen states passed laws to limit senators to twelve years and House members to anywhere from six to twelve years. The number of states with term limits increased to twenty-two after the 1994 elections.

Domestic Failures

Bush's domestic policies sent mixed signals to the nation. Conservatives were concerned about his liberal compromises, while liberals were disappointed with his conservative stands. He said he opposed abortion, but he appointed a Supreme Court justice who upheld *Roe v. Wade.* He said he opposed big government intrusion into business, but he increased the minimum wage from $3.35 to $4.25. He said he supported business, but the 1991 Clean Air Act cost businesses around $30 billion per year. He said he wanted to simplify government, but the number of pages devoted to regulations rose from 47,418 under Reagan to 67,715 under Bush. He said he supported traditional values, but he became the first president to invite homosexuals to visit the White House when he signed the Hate Crimes Statistics Act.

The "Education President"—Ronald Reagan had campaigned against Washington's control of education, but his promise to disband the cabinet position went unfulfilled. In contrast, George Bush promised to become the "education president." The federal government's involvement in education grew rapidly under his administration. His favorite program was Head Start, begun by Lyndon B. Johnson in the 1960s. Even though studies indicate that the advantages of early education fade away by second or third grade, spending for this federal program grew dramatically under Bush: from $600 million to $2.8 billion.

An Education Summit in 1989 agreed on six national goals that American schools should meet by the year 2000. Bush proposed America 2000, a plan to bring American schools up to these goals. Bill Clinton, the governor of Arkansas who was a leader at the summit, later converted this program into Goals 2000. It set "voluntary" standards for textbooks and testing that states must meet in order to receive federal funds. Yet poor performance on standardized tests continued to embarrass the nation.

Disabilities Act—President Bush signed the **Americans with Disabilities Act,** which went into effect in 1992. The landmark law prohibited job discrimination based on disabilities. It also required local governments and businesses to provide better conditions for

Supporters look on as President Bush signs the Americans with Disabilities Act of 1990.

the disabled. Companies with fifteen or more employees were required to hire and promote people with disabilities. The greatest opposition to the act came from small businessmen, who feared that the new costs would put them out of business. Many Americans also feared the unclear definition of disability, which allowed people with AIDS and mental conditions to claim they had a "disability." The law brought a flood of expensive lawsuits.

The Los Angeles riots in response to the beating of Rodney King were the deadliest riots in modern American history.

This law aroused the ire of conservatives who opposed federal interference in business and local government. The concept of "rights" for the disabled departed from historic civil liberties and rights. The Disabilities Act encouraged a widespread movement against **unfunded federal mandates** (federal requirements that the federal government does not pay for). The law cost in excess of $60 billion in its first few years.

Los Angeles Riots—The most significant domestic crisis during the Bush administration was the **Los Angeles riots** (April 29–May 3, 1992)—the deadliest riots in modern American history. Fifty-three people died and over $1 billion in damage occurred in America's second largest city. The rioting had many similarities to the race riots of the early 1960s. (During the 1965 Watts riots in Los Angeles, thirty-four people died.)

The rioting began when a state court found four white police officers not guilty of charges that they used excessive force against a black motorist named Rodney King. King, who had been driving drunk, was chased for eight miles at 115 miles per hour. His passengers surrendered, but the 6' 4", 240-pound King knocked down two officers and continued resisting arrest. A bystander videotaped much of the scene, including an estimated fifty-six blows against King by officers wielding billy clubs and flashlights. The media aroused the anger of viewers by continually replaying segments of the beating.

The Los Angeles city police were unprepared for the havoc that followed the acquittals. Looting and murder spread through the inner city of Los Angeles, where gang and ethnic rivalries had been simmering for years. Motorists were pulled from their vehicles and killed by angry mobs. Bush promised to bring the officers to trial in federal court on charges of violating King's civil rights. (Two were convicted). The president and Congress also agreed to send more than $500 million in emergency aid. A jury later ordered the city of Los Angeles to pay King $3.8 million.

The 1990 Budget Deal and Economic Recession—The greatest concern among economists during the Reagan-Bush years was mounting national deficits. (A deficit is a shortage in the amount of tax money that the government makes each year in order to pay its expenses. The government creates a deficit when it spends more money than it makes in one year.) The inability of Congress and the White House to harness big spending led Bush to make the most disastrous decision of his career. Democratic leaders in Congress promised to cut spending if he would accept a large tax increase. So Bush abandoned his campaign pledge of "no new taxes." **The 1990 budget deal** did not tame the deficit, but it did ruin Bush's credibility.

Continued government spending, new taxes, and the high cost of regulations helped bring an end to the "Reagan Revolution." Even though the country enjoyed low interest rates, low inflation, and low gas prices, a recession gripped America (and the rest of the world). While Bush focused on foreign diplomacy after the breakup of the Soviet Union, Americans wanted action to help the slow economy at home. Not until his State of the Union Address in January of the election year did Bush outline his domestic policy. Although he borrowed many proposals from conservatives, his past practices did not match his new talk. His re-election campaign blamed Congress for the country's troubles and asked Americans to kick the Democrats out so that the Republicans could have a chance. He defended "family values" and attacked the character and "tax-and-spend" policies of his Democratic opponent, Bill Clinton. But voters did not listen to him.

SECTION REVIEW

1. What historical record was set with Bush's election?

2. Where did Chinese students hold a major protest? What was Bush's response to the demonstration?

3. What action caused the United States to declare war on Iraq?

4. Congressional scandals led to public support for laws that would do what?

5. The Los Angeles riots were in response to a trial surrounding the beating of what black motorist?

 Some conservatives argued that Bush did more harm than good to the cause of conservatives. Why would they say this?

SUMMARY

The United States entered its third century carrying a heavy load. The Watergate scandal had left the presidency weak. Growing national debt and inflation threatened the economy. The communists made advances in Southeast Asia and Latin America, and terrorists stalked the Middle East. But the election of Ronald Reagan marked the beginning of a new era of hope for America. While struggles continued between liberals and conservatives, it appeared that traditional values might take new root in America soil.

Chapter Review

People, Places, and Things to Remember

Bicentennial
Jimmy Carter
amnesty
deregulation
Three Mile Island
Panama Canal Treaty
Camp David Accords
Ayatollah Khomeini
Iranian hostage crisis
Ronald Reagan

supply-side economics
Sandra Day O'Connor
William H. Rehnquist
Star Wars
Mikhail Gorbachev
Muammar Qaddafi
Sandinistas
Contras
George Bush
Saddam Hussein

Persian Gulf War
term limits
Americans with
   Disabilities Act
unfunded federal man-
   dates
Los Angeles riots
1990 budget deal

Review Questions

Answer these questions.

1. What two bicentennial celebrations did America have during the 1970s and 1980s?

2. What was President Carter's greatest foreign relations triumph?

3. What two groups were fighting against each other in Nicaragua in the 1980s?

4. Who was the first woman appointed to the Supreme Court?

5. What was the most significant domestic crisis during the Bush administration?

Match these men with their descriptions.

6. Mikhail Gorbachev   a. Iranian Muslim ruler

7. Saddam Hussein   b. Libyan leader

8. Ayatollah Khomeini   c. Soviet leader

9. Muammar Qaddafi   d. Iraqi leader

10. William Rehnquist   e. chief justice appointed by Reagan

Indicate whether each of the following items is most closely associated with (A) President Ford, (B) President Carter, (C) President Reagan, or (D) President Bush.

11. pardon of Richard Nixon

12. Persian Gulf War

13. supply-side economics

14. Grenada invasion

15. Iranian hostage crisis

Questions for Discussion

16. Compare and contrast Reagan and Bush.

17. Should the United States have become involved in the Persian Gulf War? Would it have been better to remove Saddam Hussein from power?

30

Bridge to the 21st Century

Americans were expecting a rosy future after the death of communism in Europe. Yet the next few years severely tested the nation's ability to adjust to the new world. As events unfolded, Americans worried that moral corruption was eating away at the heart of the republic, posing a greater threat to the country than Soviet tanks ever had.

A New Face in Washington

The year 1992 came during a period of great transition in America. The Cold War had just ended. Around the world, socialists were in full retreat. Americans finally saw the fail-ure of Franklin D. Roosevelt's New Deal and Lyndon B. Johnson's War on Poverty. These ideas now looked dated and unsuited for the challenges of the twenty-first century.

The 1992 Election

The Democratic Party began searching for a way to break the party's liberal image after Ronald Reagan's landslide victories. Governor Bill Clinton of Arkansas and other young Democrats met to discuss new ideas in a forum called the **Democratic Leadership Council.** They got an opportunity to test their ideas in the election of 1992 when it became obvious that the "Reagan Revolution" had fallen apart under George Bush.

Bill Clinton won the Democratic Party's nomination in spite of incredible obstacles, including accusations of adultery, marijuana use, and draft dodging. Clinton hammered away at Bush's domestic policies, hoping to

Ross Perot (on the right) charmed audiences with his folksy humor during the three-way debates of the 1992 election.

draw attention away from his foreign successes. Daily the media reported the latest bad economic news. Clinton's campaign headquarters boldly stated his message: "It's the economy, stupid." He successfully portrayed

himself as a moderate "New Democrat" who wanted to change America.

Conservatives, led by columnist Pat Buchanan, also attacked Bush's mixed record. Bush apologized for breaking his "no new taxes" pledge in 1990, promising to fight taxes in the future. But he never convinced voters of his sincerity. Suspicious of both major candidates' promises to cut spending, a billionaire named **Ross Perot** entered the race as an independent candidate. He promised drastic measures to wipe out the deficit. Many voters turned to this outsider, who even took the lead temporarily in opinion polls.

On election day, Clinton won by a large margin in the electoral college (370 to 168), but he lacked deep support. Ross Perot gained the largest number of third-candidate votes since Teddy Roosevelt in 1912. Democrats won no seats in the Senate, and they lost nine in the House. Also, Clinton failed to attract a majority of the popular vote (43% Clinton, 37% Bush, 19% Perot). Democrats credited their win to Clinton's campaign skills and the country's anger against the "failed trickle-down policies of the 1980s"; Republicans blamed a weak economy, bad press, and Bush.

Controversial Nominations

Like his idol, John F. Kennedy, President Bill Clinton began his administration with grand (and sometimes contradictory) dreams, which he called a "New Covenant" with the American people. But like JFK, Clinton found himself mired in controversy and unable to push his programs through Congress.

Once elected, Bill Clinton had to choose between old liberal ideas or the new ideas of the Democratic Leadership Council. Clinton quickly made his decision. He decided to work with the old liberal establishment, and he began by nominating controversial liberals to government posts. Clinton said he wanted to

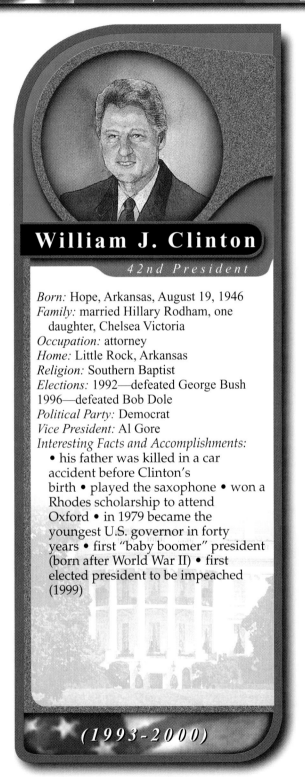

William J. Clinton

42nd President

Born: Hope, Arkansas, August 19, 1946
Family: married Hillary Rodham, one
  daughter, Chelsea Victoria
Occupation: attorney
Home: Little Rock, Arkansas
Religion: Southern Baptist
Elections: 1992—defeated George Bush
1996—defeated Bob Dole
Political Party: Democrat
Vice President: Al Gore
Interesting Facts and Accomplishments:
  • his father was killed in a car
  accident before Clinton's
  birth • played the saxophone • won a
  Rhodes scholarship to attend
  Oxford • in 1979 became the
  youngest U.S. governor in forty
  years • first "baby boomer" president
  (born after World War II) • first
  elected president to be impeached
  (1999)

(1993-2000)

create a diverse cabinet of women and minorities that reflected the mix in American society. But his liberal appointments contradicted this description. The only moderate in the cabinet was his treasury secretary.

Along with his efforts to include minorities and women in government, Clinton promised "to make a real effort to include in my administration members of the gay and lesbian community." In the first year he appointed almost thirty open homosexuals to key posts. Controversy over these and other nominations plagued Clinton throughout his first term in office.

Controversial New Social Policies

Clinton claimed that the 1992 election gave him a mandate (a command by the people) for change. However, his first acts as president were to promote social change, not economic change, and these acts caused an uproar that would not die down. Two days after assuming office he removed several limits that Reagan had placed on how government money was used to pay for abortions. Days later he kept a campaign promise to end a ban on homosexuals in the military. Such actions angered conservatives and distracted attention from his efforts to help the economy.

All of Clinton's cabinet members supported liberal social policies. His health secretary Donna Shalala was a prime example. One of her first actions was to push "children's rights." These so-called rights are laid out in the **UN Convention on the Rights of the Child,** a treaty passed in 1989 but never signed by the United States. It grants every child freedom of religion, freedom of association, the right to family planning (including abortion), the right to use his own language, and the right to have "rest and leisure." The administration made an intense effort to get the Senate to sign, but conservative Senators defeated this threat to the authority of parents.

The leading cheerleader for the president's social policies was his surgeon general, Dr. Joycelyn Elders. She was well known for her support of homosexuals and her attack on what she called the pro-life "love affair with the fetus." Elders used her office to promote controversial views, such as sex education beginning in kindergarten. In 1993 she even suggested that the government consider legalizing drugs to reduce violent crime. The president later fired Elders when her public statements became too embarrassing.

Clinton made two other appointments in his first year that showed his liberal priorities. The first was a feminist on the Supreme Court named Ruth Ginsburg, who opposed all limits on abortion. The second appointment was his attorney general, **Janet Reno,** the first woman ever to head the Justice Department. She believed crime could be solved if the government would help children to grow up in a good environment. In her view, the "war on crime" should emphasize social programs that prevent people from becoming criminals.

After taking office, Reno showed her liberal colors. Her first priority was to clamp down on pro-life sit-ins at abortion clinics. With her backing, Democrats in Congress passed the **Freedom of Access to Clinic Entrances** (FACE) law, making most abortion protests a federal crime.

A new controversy erupted soon after Reno's appointment. On February 28, 1993, the Bureau of Alcohol, Tobacco, and Firearms (ATF) raided a seventy-seven-acre compound in Waco, Texas, because it believed cult leader **David Koresh** was stockpiling illegal arms. The poorly organized raid failed, leaving four

agents dead. After a fifty-one-day standoff, Reno ordered tanks to break into the compound and spread tear gas. The compound went up in flames, killing Koresh and seventy-two of his followers. Conservatives ridiculed the handling of the initial raid and Reno's

The compound of cult leader David Koresh went up in flames when federal officials tried to force their way in.

decision to force a violent end to the standoff. Bitter over the ATF's actions, a radical named Timothy McVeigh marked the second anniversary of Koresh's death by bombing a federal office building in Oklahoma City. The huge blast killed 168 people.

Controversial New Programs

With Democrats controlling the White House and both houses of Congress, Clinton declared "an end to the deadlock and drift and a new season of American renewal." During the election, Clinton had set three priorities for the first one hundred days of his administration. First, he wanted a new budget that slashed spending and raised taxes only on the rich. Second, he wanted to reform welfare so that people went back to work after two years. Third, he wanted to reform the health care system to stop spiraling prices and to guarantee insurance for everyone. Clinton also made many side promises.

Higher Taxes—By the time of his inauguration, Clinton had already begun to backpedal on his pledges. When he finally presented his first budget, it called for new government programs, higher taxes for everyone, and few spending cuts (except in the military). Clinton proposed a record-breaking $496 billion increase in taxes. The budget barely passed Congress without a single Republican vote. This "deficit-reduction" plan did not reduce anything except the rate of growth of the national deficit. Government spending, along with taxes, grew significantly. Nevertheless, the president claimed a victory and moved on.

Bigger Government—During the election, Clinton preached against waste and inefficiency in government. But regulations grew rapidly under his leadership. Immediately after taking office, Clinton signed a backlog of big-government legislation that past Republican presidents had vetoed. The Family and Medical Leave Act forced businesses to give employees twelve weeks of unpaid leave to care for newborn babies or seriously ill family members. Another intrusive law was the Brady Bill. States had to complete background checks before customers could buy guns.

Clinton also took up the banner of the environmentalists. His secretary of the interior imposed stiff restrictions on the use of government lands in the West. To protect the threatened spotted owl in the Pacific Northwest, Clinton held a Forest Conference "to build a consensus on a balanced policy to preserve jobs and to protect the environ-

ment." His compromise literally shut down logging in federal forests, and thirty thousand loggers lost their jobs.

Clinton kept one of his most popular campaign pledges, designed to promote community service. Similar to Kennedy's Peace Corps, **AmeriCorps** offered federal money to stu-

Over one hundred thousand young people have served their communities through AmeriCorps.

dents who wished to work off their school bills through community service. In return for two years of full-time work, volunteers received $14,800 in living expenses, a $9,500 credit toward higher education, and free health care and child care benefits. Their hourly wage, excluding benefits, was $7.27. AmeriCorps "brought the taxpayer the $30,000 'volunteer,'" complained one senator.

Health-Care Disaster—The issue that proved to be the supreme test of President Clinton's ability to pass a liberal agenda was health-care reform. He set his wife, **Hillary Rodham Clinton,** over a task force to develop a plan. In November 1993 he introduced her massive 1,342-page plan to Congress.

Hillary Rodham Clinton's active involvement in politics defied the traditional role of the First Lady.

At first Americans were attracted by the promises of making insurance available to everyone at low costs. By January 1994, however, the national mood had shifted. The economy was booming, and the annual rise in medical costs had fallen. Support waned as taxpayers began to see how Clinton's plan would create a huge program, eventually costing more than Social Security.

In spite of growing opposition, the president refused to compromise. In the end no measures came to the floor for a vote.

SECTION REVIEW

1. What independent candidate won wide support during the 1992 election?

2. What did Clinton indicate would be his priority if elected?

3. List four women whom Clinton nominated for high office and their positions.

4. Who led President Clinton's task force on health care reform?

 What are the advantages and disadvantages of having health care paid for by the government?

The Republican Revolution of 1994

Clinton faced many problems in his first two years, but voters were most upset by his failure to meet his goals. Smoking and drug use were on the rise. Crime became so bad that it moved ahead of the economy as Americans' greatest concern. The country wanted action.

Contract with America

An outspoken Republican in the House named **Newt Gingrich** came up with a plan that he hoped would help his party win big in the 1994 midterm elections. Republicans in the House joined together to sign a **Contract with America,** promising to bring up ten pop-

Newt Gingrich, the first Republican Speaker of the House in forty years, actively sought support for his revolutionary ideas.

ular bills for a vote—if elected—in the first 100 days of the next Congress.

As the numbers came in on election night, analysts were astounded by the clear rebuff of the president. For the first time in forty years, voters handed control of the House over to the Republicans, by a comfortable margin of 230-204 (with one independent). The GOP also won control of the Senate (52-48) and most governorships.

First Hundred Days of the 104th Congress

The newly elected Republicans knew that voters wanted results. Gingrich, who was elected Speaker of the House, moved quickly to put his supporters in positions of power. By overlooking senior congressmen, he proved his dedication to renew Congress and to push through his conservative program.

Bob Dole, who became the majority leader in the Senate, was less dedicated to change. Like his colleagues in the Senate, Dole had not signed the Contract with

America, and he did not feel obligated to support it.

Realizing that his first actions would set the tone of the next two years, Gingrich began fulfilling the Contract on the very first day. In addition to the ten bills that it promised to bring up for a vote in the first hundred days, the Contract promised eight reforms in the way the House ran. After working fourteen hours on the first day, congressmen passed all eight of them. For example, one reform required Congress to obey the regulations that it had imposed on the rest of the nation.

The remainder of the first hundred days was no less hectic. Every one of the promised bills was brought to the floor for a vote. The three most important bills would have radically changed the balance of power established by the Constitution. Two were amendments to the Constitution. The **balanced budget amendment** would make Congress balance the budget by the year 2002, and the term limits amendment would limit congressmen to twelve years of office in each house of Congress. The third major bill instituted the **line-item veto.** It gave the president the right to cut individual items in the federal budget without approval from Congress.

The energy with which the House pushed the Contract was impressive. The line-item veto passed the House and Senate with ease. Term limits got a majority of votes, but not the two-thirds it needed. The balanced budget amendment passed in the House but failed in the Senate by only one vote. All of the other bills in the Contract passed the House in some form.

Budget Battles

The initial success of the House was mostly symbolic. The legislation still had to go to the Senate and receive the president's signature. The only bill that had become law was a restriction on future unfunded mandates. The greatest test of the Republican Congress was its effort to prepare a serious plan to balance the budget. Gingrich acknowledged that every other issue was secondary to his primary goal—to balance the budget by the year 2002.

The Uncompromising Freshman Class— The Republicans had no illusions about the battles that lay ahead. In the face of hostile media attacks, they would have to convince Americans to accept large cuts in government benefits and services. Yet the seventy-three members of the House freshman class felt up to the challenge.

In February 1995 the president unveiled a $1.6 trillion budget that—even Democratic leaders conceded—failed to make the tough choices needed to stop the rising deficit. To the world's amazement, the House drafted an alternative plan that would really balance the budget. As anticipated, Democrats condemned the Republicans as "extremists" who wanted to balance the budget on the backs of the aged and poor.

Two Train Wrecks—As the Republican spending bills (thirteen in all) began moving through Congress, Clinton started vetoing them. As the summer wore on without a budget agreement, the nation prepared for a "train wreck," or a **government shutdown.** Under the Constitution, the federal government can spend money only when Congress has approved it by law. If the government failed to pay its debts, it would wreak havoc on world finances. Both the president and Congress hoped that the other side would accept a compromise before the shutdown.

Despite the pressure, House freshmen would not give in. Either the president would accept a real balanced budget, or he would get no budget at all. As the train wreck loomed in November 1995, the Senate leaders flinched. They passed a "continuing resolution" that would keep the government running under the old budget. But the House demanded some cuts first, and the president vetoed the resolution. As a result, all "nonessential" government services, such as parks, shut down. For six days the treasury department juggled money to keep the government paying its bills, but it could not keep up for long.

The House finally agreed to a compromise, but not until the president signed a pledge to seek a serious balanced budget in seven years. But the president's next budget proved to be another sham. When the House rejected Clinton's budget, the government shut down again just before Christmas. Again the Senate, led by Republican Bob Dole, caved in. Outmaneuvered by moderates in their own party, Republicans in the House gave up. The Republican "revolution" never recovered from this blow. Republicans needed a Republican president to sign their revolution into law.

The Resignation of Newt Gingrich— Republican leaders took many hits from Democrats. House Speaker Newt Gingrich came under fire when he signed a $4.5-million book deal with a company that stood to benefit from a bill under debate in the House. Democrats also accused Gingrich of improperly using tax-deductible money to fund a college course he taught. The attacks weakened Gingrich's power as speaker. After the Republicans did poorly in the 1998 midterm elections, Gingrich stepped down, and no charismatic leaders rose up to take his place.

SECTION REVIEW

1. What did the Contract with America promise?

2. What were the three most important bills of the Contract? Name one that passed both the House and the Senate.

3. What was the result of the standoff between the House and Clinton over the budget?

 Why does the federal debt tend to grow, and why is reducing it so difficult?

Culture Wars

While politicians were arguing over balanced budgets and taxes, another set of issues was moving to the forefront of national concerns. For the first time since the Roaring Twenties, the economy was booming and the country faced no major foreign threats. Polls showed that the nation's concerns had shifted from the economy and foreign affairs to social issues, such as welfare reform, education standards, and juvenile crime.

Recognition of Moral Decline

Lifestyles changed rapidly in America during the Nineties. People had more time and money for play and recreation. Modern technology provided novel ways to fill time. Computers, compact discs, and cellular phones were commonplace by the end of the decade. Yet evidence was mounting that something was missing.

The decline in America's "traditional values" became a topic of national debate after Vice President Dan Quayle gave his famous "Murphy Brown speech" during the 1992 election campaign. In that speech, he blamed America's woes on its moral decline, symbolized by the television sitcom Murphy Brown, which glorified unwed mothers. At the time, the liberal media scoffed at him. But Americans started to reconsider their views.

Most Americans are pragmatists who care whether a system works, not about the philosophy behind it. Taxpayers could tolerate spending of their money on noble programs; however, they became angry when the programs did not work. Democrats had spent $3.5 trillion of taxpayers' money in their war on poverty, while the poor had grown poorer. Americans, who had spent 2 percent of their income on federal taxes in 1960, now spent 24 percent. "We're getting a very bad buy for our money," Gingrich concluded, and Americans seemed to agree.

Even the liberals acknowledged that thirty years of government spending had not produced the kind of country they had hoped for. Crime and poverty were up. Rap and rock music were increasingly violent. Television lost all sense of modesty. In 1993 two influential articles in the *Atlantic Monthly* and the *Wall Street Journal* blamed illegitimate births for ruining America. The percentage of illegitimate births had risen from 5 percent in 1960 to over 26 percent in 1990, and the numbers

The nation was shocked by the random violence on April 20, 1999, when two teens gunned down twelve fellow students and a teacher at Columbine High School in Littleton, Colorado.

kept getting worse. The articles argued that the breakup of the family led to most other social ills, such as poverty, crime, drugs, and even homelessness.

Proposed Solutions to Moral Decay

Now that everyone agreed about the existence of a problem, the debate shifted to understanding its cause and finding a solution.

Liberal Solutions—Many liberals, including Bill Clinton, sounded almost conservative in their proposals. They talked about the importance of "family," "community," and "traditional values." First lady Hillary Rodham Clinton even published a book on child rearing entitled *It Takes a Village*. The

title was taken from an old African proverb, "It takes a village to raise a child." But her views were, in fact, anything but conservative. **Communitarians** hold the old socialist idea that the whole community shares responsibility for the lives of its members. "How dare you believe you have the right to raise your children by yourself," said a leader in the Children's Defense Fund, a children's rights organization once headed by the first lady.

Communitarians believe that the answer to the culture wars is for governments and communities to promote love and acceptance of all minority groups—whether based on religion, ethnic background, lifestyle, or "sexual orientation." In their view, society will improve when people are free to discuss their beliefs openly and to make choices without fear of disapproval.

New Right Solutions—After abortion was legalized in 1973, a faction called the **New Right** began swelling the ranks of the Republican Party. Religious people from all denominations were worried that the government was defending and promoting wickedness. The New Right was credited with helping Ronald Reagan win the 1980 election. Members of the New Right believed that families, not the government or the "community," must solve America's moral decline. Indeed, this group attacked big government as a major cause of America's problems.

A leader of the New Right was **Rush Limbaugh.** Although the liberal media branded him as an extremist, his radio show attracted twenty million listeners each week. His first book, *The Way Things Ought to Be* (1992), was the most popular nonfiction book in over ten years, selling 4.5 million copies in its first year. Rush—as his listeners called him—attracted a large audience of "pocketbook conservatives" who were tired of the government taking their money and giving nothing in return. Although he supported some good positions, his pride, profanity, and sarcasm dismayed many Christians. He was concerned not so much with moral standards as with freedom to get rich without interference.

Solutions from the Religious Right—The conservative group that caused the most controversy was the **religious right,** comprised of various Christian leaders and organizations. This branch of the New Right believed that the country needed to return to traditional, "Judeo-Christian" values. The best-known organization in the

Promoting a no-nonsense conservative message, Rush Limbaugh became the most popular talk-show host in America.

1970s was the Moral Majority, headed by the Rev. Jerry Falwell. The religious right receded into the background after the election of Reagan in 1980, but it gained new strength when the party began looking for Reagan's successor. Pat Robertson, the Charismatic host of television's 700 Club, campaigned for president in 1988. Although he lost, he started a grassroots movement called the **Christian Coalition.** Members became heavily involved in politics, seeking to elect conservatives to local offices and school boards. They wanted to revitalize America from the ground up.

Evaluation of the Culture Wars—Most Bible-believing Christians agree on the cause of America's problems: Americans have rejected God's truth and cannot find a substitute. But Christians do not agree on the solution to the moral crisis.

Conservative Christians known as New Evangelicals believe that they need to join Roman Catholics and other Protestant groups to combat a common enemy—immorality and secular humanism. A rival group of Christians, known as Fundamentalists, offers an old-fashioned solution to society's problems. Like many of the nation's forefathers, they believe the nation's only hope is the salvation of souls by God's grace through faith in the Son of God, who shed His blood for man's sins. Fundamentalists are not seeking to restore "culture" or "tradition," which has changed throughout American history. They believe God's people should be salt and light in a sin-cursed world by proclaiming the truth of Scripture and by separating from sin (II Cor. 6:14-15).

Although most Fundamentalists believe voting is a civic duty, they oppose the view that it is their duty to join with false denominations against evil. Religious compromise harms the one institution that has the answers for America—the church. The effort of Evangelicals to influence politics has confused Americans about the true meaning of "Christian." The religious right advocates civic virtue and moral laws, whereas the Bible teaches that the letter of the law kills (II Cor. 3:6-17). Only the gospel brings life and true "liberty," as people are changed from the inside out.

Generation X

A generation is a group of people born and living around the same time. Because they share similar experiences, members of a generation are alike in many ways. You have already read about the youth of the Roaring Twenties. You also read about the Baby Boomers, the first generation born after World War II. But what of the generation after that? The Baby Boomers received so much attention that those who came after were nearly forgotten. As Boomers aged, however, people began wondering about the next generation. What were they like? How did they live? Suddenly, everyone was talking about this unknown group. Advertisers, not knowing how to describe them, borrowed the generic term "Generation X".

Generation X is made up of Americans who were born in the 1960s and the 1970s. The members of Generation X often were home alone. Mothers worked in increasing numbers, and divorce was on the rise. These children took part-time jobs in record numbers when they reached their teen years. They also had more schooling as a group than any previous generation. But when they entered the job force, they had trouble finding really good jobs. Faced with an uncertain job market and the prospect of supporting the large, aging Baby Boomer population, many Xers grew pessimistic about the future.

Generation X looked at society differently from the way their parents had. Their lonely childhood caused a craving for relationships. Wanting to make a difference for others, many volunteered for community service. They turned away from the pursuit of money; money was a means and not an end. At the same time, they liked the luxuries that money could buy. They lived at home longer and married later. Finally, they were the first generation to grow up with advanced technology, experiencing its blessings as well as its problems.

Most significantly, Generation X rejected absolute truth. No one could say he had the truth because truth was different for each person and situation. America became a land of diversity, not just of races and cultures but also of philosophies. Public schools taught that each new idea was acceptable. Tolerance was the theme of the day. People forgot that God's standards of right and wrong apply to everyone (Rom. 3:10-12), and the only way anyone will reach heaven is to trust in Jesus Christ alone (Acts 4:12).

Generation X enjoyed a series of activities that came to be known as extreme sports. Involving everything from skateboarding to skydiving, this new brand of sport tested the limits of human ability. Its fans saw extreme sports as a way to put adventure back into American life. But it also makes sense that people with few guidelines for their behavior and pessimism about the future would have little fear of risking their lives.

Even though you are technically not part of Generation X, maybe you can see some of its characteristics in your own generation. How would you describe your generation, and what do you think its members will be like in the future? Think about how you can reach your generation for Christ.

SECTION REVIEW

1. According to communitarians, who makes sure that children are brought up right?

2. What event in 1973 gave rise to the New Right?

3. Name a leading figure of the New Right.

4. What do Fundamentalists see as the only solution to society's problems?

 Should Fundamentalists join the Christian Coalition? Explain your answer.

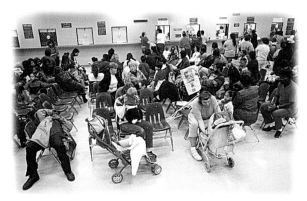
Welfare lines were cut in half soon after the passage of the Welfare Reform Act.

Confronting Society's Problems

After the budget battles of 1995, the Senate went to work on other bills, beginning with the House's Contract with America. The Senate approved the line-item veto, and the president signed the bill (although the Supreme Court later declared this law unconstitutional).

Congress passed some significant new legislation, too. The Telecommunications Bill deregulated the cable, telephone, and television industries. Republicans hoped the bill would spur new competition, cheaper rates, and the construction of a private "information superhighway." Another major overhaul of government regulations was the "Freedom to Farm Act." It phased out several New Deal programs that had paid farmers not to plant crops. Moderate Republicans joined Democrats to pass a bill raising the minimum wage from $4.25 to $5.15.

Welfare Reform

The Republican Congress also wanted to overhaul the federal government's welfare system. The president had already vetoed two bills. But to the surprise of conservatives and the dismay of liberals, he signed the **Welfare Reform Act** in 1995. For the first time since FDR's New Deal, the government rolled back its guarantee of financial aid for the poor. The law required welfare recipients to go back to work within two years, and it put a lifetime cap of five years for assistance. Rather than continuing to run the welfare system from Washington, the law gave states freedom to spend the money as they chose.

National Education Standards

After Clinton failed to take over the health care industry in 1993, he sought another cause to champion. He picked education. Costs kept going up, while student performance was going down. In his 1997 State of the Union Address he claimed, "My number one priority as president for the next four years is to insure that Americans have the best education in the

Home schools became increasingly popular during the 1990s.

world." He pushed for a long list of government programs to improve education.

Clinton's interest in education went back to his days as governor of Arkansas, when he helped produce Bush's Education 2000 proposal (see p. 619). After becoming president, Clinton signed a bill that he hoped would become a watershed in American history. The **Goals 2000**: Educate America Act established a new bureaucratic system that set "voluntary" standards that states must meet to receive federal funds.

Conservative Republicans believed that states and local communities should handle education and most other social issues, as they had been doing for hundreds of years. They argued that lack of money was not the problem, and more money was not the solution. The Republican Congress took out some parts of Goals 2000, but they feared to repeal it outright. In fact, yearly spending on Goals 2000 increased to over half a billion dollars.

Meanwhile, support grew for alternative solutions. One of the most popular ideas was **educational vouchers.** Instead of the government's deciding where students would attend school, the government would give parents vouchers (or scholarships) that they could "spend" at any school of their choice. But the leaders in public education fought the voucher system, calling it a threat to public schooling in America.

Efforts to Stop Social Evils

Republicans passed a series of bills on serious social issues. Perhaps the most significant was a ban on **partial birth abortions.** Even some feminists agreed that this cruel procedure went too far. (The doctor draws the baby's body out feet first, inserts an instrument into the base of its head, and suctions out the brain.) Sadly, President Clinton vetoed the bill in the name of "the right to choose."

Republicans passed a major bill on another issue of concern—homosexuality. Courts in Hawaii were attempting to legalize homosexual marriages in their state. If such marriages became legal, the Constitution would require all other states to recognize homosexual marriages. In response, Congress passed a bill limiting benefits, such as health insurance, to traditional marriages between men and women. The president publicly ridiculed the bill as "gay-baiting." But when it reached his desk, he quietly signed it late at night.

SECTION REVIEW

1. Name two acts of Congress that rolled back New Deal programs.

2. What law created "voluntary" standards for schools across America?

3. Name two social issues that revealed President Clinton's true liberal character.

 Are educational vouchers a good idea? Defend your answer.

Clinton's Trials

After the Democrats lost in the 1994 election, President Clinton began an all-out effort to raise money to win the next election. His party blanketed the nation with expensive television advertisements. During the campaign, Clinton spent more money on advertising than any other candidate in history had. But his reelection did not bring an end to his hardships.

The Never-Ending 1996 Campaign

Clinton ran a brilliant campaign. He stayed focused on a few important ideas, and he avoided any controversies. He presented himself as a New Democrat, again declaring, "The era of big government is over." Rather than presenting his own programs, he let others attack him on both sides—the liberals on the left and the "radical" Republicans on the right. He wanted Americans to see him as someone they could trust in the middle. Clinton took advantage of the president's "bully pulpit" to push small, popular reforms, such as recommending school uniforms and limits on teen smoking.

The Republicans' choice for president was Senate Majority Leader Bob Dole of Kansas—another pragmatist like George Bush. During his many years in the Senate, he had made friends around the country. His political connections made it easy for him to

Communications Technology

Communication became an obsession in the last part of the twentieth century. More people were exchanging more information at faster rates than ever before. Drivers took their phones with them in their cars. Important documents crossed the country instantly through fax machines. Cable and satellite subscribers had hundreds of television channels to watch. And people carried pagers for both business and personal use.

Possibly the greatest change in communications was the introduction of the Internet, a system that allows computers to share information over phone lines or cables. Government researchers developed the Internet in 1969 to connect computer scientists and engineers working on military projects. Large universities and research companies soon joined up. For several years, government and education kept the Internet to themselves, and the system was difficult to use. But two developments changed the Internet into an information highway for the entire nation.

The first development was the creation of tools for finding information. Regardless of how much data it held, the Internet would not be valuable without a practical way to look up a topic. Two tools helped organize the Internet. Browsers allowed users to view documents easily, and hypertext joined together documents on related topics through underlined words or phrases. (The researcher could use his mouse to click on one of the underlined portions and be taken to a document on that subject.)

The second development was a change of control. Though the government had developed the concept of the Internet, it gradually stepped back and let private companies take leadership. The Internet developed from a center for professional research and communication into a marketplace and a high-tech post office. Advertisements popped up along with information; consumers made on-line purchases with their credit cards (yearly sales were estimated to grow from $272 million in 1993 to $108 billion ten years later); and people from all over sent personal notes via e-mail or joined strangers in "chat room" discussions.

The Internet has become a growing part of American life, so Christians, like others, are trying to determine how to deal with it. They do not want to miss the opportunity to influence large numbers of people easily. At the same time the Internet can be dangerous. Large amounts of ungodly material confront the user (though tools to block objectionable sites are available), and Internet browsing can waste a great deal of time. So how should a Christian handle the Internet? Whether on the Internet or off, the key is to follow Ephesians 5:15-16: "See then that ye walk circumspectly, not as fools, but as wise, Redeeming the time, because the days are evil."

raise money and to win the Republican nomination. But he had several handicaps. He had a sharp tongue, he was old (over seventy), and he was unable to express a clear vision for America's future. Furthermore, Dole had offended conservatives in his own party by compromising during the budget battles.

For months, the media had predicted that Clinton would win by a landslide. But when the votes were finally tallied, he failed to win even a majority (receiving only 49 percent of the votes). Dole took 41 percent. Ross Perot, who again ran as an independent, got 8 percent. The races for Congress were close, but the Republicans held on to their majority.

Balanced Budget at Last?

Despite all of the accomplishments of the Republican Congress, their most basic need remained unchanged: balancing the budget.

After weeks of talks, the president and Congress hammered out a compromise. Unlike the revolutionary 104th Congress, the new congress did not propose to eliminate any major government programs or departments. In fact, spending for the Education Department jumped 34% in the first year of the new budget plan.

The booming economy made the budget deal possible. At the last moment, the Congressional Budget Office found $225 billion in unexpected money. The so-called budget deal spent more than if Congress had kept the old budget and never reached a deal!

In spite of the budget's shortcomings, it created a surplus in 1998, the first surplus in thirty years. This surplus was possible only because the government included income from Social Security taxes, although this money was supposed to be set aside to pay future retirement costs. The "surplus" completely changed the debates in Washington. No longer did representatives argue about spending cuts; the question became how to spend the extra money.

No End to Scandals

While President Clinton was busy trying to assure his place in history, a steady stream of scandals undermined his ability to lead the nation. Questions about his character had plagued him since before he became president. In 1992 he promised to appoint "the most ethical administration in the history of the Republic." But ethical questions hurt his party in the 1994 midterm elections and later in the 1996 campaign.

Scandals in the Cabinet—Three members of Clinton's cabinet came under criminal investigation during the first four years of Clinton's administration. Judges appointed an **independent counsel** in each case. (A "counsel" is a lawyer who gives legal advice or conducts a court case.) Democrats had created the first independent counsel during Nixon's Watergate scandal so that someone outside the administration could investigate wrongdoing within the administration.

Scandals in the White House—Clinton's past came back to haunt him in office. One scandal involved his past investment in a resort in northeastern Arkansas, called Whitewater Development Corporation. The **Whitewater scandal** was a complicated web of questionable relationships between politicians, law firms, and businessmen while Clinton was governor of Arkansas. As the investigation wore on, over a dozen people pleaded guilty to various crimes. The most

Instead of "Building a bridge to the twenty-first century," President Clinton left a legacy of scandal.

embarrassing confession came from Webster Hubbell, a former law partner with Hillary Clinton. The president had appointed Hubbell to a high position in the Justice Department. Unable to put the scandal behind him, Clinton asked the Justice Department to hire an independent counsel in 1994.

Another scandal hit the papers in the 1996 election season. The press learned that the White House had obtained confidential files from the FBI on hundreds of Republicans. The president called the incident an innocent mistake, but Filegate embarrassed the administration.

Campaign Finance Scandals—A whole new scandal began to pour out after the 1996 election. It involved the way Democrats—and the president in particular—had raised funds for the campaign.

The president had been consumed with raising money. Clinton knew that raising campaign money on government property was illegal. (This law was intended to keep people from bribing politicians.) Nevertheless, the Clintons and the Gores invited wealthy contributors to over a hundred "coffees" at the White House, and they opened the Lincoln Room for overnight stays.

The public was deeply troubled by reports that some of the campaign money had come illegally from foreigners in Asia who were trying to influence votes. The Democratic Party promised to send back over $1.5 million from questionable sources, but the party did not even know where to send some of the money. One of the money raisers, John Huang, later told investigators that Communist China had contributed to the president's campaign indirectly through Asian companies. The Clinton administration was further embarrassed by reports that China had acquired American computer and missile technology which it was using to develop long-range nuclear missiles.

Impeachment of the President

The scandal that led to the impeachment of President Clinton came from an unexpected source. A former beauty queen from Arkansas, Paula Jones, sued him in 1994 for sexual harassment—and she had witnesses. The president raised over a million dollars for a "legal defense fund," and he used the money to delay the case until after his 1996 reelection. He appealed to the Supreme Court, claiming that his duties as president gave him special privileges to avoid such trials while in office. But he lost his appeal in 1997.

The trial attracted much publicity. Defense attorneys called many witnesses to testify about the president's character. The case took an unexpected turn when a young woman named Monica Lewinsky appeared. At first she claimed under oath that she had committed no immoral acts with the president. Secret audio tape recordings by a friend of Lewinsky later showed that she had lied and was covering up. President Clinton himself appeared on national television waving his finger at the camera and declaring his innocence.

A judge eventually dismissed the Jones case, but not before the damage had been done. **Kenneth Starr,** the independent counsel investigating the Whitewater scandal, received court approval to investigate the president's part in lying to the grand jury and the attempted cover-up. The president refused to admit any wrongdoing, and he made every legal effort to block Starr's investigation. For nine months he kept up the lies, deceiving his cabinet and his friends, as well as the American people. The president's denials forced Starr to dig deeper into embarrassing, personal details. Finally, after great expense and time, Starr uncovered undeniable evidence that contradicted the president's version of the story. Starr sent his evidence to the House, listing thirteen impeachable offenses.

Four articles of impeachment came to the floor of the House for a vote on December 19, 1998, and two passed. The two articles claimed that the president had committed perjury (lied before a court) and had obstructed justice (hidden evidence from a court). President Clinton became only the second president ever impeached.

The Senate then heard the case for the removal of the president from office. When it came time to cast votes, not one Democrat voted in favor of the articles of impeachment. Robert Byrd, a respected senator from West Virginia, admitted on television that the evidence was clear, but he voted against conviction anyway. The Democrats argued that removal from office was too extreme a punishment. Several "moderate" Republican senators voted with the Democrats, too. But the vast majority of Republicans voted for conviction, even though most Americans were against them and the vote might hurt their party. The number of senators voting in favor of conviction fell below even a simple majority of 50. (The Constitution requires a two-thirds majority—67 of 100—to remove the president from office.)

Polls showed that 70 percent of Americans approved of the president's performance, a higher rating than President Reagan ever received. Polls also showed that respect for his character had fallen lower than respect for Nixon's had at any time during the Watergate scandal. Americans apparently did not care that the president broke the law, violated his sacred marriage vows, took advantage of a twenty-one-year-old employee, and lied repeatedly, as long as the economy was performing well. Conservatives in the New Right lamented the "collapse of

American civilization." President Clinton had promised a "bridge to the twenty-first century," but his actions raised questions as to whether he was instead leading the American republic to its destruction.

SECTION REVIEW

1. What strategy did President Clinton use to win the 1996 election?
2. What scandal involved Bill Clinton's business investment in northeastern Arkansas?
3. What independent counsel presented evidence for Clinton's impeachment?
4. On what two counts was President Clinton impeached?

 Why do you think so many people supported Clinton during his scandals?

Foreign Policy in the 21st Century

"Character doesn't matter," boasted Clinton's defenders. But in foreign affairs, America soon saw how much character really does matter. Bad judgment can threaten peace around the world, bringing a quick end to the nation's prosperity and balanced budgets. Clinton's lack of character ended up aiding America's potential enemies, offending America's allies, and destabilizing the world. In the view of many analysts, President Clinton failed to follow a clear set of principles to guide his foreign policy. He made quick decisions as emergencies arose, rather than taking preventative measures.

The president was fortunate to avoid several potential disasters in his first term. He hoped to shine during his second term. He selected a whole new team of foreign advisors after several cabinet members quit. **Madeleine Albright,** the first

Secretary of State Madeleine Albright

woman to serve as secretary of state, made an aggressive effort to solve the world's problems with the help of the U.S. military.

Battling the Military

Having avoided the draft and joined demonstrations against the Vietnam War in his youth, Clinton faced a difficult task earning the respect of the military. Yet his first act as commander in chief—to end the ban on homosexuals—angered generals and privates alike. His second act was to speed up the reduction in the size of the military. He hoped that improved efficiency would enable a smaller army to continue its preparedness for two wars at once. His layoffs, wage freezes, base closures, and homosexual policy caused a mass exodus of good soldiers. Poor planning in foreign actions—along with the unnecessary deaths of servicemen—discouraged new recruits.

Dealing Softly with Communists

When Clinton assumed office, communism appeared to be in its death throes. Only four countries remained under its shadow. But by failing to adopt a clear policy toward

Bill Clinton often met with Boris Yeltsin of Russia to discuss the future of democracy in Russia.

regions once dominated by communism, the president allowed a host of new dangers to take root.

Resurgence of Communist China—After the fall of the Soviet Union, Mainland China became the dominant communist power in the world. During the 1992 election campaign,

Shanghai became a prosperous port city after China's communist leaders opened the door to free enterprise.

Clinton attacked Bush for keeping the Most Favored Nation (MFN) trade status with China despite its human rights abuses at Tiananmen Square. Though China openly increased its abuses against Christians and dissenters, Clinton renewed MFN status anyway. He said he feared that American businesses might lose a chance to get rich in one of the world's fastest growing markets.

In the meantime, China continued a massive buildup of arms and began to make threatening gestures toward America's friends in the Far East. One of the touchiest issues was the status of Taiwan, which China considered a rebel province. Clinton responded with a policy of "strategic ambiguity," unlike in the past, when the United States had made plain its intention to protect its trading partner with force, if necessary.

The NATO Alliance

Current Members
(also includes the U.S., Canada, and Iceland)

New Members in 1998

Possible Future Members

Nuclear Threat in North Korea—Communist North Korea was another embarrassment. In 1993 it threatened to withdraw from the **Non-Proliferation of Nuclear Weapons Treaty (NPT).** Under this treaty, the five nations with nuclear weapons agreed to prevent any new countries from developing or buying nuclear weapons. The other nations of the world agreed to this treaty only so long as they felt relatively safe. But the development of a nuclear bomb in North Korea could touch off a nuclear arms race in Southeast Asia with deadly results. American allies begged for a tough stance, but Clinton was more casual. He eventually agreed to help North Korea build two nuclear power plants if it promised to stop trying to make nuclear weapons. Unfortunately, the delay gave the communists extra time to collect material to build nuclear weapons without any guarantee that

the weapons program had stopped.

The NPT, first signed in 1968, came up for renewal in 1995. Fearing a new arms race, President Clinton convinced many countries to make the treaty permanent. In return, the five declared nuclear powers—Russia, the United States, China, Britain, and France— promised to work harder to reduce their stockpiles. But some of the most dangerous countries in the world, such as Iran and Pakistan, refused to sign.

Expanding NATO into Eastern Europe—Clinton also failed to develop a consistent approach toward the formerly communist countries of Eastern Europe and the former Soviet Union. He almost blindly put his support behind the Russian reformer Boris Yeltsin. When Yeltsin used Russian troops to force his will on the former republics, Clinton remained silent.

The countries of Eastern Europe, who feared new Russian aggression, looked to the West for help. The expansion of NATO remained a touchy issue. Russian nationalists hated the thought of NATO troops at their doorstep. After years of talks, Russia signed a historic agreement in 1997 that gave it a voice in NATO in return for allowing Eastern European nations to join. In 1999 three new members joined NATO—Poland, the Czech Republic, and Hungary.

The radical changes in the NATO alliance took place without public debate at home. The shift in policy raised grave concerns. Would NATO be able to respond to local wars? What if dictators rose to power within the alliance itself? One of the new NATO members—Hungary—did not even share a border with the rest of the NATO alliance.

Working with the United Nations

When he took office, Clinton wanted the United Nations (UN) to become the policeman of the world. He adopted a policy of **multilateralism**—listening to many nations before making decisions that every side can agree on. Conservative Republicans accused him of shirking his responsibilities. They preferred a policy of unilateralism—making decisions alone in America's clear national interest. With so many conflicting voices, the UN proved that it could not take timely action. Events showed the world just how ineffective the UN-U.S. alliance was.

Somalia—The first failure occurred in the famine-stricken African country of Somalia. Without public approval, President Bush had sent American troops to Somalia in December 1992 to help the UN protect aid shipments and to restore order. When the UN decided to disarm the warring factions, the most powerful "warlord," General Aidid, fought back. As the killing of UN troops mounted, the UN and the United States began a fruitless effort to capture Aidid. Chief of Staff Colin Powell requested tanks and heavy armament to protect his troops, but Secretary of Defense Les Aspin turned him down, fearing that this move would be too provocative. Clinton eventually sent army specialists called Rangers to track Aidid down. But Americans watched in horror as Somalians shot down a helicopter, captured the pilot, and dragged a soldier's body through the streets. The failed raid cost eighteen lives. As a result, Clinton ordered the withdrawal of American forces from the country.

Haiti—Watching the catastrophe in Somalia were other rogue leaders of the world.

Among them was a military regime in the poverty-stricken Caribbean island of Haiti. Haiti's military leaders decided to back out of negotiations to reinstate President **Jean-Bertrand Aristide,** whom they had overthrown in a 1991 coup. For a year Clinton blustered about armed intervention if the military rulers refused to return to negotiations.

In the fall of 1994 Clinton ordered an invasion. He appeared on television to defend his decision, condemning the murderous "thugs" who had established the "most violent regime in our hemisphere." Even as the warplanes were in the air, however, Clinton allowed a three-man team to negotiate with the head of these murderers, Lt. Gen. Raoul Cedras. The negotiators—which included former president Jimmy Carter—convinced Cedras to accept generous terms of resignation. The U.S. even paid the general $10,000 per month in return for the use of his home and other buildings in Haiti. Later when American troops handed the mission over to the UN, Clinton declared the mission a "remarkable success." After an operation that cost more than $1 billion however, Haiti remained a bloody, poverty-stricken land.

Civil War in Former Yugoslavia—After the end of the Cold War, the most explosive region in the world was the Balkan Peninsula in Eastern Europe. The former Communist country of Yugoslavia, which consisted of a complex variety of competing ethnic groups, broke up into five countries. A bitter civil war erupted in 1992 in Bosnia, one of the former republics of Yugoslavia. Three ethnic groups—Muslims, Serbs, and Croats—savagely fought each other in a three-way war. The UN sent in 23,000 "peacekeeping" troops, but they were powerless to stop the bloodshed. George Bush, who was president at the time, refused to involve American troops. During the 1992 election campaign,

Clinton ridiculed him for not taking action to stop the "ethnic cleansing," or systematic murder of ethnic minorities. But Clinton softened his stance after he became president. For the next three years Clinton shifted back and forth between threatening to bomb and silence.

Meanwhile, American advisors secretly trained Croatian troops. These troops launched a surprise attack in 1995 that drove

Bombed-out homes were a common sight after the violent breakup of Yugoslavia.

out the Serbs living in the eastern part of Croatia and threatened the Serbs living in Bosnia. Clinton finally decided to send U.S. jets to bomb the Serbs. Now the Serbs were ready to come to the peace table. In November 1995 President Clinton invited the warring factions to meet at a military base in Dayton, Ohio. To encourage the peace negotiations, he promised to send 20,000 American troops to Bosnia to keep the peace.

The warring leaders signed the **Dayton Accords,** and an uneasy peace settled over the Balkan Peninsula. But the accords had many embarrassing flaws. The new "unified" government in Bosnia would have two separate armies, two legislatures, and two courts. To avoid criticism, President Clinton promised that the troops would stay only "about one year." Four years later they were still there.

Air War in Kosovo—In fact, Clinton increased U.S. commitments in the Balkan region. When rebels took up arms in Yugoslavia's southern province of Kosovo, the president demanded that Yugoslavia make peace with them or suffer the wrath of NATO bombs. When the Yugoslav government refused to back down, the president sent warplanes and cruise missiles to bomb the country. It was the first time NATO had ever attacked a sovereign nation. After over fifty days of bombing, the Yugoslav leader caved in. But by then, Serb attacks had forced approximately one million Kosovars from their homes. The U.S. military had yet another costly "peace" to enforce.

Increasing World Trade

Clinton claimed two major successes in foreign trade. One was the passage of an agreement with Mexico and Canada, called the North American Free Trade Agreement (**NAFTA**). During the election, Clinton ridiculed the free trade agreement signed by Bush and the other heads of state. But after taking office, he decided to support NAFTA if it included labor and environmental guarantees. With strong Republican support, Congress passed NAFTA late in 1993.

The president's other success in world trade was the passage of the eighth round of GATT (General Agreement on Tariffs and Trade). After World War II, the nations of the world held seven "rounds" of negotiations to make trade easier. By 1990, tariffs (taxes on trade) had fallen from 40 to 5 percent, and the volume of world trade had exploded. An eighth round of talks in Uruguay, begun in 1987, sought to reduce tariffs by another third. It also addressed unfair trade practices. But the nations could not come to an agreement. Clinton changed the basic purpose of the agreement, as he had done with NAFTA, to include new environmental standards and a

World trade reached record levels in the 1990s.

large bureaucracy. The member nations finally approved a permanent **World Trade Organization** (WTO) in 1994 to enforce GATT. Ironically, Clinton had changed free trade into "managed free trade" under international bureaucrats.

SECTION REVIEW

1. Who was the first woman to serve as secretary of state?
2. Name two Communist countries in Asia with which President Clinton failed to deal firmly. What threat did each of them pose to the United States?
3. What three new members joined NATO in 1999? What danger did this expansion of NATO pose to the United States?
4. What three ethnic groups fought each other in Bosnia? What peace agreement tried to calm the conflict?
5. What two successes did Clinton claim in foreign trade?

 In Clinton's view, what role should the UN and NATO play in promoting peace in the post–Cold War era? Do you agree with him?

SUMMARY

The end of the Cold War brought a sigh of relief to all nations. The people of the United States hoped the country would enter a new century of peace and unprecedented prosperity. But their election of President Clinton proved that prosperity requires much more than the right laws. The people need to honor righteousness, and their leaders need to be men of good character. The future success of America remained in question as the twenty-first century dawned.

Chapter Review

People, Places, and Things to Remember

Democratic Leadership
  Council
Bill Clinton
Ross Perot
UN Convention on the
  Rights of the Child
Janet Reno
Freedom of Access to
  Clinic Entrances
David Koresh
AmeriCorps
Hillary Rodham Clinton
Newt Gingrich

Contract with America
balanced budget amend-
  ment
line-item veto
government shutdown
communitarians
New Right
Rush Limbaugh
religious right
Christian Coalition
Welfare Reform Act
Goals 2000
educational vouchers

partial birth abortions
independent counsel
Whitewater scandal
Kenneth Starr
Madeleine Albright
Non-Proliferation of
  Nuclear Weapons
  Treaty (NPT)
multilateralism
Jean-Bertrand Aristide
Dayton Accords
NAFTA
World Trade Organization

Review Questions

Identify each of the following people.

1. This independent counsel presented evidence for impeaching Bill Clinton.

2. This was the first woman to serve as secretary of state.

3. This man became speaker of the House after Republicans took control in the 1994 elections.

4. This independent presidential candidate promised serious measures to fix the economy.

5. This conservative broadcaster gained a large following through his radio show and books.

Match these terms to their definitions.

6. consulting many nations about decisions

7. power to cut individual budget items

8. lawyer who investigates government corruption

a. independent counsel

b. line-item veto

c. multilateralism

Answer these questions.

9. What was the 1994 Republican campaign promise to take prompt action on popular legislation?

10. What peace agreement was signed by parties fighting over Bosnia?

11. What was President Clinton's solution to America's education problems?

12. What was the grassroots political movement of the religious right?

13. What organization was created to enforce fair trade practices?

Questions for Discussion

14. Is America a Christian nation? Explain your answer.

15. Should governments attempt to "legislate morality"? Why or why not?

WASHINGTON
Olympia •
▲ Mt. Rainier
▲ Mt. St. Helens
• Salem

OREGON

Columbia R.

• Helena
MONTANA

NORTH DAKOTA
• Bismarck

IDAHO
• Boise

Badlands

SOUTH DAKOTA
• Pierre

Black
Hills

WYOMING

NEVADA

Carson City •
Salt Lake City •
• Cheyenne
Platte River

NEBRASKA

Sacramento •

Sierra Nevada

UTAH

Rocky Mountains

• Denver

▲ Pikes Peak

COLORADO

KANSAS

Lincoln •

Topeka •

Arkansas River

CALIFORNIA

Colorado R.

Grand
Canyon

ARIZONA

Santa Fe •

NEW MEXICO

OKLAHOMA

Oklahoma City •

PACIFIC
OCEAN

• Phoenix

Red River

Rio Grande

TEXAS

• Honolulu

HAWAII

same scale as large map

Yukon River

ALASKA

Austin •

• Juneau

0 100 200 300 400 500

scale in miles

Lake Superior

MICHIGAN

Lake Huron

Lake Michigan

MAINE

•Augusta

Green Mtns.

White Mts.

•Montpelier

NEW HAMPSHIRE

Concord• VERMONT

L. Ontario

Albany• Boston• MASSACHUSETTS

NEW YORK

Providence• RHODE ISLAND

Hartford• CONNECTICUT

Lake Erie

•Trenton

NEW JERSEY

PENNSYLVANIA

Harrisburg•

•Dover DELAWARE

Annapolis•

MARYLAND

SOTA

OWA

s Moines

aul•

WISCONSIN

Madison•

Lansing•

OHIO

INDIANA

Columbus•

ILLINOIS

Indianapolis•

Springfield•

Charleston• WEST

Ohio River

VIRGINIA

Washington, D.C.

Richmond•

Jefferson City•

Frankfort•

KENTUCKY

VIRGINIA

MISSOURI

Appalachian Mountains

Raleigh•

Mississippi River

Nashville•

Great Smoky Mts.

ARKANSAS

NORTH CAROLINA

TENNESSEE

Little Rock•

SOUTH

•Columbia

Atlanta• CAROLINA

Montgomery•

GEORGIA

Jackson• ALABAMA

MISSISSIPPI

Baton Rouge•

LOUISIANA

•Tallahassee

GULF OF MEXICO

FLORIDA

ATLANTIC
OCEAN

N
W   E
S

FEET

12,000

9,000

5,000

2,000
1,000
500
0

0   100   200   300   400   500

scale in miles

647

ARCTIC OCEAN

BEAUFORT SEA

Baffin Bay

GREENLAND

ICELAND

BERING SEA

Hudson Bay

LABRADOR SEA

Gulf of Alaska

CANADA

IRELAND

ENG

NORTH ATLANTIC OCEAN

NORTH PACIFIC OCEAN

UNITED STATES OF AMERICA

PORTUGAL

SPA

MOROCCO

CANARY ISLANDS

Gulf of Mexico

MEXICO

THE BAHAMAS

CUBA

HAITI DOM. REP.

WESTERN
SAHARA

MAURITANIA

MA

BELIZE

JAMAICA

GUATEMALA

HONDURAS

CARIBBEAN SEA

SENEGAL

GAMBIA

EL SALVADOR

NICARAGUA

GUINEA BISSAU

GUINEA

BUR
FA

COSTA RICA

PANAMA

VENEZUELA

GUYANA

SIERRA LEONE

COTE
D'IVOIRE

COLOMBIA

SURINAME

FRENCH GUIANA

LIBERIA

GHANA

ECUADOR

PERU

BRAZIL

BOLIVIA

PARAGUAY

ARGENTINA

URUGUAY

SOUTH PACIFIC OCEAN

CHILE

FALKLAND ISLANDS

SOUTH GEORGIA ISLAND

648

NEGIAN
EA

SWEDEN FINLAND
ESTONIA
LATVIA
LITHUANIA
RK
BELARUS
MANY POLAND
CZECH
SLOVAKIA UKRAINE
AUSTRIA HUNGARY MOLDOVA
CROATIA ROMANIA
BOSNIA YUGO BULGARIA BLACK SEA
ITALY GREECE TURKEY
ALBANIA
UNISIA
MEDITERRANEAN
SEA
CYPRUS SYRIA
LEBANON
ISRAEL
JORDAN
IRAQ
IRAN
KUWAIT
QATAR
U.A.E.
LIBYA EGYPT SAUDI ARABIA
RED
SEA
OMAN
GER CHAD
ERITREA YEMEN
RIA SUDAN DJIBOUTI
SOMALIA
CENTRAL AFRICAN ETHIOPIA
REPUBLIC
CAMEROON UGANDA
GABON RWANDA KENYA
CONGO DEMOCRATIC BURUNDI
REPUBLIC
OF CONGO TANZANIA

RUSSIA

SEA OF OKHOTSK

KAZAKHSTAN
ARAL
SEA
CASPIAN
SEA
UZBEKISTAN KYRGYZSTAN
GEORGIA
ARMENIA AZERBAIJAN
TURKMENISTAN
TAJIKISTAN

MONGOLIA

SEA OF
JAPAN
NORTH KOREA
SOUTH KOREA JAPAN

AFGHANISTAN
CHINA
EAST
CHINA SEA
NORTH PACIFIC OCEAN

PAKISTAN
NEPAL
BHUTAN
Gulf of Oman
INDIA
TAIWAN
ARABIAN SEA
MYANMAR LAOS
BANGLADESH
SOUTH
CHINA SEA
PHILIPPINE SEA
THAILAND
Gulf of Aden
ANDAMAN
SEA
CAMBODIA
PHILIPPINES
SRI LANKA
Gulf
of
Thailand VIETNAM
BRUNEI
MALAYSIA

INDONESIA
JAVA SEA
PAPUA
NEW GUINEA
ANGOLA
ZAMBIA MOZAMBIQUE
ZIMBABWE MADAGASCAR
NAMIBIA MALAWI
BOTSWANA
SWAZILAND
SOUTH AFRICA LESOTHO

INDIAN OCEAN

ARAFURA SEA
TIMOR SEA
Gulf of
Carpentaria
CORAL SEA

NEW CALEDONIA

AUSTRALIA

Great
Australian
Bight
TASMAN SEA

NEW ZEALAND

ANTARCTICA

649

Index

Photo Credits

The following agencies and individuals have furnished materials to meet the photographic needs of this textbook. We wish to express our gratitude to them for their important contribution.

ADN-Zentralbild
Suzanne R. Altizer
American Red Cross
Architect of the Capitol
Agence France Presse (AFP)
Associated Press
Chessie System
Kindra Clineff
George R. Collins
Colonial Williamsburg Foundation
Corbis-Bettmann
Corel Corporation
Cumberland Gap National Historical Park
Department of State, U.S.A.
Digital Stock
Dover Publications, Inc.
Thomas DuRant
Eastman Chemicals Division
Michael Evans
Gene Fisher
Ford Motor Company
Franklin D. Roosevelt Library
Richard Frear
Kenneth Frederick
George Bush Presidential Library
George Bush Presidential Materials Project
GeoSystems Global Corporation
The Gingrich Group
Harpers Ferry Center
Harry S. Truman Library
Historical Documents Company
Imperial War Museum
Jimmy Carter Library

John F. Kennedy Library
Brian D. Johnson
Tim Keesee
W.S. Keller
Reed Kelley
Jack Kightlinger
Bob Krist
Library of Congress
Lyndon Baines Johnson Library
Mr. & Mrs. Albert Maghan
Fred Mang, Jr.
Robert Matthews
Metropolitan Museum of Art, New York
J. Strider Moler
Montana Department of Commerce
Mt. Vernon Ladies Association
Museum of the City of New York
National Aeronautics & Space Administration (NASA)
National Archives
National Cotton Council of America
National Park Service (NPS)
New York Convention and Visitors Bureau (NYCVB)
New York Public Library
New York State Department of Commerce
North Carolina Division of Tourism, Film & Sports Development
Oregon Economic Development Department
Argyle Paddock
Pana-View Slides
Pennsylvania Division of Travel Marketing

Pennsylvania Historical Museum and Commission
Philadelphia Convention & Visitors Bureau
Photo Disc, Inc.
Premiere Radio Networks
Princeton University
Puerto Rico Tourism
Wade Ramsey
Ed Richards
Abbie Rowe
Phyllis Schlafly
South Carolina Department of Parks, Recreation & Tourism
Pete Souza
Tennessee Tourist Development
Texas Tourist Development Agency
Brad Trent
Peter Turnley
Unicorn Stock Photo
Union Pacific Railroad
United Press International (UPI)
United States Air Force
United States Capitol Art Collection
United States Marine Corps
Unusual Films
Virginia Tourism Corporation
The White House
Woolaroc Museum, Bartlesville, Oklahoma
www.arttoday.com
Young Americans Foundation
Zion National Park, Utah

Cover/Title Page Collage
Digital Stock (Statue of Liberty), (Chrysler Building); Eastman Chemicals Division (Ronald Reagan); Library of Congress (Robert E. Lee), (planes); NASA (astronaut); National Archives (Iwo Jima), (Sitting Bull, covered wagon); Photo Disc, Inc. (internet), (space shuttle, Mount Rushmore); United States Air Force (atomic bomb); United States Capitol Art Collection (Surrender of Lord Cornwallis); Unusual Films (ship); www.arttoday.com (duel, Frederick Douglass)

Pronunciation Guide & Introduction Page
Digital Stock (backgrounds)

Unit 1 Opener
Library of Congress x(top), xi(top); United States Capitol Art Collection x-xi

Chapter 1
Digital Stock 2; Argyle Paddock 3; Library of Congress 4; Photo Disc, Inc. 6; Unusual Films 8; George R. Collins 10, 11(both)

Chapter 2
NPS, photo by Richard Frear 14; Unusual Films 15; Corel Corporation 17; George R. Collins 19, 20(both), 21, 29(top), 31(top); Rare Book Division, New York Public Library 27(left); Library of Congress 27(right), 28; Wade Ramsey 29(bottom)

Chapter 3
Unusual Films 34; Dover Publications, Inc. 36; Pennsylvania Division of Travel Marketing 37; George R. Collins 39(top), 40; NPS, photo by Richard Frear 39(bottom); Wade Ramsey 41, 45; Virginia Tourism Corporation 42, 44; Colonial Williamsburg Foundation 43

The Northeast
Photo Disc, Inc. 51(all); ©1998 GeoSystems Global Corporation 51(map)

Chapter 4
Wade Ramsey 52, 68(bottom); Dover Publications, Inc. 53, 64; Gene Fisher 55(both); George R. Collins 56, 67, 68(top); Library of Congress 58, 65; Princeton University, photo by Robert Matthews 60; Unusual Films 63, 70

Chapter 5
George R. Collins 74, 89, 90; Library of Congress 77(both), 78, 82, 83, 85(both); National Archives 87; Photo Disc, Inc. 88

Unit 2 Opener
Unusual Films 92-93(Constitution); United States Capitol Art Collection 92-93(Surrender of Lord Cornwallis); Mt. Vernon Ladies Association 93(top)

Chapter 6

NPS, photo by Richard Frear 95, 103, 104; www.arttoday.com 96, 98, 102, 105; George R. Collins 97; Architect of the Capitol 99; Metropolitan Museum of Art, New York 101; National Archives 107; U.S. Capitol Art Collection 109

Chapter 7
George R. Collins 112; ©1995 Historical Documents Company 118; National Archives 120; Digital Stock 121; Architect of the Capitol 122; Library of Congress 123, 124; www.arttoday.com 128; Mt. Vernon Ladies Association 130

Chapter 8
Unusual Films 133; NPS, photo by Richard Frear 141; Architect of the Capitol 146; Photo Disc, Inc. 148, 152, 156, 158, 167; Digital Stock 150, 160, 164; Library of Congress 162

Chapter 9
NPS, photo by Richard Frear 170; Digital Stock 171, 185(backgrounds); Virginia Tourism Corporation 175; www.arttoday.com 176, 178, 179, 180(inset), 182; National Archives 177; Photo Disc, Inc. 180, 188; Library of Congress 181, 186, 187, 189; ©1999 Kindra Clineff 183

Unit 3 Opener
Chessie System 192(top); George R. Collins 192(bottom); Library of Congress 193(both)

Chapter 10
NPS, Harpers Ferry Center 195, 212; Digital Stock 196, 206(backgrounds); www.arttoday.com 199(both), 203; Oregon Economic Development Department 201; NPS, photo by J. Strider Moler 204, photo by Richard Frear 210(left); Virginia Tourism Corporation 207(top); Library of Congress 207(bottom); George R. Collins 210(right); National Archives 213

The Midwest
Photo Disc, Inc. 217(all); ©1998 GeoSystems Global Corporation 217(map)

Chapter 11
Unusual Films 218; Digital Stock 219, 227(backgrounds); Dover Publications, Inc. 220; Library of Congress 222, 228(background), 229; ©1999 Kindra Clineff 228(top); Photo Disc, Inc. 230

Chapter 12
Tennessee Tourist Development 234; Digital Stock 235, 246, 248, 249(backgrounds); Woolaroc Museum, Bartlesville, Oklahoma 237; Library of Congress 241, 242; www.arttoday.com 243; Philadelphia Convention & Visitors Bureau 244

Chapter 13
Library of Congress 254, 260, 267(both); Corel Corporation 256(left); Cumberland Gap National Historical Park 256(right); National Archives 259; New York State Department of Commerce 262; Chessie System 265; Unusual Films, courtesy of Tim Keesee 266

Chapter 14
Pana-View Slides 269; Corel Corporation 270; National Cotton Council of America 271; Library of Congress 273, 276, 281; www.arttoday.com 278; Unusual Films 280

Chapter 15
Zion National Park, Utah, photo by Reed Kelley 284; National Archives 286, 288(right); Kenneth Frederick 288(left); Corel Corporation 289; George R. Collins 292; Library of Congress 293, 296; Texas Tourist Development Agency 294(top); Unusual Films, courtesy of Tim Keesee 294(bottom); Digital Stock 295, 303, 304, 305(backgrounds); www.arttoday.com 297, 299, 301

Unit 4 Opener
NPS, photo by Richard Frear 308-9; Library of Congress 308, 309

Chapter 16
NPS, photo by Thomas A. DuRant 311; Library of Congress 312, 315, 318(bottom), 319, 323, 325, 328; www.arttoday.com 318(top); Digital Stock 320, 324(backgrounds); National Archives 321; South Carolina Department of Parks, Recreation & Tourism 325(inset); Unusual Films 328(background), 329

The South
Photo Disc, Inc. 333(middle, right); Digital Stock 333(left); ©1998 GeoSystems Global Corporation 333(map)

Chapter 17
NPS, photo by Richard Frear 334, 340, 348(both), 354(bottom), 355(top), 356; Library of Congress 336, 338(top), 341(both), 343, 346, 349, 352, 354(top), 355(bottom); National Archives 338(bottom), 339, 351; Corel Corporation 357

Chapter 18
National Archives 360, 369(top); Unusual Films, courtesy of Tim Keesee 361(top); Library of Congress 361(bottom), 363, 366(right), 367(background), 368, 369(bottom), 370, 371, 373, 377; Digital Stock 365, 372, 375(backgrounds); www.arttoday.com 366(left), 375

Unit 5 Opener
NPS, photo by W.S. Keller 384(top); Library of Congress 384(bottom), 385(top); Union Pacific Railroad 385(bottom)